34TH CONGRESS, 1st Session. } SENATE. { Ex. Doc. No. 107.

REPORT

ON THE

COMMERCIAL RELATIONS OF THE UNITED STATES

WITH

ALL FOREIGN NATIONS.

EDMUND FLAGG,
SUPERINTENDENT.

PREPARED AND PRINTED UNDER THE DIRECTION OF THE SECRETARY OF STATE, IN ACCORDANCE WITH RESOLUTIONS OF THE HOUSE OF REPRESENTATIVES.

VOLUME II.

WASHINGTON:
A. O. P. NICHOLSON, PRINTER.
1857.

RESOLUTIONS.

CONGRESS OF THE UNITED STATES.

THIRTY-FOURTH CONGRESS: FIRST SESSION.

IN THE SENATE.

Thursday, August 14, 1856.

Mr. SLIDELL submitted the following resolution; which was considered by unanimous consent, and referred to the Committee on Printing:

Resolved, That the Committee on Printing be instructed to report on the expediency of printing in quarto form five thousand copies of the message of the President to the House of Representatives on Commercial Statistics, with the accompanying documents, for the use of the Senate.

Friday, August 15, 1856.

Mr. FITZPATRICK, from the Committee on Printing, to whom was referred the resolution of the 14th instant, to inquire into the expediency of printing, for the use of the Senate, five thousand copies of the message of the President to the House of Representatives on Commercial Statistics, reported the following resolution, which was considered by unanimous consent, and agreed to:

Resolved, That there be printed, for the use of the Senate, the usual number, and five thousand additional copies of the message of the President to the House of Representatives on Commercial Statistics of different nations, with the accompanying documents.

COMMERCIAL REPORT.

PART SECOND.

COMPARATIVE TARIFFS.

EXTRACT FROM THE LETTER OF THE SUPERINTENDENT SUBMITTING THE REPORT. (a)

THIS branch of the work comprises tables exhibiting a comparative statement of the tariff of the United States with the tariffs of all other nations, numbering, with those of their dependencies, more than forty—tariffs of exportation as well as of importation being given were found to exist; the denominations of foreign moneys, weights, and measures, being, in all instances, reduced to the federal standard of the United States, (b) and each tariff being preceded by an explanatory preface.

In addition to these comparative statements of the tariffs of separate nations with that of the United States, others are given, which, grouping the tariffs of countries contiguous to each other, and having similar trade, the customs rates of these countries are presented at a glance, in comparison with those of the tariff of the United States, as regards the most important staples of commerce. In one tabular group, for example, are compared the customs rates of the nations of northern Europe; in another, those of southern Europe; in a third, those to which our indirect trade with central Europe is subjected; a fourth presents the tariff rates of the South American republics; a fifth, those of the States of Central America; and a sixth, those of Hayti and the Dominican republic. A like course has been pursued with the colonial and other possessions of Great Britain, forming four such tabulated groups—East Indies, West Indies, North America, and one composed of Gibraltar and Malta.

Another similar comparative statement exhibits, at a glance, the import duties levied by twelve of the principal commercial nations, respectively, on thirty-five of the staple products of the United States. Another statement exhibits, at a glance, the per centage increase or decrease of the rates of duty on prominent articles of commerce by the customs tariffs of the principal commercial countries of Europe for a period of eight years, from 1846 to 1853, both inclusive, showing the changes within that period, during which no change occurred in the tariff of the United States; while still another exhibits the rates of duty imposed on principal imports for a

(a) Vol I, p. x.

(b) The pound sterling excepted, which, for reasons given in the preface to the tariff of Great Britain, is estimated at $4 80, instead of 4 484.

period of nearly fifty years, under each of the eighteen different tariffs of the United States, from that of 1789 to that of 1846, both inclusive, with the increase or decrease of the rates for that period.

Following the series of Comparative Tariffs is presented a series of tabular statements, preceded by an explanatory introduction, illustrated by numerous tables, exhibiting the quantities and values of thirty of the staple products exported from the United States to thirteen of the principal commercial countries, together with the amounts of duties paid thereon, during the commercial years 1851, 1852, and 1853; and, also, a summary statement exhibiting the *aggregate* value of the staple and other domestic products exported to the same countries during the same years, with the aggregate amount of duties paid on the staple products exported; and a summary statement exhibiting the *average* value of the same, to the same countries, for the same years, with the average amount of duties thereon accruing to each country in each of the years specified.

An elaborate series of tabular statements is next given, exhibiting, in detail, the import duties levied by the tariffs of all nations, and by those of their dependencies, on the staple or principal productions of the United States—products of the sea, of the soil, of the forest, of manufactures, &c., being specified in distinct tables—columns being added to show the rates of duty levied on the same articles imported from other countries, and the discrimination in favor of or against the United States, where such may exist. A statement exhibiting the same facts with regard to all portions of the British empire follows; while detailed statements of the privileges afforded, and the restrictions imposed, by all nations and their dependencies on commercial intercourse with the United States, whether by treaty or local legislation, by duties on imports or on exports, by bounties or drawbacks, or in any other way, in distinct tables; together with their tonnage charges, whether by treaty or legislation, their modes of measuring tonnage, their sanitary regulations, and the regulations of their colonial trade, also in distinct tables, complete the second part of the Report.

The preparation of the Comparative Tariffs has proved a tedious and toilsome task; while there can be none, perhaps, in which, despite all possible care, there is a greater liability to error. The latest official publications, in the original languages, have alone, in all instances, been relied on as authority; and the work has been repeatedly subjected to vexatious delay by the difficulty in procuring them from abroad. Changes and modifications also in foreign customs rates have been so frequent and so important the last year or two, that it has been found by no means easy to keep pace with them, even by constant alterations in the work performed; while, in several instances, the unlooked for appearance of entirely new tariffs has rendered worthless long and labored tabular statements already prepared, and complete substitution indispensable.

NOTE.

In revising this volume for the press, all changes in the tariff of the United States caused by the act of March 3, 1857, have been noted, and a comparison between the rates of this tariff and that of July 30, 1846, has, at the same time, been instituted by placing the customs rates of the two acts in adjacent parallel columns; while all material modifications which have taken place in the tariffs of other nations have, with more or less minuteness, been detailed. The delay, however, which the Report had unavoidably sustained in the course of printing, and a solicitude to have it, as speedily as possible, completed, have tended to rende impracticable that thorough and critical revision of the volume which had been designed. For changes and modifications in the tariffs of foreign nations since they were prepared, general reference is invited to Consular Returns embraced in volumes III and IV of this work, and to the An ual Reports of the Secretary of State on Foreign Commerce. As a customs guide, or a hand book, for daily use by the merchant, a volume comprehending statements of "The Tariffs of all Nations," can never, it is evident, be deemed so reliable as the quotations of his foreign correspondence from the rates prescribed by the latest customs act, or imperial decree, or royal order, or order in council, affording the precise current duties on merchandise in the export of which he may have interest. To present a printed volume containing the tariff rates on all articles of import or export, in all countries, actually in force on the day the volume is published, is, of course, in the very nature of customs regulations, impossible. Granted that the very latest tariff in force in a distant country had been procured, translated, and prepared for the press, it is probable that long before the last of the orty or fifty tariffs which the volume would contain was in type, ma rial changes would have taken place, not only in the tariff first obtained and prepared, but even in the latest. Were it possible, however, that, on the day of publication, each tariff statement in the volume should present the precise current rates actually in force on each article of merchandise in each of all commercial nations on that day, there is not the slightest probability that these rates would continue thus exact six months later, or even one month later, so incessant are the executive, legislative, or provisional modifications in the rates of foreign tariffs, and so unlooked for, so varied, and so apparently insignificant oftentimes are the contingencies from which such modifications arise. As an aid, however, to the commercial statesman or the political economist in ascertaining the tariff *policy* of different nations, and of comparing or contrasting such policy with that of the United States—a policy which may outlive a century, and which may be ascertained quite as well from a tariff law enacted ten years since, (as that of Spain) no change of policy having occurred, as in one of latest date—a volume of tariffs can but prove of invaluable service. Causes of ephemeral influence may affect the minor details in tariff rates but changes in tariff policy are of slow growth and unfrequent occurrence.

CONTENTS.

□ 2

CONTENTS

OF

PART II.—COMPARATIVE TARIFFS.

TARIFFS NOT STATED IN THIS VOLUME.

GIBRALTAR.—No import duties are levied, except on wines, cordials, and spirituous liquors generally.—(See vol. 1 "Digests," p. 91; also vol. 3 "Returns," p. 45.)

MALTA.—Duties are levied on but few articles, as follows: breadstuffs, cattle, seeds, beans, potatoes, olive oil, wines, and spirits.—(See vol. 3 "Returns," p. 46.) (*a*)

EGYPT.—*Import duties:* 5 per cent. ad valorem. Deducting one-fifth, however, which is returned to the importer, the net rate of duty is only 4 per cent. ad valorem.

Prohibited: Arms and ammunition.

Export duties: 12 per cent. ad valorem. Deducting one-sixth, however, which is returned to the importer, the net rate of duty is only 10 per cent. ad valorem.

Transit duties: 3 per cent. ad valorem. Those goods, however, which pass between Europe and India, pay only ½ per cent. ad valorem.

LIBERIA.—*Import duties:* On beer, cordials, spirituous liquors, wines, $1 per gallon, and on all other articles, 8 per cent. ad valorem. Export duties, none.

PERSIA.—Import duties, 6 per cent. ad valorem.

SIAM.—For tariff regulations, bearing date April 18, 1855, see vol. 1 "Digests," pp. 494, *et seq.*

SANDWICH ISLANDS.—For a tariff of May, 1855, see vol. 1 "Digests," pp. 547, *et seq.*

Its main features, compared with the former tariffs, are as follows: 1st. It reduces the duty on liquor from $5 to $3 per gallon; 2d. It imposes a duty of $1 per gallon on wines of a strength between 18 and 30 per cent. of alcohol, which now pay a duty of 5 per cent. ad valorem; 3d. Instead of a uniform duty of 5 per cent. ad valorem on all other merchandise, this act admits a class of free goods, and three other classes at 5, 10, and 15 per cent. ad valorem. It was to have gone into effect May, 1856, "provided it was in violation of no treaty existing at that time:" but, being supposed to conflict with the 6th article of a treaty of 1846 with France, it has not yet superseded the former tariff.

NICARAGUA.—For tariff of July 21, 1856, see vol. 1 "Digests," pp. 599, *et seq.*

PARAGUAY.—For the tariff of January 2, 1846, see vol 1 "Digests," pp. 761, *et seq.* Changes, however, have since taken place; the latest being by virtue of a law of October 31, 1856, which came into force January 1, 1857, declaring coals and lime free, and imposing a duty on furs and raw wool of 15 per cent. ad valorem, and on silk, raw, sewing, and manufactures of, 8 per cent.

(*a*) The simplicity of the customs rates at Gibraltar and Malta has caused the omission in printing of a comparative statement prepared for this volume, in which the import duties of the respective tariffs are combined in a tabular group.

ERRATA.

"To one familiar with commercial statistics, it is unnecessary to suggest, that, in a work so complicated and so comprehensive as the present, involving facts and figures almost without number, derived from authorities numerous, and often conflicting, in various languages, errors, notwithstanding the most unsleeping vigilance and the most toilsome scrutiny, are unavoidable."

The above sentence appears prefixed to the first volume of this work, devoted to "Digests;" and, if its significance has been recognized in that connexion, much more ought it to be acknowledged as prefixed to the present volume, devoted to a subject far more intricate and involved, especially when it is considered that to the "Digests," consisting mainly of letter press, printed in comparatively large type, were accorded nine months for conduct through the press, while to the "Tariffs," made up almost entirely of tabular statements, and printed in smaller type, have been accorded scarcely three. Material "corrections and additions, found requisite in the course of printing," were, it is true, made in the "Digests," as authorized by the House resolution ordering the printing; but "corrections and additions" yet more "requisite" have been made in the "Tariffs." The second volume is, however, less voluminous than was the first.

A few errors have chanced to arrest the eye since the sheets left the press; but it is deemed advisable to leave their correction, as well as that of all others, to the pencil of the reader.

PART II.

COMPARATIVE TARIFFS.

GREAT BRITAIN

AND

HER POSSESSIONS.

GREAT BRITAIN.

THE tariff is that of 1854, with changes and modifications down to 1855.(*a*) The whole of the imperial duties heretofore levied in the British possessions abroad, and in force when the last Commercial Report from this Department was prepared, are now repealed; consequently, the only duties to which importations into such possessions are subject are those assessed by colonial legislation, differing, as they frequently do, in the different colonies, and ranging from 3 to 30 per cent. ad valorem. This exemption from imperial duties in our commercial intercourse with British colonial possessions will explain the absence in the following tables of the separate columns appropriated to such possessions in the Report of 1842. The omission, however, is supplied by a comprehensive view of our present commercial relations with British colonial possessions, in all parts of the world, presented in a series of supplemental tables prepared from the most authentic documents. In all cases, in which there appears to be any discriminating duty on articles imported into Great Britain in favor of the colonies, the differential duty is noted in the column headed "Into Great Britain from the British Colonies."

Money.—4 farthings = 1 penny = 2 cents; 12 pence = 1 shilling = 24 cents; 20 shillings = 1 pound = $4 80.

The reasons for estimating the value of the pound sterling at $4 80 instead of at the intrinsic value $4 87, or at the legal and United States custom-house value, by the act of Congress of July 27, 1842, $4 84, or at the par value $4 44, are chiefly these: 1st. In the Report of 1842, on which the present is required to be framed, the value of the pound is estimated at $4 80. 2d. By estimating the pound at $4 80 fractions are avoided; while at $4 84 they would be of constant occurrence. When an estimate of duties at the legal value of the pound sterling ($4 84) is desired, there must be added to each rate of duty given in the tables $\frac{1}{120}$th, or to the aggregate of any amount of duties on articles calculated at those rates $\frac{1}{120}$th, or $\frac{5}{6}$ths (nearly) of 1 per cent. on that aggregate; and, when it is desired to estimate duties at the par value of the pound sterling, ($4 44,) there must, in the same manner, be deducted from each given rate, or from the aggregate of the amounts of duties calculated in the tables, $\frac{1}{11}$th of said rate on the aggregate of the amounts, or about 9 per cent.

Weights and measures.—The same as in the United States. The imperial gallon = 1. 20 gallons United States custom-house standard. The imperial bushel = 8 imperial gallons = 1. 03 bushels United States custom-house standard.

(*a*) CHANGES.—For changes made in the tariff of Great Britain in 1855, by the act of Parliament 18 and 19 Vict., chap. 97, after this work was prepared, see Appendix. For changes subsequent to those, whether in the tariffs of Great Britain, or in the tariffs of her colonial possessions, reference is invited to the Annual Reports of the Secretary of State on Foreign Commerce.

COMPARATIVE TARIFFS.

UNITED STATES AND GREAT BRITAIN.

DENOMINATION OF MERCHANDISE.	DUTIES ON IMPORTS.			
	Into the United States from foreign nations, per cent. ad valorem, under the act of—		Into Great Britain from foreign nations.	Into Great Britain from the British colonies.
	184	1857.		
Absynth, oil of	30	24	24 cents per pound	24 cents per pound
Acetate of lead	20	15	Free	Free
of morphia	30	24	$1 20 per pound	$1 20 per pound
of potash	20	15	Free	Free
of mercury	20	15	Free	Free
Accordeons	20	15	Chinese, 24 cents per 100 notes; other sorts $1 20 do	No discrimination in favor of the colonies
Acid, acetic		4	Free	Free
sulphuric	10	4	Free	Free
All other acids used for chemical or medical purposes, or for manufacturing or in the fine arts, not otherwise provided for	10	4	Free	Free
Adhesive felt, for ships' bottoms	Free	Free	Free	Free
plaster	30	24	20 per cent. ad valorem	No discriminating duty defined
Adzes	30	24	60 cents per cwt	do do
Agate mortars	30	24	10 per cent. ad valorem	do do
Agates, precious stones	10	4	Not set, free; set, 10 per cent	do do
Alabaster ornaments	40	30	10 per cent. ad valorem	10 per cent
Alba canella	20	15	Free	Free
Alcornoque bark	5	8	Free	Free
Ale, in bottles (*a*)	30	24	Not defined	Not defined
otherwise than in bottles	30	24	$4 80 per barrel (of 32 gallons)	No discriminating duty defined
Almonds	40	30	Bitter, free; others $2 40 per cwt	do do
paste of	30	24	4 cents per pound	do do
oil of, sweet or bitter	30	24	2 cents per pound	do do
Aloes	20	4	Free	Free
Alspice, oil of	30	24	24 cents per pound	No discriminating duty defined
Alum	20	15	Free	Free

(*a*) No ale, beer, or porter shall be brought into the United States by sea, from any foreign place, except in casks, or vessels the capacity of which shall not be less than 40 gallons beer measure, or packages containing not less than six dozen bottles each, on pain of forfeiture of such ale, beer, and porter, and the vessel in which the same shall be brought.—(Act March 2, 1799.)

TARIFFS—Continued.

Denomination of merchandise.	Duties on imports. Into the United States from foreign nations, per cent. ad valorem, under the act of— 1846.	1857.	Into Great Britain from foreign nations.	Into Great Britain from the British colonies.
Amber	20	4	Free	Free
beads of	30	24	4 cents per pound	No discriminating duty defined
oil of	30	24	24 cents per pound	do do
Ambergris	20	4	Free	Free
Amethyst	10	4	Free	Free
Ammonia, sal	10	8	Free	Free
Ammoniac, crude	20	8	Free	Free
Ammunition, balls and shot of all kinds	30	24	Of lead, (large or small,) 48 cents per cwt	No discriminating duty defined
gunpowder		15	Free	Free
musket balls	20	15	Of lead, (large or small,) 48 cents per cwt	No discriminating duty defined
Anchors, and all parts thereof	30	24	60 cents per cwt	No discrimination
Anchovies, in oil	40	30	Free	Free
salt	20	15	Free	Free
Angelica root	20	15	Free	Free
Angora goat's hair	20	24	Free	Free
gloves and hosiery	30	24	6 cents per dozen pairs	5 per cent. ad valorem
Animals imported for breed	Free	Free	Free	Free
Animal oil	20	15	Free	Free
carbon	20	Free	Free	Free
Annatto, or rocoa	10	4	Free	Free
extract	20	15	20 per cent. ad valorem	No discriminating duty defined
Aniseed (the seed)	20	4	Free	Free
oils of	30	24	24 cents per pound	No discriminating duty defined
Anthos, oil of	30	24	do	do do
Antimony, crude	20		Free	Free
Antiquities	Free	Free	Free	Free
Anvils	30	24	60 cents per cwt	No discriminating duty defined
Aqua ammonia (hartshorn)	20	24	20 per cent. ad valorem	do do
Aquafortis	20	15	Free	Free
Arabic, gum	10	8	Free	Free
Archil (orchelia)	20	15	Free	Free
Argol, or wine lees	5	Free	Free	Free
Armenian, bole	20	15	Not defined	Not defined
stone	20	15	do	do
Arms, fire	30	24	10 per cent. ad valorem (a)	No discriminating duty defined
side	30	24	60 cents per cwt	do do
Arrow root	20	15	9 cents per cwt	do do

(a) Arms, ammunition, or any other goods, may be prohibited by proclamation or order in council.

TARIFFS—Continued.

DENOMINATION OF MERCHANDISE.	DUTIES ON IMPORTS.			
	Into the United States from foreign nations, per cent. ad valorem, under the act of—		Into Great Britain from foreign nations.	Into Great Britain from the British colonies.
	1846.	1857.		
Arsenic	15	4	Free	Free
Articles, not in a crude state, used in dyeing or tanning, not otherwise provided for	20	Free	Free	Free
Artificial flowers	30	24	$2 88 per cubic foot as packed	$2 88 per cubic foot as packed
feathers	30	24	10 per cent. ad valorem	No discriminating duty defined
Assafœtida	20	4	Free	Free
Asphalta, or chapapote	20	4	Free	Free
Asses' skin, imitation, (or parchment)	30	24	10 per cent. ad valorem	No discriminating duty defined
Augers	30	24	60 cents per cwt	do do
Ava root	20	15	Free	Free
Awl hafts of wood, and awls	30	24	Awls 60 cents per cwt	No discriminating duty defined
Axes	30	24	60 cents per cwt	60 cents per cwt
Bacon	20	15	Free	Free
Baggage, personal, in actual use	Free	Free	See "Digests," vol. 1, p. 42	See "Digests," vol. 1, p. 42
Bags of flax	20	15	5 per cent. ad valorem	No discriminating duty defined
of grass	20	24	10 per cent. ad valorem	10 per cent. ad valorem
Baizes	25	19	Free	Free
Balls, bone or ivory	30	24	10 per cent. ad valorem	No discriminating duty defined
Balsams, cosmetic	30	24	As perfumery, 4 cents per pound	do do
medicinal	30	24	Free	Free
Bamboos, unmanufactured	10	Free	Free	Free
Band iron, slit or rolled	30	24	Free	Free
Bandannas	25	19	In pieces not exceeding 6¼ yards in length, 12 cents; exceeding 6¼ yards, and not exceeding 7¼ yards, 16 cents; exceeding 7¼ yards, and not exceeding 12 yards, 20 cents per piece	No discriminating duty defined
Barege, cotton	25	24	Free	Free
wool	30	24	Free	Free
Barilla	10	4	Free	Free
Barley, hulled, pearl or other	20	15	9 cents per cwt	9 cents per cwt
Bar, iron	30	24	Unwrought, free	Free
			Wrought or manufactured, viz: machinery, wrought castings, tools, cutlery, and other manufactures of iron not enumerated, 60 cents per cwt	No discriminating duty defined
wood	5	Free	Free	Free

TARIFFS—Continued.

DENOMINATION OF MERCHANDISE.	DUTIES ON IMPORTS.			
	Into the United States from foreign nations, per cent. ad valorem, under the act of—		Into Great Britain from foreign nations.	Into Great Britain from the British colonies.
	1846.	1857.		
Bark, cork tree, unmanufactured	15	4	Free	Free
Jesuits' or Peruvian	15	Free	Free	Free
Barytes, sulphate of	20	15	Free	Free
Bassoons	20	15	10 per cent. ad valorem	No discriminating duty defined
Bastard files	30	24	60 cents per cwt	60 cents per cwt
Battledoors and shuttlecocks	30	24	8 cents per cubic foot	No discriminating duty defined
Beads of metals	30	24	4 cents per pound	4 cents per pound
all others unenumerated	30	24	4 cents per pound, (except coral,) which is subject to 36 cents per pound	
Beams, for scales	30	24	60 cents per cwt	60 cents per cwt
Beans, vanilla	20	15	Free	Free
tonka or tonqua	20	15	Free	Free
Beaver fur, undressed	10	8	Free	Free
Bed screws	30	24	60 cents per cwt	60 cents per cwt.
ticking, linen	20	15	5 per cent. ad valorem	5 per. cent. ad valorem
cotton	25	24	do do	do do
Beef, in barrels or otherwise	20	15	Free	Free
Beer, ale, and porter, in bottles	30	24	Not defined when bottled; in barrels, $4 80 per barrel, each barrel to contain 32 gallons	No discriminating duty in favor of colonial importation.
otherwise	30	24		
Bells	30	24	As goods manufactured, 10 per ct.	10 per cent. ad valorem
when old	5	Free	Free	Free
fit only to be remanufactured	5	Free	Free	Free
Belts, of leather	30	24	10 per cent. ad valorem	10 per cent. ad valorem
Benzoates	30	24	Free	Free
Benzoin acid	20	4	Free	Free
gum	30	8	Free	Free
Bergamot, oil and essence	30	24	24 cents per pound	24 cents per pound
Berries, nuts, and vegetables, used exclusively in dyeing, in a crude state	5	Free	Free	Free
Berries, vegetables, flowers, and barks, not otherwise provided for	20	15	Free	Free
Binding, cotton	25	24	5 per cent. ad valorem	5 per cent. ad valorem
silk, or silk and cotton	25	19	15 per cent. ad valorem	do do
thread or flax	20	15	5 per cent. ad valorem	No discriminating duty defined
wool, or flax and cott n	30	24	do do	do do
worsted, or flax and cotton	25	19	do do	do do
Birds	20	Free	Free	Free
Bismuth	20	Free	Free	Free

TARIFFS—Continued.

DENOMINATION OF MERCHANDISE.	DUTIES ON IMPORTS.			
	Into the United States from foreign nations, per cent. ad valorem, under the act of—		Into Great Britain from foreign nations.	Into Great Britain from the British colonies
	1846.	1857.		
Bismuth, oxide of	20	15	Free	Free
Bitter apple	20	Free	Free	Free
Bitumen or aspaltum	20	15	Free	Free
Black, ivory, lamp, and lead or plumbago	20	15	Free	Free
crucibles, retorts or pots	30	24	Free	Free
lead pencils	30	24	Free	Free
Blacking	20	15	Free	Free
Blacksmiths' hammers and sledges	30	24	60 cents per cwt	60 cents per cwt
Bladders	20	15	Free	Free
Blankets of all kinds	20	15	5 per cent. ad valorem	No discriminating duty defined
Bleaching powders	10	4	Free	Free
Blue, Prussian	20	4	Free	Free
vitriol	20	15	Free	Free
Boards, rough or dressed	20	15	$2 40 per load of 50 cubic feet	48 cents per load of 50 cubic feet.
Bobbin, cotton	25	24	As "manufactures of cotton," 5 per cent	No discriminating duty defined
Bocking, baize	25	19	Free, as goods manufactured of wool or of wool mixed with cotton, not particularly enumerated	Free
Bodkins, ivory, bone, silver, gold, plated, gilt	30	24	10 per cent., as manufactured goods	No discriminating duty defined
iron, steel	30	24	60 cents per cwt	do do do
brass, copper	30	24	$2 40 per cwt	$2 40 per cwt
Boilers, iron	30	24	60 cents per cwt	60 cents per cwt
Bologna sausages	30	24	Free	Free
Bolts, iron	30	24	60 cents per cwt	No discriminating duty defined
copper	20	15	$2 40 per cwt	do do do
composition or brass	30	24	$2 40 per cwt	do do do
Bolt ropes, as cordage	25	19	Free	Free
Bone, whale, produce of foreign fisheries	20	15	Free	Free
all manufactures of	30	24	10 per cent. ad valorem	No discriminating duty defined
Bones and bone tips	5	4	Free	Free
Bonnets and hats for men, women, and children, of straw, silk or satin, chip, grass, palm leaf, willow, cotton, bone, or other material, not otherwise provided for	30	24	As silk millinery, $1 68 each.	No discriminating duty defined

TARIFFS—Continued.

DENOMINATION OF MERCHANDISE.	DUTIES ON IMPORTS.			
	Into the United States, from foreign nations, per cent. ad valorem, under the act of—		Into Great Britain from foreign nations.	Into Great Britain from the British colonies.
	1846.	1857.		
Bonnets and hats, &c—Continued.	30	24	Other kinds enumerated, coming under class of "goods manufactured," 10 per cent. ad val., except chip, baste, cane, horse-hair, or straw, which are rated at 60 cents per pound	No discriminating duty defined.
Bonnets, braids, plats, and sparterre, and willow squares	30	24	Braids, plats, and sparterre, from 12 cents to 48 cents per pound; willow squares $2 40 per cwt.	do. do.
Bonnets, wire for, called bonnet wire	30	24	Free	Free
Books, blank, bound or unbound.	20	15	10 per cent. as "manufactured goods." Being of editions printed prior to the year 1801, bound or unbound, free(a)	No discriminating duty defined.
Books, printed magazines, pamphlets, periodicals, and illustrated newspapers, bound or unbound, not in the course of republication in the U. States	10	8	Printed in or since the year 1801, $7 20 per cwt	do. do.
Books, periodicals and other works in the course of printing in the United States, or of republication	20	15	Books admitted under treaties of international copy-right, $3 60 per cwt	do. do.
Books imported by schools, libraries, and institutions of learning	Free	Free	Being presents to the several learned societies, free	No discrimination
Books, obscene, and containing obscene pictures	Prohib.	Prohib.	Prohibited	Prohibited
Books, professional, of persons arriving in the United States	Free	Free	No exemption in such cases	No exemption in such cases

(a) Books, wherein the copy-right shall be first subsisting, first written or printed in the United Kingdom, and printed or reprinted in any other, as to which the proprietor of such copy-right or his agent shall have given to the commissioners of customs a notice, in writing, that such copy-right subsists, such notice also stating when such copy-right shall expire, are prohibited. The privilege of copy-right in England is extended to the following countries and States, viz: Saxony, Brunswick, The Thuringian Union, Hanover, Oldenburgh, France, Anhalt Dessau and Anhalt Bernburgh, and Hamburgh. Books printed abroad to be first published in the United Kingdom, although stamped, are deemed liable to the duty of $7 20 per cwt.—(4th March, 1854, Beedell's British Tariff, 1854-'55, p. 8.)

TARIFFS—Continued.

DENOMINATION OF MERCHANDISE.	DUTIES ON IMPORTS.			
	Into the United States, from foreign nations, per cent. ad valorem, under the act of—		Into Great Britain from foreign nations.	Into Great Britain from the British colonies.
	1846.	1857.		
Books, maps, and charts, imported by authority of the Joint Library Committee of Congress (a)	Free	Free	Maps and charts, free	Maps and charts, free
Boots, laced, or bootees, for men, women, or children, of leather, or any material	30	24	See note (b)	See note (b)
Borax	25	4	Free	Free
Botany, specimens in	Free	Free	Free	Free
Bottles, glass	30	24	Cut, engraved, or otherwise ornamented, $2 40 per cwt	No discrimination
			All other kinds free	Free
Bougies, elastic	30	24	8 cents per pound	No discriminating duty defined
Boxes, gold or silver	30	24	10 per cent. ad valorem	No discrimination
japanned on wood, metal, or paper	30	24	$4 80 per cwt	$4 80 per cwt
of cedar, grenadilla, ebony, mahogany, rosewood, and satin wood, solid or veneered	40	30	10 per cent. ad valorem	10 per cent. ad valorem
all other wood	30	24	do do	do do
shell, horn, or ivory	30	24	do do	do do
musical	20	15	Small, not exceeding 4 inches in length: the air, 6 cents; large, 16 cents. Overtures, or extra accompaniments: the air, 60 cents	No discriminating duty defined
Braces and bits, carpenters'	30	24	60 cents per cwt	do do
or suspenders, cotton or linen	30	24	5 per cent. ad valorem	5 per cent. ad valorem
of leather	30	24	10 per cent. ad valorem	do do
of silk	30	24	15 per cent. ad valorem	do do
of worsted or wool	30	24	5 per cent. ad valorem	No discriminating duty defined

(a) The exemption from duty of books, maps, charts, &c., imported into the United States, is governed by the following synopsis: Free—*Provided*, That if in any case a contract shall have been made with any bookseller, importer, or other person, for books, maps, or charts, in which contract the bookseller, importer, or other person aforesaid, shall have paid the duty, or included the duty in said contract; in such case the duty shall not be remitted.

All philosophical apparatu, sinstruments, books, and charts; statues, statuary, busts and casts of marble, bronze, alabaster, or plaster of Paris; paintings, drawings, etchings, specimens of sculpture, cabinets of coins, medals, gems, and all collections of antiquities; provided the same be specially imported in good faith for the use of any society incorporated or established for philosophical or literary purposes, or for the encouragement of the fine arts; or for the use and by the order of any college, academy, school, or seminary of learning in the United States, and all articles whatever imported for the use of the United States, free.—(Treasury Circular, No. 18, August 19, 1848.)

(b) According to character, quality, dimensions, and materials of which composed, &c. Such is the extent and variety of the nomenclature, and of the corresponding rates of duties, set down under this head in the tariffs of Great Britain, that anything like a summary view of those rates, in comparison with the rate of the single item in the United States tariffs, seems impracticable in a condensed statement like the present.

TARIFFS—Continued.

Denomination of merchandise.	Duties on imports. Into the United States from foreign nations, per cent. ad valorem, under the act of— 1846.	1857.	Into Great Britain from foreign nations.	Into Great Britain from the British colonies.
Braces, composed wholly or in part of India rubber	30	24	8 cents per pound	No discriminating duty defined
Bracelets, hair	30	24	10 per cent. ad valorem	do do
of gold, gilt, or set	30	24	10 per cent. ad valorem	do do
Brads of all sizes	30	24	60 cents per cwt	
Braids, hair, or of which hair is a component part	30	24	10 per cent. ad valorem	10 per cent ad valorem
Braids for hats or bonnets	30	24	48 cents per pound	48 cents per pound
of cotton or worsted	25	24	5 per cent. ad valorem	No discriminating duty defined
of silk	25	24	15 per cent. ad valorem	5 per cent ad valorem
Brandy	100	30	For every gallon of any strength not exceeding the strength of proof by Sykes' hydrometer, and so in proportion for any greater or less strength than the strength of proof, and for any greater or less quantity than a gallon, $3 60 per gallon	
Brass, all manufactures of, not otherwise defined	30	24	$2 40 per cwt	No discriminating duty defined
Brass, in plates, sheets, or rolled	20	24	Free	Free
in bars, blocks, or pigs	5	Free	Free	Free
wire	30	24	Free	Free
runners and tips for umbrellas	30	24	$2 40 per cwt	$2 40 per cwt
nails, screws, and studs	30	24	$2 40 per cwt	do
old, and fit only to be remanufactured	5	Free	Free	Free
Braziers' rods	30	24	$2 40 per cwt	No discriminating duty defined
copper	20	15	$2 40 per cwt	do do
Brazil, pebbles of, for spectacles	30	24	Free	Free
wood in sticks	5	Free	Free	
paste	15	12	4 cents per pound	4 cents per pound
Bread baskets, silver, plated, &c	30	24	Made of rods, 8 cents per cubic foot; others, 10 per cent	No discriminating duty defined
Bricks	20	15	Free	Free
Bridles	30	24	According to material	According to material
Bridle bits, brass, plated, or polished steel	30	24	Of brass, $2 40 per cwt.; of steel, 60 cents per cwt	No discriminating duty defined

TARIFFS—Continued.

DENOMINATION OF MERCHANDISE.	DUTIES ON IMPORTS.			
	Into the United States from foreign nations, per cent. ad valorem, under the act of—		Into Great Britain from foreign nations.	Into Great Britain from the British colonies.
	1846.	1857.		
Brimstone, rolled, refined, or in packages	20	15	Every description free	Free
Brimstone, crude, in bulk	15	4	Free	Free
Bristles	5	4	Free	Free
Bristol stones	20	15	Free	Free
pasteboards	30	24	5 cents per pound	No discriminating duty defined
Bronze, powder, leaf or liquor	20	15	Manufactures of, $2 40 per cwt.; powder, &c., free	No discrimination
casts and manufactures of	30	24	All works of art thereof, (not merchandise,) free	do
Brooms of all kinds	30	24	10 per cent. ad valorem as "manufactured goods"	do
Brown holland and cotton	25	15	Free	Free
linen	20	15	Free	Free
rolls	20	15	Free	Free
Spanish, in oil	30	24	Not defined	Not defined
smalts	20	15	Free	Free
Brucine	20	15	Free	Free
Brushes of all kinds	30	24	10 per cent. ad valorem as "manufactured goods"	No discriminating duty defined
paint	30	24	Free	Free
Buckles of copper, brass, iron, steel, pewter, tin, lead, or of which any of those articles is a component part	30	24	Of brass, copper, and tin, $2 40 per cwt.; of iron and steel, 60 cents per cwt.; of pewter and lead, 48 cents per cwt	No discrimination
Buckles, chiefly of gold or silver	30	24	10 per cent. ad valorem	No discriminating duty defined
Buckram, cotton	25	15	Free	Free
Bugles, musical instruments	20	15	18 cents per pound	18 cents per pound
glass, not cut	30	24	Free	Free
cut	40	30	Free	Free
Building stones	10	8	Free of every description	Free
Bulbous roots	Free	Free	Free	Free
Bullion	Free	Free	Free	Free
Bunting	25	19	Free	Free
Burr stones, wrought or unwrought	10	Free	Free	Free
Butter	20	15	$1 20 per cwt	60 cents per cwt
Buttons and button moulds	25	19	Buttons of all kinds, free	Free
of all kinds	25	19	Moulds, according to material	According to material

TARIFFS—Continued.

DENOMINATION OF MERCHANDISE.	DUTIES ON IMPORTS.			
	Into the United States from foreign nations, per cent. ad valorem, under the act of—		Into Great Britain from foreign nations.	Into Great Britain from the British colonies.
	1846.	1857.		
Butchers' knives	30	24	60 cents per cwt	No discriminating duty defined
Butt hinges, wrought or unwrought	30	24	60 cents per cwt	do do do
Cabinet wares	30	24	10 per cent., as "manufactured goods"	do do do
Cables, cordage, tarred or untarred	25	19	Free	Free
made of grass	25	19	Free	Free
iron chain, or parts	30	24	60 cents per cwt	No discriminating duty defined
Cadmium	20	15	Free	Free
Cajeput, or cajeputa, oil of	30	24	24 cents per pound	24 cents per pound
Calamine	20	15	Free	Free
Calcined magnesia	30	24	20 per cent. ad valorem	No discriminating duty defined
Calomel	25	19	20 per cent. ad valorem	do do do
Calf skins, tanned	20	19	Free	Free
raw, salted, or pickled	5	4	Free	Free
Camlets or camblets, worsted	25	19	Free	Free
Cameos, real, unset	10	4	Free	Free
imitation, unset	10	8	Free	Free
set	30	24	10 per cent. ad valorem	No discriminating duty defined
Camels' hair, in the raw state	10	8	Free	Free
shawls of	30	24	5 per cent. ad valorem	No discriminating duty defined
Camels' hair pencils	30	24	Free	Free
Camphor, crude	25	8	Free	Free
refined	40	30	Free	Free
Camwood, in sticks	5	Free	Free	Free
ground	20	Free	Free	Free
Canary seed	Free	Free	Free	Free
Candles, spermaceti	20	15	56 cents per cwt	56 cents per cwt
stearine	20	15	Until the 5th April, 1858, unless the duty on tallow shall be repealed at an earlier day, in which case, or after the 5th April, 1858, this duty shall be reduced to the same rate as tallow candles, 84 cents per cwt., and no discrimination in favor of colonial importation	
tallow, wax or other	20	15	56 cents per cwt	No discriminating duty defined
Candlesticks, spar, alabaster or cut glass	40	30	Articles of cut or fancy glass, $2 40 per cwt.; spar and alabaster candlesticks, 10 per cent.	do do do
all other	30	24	According to material	According to material
Canella alba	20	15	Free	Free
Canes, walking or fishing	30	24	When mounted, painted, or otherwise ornamented, $1 44 = 100.	No discriminating duty defined
			Otherwise, free	Free

TARIFFS—Continued.

DENOMINATION OF MERCHANDISE.	DUTIES ON IMPORTS.			
	Into the United States from foreign nations, per cent. ad valorem, under the act of—		Into Great Britain from foreign nations.	Into Great Britain from the British colonies
	1846.	1857.		
Cantharides	20	8	Free	Free
Canton crapes	25	19	Free	Free
Canvas, hemp, or flax	20	15	Free	Free
of cotton	25	19	Free	Free
Capers	30	24	Including the pickle, 3 cents per pound	No discriminating duty defined
Caps, women's, embroidered or trimmed	30	24	According to the material of which the several sorts are composed	do do do
fur, leather, wool, silk, lace, worsted, or other materials	30	24	do do do	do do do
Cap wire, covered with silk	30	19	Free	Free
cotton	30	24	Free	Free
Caps, percussion	30	24	2 cents per 1,000	No discriminating duty defined
Capsules	30	24	Free	Free
Carbonate of ammonia	20	8	Free	Free
of soda	20	8	Free	Free
of magnesia	30	24	20 per cent. as a medicinal preparation	No discriminating duty defined
of iron	20	15	do do do	do do do
Carboys	30	24	Free	Free
Carbuncles	10	4	Free	Free
Cardamon seed	Free	Free	Free	Free
Cards, blank, playing, and visiting	30	24	Card paper, all fancy kinds 5 cents per pound, playing cards $3 60 per dozen packs	No discriminating duty defined
for carding wool or cotton	30	24	10 per cent. ad valorem	do do do
Card cases	30	24	10 per cent. ad valorem	No discriminating duty defined
Carmine	30	24	Free	Free
Carpets or carpeting of all kinds	30	24	12 cents per square yard	No discriminating duty defined
oil cloth	30	24	(For table covers,) 3 cents per square yard	do do
bindings	25	24	Of cotton or wool, 5 per cent	5 per cent. ad valorem
Carriages of all kinds, and parts thereof	30	24	Free	Free
Carriage springs	30	24	60 cents per cwt	60 cents per cwt
Cascarilla bark	20	8	Free	Free
Casement rods	30	24	Of iron, 60 cents per cwt.; of brass, $2 40 per cwt	No discriminating duty defined

TARIFFS—Continued.

Denomination of merchandise.	Duties on imports. Into the United States, from foreign nations, per cent. ad valorem, under the act of— 1846.	1857.	Into Great Britain from foreign nations.	Into Great Britain from the British colonies.
Cashmere of Thibet	25	19	5 per cent. ad valorem, (being not otherwise defined.)	wholly or in part made up, and
shawls of camels' hair	30	24	5 per cent. ad valorem	5 per cent. ad valorem
Cassada, or meal of	20	15	9 cents per cwt	No discriminating duty defined
Cassia, Chinese, Calcutta or Sumatra	40	4	Cassia lignea 2 cents per pound	do do
buds and fistula of	20	15	Free	Free
oil of	30	24	24 cents per pound	24 cents per pound
Cassimere, wool, and wool and cotton	30	24	Free	Free
cotton	25	24	Free	Free
Castania nuts	30	24	Small nuts and walnuts 24 cents per bushel	No discriminating duty defined
Castings, brass, iron, or other metal	30	24	Of brass, $2 40 per cwt; of iron, viz: rough castings, free; wrought castings, 60 cents per cwt	do do
plaster of Paris	30	24	Of busts, statues, or figures, (not merchandise,) free	Free
Castorum, or castor bean or oil	20	15	Free	Free
Castors, brass or iron, or other metal	30	24	$2 40 per cwt. of brass; 60 cents per cwt. of iron	No discrimination
lignum-vitæ, with metal shanks	30	24	10 per cent. ad valorem	No discriminating duty defined
Casts, bronze	30	24	Works of art, free	Free
Catechu, or terra japonica	10	Free	Free	Free
Catgut strings	20	15	Not defined	Not defined
Catsup	30	24	2 cents, (as sauces,) per pound	No discriminating duty defined
Cayenne pepper	30	4	12 cents per pound, and 5 per cent. additional	No discrimination
Cedar wood	20	8	Free	Free
Cement, Roman	20	15	Free	Free
Chafing dishes, copper, iron, or tin	30	24	$2 40 per cwt.; iron, 60 cents per cwt.; tin, $2 40 per cwt	$2 40 per cwt; iron, 60 cents per cwt.; tin, $2 40 per cwt
Chains and chain cables, or parts thereof	30	24	60 cents per cwt	No discrimination
hair, or of which hair is a component part	30	24	5 per cent. ad valorem	No discriminating duty defined
trace, ox, dog, or other	30	24	(Of iron or steel,) 60 cts. per cwt	do do

TARIFFS—Continued.

DENOMINATION OF MERCHANDISE.	DUTIES ON IMPORTS. Into the United States, from foreign nations, per cent. ad valorem, under the act of— 1846.	1857.	Into Great Britain from foreign nations.	Into Great Britain from the British colonies.
Chairs	30	24	10 per cent. ad valorem	No discriminating duty defined
Chalk, white	4	4	Free	Free
red	20	4	Free	Free
red pencils	30	24	Free	Free
French do	20	4	Free	Free
Chambrays, cotton	25	24	Free	Free
cotton and wool	30	24	Free	Free
silk	25	19	15 per cent. ad valorem	5 per cent. ad valorem
Chamomile flowers	20	15	Free	Free
Charts, and books of	10	Free	Free	Free
Cheese	30	24	60 cents per cwt	36 cents per cwt
Chemical preparations, medicinal, not otherwise defined	30	15	20 per cent. ad valorem	No discriminating duty defined
Chenille silk	25	24	15 per cent. ad valorem	5 per cent. ad valorem
Chesnuts	30	24	Free	Free
Chessmen, of ivory, bone, or wood	30	24	10 per cent. ad valorem	No discriminating duty defined
Chicory	20	Free	Roasted and ground, 8 cents per pound; raw or kiln-dried, up to October 10, 1854, 96 cents per pound; from and since October 10, 1854, free	do do
Chinchilla skins, dressed	20	15	Free	Free
undressed	10	8	Free	Free
China ware	30	24	$2 40 per cwt	No discriminating duty defined
Chip hats or bonnets	30	24	60 cents per pound	do do
Chisels, socket, and other	30	24	60 cents per cwt	do do
Chloride of lime	10	4	Free	Free
Chocolate	20	15	4 cents per cwt	No discriminating duty defined
Chromate of potash	20	15	Free	Free
of lead	20	15	Free	Free
Chrome, yellow	20	24	Free	Free
green	20	24	Free	Free
Choppa romals, (including corahs, chappas, bandannas, and tussone cloths)	25	19	In pieces not exceeding 6¼ yards in length, 12 cents per piece; exceeding 6¼, and not exceeding 7¼ 16 cents; exceeding 7¼ and not exceeding 12 yards, 20 cents per piece	No discriminating duty defined
Crystals	10		Cut, and all kinds of fancy glass, $2 40 per cwt	do do

TARIFFS—Continued.

DENOMINATION OF MERCHANDISE.	DUTIES ON IMPORTS.			
	Into the United States, from foreign nations, per cent. ad valorem, under the act of—		Into Great Britain from foreign nations.	Into Great Britain from the British colonies.
	1846.	1857.		
Crystals, for watches	30	24	(Not cut,) free	No discriminating duty defined
of tin	20	15	$2 40 per cwt	do do
Ciar or coir rope	25	19	Also twine and strands, free	Free
Cicuta	20	15	Free	Free
Cigars	40	30	$2 16 per pound, and 5 per cent. additional thereon (a)	No discrimination
Cinchona, Peruvian	15	Free	Free	Free
Cinnabar	25	19	Free	Free
Cinnamon	30	4	4 cents per pound	4 cents per pound
oil of	30	24	24 cents per pound	24 cents per pound
Citrate of lime	20	15	Free	Free
Citron, oil of	30	24	24 cents per pound	No discriminating duty defined
fruit of	20	8	Preserved with salt, free; raw, not otherwise enumerated, 4 cents per bushel	Free
Civet, oil of	30	24	24 cents per pound	No discriminating duty defined
Clay, unwrought	5	4	Free	Free
ground	20	15	Free	Free
Clocks and parts of clocks	30	24	Not exceeding the value of $1 20 each, 96 cents per dozen; exceeding $1 20, and not exceeding $3 each, $1 92 per dozen; exceeding $3, and not exceeding $14 40 each, 48 cents each; exceeding $14 40, and not exceed ing $48 each, 96 cents each; exceeding $48 each, $2 40 each	
Cloth, oil, floor, patent printed or painted	30	24	3 cents per square yard	3 cents per square yard
Cloth, India rubber	30	24	$1 20 per cwt	$1 20 per cwt
Cloths, all of wool	30	24	Free	Free
Clothing, ready made	30	24	From 5 to 10 per cent. ad valorem, according to the materials of which they are composed, clothing composed in whole or in part of silk, or ladies' clothing, excepted	
Cloves	40	4	4 cents per pound	4 cents per pound
oil of	30	24	24 cents per pound	No discriminating duty defined
Coaches and parts thereof	30	24	Free	Free
Coach and harness furniture of all kinds	30	24	10 per cent. ad valorem, generally, and according to material	
Coal	30	24	Free	Free
hods, copper	30	24	$2 40 per cwt	$2 40 per cwt
iron	30	24	60 cents per cwt	60 cents per cwt
Coatings, mohair, alpaca, and worsted	25	19	Free	Free

(a) Prohibited unless imported in ships of not less than 120 tons burden, in packages not less than eighty pounds, net weight, and into ports approved by the commissioners of customs.—(See Tobacco, *postea*.)

TARIFFS—Continued.

DENOMINATION OF MERCHANDISE.	DUTIES ON IMPORTS.			
	Into the United States from foreign nations, per cent. ad valorem, under the act of—		Into Great Britain from foreign nations.	Into Great Britain from the British colonies.
	1846.	1857.		
Cobalt	20	15	Free	Free
Cochineal	10	4	Free	Free
Cocoa	10	4	2 cents per pound	2 cents per pound
nuts	20	4	Free	Free
shells	10	4	(And husks,) 1 cent per pound	1 cent per pound
matting	25	4	Free	Free
Coculus Indicus	20	15	$1 20 per cwt	$1 20 per cwt
Codfish, dry or salted	20	15	Free	Free
Codilla, or tow of hemp or flax	15	12	Free	Free
Coffee	20(a)	15	6 cents per pound	6 cents per pound
mills	30	24	10 per cent. ad valorem	10 per cent. ad valorem
Coins of gold, silver, and copper	Free	Free	Free, (counterfeit prohibited)	Free
Coir rope	25	19	Free	Free
Coke and culm of coal	30	24	Free	Free
Colocynth, bitter apple	20	Free	Free	Free
Cologne water	30	24	The flask—30 of such flasks containing not more than 1 gallon each, 16 cents; when not in flasks, as perfumed spirit, $4 80 per gallon	No discriminating duty in favor of colonial importation
Coloquintida	20	24	Free	Free
Colombo root	20	15	Free	Free
Combs, brush-makers'	30	24	10 per cent. ad valorem	10 per cent. ad valorem
curry	30	24	60 cents per cwt	60 cents per cwt
gilt, iron, steel	30	24	If fancy and ornamental, $3 60 per cwt; otherwise, 60 cents per cwt	do
lead	30	24	24 cents per cwt	24 cents per cwt
ivory, shell, horn, and all others	30	24	10 per cent. ad valorem	10 per cent. ad valorem
Comfits of all kinds	40	30	4 cents per pound	4 cents per pound
Coney wool, or hair for hatters	10	8	Free	Free
Copper bolts, rods, nails, spikes, and bottoms	20	15	$2 40 per cwt	$2 40 per cwt
old, fit only to be remanufactured	5	Free	Free	Free
pigs or bars	5	Free	Free	Free
Copper plates for engravers, if polished and finished	30	24	$2 40 if engraved; otherwise, free.	No discriminating duty defined

(a) From the place of its growth or production, in American or equalized vessels, or of the growth of Netherlands colonies, from the Netherlands—free.

TARIFFS—Continued.

DENOMINATION OF MERCHANDISE.	DUTIES ON IMPORTS.			
	Into the United States, from foreign nations, per cent. ad valorem, under the act of—		Into Great Britain from foreign nations.	Into Great Britain from the British colonies.
	1846.	1857.		
Copper sheathing for ships, 14 × 48 inches, weighing from 14 to 34 ounces per square foot	Free	Free	Free	Free
vessels, scales, and rivets of	30	24	$2 40 per cwt	$2 40 per cwt
wire	30	Free	Free	Free
for the use of the mint	Free	Free	Free	Free
all other manufactures of	30	24	$2 40 per cwt	$2 40 per cwt
sulphate of	20	15	Free	Free
Copperas	20	15	(Blue, green, white.) Free	Free
Coral, beads	30	24	36 cents per pound	36 cents per pound
negligèes	30	24	24 cents per pound	24 cents per pound
marine, unmanufactured	20	15	Free	Free
Cordage, tarred and untarred	25	19	Free	Free
Cordials of all kinds	100	30	$4 80 per gallon	No discrimination
Coriander seed	Free	Free	Free	Free
Cork tree, bark of, unmanufactured	15	4	Free	Free
Cork, manufactures of	30	24	10 per cent. ad valorem	10 per cent. ad valorem
Corks, ready made	30	24	12 cents per pound	12 cents per pound
Carnelian, unset, (real or imitation)	10	4	Free	Free
rings	20	15	10 per cent. ad valorem	10 per cent. ad valorem
Cosmetics	30	24	4 cents per pound	4 cents per pound
Cotton, raw	Free	Free	Free	Free
bagging, of any weight or width	25	15	Free	Free
cords, gimps, and galloons	30	24	5 per cent. ad valorem	5 per cent. ad valorem
laces, insertings, trimming laces, laces and braids, coach, and other	25	24	do do	do do
stockings	20	24	12 cents per dozen pairs	12 cents per dozen pairs
gloves and mits	20	24	6 cents per dozen pairs	6 cents per dozen pairs
caps, shirts, and drawers	20	24	5 per cent. ad valorem	5 per cent. ad valorem
twist, yarn, or thread	25	24	Free	Free
braces or suspenders	30	24	5 per cent. ad valorem	5 per cent. ad valorem
Cowage or cowitch	20	14	Free	Free
Cranks, mill, wrought iron	30	24	60 cents per cwt	60 cents per cwt
Crash, Russia linen	20	15	Free	Free
Crayons, of all kinds	30	24	Free	Free
Cream of tartar	20	4	Free	Free

TARIFFS—Continued.

DENOMINATION OF MERCHANDISE.	DUTIES ON IMPORTS.			
	Into the United States, from foreign nations, per cent. ad valorem, under the act of—		Into Great Britain from foreign nations.	Into Great Britain from the British colonies.
	1846.	1857.		
Crea's linen	20	15	Free	Free
cotton	25	24	Free	Free
Crucibles, sand and black lead	30	24	Free	Free
Crocus martis	20	15	Free	Free
Cubebs	20	15	Free	Free
Cudbear	10	4	Free	Free
Cummin seed	Free	Free	Free	Free
Currants	40	8	$3 60 per cwt., and 5 per cent. ad valorem additional	No discriminating duty defined
Curriers' knives	30	24	60 cents per cwt	60 cents per cwt
Cut glass, all wares of, not otherwise defined	40	30	$2 40 per cwt	$2 40 per cwt
Cutch	10	Free	Free	Free
Cutlasses	30	24	When not prohibited, 60 cents per cwt	60 cents per cwt
Cutlery of all kinds	30	24	60 cents per cwt	do
Cutting knives	30	24	do	do
Cyanite of potassum	30	24	Free	Free
of zinc	30	24	Free	Free
of any other metal	30	24	Free	Free
Dates	40	4	$2 40 per cwt	$2 40 per cwt
Decanters, cut	40	30	do	do
plain	30	24	Free	Free
Delf ware	30	24	$2 40 per cwt	$2 40 per cwt
Demijohns, all sizes	30	24	Free	Free
Denmark satins, silk and stuff	25	19	$1 20 per pound	$1 20 per pound
Devonshire kerseys	30	24	Free	Free
Diamonds, when not set	10	4	Free	Free
when set	30	24	10 per cent. ad valorem	10 per cent. ad valorem
Diapers, linen	20	15	Free	Free
cotton	25	24	Free	Free
Dice, bone or ivory	30	24	$5 04 per pair	$5 04 per pair
Dimities, furniture, cambric, and other	25	24	Free	Free
Dirks and daggers	30	24	When not prohibited, 60 cents per cwt	60 cents per cwt
Dishes, pewter	30	24	48 cents per cwt	48 cents per cwt
copper and tin	30	24	$2 40 per cwt	$2 40 per cwt
iron	30	24	60 cents per cwt	60 cents per cwt
Diuretic salt	20	15	Free	Free
Divi divi, a bean used in tanning	20	Free	Free	Free

TARIFFS—Continued.

DENOMINATION OF MERCHANDISE.	DUTIES ON IMPORTS. Into the United States from foreign nations, per cent. ad valorem, under the act of— 1846.	1857.	Into Great Britain from foreign nations.	Into Great Britain from the British colonies
Down of all kinds	25	19	Free	Free
tippets, muffs, victorines	30	24	If manufactured of skins or furs, free; otherwise, according to material	
Dowlas, flax	20	15	Free	Free
Doyleys, linen	20	15	Free	Free
cotton and worsted	25	24	Free	Free
wool	30	24	Free	Free
Dragons' blood	15	Free	Free	Free
Drawing knives	30	24	60 cents per cwt	60 cents per cwt
Drawing paper	30	24	5 cents per pound	5 cents per pound
pencils	30	24	Free	Free
Drawings	10	15	Plain or colored, 6 cents per lb	No discrimination
Dried pulp	20	15	Free	Free
Drillings, linen	20	15	Free	Free
cotton	25	24	Free	Free
Drugs, for dyes, not otherwise enumerated	20	Free	Free	Free
not otherwise enumerated	30	15	Free	Free
Duck, Holland, Raven's, Russia, sail	20	15	Free	Free
Dutch pink	20	15	Free	Free
Dyeing articles, not otherwise defined	20	Free	Free	Free
Dye woods, in sticks	5	Free	Free	Free
Earthen ware, not otherwise described	30	24	$2 40 per cwt	$2 40 per cwt
Ebony, unmanufactured	20	8	Free	Free
manufactures of	40	30	10 per cent. ad valorem	10 per cent. ad valorem
Elephants' teeth	5	Free	Free	Free
Elastic, gum, in bottles, slabs and sheets	10	4	All manufactures of, not moulded, $1 20 per cwt; moulded, 4 cents per pound	
web	30	24	Moulded, 8 cents per pound	
garters	30	24	do do do	
Emery	20	8	Free	Free
Emetic, tartar	30	24	As a medicinal preparation, 10 per cent	No discrimination
Enamel	20	Free	Free	Free
Engravers' copper plates, polished and finished	30	24	If engraved, $2 40 per cwt.; otherwise, free	No discriminating duty defined

TARIFFS—Continued.

DENOMINATION OF MERCHANDISE.	DUTIES ON IMPORTS.			
	Into the United States from foreign nations, per cent. ad valorem, under the act of—		Into Great Britain from foreign nations.	Into Great Britain from the British colonies.
	1846.	1857.		
Epaulets, cotton	25	24	As "manufactures of cotton," 5 per cent	5 per cent. ad valorem
gold, silver, or other metal	30	24	As "manufactured goods," 10 per cent. ad valorem	10 per cent. ad valorem
silk	25	24	15 per cent. ad valorem	5 per cent. ad valorem
worsted	25	24	5 per cent. ad valorem	do do
Epsom salts	20	15	Free	Free
Essences as perfumery	30	24	4 cents per pound	4 cents per pound
for medicinal purposes	30	24	20 per cent. ad valorem	20 per cent. ad valorem
Estopillas, linen	20	15	Free	Free
Etchings or engravings	10	8	As merchandise, 10 per cent.;	otherwise, free
Ether	20	15	20 per cent. ad valorem	20 per cent. ad valorem
Extracts for the toilet	30	24	4 cents per pound	4 cents per pound
for medicinal purposes	30	24	Extract of cardamoms, coculus indicus, Guinea grains and grains of Paradise, liquorice, nux vomica, opium, Guinea pepper, Peruvian, or Jesuits' bark, quassia, radix rhataniæ, vitriol, viz: 20 per cent. Extract of chesnut bark, quercitron bark, logwood, safflower, and all extracts of bark, or other vegetable substances used for tanning, or other manufacturing purposes, free. All other extracts and preparations not otherwise defined, 20 per ct.	
Extract of indigo, logwood, and other dye wood, of madder	20	4	Free	Free
Fancy boxes	30	24	10 per cent. ad valorem	10 per cent. ad valorem
or perfumed soaps	30	24	4 cents per pound	4 cents per pound
bottles, if cut glass or alabaster	40	24	Cut glass, $2 40 per cwt.; alabaster, 10 per cent. ad valorem	No discrimination
Fans of all descriptions	30	24	10 per cent. ad valorem	10 per cent. ad valorem
Feathers, for beds	25	19	Free	Free
ornamental	30	24	Dressed, 72 cents per pound; undressed, free	Dressed, 72 cents per pound; undressed, free
Feldspar	20	15	Free	Free
Felts, or hat bodies, made wholly or in part of wool	20	15	5 per cent. ad valorem	5 per cent. ad valorem
wholly of cotton	30	24	do do	do do
Ferri, rubigo	20	15	Free	Free
Fiddles	20	15	10 per cent. ad valorem	10 per cent. ad valorem
Fifes, wood, bone, or ivory	20	15	do do	do do
Fig blue	20	15	Free	Free

TARIFFS—Continued.

DENOMINATION OF MERCHANDISE.	DUTIES ON IMPORTS.			
	Into the United States from foreign nations, per cent. ad valorem, under the act of—		Into Great Britain from foreign nations.	Into Great Britain from the British colonies.
	1846.	1857.		
Figs	40	8	$3 60 per cwt , and 5 per cent additional	$3 60 per cwt., and 5 per ct. add'l.
Filberts	30	24	24 cents per bushel	24 cents per bushel
Files of all kinds	30	24	60 cents per cwt	60 cents per cwt
Filtering stones, unmanufactured	20	15	Free	Free
Fire-arms of all kinds	30	24	10 per cent. ad valorem, if not prohibited	10 per cent. ad valorem
Fire crackers	30	24	do do	do do
irons, wrought	30	24	60 cents per cwt	60 cents per cwt
works	30	24	10 per cent. ad valorem	10 per cent. ad valorem
wood	30	24	Fathom of 216 cubic feet, $1 44	Free
Fish, foreign, whether fresh, smoked, salted, dried, or pickled, not otherwise provided for	20	15	Free(*a*)	Free
salmon, preserved	30	24	Free	Free
in oil	40	30	Free	Free
glue	20	15	Free	Free
hooks	30	24	60 cents per cwt	60 cents per cwt
skins	20	15	Free	Free
Flannels, all	25	19	Not made up, wholly or in part	Free, and no discrimination
Flasks, powder, copper, or brass	30	24	$2 40 per cwt	$2 40 per cwt
japanned	30	24	$4 80 per cwt	$4 80 per cwt
Flat irons, or sad irons	30	24	60 cents per cwt	60 cents per cwt
Flats for hats or bonnets, straw	30	24	Of chip, not being of greater value than 12 cents per piece of 60 yards, 12 cents per pound.	
Flax, unmanufactured, and codilla of	15	Free	Free	Free
all manufactures of, not otherwise specified	20	15	Not made up, free ; made up, 5 per cent	No discriminating duty defined
carpeting	30	24	5 per cent. ad valorem	5 per cent. ad valorem
sewing thread	20	15	Free	Free
seed	20	15	Free	Free
Fleams, steel, lancet	30	24	60 cents per cwt	60 cents per cwt
Flies, Spanish, or cantharides	20	8	Free	Free
Flints	5	4	Free	Free
Floor cloths, stamped, printed, or painted	30	24	3 cents per yard	3 cents per yard

(*a*) Prior to 1850, the importation of fish of foreign taking or curing, and in foreign vessels, was either totally prohibited or burdened with such restrictions and duties as were equivalent to a prohibition. Since 1850, the British policy with respect to this necessary article of food has entirely changed ; and fish, no matter where or by whom taken or cured or in what bottoms imported are now admitted free of duty.—(The Customs Tariff Ac 1853, 16 and 17 Vict. chap. 106.)

TARIFFS—Continued.

DENOMINATION OF MERCHANDISE.	DUTIES ON IMPORTS. Into the United States from foreign nations, per cent. ad valorem, under the act of— 1846.	1857.	Into Great Britain from foreign nations.	Into Great Britain from the British colonies.
Floor cloths, of baize or bocking	25	24	12 cents per square yard	No discriminating duty defined
Floor matting, of flags, jute or grass, or cocoa	25	19	10 per cent. ad valorem, as "manufactured goods." (a)	do do
Floss silks	25	19	15 per cent. ad valorem	5 per cent. ad valorem
Flour, wheat, or other grain	20	15	9 cents per cwt. (b)	
brimstone or sulphur	20	15	Free	Free
Flushings	30	24	Free	Free
Flutes and fifes of all kinds	20	15	10 per cent. ad valorem	10 per cent. ad valorem
Foils, gold, silver, and copper	30	24	do do	do do
tin	15	12	$2 40 per cwt	$2 40 per cwt
Forks of all kinds	30	24	Silver, 10 per cent. ad valorem Steel, 60 cents per cwt	10 per cent ad valorem 60 cents per cwt
Forte pianos	20		Horizontal or grand, $14 40 each Upright or square, $9 60 each	Horizontal or grand, $14 40 each Upright or square, $9 60 each
Fossils	Free	Free	Free	Free
Frames and sticks for parasols or umbrellas	30	24	72 cents per cwt	72 cents per cwt
Frankfort black	20	15	Free	Free
Frankincense, a gum	20	8	Free	Free
Frizettes, hair	30	24	5 per cent. ad valorem	5 per cent. ad valorem
silk	30	24	15 per cent. ad valorem	do do
Frocks, Guernsey, and all ready made	30	24	5 per cent. ad valorem	do do
Fruits, green or ripe, not otherwise provided for	20	8	4 cents per bushel	4 cents per bushel
Fruits, pickled	30	24	10 per cent. ad valorem	10 per cent. ad valorem
Frying pans	30	24	60 cents per cwt	60 cents per cwt
Fuller's earth	10	8	Free	Free
boards	30	24	10 per cent. ad valorem	10 per cent. ad valorem
Fulminates or fulminating powders	20	15	do do	do do
Furniture, cabinet and household	30	24	10 per cent. ad valorem	do do
brass, gilt or plated, and copper	30	24	$2 40 per cwt	$2 40 per cwt
iron and steel	30	24	60 cents per cwt	
oil cloth for	30	24	3 cents per square yard	3 cents per square yard
Furs, dressed on the skin	20	15	Free	Free
undressed on the skin	10	8	Free	Free
hatters', dressed or undressed, not on the skin	10	8	Free	Free

(a) "Mats and matting" are entered in the British tariff as "free goods;" but this, doubtless, refers to common entrance mats.

(b) The duties upon corn, grain, meal, and flour, are to be paid on importation, and such goods may not be warehoused, either for home consumption or exportation.—(16 and 17 Vict., ch. 107, s. 41.)

TARIFFS—Continued.

Denomination of merchandise.	Duties on imports. Into the United States from foreign nations, per cent. ad valorem, under the act of— 1846.	1857.	Into Great Britain from foreign nations.	Into Great Britain from the British colonies.
Furs, caps, hats, muffs, tippets, coats, and gloves, hat bodies or felts	30	24	Not being otherwise defined, these articles are classed with "manufactured goods," at 10 per cent. ad valorem (a)	No discriminating duty defined
Fustic, in the stick	5	Free	Free	Free
Galls, nut	5	Free	Free	Free
Garters, elastic and all others	30	24	Elastic, 8 cents per pound; others according to material	Elastic, 8 cents per pound; others according to material
Gelatine	30	24	Free	Free
Gems, not set	10	4	Free	Free
set	30	24	10 per cent. ad valorem	10 per cent. ad valorem
Gentian root	20	15	Free	Free
German silver, alabata, or argentine	30	24	Free	Free
Gig hames, japanned	20	24	10 per cent. ad valorem	10 per cent. ad valorem
Gilt wares of all kinds	30	24	According to solid material	According to solid material
Gimlets	30	24	60 cents per cwt	60 cents per cwt
Gimp, cotton	30	24	Free	Free
wire	30	24	Free	Free
silk, or silk and cotton	25	19	15 per cent. ad valorem	5 per cent. ad valorem
Gin	100	30	$3 60 per gallon	
cases of wood, empty, or with bottles	30	24	As "goods manufactured," 10 per cent	No discriminating duty defined
Ginger, ground	30	15	$1 20 per cwt	$1 20 per cwt
root, dried, or green, or preserved	40	15	3 cents per pound	3 cents per pound
oil and essence	30	24	24 cents per pound	24 cents per pound
Ginseng	20	15	Free	Free
Glass, vials and bottles	30	24	Free	Free
demijohns	30	24	Free	Free
cut, not otherwise specified	40	30	$2 40 per cwt	$2 40 per cwt
window, broad, crown, or cylinder	20	15	Until April, 1857, 36 cents per	cwt; afterwards free
colored, stained, or painted	30	24	$2 40 per cwt	$2 40 per cwt
Glass, paintings on	30	24	$2 40 per cwt	$2 40 per cwt
looking, silvered or unsilvered	30	24	Free	Free

(a) Skins and furs, or pieces of skins or furs, raw and undressed, or tanned, tawed, curried, or in any way dressed, and all articles manufactured of skins and furs, are admitted free of duty.—(16 and 17 Vic., chap. 106.)

TARIFFS—Continued.

DENOMINATION OF MERCHANDISE.	DUTIES ON IMPORTS. Into the United States from foreign nations, per cent. ad valorem, under the act of— 1846.	1857.	Into Great Britain from foreign nations.	Into Great Britain from the British colonies.
Glass, all other manufactures of	30	24	Free	Free
Glauber salts	20	15	Free	Free
Globes	30(a)	24	10 per cent. ad valorem	10 per cent. ad valorem
Gloves, cotton and Lisle	20	24	5 per cent. ad valorem	5 per cent. ad valorem
of leather	30	24	Men's, 84 cents per dozen pairs, and 5 per cent. additional; women's, $1 08 per dozen pairs, and 5 per cent. additional	
of silk	30	24	15 per cent. ad valorem	5 per cent. ad valorem
of thread	30	24	6 cents per dozen pairs	6 cents per dozen pairs
wool, and all others	30	24	Of wool, 6 cents per dozen pairs	do do
Glue	20	15	Free	Free
Goats' hair or wool	20	Fr e	Free	Free
skins, raw	5	4	Free	Free
tanned	20	19	Free	Free
Gold, all articles composed wholly or chiefly of	30	24	10 per cent., as manufactured goods	10 per cent. ad valorem
Gold beaters' skins	10	8	Free	Free
Gold, bullion, coin, or dust	Free	Free	Free	Free
epaulets, lace and embroideries	30	24	10 per cent. ad valorem; if the lace be silk, 15 per cent. ad valorem	10 per cent. ad valorem; if the lace be silk, 5 per cent. ad valorem
Gold leaf	15	12	Free(b)	Free
watches	10	8	Watches of gold or silver, or of any other metal, exceeding the value of $48, $4 80 each; other watches, viz: gold, open faces, $1 20 each; hunters', $1 80 each; repeaters, $3 60 each	No discriminating duty
muriate of	20	....	Free	Free
Goods of American produce(c)	Free	Free	According to character, &c	According to character, &c
Gouges	30	24	60 cents per cwt	60 cents per cwt
Granella, cochineal	10	4	Free	Free
Grass cloth	25	19	10 per cent. ad valorem	10 per cent. ad valorem
baskets	30	24	8 cents per cubic foot	8 cents per cubic foot

(a) By act of August 12, 1848, globes are exempted from duty, provided they be "specially imported in good faith for the use of any society incorporated or established for philosophical or literary purposes, or for the encouragement of the fine arts; or for the use or by the order of any college, academy, school, or seminary of learning in the United States."

(b) Clocks and watches, of any metal, impressed with any mark or stamp appearing to be or to represent any legal British assay mark or stamp, or purporting by any mark or appearance to be of the manufacture of the United Kingdom, are prohibited.—(Beedell's British Tariff, 1854-'55, p. 3.)

(c) Goods, wares, and merchandise of American produce or manufacture exported to a foreign country and brought back to the United States in the same condition as when exported, upon which no drawback or bounty has been allowed, are admitted free. Such goods, wares, and merchandise must be in *precisely* the same condition as when exported; otherwise they will be liable to their appropriate duties respectively.—(Treasury decision.)

TARIFFS—Continued.

DENOMINATION OF MERCHANDISE.	DUTIES ON IMPORTS. Into the United States from foreign nations, per cent. ad valorem, under the act of— 1846.	1857.	Into Great Britain from foreign nations.	Into Great Britain from the British colonies.
Grass, flags and mats	25	19	Free	Free
hats or bonnets	30	24	10 per cent. ad valorem	10 per cent. ad valorem
ropes or cordage	25	19	Free	Free
Grease and tallow for soap stock	10	8	Free	Free
Green Battersea, (paint)	20	15	Free	Free
Grindstones, wrought or unwrought	5	4	Free	Free
Guano	Free	Free	Free	Free
Guernsey frocks	30	24	5 per cent. ad valorem	5 per cent. ad valorem
Guitar, or gut strings for	20	15	10 per cent. ad valorem	10 per cent. ad valorem
Gum, Arabic, Senegal, tragacanth	10	8	In the British tariff the following gums are free, viz: animi, copal, Senegal, lac dye, seedlac, shel lac, sticklac, ammiacum, asafœtida, euphorbium, guiacum, kino, mastic, tragacanth, unenumerated	
Barbary, East India, Jedda	10	8		
Benzoin or Benjamin	30	24		
perdu and kino	20	15		
lac	20	15		
substitute, or British starch	10	8		
all other for dyeing	20	8		
medicinal	20	15		
Gunny cloth and bags	20	15	Gunny cloth, free; bags not defined, except as "manufactured goods," 10 per cent	
Gunpowder	20	15	Free	Free
Gun wadding, of paper	30	24	10 per cent. ad valorem	10 per cent. ad valorem
Guns and parts thereof	30	24	10 per cent. ad valorem, (comprising muskets, rifles, carbines, fowling pieces, or guns of any sort not otherwise enumerated, and pistols)	
Gutta percha, unmanufactured	10	4	Free	Free
manufactures of	20	15	$1 20 per cwt	$1 20 per cwt
Gypsum, unground	Free	Free	Free	Free
Haarlem oil	30	24	Free	Free
Hair, bracelets, braids, and head dresses	30	24	10 per cent. ad valorem	5 per cent. ad valorem and 5 per cent. additional
Hair, goats', Thibet and alpaca raw	20	Free	Free	Free
curled, for beds and mattresses	20	15	Free	Free
human, prepared for use	30	24	Free	Free
pencils	30	24	Free	Free
pins	30	24	10 per cent. ad valorem	10 per cent. ad valorem
Halter chains	30	24	60 cents per cwt	60 cents per cwt
Hammers, blacksmiths', and all others	30	24	60 cents per cwt	60 cents per cwt
Hams	20	15	Free	Free

TARIFFS—Continued.

DENOMINATION OF MERCHANDISE.	DUTIES ON IMPORTS. Into the United States from foreign nations, per cent. ad valorem, under the act of— 1846.	1857.	Into Great Britain from foreign nations.	Into Great Britain from the British colonies.
Handkerchiefs, (linen)	20	15	Cambric, hemmed or hemmed-stitched, not trimmed, 60 cents per dozen	No discriminating duty defined
			Bordered, not trimmed, free	Free
silk	25	19	Plain and damask, 72 cents per pound; embroidered, $1 20 per pound; pongees, (including twilled handkerchiefs,) plain and figured, in pieces not exceeding 9 yards in length, 36 cents per piece; exceeding 9 yards and not exceeding 18 in length, 72 cents per piece	No discrimination
Hangers, or side-arms	30	24	When not prohibited, 60 cents per cwt	60 cents per cwt
Hangings, paper	20	15	Printed, painted, or stained, or flock paper, 6 cents per pound	No discriminating duty defined
Hares' hair or fur	10	8	Free	Free
skins undressed	10	8	Free	Free
dressed	20	15	Free	Free
Harness, as manufactures of leather	30	24	10 per cent. ad valorem	10 per cent. ad valorem
Harps and harpsichords	20	15	10 per cent. ad valorem	10 per cent. ad valorem
strings, gut	20	15	10 per cent ad valorem; harp and lute strings, silvered	Free
Hartshorn	30	24	As a medicinal preparation, 20 per cent	20 per cent. ad valorem
Hatchets	30	24	60 cents per cwt	60 cents per cwt
Hats or bonnets, of all kinds	30	24	Chip, baste, cane, horse hair, or straw, 60 cents per pound; felt, hair, wool, beaver, silk, or silk shag laid upon felt, linen, or other material, 24 cents each	No discriminating duty defined
Hat bodies or felts, in whole or in part of wool	20	15	5 per cent. ad valorem	5 per cent. ad valorem
of cotton	30	24	do do	do do
Hearth rugs	30	24	12 cents per square yard	12 cents per square yard
Hellebore root	20	15	Free	Free
Hemlock, cicuta	20	4	Free	Free
Hemp, unmanufactured	30	24	Free	Free
carpeting	30	24	5 per cent. ad valorem	5 per cent. ad valorem
Manila, or Sisal grass	25	19	Free	Free
seed	10	8	Free	Free

TARIFFS—Continued.

DENOMINATION OF MERCHANDISE.	DUTIES ON IMPORTS.			
	Into the United States from foreign nations, per cent. ad valorem, under the act of—		Into Great Britain from foreign nations.	Into Great Britain from the British colonies.
	1846.	1857.		
Hemp seed, oil of	20	15	Free	Free
Herrings, pickled, smoked, or dried	20	15	Free	Free
Hessians, linens	20	15	Free	Free
Hides, raw, dried, or salted	5	4	Free	Free
tanned	20	15	Free	Free
Hinges, brass, iron, or other metal	30	24	Brass, $2 40 per cwt.; iron or steel, 60 cents per cwt.	Brass, $2 40 per cwt.; iron or steel, 60 cents per cwt
Ho by horses	30	24	10 per cent. ad valorem	10 per cent. ad valorem
Hods, coal, iron	30	24	60 cents per cwt	60 cents per cwt
copper	30	24	$2 40 per cwt	$2 40 per cwt
Hoes	30	24	60 cents per cwt	60 cents per cwt
Holland flax	20	15	Free	Free
Honey	30	24	Free	Free
Hooks, reaping	30	24	60 cents per cwt	60 cents per cwt
fish, dress, horn	30	24	10 per cent. ad valorem	10 per cent. ad valorem
Hoop iron and hoops	30	24	Free	Free
Hops	20	15	Until August 1, 1855, $4 80 per cwt.; from and after that date, $10 80 per cwt	No discriminating duty defined
Horns and horn tips	5	4	Free	Free
Horse hair	10	8	Free	Free
Hose, Angora, wool, worsted	30	24	5 per cent. ad valorem	5 per cent. ad valorem
silk and linen	30	24	Linen, 5 per cent. ad val.; silk, 15 per cent	Linen, 5 per cent.; silk, 5 per ct.
cotton	20	24	12 cents per dozen pairs	12 cents per dozen pairs
embroidered	30	24	10 per cent. ad valorem	5 per cent. ad valorem
Lisle thread	20	24	12 cents per dozen pairs	12 cents per dozen pairs
Ice	20	Free	Free	Free
Images, alabaster	40	30	10 per cent. ad valorem	10 per cent. ad valorem
brass and copper	30	24	$2 40 per cwt	$2 40 per cwt
China, marble, and wood, or plaster of Paris	30	24	10 per cent. ad valorem	10 per cent. ad valorem
Implements of trade of persons arriving in the United States	Free	Free	See "Digests," Vol. I, p. 42	See "Digests," Vol. I, p. 42
India rubber, in bottles, slabs, sheets, unmanufactured	10	4	$1 20 per cwt	Free
cloth, web, or shoes	30	24	4 cents per pound	8 cents per pound
suspenders, garters	30	24	do do	do do
Indigo	10	4	Free	Free

TARIFFS—Continued.

DENOMINATION OF MERCHANDISE.	DUTIES ON IMPORTS. Into the United States from foreign nations, per cent. ad valorem, under the act of— 1846.	1857.	Into Great Britain from foreign nations.	Into Great Britain from the British colonies.
Indian corn and corn meal	20	15	Corn meal 9 cents per cwt. (a)	Corn meal 9 cents per cwt (a)
Ink, India	30	24	Free	Free
printing, all kinds	30	24	Free	Free
powder	30	24	Free	Free
Ink-stands, cut glass	40	30	$2 40 per cwt	$2 40 per cwt
all other	30	24	10 per cent. ad valorem	10 per cent. ad valorem
Instruments, philosophical	30	24	According to component material	According to component material.
mathematical, in cases	30	24	10 per cent. ad valorem	10 per cent. ad valorem
surgical	30	24	60 cents per cwt	60 cents per cwt
musical	20	15	Not otherwise defined, 10 per ct	10 per cent. ad valorem
Inventions, models of	Free	Free	(Not merchandise.) Free	Free
Iodine	20	15	Free	Free
salts of	20	15	20 per cent. ad valorem	20 per cent. ad valorem
Ipecacuanha	20	15	Free	Free
Iridium, (a metallic ore)	20	15	Free	Free
Iris, or orris root	20	15	Free	Free
Iron, all manufactures of, or of which it is a component material	30	24	60 cents per cwt	60 cents per cwt
carbonate of	20	15	As a medicinal preparation, 20 per cent	20 per cent
sulphate of	20	15	do do	do
old, and only fit to be re-manufactured	30	24	Free	Free
pig, bar, sheet, and all other	30	24	Free	Free
wire	30	24	Free	Free
isinglass, or gelatine	20	15	Free	Free
Ivory, unmanufactured	5	Free	Free	Free
Ivory balls, chessmen, combs, and scales	30	24	10 per cent. ad valorem	10 per cent. ad valorem
Ivory black	20	15	Free	Free
vegetable, manufactures of	30	24	10 per cent. ad valorem	10 per cent. ad valorem
nuts, or vegetable ivory	5	4	Free	Free
Jack screws and chains	30	24	60 cents per cwt	60 cents per cwt
Jalap	20	15	Free	Free
Jars, China, earthen ware, or stone ware	30	24	$2 40 per cwt	$2 40 per cwt
Jean, cotton	25	24	Free	Free
Jerked beef	20	15	Free	Free

(a) Indian corn 24 cents per quarter, or 8 bushels.

TARIFFS—Continued.

Denomination of merchandise.	Duties on imports.			
	Into the United States from foreign nations, per cent. ad valorem, under the act of—		Into Great Britain from foreign nations.	Into Great Britain from the British colonies.
	1846.	1857.		
Jessamine, oil of	30	24	24 cents per pound	24 cents per pound
Jet, and manufactures of jet, and imitations	30	24	Manufactures of, 10 per cent.; unmanufactured, free	Manufactures of, 10 per cent.; unmanufactured, free
Jewelry	30	24	10 per cent ad valorem	10 per cent. ad valorem
Jostic, or joslight	20	15	Free	Free
Juice, lemon, and lime	10	8	Free	Free
oranges	20	15	Free	Free
Juniper berries	20	15	Free	Free
oil of	30	24	24 cents per pound	24 cents per pound
Junk, old	Free	Free	Free	Free
Jute, unmanufactured	25	19	Free	Free
twist	20	15	Free	Free
matting	25	24	Free	Free
Kelp	10	8	Free	Free
Kerseys and kerseymere	30	24	Free	Free
Kettles, brass, iron, copper, or other metal	30	24	Of brass or copper, $2 40 per cwt.; of iron, 60 cents per cwt	Of brass or copper, $2 40 per cwt.; of iron, 60 cents per cwt
Keys, watch, brass, steel, or other metal	30	24	Brass, $2 40 per cwt.; iron, 60 cents per cwt	Brass, $2 40 per cwt.; iron, 60 cents per cwt
Knitting needles	20	15	Of iron, 60 cents per cwt.; of wire, 10 per cent	Of iron, 60 cents per cwt.; of wire, 10 per cent
Knives, cutting, drawing, and all other	30	24	60 cents per cwt	60 cents per cwt
Knobs, brass or plated	30	24	$2 40 (brass) per cwt	$2 40 per cwt
coach and commode	30	24	60 cents (iron) per cwt; $2 40 (cut glass) per cwt	No discriminating duty defined
Kreosote	30	24	Free	Free
Labels, porcelain	30	24	$2 40 per cwt	$2 40 per cwt
Lac dye, a gum	5	4	Free	Free
sulphur	20	4	Free	Free
Lace, gold, silver, or plated	30	24	10 per cent. ad valorem	10 per cent. ad valorem
cotton	25	24	The classification of laces, in the British tariff, seems to be predicated not so much upon the quality of the different articles compre- hended under the general term "laces," as upon the mode of man-	
silk	25	19		
worsted	25	19		

TARIFFS—Continued.

DENOMINATION OF MERCHANDISE.	DUTIES ON IMPORTS. Into the United States from foreign nations, per cent. ad valorem, under the act of— 1846.	1857.	Into Great Britain from foreign nations.	Into Great Britain from the British colonies.
			ufacturing them: silk lace, for example, if made in the loom, is subject only to a duty of 15 per cent., whilst the same article, if made by the hand, pays $7 20 per pound.	
Laces, silk, or other	25	19	Silk, 15 per cent. ad val.; cotton, 5 per cent. ad valorem	5 per cent. ad valorem
Lacquered ware	30	24	$4 80 per cwt	$4 80 per cwt
Lake, water color	30	24	Free	Free
Lamp black	20	15	Free	Free
Lamps, copper, tin, or brass	30	24	$2 40 per cwt	$2 40 per cwt
cut glass	40	30	do	do
Lanterns, horn, tin, wire, and all others	30	24	Tin, $2 40 per cwt; All others, 10 per cent. ad valorem	$2 40 per cwt; 10 per cent. ad valorem
Lard	20	15	Free	Free
Lastings suitable for shoes, boots, bootees, or buttons	5	4	5 per cent. ad valorem	5 per cent. ad valorem
Lath	20	15	$2 88 per fathom, or 2 yards = 6 feet	24 cents per fathom, or 2 yards = 6 feet
Laurel, oil of	30	24	Free	Free
Lavender, essence, oil, or water of	30	24	24 cents per pound	24 cents per pound
Laudanum	30	24	20 per cent. ad valorem	20 per cent. ad valorem
Lavender flowers	20	15	Free	Free
Lawns, cotton cambric	25	24	Free	Free
linen cambric	20	15	Free	Free
Lead black	20	15	Free	Free
crucibles and pots	30	24	Free	Free
nitrate of	20	15	Free	Free
old and scrap	20	15	Free	Free
pencils	30	24	Free	Free
pigs, bars, or sheets	20	15	Free	Free
red and white, ground in oil or dry	20	15	Free	Free
shot	20	15	48 cents per cwt	48 cents per cwt
sugar of	20	15	Free	Free
pipes	20	15	48 cents per cwt	48 cents per cwt
all manufactures of, or of which it is a material, not otherwise specified	30	24	48 cents per cwt	48 cents per cwt
Leaf, gold and silver	15	12	Free	Free
Leaves, medicinal, in a crude state	20	15	Free	Free
Leather, caps or hats of, patent or japanned	20	19	10 per cent. ad valorem	10 per cent. ad valorem

TARIFFS—Continued.

Denomination of merchandise.	Duties on imports. Into the United States from foreign nations, per cent. ad valorem, under the act of— 1846.	1857.	Into Great Britain from foreign nations.	Into Great Britain from the British colonies.
Leather, all other manufactures of not otherwise specified	30	24	10 per cent. ad valorem	10 per cent. ad valorem
Leeches	20	15	Free	Free
Lees of wine, liquid	20	15	$1 32 per gallon and 5 per cent. additional	66 cents per gallon and 5 per cent. additional
of argols	5	4	Free	Free
Leghorn hats or bonnets, and all hats or bonnets of straw, chip, or grass	30	24	60 cents per pound	60 cents per pound
Lemons	20	8	16 cents per bushel	16 cents per bushel
essence of or oil	30	24	24 cents per pound	24 cents per pound
juice of	10	8	Free	Free
peel of	20	15	Free	Free
Limes	20	8	16 cents per bushel	16 cents per bushel
juice of	10	8	Free	Free
Lines, fishing	30	24	5 per cent. ad valorem as "manu	factured goods," generally, though the precise duty on *fishing lines* can be ascertained only by knowing their component material
worsted	25	19	5 per cent. ad valorem	5 per cent. ad valorem
Linen, manufactures of	20	15	5 per cent. ad valorem	5 per cent. ad valorem
in strips, fit only for buttons or shoes	5	4	Free	Free
bags	20	15	5 per cent. ad valorem	5 per cent. ad valorem
lawn	30	24	5 per cent ad valorem	5 per cent. ad valorem
Linseed	10	Free	Free	Free
oil, cakes or meal	20	15	Free	Free
Linsey woolsey	30	24	Free	Free
Lint, patent	20	15	5 per cent. ad valorem	5 per cent. ad valorem
Liquor cases, with or without bottles	30	24	10 per cent. ad valorem	
Licorice root	20	15	Until 5th April, 1857, inclusive,	$1 20 per cwt. From and after the 5th April, 1857, free
paste of	20	15	$4 80 per cwt	$2 40 per cwt
Litharge	20	15	Free	Free
Lithographic stones	20	15	Free	Free
Macaroni and vermicelli	30	24	24 cents per cwt	24 cents per cwt
Macassar oil	30	24	24 cents per pound	24 cents per pound
Mace	40	4	24 cents per pound	24 cents per pound
oil of	30	42	24 cents per pound	24 cents per pound
Machines, models of	Fr e	Free	Free	Free
Mackerel	20	15	Free	Free

TARIFFS—Continued.

DENOMINATION OF MERCHANDISE.	DUTIES ON IMPORTS.			
	Into the United States from foreign nations, per cent. ad valorem, under the act of—		Into Great Britain from foreign nations.	Into Great Britain from the British colonies.
	1846.	1857.		
Madder, or madder root	5	Free	Free	Free
Magic lanterns	30	24	10 per cent. ad valorem	10 per cent. ad valorem
Magnesia, lump or calcined	30	24	Calcined, as a medicina preparation, 20 per cent	No discriminating duty defined
carbonate of	30	24	Calcined, as a medicinal preparaon, 20 per cent	No discriminating duty defined
sulphate of	20	15	Free	Free
Mahogany	20	8	Free	Free
Manganese	20	15	Free	Free
Manna	20	8	Free	Free
Mantles and mantillas	30	24	According to material	According to material
Manila matting	25	19	Free	Free
Manufactures of tobacco	40	30	Tobacco imported into Great rates of duty, with 5 per cent.	Britain is subject to the following additional thereon, viz:
			Unmanufactured, stemmed, or 5 per cent	stripped, 72 cents per pound, and
			Unstemmed, 72 cents per pound,	and 5 per cent
			Manufactured, or cigars, $2 16	per pound, and 5 per cent
			Snuffs, $1 44 per pound, and 5 per	cent
			Stalks and flour of, snuff works,	prohibited
			Manufactured in the United King carrot tobacco or cigars; such dise, being packed in cases con pounds net weight, a drawback shipment as stores of 63 cents	dom, made into cut, shag, roll or cigars, when exported as merchantaining not less than one hundred shall be allowed on exportation or per pound
Maps and charts	10	Free	(Or parts thereof, plain or colored,) free	Free
Marble, unmanufactured	20	15	Free	Free
manufactures of	30	24	10 per cent. ad valorem	10 per cent. ad valorem
marbles	30	24	8 cents per cubic foot	8 cents per cubic foot
Marmalade	40	30	4 cents per pound	4 cents per pound
Marrow	10	8	Free	Free
Mastic gum	20	15	Free	Free
Matches, wax	30	24	In boxes not exceeding 1,000 matches, dozen boxes, 12 cents	12 cents per dozen boxes
			In boxes exceeding 1,000 matches, 1,000 matches 1 cent	1 cent per 1,000 matches
Matting, China and other floor, and mats made of flags, jute, or grass	25	15	Free	Free
of cocoa fibres	30	15	Free	Free
Mats, sheepskin	30	24	Free	Free

TARIFFS—Continued.

DENOMINATION OF MERCHANDISE.	DUTIES ON IMPORTS. Into the United States from foreign nations, per cent. ad valorem, under the act of— 1846.	1857.	Into Great Britain from foreign nations.	Into Great Britain, from the British colonies.
Mats, table, of grass, straw or flag	25	19	Free	Free
oil cloth, or japanned	30	24	3 cents per square yard	3 cents per square yard
wool, zephyr and fancy	30	24	12 cents per square yard	12 cents per square yard
Meats, prepared	40	30	Free	Free
Medals	Free	Free	Of gold, silver, or any other sort, free	Of gold, silver, or any other sort, free
Medicinal preparations not otherwise provided for	30	24	20 per cent. ad valorem	20 per cent. ad valorem
drugs, roots, and leaves in a crude state, not otherwise provided for	20	15	Free	Free
Melting pots, earthenware or glue pots	30	24	Of any material, free	Free
Mercury	20	15	Free	Free
Merino wool, and manufactures of	30	24	Shawls, scarfs, and handkerchiefs	No discriminating duty defined.
shawls	30	24	plain, 8 cts. per lb	
worsted body	30	24	printed, 16 cts. per lb	
of combed wool, manufactured	25	19	Gloves, 6*d.* dozen pairs	
in whole or part of wool	30	24	Free	Free
Metals, all manufactures of, not provided for	30	24	10 per cent. ad valorem	10 per cent. ad valorem
Mica	20	15	Free	Free
Millinery of all kinds	30	24	According to material	According to material
Mill cranks, of wrought iron	30	24	60 cts. per cwt	60 cts. per cwt
irons, do do	30	24	do	do
saws	30	24	do	do
Mills, coffee	30	24	10 per cent. ad valorem	10 per cent. ad valorem
Mineral and bituminous substances in a crude state, not otherwise provided for	20	15	Free	Free
green	20	15	Free	Free
waters	30	24	Free	Free
salt	20	15	Free	Free
Mineralogy, specimens of	Free	Free	Free	Free
Mirrors	30	24	As manufactured goods, 10 per ct.	10 per cent. ad valorem
Mittens or mitts of silk	30	24	15 per cent. ad valorem	5 per cent. ad valorem
wool and Angora	30	24	6 cts. per dozen	6 cts. per dozen
cotton	20	24	5 per cent. ad valorem	
linen thread	30	24	do do	5 per cent. ad valorem
leather	30	24	Habit mitts, 56 cts. dozen pairs Women's mitts, $1 08 do	And 5 per cent. additional

TARIFFS—Continued.

DENOMINATION OF MERCHANDISE.	DUTIES ON IMPORTS. Into the United States from foreign nations, per cent. ad valorem, under the act of— 1846.	1857.	Into Great Britain from foreign nations.	In from the British colonies.
Models of inventions, machines, &c.	Free	Free	Free (a)	Free (a)
Mohair or Angora, wool or hair	20	15	Free	Free
cloth in strips, fit only for buttons or shoes	5	4	Free	Free
manufactures of, not otherwise provided for	25	24	If made up, 5 per cent.; otherwise, free	No discriminating duty defined
Molasses	30	24	$1 02 per cwt	Free
Morphia, acetate, and sulphate of	30	24	$1 20 per lb	$1 20 per lb
Mortars and pestles, of brass or other metals	30	24	Of brass or copper, $2 40 per cwt	$2 40 per cwt
marble or stone	30	24	10 per cent. ad valorem	10 per cent. ad valorem
Moss, Iceland, Irish, or other	20	15	Free, (including moss known as lichen islandicus and rock, for dyers' use)	No discriminating duty defined
Mother-of-pearl shell	5	4	Free	Free
studs, and all manufactures of	30	24	10 per cent. ad valorem	10 per cent. ad valorem
Mouse traps	30	24	10 per cent. ad valorem	do do
Munjeet, a dye	5	Free	Free	Free
Muriate of potash, barytes, gold, silver, tin, strontian	20	15	These muriates being chiefly applied in the arts, are admitted free	No discriminating duty defined
Musical instruments of all kinds	20	15	According to character. Those not otherwise enumerated or described, 10 per cent. ad val. (b)	
strings of whipgut or catgut, and all other strings of the same material	20	15	As "manufactured goods," 10 per cent	No discrimination
			Harp and lute strings, silvered	Free
Mushrooms, prepared	40	30	10 per cent. ad valorem	10 per cent. ad valorem
sauce or catsup	30	24	2 cents per pound	2 cents per pound
Musk	30	24	Free	Free
Muskets and parts	30	24	10 per cent. ad valorem	No discrimination
Muslins	25	24	Free	Free
embroidered with the needle	30	24	10 per cent. ad valorem	5 per cent. ad valorem
collars, sleeves, chemisettes	30	24	5 per cent. ad valorem	No discriminating duty defined
Mustard, flour of	20	15	36 cents per cwt	do do
Myrabalans, (a nut for dyeing)	5	Free	Free	Free
Nails, brads, sprigs, and tacks	30	24	If of iron, 60 cents per cwt.; others according to component material.	

(a) If imported as merchandise, they are charged according to material.

(b) See note, p. 18.

TARIFFS—Continued.

DENOMINATION OF MERCHANDISE.	DUTIES ON IMPORTS.			
	Into the United States from foreign nations, per cent. ad valorem, under the act of—		Into Great Britain from foreign nations.	Into Great Britain from the British colonies.
	1846.	1857.		
Nails, brass	30	24	$2 40 per cwt	$2 40 per cwt
iron, cast or wrought	30	24	60 cents per cwt	60 cents per cwt
Nail rods or nail plates	30	24	Free	Free
Nankeens, cotton	25	24	Free	Free
Napkins, cotton	25	24	5 per cent. ad valorem	5 per cent. ad valorem
Naples, and all other soap	30	24	Except scented or fancy soap, 16 cents per cwt.; scented and fancy soap, 4 cents per lb	Common soap, 16 cents per cwt.; scented and fancy, 4 cents per pound
Narcotine	20	15	Free	Free
Natron	10	8	Free	Free
Natural history, specimens of	F ee	Free	Free	Free
Needles of all kinds	20	15	Iron or steel, 60 cents per cwt	60 cents per cwt
crotchet	30	24	do do	do do
Nests, brass kettles	30	24	$2 40 per cwt	$2 40 per cwt
Nets, fishing, of hemp or flax	30	24	5 per cent. ad valorem	5 per cent. ad valorem
Nutria skins, undressed	10	8	Free	Free
Newspapers and periodicals not in course of re-publication here	10	8	Newspapers, unbound, free Bound, 10 per cent. ad valorem	No discrimination do
Nickel	10	4	Ore of, metallic and oxide of, ar seniate of, in lumps or powder, being unrefined, free	
Nitre, not refined	10	4	Free	Free
refined or partially refined	10	8	20 per cent. ad valorem	20 per cent. ad valorem
Nitrate of lead, iron, tin	20	15	Such of these nitrates as are ap plied to medicinal purposes are charged as "medicinal prepa rations," 20 per cent. ad valorem. Those used in the arts are ad mitted free	
Nutmegs	40	4	Except those commonly called wild, 24 cents per pound	No discriminating duty defined
			Wild in the shell, 6 cents per pound	do do
			Not in the shell, 10 cents per pound	do do
Nuts, not otherwise provided for	30	24	Fre	Free
pea or ground	20	15	24 cents per bushel	24 cents per bushel
oil of	30	24	Free	Free
used exclusively in dyeing	5	Free	Free	Free
Nutgalls	5	Free	Free	Free
Nux vomica	10	8	48 cents per cwt	48 cents per cwt
Oakum or junk	Free	Free	Free	Free
Oatmeal	20	15	9 cents per cwt	9 cents per cwt

TARIFFS—Continued.

DENOMINATION OF MERCHANDISE.	DUTIES ON IMPORTS. Into the United States from foreign nations, per cent. ad valorem, under the act of— 1846.	1857.	Into Great Britain from foreign nations.	Into Great Britain from the British colonies.
Oats	20	15	24 cts. pr. quarter, or 8 bushels(a)	24 cents per quarter, or 8 bushels.
Ochre, brown, blue, and yellow, and all ochry earths as paints, in oil	30	24	Free	Free
Oil of abysynth	30	24	24 cents per pound	24 cents per pound
cloth of every description	30	24	3 cents per square yard	3 cents per square yard
castor or recine; linseed, hemp seed, and rape seed, and all other oils used in painting; neatsfoot and other animal oil	20	15	Free	Free
vitriol	10	4	Free	Free
spermaceti, whale, and other fish oil of American fisheries	Free	Free	Free	Free
whale, or other fish oil, of foreign fisheries	20	15	Free	Free
volatile, essential or expressed, not otherwise provided for	30	24	24 cents per pound	24 cents per pound
palm	10	4	Free	Free
Old iron	30	24	Free	Free
Old brass, copper, or pewter, only fit to be remanufactured	5	Free	Free	Free
Olives	30	8	Free	Free
Opium	20	15	24 cents per pound	24 cents per pound
Orange mineral	20	15	Free	Free
Oranges	20	8	(and lemons) 16 cents per bushel	16 cents per bushel
flower water	30	24	Free	Free
peel	20	15	Free	Free
Orchille weed, for dyeing	5	Free	Free	Free
Ore, metallic, not otherwise provided for	20	15	Free	Free
Ornamental feathers	30	24	72 cents per pound	72 cents per pound
Orpiment	10	8	Free	Free
Orris root	20	15	Free	Free
Osnaburgs	20	15	Free	Free
Ostrich feathers, undressed	30	24	Free	Free
prepared	30	24	72 cents per pound	72 cents per pound
Oxalic acid	20	4	Free	Free
Oxide of bismuth	20	15	Free	Free
Packthread	30	24	Free	Free

(a) The duties upon corn, grain, meal, and flour, are to be paid on importation; and such goods may not be warehoused either for home consumption or exportation—(16 and 17 Vict., chap. 107, § 41.)

TARIFFS—Continued.

DENOMINATION OF MERCHANDISE.	DUTIES ON IMPORTS. Into the United States, from foreign nations, per cent. ad valorem, under the act of— 1846.	1857.	Into Great Britain from foreign nations.	Into Great Britain from the British colonies.
Padding	30	24	Free	Free
Paddy, or rice in the hull	20	15	Rough, or in the husk, 18 cents per quarter, or 8 bushels	No discrimination
Painted floor cloths	30	24	3 cents per square yard	3 cents per square yard
Paint brushes of all kinds	30	24	Free	Free
Paintings	Free	Free	If imported in good faith as merchandise, free	objects of taste and not of merchandise
otherwise	20	15	10 per cent. ad valorem	10 per cent. ad valorem
on glass or porcelain	30	24	10 per cent. ad valorem	10 per cent. ad valorem
Paints, not otherwise enumerated, dry or ground in oil	20	15	Free	Free
water colors	30	24	Free	Free
Palm leaf baskets	30	24	8 cents per cubic foot	8 cents per cubic foot
brooms, fans, and hats	30	24	Hats (chip) 60 cents per pound. Broom and fans 10 per cent. ad valorem	Hats (chip) 60 cents per pound. Brooms and fans 10 per cent. ad valorem
leaves, unmanufactured	10	Free	Free	Free
oil	10	4	Free	Free
Paper of all kinds, not otherwise provided for	30	24	Brown paper made of old ropes or cordage only, without separating the pitch or tar therefrom, and without any mixture of other materials therewith, 5 cents per pound	5 cents per pound
foolscap, all drawing and writing	30	24	5 cents per pound	5 cents per pound
Paper, envelopes	30	24	As "manufactured goods," 10 per cent	10 per cent. ad valorem
printing, copper plate, and stainers'	30	24	5 cents per pound	5 cents per pound
all manufactures of not otherwise provided for	30	24	10 per cent. ad valorem	10 per cent. ad valorem
colored, such as is used for lining book covers, for ornamental boxes, card racks	30	24	5 cents per pound	5 cents per pound
hangings, or paper for screens or fireboards	20	15	6 cents per pound	6 cents per pound
boxes of all kinds	30	24	10 per cent. ad valorem	10 per cent. ad valorem

TARIFFS—Continued.

DENOMINATION OF MERCHANDISE.	DUTIES ON IMPORTS. Into the United States from foreign nations, per cent. ad valorem, under the act of— 1846.	1857.	Into Great Britain from foreign nations.	Into Great Britain from the British colonies.
Paper cigars	40	30	$2 16 per pound and 5 per cent. ad valorem	$2 16 per pound and 5 per cent. ad valorem
Papier maché manufactures	30	24	10 per cent. ad valorem	10 per cent. ad valorem
Parasols and sun shades	30	24	According to material	According to material
frames or sticks for	30	24	72 cents per 100 (sticks)	72 cents per 100 (sticks)
Parchment	30	24	Free	Free
Paris white	20	15	Free	Free
Pasteboard	30	24	5 cents per pound	5 cents per pound
Pastes for the toilet	30	24	(As perfumery,) 5 cents per pound	(As perfumery,) 5 cents per pound
for medicinal purposes	30	24	20 per cent. ad valorem	20 per cent. ad valorem
unset	10	8	Free	Free
work set in gold or silver	30	24	10 per cent. ad valorem	10 per cent. ad valorem
almond	30	24	4 cents per pound	4 cents per pound
Brazil, a dye	15	4	4 cents per pound	4 cents per pound
Pastel or woad	10	4	Free	Free
Patent floor cloths, stamped, printed, or painted	30	24	If oil cloth, 3 cents per square yard; otherwise according to material	If oil cloth, 3 cents per sq. yard; otherwise according to material.
Paving stones	20	15	Free	Free
Peanuts	20	15	24 cents per bushel	24 cents per bushel
Pearl, all articles composed wholly or chiefly of	30	24	The duty to be levied on the setting only as goods manufactured; 10 per cent. ad valorem	No discriminating duty defined
Pearl, mother of	5	4	Free	Free
Pearls, not set	10	4	Free	Free
real, set	30	24	10 per cent. ad valorem	10 per cent. ad valorem
Peas	20	15	Free	Free
Pencil cases	30	24	10 per cent. ad valorem	10 per cent. ad valorem
Pencils, black lead	30	24	Free	Free
camels' hair, red chalk, slate	30	24	Of all kinds free	Free
Penknives	30	24	60 cents per cwt	60 cents per cwt
Pens, metal or quill	30	24	Free	Free
Pepper, black or white, Cayenne, Chili, or African	30	24	12 cents per pound and 5 per cent. additional	12 cents per pound and 5 per cent. additional

TARIFFS—Continued.

DENOMINATION OF MERCHANDISE.	DUTIES ON IMPORTS.			
	Into the United States from foreign nations, per cent. ad valorem, under the act of—		Into Great Britain from foreign nations.	Into Great Britain from the British colonies.
	1846.	1857.		
Peppers, pickles	30	24	2 cents per gallon	2 cents per gallon
Percussion caps	30	24	2 cents per 1,000	2 cents per 1,000
Perfumes of all kinds	30	24	4 cents per pound	4 cents per pound
Perfumery, bottles and fancy bottles, or vials	30	24	If of flint cut glass, flint colored glass, or fancy ornamental glass, $2 40 per cwt.; all other kinds, free	No discriminating duty defined
Perfumed or fancy, shaving, or other soap	30	24	4 cents per pound	4 cents per pound
Peruvian bark	15	Free	Free	Free
Petershams, woollen cloth	30	24	Free	Free
Pewter, all manufactures of	30	24	48 cents per cwt	48 cents per cwt
old, and fit only to be remanufactured	5	4	Free	Free
Phosphate, and phosphuret of lime	20	15	Free	Free
Phosphorus	20	15	Free	Free
Pickled fish, of all descriptions	20	15	Free	Free
Pickles	30	24	Preserved in vinegar, 2 cents per gallon; in salt, free	Preserved in vinegar, 2 cents per gallon; in salt, free
Pigs, of brass, copper, tin	5	Free	Free	Free
iron	30	24	Free	Free
lead	20	15	Free	Free
Pimento	40	4	$1 20 per cwt	$1 20 per cwt
oil of	30	24	24 cents per pound	24 cents per pound
Pine apples	20	8	4 cents per bushel	4 cents per bushel
Pink, Dutch	20	15	Free	Free
root	20	15	Free	Free
rose	20	15	Free	Free
saucers	20	15	Free	Free
Pins, of all kinds	30	24	10 per cent. ad valorem	10 per cent. ad valorem
Pipes, china and clay	30	24	Of clay, free	Of clay, free
iron	30	24	60 cents per cwt	60 cents per cwt
lead	20	15	48 cents per cwt	48 cents per cwt
wood	30	24	10 per cent. ad valorem	10 per cent. ad valorem
Pistols	30	24	do do	do do
Pitch	20	15	Free	Free
Burgundy	25	19	Free	Free
Plaids, cotton	25	24	Free	Free
Plaiting of straw	30	24	24 cents per pound	24 cents per pound
Planes, and plane irons	30	24	60 cents per cwt	60 cents per cwt

TARIFFS—Continued.

DENOMINATION OF MERCHANDISE.	DUTIES ON IMPORTS.			
	Into the United States from foreign nations, per cent. ad valorem, under the act of—		Into Great Britain from foreign nations.	Into Great Britain from the British colonies
	1846.	1857.		
Plank, rough or dressed	20	15	$2 40, load of 50 cubic feet	48 cents, load of 50 cubic feet
Plants, not otherwise provided for	Free	Free	Free, (including shrubs, trees, &c., alive)	
Plaster, court	30	24	As "manufactured goods," 10 per cent. ad valorem	As "manufactured goods," 10 per cent
Plaster of Paris, unground	Free	Free	Free	Free
ground	20	15	Free	Free
all manfactures of	30	24	10 per cent. ad valorem(a)	10 per cent. ad valorem(a)
Plated saddlery, of all descriptions	30	24	do do	do do
Plated metal	30	24	Free	Free
wares, of all kinds	30	24	10 per cent. ad valorem	10 per. cent. ad valorem
Plates, copper, for engravers, if polished and finished	30	24	If engraved, $2 40 per cwt	$2 40 per cwt., (if engraved)
Plates, iron	30	24	If manufactured for use, 60 cts. per cwt	If manufactured for use, 60 cents per cwt
Platina, unmanufactured	Free	Free	Free	Free
manufactures of	30	24	10 per cent. ad valorem	10 per cent. ad valorem
Plaits of all kinds, for making hats and bonnets	30	24	Of chip, not being of greater value than 12 cents per piece of 60 yards, 12 cents per lb	No discriminating duties defined.
Playing cards	30	24	$3 60 per dozen packs (b)	$3 60 per dozen packs(b)
Ploughs	30	24	60 cents per cwt	60 cents per cwt
Plumbago	20	15	Free	Free
Plumes, ornamental	30	24	Dressed, 72 cents per lb	Undressed, free
Plush, worsted	25	19	Free	Free
Polishing stones	10	8	Free	Free
Pomatum	30	24	4 cents per lb	4 cents per lb
Pongees	25	19	In pieces not exceeding 15 yards in length, 48 cents per piece; exceeding 15 yards and not exceeding 21 yards, 72 cents per piece; exceeding 21 yards and not exceeding 31 yards, $1 20 per piece	
Poplins, silk and worsted	25	19	15 per cent. ad valorem	5 per cent. ad valorem

(a) When manufactured into busts or models, as objects of taste and not of merchandise, free.

(b) Under the stamp duties act, s. 114, the importation into Great Britain of playing cards, and the sale thereof, are prohibited, unless the packs are separately enclosed in wrappers provided by the commissioners of inland revenue, with such devices as they may direct, and securely fastened round or over by means of some adhesive substance, so that such wrappers cannot be opened without being destroyed. Many other restrictions and provisions prevail; but, as no such discriminations are recognized in the United States tariff, it is deemed unnecessary to refer to them more particularly.

TARIFFS—Continued.

Denomination of merchandise.	Duties on imports. Into the United States, from foreign nations, per cent. ad valorem, under the act of— 1846.	1857.	Into Great Britain from foreign nations.	Into Great Britain from the British colonies.
Porcelain	30	24	$2 40 per cwt	$2 40 per cwt
slates	25	19	do	do
Pork	20	15	Fresh or salted, free	Free
Portable desks	30	24	10 per cent. ad valorem	10 per cent. ad valorem
Porter in casks or bottles	30	24	$4 80 per barrel, of 32 gallons	$4 80 per barrel, of 32 gallons
Potash, of all kinds	20	15	Being used chiefly in the arts, free	Free
Potassium	20	15	Free	Free
Potatoes	30	24	Free	Free
Pots, copper	30	24	$2 40 per cwt	$2 40 per cwt
earthenware	30	24	do	do
iron, cast	30	24	60 cents per cwt	60 cents per cwt
tin	30	24	$2 40 per cwt	do
all other	30	26	10 per cent. ad valorem	10 per cent. ad valorem
Powder, bleaching	10	4	Free	Free
hair, perfumed	30	24	4 cents per lb	4 cents per lb
ink	30	24	Free	Free
tooth, and cosmetics	30	24	4 cents per lb	4 cents per lb
bronze	20	15	Free	Free
gun	20	15	When not prohibited, free	Free
Precious stones, of all kinds, set	30	24	10 per cent. ad valorem	10 per cent. ad valorem
not set	10	4	Free	Free
Prepared vegetables, meats, poultry, and game	40	30	Free	Free
Preserves, in sugar, brandy, or molasses	40	30	In sugar or molasses, 4 cents per pound	4 cents per pound
			In brandy 10 per cent. on the fruit, and the spirit duty on the quantity of spirits	No discriminating duty defined
Pressing boards	30	24	10 per cent. ad valorem	10 per cent. ad valorem
Printing ink	30	24	Free	Free
types, new or old	20	15	10 per cent. ad valorem	10 per cent. ad valorem
paper	30	24	5 cents per pound	5 cents per pound
Prisms, cut glass	40	30	Free	Free
of cut glass and metal	30	24	$2 40 per cwt	$2 40 per cwt
Preparations, medicinal, not otherwise provided for	30	24	20 per cent. ad valorem	20 per cent. ad valorem
Prunella, suitable for boots, shoes, bootees, exclusively	5	4	5 per cent. ad valorem	5 per cent. ad valorem
otherwise	25	19	Free	Free
Prunes	40	8	$1 68 per cwt	$1 68 per cwt
Prussian blue	20	4	Free	Free
Prussiate of potash	20	15	Free	Free

TARIFFS—Continued.

DENOMINATION OF MERCHANDISE.	DUTIES ON IMPORTS. Into the United States, from foreign nations, per cent. ad valorem, under the act of— 1846.	1857.	Into Great Britain from foreign nations.	Into Great Britain from the British colonies.
Pumice stone and pumice	10	8	Free	Free
Pumpkins	20	15	Free	Free
Quadrants, sextants, and frames	30	24	10 per cent. ad valorem	10 per cent. ad valorem
Quality, binding	25	19	According to material	According to material
Quassia wood	20	15	24 cents per cwt	24 cents per cwt.
Quercitron bark	20	15	Free	Free
Quicksilver	20	15	Free	Free
Quilla bark	15	12	Free	Free
Quills	20	15	Free	Free
Quilts, cotton	25	24	5 per cent. ad valorem	5 per cent. ad valorem
Quinine, sulphate of	20	15	12 cents per ounce	12 cents per ounce
Rags, of whatever material	5	Free	Free	Free
of wool	5	4	Free	Free
Railroad iron	30	24	60 cents per cwt	60 cents per cwt
Raisins, of all kinds	40	8	$2 40 per cwt	$2 40 per cwt
Rape seed	10	Free	Free	Free
oil	20	15	Free	Free
Rattans and reeds, unmanufactured	10	Free	Free	Free
split	20	15	Free	Free
Ravens' duck, hemp, or flax	20	15	Free	Free
Raw hides of all kinds, and skins, whether dried, salted, or pickled, not otherwise provided for	5	4	Free	Free
Raw silk, not more advanced than singles, tram, and thrown, or organzine	15	12	Free	Free
Razors	30	24	60 cents per cwt	60 cents per cwt
Razor cases, paper, leather and wood	30	24	10 per cent. ad valorem	10 per cent. ad valorem
strops	30	24	do do	do do
Ready-made clothing	30	24	According to material	According to material
Reaping hooks, of iron or steel	30	24	60 cents per cwt	60 cents per cwt
Red lead, dry, or ground in oil	20	15	Free	Free
tartar	5	Free	Free	Free
Venetian, as ochre	30	15	Free	Free
wood, in sticks or sanders	5	Free	Free	Free
Reeds, unmanufactured	10	Free	Free	Free
weavers' and manufactured	30	24	10 per cent. ad valorem	10 per cent. ad valorem
Regulus of antimony	20	8	Free	Free
Rhodium	30	15	Free	Free
Rhubarb	20	15	Free	Free

TARIFFS—Continued.

Denomination of merchandise.	Duties on imports. Into the United States from foreign nations, per cent. ad valorem, under the act of— 1846.	1857.	Into Great Britain from foreign nations.	Into Great Britain from the British colonies.
Rice	20	15	Not rough, in the husk, 9 cents per cwt.; rough, and in the husk, 18 cents per quarter, or eight bushels	
Rice fans	30	24	10 per cent. ad valorem	10 per cent. ad valorem
Rivets, iron or steel	30	24	60 cents per cwt	60 cents per cwt
Rochelle salts	20	15	Free	Free
Rods, copper	20	15	$2 40 per cwt., as "manufactures of copper"	$2 40 per cwt., as "manufactures of copper"
fishing, manufactured	30	24	10 per cent. ad valorem	10 per cent. ad valorem
unmanufactured	20	15	Free	Free
Rolled iron, in nails or spikes, rods, or nail plates, for band iron, scroll iron, or casement rods	30	24	Free	Free
Roman cement	20	15	Free	Free
vitriol	20	15	Free	Free
Root, arrow	20	15	9 cents per cwt	9 cents per cwt
colombo	20	15	Free	Free
medicinal, not enumerated	20	15	Free	Free
madder	5	Free	Free	Free
Ropes	25	19	According to material; cordage, tarred and untarred, free	
Rose, pink	20	15	Free	Free
water	30	24	Free	Free
wood	20	8	Unmanufactured, free	Free
Rosin	20	8	Free	Free
Rotten stone	10	8	Free	Free
Rouge, a cosmetic	30	24	4 cents per pound	4 cents per pound
Rubies, not set	10	4	Free	Free
set	30	24	10 per cent. ad valorem	10 per cent. ad valorem
Rubber, India, unmanufactured	10	4	Free	Free
Rugs, woolen and hearth	30	24	12 cents per square yard	12 cents per square yard
horse or blanket	30	24	5 per cent. ad valorem	5 per cent. ad valorem
Rules, iron or steel	30	24	60 cents per cwt	60 cents per cwt
Russia sheetings, and other linen	20	15	Free	Free
Rye and rye flour	20	15	Rye, 24 cents per quarter of 8 bushels	No discrimination
			Rye flour, 9 cents per cwt	do
Sabres	30	24	When not prohibited, 60 cents per cwt	60 cents per cwt
Saddles and saddle trees	30	24	10 per cent. ad valorem	10 per cent. ad valorem
Saddlery of all kinds, not otherwise provided for	30	24	do do	do do

TARIFFS—Continued.

DENOMINATION OF MERCHANDISE.	DUTIES ON IMPORTS. Into the United States from foreign nations, per cent. ad valorem, under the act of—			
	1846.	1857.	Into Great Britain from foreign nations.	Into Great Britain from the British colonies.
Saddlery, common tinned and japanned, of all descriptions	20	15	10 per cent. ad valorem	10 per cent. ad valorem
Sad irons	30	24	60 cents per cwt	60 cents per cwt
Safflower	5	Free	Free	Free
Saffron and saffron cake	20	15	Free	Free
Sago	20	15	9 cents per cwt	9 cents per cwt
Sail duck	20	15	Free	Free
Sal ammoniac	10	8	Free	Free
Salempores, cotton	25	24	5 per cent. ad valorem	5 per cent. ad valorem
Salad oil	30	24	Free	Free
Salacine, a medicinal preparation	30	24	6 cents per ounce	6 cents per ounce
Salmon, pickled, dried, or smoked	20	15	Free	Free
preserved	30	24	Free	Free
Salt	20	15	Free	Free
Salted skins, skivers, pelts, and roans	5	4	Free	Free
Salts, Epsom, Glauber, and Rochelle	20	15	Free	Free
Saltpetre, or nitrate of soda or potash, refined or partially refined	10	8	Free	Free
Saltpetre, or nitrate of potash or soda, crude	5	4	Free	Free
Sand stones	20	15	Free	Free
Sandal wood	30	8	Free	Free
Sardines, in oil	40	30	Free	Free
pickled	20	15	Free	Free
Sarsaparilla	20	15	Free	Free
Sassafras, oil	30	24	24 cents per pound, if classed fumed oils; otherwise, free	with chemical, essential, or perfumed oils
Satins, silk	25	19	Plain, striped, figured, or bro pound; articles not otherwise and at the option of the officers valorem	caded, viz: broad stuffs, $1 20 per enumerated, $1 44 per pound, or, of the customs, 15 per cent. ad
Satin wood, unmanufactured	20	8	Free	Free
Sauces of all kinds	30	24	(Not otherwise enumerated,) 2 cents per pound	(Not otherwise enumerated,) 2 cents per pound
Sausage skins	20	15	Free	Free
Sausages, Bologna	30	24	Free	Free
Saws, all kinds	30	24	60 cents per cwt	60 cents per cwt
Scale beams	30	24	60 cents per cwt	60 cents per cwt

TARIFFS—Continued.

Denomination of merchandise.	Duties on imports. Into the United States from foreign nations, per cent. ad valorem, under the act of— 1846.	1857.	Into Great Britain from foreign nations.	Into Great Britain from the British colonies.
Scales, brass, copper	30	24	$2 40 per cwt	$2 40 per cwt
iron or steel	30	24	60 cents per cwt	60 cents per cwt
Gunter and others, wood, ivory, or bone	30	24	10 per cent. ad valorem	10 per cent. ad valorem
Scissors	30	24	60 cents per cwt	60 cents per cwt
Scrap iron and old iron	30	24	Free	Free
lead	20	15	Free	Free
Screws of iron and other metal	30	24	60 cents per cwt	60 cents per cwt
Seedlac	5	4	Free	Free
Seeds, garden, and all others not specified	Free	Free	Free	Free
Seines of hemp or flax	20	15	10 per cent. ad valorem	10 per cent. ad valorem
Seltzer water	30	24	Free	Free
Seneca, or radix root	20	15	Free	Free
Senegal, gum	10	8	Free	Free
Senna leaves	20	15	Free	Free
Sepia, or sepic, or cuttle fish bone	20	15	Free	Free
Serge, woolen	30	24	Free	Free
worsted	25	19	Free	Free
Sewing silk, in the gum or purified	30	24	Prepared for use, 15 per ct. ad val.	Prepared for use, 5 per ct. ad val.
Sextants	30	24	10 per cent. ad valorem	10 per cent. ad valorem
Shawls, merino, of wool	30	24	Plain, 8 cents per lb.; printed, 16 cents per lb	Plain, 8 cents per lb.; printed, 16 cents per lb
cashmere, of camels' or goats' hair	30	24	5 per cent. ad valorem	5 per cent. ad valorem
cotton	30	24	do	do
silk and worsted	30	24	15 per cent. ad valorem	do
Shears	30	24	60 cents per cwt	60 cents per cwt
Sheathing copper for ships, sheathing metal, and sheathing felt	Free	Free	Free	Free
paper	20	15	5 cents per lb	5 cents per lb
Sheet brass	30	24	Manufactured, $2 40 per cwt	Manufactured, $2 40 per cwt.
lead	20	15	Free	Free
Sheetings, Russia, Irish, & German	20	15	In the piece, free	Free
Shells and turtle shell	5	4	Free	Free
Shell boxes	30	24	10 per cent. ad valorem	10 per cent. ad valorem
Shellac, gum	5	4	Free	Free
Shingles	20	15	Shingles, $2 40 per load of 50 cubic feet	48 cents per load of 50 cubic feet, and 5 per cent. additional

TARIFFS—Continued.

DENOMINATION OF MERCHANDISE.	DUTIES ON IMPORTS.			
	Into the United States, from foreign nations, per cent. ad valorem, under the act of—		Into Great Britain from foreign nations.	Into Great Britain from the British colonies.
	1846.	1857.		
Shirtings, cotton, unbleached	25	19	Free	Free
linen	20	15	Free	Free
Shoe bills, cast or cut	30	24	60 cents per cwt	60 cents per cwt
Shoes and slippers of nankeen, prunella, or other stuff	30	24	10 per cent. ad valorem	10 per cent. ad valorem
silk	30	24	15 per cent. ad valorem	5 per cent. ad valorem
composed wholly of India rubber	30	24	8 cents per lb	8 cents per lb.
horse	30	24	60 cents per cwt	60 cents per cwt
Shoe knives, rasps, and horns	30	24	Shoe knives and rasps, 60 cents per cwt Horns, 10 per cent. ad valorem	Shoe knives and rasps, 60 cents per cwt. 10 per cent. ad valorem
Shot, iron	30	24	60 cents per cwt	60 cents per cwt.
lead	20	15	48 cents per cwt	48 cents per cwt
Shovels, all kinds	30	24	60 cents per cwt	60 cents per cwt
Shrubs, not otherwise provided for	Free	Free	Free	Free
Shumac, or Sumac	5	4	Free	Free
Shuttlecocks and battledores	30	24	10 per cent. ad valorem	10 per cent. ad valorem
Sickles of iron or steel	30	24	60 cents per cwt	60 cents per cwt
Side-arms of every description	30	24	When not prohibited, 60 cents per cwt	When not prohibited, 60 cents per cwt
Sieves, hair, wire, and other	30	24	10 per cent. ad valorem	10 per cent. ad valorem
Silk, raw, and not more advanced in manufacture than singles, tram, and thrown or organzine	15	12	Free	Free
Silk, sewing	30	24	15 per cent. ad valorem(a)	5 per cent. ad valorem(a)
all manufactures of silk, or of silk mixed with any other material not otherwise specified	25	19	do do	do do
Silver, bullion and coin	Free	Free	Free	Free
plated ware	30	24	10 per cent. ad valorem	10 per cent. ad valorem
German	30	24	Unmanufactured, free; manufactured, 10 per cent	Unmanufactured, free; manufactured, 10 per cent. ad valorem.
thread	30	24	Free	Free
watches, and parts of	10	8	Silver, or any other metal not each; hunters', 84 cents each;	gold, viz: Open faces, 60 cents repeaters, $1 92 each
all manufactures of	30	24	10 per cent. ad valorem	10 per cent. ad valorem

(a) See note p. 18.

TARIFFS—Continued.

Denomination of merchandise.	Duties on imports. Into the United States from foreign nations, per cent. ad valorem, under the act of— 1846.	1857.	Into Great Britain from foreign nations.	Into Great Britain from the British colonies.
Sisal grass, unmanufactured	25	19	Free	Free
Skates	30	24	60 cents per cwt	60 cents per cwt
Skins of all kinds not otherwise provided for	20	15	Free(a)	Free(a)
Skins, sheep, with the wool on	20	15	Free	Free
sheep, salted or pickled	5	4	Free	Free
fish	20	15	Free	Free
Slates of all kinds	25	19	Of tin, covered with composition, 10 per cent. ad valorem	10 per cent. ad valorem
			All others fit for use, 10 per cent. ad valorem	10 per cent. ad valorem
Slate pencils	20	15	Free	Free
Sledges, blacksmiths'	30	24	60 cents per cwt	60 cents per cwt
Slit iron, in nail or spike rods, or nail plates	30	24	Free	Free
Smelling bottles, cut glass, with metal or silver tops	40	30	$2 40 per cwt	$2 40 per cwt
Snake root	20	15	Free	Free
Snuff	40	30	$1 44 per pound, and 5 per cent. additional	$1 44 per pound, and 5 per cent. additional
Snuff boxes	30	24	10 per cent. ad valorem	10 per cent. ad valorem
Soap, Castile	30	24	16 cents per cwt	16 cents per cwt
common	30	24	16 cents per cwt	16 cents per cwt
fancy and perfumed	30	24	4 cents per pound	4 cents per pound
shaving and others, including Windsor and wash-balls	30	24	All scented and perfumed soaps, 4 cents per pound; when not scented, shav'g soap is charged 10 per cent	No discriminating duty defined
Socket chisels	30	24	60 cents per cwt.	
Socks, wool, silk, worsted and linen	30	24	5 per cent. ad valorem, except silk, which is 15 per cent. ad valorem	No discriminating duty defined; 5 per cent. ad valorem
cotton	20	15	6 cents per dozen pairs	6 cents per dozen pairs
Soda ash	10	4	Free	Free
Soy, a sauce	30	24	12 cents per gallon	12 cents per gallon

(a) The British Tariff enumerates sixty different kinds of skins, all of which are free, dressed or undressed.

TARIFFS—Continued.

DENOMINATION OF MERCHANDISE.	DUTIES ON IMPORTS. Into the United States from foreign nations, per cent. ad valorem, under the act of— 1846.	1857.	Into Great Britain from foreign nations.	Into Great Britain from the British colonies.
Spades of iron or steel, with or without handles	30	24	60 cents per cwt	60 cents per cwt
Spanish brown, dry	30	15	Free	Free
ground in oil	30	24	Free	Free
Spanish flies, or cantharides	20	8	Free	Free
Spar ornaments	40	30	10 per cent. ad valorem	10 per cent. ad valorem
Specimens of botany, mineralogy, or natural history	Free	Free	Free	Free
Spelter, in sheets	15	12	Free	Free
unmanufact'd, not otherwise provided for	5	4	Free	Free
Spermaceti candles	20	15	56 cents per cwt	56 cents per cwt
oil, foreign fisheries	20	15	Free	Free
Spider nets, as cotton cloths	25	24	Free. (If made ready for use 5 per cent.)	Free
Spikes, copper	20	15	$2 40 per cwt	$2 40 per cwt
composition	30	24	10 per cent. ad valorem	10 per cent. ad valorem
iron	30	24	60 cents per cwt	60 cents per cwt
Spike rods	30	24	Free	Free
Spindles, iron	30	24	60 cents per cwt	60 cents per cwt
Spirits, alcoholic, of all kinds	100	30	According to character, origin, &c. (a)	
Spirits of turpentine	20	15	Free	Free
Sponges	20	8	Free	Free
Spoons, horn, gold, silver, and all other	30	24	10 per cent. ad valorem	10 per cent. ad valorem
Sprigs of all kinds	30	24	60 cents per cwt	60 cents per cwt
Springs of steel, or other metal	30	24	60 cents per cwt.; if copper or brass, $2 40 per cwt	60 cents per cwt.; if copper or brass, $2 40 per cwt
Spunk	20	15	Free	Free
Spurs, gold or silver, gilt or plated	30	24	10 per cent. ad valorem	10 per cent. ad valorem
polished steel	30	24	60 cents per cwt	60 cents per cwt
brass	30	24	$2 40 per cwt	$2 40 per cwt
Squares of iron, steel	30	24	60 cents per cwt	60 cents per cwt
of brass	30	24	$2 40 per cwt	$2 40 per cwt
Square wire, for manufacture of stretchers for umbrellas	30	24	Free	Free
Squills	20	15	Dried and undried, free	Dried or undried, free

(a) See note page 13.

TARIFFS—Continued.

DENOMINATION OF MERCHANDISE.	DUTIES ON IMPORTS.			
	Into the United States from foreign nations, per cent. ad valorem, under the act of—		Into Great Britain from foreign nations.	Into Great Britain from the British colonies.
	1846.	1857.		
St. Lucar wine	40	30	$1 32 per gallon, and 5 per cent. additional	No discriminating duty(a)
Starch	20	15	9 cents per cwt	9 cents per cwt
Statuary, imported in good faith as objects of taste	Free	Free	Free	Free
Statues, and works of alabaster	40	Free	10 per cent. ad valorem	10 per cent. ad valorem
all others	30	Free	do do	do do
Staves, rough or dressed	20	15	Exceeding 72 inches in length, 7 thickness, the load of 50 cubic in length, nor 7 in. in breadth,	inches in breadth, or 3¼ inches in feet $2 16 ; not exceeding 72 inches nor 3¼ inches in thickness, free
Stearine candles and tapers	20	15	Until the 5th April, 1858, unless repealed, in which case the du cwt; after the 5th April, 1858,	the duty on tallow shall be sooner ty shall cease, viz: 84 cents per free
Steel, not otherwise provided for	20	15	Not manufactured, free; manufactures of, 60 cents per cwt	Not manufactured, free; manufactures of, 60 cents per cwt
cast, shear and German, in bars	15	12	Free	Free
beads	30	24	4 cents per pound	4 cents per pound
cutting knives, reaping hooks, scythes, and sickles	30	24	60 cents per cwt	60 cents per cwt
Steel saddlery, polished, all descriptions	30	24	60 cents per cwt	60 cents per cwt
Steel wire	30	24	Free	Free
all manufactures of not otherwise specified, or of which steel is a component material	30	24	60 cents per cwt	60 cents per cwt
Steelyards	30	24	60 cents per cwt	60 cents per cwt
Stereotype plates	20	15	Copper plates are marked free; if engraved, $2 40 per cwt	Copper plates, free; if engraved, $2 40 per cwt
Sticks or frames for umbrellas or parasols	30	24	72 cents per 100	72 cents per 100
Stills, copper, and still worms	30	24	$2 40 per cwt	$2 40 per cwt
bottoms for, of copper	20	15	$2 40 per cwt	$2 40 per cwt
Stirrups, plated, brass, and polished steel	30	24	$2 40 per cwt; polished steel, 60 cents per cwt	$2 40 per cwt; polished steel, 60 cents per cwt

(a) Unless it be the growth and produce of a British possession, and imported direct from thence. The duty in that case is reduced one-half, with the same additional per centage.

TARIFFS—Continued.

DENOMINATION OF MERCHANDISE.	DUTIES ON IMPORTS. Into the United States from foreign nations, per cent. ad valorem, under the act of— 1846.	1857.	Into Great Britain from foreign nations.	Into Great Britain from the British colonies.
Stockings, or half stockings, angora silk, thread, woolen or	30	24	5 per cent. ad valorem	5 per cent. ad valorem
worsted	30	24	Silk, 15 per cent ad valorem; thread, full, 12 cents per dozen; half, 6 cents per dozen.	Silk, 5 per cent. ad valorem; thread, full, 12 cents per dozen; half, 6 cents per dozen
Stones, ballast	20	15	Free	Free
Brazil pebbles	30	8	Free	Free
Bristol	20	15	Free	Free
polishing	10	8	Free	Free
building	10	8	Free	Free.
burr and mill stones, wrought or unwrought	10	Free	Free	Free
grind, wrought or unwrought	5	4	Free	Free
oil	20	15	Free	Free
precious stones, set	30	24	10 per cent. ad valorem	10 per cent. ad valorem
unset	10	4	Free	Free
rag, sand, and whet	20	15	Free	Free
rotten and pumice	10	8	Free	Free
paving	20	15	Free	Free
stone or earthenware	30	24	$2 40 per cwt	$2 40 per cwt
carnelian or other	10	4	10 per cent. ad valorem	10 per cent. ad valorem
rings	20	15	do do	do do
Storax, a balsam	30	24	Free	Free
Straining web, hemp or flax	20	15	5 per cent. ad valorem	5 per cent. ad valorem
Straw bonnets or hats	30	24	60 cents per pound	60 cents per pound
baskets, plats, flats, or braids	30	24	Baskets, 8 cents per cubic foot; braids, 48 cents; of chip, not per piece of 60 yards, 12 cents	flats, 60 cents per pound; plats or being of greater value than 12 cents per pound
twist	30	24	12 cents per pound	12 cents per pound
knives	30	24	60 cents per cwt	60 cents per cwt
Strychnine	30	24	20 per cent. ad valorem	20 per cent. ad valorem
Studs of gold, ivory, or pearl	30	24	Free	Free
Succini oil, drug	30	24	24 cents per pound	24 cents per pound
Sugar of all kinds, raw, clayed, or refined	30	24	According to quality, character,	&c., &c. (a)
Sugar of lead	20	15	Free	Free
Sulphate of barytes, crude or refined	20	15	Free	Free
magnesia, Epsom salts	20	15	Free	Free

(a) See note p. 18.

TARIFFS—Continued.

Denomination of merchandise.	Duties on imports. Into the United States from foreign nations, per cent. ad valorem, under the act of— 1846.	1857.	Into Great Britain from foreign nations.	Into Great Britain from the British colonies.
Sulphate of quinine	20	15	12 cents per ounce	12 cents per ounce
morphia	30	24	$1 20 per pound	$1 20 per pound
Sulphur, roll or flour	20	15	Free	Free
Sulphuric acid, or oil of vitriol	10	4	Free	Free
Sumac, or shumac	5	4	Free	Free
Surgical instruments	30	24	60 cents per cwt	60 cents per cwt
Suspenders, cotton and wool	30	24	5 per cent. ad valorem	5 per cent. ad valorem
gum, or part gum and webbing, India rubber	30	24	8 cents per pound	8 cents per pound
Swansdown, real	25	19	If made on silk body, 15 per ct.	No discriminating duty defined.
vestings and cloths, woollen	30	24	If made on cotton body, free	Vestings, cloths, &c , not made up, free
Sweetmeats, of all descriptions	30	40	Free	Free
preserved in sugar, brandy, or molasses	40	30	Preserved in sugar, 4 cents per lb. Preserved in brandy, the spirit	4 cents per pound duty on the quantity thereof
Sword knots, metal, lace	30	24	10 per cent. ad valorem	10 per cent. ad valorem
Table cloths or covers, cotton or worsted	25	24	5 per cent. ad valorem	5 per cent. ad valorem
linen	20	15	5 per cent. ad valorem	5 per cent. ad valorem
oil cloth and mats	30	24	Oil cloth 3 cents per yard, mats free	Oil cloth 3 cents per yard, mats free
woollen	30	24	5 per cent. ad valorem	5 per cent. ad valorem
Table tops of scagliola	40	30	10 per cent. ad valorem	10 per cent. ad valorem
Table tops of marble	30	24	Free	Free
Tables	30	24	10 per cent. ad valorem	10 per cent. ad valorem
Tacks, brads, and sprigs of all kinds	30	24	60 cents per cwt	60 cents per cwt
Tailor's irons	30	24	60 cents per cwt	60 cents per cwt
Tallow, marrow, and all other grease and soap stuffs, not otherwise provided for	10	8	36 cents per cwt., except vegetable tallow, which is free	2 cents per cwt., except vegetable tallow, which is free
candles	20	15	56 cents per cwt	No discriminating duty defined
Tamborines	20	15	10 per cent. ad valorem	10 per cent. ad valorem
Tannin	30	24	Free	Free
Tapers, wax	20	15	56 cents per cwt	56 cents per cwt
Tapes, cotton	25	24	5 per cent. ad valorem	5 per cent. ad valorem
linen	20	15	5 per cent. ad valorem	5 per cent. ad valorem
Tapioca	20	15	9 cents per cwt	9 cents per cwt

TARIFFS—Continued.

Denomination of merchandise.	Duties on imports. Into the United States from foreign nations, per cent. ad valorem, under the act of— 1846.	1857.	Into Great Britain from foreign nations.	Into Great Britain from the British colonies.
Tar	20	15	Free	Free
Tartaric acid	20	4	Free	Free
Tarred cables and cordage	25	19	Free	Free
Tartar, cream of	20	4	Free	Free
crude or raw	5	Free	Free	Free
Teas, of all kinds, imported direct from place of production in American or equalized vessels		Free	All teas pay:	
all other	20	15	Until 5th April, 1856, 30 cents per pound; after 5th April, 1856, 24 cents per pound	No discriminating duty defined
Teazles	20	15	Free	Free
Telescopes	30	24	Free	Free
Terne, tin plates	15	8	As manufactures of tin, $2 40 per cwt	$2 40 per cwt
Terra japonica, a dye	10	Free	Free	Free
Thread, cotton, yarn, or twist	25	24	Free	Free
Thread, sewing, of flax or shoe thread	20	15	Free	Free
gloves, stockings, or socks	30	24	5 per cent. ad valorem	5 per cent. ad valorem
laces and insertings	20	15	Not being Brussels, point, or Saxon bone lace, not exceeding one inch in width, $4 80 per lb.; exceeding one inch in width, $9 60 per lb	No discriminating duty defined
pack	30	24	Free	Free
Thibet and other goats' hair, unmanufactured	20	15	Free	Free
shawls	30	24	5 per cent. ad valorem	5 per cent. ad valorem
Thimbles, steel and other	30	24	60 cents (steel) per cwt	60 cents (steel) per cwt
brass	30	24	$2 40 per cwt	$2 40 per cwt
gold and silver	30	24	10 per cent. ad valorem	10 per cent. ad valorem
Thyme, essence or oil of	30	24	24 cents per lb	24 cents per lb
Tiles, paving and roofing	20	15	Free	Free
marble	30	24	Free	Free
Tin, in blocks, pigs, or bars	5	Free	Free	Free
granulated and powdered	20	15	$2 40 per cwt	$2 40 per cwt
all manufactures of tin not specified, or of which tin is a component material	30	24	do	do
Tinned saddlery, common	20	15	10 per cent. ad valorem	10 per cent. ad valorem

TARIFFS—Continued.

DENOMINATION OF MERCHANDISE.	DUTIES ON IMPORTS.			
	Into the United States, from foreign nations, per cent. ad valorem, under the act of—		Into Great Britain from foreign nations.	Into Great Britain from the British Colonies.
	1846.	1857.		
Tinned wire	30	24	Free	Free
Tincal or borax	25	4	Free	Free
Tinctures, medicinal	30	24	20 per cent. ad valorem	20 per cent. ad valorem
perfumery	30	24	4 cents per lb	4 cents per lb
Tips for umbrellas, parasols, of brass or plated	30	24	Brass, $2 40 per cwt Plated, 10 per cent. ad valorem	$2 40 per cwt 10 per cent. ad valorem
bone, horn, or ivory	30	24	10 per cent. ad valorem	do
Tippets and muffs of fur	30	24	Free	Free
Tobacco, unmanufactured	30	24	72 cents per lb., and 5 per cent. additional (a)	72 cents per lb., and 5 per cent. additional
manufactured, or segars	40	30	$2 16 per lb., and 5 per cent. additional	$2 16 per lb., and 5 per cent. additional
snuff	40	30	$1 44 per lb., and 5 per cent. additional	$1 44 per lb., and 5 per cent. additional
Tobacco pipes, of clay, china, or other material	30	24	Free $2 40 per cwt	Free $2 40 per cwt
seed	Free	Free	Free	Free
stems and scraps	30	24	72 cents per lb., as tobacco unmanufactured	72 cents per lb., as tobacco unmanufactured
Tolu, balsam of	30	24	Free	Free
Tokay wine	40	30	$1 32 per gallon, and 5 per cent. additional	No discriminating duty, not being of colonial production
Tongues, neat's, sounds, and rein-deer	20	15	Free	Free
Tonka, or tonqua, or tonca beans	20	15	Free	Free
Tooth brushes	30	24	10 per cent. ad valorem	10 per cent. ad valorem
Tortoise and other shells, unmanufactured	5	4	Free	Free
shell, all manufactures of	30	24	10 per cent. ad valorem	10 per cent. ad valorem
Tow carpets and carpeting	30	24	5 per cent. ad valorem	5 per cent. ad valorem
Tragacanth, gum	10	8	Free	Free
Traces, chain	30	24	60 cents per cwt.	60 cents per cwt
leather	30	24	10 per cent. ad valorem	10 per cent. ad valorem
Traps, of iron	30	24	60 cents per cwt	60 cents per cwt
of iron and wood, or wire	30	24	10 per cent. ad valorem	10 per cent. ad valorem

(a) Tobacco, and manufactures of, are prohibited by the British Tariff, unless imported in ships of not less than 120 tons burden, and into ports approved by the commissioners of customs. The packages must contain a quantity not less than 80 lbs. net weight.—("Digests," Vol. I, p. 43.)

TARIFFS—Continued.

DENOMINATION OF MERCHANDISE.	DUTIES ON IMPORTS.			
	Into the United States, from foreign nations, per cent. ad valorem, under the act of—		Into Great Britain from foreign nations.	Into Great Britain from the British colonies.
	1846.	1857.		
Trays, japanned	30	24	$4 80 per cwt., as japanned ware.	$4 80 per cwt., as japanned ware.
Trowels	30	24	60 cents per cwt	60 cents per cwt.
Tresses	30	24	10 per cent. ad valorem	10 per cent. ad valorem
Tubes, bone or ivory	30	24	do do	do do
Tubs, wooden	30	24	do do	do do
Turkey carpets and carpeting	30	24	12 cents per square yard	12 cents per square yard
Turmeric	5	4	Free	Free
Turpentine, spirits of	20	15	Free	Free
Turtles	20	15	Free	Free
shell	5	4	Free	Free
Turquoises, unset	10	4	Free	Free
set	30	24	10 per cent. ad valorem	10 per cent. ad valorem
Twines and packthread	30	24	Free	Free
Twist, cotton	25	24	5 per cent. ad valorem	5 per cent. ad valorem
silk	25	24	15 per cent. ad valorem	do do
worsted	25	19	5 per cent. ad valorem	do do
straw	30	24	12 cents per pound	12 cents per pound
Ultramarine, a sky blue color	20	15	Free	Free
Umbrellas and parasols, of all kinds	30	24	Silk, each, 24 cents; cotton, 5 per cent	No discriminating duty defined
frames or sticks	30	24	Of cane, 72 cents per 100	Of cane, 72 cents per 100
Unbleached linens	20	15	Free	Free
Undressed furs, on the skin	10	8	Free	Free
Unmanufactured cork	15	4	Free	Free
flax	15	Free	Free	Free
ivory	5	Free	Free	Free
marble	20	15	Free	Free
Untarred cordage	25	19	Free	Free
Unwrought burr-stones	10	Free	Free	Free
clay	5	4	Free	Free
Valonia, a nut for dyeing	5	Free	Free	Free
Vanilla beans	20	15	Free	Free
Varnishes of all descriptions	20	15	Containing any quantity of spirits or alcohol, $2 88 per gallon	
Vases, china, earthenware, or stone	30	24	$2 40 per cwt	$2 40 per cwt
plaster of Paris	30	24	10 per cent. ad valorem	10 per cent. ad valorem
Vegetable substances unmanufactured, not otherwise provided for	20	15	Free	Free
Vegetables used in dyeing or in composing dyes, not otherwise provided for, crude	5	Free	Free	Free

TARIFFS—Continued.

DENOMINATION OF MERCHANDISE.	DUTIES ON IMPORTS.			
	Into the United States from foreign nations, per cent. ad valorem, under the act of—		Into Great Britain from foreign nations.	Into Great Britain from the British colonies.
	1846.	1857.		
Veils, lace, cotton	25	24	All manufactures of cotton are marked in the British tariff at 5 per cent. ad valorem, whilst thread or cotton pillow lace is rated at a duty of $4 80 per pound.	
silk	25	24	15 per cent. ad valorem	5 per cent. ad valorem
Vellum	30	24	Free	Free
Velvets, cotton	20	15	5 per cent. ad valorem	5 per cent. ad valorem
silk	25	19	Plain or figured, viz: broad stuffs, $2 16 per pound	Plain or figured, viz: broad stuffs, $2 16 per pound
ribbons	25	19	Not exceeding 9 inches in width, viz: plain, or embossed by depression, without satin or fancy edge, $1 20 per pound	No discrimination
			Figured, brocaded, striped, or spotted, or with fancy or satin edge, and silk ribbons in any way mixed or ornamented with velvet or plush, $2 40 per pound.	
in strips, fit only for shoes or buttons	5	4	72 cents per pound	72 cents per pound
Velveteens, cotton	25	15	5 per cent. ad valorem	5 per cent. ad valorem
Venetian carpets and carpeting	30	24	12 cents per square yard	No discriminating duty defined
red, dry	30	24	Free	Free
Venice turpentine	20	15	Of Venice, Scio, or Cyprus, free	Free
Verdigris	20	15	Free	Free
Vermicelli and macaroni	30	15	24 cents per pound	24 cents per cwt
Vermilion	20	15	Free	Free
Vessels of copper	30	24	$2 40 per cwt	$2 40 per cwt
of cast iron	30	24	60 cents per cwt	60 cents per cwt
Vestings, cotton	25	24	Free	Free
silk	25	19	15 per cent. ad valorem	5 per cent. ad valorem
wool, or part wool	30	24	Free	Free
Vests, wove, cotton	20	24	5 per cent. ad valorem	5 per cent. ad valorem
Vials and bottles	30	24	Except cut glass, free	Except cut glass, free
Vices	30	24	60 cents per cwt	60 cents per cwt
Vinegar	30	24	9 cents per gallon	9 cents per gallon
Violins	20	15	10 per cent. ad valorem	10 per cent. ad valorem
Vitriol, blue or Roman	20	15	Free	Free
oil of	10	4	Free	Free
white and green	20	15	Free	Free
Wadding paper	30	24	If ready for use, 10 per cent	No discriminating duty defined
Wafers	30	24	Free	Free
Wagon boxes	30	24	10 per cent. ad valorem	10 per cent. ad valorem

TARIFFS—Continued.

DENOMINATION OF MERCHANDISE.	DUTIES ON IMPORTS.			
	Into the United States from foreign nations, per cent. ad valorem, under the act of—		Into Great Britain from foreign nations.	Into Great from the British colonies.
	1846.	1857.		
Waiters, gilt, plated, or japanned	30	24	Japanned, $4 80 per cwt	Japanned, $4 80 per cwt
Walking canes, or sticks	30	24	Mounted, painted, or otherwise ornamented, $1 44 per 100	Mounted, painted, or otherwise ornamented, $1 44 per 100
Walnuts	30	24	24 cents per bushel	24 cents per bushel
Wares, cabinet and household	30	24	10 per cent. ad valorem	10 per cent. ad valorem
Ware, china, earthen, and stone	30	24	$2 40 per cwt	$2 40 per cwt
glass, uncut	30	24	Free	Free
cut	40	30	$2 40 per cwt	$2 40 per cwt
gilt plates, wood	30	24	10 per cent. ad valorem	10 per cent. ad valorem
iron	30	24	60 cents per cwt	60 cents per cwt
japanned, all kinds not otherwise specified	30	24	$4 80 per cwt	$4 80 per cwt
Warming pans, brass or copper	30	24	$2 40 per cwt	$2 40 per cwt
Wash balls	30	24	If perfumed, 4 cents per pound; other soap, 16 cents per cwt	If perfumed, 4 cents per pound; other soap, 16 cents per cwt
Washes, cosmetic, and perfumes	30	24	4 cents per pound	4 cents per pound
Watches, and parts thereof	10	8	See silver watches, page 51	See silver watches
Water colors	30	24	Free	Free
rose, bay, honey and other	30	24	Free	Free
Wax, bees	20	15	Free	Free
beads	30	24	4 cents per pound	4 cents per pound
candles	20	15	56 cents per cwt	56 cents per cwt
sealing	30	24	Free	Free
shoemakers'	20	15	Free	Free
tapers and matches	20	15	10 per cent. ad valorem	10 per cent. ad valorem
all other manufactures of	20	15	do do	do do
Web, diaper, flax, or hempen	20	15	Free	Free
worsted or cotton	25	19	Free	Free
silk	25	19	15 per cent. ad valorem	5 per cent. ad valorem
Webbing, India rubber	30	24	Manufactures of India rubber, 8 cents per pound	Manufactures of India rubber, 8 cents per pound
Weights, brass and copper	30	24	$2 40 per cwt	$2 40 per cwt
of iron	30	24	60 cents per cwt	60 cents per cwt
of lead	30	24	48 cents per cwt	48 cents per cwt
Weld	5	4	Free	Free
Whalebone, the product of foreign fishery	20	15	Free	Free
Whale oil, of foreign fishing	20	15		
Wheat	20	15	24 cents per quarter, or 8 bushels.	No discriminating duty defined

TARIFFS—Continued.

DENOMINATION OF MERCHANDISE.	DUTIES ON IMPORTS. Into the United States from foreign nations, per cent. ad valorem, under the act of— 1846.	1857.	Into Great Britain from foreign nations.	Into Great Britain from the British colonies
Wheat flour	20	15	9 cents per cwt	9 cents per cwt
Whetstones	20	15	Free	Free
Whips	30	24	10 per cent. ad valorem	10 per cent. ad valorem
White Paris	20	15	Free	Free
Whiting, dry or ground, in oil	20	15	Free	Free
Wigs, hair	30	24	5 per cent. ad valorem	5 per cent. ad valorem
Willow baskets	30	24	8 cents per cubic foot	
or osiers prepared for basket makers' use	20	15	Free	Free
Wine lees, liquid	20	15	$1 32 per gallon, and 5 per cent. additional	66 cents per gallon, and 5 per cent. additional
Wines, Burgundy, Champagne, Claret, Madeira	40	30	$1 32 per gallon, and 5 per cent. additional	If of colonial produce, and imported thence, 66 cents per gallon, and 5 per cent. ad valorem
Wines, port	40	30	$1 32 per gallon, and 5 per cent. additional	No discriminating duty defined
sherry	40	30	$1 32 per gallon, and 5 per cent. additional	$1 32 per gallon, and 5 per cent. additional
of all other kinds	40	30		
Wine bottles	30	24	Free	Free
Wire of all kinds	30	24	Free	Free
Woad or pastel	10	4	Free	Free
Wood, unmanufactured, not enumerated	30	24		
cedar, grenadilla, ebony, mahogany, rose, and satin, unmanufactured	20	15	Timber or wood, not being deals, spikes, oars, lath wood, or other otherwise dressed, except	battens, boards, staves, hand- timber or wood, sawn, split, or hewn, and not being otherwise
boards or plank	20	15	charged with duty, $1 80 per	load of 50 cubic feet
Brazil wood, braziletto, log, fustic, Nicaragua, and all dye wood in sticks	5	Free.	Of and from British possessions, and 5 per cent. ad valorem Deals, battens, boards, or other	24 cents per load of 50 cubic feet, additional timber or wood, sawn or split,
all dye woods, chipped or ground	20	15	and not otherwise charged with feet	duty, $2 40 per load of 50 cubic
screws	30	24	Of and from British possessions,	48 cents per load of 50 cubic feet,
quassia	20	15	and 5 per cent. additional	
manufactures of cedar, grenadilla, ebony, mahogany, rose, and satin	40	30	Staves, exceeding 72 inches in inches in thickness, $2 16 per Of and from British possessions,	length, 7 inches in breadth, or 3¼ load of 50 cubic feet 48 cents per load of 50 cubic feet,
bar, a dye wood	5	Free.	and 5 per cent. additional	

TARIFFS—Continued.

DENOMINATION OF MERCHANDISE.	DUTIES ON IMPORTS. Into the United States, from foreign nations, per cent. ad valorem, under the act of— 1846.	1857.	Into Great Britain from foreign nations.	Into Great Britain from the British colonies.
Wood, all manufactures of, not otherwise specified	30	24	Staves not exceeding 72 inches nor 3¼ inches in thickness,	in length, nor 7 inches in breadth, free, per load. (a)
Wool, unmanufactured	30	24 (b)	Free	Free
clothing	30	24	5 per cent. ad valorem	5 per cent. ad valorem
caps, or hats	30	24	5 per cent. ad valorem	5 per cent. ad valorem
gloves, mitts, hosiery	30	24	6 cents per dozen pair	6 cents per dozen pair
baizes, bockings	25	19	Free	Free
floor-cloths	25	24	5 per cent. ad valorem	5 per cent. ad valorem
cloths, cassimeres, cassinets	30	24	Free	Free
flannels	25	19	Free	Free
rugs	30	24	12 cents per square yard	No discrimination
yarn	25	24	Cable yarn; camel or mohair; linen or raw; of silk and worsted spun together and not dyed; woollen; free. Worsted yarn, fit and proper for embroidery, 12 cents per pound. Worsted yarn, for fancy purposes, of two or more threads, not fit and proper for embroidery, 6 cents per pound. Worsted yarn, raw, not dyed, or only partially dyed, and not being fit or proper for embroidery, or other purposes, free	
all other manufactures of, or of which wool is a component part	30	24	Free	Free
manufactures of embroidered or tamboured	30	24	10 per cent. ad valorem	5 per cent. ad valorem
and cotton or silk	30	24	(and cotton) free; (and silk) 15 per cent	(and cotton) free; (and silk) 5 per cent
flocks	5	4	Free	Free
Wormseed oil	30	24	20 per cent. ad valorem	20 per cent. ad valorem
Wormwood oil	30	24	20 per cent. ad valorem	20 per cent. ad valorem
Worsted bindings	25	19	5 per cent. ad valorem	5 per cent. ad valorem
shawls	30	24	Plain, 8 cents per pound; printed, 16 cents per pound	No discrimination
braces, hose, gloves, shirts and drawers	30	24	Gloves, 6 cents per dozen pairs	No discrimination
			Braces, shirts, hose, and drawers, 5 per cent. ad valorem	No discrimination
plush	25	19	Free	Free
manufactures of	25	19	(Not made up) free	(Not made up) free
Yams	20	15	4 cents per pound	4 cents per pound

(a) See note, p. 13.

(b) By the tariff of 1857, wool unmanufactured, the value of 20 cents per pound, or less, at the port of exportation, provided it is imported in ordinary condition, is declared free.

TARIFFS—Continued.

Denomination of merchandise.	Duties on imports. Into the United States, from foreign nations, per cent. ad valorem, under the act of—		Into Great Britain from foreign nations.	Into Great Britain from the British colonies.
	1846.	1857.		
Yarns, cordage	25	19	Free	Free
cotton	25	24	Free	Free
flax or hemp	20	15	Free	Free
Yellow berries	5	Free	Free	Free
Zinc, in blocks	5	4	Free	Free
valerianate of	30	24	As an extract, &c., 20 per cent.	ad valorem
sulphate and oxide of	20	15	As an extract, &c., 20 per cent.	ad valorem
manufactured into sheets	15	12	Free	Free
manufactures of	30	24	10 per cent. ad valorem	10 per cent. ad valorem

APPENDIX.

TARIFF DUTIES.

Changes in Tariff Duties made by Act of Parliament, 18 *and* 19 *Vict.*, *Chap.* 97, 1855.

Description of merchandise.	Foreign.	Colonial.
Arms, viz: gun barrels	60 cents per cwt	60 cents per cwt
Boxes, viz: brass	$7 20 per cwt	$7 20 per cwt
not otherwise described	10 per cent. ad valorem	10 per cent
Chloroform	72 cents per pound	72 cents per pound
Corn, and groats	9 cents per cwt	9 cents per cwt
Embroidery on silk, or silk mixed with other materials, not being silk net	15 per cent. ad valorem	5 per cent
Leather: any article made of leather, or any manufacture whereof it is the most valuable part, not otherwise enumerated or described	10 per cent. ad valorem	10 per cent
Licorice root	$1 20 per cwt	$1 20 per cwt
Nutmegs, &c., ground	24 cents per pound	24 cents per pound
Opera glasses, single	24 cents each	24 cents each
double, and all marine and race glasses, telescopes excepted	60 cents each	60 cents each
Silk, romals and taffetas, viz: in pieces not exceeding 6¼ yards	12 cents each	12 cents each
6¼, not over 7¼ yards	16 cents each	16 cents each
7¼, not over 12 yards	20 cents each	20 cents each
and for every additional yard	3 cents	3 cents
Beer, spruce, barrel of 32 gallons	$7 20	$7 20
Cocoa, husks and shells	24 cents per cwt	24 cents per cwt
Ginger	$1 20 per cwt	$1 20 per cwt
preserved	5 cents per pound	5 cents per pound
Hops	$10 80 per cwt	$10 80 per cwt
Morphia, and its salts	$2 40 per pound	$2 40 per pound
Musical instruments, viz: harmoniums or seraphines	$2 88 each	$2 88 each
Prints, &c , admitted under treaties of international copyright, and at the option of the importer, single	1 cent each	1 cent each
Bound	3 cents per dozen	3 cents per dozen
Silk: manufactures of silk, or of silk mixed with any other material called plush, not being ribbons	72 cents per pound	72 cents per pound
Spirits or strong waters, viz: not being sweetened or mixed with any article, so that the degree of strength thereof cannot be ascertained by Sykes' hydrometer, for every gallon of the strength of proof by such hydrometer, and so in proportion for any greater or less strength than the strength of proof, and for any greater or less quantity than a gallon	$3 60	

TARIFFS—Continued.

Description of merchandise.	Foreign.	Colonial.
Of and from a British possession in America or the island of Mauritius, and rum of and from any British possession within the limits of the East India Company's charter, in regard to which the conditions of the act 4 Victoria, c. 8, have or shall have been fulfilled, if imported into England		$1 96 per gallon
If imported into Scotland		$1 96 per gallon
If imported into Ireland		$1 52 per gallon
Rum, shrub, liqueurs, and cordials of and from a British possession in America, or the island of Mauritius, or a British possession within the limits of the East India Campany's charter, qualified as aforesaid, if imported into England		$1 96 per gallon
If imported into Scotland		$1 96 per gallon
If imported into Ireland		$1 52 per gallon
Other spirits, being sweetened or mixed, so that the degree of strength cannnot be ascertained as aforesaid, and perfumed spirits, to be used as perfumery only	$4 80 per gallon	$4 80 per gallon
Spirits or strong waters mixed with any ingredient, though coming under some other denomination, except varnish, shall be subject to duty as spirits.		
Sugar and molasses:		
Upon refined sugar, in loaf or lumps duly refined, having been perfectly clarified and thoroughly dried in the stove, and being of an uniform whiteness throughout, or sugar candy, or sugar refined by the centrifugal machine, not in any way inferior to the export standard No. 3, approved by the lords of the treasury	$4 50 per cwt	$4 50 per cwt
Upon such sugar, if pounded, crushed, or broken, in a warehouse approved by the commissioners of customs, such sugar having been there first inspected by the officers of the customs, in lumps, or loaves, as if for immediate shipment, and then packed for exportation in the presence of such officers	$4 50 per cwt	$4 50 per cwt
Upon bastard or refined sugar unstoved, broken in pieces, or being ground, powdered, or crushed, not in any way inferior to the export standard sample No. 2, approved, &c	$3 96 per cwt	$3 96 per cwt
Upon bastard or refined sugar, being inferior in quality to the said export standard No. 2	$3 30 per cwt	$3 40 per cwt
Tobacco, (manufactured in the united kingdom,) made into cut, shag, roll, or carrot tobacco or cigars, such cigars, when exported as merchandise, being packed in cases containing not less than 80 pounds net, a drawback shall be allowed on exportation or shipment, as stores, of 63 cents per lb		
Worsted or woollen yarn, commonly called Berlin wool or zephyr yarn, and woollen and worsted yarn of two or more threads, scoured, bleached, or colored	12 cents per pound	12 cents per pound
not scoured, bleached, or colored	6 cents per pound	6 cents per pound

TARIFFS—Continued.

ARTICLES EXEMPT FROM DUTY.

Art, works of, of whatever metal; ammonia, liquid; ammonia, sulphate of; beer, produce of the Isle of Man; chicory, or any other vegetable matter applicable to the uses of chicory or coffee, raw, or kiln dried; coir rope, twine, and strands; cordage; marble, sawn, in slabs, or otherwise manufactured; silk, ribbons of, and from a British possession; soda, sulphate of.

Section 11 provides that, if any ship having cargo on board shall depart from any port without being duly cleared, the master shall forfeit the sum of $500.

Section 38 imposes a penalty of $500 on any person making a false declaration in any matter relating to the customs.

NOTE.

Beedell, in the preface to his edition of "The British Tariffs" for 1856–'57, says:

"This edition of 'The British Tariffs' contains but few important changes effected in the laws and duties of customs since the appearance of the former volume. The compiler, partly by reason of this dearth of fiscal legislation, had not intended to reproduce his publication in the present year."

COMPARATIVE TARIFFS.

UNITED STATES AND BRITISH COLONIAL POSSESSIONS.

NORTH AMERICA.(a)

Denomination of merchandise.	Duties on imports. Into— The United States from foreign nations, per cent. ad valorem, under the act of— 1846.	1857.	Newfoundland.(b)	New Brunswick.	Nova Scotia.(b)	Prince Edward's Island.	Canada.
Ale and porter	30	24	In bottles, per doz., 18 cts.; in casks, per gallon, 6 cents.	12 cents per gallon	6¼ per cent. ad valorem	6 cents per gallon	12½ per cent. ad val.
Apples	20	8	36 cents per barrel	12 cents per bushel	96 cents per barrel	5 per cent. ad valorem	30 per cent. ad val.
Apothecaries' ware	30	24	10 per cent. ad valorem	7½ per cent. ad valorem	6¼ per cent. ad valorem	do do	12½ per cent. ad val.
Bacon and hams	20	15	$1 80 per cwt	$1 96 per cwt	$2 16 per cwt	$1 44 per cwt	20 per cent. ad val.
Beef, salted	20	15	48 cents per barrel	do	$1 44 per cwt	do	do do
Biscuit and bread	20	15	6 cents per cwt	10 per cent. ad valorem	(Fine,) 80 cents.; other, free.	$1 56 per cwt	12½ per ct. ad val.; from United Kingdom, free.

(a) This supplement (as well as those which follow) was compiled from the latest imperial and colonial authorities received at the Department of State; but, as many of the articles enumerated have since been exempted from duty by the provisions of the reciprocity treaty of 1854, a list of such articles, together with article 3 of said treaty, is appended:

ARTICLE 3. It is agreed that the articles enumerated in the schedule hereunto annexed, being the growth and produce of the aforesaid British colonies or of the United States, shall be admitted into each country, respectively, free of duty:

Schedule.—Grain, flour, and breadstuffs, of all kinds; animals of all kinds; fresh, smoked, and salted meats; cotton-wool, seeds, and vegetables; undried fruits, dried fruits; fish of all kinds; products of fish, and of all other creatures living in the water; poultry, eggs; hides, furs, skins, or tails, undressed; stone or marble, in its crude or unwrought state; slate; butter, cheese, tallow; lard, horns, manures; ores of metals, of all kinds; coal; pitch, tar, turpentine, ashes; timber and lumber of all kinds, round, hewed, and sawed, unmanufactured in whole or in part; firewood; plants, shrubs, and trees; pelts, wool; fish oil; rice, broom corn, and bark; gypsum, ground or unground; hewn, or wrought, or unwrought burr or grindstones; dye stuffs; flax, hemp, and tow, unmanufactured; unmanufactured tobacco; rags.

For later changes, reference is invited to the Annual Report of the Secretary of State on Foreign Commerce.

(b) On the 21st July, 1855, a new tariff was adopted for Newfoundland, and on the 12th May, 1856, an act was passed raising the scale of import duties, which latter act expired by limitation May 12, 1857. A similar act, passed March 31, 1856, by the provincial parliament of Nova Scotia, expired by limitation April 1, 1857.

NORTH AMERICA—TARIFFS—Continued.

DENOMINATION OF MERCHANDISE.	DUTIES ON IMPORTS. INTO— The United States from foreign nations, per cent. ad valorem, under the act of—						
	1846.	1857.	Newfoundland.	New Brunswick.	Nova Scotia.	Prince Edward's Island.	Canada.
Butter	20	15	72 cents per cwt	$2 24 cents per cwt	$1 92 per cwt	$2 16 per cwt	20 per ct. ad val.; if from United Kingdom, free.
Cabinet ware	30	24	10 per cent. ad valorem	20 per cent. ad valorem	6¼ per cent. ad valorem	5 per cent. ad valorem	12½ per cent. ad val.
Candles, tallow	20	15	7½ per cent. ad valorem	8 cents sperm, and 2 cts. all others, per pound.	2 cents, and all others 6 cents per pound.	do do	do do
Cheese	30	24	$1 20 per cwt	$3 36 per cwt	$1 20 per cwt	$1 92 per cwt	20 per cent. ad val.
Chocolate	20	15	do	7½ per cent. ad valorem	2 cents per pound	2 cents per pound	12½ per cent. ad val.
Coffee	Free(a)	Free	2 cents per pound	3 cents per pound	Green, 2 cents; roasted, &c., 4 cents per lb.	3 cents per pound	Green $1 12 per cwt., and 12½ per ct. ad valorem; roasted, &c., $3 36 per cwt., and 12½ per cent. ad valorem.
Corn, Indian	20	15	5 per cent. ad valorem	Free	Free	5 per cent. ad valorem	Free
meal	20	15	12 cents per barrel	24 cents per barrel, (196 pounds.)	Free	do do	12½ per cent. ad val.
Cotton manufactures	25	24	7½ per cent. ad valorem	7½ per cent. ad valorem	6¼ per cent. ad valorem	do do	do do
Drugs, medicinal	20	15	do do	do do	do do	do do	12½ per cent.; drugs for dyeing, 2½ per cent.
Earthen and china ware	30	24	10 per cent	do do	do do	do do	12½ per cent. ad val.
Fish	20	15	Oysters, 5 p. c.; fish, free	do do	Free	48 cts. per bbl.; dried, 36 cents per 100 pounds.	12½ per ct.; from United Kingdom, free.

(a) When not imported direct from the place of its growth or production, in American or equalized vessels, 20 per cent. ad valorem by the tariff of 1846, and 15 per cent. by that of 1857.

NORTH AMERICA—TARIFFS—Continued.

DENOMINATION OF MERCHANDISE.	DUTIES ON IMPORTS. INTO— The United States from foreign nations, per cent. ad valorem, under the act of—						
	1846.	1857.	Newfoundland.	New Brunswick.	Nova Scotia.	Prince Edward's Island.	Canada.
Fruits	20	8	Fruit, 10 per ct. ad val.; vegetables, fresh, free.	(Dried,) $2 24 per cwt	96 cents per barrel	5 per cent. ad valorem	30 per cent., preserved.
Feathers, for beds	25	19	10 per cent. ad valorem	7½ per cent. ad valorem	6¼ per cent. ad valorem	do do	12½ per cent. ad val.
Furniture	30	24	do do	20 per cent	do do	do do	do do
Flour, wheat	20	15	36 cents per barrel	72 cents per barrel, of 196 pounds.	Free	$1 20 per barrel of 196 pounds.	20 per cent. ad val.; from United Kingdom, free.
Glass ware	30	24	10 per cent. ad valorem	7½ per cent.; looking-glasses, 20 per cent.	6¼ per cent. ad valorem	5 per cent. ad valorem	12½ per cent. ad val.
Grain, wheat	20	15	do do	4 cents per bushel	Free	do do	Free
Hardware and cutlery	30	24	do do	7½ per cent. ad valorem	6¼ per cent. ad valorem	do do	12½ per cent. ad val.
Hats	30	24	do do	20 per cent	do do	do do	do do
Iron manufactures	30	24	5 per cent	7½ and 15 per cent.	2¼ per cent. ad val. (a)	5 per cent., (chain cables free.)	2½ per ct., (of all kinds.)
Leather	20	15	7½ per cent. ad valorem	5 cts. per lb.; (manufactures of, 20 per cent.)	10 per cent. ad val. if manufactured; sole and upper, 2 and 4 cts. per pound.	From 2 to 6 cts. per lb	12½ per cent. ad val.
Lumber	20	15	30 cents per M feet, 1 inch thick.	From 7¼ to 15 per cent.	Free	Boards, 60 cents per M feet; other, free.	2½ per cent. ad val.
Meat, salted and cured	20	15	90 cents per bbl.; prime American pork, 72 cts. per barrel.	$1 96 per cwt	$1 44 per cwt	$1 44 per cwt	Mess pork, 12½ per ct.; all other kinds, 20 per ct.

(a) Unwrought or pig iron, ores of iron of all kinds, iron rails for railroads, boilers, plates, and plough moulds, are admitted free.

NORTH AMERICA—TARIFFS—Continued.

DENOMINATION OF MERCHANDISE.	DUTIES ON IMPORTS. INTO— The United States from foreign nations, per cent. ad valorem, under the act of—						
	1846.	1857.	Newfoundland.	New Brunswick.	Nova Scotia.	Prince Edward's Island.	Canada.
Molasses	30	24	5 cents per gallon	2 cents per gallon	5 cents per gallon	4 cents per gallon	4 cts. per gallon, and 12½ per cent. ad valorem.
Musical instruments	20	15	10 per cent. ad valorem	7½ per cent. ad valorem	6¼ per cent. ad valorem	5 per cent. ad valorem	12½ per cent ad val. (a)
Segars	40	30	$2 40 per 1,000	20 per cent. ad valorem	10 per cent. ad valorem	8 cents per lb	36 cents per lb., and 12½ per cent. ad valorem.
Snuff	40	30	6 cents per lb	do do	do do	do do	8 cents per lb., and 12½ per cent. ad valorem.
Shingles	20	15	24 cents per 1,000	Cedar, spruce pine, and hemlock, 7½ per cent. ad valorem; other kinds, free.	Free	5 per cent. ad valorem	12½ per cent. ad valorem.
Soap	30	24	10 per cent. ad valorem	1 cent. per lb	6¼ per cent. ad valorem	do do	do do
Spirits	100	30	All other than rum, 96 cents; rum, 36 cents per gallon.	80 cents per gall. brandy; 24 cts. per gallon rum.	From 22 cents to 64 cents per gallon.	72 cents per gallon	Whiskey, 6 cents per gallon, and 12½ per cent. ad. val.; rum, 30 cts. per gall., and 25 per cent. ad val.; brandy, 48 cents per gallon, and 25 per cent. ad valorem
Sugar, refined	30	24	$2 88 per cwt	Loaf, 3 cents per lb.; refined, $2 24 per cwt.	Best quality, $3 36; 2d do., $2 40 per cwt.	4 cents per lb	$2 40 per cwt., and 12½ per cent. ad valorem.

(a) For the use of military bands, free.

NORTH AMERICA—TARIFFS—Continued.

Denomination of merchandise.	DUTIES ON IMPORTS. INTO— The United States from foreign nations, per cent. ad valorem, under the act of— 1846.	1857.	Newfoundland.	New Brunswick.	Nova Scotia.	Prince Edward's Island.	Canada.
Sugar, brown	30	24	$1 80 per cwt	$1 44 per cwt	$1 68 per cwt	$1 44 per cwt	$1 44 per cwt., and 12½ per cent. ad valorem.
Tallow	10	8	10 per cent. ad valorem.	1 per cent. ad valorem.	Free	Free	2½ per cent. ad valorem.
Tar	20	15	5 per cent. ad valorem.	do. do.	2½ per cent. ad valorem	2 per cent. ad valorem.	do. do.
Tea	Free(*a*).	Free.	8 cents per lb	4 cents per lb	From 4 to 8 cts. per lb., (according to quality.)	6 cents per lb	2 cents per lb., and 12½ per cent.
Tobacco, manufactured	40	30	6 cts. per lb.; stems, 48 cents per cwt.	3 cents per lb.; unmanufactured, 1 per cent. ad valorem.	3 cents per lb	8 cts. per lb.; (unmanufactured, 4 cts. per lb.	
Turpentine	20	15	5 per cent. ad valorem.	7½ per cent. ad valorem.	Free	5 per cent. ad valorem.	12½ per cent. ad valorem.
Vinegar	30	24	6 cents per gallon	do. do.	6¼ per cent. ad valorem.	do. do.	do. do.
Wine	40	30	In bottles, $1 20; all others, $1 per gall.	60 cents per gallon, and 10 per ct. in addition.	From 30 to 72 cents per gallon.	84 cents per gallon	12 cents per gallon, and 30 per cent.

NOTES.—*Newfoundland.*—There are no export duties levied in Newfoundland. In the port of St. John's an additional duty of 10 per cent. is levied on the amount of duties as noted in the tariff.

New Brunswick.—An additional duty of 1 per centum is levied in this province on all articles of foreign manufacture, or the manufacture of the United Kingdom. This per cent. additional duty is levied on the total amount of the entry, (and not added to the rate,) being computed as follows:

500	lbs. tobacco, at a duty of 3 cents per lb.
3	
15 00	amount of rated duty.
15	amount thereon at 1 per cent.
$15 15	total duties.

Nova Scotia and Canada.—No export duties.

Prince Edward's Island.—An export duty is levied on juniper knees of 24 cents each.

(*a*) When not imported direct from place of production, in American or equalized vessels, 20 per cent. ad valorem by the tariff of 1846, and 15 per cent. by that of 1857.

TARIFFS—Continued.

EAST INDIES AND OTHER COLONIES.

DENOMINATION OF MERCHANDISE.	DUTIES ON IMPORTS. INTO— The United States, from foreign nations, per cent. ad valorem, under the act of— 1846.	1857.	East Indies.	South Australia.
Bread and biscuit	20	15	In British vessels, 5 per cent. ad valorem; in foreign, 10 per cent.	14 cents per cwt
Butter	20	15		72 cents per cwt
Candles	20	15		Tallow, 72 cts.; others, $2 88
Cheese	30	24		72 cents per cwt
Clocks	30	24		10 per cent. ad valorem
Cutlery	30	24		5 per cent. ad valorem
Earthen and china ware	30	24		do do
Furniture	30	24		10 per cent. ad valorem
Glass, manufactures	30	24		do do
Hides, dressed	20	15		72 cents per cwt
Lead, manufactures of	30	24		5 per cent. ad valorem
Leather, manufactures of	30	24		do do
Musical instruments	20	15		10 per cent. ad valorem
Pitch and tar	20	15		24 cents per barrel
Rosin	20	15		12 cents per barrel
Tallow	10	8		48 cents per cwt

TARIFFS—Continued.

EAST INDIES AND OTHER COLONIES.

DENOMINATION OF MERCHANDISE.	DUTIES ON IMPORTS. INTO— The United States, from foreign nations, per cent. ad valorem, under the act of—			
	1846.	1857.	Natal.	Cape of Good Hope. (a)
Bread and biscuit	20	15	Of British produce, 5 per cent. ad valorem; of foreign, 12 per cent.	Of British produce, 5 per cent. ad valorem; of foreign, 12 per cent.
Butter	20	15		
Candles	20	15		
Cheese	30	24		
Clocks	30	24		
Cutlery	30	24		
Earthen and china ware	30	24		
Furniture	30	24		
Glass, manufactures	30	24		
Hides, dressed	20	15		
Lead, manufactures of	30	24		
Leather, manufactures of	30	24		
Musical instruments	20	15		
Pitch and tar	20	15		
Rosin	20	15		
Tallow	10	8		

(a) On the 4th of May, 1855, a tariff was adopted by the assembly of the Cape of Good Hope—the rates on a few of the articles in which are as follows: cheese, per cwt, $2 40; coffee, per cwt., $3 20; currants, per cwt., $1 20; flour, per barrel, 74 cents; meat, per cwt., 74 cents; rice, per cwt., 50 cents; sugar, unrefined, per cwt., 86 cents; sugar, refined, per cwt., $1 20; tea, per pound, 12 cents; tobacco, unmanufactured, per cwt., $6 75; tobacco, manufactured, (not cigars,) per cwt, $18 50.

TARIFFS—Continued.

WEST INDIES.

Denomination of merchandise.	Duties on imports. Into the United States from foreign nations, per cent. ad valorem, under the act of— 1846.	1857.	Into Antigua.	Into Bahamas.
Ale and beer	30	24	$7 20 per tun, 18 cents per dozen quart bottles.	8 cents per gallon, 24 cents per dozen quart bottles
Beef and pork	20	15	$3 84 per barrel of 200 pounds	$1 20 per cwt
Bread or biscuit	20	15	60 cents per cwt	48 cents per cwt
Butter	20	15	$2 40 per cwt	$2 88 per cwt.
Barley	20	15	6 cents per bushel	Not defined
Candles	20	15	Tallow, 2; others, 6 cts. per lb	Tallow, $1 20 per cwt.; sperm and wax, $2 88 per cwt
Cheese	30	24	$1 92 per cwt	$2 16 per cwt
Cigars	40	30	$2 40 per 1,000	96 cents per 1,000, and 15 per cent. ad valorem
Coffee	Free(a)	Free	4½ per cent. ad valorem	96 cents per cwt
Corn, Indian	20	15	6 cents per bushel	Free
Flour, wheat	20	15	$1 20 per barrel of 196 pounds	72 cents per barrel, (196 pounds.)
Hams and bacon	20	15	$1 92 per cwt	$1 20 per cwt
Ice	20	Free	Free	Free
Lard	20	15	$1 20 per cwt	$1 44 per cwt
Meat, salted and cured	20	15	$3 84 per barrel of 200 pounds	$1 20 per cwt
Molasses	30	24	4½ per cent. ad valorem	4 cents per gallon
Nails of iron	30	24	4½ per cent. ad valorem	72 cents per cwt
Pitch	20	15	4½ per cent. ad valorem	Tar and turpentine, 24 cts. per bl.
Potatoes	30	24	24 cents per barrel	Free
Rice	20	15	48 cents per cwt	36 cents per cwt
Rosin, tar, turpentine	20	15	4½ per cent. ad valorem	Spirits of turpentine, 6 cents per gallon. (See pitch)
Rum	100	30	48 cents per gallon	From 48 to 72 cents per gallon
Shingles, cypress	20	15	$1 50 per 1,000	48 cents per 1,000
other than cypress	20	15	50 cents per 1,000	24 cents per 1,000
Soap, common	30	24	1 cent per pound	96 cents per cwt
Sugar, refined	30	24	12 cents per pound, (refined in bond in the United Kingdom).	$2 40 per cwt
unrefined	30	24	Not defined	$1 20 per cwt
Spirits	100	30	From 48 to 60 cents per gallon	60 cts. per gal.; rum, from 48 to 72 cts. per gal.; brandy, $1 20 do.
Tobacco, unmanufactured	30	24	4 cents per pound	$1 20 per cwt
manufactured, not cigars	40	30	8 cents per pound	$3 36 per cwt
Turpentine, spirits of	20	15	4½ per cent. ad valorem	6 cents per gallon
Wines	40	30	15 per cent. ad valorem	Of all kinds, 12 cents per gallon and 20 per cent. ad valorem

(a) Except as before noted, p. 69.

TARIFFS—Continued.

WEST INDIES.

DENOMINATION OF MERCHANDISE.	DUTIES ON IMPORTS. Into the United States from foreign nations, per cent. ad valorem, under the act of— 1846.	1857.	Into Barbadoes.	Into British Guiana.
Ale and beer	30	24	$1 per cask of 64 gallons; 6 cents per dozen bottles	$2 per hogshead
Beef and pork	20	15	50 cents per barrel of 200 pounds	Pickled, $1 50 per barrel; dried, 4 cents per pound
Bread or biscuit	20	15	White, 16 cents per bbl; brown, 12 cents per cwt	50 cents per 100 pounds
Butter	20	15	$1 per cwt., (salted)	3 cents per pound
Barley	20	15	12 cents per bushel	5 cents per bushel
Candles	20	15	Tallow, 50 cents; and others $2 per cwt	Tallow, 3; others 5 cts. per lb
Cheese	30	24	$1 per cwt	3 cents per pound
Cigars	40	30	Free, (under acts of limited duration)	$2 per 1,000
Coffee	Free(a)	Free	50 cents per cwt	$2 50 per 112 pounds
Corn, Indian	20	15	6 cents per bushel	5 cents per bushel
Flour, wheat	20	15	36 cents per barrel of 196 pounds	$1 per barrel of 196 pounds
Hams and bacon	20	15	50 cents per cwt	2 cents per pound
Ice	20	Free	50 cents per ton	Free
Lard	20	15	50 cents per cwt	1 cent per pound
Meat, salted and cured	20	15	50 cents per barrel of 200 pounds	$1 50 per barrel of 200 pounds
Molasses	30	24	3 per cent. ad valorem	18 cents per gallon
Nails of iron	30	24	3 per cent. ad valorem	4 per cent. ad valorem
Pitch	20	15	3 per cent. ad valorem	50 cents per barrel
Potatoes	30	24	Free	8 cents per bushel
Rice	20	15	12 cents per cwt	25 cents per 100 pounds
Rosin, tar, turpentine	20	15	Turpentine, $1 per 100 gallons	50 cents per barrel; spirits of turpentine, 18 cents per gallon
Rum	100	30	Free	From 6 cents to $1 20 per gallon
Shingles, cypress	20	15	3 per cent. ad valorem	Of all kinds, 50 cents per 1,000
other than cypress	20	15	3 per cent. ad valorem	
Soap, common	30	24	24 cents per cwt	1 cent per pound
Sugar, refined	30	24	$1 per cwt	$4 per 112 pounds
unrefined	30	24	do	$4 per 112 pounds
Spirits	100	30	Free	From 6 cents to $1 20 per gallon
Tobacco, unmanufactured	30	24	Free	5 cents per pound
manufactured, not cigars	40	30	Free	5 cents per pound
Turpentine, spirits of	20	15	$1 per 100 gallons	18 cents per gallon
Wines	40	30	Temporary acts, free; under permanent act, 5 per cent.	$1 per dozen quart bottles; in wood, 54 cents per gallon

(a) Except as before noted, p. 69.

TARIFFS—Continued.

WEST INDIES.

Denomination of merchandise.	Duties on imports. Into the United States from foreign nations, per cent. ad valorem, under the act of— 1846.	1857.	Into Turk's Island. (a)	Into Jamaica.	Into Trinidad.
Ale and beer	30	24	In quart bottles, 12 cts. per doz.; in wood, free.	$20 88 (sterling value) per tun.	$2 40 per cask of 64 gls.; 12 cts per doz. qt. btls.
Beef and pork	20	15	$1 12 per cwt	$2 40 per bbl. of 200 lbs.	$2 per bbl.; $1 per 100 pounds.
Bread or biscuit	20	15	36 cents per cwt	$1 44 per cwt	15 cents per barrel
Butter	20	15	$2 24 per cwt	$2 16 per cwt	2 cents per pound
Barley	20	15	4 cents per bushel	6 cents per bushel	3½ per cent. ad valorem, (not enumerated.)
Candles	20	15	Tallow, 72 cts. per cwt.; others, from $1 50 to $2 88 do.	Tallow, 60 cts. per 56 lbs.; spermaceti, $1 92 do.	Tallow, 50 cts.; sperm and others, $1 44 per 100 pounds.
Cheese	30	24	$1 92 per cwt	$2 40 per cwt	$1 20 per 100 pounds
Cigars	40	30	$2 40 per 1,000	16 cts. per lb., and 20 per ct. ad valorem.	6 cents per pound
Coffee	Free(b)	Free	$1 44 per cwt	$4 80 (sterling value) per cwt.	$1 20 per 100 pounds
Corn, Indian	20	15	4 cents per bushel	6 cents per bushel	5 cents per bushel
Flour, wheat	20	15	90 cts. per bbl.; other than wheat, 36 cts. do.	Wheat, $1 44; rye, 48 cents per bbl.	$1 20 per bbl. of 196 lbs.
Hams and bacon	20	15	$1 12 per cwt	$2 40 per cwt	Not defined.—(See beef and pork.)
Ice	20	Free	Free	Free	Not defined
Lard	20	15	96 cents per cwt	$1 20 per cwt	60 cents per 100 pounds.
Meat, salted and cured	20	15	$1 12 per cwt	$2 40 per bbl. of 200 lbs.	$2 per bbl.; $1 per 100 pounds.
Molasses	30	24	4 cents per gallon	72 cents per cwt	12 cents per gallon
Nails of iron	30	24	72 cents per cwt	12½ per ct. ad valorem.	5 per cent. ad valorem.
Pitch	20	15	Tar, rosin, and turpentine, 48 cents per bbl.	12½ per ct. ad valorem.	12 cents per barrel
Potatoes	30	24	Free	Free	3½ per cent. ad valorem.
Rice	20	15	24 cents per cwt	48 cents per cwt	48 cents per 100 pounds.
Rosin, tar, turpentine	20	15	48 cents per barrel	Not defined; resins, free	12 cents per barrel
Rum	100	30	From 60 to 72 c. per gall.	$1 92 per gallon; British colonial, $1 44 per gal.	96 cents per gallon
Shingles, cypress	20	15	48 cents per 1,000	Larger than 12 inches, $1 44 per 1,000	24 cents per 1,000
other than cypress	20	15	24 cents per 1,000 (c)	72 cents per 1,000	24 cents per 1,000

(a) A new tariff of Turk's and Caicos islands was adopted to take effect January 1, 1856, and "thence to the end of the next session of the legislative council."

(b) Except as before noted, p. 69.

(c) Over 18 inches in length, 48 cents per thousand.

TARIFFS—Continued.

WEST INDIES.

DENOMINATION OF MERCHANDISE.	DUTIES ON IMPORTS.				
	Into the United States from foreign nations, per cent. ad valorem, under the act of— 1846.	1857.	Into Turk's Island.	Into Jamaica.	Into Trinidad.
Soap, common	30	24	72 cents per cwt	48 cts. per box of 56 lbs.	24 cents per 100 pounds.
Sugar, refined	30	24	$4 08 per cwt	4 cents per pound	$2 40 per 100 pounds
unrefined	30	24	$1 12 per cwt	$2 40 per cwt	$2 40 per 100 pounds
Spirits	100	30	5 cents per gallon	Not otherwise described, $1 92 per gallon(a)	48 cents per gallon
Tobacco, unmanufactured	30	24	$1 per cwt	4 cents per pound	9 cents per pound
manuf., not cigars	40	30	$2 per cwt	6 cents per pound and 30 per ct. ad valorem.	9 cents per pound
Turpentine, spirits of	20	15	6 cents per gallon	12½ per ct. ad valorem.	2 cents per gallon
Wines	40	30	Champagne, $1 20 per dozen quart bottles; other, 96 cents; in wood, from 36 to 60 cents per gallon.	$48 (in wood or bottles) per ton, and 10 per cent. ad valorem.	In quart bottles, from 96 cents to $1 44 per dozen; in wood, from 16 to 48 cts. per gal.

(a) By new tariff of 22d December, 1854, to continue in force to 31st day of December, 1856, brandy is charged $1 44 per gallon; gin, $1 20 per gallon; whiskey, $1 20 per gallon; all other spirits, cordials, or compounds, $1 92 per gallon.

FRANCE

AND

HER POSSESSIONS.

FRANCE AND HER POSSESSIONS.

The tariff is that of 1844, with supplements and modifications up to 1855.(a)

The prohibitions and duties are applicable to all ports of entry of the empire. The foreign ministers and other members of the diplomatic corps are the only persons enjoying the privilege of immunity from all custom-house duties.

All merchandise imported from foreign countries is considered as "foreign," and, therefore, subject to the duty on foreign goods.

Merchandise, the import duty on which exceeds twenty francs ($3 72) per 100 kilogrammes, (220 pounds,) is admissible only at certain ports; the same is true as regards exports. From this restriction, however, small quantities carried by travellers are exempted.

Products of the French colonies enjoy important modifications of duty under the title of "colonial privileges."

Products of the East Indian archipelago (the islands beyond the Straits of Sunda) pay, with the exception of sugar, one-fifth less duty on all imports than those countries which, after the colonies, are the most favored as regards duties.

Products of the Levant are treated as those of countries out of Europe, if imported direct, and consist, for the most part, of yellow wax, copper in masses, fish oil, gall-nuts, hides, and potash, coming from the ports of the Black Sea.

American vessels, on direct voyage to France, compelled to run into a foreign port by inclemency of weather, will, if they procure a certificate of the fact from the French consul residing at that port, be considered as on direct voyage and enjoy all the privileges attached thereto.

Besides the custom-house dues, there is levied ten per cent. on the amount of the total duty, (exclusive of the sanitary dues,) called "*décime additionnel;*" but American vessels are exempted from this.

An extra duty (*surtaxe*) of twenty francs ($3 72) on the ton of merchandise was levied after the conclusion of the treaty of June 24, 1822, on American vessels in French ports and on French vessels in American ports. This charge, however, ceased by limitation the 1st of October, 1827. It may be remarked that the abolition has reference not only to the *direct*, but also to the indirect importation of the two countries, as appears from a letter of the Secretary of the Treasury to the French minister at Washington, dated July 6, 1849. French vessels have, however, in this case to pay the differential duties, as prescribed in the American tariff, and amounting to from ten to twenty per cent. ad valorem.

Every false declaration of the value of goods at the custom-house entails the right of "pre-emption"—that is, the merchandise is retained at the custom-house, and to the owner there is paid, a fortnight after he has received notice of the seizure, a sum equal to the value of the merchandise, with an addition of ten per cent. ad valorem. Articles of which the declaration of the value must be controlled by the "*comité consultatif des arts et manufactures,*" as engraved plates, optical instruments, &c., are not liable to pre-emption. All merchandise taxed by the pound must pay the duty on the gross pound—that is, the weight of the boxes, casks, *emballage*, &c., are not deducted from the real weight of merchandise. From this, however, are excepted those goods the duty on which exceeds forty francs ($7 44) per 100 kilogrammes (220 pounds.) They pay, in conformity with article 7th of the decree of March 27, 1817, only the duty on the net pound.

A later decree also exempts silk work mixed with gold or silver, raw and dyed silks, gold and silver bullion, machines, laces, prepared quills, Indian nankin, raw cotton, sugar, coffee, cocoa, pepper, indigo, potash, sulphate of soda, cream of tartar, and carbonate of potash, which also pay the duty on the net pound. Double cases, coverings, casks, &c., are not estimated in the weight when the duty is charged on the gross weight.

The net pound is either *effective* or *legal*. It is *effective* or really net if the merchandise has been taken out of the boxes, wrappers, &c., and weighed alone. It is *legal* when a deduction or tare for the weight of the cases, coverings, boxes, &c., as defined by law, has been made. The tares of the principal articles of the commerce between the United States and France are as follows:

(a) CHANGES.—For changes in the tariff rates of France and her Possessions since this work was prepared, reference is invited to the Appendix and to the Annual Reports of the Secretary of State.

Rates of tare allowed for the weight of packages.

Denomination of merchandise.	Denomination of the wrapping or packing material.	Rates of Tare.
Sugar	Barrels, from the French colonies	13 per cent
	Barrels, from foreign countries	12 do
	Cases or boxes	12 do
	Bales or bags, several coverings	5 do
	Bales or bags, one covering	2 do
Coffee, Cocoa, Pepper and pimento	In boxes or casks	12 do
	In bales or bags	3 do
Indigo	In boxes or bags, containing bags of linen	14 do
	In boxes or bags, " " of skin	21 do
	In boxes or bags, containing the indigo, without bags of linen or skin	12 do
	In seroons, leather bags	9 do
	In linen bags	2 do
Cotton, raw, from Turkey	In double coverings of matting, or of goats' hair tissues	10 do
Cotton, raw, of all other origin	In bales of under 50 kilogrammes (110 pounds	8 do
	In bales of above 50 kilogrammes, (110 pounds)	6 do
All other merchandise charged with duty, according to net weight	In boxes or casks	12 do
	In bales, boxes, bags, baskets, or hampers	2 do

On tin cases, in which goods are sometimes packed, is charged the duty on tin, and the actual tare of the box is deducted from the articles the box contains.

The net weight of such liquids as are taxed by weight, as acids, fluids, oils, preserves, syrups, &c., is ascertained by deducting the tare allowed on the vessel containing them; on the bottles and jars duty is also paid. Metal vessels pay 10 per cent. ad valorem.

Merchandise injured by storms and other accidents, and depreciated in the value fixed in the price currents, enjoys, if sold at public sale, a reduction of duty in proportion to the depreciation.

Corsica and Algiers have, with the exception of some articles given in the tariff, the same custom-house regulations and duties as France.

The direct trade between France and her colonies is confined to French vessels(a) measuring 40 tons, at least.

As French colonies are considered in the tariff the Island of Bourbon, French Guiana, the French Antilles, Martinique, and Guadalupe, (with its dependencies, viz: Marie Galante, Dĕsirade,) and the French part of St. Martin, all the other French colonial establishments, as Senegal and Gorĕe, St. Pierre and M quelon, the Islands Ste. Marie de Madagascar, Mayotte, Nossi-Bĕ, Tahite, Mukahira, are only regarded as "settlements," and enjoy less privileges than the colonies proper.

France has with almost all nations distinct and separate treaties, which circumstance renders more complicated the French custom-house system.

American produce imported *direct* into France, and in American bottoms, will, with the exception of the raw products of fisheries and crude tin, pay the duty given in the tariff, under the head "*In national vessels.*" If, however, imported *indirectly*, they are, with the exception of raw cotton, subject to the duty given under the head "*In foreign vessels.*"

Moneys, weights, and measures.

1 franc = 100 centimes = 18.6 American cents.
5 francs = 93 cents
1 American dollar = 5 francs 42 centimes.
1 American cent = 5.4 centimes.
1 mĕtre = 3.28 feet. 1 decimĕtre = 3.94 inches.
1 millimĕtre = 0.0394 of an inch.
1 hectolitre, liquid capacity, = 26.42 gallons.
1 " dry capacity, = 2.84 bushels.

1 decalitre, liquid capacity, = 2.64 gallons.
1 " dry capacity, = 9.08 quarts.
1 litre = 2.11 pints.
1 kilogramme = 2.22 l s.
100 kilogrammes, or 1 quintal, = 220 lbs.
1 stĕre = 35.31 cubic feet.
1 aune = 1.30 yards.

(a) For modifications of this law see Vol. I, "Digests," France.

APPENDIX.

THE nature of the changes and modifications sustained by the tariff of France since the preceding pages were prepared, as well as the character and frequency of changes and modifications in that tariff generally, may be inferred from a synopsis of the more important imperial decrees, ministerial circulars, &c., which have been put forth during the two years ending September, 1856, which is subjoined. It affords a convincing exemplification of the impossibility of presenting in print a statement which shall afford the exact rates of the French tariff, current and in force on the day of publication. It may be doubted whether the Director General of the Customs of France could himself present such a work. Long before the last sheets of his thick quarto, embodying the existing tariff, had left the press, the rates noted in the columns of the first pages would, doubtless, have experienced material modifications, by virtue of the decrees, ordinances, circulars, decisions, &c., &c., which are daily looked for from that department of the public service. And the remark is not inapplicable to the tariffs of other countries besides France.

September 22, 1854, a decree was issued fixing the duties on all foreign brandies at 15 francs per hectolitre, (26½ gallons United States custom-house measurement,) of the strength of 100 degrees.(a)

October 3 the duty on leeches of 50 centimes per 1,000 was abolished by decree.

October 5 a decree was issued reducing the duties on all foreign wines, both in casks and bottles, to 25 centimes per hectolitre; and on all salted meats 50 centimes (9½ cents) per 100 kilogrammes, (220 pounds United States weight) (b)

October 7 a decree was issued by which the time specified in the decree of June 24th was extended till 31st July, 1855.

The decree of June 24, 1854, provided as follows:

1st. That flour and grain should be admitted on the same terms when imported in foreign ships as when imported in French ships.

2d. That the duties on grain, &c., be reduced to the minimum established by the law of 1832, namely: to 25 centimes per 100 kilogrammes on rice, flour, dried vegetables, and meal of all descriptions.

3d. A prohibition of the export of grain, potatoes, and dried vegetables.

4th. An exemption from tonnage dues of foreign vessels arriving with flour, grain, rice, dried vegetables, and potatoes.

5th. Permission granted foreign vessels to carry the above articles from one port in France to another, and also between ports in France and Algeria.

6th. Prohibition of the export of potatoes from Algeria, and export from France to Algeria permitted.

By a decree of the 25th October the importation duty on medicinal leaves was fixed as follows:

Orange, ivy, (stems and branches included.)

Betel; clove; senna, (leaves and follienas, whole or broken;) and others not enumerated:

By French ships.—From countries out of Europe, free.

From entrepots, 10 francs per 100 kilogrammes.

By foreign ships, 20 francs per 100 kilogrammes.

(a) There are no spirits of the above strength, 90 degrees being about the maximum distilled. Sixty-three degrees, French standard, corresponds with the fourth-proof United States, and is the usual strength at which brandies are bought and sold.

(b) The increase in the price of meats in France has been very great since 1848; so much so, that general complaint exists on the subject. From 1852 to 1854 there has been an increase of price from 40 to 45 per cent. The attention of the government of France having been called to this fact, its efforts have been not only to prevent a further increase, but to effect a diminution from present prices. To this end the tariffs have been revised, and very great reductions have been made upon the importation of foreign cattle, to wit: from $10 23 to 74 cents a head on beef, &c. Not only so, but the direct attention of the people of France has been called to the use of salt meat, and the experiment of opening the market is being made with much success. The duty upon this article has been successively reduced from $5 58 to $3 72, to $1 86, and, in the month of October last, to 9⅓ cents the 220 pounds, or 100 kilogrammes. Under these reductions there has been an astonishing development in its importation. In 1854 the importation of meats, fresh and salt, reached only 3,527 quintaux, or 777,844 58-100 pounds; while, in the first month of 1855, the importation reached 3,720 quintaux, being more than in the whole year of 1854 by 193 quintaux, or 44,769 62-100 pounds.—*Consular Return.*

The distillation of any substance whatsoever that could be distilled was carried on to such a degree that a decree was issued on the 26th of October forbidding the distillation of cereals and of all other alimentary substances.

By a decree of the 1st of November the exportation from France of cereals—wheat, flour, &c.—was prohibited; and on the 6th a similar decree allowed the free admission of quercitron bark, imported by French vessels from countries out of Europe, and reduced the existing duty of 40 francs on that article, arriving by French vessels from the entrepots of Europe, to 20 francs, and from 60 francs to 30 francs when imported by foreign vessels having no commercial treaty with France.

On the 16th November notice was communicated by circular that, by a treaty concluded between France and Belgium, the former admitted geographical and marine charts, linen, printing ink, types, thread and hemp yarn, straw plait, slate, stone, and other raw materials, without a certificate of origin—Belgium conceding to France a similar privilege on charts, types, printing ink, clothes, pasteboard in sheets, paper of all descriptions, (except colored or morocco,) slates, prepared plaster, Bordeaux, Burgundy, and Champagne wines, and also those of Tours and Bayonne, in cask.

November 29 a decree was issued prohibiting the export from France, till July 31, 1855, of flour, and all kinds of grain.

On the 5th December a declaration was promulgated between the emperor of the French and the prince of Monaco, by which the former reduced the then existing duty on olive oil, (not exceeding 180,000 kilogrammes in quantity,) when imported by French vessels, or those of the prince of Monaco, to a uniform duty of 15 francs per 100 kilogrammes—the vessels of the principality being assimilated to those of Sardinia for payment of tonnage dues—the duty on French wines imported into the territory of the prince of Monaco, in cask, being fixed at 3f. 30c. per hectolitre, and at 10 centimes in bottle not containing more than a litre.

By a decree, dated 20th December, molasses from the French colonies, arriving by French vessels, was admitted free; when imported from countries out of Europe, at a duty of 3 francs, and from the entrepots at a duty of 8 francs per 100 kilogrammes. When imported by foreign vessels, it was fixed at 13 francs per 100 kilogrammes.

On the same day a decree was issued fixing the duties on sugar as follows: On brown sugars, when imported from French colonies in French ships, no charge; from China, Cochin-China, Philippine Islands, and Siam, when imported in French vessels, 48 francs per 100 kilogrammes; from other ports out of Europe, when in French vessels, 53 francs per 100 kilogrammes. On those already stored in government warehouses, 63 francs per 100 kilogrammes; when imported in foreign vessels, 68 francs per 100 kilogrammes. On clayed sugars, the duties to be 3 francs per kilogramme higher than the above rates.

Also a decree fixing the duties on dried raisins at 25 centimes per 100 kilogrammes when imported in French vessels, and 2 francs when in foreign vessels.

Also a decree fixing the duties on molasses when intended for distillation, as follows:

From French colonies, in French ships, free; from countries out of Europe, in French ships, 3 francs per 100 kilogrammes. On that in government warehouses, 8 francs; when imported in foreign vessels, 13 francs per 100 kilogrammes.

Also a decree fixing the duties on all animal greases, as follows:

When imported in French vessels from India, 2 francs per 100 kilogrammes; from other countries, 5 francs per 100 kilogrammes; when imported in foreign vessels, 8 francs. Fish oil, when imported in French vessels from beyond Cape Horn and the Cape of Good Hope, 10 francs per 100 kilogrammes; from other places out of Europe, 15 francs. On that in government warehouses, 20 francs; when imported in foreign vessels, 30 francs.

On the 6th January, 1855, three decrees were published; one permitting the temporary importation of sheet copper into France by French vessels, or direct from the country where it is produced, free of duty; when intended for the manufacture of boilers or machinery, its origin to be certified by the French consul at the place of its departure. Immediately on its arrival, the importer is bound to make a declaration at the custom-house of the number and weight of the sheets, as well as of their length, breadth, and thickness. The custom-house, after having ascertained the correctness of such declaration, is enjoined to cause a stamp to be put on each sheet, in order to assure the exportation of the same copper; and a charge of 5 centimes for stamping, including the cost of the stamp, is made for every sheet so stamped. Bond must be given that the whole quantity of copper imported shall be used, and re-exported, or placed in the public stores, (excepting such parts as may remain from cuttings or corners of sheets, on which the duty must be paid in the same proportion as if they were whole sheets,) within six months; and the custom-house is enjoined to assure itself that the articles so manufactured are equal in quantity, kind and quality, so that, temporarily admitted, sheet copper can only be exported from ports or places having public warehouses, or from places to which such articles are allowed to be sent in *transit*. By another, the temporary introduction of old cast iron belonging to foreign built steamboats, which may put into France for repairs, is also admitted free of duty, the importers giving sufficient security for replacing in the entrepots of France, within six months, an equal quantity of iron, proper for ships' use, to that which may have been employed in such repairs. Iron imported under this decree, and the article manufactured therefrom, can only be exported from places having government warehouses; and the custom-house is charged to see that the iron imported and not used be broken up in such way as to render it impossible of being used otherwise.

The third decree subjects foreign vessels at the Island of Senegal to a simple tax of 50 centimes per ton, without the additional

10 per cent. ; but this is limited to the port of Gorée. A decree relative to French and foreign emigration was promulgated on the 15th January. A circular bearing the same date exempts from the tax of *stombage*, or *leading*, certain articles of French origin, or foreign goods, on which the duty imposed by law has been paid, when they are sent by water from one part of the empire to another, precautions being taken to assure the identity of the goods on their arrival at the port of destination.

By a circular, dated 16th January, the decree of 20th December, prohibiting the importation of foreign molasses, extends only to such as is intended for distillation ; and the exemption from duty on French molasses equally applies to such as is imported solely for distillation. Molasses so imported is always under the surveillance of the customs till after its completion, at the place of distillation.

By another circular, of the 27th of the same month, alcohol produced in Corsica from the distillation of the bulbs of daffodils, figs of the cactus, (prickly pears?) juniper and myrtle berries, and all other substances, with the exception f farinaceous, (which the distillation from these substances the circular continues to prohibit,) are added to the number of articles admitted free of duty. A decree of the same date modifies the duty on juniper and myrtle berries, and also on table fruits, and equalizes the duty on the bulbs of daffodils and figs of the cactus.

By a decree of the 31st January foreign wines of every description were admitted into the islands of Martinique, Guadalupe, Guiana, Réunion, and Senegal, subject to a duty, when imported by French ships, of 25 centimes per hectolitre, and to that of 5 francs when imported by foreign vessels.

A circular of the 1st February exempts from examination, at the custom-houses of France, the baggage of foreigners arriving from foreign parts to embark for places abroad ; and a decree of the 10th allows the free importation of salt (foreign) intended for the mackerel fishery, which heretofore was confined to that of France, from the 15th February of every year ; and another decree of the 14th extends the period for its introduction from the 1st March to the 15th June. Previously to the date of that decree, it was only admitted between the 10th March and 15th June.

February 11 a decree was issued by which the mackerel fishery can commence on the 1st of March, instead of on the 10th, as heretofore.

On the 14th a decree was issued by which flour and grain from Algeria are admitted free of duty ; and on the same day the importation duty upon spermaceti from the whale and "cachelot" of foreign fisheries was provisionally established as follows : Raw :

By French vessels.—From countries situated beyond Cape Horn and the Cape of Good Hope, 5 francs per 100 kilogrammes.
From elsewhere out of Europe, 7.50 francs per 100 kilogrammes.
From the entrepots, 10 francs per 100 kilogrammes.

By foreign vessels, 15 francs per 100 kilogrammes.

Pressed, 20 francs per 100 kilogrammes.

Refined, 50 francs per 100 kilogrammes.

By a decree of February 17 it is provisionally established that, from the first of March next, the rate of drawback allowed on the exportation of soap shall be as follows :

White or mottled soap, composed of alkali and olive oil, or of oleaginous seeds, or mixed with animal fat :

1s. The oil entering by one-half, at least, in the mixture of greasy matter, 8.20 francs per 100 kilogrammes.

2d. The oil entering for less than one-half, 6 francs per 100 kilogrammes.

Soap of animal fat :

3d. Pure, 6 francs per 100 kilogrammes.

4th. Mixed with rosin, 6 francs per 100 kilogrammes.

Soap of palm or cocoa oil, mixed with animal fat or rosin, 4 francs per 100 kilogrammes.

By a ministerial decision of the 22d of February filaments of cocoa, in the shape of tresses or twists, were assimilated to the coarse tresses for matting, and admitted as such at the duty of 2f. and 2f. 20c., according to the mode of importation.

A circular of the 28th February specifies the objects which shall be considered as coming within the meaning of the treaty concluded with Spain on the 15th November, 1853, which are : books, dramatic and musical compositions, paintings, drawings, engravings, lithographs, sculptures, geographical maps, and all other similar productions, with the exception of works of art applicable to agriculture and industrial manufactures ; and prohibits the reproduction of the works of either in the country of the other, and indicates the ports in France by which alone such works can be introduced.

By a decree of the 10th March salted meats of all sorts of foreign origin, imported from any country whatsoever, or by any flag, into the colonies of Martinique, Guadalupe, Guiana, and La Réunion, will pay on entry a duty of 50 centimes per 100 kilogrammes. The importation of these same meats, on the payment of a duty of 50 centimes per 100 kilogrammes, is also permitted into St. Louis, (Senegal,) but by French vessels only, either direct from abroad or by extraction from the entrepot at Gorée. Those which arrive at Senegal under a foreign flag continue subject to the same regulations that exist.

By a ministerial decision of the 15th March the icaco or American prune will in future pay an entry duty similar to the ground and Taulmouna nut, either 1, 2, 3 francs, or 3f. 50c. the 100 kilogrammes, according to the source from whence it comes and mode of importation.

By a decree of the 14th April the duty on "liqueurs" imported from the French colonies is fixed at 15 francs the hectolitre of liquid.

By a decree of the 14th April the importation duties on raw wool were modified as follows, viz:

Wool in bulk, imported direct, by French ships, from countries situated beyond Cape Horn and the Cape of Good Hope:

From Australia and the Colony of the Cape, including Cape Town, present duties.

From elsewhere—In the grease, 10 centimes per kilogramme.

Cold washed: In whole fleeces, 20 centimes per kilogramme.

(a) Offal or refuse, 10 centimes per kilogramme.

Hot-washed: In whole fleeces, 30 centimes per kilogramme.

Offal or refuse, 15 centimes per kilogrammes.

From elsewhere, present duties.

Another decree of the same date repeals the export duty of 5 centimes per 100 kilogrammes on lime.

By a decree of the 23d April the importation duties on nitrate of soda and of potash were established as follows:

By French ships—From countries situated beyond Cape Horn and the Cape of Good Hope, 1 franc per 100 kilogrammes.

From other countries out of Europe, 6 francs per 100 kilogrammes.

From entrepots, 8 francs per 100 kilogrammes.

By foreign ships, 11 francs per 100 kilogrammes.

The premiums allowed by the laws of 6th May, 1841, and 11th June, 1845, on exportation of nitric and sulphuric acids, are: for nitric acid, 5 francs the 100 kilogrammes net of acid; and for sulphuric acid, 20 centimes the 100 kilogrammes net of acid. By a decree of the 23d of April, citric acids of all sorts, imported from the colonies of France, in French ships, are admitted free of duty; and by foreign vessels, at a duty of 11 francs per 100 kilogrammes.

On the same day an allowance of 5 per cent. for loss in weight, whether from water or decay, was authorized by decree on refined salt, if imported by sea and shipped in bulk at the place of production; and a third decree of the same date establishes the inward duty on nitrates of soda and potashes arriving by French vessels from countries situated beyond Cape Horn and the Cape of Good Hope, at 1 franc per 100 kilogrammes; from places in Europe, 6 francs per 100 kilogrammes; from entrepots, 8 francs per 100 kilogrammes.

On the 24th April a circular was issued authorizing the temporary free admission into France of machinery, glass, (for resilvering,) bronzes, and other similar works, and books, when imported separately, or in small quantities, for the purpose of being repaired or finished, on condition of their being re-exported within six months.

By a decree of the 28th of April, iron work, in bars or sheets, (without distinction of origin,) fit for the construction of edifices or dwelling-houses, is allowed to be imported into Senegal by French vessels, free of duty, whether coming from the entrepots of the metropolis or that of Gorée. Another decree of the same date fixes the duty on old worn-out type at 5 francs per 100 kilogrammes.

An *arreté* of May 5th orders the withdrawal from circulation of all gold pieces of the value of ten francs bearing the effigy of the present emperor, to take place on the 15th of October, 1855.

By *ordonnance* of the 31st July and 4th December, 1816, all vessels arriving in France in ballast, to take in salt, were exempted from tonnage dues. By a decree of the 16th of May, 1855, foreign vessels arriving with cargo enjoy the same privilege, but only in proportion to the quantity of salt taken by them; and by a circular of the 2d of June the export duty on salt is suppressed.

Alcohol distilled from daffodils in Algeria is admitted into France free of duty by decree of May 23d.

By a decree of the 2d of June the delay fixed for the introduction of provisions into France is prolonged to the 31st of December, 1855; by another of the 5th the free admission of ships importing grain, flour, rice, &c., is extended; and by a circular of the 11th the exportation of these articles is prohibited during the same period.

By a decree of the 5th June the exemption of navigation dues accorded up to the 31st July, 1855, on cargoes of grain, flour, rice, potatoes, and dry vegetables, is extended to the 31st December, 1855.

A decree of the 23d of June accords the privilege of transporting grain and flour between Algeria and France to foreign vessels having left their port of loading on or before the 31st December, 1855. By another decree of the same date the exportation of corn and barley from Algeria to foreign countries is prohibited; and by a third decree the importation of carol beans by French vessels is admitted at a duty of 25 centimes per 100 kilogrammes, and of one franc per foreign vessels.

By a decree of the same date the importation duty on locust trees is fixed as follows: by French ships, 25 centimes the 100 kilogrammes; by foreign ships, one franc the 100 kilogrammes.

(a) Wool from the neck, legs, and tail, to be counted offal and refuse.

A decree of the 7th July admits, free of duty, vanilla imported by French vessels arriving direct from the French colonies, Cayenne and Mayottel.

A circular of the 10th July imposes a double *décime* on the amount of all government taxes, to remain in force till the 1st January, 1858; increases the excise consumption duty on brandies, spirits, liquors, and brandy fruits, from 34 francs to 50 francs per hectolitre of alcohol, and from 50 francs to 66 francs, exclusive of the double *décime*, the tax on these articles on their admission into Paris, and further imposes a tax of 10 per cent. on the receipts of passenger money by railroad, and also on the conveyance of goods by fast or express trains.

By a decree of the 14th July the regulation for the admission of molasses intended for distillation is fixed as follows, until it shall be otherwise ordained:

Molasses imported to be converted into alcohol, according to the regulation determined by the decree of the 20th December, 1854.

By French vessels—

From French colonies, exempt.

From the East Indies, exempt.

From South America, exempt.

From the West Indies, exempt.

From elsewhere, 2 francs the 100 kilogrammes.

By foreign vessels, 3 francs the 100 kilogrammes.

By a decree of the 16th July the importation duties are maintained or modified for the several articles designated as follows:

ARTICLE I.

Amomes, or cardamoms.—Same duties as medicinal fruits not denominated.

Bole, armenian, and limnas earth.—Same duty as stones and earths not denominated.

Bulbous roots.—Same duties as green vegetables.

Cadmium, raw.—Two francs per 100 kilogrammes.

Flint stones and glass.—Same duties as on stones and earth not denominated.

Earthenware and porcelain sand.—Same duties as on stones and earth not denominated.

Camphor, raw.—By French ships—

From India, 20 francs per 100 kilogrammes.

From countries out of Europe, 30 francs per 100 kilogrammes.

From entrepots, 40 francs per 100 kilogrammes.

By foreign ships, 50 francs per 100 kilogrammes.

India rubber or gutta percha, raw or remelted in bulk.—By French ships—

From countries out of Europe, exempt.

From entrepots, 5 francs per 100 kilogrammes.

By foreign ships, 10 francs per 100 kilogrammes.

India rubber or gutta percha manufactures, except surgical instruments.—Simply pure, 20 francs per 100 kilogrammes.

Remelted, mixed with other matter, 50 francs per 100 kilogrammes.

Combined with or applied on other matter, except tissues in the piece, 200 francs per 100 kilogrammes.

Cassia unprepared and tamarinds, (pods and pulp.)—Same duties as medicinal fruits not denominated.

Goldsmiths' dust and refuse.—Same duties as stones and earth not denominated.

Pearly shells.—Mother of pearl, without distinction of the pearl called "French or Bastard."

In shells in the rough:

By French ships—From countries situated beyond Cape Horn and the Cape of Good Hope, exempt

Elsewhere, 15 francs per 100 kilogrammes.

By foreign ships, 25 francs per 100 kilogrammes.

Sawed, or divested of the crust, double the above duty.

Haliosides, called "Sea-Ears:

By French ships, exempt.

By foreign ships, 3 francs per 100 kilogrammes.

Chalk.—Same duties as stones and earth not enumerated.

Elephants' teeth.—Tusks, whole, or in pieces:

By French ships—From countries out of Europe, exempt.

From elsewhere, 50 francs per 100 kilogrammes

By foreign ships, 60 francs per 100 kilogrammes.

Jaw teeth:

By French ships—From countries out of Europe, exempt.

From elsewhere, 5 francs per 100 kilogrammes.

By foreign ships, 10 francs per 100 kilogrammes.

Wolves' teeth.—Same duties as the bones and hoofs of cattle.

Porcelain clay or earth.—Same duty as stones and earth not enumerated.

Old rags.—By French ships, exempt.

By foreign ships, 1 franc per 100 kilogrammes.

Tortoise shell.—Carapaces and claws:

By French ships—From countries out of Europe, exempt.

Elsewhere, 50 francs per 100 kilogrammes.

By foreign ships, 60 francs per 100 kilogrammes.

Cuttings, half the above duty.

Barks, medicinal, not enumerated.—Same duties as Jesuits' bark.

Bark, pine, alder, pomegranate, and blackberry.—Same duty as tan-bark.

Manure, not denominated:

By French vessels and by land, exempt.

By foreign ships, 50 centimes per 100 kilograemms.

Tin, raw.—By French ships from India, exempt.

Hay, straw, and meadow grass:

By French ships and by land, exempt.

By foreign ships, 50 centimes per 100 kilogrammes.

Medicinal flowers, not denominated:

By French ships.—From countries out of Europe, exempt.

From entrepots, 10 francs per 100 kilogrammes.

By foreign ships, 20 francs per 100 kilogrammes.

Medicinal fruits, not denominated:

By French ships.—From countries out of Europe, exempt.

From entrepots, 10 francs per 100 kilogrammes.

By foreign ships, 20 francs per 100 kilogrammes.

Mustard seed.—Same duty as oleaginous seeds not denominated.

Groisit:

By French ships and by land, exempt.

By foreign ships, 1 franc per 100 kilogrammes.

Groison.—Same duty as stones and earth not denominated.

Medicinal herbs not denominated, and lemon grass:

By French ships.—From countries out of Europe, exempt.

From elsewhere, 10 francs per 100 kilogrammes.

By foreign ships, 20 francs per 100 kilogrammes.

Manganese.—Same duties as stones and earth not denominated.

Hops.—45 francs per 100 kilogrammes.

Marble statuary, when the produce of, and imported from Italy.—Same duties as marble of its origin imported from Italy.

Marl	Same duties as stones and earth not denominated.
Materials not denominated, except chalk, for manure; and shingles, rough or squared, otherwise than by the saw, which remains subject to the present duty	
Mineral black, native	
Ochre	
Oxide of iron	
Stones, sharpening, rough	

Stones and earth not denominated:

By French ships and by land, exempt.

By foreign ships, 1 franc per 100 kilogrammes.

Stones.—Ferruginous, except emery	Same duties as stones and earth not enumerated.
Flint	
Chalk, rough	
Pumice	
French stone	

Pistachio nuts.—Same duty as dry or pressed fruit.

Pepper and pimento from the French colonies other than Guiana.—Same duties as pepper and pimento from Guiana.

Quercitron bark :

By French ships—From countries out of Europe, 2 francs the 100 kilogrammes.
From entrepots, 4 francs the 100 kilogrammes.

By foreign ships, 6 francs the 100 kilogrammes.

Roots, medicinal, not denominated :

By French ships—From countries out of Europe, exempt.
From entrepots, 10 francs the 100 kilogrammes.

By foreign ships, 20 francs the 100 kilogrammes.

Rhubarb :

By French ships—From India, 35 francs the 100 kilogrammes.
From elsewhere, out of Europe, 45 francs the 100 kilogrammes.
From Europe, 55 francs the 100 kilogrammes.

By foreign ships, 65 francs the 100 kilogrammes.

Sand for building.—Same duty as stones and earths not denominated.

Sago and salep :

By French ships—From India, 5 francs per 100 kilogrammes.
From elsewhere, out of Europe, 10 francs per 100 kilogrammes.
From entrepots, 15 francs per 100 kilogrammes.

By foreign ships, 20 francs per 100 kilogrammes.

Spar	Same duties as stones and earth not denominated.
Sulphate of barytes	
Isinglass stone, (talc,) raw, in bulk	
Pipe clay	
Tripoli or manna	

ART. 2. The following merchandise shall be admitted free of duty, whatever may be the source or mode of importation, viz : Absinthe, (wormwood ;) acetate of iron, (liquid ;) agates, rough ; agaric, oak or touchwood, rough ; agaric, larch ; amurca ; asses, male and female ; animals, not denominated ; antalus ; arsenic, (metal ;) wormseed ; bezoar ; fire-wood, in logs or sticks ; fire-wood, in faggots ; fustic, (young,) *fushet ;* goats, male and female ; wool, flock ; guts, fresh or salted ; nut-shells or peel ; broom, for making wisps, raw ; calabashes, empty ; ash, vegetable, live or for ley ; mushrooms ; carding thistles ; hair, human ; kids ; dogs ; woodlice, dried ; horns, stags' and snacks ; rock crystal, rough ; diamonds, rough ; bleak scales ; peel, lemon and orange ; tan bark, unground ; lime bark for cordage ; leaves, fit for dyeing and tanning, not denominated ; flowers, lavender and orange, even resalted ; garon, (root ;) dyers' weed ; dyers' broom ; game ; bird-lime, (glue, bot. ;) gums, European, pure ; black olives ; misletoe of oak ; jet ; canes and reed, European, of gardens, and not denominated ; kerms in grain, or scarlet seeds ; vegetables, green ; yeast of beer ; lichens, except those fit for dying ; lees of wine ; lycopodium ; rose leaves, pressed, residue of ; mill-stones of all sizes ; hart's marrow ; turf for burning ; pizzles, bull's and other animals ; nickel, raw ; collections, articles not for trading ; silk worms' eggs ; eggs of fowl and game ; orcanet ; bones of stags, hart, and of cuttle-fish ; osier in bundles ; oxyde of cobalt, pure or silicious ; oxyde of tin ; oxyde of copper ; oxyde of zince, gray, (fustic and cadmic ;) dyers' wood, stems and leaves of ; rabbit skins, raw ; hare skins, raw ; pearls, fine ; elks' feet ; precious stones, rough ; plants of trees ; massina hair ; fresh water fish, fresh ; apples and pears, crushed ; preste, (shave grass, bot. ;) rennett ; roots for rods ; raspings of stags' horns and ivory ; wax, residue of ; bee-hives, with living swarms ; cattles' blood ; blood of he goats, dried ; sawwort, (bot. ;) cobalt salt of all kinds ; silk in cocoons ; yellow amber ; millet twigs, for brooms ; tortoises.

A decree of the 31st August accords the free admission of game, poultry, and shell-fish, (*tortue ;*) and one of the 22d September prolongs to the 31st December, 1856, the exemption from tonnage duty all vessels laden with grain, flour, rice, potatoes, and dried vegetables.

By a decree of October 10 foreign vessels which have imported, from countries in the north of Europe, into the ports of

Algiers, lumber, in proportion to three-fourths of their legal tonnage, and which shall subsequently leave such ports with cargoes consisting of French or Algerine produce, are exempted from tonnage dues. In case the quantity of lumber does not amount to three-fourths, duties will be levied on the tonnage unemployed, or used for other merchandise ; and so with reference to the produce taken, provided one-half, at least, of the tonnage shall not be so used.

By a decree issued October 17 lumber, wood for cabinet work, in logs or sawed, more than three decimetres (one English foot) in thickness ; pig iron, bar iron, sheet iron, and fashion pieces ; copper and zinc, unmanufactured ; hemp and flax, hatcheled or unhatcheled ; resin and tar, and tallow and other animal fats used in naval construction, are ordered to be admitted free of duty for a period of three years from date, on condition that the importer, within a year after the importation, gives satisfactory proof that said articles have been devoted to the purpose designated. And for one year from date vessels of every kind, whether sailing or propelled by steam, are to be admitted to all the privileges of naturalization, (*francisation*,) by paying a duty of 10 per cent. ad valorem ; the same to be estimated by the Board of Arts and Manufactures. By the same decree the duties on the exportation of wood for cabinet makers, and also on iron scalings, are abolished.

By a decree of December 10 the importation duties on the under-mentioned merchandise were established as follows :

Description of merchandise.	Quantity.	Flag.	Duty.
Almonds, in the shell or broken	220 pounds	French	\$0 $18\frac{3}{5}$
		Foreign	$55\frac{4}{5}$
Antimony, sulphureted	do	French	$18\frac{3}{5}$
		Foreign	$55\frac{4}{5}$
Argentan, (nickel alloyed,) in bulk	do	French	$18\frac{3}{5}$
		Foreign	$37\frac{1}{5}$
Bitumen, liquid and mineral, tar produced by the distillation of coal.	do	French	$00\frac{9}{10}$
		Foreign	$18\frac{3}{5}$
Wood, of all sorts, from the French colonies and Senegal	do		Free.
Wood, in splints	1,000	French	$1\frac{4}{5}$
Wood, hoop	do	French	$1\frac{4}{5}$
		Foreign	28
Wood, stave, of all sorts	do	French	$1\frac{4}{5}$
		Foreign	28
Wood, pine, fir, elm, and other common wood, viz :			
In rough, squared with the axe or sawed, of more than 80 millimetres (*a*) in thickness.	Per stere, or 35.316 cubic feet.	French	$00\frac{9}{10}$
		Foreign	$1\frac{4}{5}$
Sawn, of 80 millimetres thick, or less, except planks and plates of walnut, denominated in the tariff.	Per 1,000 metres, or 3,280.899 feet.	French	$00\frac{9}{10}$
		Foreign	$18\frac{3}{5}$
Heath, for whisks, stripped of its barb	220 pounds	French	$9\frac{3}{10}$
		Foreign	94
Safflower	220 pounds	French: countries out of Europe.	$18\frac{3}{5}$
		From entrepots	1 $11\frac{3}{5}$
		Foreign	1 86
Lime, slacked, and limestones, calcined or crushed	220 pounds	French	$00\frac{19}{100}$
		Foreign	$18\frac{3}{5}$
Wax, unmanufactured, yellow or brown	220 pounds	French	$18\frac{3}{5}$
Citrate of lime	2.20 pounds	French	$00\frac{19}{100}$
		Foreign	$00\frac{9}{10}$
Horns, (cattle,) in the rough	220 pounds	French, and by land.	$1\frac{4}{5}$
		Foreign	$18\frac{3}{5}$
Spars			Free.
Seeds : sowing, garden ; flower, madder ; pastel, cardamom ; thistle, cotton, forest, and meadow.	220 pounds	French	$1\frac{4}{5}$
		Foreign	$18\frac{3}{5}$

(*a*) 1,000 millimetres equal $39\frac{3}{8}$ inches.

DUTIES—Continued.

Description of merchandise.	Quantity.	Flag.	Duty.
Graphite or plumbago	220 pounds	French	$0 18⅗
		Foreign	55⅘
Canes and reeds, exotic	220 pounds	French	1 86
		Foreign	3 72
Lemon juice, natural or concentrated, at 35° and under	220 pounds	French	00$\frac{19}{100}$
		Foreign	00$\frac{9}{10}$
Cork, rough, with its cracked coating	220 pounds	French	9$\frac{3}{10}$
		Foreign	93
Boat-hook poles, from 6 centimetres(a) to 11 centimetres, exclusively, in diameter.			Free.
Handles, pitchfork or harpoon, and tar brush handles			Free.
Chestnuts, and their flour	220 pounds	French	18⅗
		Foreign	55⅘
Masts and small masts			Free.
Mercury (native) or quicksilver	220 pounds	French	18⅗
		Foreign	93
Grindstones	Each	French	1⅘
		Foreign	5⅖
Honey	220 pounds	French	18⅗
		Foreign	1 11⅗
Lampblack	220 pounds	French	18⅗
		Foreign	55⅘
Spanish black, (as lampblack)			
Walnuts, small nuts, and filberts	220 pounds	French	18⅗
		Foreign	55⅘
Skin parings, or cuttings for making glue	220 pounds	French	1⅘
		Foreign	18⅗
Cattle bones and hoofs	220 pounds	French, (and by land)	1⅘
		Foreign	18⅗
LARGE SKINS, RAW. DRIED: By sea	220 pounds	French, countries out of Europe	1⅘
		From entrepot	55⅘
		Foreign	1 86
LARGE SKINS, RAW. DRIED: By land, not of European origin	220 pounds		1 86
LARGE SKINS, RAW. GREEN: By sea		French, from countries out of Europe.	1⅘
LARGE SKINS, RAW. GREEN: By land, the growth of neighboring countries.			1⅘
Sea-dog skins, raw, green, or dried	220 pounds	French	1⅘
		Foreign	93
Lamb skins, raw, green, or dried, except those covered with their wool.	220 pounds	French	1⅘
		Foreign	18⅗
Kid skins, green or dried, and other small raw skins not denominated.	220 pounds	French	1⅘
		Foreign	18⅗
Pigouélles, of 11 centimetres, inclusively, to 15 centimetres, exclusively, in diameter.			Free.

(a) 100 centimetres equal 39⅜ inches.

DUTIES—Continued.

Description of merchandise.	Quantity.	Flag.	Duty.
Quills, writing, raw	220 pounds	French	$0 01$\frac{4}{5}$
		Foreign	1 86
Hair, raw	220 pounds	French	1$\frac{4}{5}$
		Foreign	18$\frac{3}{5}$
combed, or in bundles of assorted lengths	220 pounds	French	1 86
		Foreign	2 04$\frac{3}{5}$
Leeches			Free.
Sarcocolla, kino, and other dried vegetable juices		Same duties as resinous exotics not denominated.	
Bran	220 pounds	French	0$\frac{9}{10}$
Esparto, (or Spanish broom,) in rough stems or beaten	220 pounds	French	0$\frac{9}{10}$

By a decree, dated December 29, the importation duties on sugars were fixed as follows, viz:

Sugar of a color equal, at most, to the first (present) type, by French vessels, from the French colonies, beyond the Cape of Good Hope, and of America, the present duties.

Sugars from China, Cochin China, the Philippine Islands, and from Siam, 220 pounds		$8 37
From other countries of India	do.	8 74
From elsewhere, out of Europe	do.	9 30
From entrepots	do.	11 16
By foreign vessels	do.	12 09

Sugar, of a superior color to the present, first type, the above duties, with the addition of three francs per 220 pounds.

By a decree of the same date it is enacted that, from the 1st day of January, 1856, Dutch vessels coming direct from ports of Holland laden, or from any port whatever in ballast, shall be exempt, both inwards and outwards, from the tonnage duties established by the ordinance of June 26, 1841; nevertheless, and in conformity with the regulations of the said ordinance, Dutch vessels coming without cargo from the ports of Great Britain to continue to pay, like French vessels, 18 3-5 cents (1 franc) per ton each voyage.

By a decree published the 5th January, 1856, the importation duty on prepared skins was fixed as follows, until further order:

				Quantity.	Duty.
Prepared skins	With tan	Simply tanned for soles or other uses	Hog	220 lbs.	$37 20
			Others—Large	do.	8 37
			Others—Small(a)	do.	22 32
		Curried	For boot-legs, upper leather, front and back	do.	37 20
			Others	do.	18 60
	With alum		In the Hungarian manner	do.	7 44
			Tawed	do.	9 30

(a) By small skins, is meant those that weigh less than 2.20 pounds.

By a decree published on the 21st January, the importation duties on wool were reduced to the following rates, viz:

			Quantity.	Flag.	Duties.
By sea	In the grease	Common	220 lbs	FRENCH, from countries out of Europe	$0 93
			do	Elsewhere	1 68
			do	FOREIGN	2 78
		Fine	do	FRENCH, from countries out of Europe	1 86
			do	Elsewhere	2 79
			do	FOREIGN	3 72
	Washed	Common		FRENCH, from countries out of Europe	1 86
				Elsewhere	3 72
				FOREIGN	4 65
		Fine		FRENCH, from countries out of Europe	4 18
				Elsewhere	6 04
				FOREIGN	6 97
By land	Of the growth of neighboring countries			Same duties as when imported in French vessels.	
	Of other growth			Same duties as when imported in foreign vessels.	

Formerly wool paid an ad valorem duty of 20 per cent.; the preceding tariff is considered to be equal to a reduction of one-half. The drawback on the exportation of woolen tissues and worsted is proportionably diminished.

By a decree of February 23 cotton, proper for the manufacture of sail duck, is admitted into France duty free.

By a decree of April 16 pieces of iron, called knees, or branches of knees, intended in ship building to bind or strengthen the frame-work, and especially to secure the beams and timbers, are added to the list of articles of which the decree of 17th of October, 1855, permits the entry free of duty.

By a decree of the 6th of May the duties on cocoa were reduced to 65 francs per 100 kilogrammes when imported by French vessels, and 75 francs by foreign vessels.

By a decree of September 29 the extension fixed by the decree of September 19, 1855, for the operation of the modifications in the tariff of customs in the colonies of Martinique, Guadalupe, the island of Réunion, and of Senegal, in all that relates to, grains, breadstuffs, and dried pulse, is further continued to December 31, 1857.

The tariff policy of the French government during the last three years, has, it will have been perceived from the preceding abstracts of decrees, &c., manifested a tendency to reduction of duties. Among the somewhat numerous changes, nearly all indicate decrease on previous rates. The per centage decrease, by virtue of these and other decrees and ordinances, on some of the articles named, when imported in foreign vessels or by land, may be noted approximately, as follows:(a)

On sago, 50; salep, 75; sugar, 1st type and above 1st type, 10; camphor, 33; ultramarine, 77; rhubarb root, 63; tamarinds, 54; fruit not otherwise described, 50; timber, lumber, &c., 24 to 33; iron, cast, plated, old, &c., 12 to 70; iron for railroads, 45 to 60; steel in sheets, 36; manganese, 10; basket work, 38 to 58; steam engines and machines, 17 to 38; other than steam, 11 to 40; detached pieces of, 17 to 38; agricultural implements, 20; files, rasps, &c., 6 to 10; other instruments, 10 to 13. Among the articles declared free, previously paying duty, are: silk in cocoons, potatoes, molasses, gums from Europe, tow of hemp or flax for sails, masts and spars of certain dimensions, carding thistles, oil cakes, iron ribs and knees for vessels, nickel, (1st fusion,) arsenic, alkalies, vegetable ashes, &c., acetate of iron, cotton (raw) for cordage, resin of all sorts.

On wool, common, fine, and washed, the duty changed from ad valorem to specific; and from skins, dressed, tanned, tawed, &c., prohibition removed.

By decree of various dates, during the first half of 1857, the per centage decrease in the rates of duties imposed on certain articles imported in foreign vessels is as follows: on fish, marinated in oil, 74 per cent; crystallized soda, 28; ginger, 10; oil palm, cocoa, &c., from India, beyond French establishments, 72; sulphur, unrefined, 33, refined, 73; flowers of, 82.

On wool, combed, dyed, duty changed from ad valorem to specific.

(a) Parliamentary Returns.

COMPARATIVE TARIFFS.

UNITED STATES AND FRANCE AND HER POSSESSIONS.

DENOMINATION OF MERCHANDISE.	DUTIES ON IMPORTS. Into the United States from foreign nations, per cent. ad valorem, under the act of—		INTO FRANCE FROM FOREIGN NATIONS.			INTO FRENCH POSSESSIONS.	REMARKS.
	1846.	1857.	Number, weight, or measure.	In national vessels.	In foreign vessels		
Acids, muriatic	20	4	100 kilogs. 220 lbs.	$11 48	$12 75½	If in French vessels into Guiana, 2 per ct. ad valorem. Into Martinique and Guadalupe the same as for France. In foreign vessels, with the exception of Algiers and Corsica, prohibited. Algiers and Corsica the same as for France.	Sulphuric acid enjoys a bounty of $1 30 per 220 pounds at its exportation.
sulphuric	10	4	do	7 59	8 50⅘		The trade between France and her colonies is confined to French vessels, measuring not less than 40 tons, and in which the officers and at least three-fourths of the crew are French.
tartaric	20	4	do	12 96	14 34		
Acorns	20	15	do	18⅗	20⅗		
Adhesive felt	Free	Free	do	18 51	20 83		
Adzes	30	24	do	25 92	27 99⅗	If direct from France into Guiana, free	
Alabaster ornaments	40	30		15 per cent.	ad valorem		All goods imported into Guiana in French vessels from France pay 2 per cent. ad valorem.
Almonds, in shell	40	30	do	1 48	1 64$\frac{7}{10}$	Algiers and Corsica the same as France; for the colonies only permitted in French vessels.	
oil of bitter	30	24	1 kilog. 2. 22 lbs.	93	1 03		
paste of	30	24	220 pounds	4 62$\frac{9}{10}$	5 15½		The French have two kinds of entrepot; one called entrepot "réel," the other entrepot "fictif;" the difference between them is, that goods placed in the former are under the supervision of public officers, while in the latter they are under the supervision and control of the depositor.
Ale, in casks	30	24	1 hectolitre, or 26 gals.	1 12⅓	1 12⅓	Ale, in Oceanica, per dozen bottles, 37½	Ale, and all other liquids in bottles, pay an additional duty of 2⅔ cents for each quart, as duty on the bottles. Empty bottles are prohibited.
in bottles	30	24	do	3 93¼	3 93¼		

FRANCE AND HER POSSESSIONS—TARIFFS—Continued.

DENOMINATION OF MERCHANDISE.	DUTIES ON IMPORTS. Into the United States from foreign nations, per cent. ad valorem, under the act of— 1846.	1857.	INTO FRANCE FROM FOREIGN NATIONS. Number, weight, or measure.	In national vessels.	In foreign vessels.	INTO FRENCH POSSESSIONS.	REMARKS.
Aloes	20	4	220 pounds	$9 $25\frac{9}{10}$	$11 $23\frac{1}{2}$	Aloes, into Algiers, free.	
Alum, crude	20	15	do	4 62	5 $24\frac{1}{3}$	If in French vessels, and direct from France into Guiana, 2 per cent. ad valorem. Into Algiers, Martinique, Guadalupe, and Corsica, the same duties as in the French tariff. In foreign vessels for Martinique and Guadalupe, prohibited.	
Ammonia, crude	20	8	2.22 pounds	$7\frac{3}{10}$	$9\frac{1}{5}$		Ammonia (the salt) enjoys a bounty of $3 per 220 pounds, if exported.
refined, or carbonate of.	20	8	do	20	26		
Amber	20	4	220 pounds	6 33	7 62		
Ambergris	20	4	2.22 pounds	11 48	12 $65\frac{9}{10}$		
Anchors, and parts thereof, of 550 lbs. and under.	30	24	220 pounds	2 77	3 $08\frac{9}{10}$		
of 550 pounds and upwards.	30	24	do	1 85	2 06		
Aniseed, seed	20	4	220 pounds	3 $70\frac{1}{4}$	4 12	do do do	
cordials	100	30	1 hectolitre, or 26 gals.	28 09	28 09	Dozen bottles of cordial in Oceanica, $74\frac{2}{5}$ cents.	
essence (oil of)	30	24	2.22 pounds	93	1 03		
Anchovies, preserved in oil	40	30	220 pounds	18 51	20 83	In foreign vessels, with the exception of Corsica, (where the duty is the same as for France,) prohibited.	
Angora goats' hair	20	24	do	$18\frac{3}{5}$	$20\frac{1}{2}$		
Animal carbon	20	Free		Prohibited.			
Animals imported for breed	Free	Free		See note (a)		Into Algiers, free; into Corsica, oxen $18\frac{3}{5}$ cents, cows $5\frac{1}{2}$ cents, heifers $5\frac{1}{2}$ cents, sheep $37\frac{1}{5}$ cents, hogs $55\frac{4}{5}$ cents each. Into Martinique and Guadalupe, 10 per cent. ad valorem. Into Guiana, free.	Animals for exhibition are exempted from both importation and exportation duties.
otherwise	20	Free					

(a) *In national or foreign vessels.*—Horses, $4 88; colts, $2 80; bulls, $9 36; cows, $4 68; rams and asses, 93 cents each; oxen, $2 80; asses, $4 68; calves, $56\frac{1}{6}$ cents; heifers, $2 34.

FRANCE AND HER POSSESSIONS—TARIFFS—Continued.

DENOMINATION OF MERCHANDISE.	DUTIES ON IMPORTS. Into the United States from foreign nations, per cent. ad valorem, under the act of— 1846.	1857.	INTO FRANCE FROM FOREIGN NATIONS. Number, weight, or measure.	In national vessels.	In foreign vessels.	INTO FRENCH POSSESSIONS.	REMARKS.
Annotto, or roucou	10	4	100 kilogs. 220 lbs.	Free	$3 44	Into Guiana, prohibited. Into Algiers and Corsica, the same as into France. Into the French West Indies, in foreign vessels, prohibited.	If exported from Guiana, subject to an additional duty (contribution fonciére) of 55$\frac{4}{5}$ cents.
extract	20	15	do	$2 77	3 08$\frac{9}{10}$		
Antiquities, if imported for national museums.	Free	Free		Free	Free	Duties on antiquities, the same as in France.	Antiquities, otherwise imported, 1 per cent. ad valorem.
Anvils	30	24	100 kilogs. 220 lbs.	9 61	10 39$\frac{1}{3}$	In Corsica and Algiers as in France. Into Guiana, Martinique, Guadalupe, in foreign vessels, prohibited.	Copper beaten or laminated, if exported, receives as bounty the same amount which has been paid on the material when imported in a crude state.
Antimony, mineral	20	8	do	Free	18$\frac{2}{5}$	In Corsica and Algiers as in France. Into Guiana, Martinique, Guadalupe, in foreign vessels, prohibited.	Antimony ore must come directly from the mines to be admitted for this duty. If submitted to any sort of preparation, it must pay the duty of sulphurated antimony, viz: $2 26½ per 220 pounds.
regulus of (crude)	20	8	do	4 81	5 29		
Apparel, wearing, and all other baggage in actual use.	Free	Free	Traveller's. Other, 30 per cent.	free. 30 per cent. ad valorem.	30 per cent. ad valorem.		Travellers' wearing apparel, free. Foreign ready made clothing, including hats and stockings, can, into Guiana in foreign vessels, only be imported into the entrepot fictif. Ready made clothing, if exported from France in quantities of at least 55 pounds, (25 kilogs.) will receive as bounty the same amount as has been levied on the importation of the raw material.
Apparatus, philosophical (according to material.)	Free	Free	30 per cent	ad valorem.	(a)		

(a) The value to be fixed by a committee of consultation of arts and manufactures.

FRANCE AND HER POSSESSIONS—TARIFFS—Continued.

DENOMINATION OF MERCHANDISE.	DUTIES ON IMPORTS. Into the United States from foreign nations, per cent. ad valorem, under the act of—		Into France from foreign nations.			Into French possessions.	REMARKS.
	1846.	1857.	Number, weight, or measure.	In national vessels.	In foreign vessels.		
Apples, pine	20	8	220 pounds	$0 74	$1 $63\frac{1}{10}$	In Algiers, free. In Corsica, the same as in France. In Guiana, prohibited. In Martinique and Guadalupe, 4 per cent. ad valorem.	
Aqua fortis	20	15	do	16 55	18 $20\frac{1}{3}$	In Corsica and Algiers as in France. In Guiana, Martinique and Guadalupe, in foreign vessels, prohibited.	Aqua fortis (nitric acid) enjoys, if exported, a bounty of $1 30 per 220 pounds.
Arabic, gum	10	8	do	3 70	5 $61\frac{2}{3}$	In Corsica and Algiers as in France. In Guiana, in foreign vessels, prohibited. In West Indies, free.	
Argol, or wine-lees	5	Free	do	3 38	3 $93\frac{1}{4}$	In Corsica and Algiers as in France. Into Guiana and the West Indies, in foreign vessels, prohibited.	
Arms, fire, for soldiers	30	24		Prohibited			*Arms:* The distinction between arms for the army and arms for commerce consists in the calibre and ornamenting. Pocket pistols, which are prohibited, may be admitted, however, in entrepot.
fire, for commerce	30	24	do	37 03	39 $79\frac{1}{2}$		
side, for soldiers	30	24		Prohibited			
side, for commerce	30	24	do	74 06	77 31		
Arrack	100	30	do	2 77	2 77	In Algiers and Corsica as in France. In West Indies, in foreign vessels, prohibited. In Oceanica, $11\frac{1}{4}$ cents per $\frac{1}{4}$ gallon. In Guiana, admitted only in entrepot fictif.	In French and Tahitian vessels, arrack imported into Oceanica pays only one-half of this duty.
Artificial flowers	30	24		12 per ct.	ad valorem	In Corsica and Algiers as in France. In West Indies and Guiana, in foreign vessels, prohibited.	
Asafœtida	20	4	do	20 22	24 40		*Asafœdita:* To the same class belong bdellium, dragons' blood, mastic, myrrh, sumac, &c., and pay the same duties.

13 □

FRANCE AND HER POSSESSIONS—TARIFFS—Continued.

DENOMINATION OF MERCHANDISE.	DUTIES ON IMPORTS.						REMARKS.
	Into the United States, from foreign nations, per cent. ad valorem, under the act of—		INTO FRANCE FROM FOREIGN NATIONS.			INTO FRENCH POSSESSIONS.	
	1846.	1857.	Number, weight, or measure.	In national vessels.	In foreign vessels.		
Axes	30	24	220 pounds	$25 92	$27 99⅗		Axes, and all implements of husbandry, imported in French vessels into Guiana, direct from France, are free.
Asses' skins, raw	30	24	do	65	84¼	In Corsica and Algiers as in France. In West Indies and Guiana, in foreign vessels, prohibited.	Asses' skins, raw, dried, or salted, if imported into France from countries east of Cape Horn, pay only one-half of the duty to which those of American product are subjected.
Arrow-root	20	15	do	2 77	4 62		Arrow-root pays, in the French tariff, the same duty as sago, being considered a farinaceous substance.
Arsenic, white	15	4	do	18⅗	20½		
Bacon and hams, salted	20	15	do	$9\frac{3}{10}$	$9\frac{3}{10}$	In Algiers as in France. Into Corsica, in French vessels, $1 86; in foreign vessels, $2 05 per 220 pounds. Into West Indies, in foreign vessels, prohibited. Into Guiana, 5 per cent. ad valorem.	Into Guiana, free, if direct from France and in French vessels. Bacon, if salted with French salt, enjoys, if exported, a bounty of $53\frac{7}{10}$ cents per 220 pounds.
Baizes	25	19	do	37 02	39 79½	In Algiers and Corsica as in France. In Guiana and West Indies, in foreign vessels, prohibited.	
Balsams, cosmetic, in powder	30	24	do	34 07	36 64⅔	In Algiers and Corsica as in France. In Guiana and West Indies, in foreign vessels, prohibited.	In Martinique and Guadalupe, if for medicinal purposes, free.
others not enumerated.	30	24	2.20 pounds	$27\frac{9}{10}$	41⅕		

FRANCE AND HER POSSESSIONS—TARIFFS—Continued.

DENOMINATION OF MERCHANDISE.	DUTIES ON IMPORTS.						REMARKS.
	Into the United States from foreign nations, per cent. ad valorem, under the act of—		INTO FRANCE FROM FOREIGN NATIONS.			INTO FRENCH POSSESSIONS.	
	1846.	1857.	Number, weight, or measure.	In national vessels.	In foreign vessels.		
Bamboos, unmanufactured	10	Free	220 pounds	Free	$7 40$\frac{1}{2}$	In Algiers and Corsica as in France. In Guiana, prohibited; in West Indies, free.	
Bananas	20	8	do	$1 48	1 64$\frac{7}{10}$	In Algiers, free. In Corsica the same as in France. In Guiana, prohibited. In Martinique and Guadalupe, 4 per cent. ad valorem.	Bananas, imported in French vessels into Guiana, are subjected to a duty of only 2 per cent. ad valorem.
Barley	20	15	Duties according to the "mercuriale" on the price of grain in the French regulating markets. (a)			In Algiers and Corsica as in France. In Guiana, 5 per cent. ad valorem. In Martinique and Guadalupe, in foreign vessels, prohibited. If for seed in Algiers, free.	
Barilla	10	4	220 pounds	1 87$\frac{4}{5}$	2 35$\frac{9}{10}$	In Algiers and Corsica as in France; in Guiana and West Indies, prohibited.	Barilla, (soda,) of less than 33 degrees, enjoys, if exported from France, a bounty of 83$\frac{4}{5}$ cents per 220 pounds.
Bark, Jesuits', or Peruvian	15	Free	do	Free	5 58	In Corsica and Algiers as in France; in West Indies, free; in Guiana, prohib.	Bark for tanning, in Algiers, imported, if raw, 1$\frac{4}{5}$ cent; if ground, 9$\frac{3}{10}$ cents per 220 lbs.
Alcornoque	5	4	do	1 67	1 85$\frac{3}{4}$		

Barley.—The tariff on cereals of all kinds in France is regulated by the average monthly prices of *wheat* in the standard markets, which markets are divided into four classes, and which prices are published on the first day of every month by the minister of commerce. When, therefore, wheat is 28 francs, or more, per hectolitre (2 83 bushels) in markets of the first class; 26, or more, in those of the second; 24, or more, in those of the third; and 22, or more, in those of the fourth; then the import duty on barley is 12$\frac{1}{2}$ centimes (2 33 cents) per hectolitre in each of these markets, and the duty on its flour per 100 kilogrammes (220 pounds) is 30 centimes (5.50 cents) in French vessels and by land. In foreign vessels it is much higher. When wheat is 23, 21, 19, and 17 francs, respectively, in the four classes, the duty on barley is 2 francs 37$\frac{1}{2}$ centimes, (43 9-10 cents,) and on its flour 8 francs 40 centimes, ($1 57;) and when intermediate prices prevail the duty is proportional. The duty goes on increasing as the price of wheat in the standard markets *decreases* or cereals become more abundant, and *vice versa;* and when wheat is less than 22 francs in markets of the first class, less than 20 in those of the second, less than 18 in those of the third, and less than 16 in those of the fourth, per hectolitre, the duty on French vessels and by land increases by 75 centimes (13.80 cents) on each hectolitre of barley by the *decrease* of each franc in the price of wheat per hectolitre, and by 2 francs 70 centimes (50 cents) on every 100 kilogrammes of flour by the decrease of each franc in the price of flour per kilogramme. By the French customs calculation, the hectolitre of barley equals 60 kilogrammes, or 138 1-5 pounds.

FRANCE AND HER POSSESSIONS—TARIFFS—Continued.

DENOMINATION OF MERCHANDISE.	DUTIES ON IMPORTS.						REMARKS.
	Into the United States from foreign nations, per cent. ad valorem, under the act of—		INTO FRANCE FROM FOREIGN NATIONS.			INTO FRENCH POSSESSIONS.	
	1846.	1857.	Number, weight, or measure.	In national vessels.	In foreign vessels.		
Bark of the cork tree, unmanufactured.	15	4	220 pounds	\$1 11⅗	\$1 23	In Corsica and Algiers as in France; in Guiana and West Indies, prohibited, if in foreign vessels.	
Baskets, rough	30	24	do	2 77	3 09	In Corsica and Algiers the same as in France; in Guiana and West Indies, if in foreign vessels, prohibited.	
stripped of the bark	30	24	do	4 62	5 15		
Beads, coral, not set	30	24	2.20 pounds	1 85	2 06		
enamelled	30	24	do	37⅕	41⅕		
glass, pierced	30	24	do	18⅗	20½		
Beams for scales, of wood	30	24	220 pounds	44⅖	82⅓		
of iron	30	24	do	9 25	10 28½		
of copper	30	24	do	27 77	29 62		
Beef, fresh or salted	20	15	do	$9\frac{3}{10}$	$9\frac{3}{10}$	In Corsica and Algiers the same as in France; in Guiana, 5 per cent. ad val.; in Martinique and Guadalupe, \$1 86 per 220 pounds, both for French and foreign vessels, if not imported from France.	Beef, if imported into Martinique and Guadalupe direct from France, and on French vessels, \$1 48⅘ per 220 pounds; if exported from France, it enjoys a bounty of 74⅗ cts. per 220 pounds. The United States export principally to the French West Indies, and less to France proper.
Beer, in casks	30	24	Hectolitre of 26 galls.	1 12⅓	1 12⅓	Beer, in Oceanica, per dozen bottles, 37⅕ cents; in Martinique, Guadalupe, and Guiana, in foreign vessels, prohibited; in Corsica and Algiers the same as in France.	
in bottles	30	24	do	3 93¼	3 93¼		
Beeswax, yellow or brown	20	15	220 pounds	1 48⅘	2 80⅘	In Corsica and Algiers the same as in France; in Guiana, prohibited; in Martinique and Guadalupe, free.	
white	20	15	do	11 11	12 12		

FRANCE AND HER POSSESSIONS—TARIFFS—Continued.

DENOMINATION OF MERCHANDISE.	DUTIES ON IMPORTS. Into the United States from foreign nations, per cent. ad valorem, under the act of— 1846.	1857.	INTO FRANCE FROM FOREIGN NATIONS. Number, weight, or measure.	In national vessels.	In foreign vessels.	INTO FRENCH POSSESSIONS.	REMARKS.
Bismuth, crude	20	Free	220 pounds	$0 37$\frac{1}{5}$	$0 93	In Corsica and Algiers the same as in France; in Guiana and West Indies, prohibited.	In Guiana, French vessels may import pepper into the entrepot fictif. Implements of husbandry, in French vessels, if coming direct from France, are free of duty.
Benzoates	30	24	do	18 03	21 53$\frac{1}{2}$		
Bitter apples	20	Free	do	93	2 24		
Bladders, fish	20	15	do	5 55	6 17$\frac{2}{3}$		
other kinds	20	15	do	2 47	2 67$\frac{2}{3}$		
Black pepper	30	4	do	14 81	19 66$\frac{1}{3}$		
Blacksmiths' hammers and sledges.	30	24	do	9 25	10 28$\frac{1}{2}$		
Block tin	5	Free	do	37$\frac{1}{5}$	93	------------	The treaty of June 21, 1822, between France and the United States, did not comprise raw tin; therefore, it will be submitted to the duty specified under foreign vessels, although the importation may be direct from the United States to France.
Berries, juniper	20	15	do	Free	20$\frac{3}{10}$	In Corsica and Algiers same as in France; in Guiana, prohibited; in West Indies, prohibited.	
Berries, nuts, nut-galls, and vegetables for dyeing	5	Free	do	93	2 24		
Bichromate of potash	20	15	do	27 77	29 62		
Blue, Prussian	20	4	do	27 77	29 96		
				And 10 per	ct. ad val.	additional.	
vitriol	20	15	do	5 74	6 38$\frac{1}{2}$		
Bocking, baize	25	19	do	37 02	39 79$\frac{1}{2}$		
Bologna sausage	30	24	do	5 74	6 38$\frac{1}{2}$		
Bolting cloth, of silk	25	Free	2.20 pounds	2 96	3 79$\frac{1}{8}$	In Corsica and Algiers the same as in France; in Guiana and West Indies prohibited.	French vessels pay in Guiana 2 per cent. ad valorem.—(See remarks on silk and wool.)
Bolt rope, as cordage tarred	25	19	do	4 62	5 09		

FRANCE AND HER POSSESSIONS—TARIFFS—Continued.

DENOMINATION OF MERCHANDISE.	DUTIES ON IMPORTS. Into the United States from foreign nations, per cent. ad valorem, under the act of— 1846.	1857.	INTO FRANCE FROM FOREIGN NATIONS. Number, weight, or measure.	In national vessels.	In foreign vessels.	INTO FRENCH POSSESSIONS.	REMARKS.
Bombazine	25	19		Prohibited	Prohibited	In Algiers 25 per cent. ad val.; in Corsica as in France; in Guiana and West Indies, prohibited in foreign vessels.	
Bombazettes	25	19		Prohibited	Prohibited		
Boots, for men, women, and children, leather.	30	24		Prohibited	Prohibited		
Bonnets, straw, bark, chip, grass, coarse, common.	30	24	One	$0 09$\frac{3}{10}$	$0 09$\frac{3}{10}$		Straw bonnets which pay an importation duty of 23 cts. each, will receive back, if re-exported after having been ornamented with braids or otherwise trimmed, the same amount as bounty. Bonnets of wool or cotton enjoy, if exported from France, a bounty of $15 74 per 220 pounds.
Do....do....fine	30	24	One	23	20		
Bonnets, others, of wool or cotton.	30	24	220 pounds; As articles of fashion subject to a duty of 12 per cent. ad val.	37 03$\frac{4}{10}$	39 79$\frac{1}{2}$		
Books, bound or not bound, illustrated or not, in dead or foreign languages.	10	8	220 pounds	According to character, language, origin, &c. (a)			
Borax, crude, native	25	4	....do	55$\frac{4}{5}$	9$\frac{2}{3}$	In Algiers and Corsica as in France; in Guiana and West Indies, in foreign vessels, prohibited.	
artificial	25	4	....do	18 51	23 14		
half refined, (both)	25	4	....do	24 74	30 09		
Botany, specimens of	Free	Free	For museums and other scientific institutions, 1 per cent. ad valorem.			In Corsica and Algiers the same as in France; in Guiana and West Indies, in foreign vessels, prohibited.	

(a) If a book is over 50 years old it will be considered as an object of collection, and charged only 1 per cent. ad valorem. Libraries belonging to private persons intending to settle in France will pay 1 per cent. ad valorem, if proofs have been given that they are not for commercial purposes. Books imported in small quantities, by travellers, are free, if they exhibit traces of having been already used. If in the English language, they can only be imported through the ports of Bordeaux, Nantes, St. Malo, Granville, Dieppe, Boulogne, Calais, Dunquerque, Marseilles, Bayonne, and Havre.

Almanacs printed in foreign languages pay the same duty as on French works published abroad. All books published by learned associations, colleges, &c., are regarded as scientific memoirs.

FRANCE AND HER POSSESSIONS—TARIFFS—Continued.

Denomination of merchandise.	Into the United States from foreign nations, per cent. ad valorem, under the act of— 1846.	1857.	Duties on imports. Into France from foreign nations. Number, weight, or measure.	In national vessels.	In foreign vessels.	Into French possessions.	Remarks.
Box boards, paper	30	24	220 pounds	$18 51	$20 13	In Corsica and Algiers as in France. Into Guiana and West Indies, in foreign vessels, prohibited.	
Boxes, papier maché	30	24	do	37 $03\frac{7}{10}$	39 $79\frac{1}{2}$		
all other kinds	30	24	do	27 77	29 $96\frac{1}{4}$		
Brass, in plates, sheets, or rolled.	20	24	do	9 25	10 $28\frac{1}{2}$	In Algiers, in bars and plates, $27\frac{7}{10}$ cents per 220 pounds, if in foreign vessels. In Corsica as in France. Into Guiana and West Indies, prohibited, if in foreign vessels.	Brass beaten and laminated will, if exported from France, receive a bounty similar to the amount paid as duty on the importation of the crude metal (copper ore.)
in bars, pigs, or blocks	5	Free	do	$01\frac{4}{5}$	$55\frac{4}{5}$		
hammered	30	24	do	14 $81\frac{3}{5}$	16 $01\frac{4}{5}$		
wire, polished	30	24		Prohibited			
wire, polished or not, for cords for musical instruments.	30	24	do	18 51	20 13		
cooking utensils, common.	30	24	do	18 51	20 13		
cooking utensils, fine	30	24	do	37 $03\frac{7}{10}$	39 $79\frac{1}{2}$		
all other manufactures of.	30	24		Prohibited			
Brazier's rods	30	24	do	9 25	10 $28\frac{1}{2}$		
copper, first fusion	20	15	do	$1\frac{4}{5}$	$55\frac{4}{5}$		
Bracelets, hair	30	24	1 kilog. 2.20 lbs.	$37\frac{1}{5}$	$41\frac{1}{5}$	In Algiers and Corsica the same as in France. Into Guiana and West Indies, in foreign vessels, prohibited.	Bracelets, in French vessels, into Guiana, pay only 2 per cent. ad valorem.
Braces, suspenders composed wholly of India rubber.	30	24	220 pounds	3 $70\frac{1}{3}$	4 12		
suspenders in part of India rubber.	30	24	do	37 $03\frac{7}{10}$	39 $79\frac{1}{2}$		

FRANCE AND HER POSSESSIONS—TARIFFS—Continued.

DENOMINATION OF MERCHANDISE	DUTIES ON IMPORTS. Into the United States from foreign nations, per cent. ad valorem, under the act of— 1846.	1857.	INTO FRANCE FROM FOREIGN NATIONS. Number, weight, or measure.	In national vessels.	In foreign vessels.	INTO FRENCH POSSESSIONS.	REMARKS.
Braids, hair, or of which hair is a component part.	30	24	2.20 pounds	$0 37$\frac{1}{5}$	$0 41$\frac{1}{5}$	In Corsica and Algiers the same as in France. Into Guiana and West Indies, in foreign vessels, prohibited.	
of straw, bark, &c., common.	30	24	220 pounds	37$\frac{1}{5}$	41$\frac{1}{5}$		
of straw, bark, &c., fine.	30	24	2.20 pounds	93	1 02		
Brazil pebble, prepared for spectacles.	30	24	do	7$\frac{3}{5}$	9$\frac{2}{5}$		
wood, in sticks	5	Free	220 pounds	Free	1 11$\frac{1}{5}$	In Algiers and Corsica as in France. In Guiana, in foreign vessels, prohibited. In French West Indies, free.	
ground	20	12	do	3 70$\frac{1}{5}$	4 07$\frac{2}{5}$		
Bridles	30	24		Prohibited		In Corsica as in France. In Algiers, 25 per cent. ad valorem. In Guiana and West Indies, in foreign vessels, prohibited.	
bits, all kinds	30	24		do			
Bristol stones, manufactured	30	24	2.20 pounds	7$\frac{3}{5}$	9$\frac{2}{5}$	In Corsica and Algiers the same as in France. In Guiana and West Indies, in foreign vessels, prohibited.	
crude	10	15	do	3$\frac{2}{5}$	4$\frac{3}{5}$		
Bristles, rough	5	4	220 pounds	93	1 02		
assorted	5	4	do	3 70$\frac{1}{5}$	4 07$\frac{2}{5}$		Building stones imported into Algiers, free.
Bricks	20	15	1,000	74$\frac{2}{5}$	74$\frac{2}{5}$		Bronze statues and casts, as objects of taste, or the property of French artists at Rome, 1 per cent. ad valorem. Those imported for French national museums are free.
Brooms	30	24	100	$\frac{3}{5}$	4$\frac{3}{5}$		
Bronze powder	20	15	220 pounds	6 89	7 21		
casts, and manufactures of.	30	24	do	7 47	8 30		

FRANCE AND HER POSSESSIONS—TARIFFS—Continued.

Denomination of merchandise.	Duties on imports. Into the United States from foreign nations, per cent. ad valorem, under the act of— 1846.	1857.	Into France from foreign nations. Number, weight, or measure.	In national vessels.	In foreign vessels.	Into French possessions.	Remarks.
Brimstone, crude, in bulk	15	4	220 pounds	$0 18$\frac{3}{5}$	$0 27$\frac{9}{10}$	In Corsica and Algiers the same as in France. In Guiana and French West Indies, prohibited, if in foreign vessels.	Flour of brimstone, if exported in quantities of about 300 pounds, enjoys a bounty similar to the duty paid on the importation of the crude brimstone.
purified, in packages.	20	15	do	93	1 02		
Brussels carpeting	30	24	do	55 55	58 79		
Buckles, of iron or tin, for suspenders.	30	24	do	18 51	20 13		
all others, according to material.							
Bullion, gold	Free	Free	Hectogram. or $\frac{1}{4}$ pound.	4$\frac{3}{5}$	4$\frac{3}{5}$	In Corsica and Algiers the same as in France. In Guiana and West Indies, free.	
silver	Free	Free	Kilogram., or 2.20 lbs.	0$\frac{9}{10}$	0$\frac{9}{10}$		
Bulbous roots	Free	Free	220 pounds	93	1 02	In Corsica as in France. In Algiers, if green, free. In West Indies, as dried vegetables, per 2$\frac{4}{5}$ bushels, 64$\frac{4}{5}$ cents. In Guiana, 5 per cent. ad valorem.	
Building stones	10	8	1,000	74$\frac{2}{5}$	74$\frac{2}{5}$	In Corsica as in France. In Algiers, free. In Guiana and West Indies, in foreign vessels, prohibited.	
Bunting, worsted stuff	25	19		Prohibited.	Prohibited.		
Button moulds	25	19	100 kilogs. 220 lbs.	2 40$\frac{9}{10}$	2 64$\frac{4}{5}$	In Corsica and Algiers the same as in France. In Guiana and West Indies, in foreign vessels, prohibited.	If French product, and in French vessels, in Guiana, only 2 per cent. ad valorem. Buttons, if of cotton and wool, are, in France, to be classed with hosiery, and enjoy on exportation a bounty of $15 74 per 220 lbs.
Buttons, all kinds, common	25	19	do	18 51	21 13		
fine	25	19	do	37 03$\frac{7}{10}$	39 79$\frac{1}{2}$		
Brushes of all kinds	30	24	do	18 51	20 13		

FRANCE AND HER POSSESSIONS—TARIFFS—Continued.

DENOMINATION OF MERCHANDISE.	DUTIES ON IMPORTS.						REMARKS.
	Into the United States from foreign nations, per cent. ad valorem, under the act of—		INTO FRANCE FROM FOREIGN NATIONS.			INTO FRENCH POSSESSIONS.	
	1846.	1857.	Number, weight, or measure.	In national vessels.	In foreign vessels.		
Butter, fresh	20	15	220 lbs	$0 56$\frac{1}{5}$	$0 61$\frac{4}{5}$	In Corsica and Algiers same as in France In Guiana and West Indies, in foreign vessels, prohibited.	Salted butter, if exported from France, enjoys a bounty of 22$\frac{1}{4}$ cents per 220 lbs.
salted	20	15	do	93	1 02		
Cabinets of coins	Free	Free	For museums and other scientific institutions, 1 per cent. ad valorem.			In Corsica and Algiers the same as in France. In Guiana and West Indies, free.	Cabinet coins for national museums, free.
Cables and cordage, tarred or untarred, hemp.	25	19	100 kilogs, or 220 lbs.	4 68	5 09$\frac{1}{5}$		
Cables and cordage, of bark, sparte, coir, or hair.	25	19	do	93	1 02		
Cables and cordage, of other vegetable substances.	25	19	do	37$\frac{1}{5}$	41$\frac{1}{5}$	In Corsica and Algiers the same as in France. In Guiana and West Indies, in foreign vessels, prohibited.	
Cables and cordage, iron cables.	30	24	do	6 94$\frac{2}{5}$	7 63		
Cajeput oil	30	24	2. 20 lbs	93	1 02		
Calcined magnesia	30	24	220 lbs	37 03$\frac{7}{10}$	39 79$\frac{1}{2}$		
Calf skins, fresh and dry	5	4	do	18$\frac{3}{5}$	20$\frac{3}{10}$	In Algiers and Corsica the same as in France. In Guiana and West Indies, in foreign vessels, free.	Calf skins, from places west of Cape Horn, pay only one-half of these duties if imported in French vessels.
tanned, and otherwise prepared.	20	19	do	Prohibited.	Prohibited.	In Algiers, 25 per cent. ad valorem. In Corsica as in France. In Guiana and West Indies, in foreign vessels, prohibited.	

FRANCE AND HER POSSESSIONS—TARIFFS—Continued.

Denomination of merchandise	Duties on imports. Into the United States from foreign nations, per cent. ad valorem, under the act of—		Into France from foreign nations.			Into French possessions.	Remarks.
	1846.	1857.	Number, weight, or measure.	In national vessels.	In foreign vessels.		
Calomel, crude	25	19	220 lbs.	\$3 70⅓	\$4 11⅔	In Algiers and Corsica the same as in France. In Guiana and West Indies, in foreign vessels, prohibited.	
Cambrics, cotton	25	24	do.	Prohibited.	Prohibited.	In Algiers, 25 per cent. ad valorem. In Corsica as in France. In Guiana and West Indies, in foreign vessels, prohibited.	In Guiana, French productions on French vessels, only 2 per cent. ad valorem.
linen	20	15	2. 20 lbs.	4 69 9/10	5 00	In Algiers and Corsica the same as in France. In Guiana and the West Indies, in foreign vessels, prohibited.	Indian handkerchiefs, called Madras, may be imported into the French West Indies for \$1 50 per piece of 8 handkerchiefs.
Camels' hair, raw	10	8	220 lbs.	18⅗	20 3/10	In Algiers and Corsica the same as in France. In Guiana and the West Indies, in foreign vessels, prohibited.	
Camphor, crude	25	8	do.	9 30	14 04½	In Corsica and Algiers the same as in France. In Guiana and West Indies, in foreign vessels, prohibited.	
refined	40	30	do.	28 09	29 96¼		
Canvas, of hemp or flax, coarse	20	15	do.	39 25	39 25	In Corsica and Algiers the same as in France. In Guiana and West Indies, in foreign vessels, prohibited.	
of cotton	25	24		Prohibited.	Prohibited.	In Corsica, prohibited. In Algiers, 25 per cent. ad valorem. In Guiana, in foreign vessels, prohibited. In French West Indies, if used for sails, made of hemp, \$11 11 per 220 pounds.	

FRANCE AND HER POSSESSIONS—TARIFFS—Continued.

DENOMINATION OF MERCHANDISE.	DUTIES ON IMPORTS.						REMARKS.
	Into the United States from foreign nations, per cent. ad valorem, under the act of—		INTO FRANCE FROM FOREIGN NATIONS.			INTO FRENCH POSSESSIONS.	
	1846.	1857.	Number, weight, or measure.	In national vessels.	In foreign vessels.		
Candles, spermaceti	20	15	220 lbs	$40 74	$43 24	In Corsica and Algiers the same as in France. In Guiana and West Indies, in foreign vessels, prohibited.	
wax, yellow	20	15	do	9 25 9/10	10 29 1/3		
white	20	15	do	15 74	17 17 1/5		
tallow	20	15	do	1 86	2 04	In Corsica and Algiers, same as in France. In Guiana, 5 per cent. ad valorem. In West Indies, in foreign vessels, prohibited.	
stearine	20	15	do	6 48	7 15	In Corsica and Algiers, same as in France. In Guiana and West Indies, in foreign vessels, prohibited.	
Caps, wool	30	24	do	20 18	37 40	In Corsica as in France. In Algiers, in French vessels, $1 27, and in foreign vessels, $1 38 per 220 lbs. In Guiana and West Indies, in foreign vessels, prohibited.	Cotton and woolen caps, if exported from France, enjoy a bounty of $15 74 per 220 lbs.
silk, white	30	24	do	22 47 1/5	23 79	In Corsica and Algiers the same as in France. In Guiana and the West Indies, in foreign vessels, prohibited.	Carpets of pure wool receive, if exported from France, a bounty of $18 51 per 220 lbs.; those mixed with linen or cotton, a bounty of $15 74. All articles prohibited importation into France may be imported into Algiers at a duty of 25 per cent. ad valorem.
colored	30	24	do	28 09	29 96 1/4		
linen	30	24	do	28 09	29 96 1/4		
fur	30	24	Each	28 4/5	28 4/5		
Carpets, half wool, half linen	30	24	220 lbs	46 81 3/5	46 81 3/5		
knotted, one side presenting a face of linen, as Brussels carpet.	30	24	do	55 55	58 79		

FRANCE AND HER POSSESSIONS—TARIFFS—Continued.

DENOMINATION OF MERCHANDISE.	DUTIES ON IMPORTS.						REMARKS.
	Into the United States from foreign nations, per cent. ad valorem, under the act of—		INTO FRANCE FROM FOREIGN NATIONS.			INTO FRENCH POSSESSIONS.	
	1846.	1857.	Number, weight, or measure.	In national vessels.	In foreign vessels.		
Carpets, of silk, and also tapestry, mixed with linen thread, or not.	30	24	220 lbs	$56 66	$59 90	In Corsica and Algiers the same as in France. In Guiana and the West Indies, in foreign vessels, prohibited.	Carpets of pure wool receive, if exported from France, a bounty of $18 51 per 220 lbs.; those mixed with linen or cotton, a bounty of $15 74. All articles prohibited importation into France may be imported into Algiers at a duty of 25 per cent. ad valorem
all others	30	24		Prohibited.	Prohibited.		
of flags, jute, or grass, common.	25	19	do	37 $\frac{1}{3}$	41 $\frac{1}{3}$		
of flags, jute, or grass, fine.	25	19	do	93	1 02		
Carriages, fine, not for agricultural and similar purposes.	30	24		Prohibited.		In Corsica as in France; in Algiers, 25 per cent. ad valorem; in Guiana, in foreign vessels, prohibited; in West Indies, 15 per cent. ad valorem.	
Carriages, common, as carts for common purposes.	30	24		15 per ct.	ad val	In Corsica and Algiers same as in France; in Guiana, free; West Indies, 15 per cent. ad valorem.	
Carriages, railroad cars, without springs.	30	24	220 pounds	4 68	5 09 $\frac{1}{3}$	Not mentioned in the tariffs.	
Carriages, laces for, cotton	25	19		5 per ct.	ad val	In Corsica and Algiers same as in France; in Guiana and West Indies, in foreign vessels, prohibited.	
Carraway oil	30	24	1 kilogram., 2 20 lbs.	93	1 02	In Algiers and Corsica same as in France; in Guiana, in foreign vessels, prohibited; in French West Indies, free.	

FRANCE AND HER POSSESSIONS—TARIFFS—Continued.

Denomination of merchandise.	Duties on imports.						Remarks.
	Into the United States from foreign nations, per cent. ad valorem, under the act of—		Into France from foreign nations.			Into French possessions.	
	1846.	1857.	Number, weight, or measure.	In national vessels.	In foreign vessels.		
Cards, blank, and visiting	30	24	100 kilogs, 220 lbs.	$55 55	$58 79	In Algiers and Corsica the same as in France; in Guiana and West Indies, in foreign vessels, prohibited.	
playing	30	24		Prohibited		In Algiers, 25 per cent. ad valorem; in Corsica, prohibited; In Guiana and West Indies, in foreign vessels, prohibited.	Playing cards, without being stamped, are prohibited exportation.
Castings, iron, as parts of machines, weighing under 25 kilogrammes.	30	24	do	18 51	20 13	In Algiers and Corsica as in France; in Guiana, in foreign vessels, prohibited; in West Indies, 15 per cent. ad valorem.	Castings, as objects of collection and not for commercial purposes, may be admitted for 1 per cent. ad valorem; castings and machines necessary for the colonial industry may be imported into Guiana free of duty.
26 to 50 kilogrammes	30	24	do	14 81	16 01		
51 to 100 kilogrammes	30	24	do	12 96	14 07		
Castor oil	20	15	do	3 70	5 61⅔	In Algiers and Corsica as in France; in Guiana, in foreign vessels, prohibited; in West Indies, free.	Cassia lignea, if product of French colonies, and in French bottoms, is only admitted in Guiana into entrepot fictif.
Cascarilla bark	20	8	do	7 03 7/10	10 95½		
Cassia lignea, from India	40	4	2.20 pounds	6 1/10	18⅗		
from other places	40	4	do	12⅕	18⅗		Oil of cassia, if for medicinal purposes, is admitted into the French West Indies, free.
oil of	30	24	do	93	1 02		
Cashmere shawls, Thibet	30	24	A piece	18 51	18 51	In Algiers and Corsica as in France; in Guiana and West Indies, in foreign vessels, prohibited.	
Casement rods	30	24		Prohibited		In Algiers, 25 per ct. ad val.; in Corsica, same as in France; in Guiana and West Indies, in foreign vessels, prohibited.	

FRANCE AND HER POSSESSIONS—TARIFFS—Continued.

DENOMINATION OF MERCHANDISE.	DUTIES ON IMPORTS. Into the United States from foreign nations, per cent. ad valorem, under the act of— 1846.	1857.	INTO FRANCE FROM FOREIGN NATIONS. Number, weight, or measure.	In national vessels.	In foreign vessels.	INTO FRENCH POSSESSIONS.	REMARKS.
Cayenne pepper, from French Guiana.	30	4	220 pounds.	1 86	Prohibited.	In Algiers the same as in France; in Corsica, one-half of the French duties; in Guiana, no importation; in West Indies, free.	Pepper from the French colonies, and in French vessels, may be imported in Guiana into the entrepot fictif.
Cayenne pepper, from other places.	30	4	....do......	14 81	19 66$\frac{1}{3}$		Colonial products are admitted into Corsica for one-half the French tariff duties.
Chalk, not otherwise provided for.	5	4	....do......	93	1 02	In Algiers, free; in Corsica as in France; in Guiana, 5 per ct. ad val.; in West Indies, in foreign vessels, prohibited.	
Chamomile flowers..........	20	15	....do......	5 55	9 25$\frac{9}{10}$	In Algiers and Corsica as in France; in Guiana, in foreign vessels, prohibited; in West Indies, free.	
Charts and maps............	10	Free...	....do......	55 55	58 79		Geographical charts placed in books as appendixes will be regarded as books.
Chinaware, common........	30	24	....do......	20 37	32 35	In Algiers and Corsica as in France; in Guiana and West Indies, in foreign vessels, prohibited.	Under common chinaware, are understood such goods as are not gilt, painted, or in any other way ornamented, but of one simple color.
fine............	30	24	....do......	60 55	63 79		
Chip hats or bonnets, coarse, common	30	24	Each	9$\frac{3}{10}$	9$\frac{3}{10}$		
Chip hats or bonnets, fine....	30	24	Each	23	23		Chip hats, which pay on importation a duty of 23 cents each, will receive back the same amount as bounty if re-exported after having been ornamented with braids or otherwise trimmed.
Cheese, Dutch..............	30	24	220 pounds	1 11$_{5}$	1 22$\frac{1}{5}$	In Corsica, in French vessels, \$1 86 per 220 pounds; in foreign, \$2 03; in Algiers as in France; in Guiana and West Indies, in foreign vessels, prohibited.	Cheese imported into France from the French colonies is free of duty.
other kinds.........	30	24	....do......	2 80$\frac{4}{5}$	3 06$\frac{1}{4}$		Dutch cheese, imported direct from Holland, either in Dutch or French vessels, is subject only to $\frac{2}{3}$ of the regular duty.

FRANCE AND HER POSSESSIONS—TARIFFS—Continued.

DENOMINATION OF MERCHANDISE.	DUTIES ON IMPORTS.						REMARKS.
	Into the United States from foreign nations, per cent. ad valorem, under the act of—		INTO FRANCE FROM FOREIGN NATIONS.			INTO FRENCH POSSESSIONS.	
	1846.	1857.	Number, weight, or measure.	In national vessels.	In foreign vessels.		
Cherry rum	100	30	1 hectolitre, 26 gall.	\$2 80$\frac{4}{5}$	\$2 80$\frac{4}{5}$	In Corsica and Algiers as in France; in Guiana and West Indies, in foreign vessels, prohibited.	In Oceanica the duty on cherry rum amounts to 11$\frac{1}{4}$ cents per $\frac{1}{4}$ gallon.
Crystals, watch, crude		24	220 pounds	1 86	2 04$\frac{3}{5}$		
polished		24	do	37 03$\frac{1}{3}$	39 79$\frac{1}{2}$		
Chocolate, simply crushed	20	15	do	28 08$\frac{9}{01}$	29 96$\frac{1}{4}$	In Algiers and Corsica the same as in France; in Guiana and West Indies, in foreign vessels, prohibited.	
Chromate of potash	20	15	do	28 08$\frac{9}{10}$	29 96$\frac{1}{4}$		
Cigars	40	30	See Tobacco.				
Cinnamon, China	30	4	2.22 pounds	06$\frac{1}{10}$	18$\frac{3}{5}$	In Corsica one-half of the French duties. In Algiers as in France. In Guiana and West Indies, in foreign vessels, prohib ted.	In Guiana, if productions of the French colonies, and in French vessels, permitt ‹ ‹ the entrepot fictif. Cinnamon of China is the common sort, and therefore subjected to one-half of the duty for French vessels.
other	30	4	do	12$\frac{1}{5}$	18$\frac{3}{5}$		
oil of	30	24	do	93	1 02	In Algiers and Corsica as in France. In Guiana, in foreign vessels, prohibited. In French West Indies, free.	
Citron, preserved in sugar or honey	40	24	220 pounds	11 23$\frac{1}{2}$	14 04$\frac{1}{2}$	In Algiers and Corsica as in France. In Guiana and West Indies, in foreign vessels, free.	
oil of	30	24	2.22 pounds	93	1 02		
fruit	20	8	220 pounds	74$\frac{2}{5}$	2 04$\frac{3}{5}$	In Algiers, free. In Corsica, one-half the French duty. In Guiana and West Indies, in foreign vessels, 4 per cent. ad valorem.	

FRANCE AND HER POSSESSIONS—TARIFFS—Continued.

Denomination of merchandise.	Duties on imports. Into the United States from foreign nations, per cent. ad valorem, under the act of— 1846.	1857.	Into France from foreign nations. Number, weight, or measure.	In national vessels.	In foreign vessels.	Into French possessions.	Remarks.
Cloth, bolting, of silk	25	Free	2.20 pounds	$2 96	$3 29½	In Algiers and in Corsica as in France. In Guiana and West Indies, in foreign vessels, prohibited.	In Guiana, however, foreign vessels may import silk, wool, and cotton tissues into the entrepot fictif, but not for consumption.
of wool	30	24	220 pounds	35 18	39 78½		
hair, and hair seating	25	19	do	28 $08\frac{9}{10}$	29 96¼		
Cloves	40	4	2.20 pounds	$33\frac{3}{10}$	$55\frac{4}{5}$	In Corsica one-half of the French duties In Algiers as in France. In Guiana and West Indies, in foreign vessels, prohibited.	In Guiana, if French product, and in French vessels, admitted into the entrepot fictif.
oil of	30	24	do	93	1 02	In Algiers and Corsica as in France. In Guiana, in foreign vessels, prohibited. In French West Indies, free.	
Cochineal	10	4	2.20 pounds	$9\frac{3}{10}$	$27\frac{9}{10}$	In Algiers and Corsica as in France. In Guiana, in foreign vessels, prohibited. In West Indies, free.	
Cocoa, beans	10	4	2.20 pounds	10 $20\frac{9}{10}$	19 66⅓	In Algiers, free. In Corsica, one-half of the French duties. In Guiana and West Indies, in foreign vessels, prohibited.	Cocoa, from French colonies and in French vessels, is, in Guiana, admitted into the entrepot fictif.
nuts	20	4	do	$18\frac{3}{5}$	1 $11\frac{3}{5}$	In Algiers, free. In Corsica, one-half of the French duties. In Guiana, in foreign vessels, prohibited. In West Indies, 4 per cent. ad valorem.	
nut oil	10	4	do	2 $59\frac{1}{5}$	2 $80\frac{4}{5}$	In Algiers and Corsica as in France. In Guiana, in foreign vessels, prohibited. In the West Indies, free.	

FRANCE AND HER POSSESSIONS—TARIFFS—Continued.

Denomination of merchandise.	Duties on imports. Into the United States from foreign nations, per cent. ad valorem, under the act of— 1846.	1857.	Into France from foreign nations. Number, weight, or measure.	In national vessels.	In foreign vessels.	Into French possessions.	Remarks.
Coffee	20	15(a)	220 pounds	$17 59	$19 66$\frac{1}{3}$	In Algiers, from the United States, in French or equalized United States vessels, on direct voyage, $2 80$\frac{4}{5}$ per 220 pounds. In other foreign or United States vessels, on indirect voyage, $3 05 per 220 pounds. In Corsica, one-half the French tariff duties. In Guiana prohibited, and only admitted, if from French colonies and in French vessels, into the intrepot fictif. In French West Indies, prohibited to all flags.	Coffe: imported into France from French colonies is less taxed than foreign, as is always the case with French colonial products. French vessels only, can trade between France and her colonies. In Guiana another duty, besides the regular exportation duty, is levied, called "contribution foncière," of $1 02 per 220 pounds, in foreign vessels.
Coins, of gold and silver	Free	Free	2.20 pounds	0$\frac{1}{5}$	0$\frac{1}{5}$	In Algiers and Corsica as in France. In Guiana and West Indies, free.	In Guiana and French West Indies, the duties here given are always for foreign vessels.
of copper, French currency	Free	Free	220 pounds		3$\frac{2}{3}$		
of copper, foreign currency.	Free	Free		Prohibited		Prohibited	French vessels, of course, have no restrictions whatever in their trading direct with the colonies. The duties on coins are applicable to all silver and gold coins, without regard to nationality. Foreign copper coins, with the exception of the Austrian 20 kreutzer pieces, are entirely prohibited. As objects of collection, 1 per cent. ad valorem.

(a) Except when imported direct from the place of its growth in American or equalized vessels, or when of the growth or production of the possessions of the Netherlands, imported from the Netherlands in the same manner, when it is free.

FRANCE AND HER POSSESSIONS—TARIFFS—Continued.

Denomination of merchandise.	Duties on imports. Into the United States from foreign nations, per cent. ad valorem, under the act of— 1846.	1857.	Into France from foreign nations. Number, weight, or measure.	In national vessels.	In foreign vessels.	Into French possessions.	Remarks.
Cokes and culm of coal	30	24	220 pounds	$0 01$\frac{2}{5}$	$0 06$\frac{1}{10}$	In Algiers, free. In Corsica as in France. In Guiana, 5 per cent. ad valorem. In West Indies, 2 cents per 220 pounds.	
Collections of antiquity	Free	Free		For museums, &c., 1 pr. ct.	ad valorem.	In Algiers and Corsica as in France. In Guiana in foreign vessels, prohibited. In West Indies, not mentioned in the tariff.	For French national museums, free.
Comfits of all kinds	40	30	do	11 23$\frac{1}{2}$	14 04$\frac{1}{2}$	In Algiers and Corsica a ce. In Guiana and West Indies, in foreign vessels, prohibited.	
Copper, ore of	Free	Free	do	Free	18$\frac{3}{5}$	In Algiers and Corsica as in France. In Guiana, in foreign vessels, prohibited. In the West Indies, free.	Copper beaten and laminated, if re-exported from France, enjoys a bounty of the same amount as has been paid as duty on the importation of the raw material. In the treaty of 1822, copper and lead ore were excluded from the privilege of paying the same duty in American as in French vessels, if imported direct into France. But in course of time the French government has ceased to regard these two exceptions, or enforce the law in relation to them.
in blocks, plates, bars, &c.	5	Free	do	1$\frac{4}{5}$	55$\frac{4}{5}$	In Algiers, in French vessels, 1 cent; in foreign, 28 cents per 220 pounds. In Corsica as in France. In Guiana and West Indies, in foreign vessels, prohibited.	
rolled, in bars and sheets, for sheathing ships.	Free	Free	do	9 25	10 29$\frac{1}{3}$	In Algiers and Corsica as in France. In Guiana and West Indies, in foreign vessels, prohibited.	
hammered	30	24	do	14 81	16 01$\frac{4}{5}$		
wire, (see wire)	30	24	do	18 51	20 13		
manufactures, simply turned, common.	30	24	do	18 51	20 13		

FRANCE AND HER POSSESSIONS—TARIFFS—Continued.

Denomination of merchandise.	Duties on imports. Into the United States from foreign nations, per cent. ad valorem, under the act of— 1846.	1857.	Into France from foreign nations. Number, weight, or measure.	In national vessels.	In foreign vessels.	Into French possessions.	Remarks.
Copper manufactures, simply turned, fine.	30	24	220 pounds	$37 $03\frac{1}{3}$	$39 $79\frac{1}{2}$		
all others	30	24		Prohibited.			
Copperas, of iron, green	20	15	do	1 $11\frac{3}{5}$	1 $22\frac{1}{5}$		
of copper, blue	20	15	do	5 74	6 $83\frac{1}{3}$		
of zinc, white	20	15	do	5 74	6 $83\frac{1}{3}$		
Coral, crude, French fishery	20	15	do	$18\frac{3}{5}$	Prohibited.		
crude, foreign fishery	20	15	do	3 $70\frac{3}{10}$	4 $07\frac{2}{5}$		
cut, but not set	30	24	2.20 pounds	1 86	2 $04\frac{3}{5}$		
Cordage, of hemp	25	19	220 pounds	4 68	5 $09\frac{1}{5}$	In Algiers and Corsica as in France. In Guiana and West Indies, in foreign vessels, prohibited.	
of bark, sparte, coir, or hair.	25	19	do	93	1 02		
of other vegetable substances.	25	19	do	$37\frac{1}{5}$	$41\frac{1}{5}$		
Cordials of all kinds	100	30	Hectolitre, or 26 galls.	28 09	28 09		In Oceanica, $11\frac{1}{4}$ cents per $\frac{1}{4}$ gallon. French vessels may import liquors into Guiana into the entrepot fictif.
Cork tree, bark of, unmanufactured.	15	4	220 pounds	1 $11\frac{3}{5}$	1 23		
bark of, manufactured.	30	24	do	10 00	10 96		
Cosmetics, for powdering	30	24	do	4 $68\frac{1}{10}$	5 15		Perfumery made of animal substances are free in the French West Indies.
others	30	24		See perfumery			
Cotton, raw, from French colonies.	Free	Free	do	Free	Prohibited.	In Algiers and Corsica as in France. In Guiana and West Indies, in foreign vessels, prohibited.	With the exception of Corsica, all the other possessions of France are cotton-growing countries. In Guiana, raw cotton, if im-
raw, from Turkey	Free	Free	do	2 $80\frac{4}{5}$	4 68		

FRANCE AND HER POSSESSIONS—TARIFFS—Continued.

Denomination of merchandise.	Duties on imports.						Remarks.
	Into the United States from foreign nations, per cent. ad valorem, under the act of—		Into France from foreign nations.			Into French possessions.	
	1846.	1857.	Number, weight, or measure.	In national vessels.	In foreign vessels.		
Cotton, raw, from East Indies.	Free	Free	220 pounds	$1 86	$6 48	In Algiers and Corsica as in France. In Guiana and West Indies, in foreign vessels, prohibited.	ported from the French colonies in French vessels, may be admitted into the entrepot fictif; if exported, it is, besides the regular duty, subject to an additional one, called "contribution foncière," of $64\frac{4}{5}$ cents, in foreign vessels. American vessels oaded with raw cotton for France, but sailing first to England to discharge other cargo there, enjoy, although they are not on direct voyage, the same privileges as if trading direct with France, and without touching at England first. In Guiana, foreign vessels may import tissues of wool, cotton, and silk into the entrepot fictif. In France, almost all cotton manufactures are prohibited. Cotton hosiery, if exported, will receive a bounty of $15 74 per 220 pounds. Tissues of cotton, mixed or not mixed with wool or silk, may be imported into Algiers (not into France) at variance with the French tariff: white, printed, or dyed calicoes; white, printed, or dyed
raw, from not European countries.	Free	Free	do	3 72	6 48		
raw, from entrepots.	Free	Free	do	5 $55\frac{1}{2}$	6 48		
in the pod, from French colonies.	Free	Free	do	Free	Prohibited		
in the pod, from Turkey.	Free	Free	do	$83\frac{3}{10}$	1 $30\frac{9}{10}$		
in the pod, from East Indies.	Free	Free	do	$60\frac{1}{10}$	1 $77\frac{1}{5}$		
in the pod, from not European countries.	Free	Free	do	1 $06\frac{2}{5}$	1 $77\frac{1}{5}$		
in the pod, from entrepots.	Free	Free	do	1 $52\frac{7}{10}$	1 $77\frac{1}{5}$		
yarn of cotton twist, of No. 143 and under, simple.	25	24	2.20 pounds	1 $30\frac{3}{10}$	1 42		
yarn of cotton twist, of No. 143 and under, threaded or twisted.	25	24	do	1 48	1 $62\frac{9}{10}$		

FRANCE AND HER POSSESSIONS—TARIFFS—Continued.

Denomination of merchandise.	Duties on imports. Into the United States from foreign nations, per cent. ad valorem, under the act of— 1846.	1857.	Into France from foreign nations. Number, weight, or measure.	In national vessels.	In foreign vessels.	Into French possessions.	Remarks.
Cotton, all other cotton threads, (without distinction of sort or No. of threads.)	25	24	-----------	Prohibited.	---------		handkerchiefs; also, tissues of cotton, nixed w h other stuffs than silk or wool, as muslins, white, dyed, or printed; laces, ns , and hoisery.
manufactures, viz: all woven, knit, or worked cottons, with the following exceptions:	25	24	-----------	Prohibited.	---------		
nankeens imported direct from India.	25	24	2.20 pounds.	$0 18$\frac{3}{5}$	Prohibited.	In Algiers and Corsica as in France. In Guiana and West Indies, in foreign vessels, prohibited.	
nankeens imported from elsewhere.	25	24	-----------	Prohibited.	---------		
lace worked by hand and with spindles, and applications of cotton thread worked on tulle or network.	25	19	-----------	5 per cent.	ad valorem		
Cream of tartar	20	4	220 pounds.	5 55	$6 10$\frac{4}{5}$	In Algiers and Corsica as in France. In Guiana and West Indies, in foreign vessels, prohibited.	
Crude tartar	5	Free	do	1 12	2 24		
Currants	40	8	do	1 86	2 04$\frac{3}{5}$	In Algiers, free. In Corsica as in France. In Guiana, in foreign vessels, prohibited. In West Indies, 4 per cent. ad valorem.	
Dates	40	8	do	1 48	1 64$\frac{7}{10}$		
Demijohns, empty	30	24	-----------	Prohibited.	Prohibited.	Prohibited.	

FRANCE AND HER POSSESSIONS—TARIFFS—Continued.

DENOMINATION OF MERCHANDISE.	DUTIES ON IMPORTS. Into the United States from foreign nations, per cent. ad valorem, under the act of—		INTO FRANCE FROM FOREIGN NATIONS.			INTO FRENCH POSSESSIONS.	REMARKS.
	1846.	1857.	Number, weight, or measure.	In national vessels.	In foreign vessels.		
Diamonds, in a crude state	10	4	1 hectogram., 0.220 lbs.	$0 09¼	$0 09¼		
Down, of all kinds, viz:							
for beds, swan, goose, and duck.	25	19	220 pounds	37 03⅓	39 79½		
eider or eider down, cleaned	25	19	2.20 pounds	93	1 02	In Algiers and in Corsica as in France; in Guiana and West Indies, in foreign vessels, prohibited.	
do....do....not cleaned	25	19	....do......	23 1/10	24		
Down, other	25	19	220 pounds	11 23½	12 26¼		
Drawings	20	15	....do......	55 55	58 79	....	As objects of collection, 1 per cent. ad val.
Drawing knives	30	24	....	Prohibited.	Prohibited.		
paper	30	24	....do......	28 09	29 96¼		
Dressed fur	20	15	....	15 per cent. ad val.			
Drugs, medical, in a crude state	20	15	....do......	7 03 7/10	10 95½	In Algiers and Corsica as in France; into Guiana, in foreign vessels, prohibited; into West Indies, free.	
prepared medicants	30	24	....	Prohibited.	Prohibited.	In Algiers and Corsica as in France; in Guiana and West Indies, in foreign vessels, prohibited.	
Duck, sail, Holland, ravens, and Prussia.	20	15	The same duties as on the tissues of which they are made.—(See the respective articles.)				
Dyeing articles, not otherwise enumerated.	20	Free.					
barks, not ground	5	Free	220 pounds	1⅘	1⅘	In Algiers, pine bark, unground, 1⅘ cent; ground, 9 3/10 cents per 220 lbs.; in Corsica as in France; in Guiana and West Indies, in foreign vessels, prohibited.	
ground	20	Free	....do......	9 3/10	9 3/10		

FRANCE AND HER POSSESSIONS—TARIFFS—Continued.

DENOMINATION OF MERCHANDISE.	DUTIES ON IMPORTS. Into the United States from foreign nations, per cent. ad valorem, under the act of—		INTO FRANCE FROM FOREIGN NATIONS.			INTO FRENCH POSSESSIONS.	REMARKS.
	1846.	1857.	Number, weight, or measure.	In national vessels.	In foreign vessels.		
Dyeing woods, in sticks, Pernambuco.	5	Free	220 pounds	Free	$0 93	In Algiers and Corsica as in France; in Guiana, in foreign vessels, prohibited; in West Indies, free,	
Dyeing woods, in sticks, sandal and Nicaragua.	5	Free	do	Free	1 11$\frac{3}{5}$		
Dyeing woods, all kinds, ground.	20	Free	do	$3 70$\frac{3}{10}$	4 07$\frac{3}{5}$		
Earthenware, pottery, common	30	24	do	1 11$\frac{3}{5}$	1 22$\frac{1}{5}$	In Algiers and in Corsica as in France; in Guiana and West Indies, in foreign vessels, prohibited.	Pottery showing traces of use, and belonging to immigrants, has to pay only 15 per ct. ad valorem. By common porcelain, is understood all that is not gilt or painted, or otherwise ornamented, and having only one color. Porcelain garnished with gilt copper is prohibited. Old porcelain, as object of curiosity, admitted at 1 per cent. ad valorem. Porcelain showing traces of use, the property of persons intending to settle in France, 15 per cent. ad valorem
of Fayence, do	30	24	do	9 07$\frac{3}{5}$	9 98		
stoneware, table, and pitcher ware.	30	24	do	2 80$\frac{4}{5}$	3 05$\frac{1}{2}$		
fine	30	24	do	Prohibited.	Prohibited.		
porcelain, com'n	30	24	do	30 37	32 35		
fine	30	24	do	60 55	63 79		
Elephants' teeth, from Senegal	5	Free	do	4 68	Prohibited.	In Algiers and Corsica as in France; in Guiana, in foreign vessels, prohibited; in the West Indies, free.	
from India	5	Free	do	4 68	12 96		
Elephants' teeth, from Africa, except Senegal.	5	Free	do	4 68	12 96		
Elephants' teeth, from all other places.	5	Free	do	10 20$\frac{9}{10}$	12 96		

FRANCE AND HER POSSESSIONS—TARIFFS—Continued.

DENOMINATION OF MERCHANDISE.	DUTIES ON IMPORTS. Into the United States from foreign nations, per cent. ad valorem, under the act of— 1846.	1857.	INTO FRANCE FROM FOREIGN NATIONS. Number, weight, or measure.	In national vessels.	In foreign vessels.	INTO FRENCH POSSESSIONS.	REMARKS.
Embroidery, with gold or silver thread.	30	24	2.20 pounds.	$5 55	$6 $11\frac{1}{10}$		
Engravings, as plates, bound or unbound.	10	8	220 pounds.	55 55	58 79		Framed engravings and lithographs are considered as furniture, and pay 15 per cent. ad valorem. Cotton epaulets, if exported from France, enjoy a bounty of $15 74 per 220 pounds.
Epaulets, cotton	25	24		Prohibited.	Prohibited.		
gold and silver	30	24	Hectogramme 0.220 lb.	1 86	2 $04\frac{3}{5}$		
silk	25	24	2 20 pounds.	2 99	3 25		
Epsom salts	20	15	220 pounds.	12 96	14 07		
Fancy soaps, perfumed	30	24	do	30 37	32 35	In Algiers and Corsica as in France; in Guiana and West Indies, in foreign vessels, prohibited.	For remarks see "Soap."
Feathers for beds, swan, goose, and duck.	25	19	do	37 $03\frac{1}{3}$	39 $79\frac{1}{2}$		
eider or eider down, cleaned.	25	19	2.20 pounds.	93	1 02		
eider or eider down, uncleaned.	25	19	do	$23\frac{1}{10}$	24		
other	25	19	220 pounds.	11 $23\frac{1}{2}$	12 $26\frac{1}{2}$		Uncleaned eider down must be in the same state as taken from the nest, still mixed with wood, straw, earth, &c.
ornamental, cock and vulture.	30	24	do	18 51	20 13		
ornamental, ostrich, white.	30	24	do	74 $07\frac{2}{5}$	77 $31\frac{2}{5}$		
ornamental, ostrich, black.	30	24	do	37 $03\frac{1}{3}$	39 $79\frac{1}{2}$		
ornam'l, of all others	30	24	do	18 51	20 13		

16

FRANCE AND HER POSSESSIONS—TARIFFS—Continued.

DENOMINATION OF MERCHANDISE	DUTIES ON IMPORTS.						REMARKS.
	Into the United States from foreign nations, per cent. ad valorem, under the act of—		INTO FRANCE FROM FOREIGN NATIONS.			INTO FRENCH POSSESSIONS.	
	1846.	1857.	Number, weight, or measure.	In national vessels.	In foreign vessels.		
Felt, for hats	20	15	Per piece	$0 27 9/10	$0 27 9/10	In Algiers and Corsica as in France. In Guiana and West Indies, in foreign vessels, prohibited.	
for ships, &c	Free	Free	220 lbs	18 51	20 13		
other manufactures	20	15	do	74 07 2/5	77 31 2/5		
Fiddles or violins	20	15	Each	55 4/5	55 4/5		
Figs	40	8	220 lbs	74	82 3/10	In Algiers, free. Corsica, as in France. In Guiana, 5 per cent. ad valorem. In West Indies, 4 per cent. ad valorem.	
Filberts	30	24	do	74	82 3/10		
Fire arms of all kinds, for soldiers.	30	24		Prohibited.	Prohibited.	Prohibited.	
Fire arms of all kinds, for commerce	30	24	do	37 03	39 79½	In Algiers and Corsica as in France. In Guiana and West Indies, in foreign vessels, prohibited.	*Arms.*—The distinction between arms for the army and arms for the trade is based upon the ornamenting and calibre. Pocket pistols, which are prohibited, may, however, be admitted into the entrepot.
Fish, of the sea, fresh, dry, salt, or smoked.	20	15	do	7 40⅔	8 14¾	In Corsica, in national vessels, $2 80⅘, and, in foreign vessels, $3 05 per 220 lbs. In Algiers, as in France. In Guiana, 5 per cent. ad valorem. In West Indies, $1 30⅕ per 220 lbs.	The French government, to encourage French fisheries, has given large bounties, since the year 1767, both for fitting out vessels and on the production of the fisheries.
Fish of the sea, fresh, from French fisheries.	20	15		Free	Prohibited.	In foreign vessels, prohibited.	The treaty of 1822 extends to American fisheries no participation in its privileges; the produce of American fisheries, therefore, is subjected to the duty assigned to all other foreign vessels; no matter if imported from the United States direct or not.

FRANCE AND HER POSSESSIONS—TARIFFS—Continued.

DENOMINATION OF MERCHANDISE.	DUTIES ON IMPORTS.						REMARKS.
	Into the United States from foreign nations, per cent. ad valorem, under the act of—		INTO FRANCE FROM FOREIGN NATIONS.			INTO FRENCH POSSESSIONS.	
	1846.	1857.	Number, weight, or measure.	In national vessels.	In foreign vessels.		
Fish of the sea, in oil or pickled	In oil, 40; Pick'd 20	30; 15	220 lbs.	$18 51	$20 13	In Corsica, in national vessels, $9 30; in foreign, $10 20 per 220 lbs. In Algiers, as in France. In Guiana and West Indies, in foreign vessels, prohibited.	
Flats, for hats and bonnets, straw, &c.	30	24				In Algiers and Corsica as in France. In Guiana and West Indies, in foreign vessels, prohibited.	
Flats, for hats and bonnets, common.	30	24	do	37⅕	41⅕		
Flats, for hats and bonnets, fine.	30	24	do	93	1 02		
Flax, in stalks, raw, green	15	Free	do	9 3/10	9 3/10		
dry	15	Free	do	11¼	11¼		
steeped	15	Free	do	13⅘	14⅘		
hackled, and tow of	15	12	do	93	1 02		
combed	15	12	do	2 80⅘	3 05½		
seed	20	15	do	46¼	81⅖		
manufactured. (See linen.)	20	15					
Flints	5	4	do	1 67⅖	1 84½		
Floor cloth, of baize or bocking.	25	24	do	37 02	39 79½		
Floor matting, of flags, jute, grass, common.	25	19	do	37⅕	41⅕		Foreign tissues of cotton, wool, or silk, may be admitted in Guiana, into the entrepot fictif.
Floor matting, of flags, jute, grass, fine.	25	19	do	93	1 02		

FRANCE AND HER POSSESSIONS—TARIFFS—Continued.

DENOMINATION OF MERCHANDISE.	DUTIES ON IMPORTS. Into the United States from foreign nations, per cent. ad valorem, under the act of— 1846.	1857.	INTO FRANCE FROM FOREIGN NATIONS. Number, weight, or measure.	In national vessels.	In foreign vessels.	INTO FRENCH POSSESSIONS.	REMARKS.
Flour, wheat, or other grain	20	15	The duty on grain and flour of every kind is regulated by the price of grain in the French markets, which are divided into four classes for that special purpose. Each of these classes issues monthly prices current, on which is based the rate of duty.—(See barley)			In Corsica and Algiers as in France, on the Mediterranean coast. In Guiana, 5 per cent. ad valorem. In West Indies, $3 94⅕ per 177½ lbs., (80 kilogrammes.)	Flour can, however, only be imported into the French West Indies if a special order by the governor, permitting the importation, has been issued; which permit can never extend beyond three months.
of brimstone or sulphur	20	15	220 lbs	$2 40	$2 64	In Corsica and Algiers as in France. In Guiana and West Indies, in foreign vessels, prohibited.	Flour of brimstone, if exported from France, in quantities of not less than 300 pounds, enjoys a bounty equivalent in amount to the duty paid on the importation of the crude brimstone.
Flowers, artificial	30	24		12 per cent.	ad valorem.		
chamomile	20	15	do	5 55	9 25$\frac{9}{10}$	In Corsica and Algiers as in France. In Guiana, in foreign vessels, prohibited. In the West Indies, free.	
medicinal	20	15	do	5 55	9 25$\frac{9}{10}$		
Folio and quarto post paper	30	24	do	18 51	20 13	In Corsica and Algiers as in France. In Guiana and West Indies, in foreign vessels, prohibited.	
Furs and skins	Dressed on the skin 20 per cent	15				In Corsica and Algiers as in France. In Guiana and West Indies, in foreign vessels, prohibited.	Skins, dry and undressed, in the French West Indies, free.
rabbit skins, dressed or undressed.	Undressed on the skin 10 per cent	8	Undressed, 220 lbs.	18⅗	18⅗		

FRANCE AND HER POSSESSIONS—TARIFFS—Continued.

DENOMINATION OF MERCHANDISE.	DUTIES ON IMPORTS. Into the United States from foreign nations, per cent. ad valorem, under the act of— 1846.	1857.	INTO FRANCE FROM FOREIGN NATIONS. Number, weight, or measure.	In national vessels.	In foreign vessels.	INTO FRENCH POSSESSIONS.	REMARKS.
Furs, castor and beaver, dressed or undressed.	10	8	Dressed, 100 pieces.	$2 $80\frac{4}{5}$	$2 $80\frac{4}{5}$	In Corsica and Algiers as in France. In Guiana and West Indies, in foreign vessels, prohibited.	Peltries, imported in French vessels into France from east of Cape Horn, are admitted for half the duty paid on those from other countries, (out of Europe.)
camel, panther, tiger, jaguar.	10	8	Each	$22\frac{3}{5}$	$22\frac{3}{5}$		
lion, lioness, zebra	10	8	do	$11\frac{1}{4}$	$11\frac{1}{4}$		
fox, white, yellow, or silver gray, of Virginia.	10	8	do	$3\frac{7}{10}$	$3\frac{7}{10}$		
fox, white, the same dyed	10	8	do		$44\frac{3}{5}$		
other	10	8	do	$8\frac{1}{3}$	$8\frac{1}{3}$		
goat, of Angora	10	8	do	$06\frac{1}{2}$	$06\frac{1}{2}$		
polecat	10	8	100 pieces	$55\frac{4}{5}$	$55\frac{4}{5}$		
muskrat, weasel, squirrel	10	8	do	$37\frac{1}{5}$	$37\frac{1}{5}$		
manufactures of	30	24		15 per cent.	ad valorem		
caps or hats of	30	24	Each	$28\frac{4}{5}$	$28\frac{4}{5}$		
Fustic, sticks, or bark and leaves.	5	Free	220 lbs	$1\frac{4}{5}$	$20\frac{1}{3}$	In Algiers and Corsica as in France. In Guiana, in foreign vessels, prohibited. In French West Indies, free.	
Fustic, sticks, ground	20	Free		2 $80\frac{4}{5}$	3 $05\frac{1}{2}$		
Gamboge, gum, crude or refined.	20	15	do	3 $70\frac{1}{3}$	5 55	In Algiers and Corsica as in France. In Guiana, in foreign vessels, prohibited. In French West Indies, free.	

FRANCE AND HER POSSESSIONS—TARIFFS—Continued.

DENOMINATION OF MERCHANDISE.	DUTIES ON IMPORTS. Into the United States from foreign nations, per cent. ad valorem, under the act of—		INTO FRANCE FROM FOREIGN NATIONS.			INTO FRENCH POSSESSIONS.	REMARKS.
	1846.	1857.	Number, weight, or measure.	In national vessels.	In foreign vessels.		
Gems—							
Diamonds, crude			1 hectogr., 0.220 lbs.	$0 9$\frac{1}{4}$	$0 9$\frac{1}{4}$		
cut, when set	30	24	do	18$\frac{3}{5}$	20		
All others, crude, not set	10	4	do	4$\frac{3}{5}$	4$\frac{3}{5}$		
cut			do	9$\frac{1}{4}$	9$\frac{1}{4}$		
Ginger root	40	15	220 pounds	3 70$\frac{1}{3}$	4 74		Ginger, in West Indies, free.
oil of	30	24	2.20 pounds	93	1 12$\frac{1}{2}$		
Glass, crystals for watches and spectacles, cut and polished.	30	24	220 pounds	37 03$\frac{1}{3}$	39 79$\frac{1}{2}$		Bottles filled and imported into France from the French colonies are free, their contents only being subjected to duty. If exported from France, whether filled or not, they will receive a bounty of 23 cents per 220 pounds. In Guiana, filled bottles, if imported from French colonies, and in French vessels, are admitted into the entrepot fictif.
bottles, empty	30	24		Prohibited		In Algiers and Corsica as in France. In Guiana and West Indies, in foreign vessels, prohibited.	
of all other kinds				Prohibited			
vitrifactions, in masses or in tubes, not cut.	30	24	2.20 pounds	55$\frac{4}{5}$	61$\frac{1}{10}$		
vitrifactions, in beads, pierced.	30	24	do	18$\frac{3}{5}$	20$\frac{1}{2}$		
vitrifactions, cut in stones, for jewelry.	40	30	do	1 11$\frac{3}{5}$	1 22$\frac{1}{3}$		
mirrors, large	30	24		According	to size		Large mirrors, on exportation from France, receive a bounty of 18$\frac{3}{5}$ cents per superficial mètre; 1 mètre = 1.09 yard.
mirrors, small, without distinction to thickness.	30	24	220 pounds	18 51	20 13		
all glasses not enumerated.	30	24		Prohibited			

FRANCE AND HER POSSESSIONS—TARIFFS—Continued.

DENOMINATION OF MERCHANDISE.	DUTIES ON IMPORTS. Into the United States from foreign nations, per cent. ad valorem, under the act of—		INTO FRANCE FROM FOREIGN NATIONS.			INTO FRENCH POSSESSIONS.	REMARKS.
	1846.	1857.	Number, weight, or measure.	In national vessels.	In foreign vessels.		
Glauber salts—							
From French colonies	20	15	220 pounds	$0 55$\frac{4}{5}$	Prohibited	In Algiers and Corsica as in France. In Guiana and West Indies, in foreign vessels, prohibited.	
From other, not European, countries.	20	15	do	1 11$\frac{3}{5}$	$2 24$\frac{7}{10}$		
Gloves, cotton	20	24		Prohibited		In Corsica as in France. In Algiers, white, in national vessels, 17½ cents, in foreign vessels, 18$\frac{9}{10}$ cents per 220 pounds. Dyed or printed, in national vessels, 31½ cents, in foreign, 33⅓ cents per 220 pounds. In Guiana and West Indies, in foreign vessels, prohibited.	
silk	30	24	2.20 pounds	2 99$\frac{2}{3}$	3 25$\frac{9}{10}$	In Corsica and Algiers as in France. In Guiana and West Indies, in foreign vessels, prohibited.	
wool	30	24	220 pounds	35 18	37 40	In Corsica as in France. In Algiers, in national vessels, $1 27; in foreign vessels, $1 38 per 2.20 pounds. In Guiana and West Indies, in foreign vessels, prohibited.	Gloves of wool and cotton enjoy in France, on exportation, a bounty of $15 74 per 220 pounds.
leather	30	24		Prohibited		In Corsica and Algiers as in France. In Guiana and West Indies, in foreign vessels, prohibited.	
Glue	20	15	220 pounds	4 68	5 09$\frac{1}{5}$	do ... do	
fish	20	15	do	29 96¼	31 57		
Goats' hair, Thibet, raw	20	15	do	1 86	1 86		

FRANCE AND HER POSSESSIONS—TARIFFS—Continued.

Denomination of merchandise.	Duties on imports. Into the United States from foreign nations, per cent. ad valorem, under the act of— 1846.	1857.	Into France from foreign nations. Number, weight, or measure.	In national vessels.	In foreign vessels.	Into French possessions.	Remarks.
Goats' hair, Thibet, combed	20	15	220 pounds	\$18 51	\$20 37	In Corsica and Algiers as in France. In Guiana and West Indies, in foreign vessels, prohibited.	
common, raw	20	15	do	$18\frac{3}{5}$	$20\frac{1}{2}$		
carpets	25	19	do	9 30	10 $20\frac{9}{10}$		
all other manufactures.	25	19		Prohibited.			
Gold, bullion	Free	Free	Hectogramme 0.220 lb.	$4\frac{3}{5}$	$4\frac{3}{5}$	In Corsica and Algiers as in France. In Guiana and West Indies, free.	These duties are applicable to all gold coins, without regard to nationality.
epaulets	30	24	do	1 86	2 $04\frac{3}{5}$	In Corsica and Algiers as in France. In Guiana and West Indies, in foreign vessels, prohibited.	All works in gold or silver, after having discharged their custom-house duties, are to be stamped with lead and placed under bonds.
jewelry, ornamented with fine pearls or precious stones.	30	24	do	3 $70\frac{3}{10}$	4 $07\frac{1}{2}$		
goldsmiths' work, in gold or vermillion.	30	24	do	1 86	2 $04\frac{3}{5}$		
jewelry and ornaments for travellers.	30	24	do	Free (*a*)	Free		Jewelry of foreign ministers is free. That of travellers, if not weighing more than 5 hectogrammes, is also free.
watches	10	8	Each (*b*)				New jewelry, if exported from France, will receive, as bounty, an amount similar to that paid on jewelry when imported.
Grapes, green	30	8	220 lbs	75	$82\frac{3}{10}$	In Algiers, free. In Corsica as in France. In Guiana, 5 per cent. ad valorem. In the West Indies, 4 per cent. ad valorem.	Fine grass bonnets, having been imported into France at a duty of 23 cents a piece, but yet in a raw state, and having been trimmed in France with braids, or otherwise ornamented, will receive back the same amount, if exported, as bounty.
preserved	40	30					
Grass, manufactured, common	25	19	do	$37\frac{1}{5}$	$41\frac{1}{5}$	In Corsica and Algiers as in France. In Guiana and West Indies, in foreign vessels, prohibited.	
fine	25	19	2.20 pounds	93	1 02		
for ropes	25	19	do	$37\frac{1}{5}$	$41\frac{1}{5}$		

(*a*) If not over 5 hectogrammes, (1.10 lb.)

(*b*) With common movement, 59 cents; with fine movement, 84 cents; repeater or alarm, common movement, 84 cents; repeater or alarm, fine movement, \$1 $12\frac{1}{2}$, with second hands, \$1 $12\frac{1}{2}$.

DENOMINATION OF MERCHANDISE.	Duties on imports. Into the United States from foreign nations, per cent. ad valorem, under the act of— 1846.	1857.	Into France from foreign nations. Number, weight, or measure.	In national vessels.	In foreign vessels.	Into French possessions.	REMARKS.
Grindstones, unwrought	5	4	220 pounds	\$0 37$\frac{1}{5}$	\$0 41$\frac{1}{5}$	In Corsica and Algiers as in France. In Guiana and West Indies, in foreign vessels, prohibited.	
wrought	5	4	do	93	1 02		
Guano, from other than European countries.	Free	Free		Free	55$\frac{4}{5}$	In Algiers and Corsica as in France. In Guiana, in foreign vessels, prohibited. In West Indies, in foreign vessels, 18$\frac{3}{5}$ cents per 220 pounds.	Guano imported into the West Indies, in French vessels, from the place of production, is free of duty.
from entrepots	Free	Free		37$\frac{3}{5}$	55$\frac{4}{5}$		
Gum Arabic	10	8	220 pounds.	3 70$\frac{1}{3}$	5 55$\frac{1}{2}$	In Algiers and Corsica as in France. In Guiana, in foreign vessels, prohibited. West Indies, free,	
Senegal, from Senegal	10	8	do	1 86	Prohibited.		
from countries not European.	10	8	do	3 70$\frac{1}{3}$	5 55$\frac{1}{2}$		
Gunpowder	20	15		Prohibited.		Prohibited.	
Gypsum, unground	Free	Free	do	1$\frac{4}{5}$	1$\frac{4}{5}$	In Algiers and Corsica as in France. In Guiana and West Indies, in foreign vessels, prohibited.	
ground	Free	Free	do	9$\frac{3}{10}$	9$\frac{3}{10}$		
Hair, human, unwrought	30	24	do	18$\frac{3}{5}$	20$\frac{1}{2}$		
camels', raw	10	8	do	18$\frac{3}{5}$	20$\frac{3}{10}$		
manufactured Cashmere shawls.	30	24	Each	18 51	18 51		
manufactured carpets	30	24	220 pounds.	9 30	10 20$\frac{9}{10}$		
Hams	20	15	Each	9$\frac{3}{10}$	9$\frac{3}{10}$	In Corsica, in national vessels, \$1 86, in foreign, \$2 05 per 220 pounds. In Algiers as in France. In Guiana and West Indies, in foreign vessels, prohibited.	Salt pork can be imported into Guiana, in foreign vessels, into the entrepot fictif; and if from France and in French vessels, it is free. Hams, if exported from France, enjoy a bounty of \$4 68 per 220 pounds.

FRANCE AND HER POSSESSIONS—TARIFFS—Continued.

Denomination of merchandise.	Duties on imports. Into the United States from foreign nations, per cent. ad valorem, under the act of— 1846.	1857.	Into France from foreign nations. Number, weight, or measure.	In national vessels.	In foreign vessels.	Into French possessions.	Remarks.
Harness, coarse pack saddles	30	24	Each	$0 09$\frac{3}{10}$	$0 09$\frac{3}{10}$	In Corsica and Algiers as in France. In Guiana and West Indies, in foreign vessels, prohibited.	Saddles and bridles, on the bodies of horses, imported into France, pay, if new, 30 per cent. ad valorem. If used, 15 per cent. ad valorem. In some instances they may be admitted free.
all the rest	30	24	do	Prohibited.			
Hartshorn	20	24	220 pounds	1 67$\frac{2}{5}$	1 82$\frac{1}{8}$	In Algiers and Corsica as in France. In Guiana and West Indies, in foreign vessels, prohibited.	
Hats and bonnets, beaver	30	24	Each	27	27		
horse hair	30	24	do	4$\frac{3}{5}$	4$\frac{3}{5}$		
of straw, bark, chip or grass, common.	30	24	Each	9$\frac{3}{10}$	9$\frac{3}{10}$		Hats of straw, which pay at their importation a duty of 23 cents each, if re-exported, trimmed with braids, or otherwise ornamented, enjoy a bounty of the same amount.
fine	30	24	do	23	23		
hat bands, bark, chip or grass.	25	24	220 pounds	According	to material.		
hat bands of cotton	25	24	do	Prohibited.			
Hempseed	10	8	220 pounds	46$\frac{1}{4}$	81$\frac{2}{5}$	In Algiers and Corsica as in France. In Guiana, in foreign vessels, prohibited. In West Indies, free.	
oil of	20	15	do	1 86	2 80$\frac{4}{5}$	In Algiers and Corsica as in France. In Guiana and West Indies, in foreign vessels, prohibited.	
Hemp, in stalks, raw, green, dried, or steeped.	30	24	do	7$\frac{2}{5}$	7$\frac{2}{5}$		
hackled, and tow of	15	12	do	1 48	1 62$\frac{9}{10}$		
combed	30	24	do	2 80$\frac{4}{5}$	3 05$\frac{1}{2}$		
cordage	25	19	do	4 68	5 09$\frac{1}{5}$		

FRANCE AND HER POSSESSIONS—TARIFFS—Continued.

Denomination of merchandise.	Duties on imports. Into the United States from foreign nations, per cent. ad valorem, under the act of— 1846.	1857.	Into France from foreign nations. Number, weight, or measure.	In national vessels.	In foreign vessels.	Into French possessions.	Remarks.
Hides, ox, cow, horse, from other than European countries, raw, dry, or salted.	5	4	220 pounds	$0 18$\frac{3}{5}$	$0 83$\frac{1}{3}$	In Algiers, free. In Corsica as in France. In Guiana, in foreign vessels, prohibited. In West Indies free.	In Guiana, ox hides are submitted to an additional export duty of 1 cent in national vessels, and 4 cents in foreign vessels, each (contribution foncière.)
from entrepots, tanned	20	15	do	64$\frac{4}{5}$	83$\frac{1}{3}$		
tanned for sole leather	20	15	do	13 88$\frac{4}{5}$	15 03$\frac{7}{10}$	In Algiers and Corsica as in France. In Guiana, in foreign vessels, prohibited. In West Indies, free.	Hides imported into France, in French vessels, from east of Cape Horn, are admitted for one-half of the duty they pay when coming from America.
Horns of cattle, raw	5	4	do	1$\frac{4}{5}$	1$\frac{4}{5}$		
prepared	30	24	do	4 68	09$\frac{1}{5}$		
manufactures of.	30	24	do	4 68	5 09$\frac{1}{5}$		
Indian corn	20	15		See barley	(a)	See barley. (b)	
meal (c)	20	15					
India rubber, from not European countries.	30	24	do	Free	1 86	In Algiers and Corsica as in France; in Guiana and the West Indies, in foreign vessels, prohibited.	
India rubber, from entrepots	30	24	do	93	1 86		
manufactures of, mixed.	30	24	do	3 70$\frac{1}{3}$	4 07$\frac{1}{2}$		

(a) The duty on grains and flour of every kind is regulated by the price of wheat in the French markets, which are divided into four classes for that purpose. Each of these markets issues a monthly price current, by which are determined the rates of duty. When wheat is 28 francs or more in the first class markets of France, 26 or more in the second, 24 or more in the third, and 22 or more in the fourth per hectolitre, (2 83 bushels,) then the duty on Indian corn is 15$\frac{3}{4}$ centimes (2.45 cents) per hectolitre in each of those markets, and the duty on meal, per 100 kilogrammes, (220 pounds,) is 30 centimes (5.63 cents.) The duty goes on increasing in like manner as the price of wheat decreases, and when wheat is 22 francs, 20, 18, and 16 in the standard markets respectively, then the duty in each of the markets increases by 82$\frac{1}{4}$ centimes (15.35 cents) on each hectolitre of corn by the decrease of each franc in the price of the hectolitre of wheat, and by 2.20 francs (40 90 cents) on every kilogramme (2.20 pounds) of meal. At the French custom-houses the hectolitre of Indian corn equals 72 kilogrammes, or 158 2-5 pounds.

(b) In Algiers and Corsica as in France; in Guiana, 5 per cent. ad valorem; in the West Indies, in foreign vessels, 87 1-5 cents per 2 4-5 bushels.

(c) In Algiers and Corsica as in France; in Guiana, 5 per cent. ad valorem; in the West Indies, 93 cents per 2 4-5 bushels.

Flour or meal can only be imported into the West Indies, in foreign vessels, when a special order has been issued by the government, permitting the importation, which permit, however, can never extend beyond the term of three months.

FRANCE AND HER POSSESSIONS—TARIFFS—Continued.

DENOMINATION OF MERCHANDISE	DUTIES ON IMPORTS.						Remarks.
	Into the United States from foreign nations, per cent. ad valorem, under the act of—		INTO FRANCE FROM FOREIGN NATIONS.			INTO FRENCH POSSESSIONS.	
	1846.	1857.	Number, weight, or measure.	In national vessels.	In foreign vessels.		
India rubber, mixed with other materials, except tissues.	30	24	220 pounds	$37 $03\frac{1}{3}$	$39 $79\frac{1}{2}$	In Algiers and Corsica as in France; in Guiana and the West Indies, in foreign vessels, prohibited.	
chirurgical instruments.	30	24		10 per cent. ad val.	10 per cent. ad val.		
Indigo, from India or other countries of production.	10	4	2.20 pounds	$9\frac{3}{10}$	$74\frac{2}{5}$	In Algiers and Corsica as in France; in Guiana, in foreign vessels, prohibited; in the West Indies, free.	
Indigo, from elsewhere out of Europe.	10	4	do	$37\frac{1}{5}$	$74\frac{2}{5}$		
Indigo, from entrepots	10	4	do	$55\frac{4}{5}$	$74\frac{2}{5}$		
Instruments, surgical and chemical.	30	24		0 per cent. ad val.	0 per cent. ad val.	In Algiers and Corsica as in France; in Guiana and West Indies, in foreign vessels, prohibited.	
Instruments, musical	20	15					
pianofortes, sq.	20	15	Each	(a)55 $55\frac{1}{2}$	55 $55\frac{1}{2}$		Old pianos, or already used ones, if imported by immigrants, pay the same duty as furniture, under the same circumstances, viz: $5 $55\frac{1}{3}$ per 220 pounds.
grand pianos	20	15	do	(b)74 $07\frac{2}{5}$	74 $07\frac{2}{5}$		
fifes and flageolets.	20	15	do	$11\frac{3}{5}$	$11\frac{3}{5}$		
flutes and triangles.	20	15	do	$13\frac{4}{5}$	$13\frac{4}{5}$		
mandolins, drums, tamborines.	20	15	do	28	28		
violins, guitars, trumpets.	20	15	do	$55\frac{4}{5}$	$55\frac{4}{5}$		

(a) Under 1,200 francs in value.

(b) Over 1,200 francs in value.

FRANCE AND HER POSSESSIONS—TARIFFS—Continued.

DENOMINATION OF MERCHANDISE.	DUTIES ON IMPORTS.						REMARKS.
	Into the United States from foreign nations, per cent. ad valorem, under the act of—		INTO FRANCE FROM FOREIGN NATIONS.			INTO FRENCH POSSESSIONS.	
	.	1857.	Number, weight, or measure.	In national vessels.	In foreign vessels.		
Instruments—clarionets and hautboys.	20	15	Each	\$0 74 2/5	\$0 74 2/5	In Algiers and Corsica as in France; in Guiana and West Indies, in foreign vessels, prohibited.	
basses and contrebasses.	20	15	do	1 38 4/5	1 38 4/5		
harmonicans, spinnets, and portable organs.	20	15	do	3 34 4/5	3 34 4/5		
harps	20	15	do	6 69 3/5	6 69 3/5		
church organs	20	15	do	74 07 2/5	74 07 2/5		
Iron, ore	20	15	220 pounds	Free	4 3/5	In Corsica, 5 cents per 220 pounds; in Algiers as in France; in Guiana and West Indies, in foreign vessels, prohib'd.	The exportation of iron from Corsica is prohibited. Iron, prohibited importation into France, has to pay in Algiers 25 p. ct. ad val. Ploughs pay, in the West Indies, \$4 65 a piece; cotton machines and boilers, 15 per cent. ad valorem; hoes and shovels, 75 cts. per dozen.
cast in blocks, not weighing less than 15 kilogrammes, 33 1/3 lbs.	30	24	do	1 30 1/5	1 42 1/2	In Corsica as in France; in Algiers, in national vessels, 64 4/5, in foreign, 70 cts. per 220 lbs.; in Guiana and West Indies, in foreign vessels, prohibited.	
purified cast iron, (or mazée,) not under 55 pounds.	30	24	do	2 24 7/10	2 44 2/5	In Corsica and Algiers as in France; in Guiana and West Indies, in foreign vessels, prohibited.	
all other cast iron	30	24		Prohibited.	Prohibited.		
plates and bars, (according to dimension.)	30	24		Fr'm \$2 80 4/5 to \$6 94 2/5.	Fr'm \$3 05 1/2 to \$7 62 9/10.		
forged, in blocks or prisms.	30	24		Prohibited.	Prohibited.		
sheet, also plates of	30	24	do	7 40 7/10	8 15		

FRANCE AND HER POSSESSIONS—TARIFFS—Continued.

DENOMINATION OF MERCHANDISE.	DUTIES ON IMPORTS. Into the United States from foreign nations, per cent. ad valorem, under the act of— 1846.	1857.	INTO FRANCE FROM FOREIGN NATIONS. Number, weight, or measure.	In national vessels.	In foreign vessels.	INTO FRENCH POSSESSIONS.	REMARKS.
Iron, sheet, tinned	30	24	220 pounds	$12 96	$14 07	In Corsica as in France; in Algiers, in national vessels, $6 48, in foreign, $7 12 per 220 lbs.; in Guiana and West Indies, in foreign vessels, prohibited.	
wire, tinned or not	30	24	do	11 23½	12 26½	-----	Utensils and implements of husbandry, especially shovels, hoes, hatchets, ploughs, pruning hooks, and harrows, if imported from France in French vessels into Guiana, are free of duty.
for instruments	30	24		12 96	14 07		
wrought, articles of cast iron.	30	24		Prohibited.	Prohibited.		
wrought, articles of sheet iron.	30	24		Prohibited.	Prohibited.		
Ivory, unmanufactured, from Senegal.	5	Free	do	4 68	Prohibited.	In Algiers and Corsica as in France; in Guiana, in foreign vessels, prohibited; in the West Indies, free.	
from India	5	Free	do	4 68	12 96		
from Africa, except Senegal.	5	Free	do	4 68	12 96		
from all other places	5	Free	do	10 20$\frac{9}{10}$	12 96		
manufactured, billiard balls and combs.	30	24	2.20 pound	74	81½	In Algiers and Corsica as in France; in Guiana and West Indies, in foreign vessels, prohibited.	
all other manufactures	30	24	do	74	81½		
Japanned saddlery	20	15		Prohibited.	Prohi ited.	In Algiers, 25 per cent. ad val.; in Corsica as in France; in Guiana and West Indies, in foreign vessels, prohibited.	Saddles and bridles on the bodies of horses, imported into France, pay, if new, 30 per cent. ad val.; if used, 15 per cent. In some cases they may even be imported free.
ware, pottery, common.	30	24	220 pounds	18 51	20 13	In Algiers and Corsica as in France; in Guiana and West Indies, in foreign vessels, prohibited.	
ware, pottery, fine	30	24	do	37 03⅓	39 79½		

FRANCE AND HER POSSESSIONS—TARIFFS—Continued.

DENOMINATION OF MERCHANDISE	DUTIES ON IMPORTS. Into the United States from foreign nations, per cent. ad valorem, under the act of— 1846.	1857.	INTO FRANCE FROM FOREIGN NATIONS. Number, weight, or measure.	In national vessels.	In foreign vessels.	INTO FRENCH POSSESSIONS.	REMARKS.
Japanned ware, all other	30	24	....	Prohibited.	Prohibited.	In Algiers, 25 per cent. ad val.; in Corsica as in France; in Guiana and West Indies, in foreign vessels, prohibited.	
Jewelry of all kinds, of gold	30	24	Hectogram., 0.22 pounds.	$1 86	$2 04$\frac{3}{4}$	In Algiers and Corsica as in France; in Guiana and West Indies, in foreign vessels, prohibited.	All works in gold or silver, after having discharged their custom-house duties, must be sealed with lead, and placed under bonds, (acquit de caution.) Jewelry of foreign ministers is free; that of travellers also, if weighing not more than 5 hectogrammes, (1$\frac{1}{3}$ pound, Troy.) New jewelry, exported from France, will receive as bounty an amount similar to that paid on jewelry when imported.
Jewelry, ornamented with fine pearls and precious stones.	30	24	....do......	3 70$\frac{3}{10}$	4 07$\frac{1}{2}$		
Jewelry, of silver	30	24	....do......	1 86	2 04$\frac{3}{4}$		
Juniper berries	20	15	220 pounds.	Free.....	20$\frac{3}{10}$		
oil of	30	24	2.20 pounds.	13$\frac{7}{13}$	14$\frac{4}{5}$		
Kermes, in grains	5	4	220 pounds.	18$\frac{3}{5}$	20$\frac{3}{10}$	In Algiers and Corsica as in France; in Guiana, in foreign vessels, prohibited; in West Indies, free.	
in powder or paste	5	4	2.20 pounds.	74$\frac{2}{3}$	1 11$\frac{3}{5}$	In Corsica and Algiers, free; in Guiana and West Indies, in foreign vessels, prohibited.	
Kettles, copper or tin, simply turned, common.	30	24	220 pounds.	18 51	20 13	In Algiers and Corsica as in France; in Guiana and West Indies, in foreign vessels, prohibited.	
fine	30	24	....do......	37 03$\frac{1}{3}$	39 79$\frac{1}{2}$		
all other	30	24	....	Prohibited.	Prohibited.	In Algiers, 25 per ct. ad val.; in Corsica as in France; in Guiana and West Indies, in foreign vessels, prohibited.	
Knives, all kinds	30	24	....	Prohibited.	Prohibited.		

FRANCE AND HER POSSESSIONS—TARIFFS—Continued.

DENOMINATION OF MERCHANDISE.	DUTIES ON IMPORTS.						REMARKS.
	Into the United States from foreign nations, per cent. ad valorem, under the act of—		INTO FRANCE FROM FOREIGN NATIONS.			INTO FRENCH POSSESSIONS.	
	1846.	1857.	Number, weight, or measure.	In national vessels.	In foreign vessels.		
Lace, cotton, worked by hand and with spindle, and applications of cotton thread worked on tulle or network.	25	19	----------	5 per cent.	ad val. ----	In Algiers, white, in national vessels, \$12 50, in foreign, \$13 57 per 2.20 lbs.; in Algiers, dyed, in national vessels, \$16 81, in foreign, \$18 11 per 2.20 lbs.; in Guiana and West Indies, in foreign vessels, prohibited; in Corsica as in France.	
Lace, linen ----------	20	15	----------	5 per cent.	ad val. ----	In Algiers and Corsica as in France; in Guiana and West Indics, in foreign vessels, prohibited.	All articles prohibited importation into France are admitted into Algiers, if coming from French entrepots, at 20 per ct., and if from foreign countries, at 25 per cent. ad val.
silk, called blondes ----	25	19	----------	15 per cent.	ad val. ----		
gold thread ----------	30	24	2.20 pounds	\$37 03⅓	\$39 79½		
silver thread ----------	30	24	----do------	18 51	20 13		
Lard ----------	20	15	220 pounds.	$9\frac{3}{10}$	$9\frac{3}{10}$	In Algiers and Corsica as in France. In Guiana, 5 p. ct. ad val.; in West Indies, free.	
Lavender, essential oil of ----	30	24	2.20 pounds.	93	1 02	In Algiers and Corsica as in France. In Guiana and West Indies, in foreign vessels, prohibited.	
Lead pencils, black, in pine wood.	30	24	220 pounds.	18 51	20 13		Lead, beaten or laminated, if exported from France, receives a bounty of the same amount as is paid as import duty on 225 pounds of raw lead. In the treaty of 1822, raw lead was not included among those articles enjoying, on direct voyage, the same privileges and duties in United States as if in French vessels. However, this exception has not been observed by the French government, and has, therefore, practically ceased to exist.
pencils, black, in cedar wood.	30	24	----do------	37 03⅓	39 79½		
mineral of every denomination.	20	15	----do------	Free ----	18⅗		
mixed with antimony --	20	15	----do------	4 81	5 29⅗		
unworked or cast, also old.	20	15	----do------	93	1 30⅕		
hammered, or in sheets.	20	15	----do------	4 44⅖	4 88⅘		
manufactures of ------	30	24	----do------	4 44⅖	4 88⅘		

FRANCE AND HER POSSESSIONS—TARIFFS—Continued.

Denomination of merchandise.	Duties on imports. Into the United States from foreign nations, per cent. ad valorem, under the act of— 1846.	1857.	Into France from foreign nations. Number, weight, or measure.	In national vessels.	In foreign vessels.	Into French possessions.	Remarks.
Lead, oxydes of, yellow, (massicot.)	20	15	220 pounds.	$6 85	$7 53	In Algiers and Corsica as in France. In Guiana and West Indies, in foreign vessels, prohibited.	
oxydes of, red, (minium.)	20	15	....do......	4 44$\frac{3}{5}$	4 88$\frac{4}{5}$		
oxydes of, litharge.....	20	15	....do......	1 86	2 04$\frac{3}{4}$		
oxydes of, orange......	20	15	....do......	6 48	7 12$\frac{9}{10}$		
white................	20	15	....do......	5 55$\frac{1}{2}$	6 11		
sugar of.............	20	15	....do......	12 97	14 07		
Leaf gold.................	15	12	2.20 pounds.	5 55	6 11$\frac{1}{4}$		
Leather, lamb and goat skins, tanned.	20	15	100 pieces..	55$\frac{4}{5}$	55$\frac{4}{5}$		
Russia calf, tanned and odoriferous, for bookbinders'.	20	15	Piece	93	93		
sole leather	20	15	220 pounds.	13 88$\frac{4}{5}$	15 03$\frac{7}{10}$		
Leghorn hats or bonnets	30	24	Each.......	23	23		Leghorn hats imported into France at a duty of 23 cents each, but yet in an unfinished state, receive back, if re-exported, trimmed with braid, or otherwise ornamented, the above amount of 23 cents each as bounty.
Lemons, preserved in sugar or honey.	40	30	220 pounds.	11 23$\frac{1}{2}$	14 04$\frac{1}{2}$	In Algiers and Corsica as in France. In Guana and West Indies, in foreign vessels, prohibited.	
oil of	30	24	2.22 pounds.	93	1 02		
fruit..............	20	8	220 pounds.	74$\frac{3}{5}$	2 04$\frac{3}{5}$	In Algiers, free. In Corsica as in France. In Guiana, 5 per cent. ad valorem. In the West Indies, 4 per cent. ad valorem.	
Lime, in stones, crude	10	4	....do......	0$\frac{1}{6}$	0$\frac{1}{6}$	In Algiers, free. In Corsica as in France. In Guiana, free. In the West Indies, in foreign vessels, prohibited.	
calcined	10	4	....do......	3$\frac{1}{3}$	3$\frac{1}{3}$		

FRANCE AND HER POSSESSIONS—TARIFFS—Continued.

DENOMINATION OF MERCHANDISE.	DUTIES ON IMPORTS.						REMARKS.
	Into the United States from foreign nations, per cent. ad valorem, under the act of—		INTO FRANCE FROM FOREIGN NATIONS.			INTO FRENCH POSSESSIONS.	
	1846.	1857.	Number, weight, or measure.	In national vessels.	In foreign vessels.		
Limes, preserved in sugar	40	30	220 pounds.	$11 23½	$14 04½	In Algiers and Corsica as in France. In Guiana and in the West Indies, in foreign vessels, prohibited.	
fruit	20	8	do	74⅗	2 04⅗	In Algiers, free. In Corsica as in France. In Guiana, 5 per cent. ad valorem. In the West Indies, 4 per cent. ad valorem.	
oil of	30	24	2.20 pounds.	93	1 02	In Algiers and orsica as in France. In Guiana and in the West Indies, in foreign vessels, prohibited.	
Linens of all kinds(a)	20	15				In Corsica, one-half o the duties paid in France. In Algiers as in France. In Guiana and the West Indies, in foreign vessels, prohibited.	Linen stuffs can be imported into Guiana, in foreign vessels, into the entrepot fictif. In the West Indies, common sail cloth (of not more than 8 threads to the 5 millimètres) is an exception to this; it pays, in national vessels, $8 88; in foreign, $11 11 per 220 pounds. Linen imported from Belgium in quantities amounting in one year to not more than 4½ millions of pounds, enjoys, by a special treaty, (of June 22, 1846,) a deduction of 15 per cent. on the regular duty.
Linseed	10	Free	do	46¼	81⅗	In Algiers, free; in Corsica as in France; in Guiana, in foreign vessels, prohibited; in West Indies, free.	

(a) Such is the extent, variety, and minuteness of the nomenclature, and the corresponding rates of duties set down under this head in the tariff of France, that anything like a summary view of those rates in comparison with the single rate appropriated to the comprehensive item in the United States tariff, seems impracticable, in a condensed statement like the present.

DENOMINATION OF MERCHANDISE.	DUTIES ON IMPORTS.						REMARKS.
	Into the United States from foreign nations, per cent. ad valorem, under the act of—		INTO FRANCE FROM FOREIGN NATIONS.			INTO FRENCH POSSESSIONS.	
	1846.	1857.	Number, weight, or measure.	In national vessels.	In foreign vessels.		
Linseed oil	20	15	220 pounds	$1 86	$2 80$\frac{4}{5}$	In Algiers and Corsica as in France; in Guiana and West Indies, in foreign vessels, prohibited.	
Litharge	20	15	...do...	1 86	2 04$\frac{3}{4}$		
Logwood, in sticks	5	Free	...do...	Free	1 11$\frac{3}{5}$	In Algiers and Corsica as in France; in Guiana, in foreign vessels, prohibited; in West Indies, free.	
ground	20	4	...do...	3 70$\frac{3}{10}$	4 07$\frac{2}{5}$		
extracts of	20	4	...do...	Prohibited.	Prohibited.	In Algiers 25 per cent. ad valorem; in Corsica as in France; in Guiana and West Indies, in foreign vessels, prohibited.	
Mace, from Bourbon and French Guiana.	40	4	...do...	18$\frac{3}{5}$	Prohibited.	In Algiers and Corsica as in France; In Guiana and West Indies, in foreign vessels, prohibited.	In Guiana admitted, in French vessels, into the entrepot fictif.
Mace, from India	40	4	...do...	27$\frac{9}{10}$	74$\frac{2}{5}$	In Algiers and Corsica as in France; in Guiana and West Indies, in foreign vessels, prohibited.	
elsewhere	40	4	...do...	37$\frac{1}{5}$	74$\frac{2}{5}$		
Machines, steam, stationary	30	24	...do...	5 55	6 11	In Algiers and Corsica the same as in France; in Guiana, all machines and similar works, necessary for the colonial industry, are free. In the West Indies, cotton machines, cast iron boilers, 15 per cent. ad valorem; all other machines, in foreign vessels, prohibited.	Machines on French steam vessels, employed for the inland navigation, are free. This immunity, however, applies only to complete machines. Steam engines of French manufacture, and used on French vessels, enjoy a bounty of the same amount as is paid as importation duty on similar foreign machinery imported in French vessels.
for navigation	30	24	...do...	8 33	9 16		
locomotives without tender.	30	24	...do...	12 03	13 09		
spinning, for flax and hemp.	30	24	...do...	12 03	13 09		
spinning, for other materials.	30	24	...do...	8 33	9 16		

FRANCE AND HER POSSESSIONS—TARIFFS—Continued.

Denomination of merchandise.	Duties on imports. Into the United States from foreign nations, per cent. ad valorem, under the act of— 1846.	1857.	Into France from foreign nations. Number, weight, or measure.	In national vessels.	In foreign vessels.	Into French possessions.	Remarks.
Machines, printing, for books and cloth.	30	24	220 pounds	$7 47$\frac{2}{3}$	$8 14	In Algiers and Corsica the same as in France; in Guiana all machines and similar works, necessary for the colonial industry, are free. In the West Indies cotton machines, cast-iron boilers, 15 per cent. ad valorem; all other machines, in foreign vessels, prohibited.	The duty on locomotives applies only to complete works; tenders have to pay a separate duty. Boilers, for sugar factories, may be imported into Guiana from France, in French vessels, free of duty. Under unenumerated machines are to be found flour-mills, sugar, tanning, dredging and flattening machines; fire engines; pumps for draining off water; combing, spinning, and weaving machines; hydraulic presses; machines for drying and cutting paper. Machines entirely of wood come under the head of "wooden manufactures."
for agricultural purposes.	30	24	do	4 68	5 09		
railroad cars, without springs.	30	24	do	4 68	5 09		
tenders, boats for rivers, apparatus for distilling spirits and manufacturing molasses, of copper.	30	24	do	11 11	12 12		
unenum'd, weighing 220 lbs. or less.	30	24	do	14 81	16 01		
220 to 440 lbs	30	24	do	11 11	12 12		
440 to 2,200 lbs	30	24	do	9 30	10 20		
2,200 to 6,500 lbs	30	24	do	7 47$\frac{2}{3}$	8 14		
6,500 to 11,000 lbs.	30	24	do	5 55	6 11		
over 11,000 lbs	30	24	do	3 70$\frac{1}{2}$	4 07		
Mackerel, French fishery	20	15		Free	Prohibited.	Prohibited	U. States vessels have to pay here the same duty as other foreign vessels, although they may be on direct voyage, as raw products of fishery are not included in the treaty of 1822.
United States fishery.	Free	Free	do	7 40$\frac{2}{3}$	8 14$\frac{3}{4}$	In Algiers and Corsica as in France; in Guiana 5 per cent. ad valorem; in the West Indies $1 30 per 220 pounds.	

FRANCE AND HER POSSESSIONS—TARIFFS—Continued.

Denomination of merchandise.	Duties on imports. Into the United States from foreign nations, per cent. ad valorem, under the act of— 1846.	1857.	Into France from foreign nations. Number, weight, or measure.	In national vessels.	In foreign vessels.	Into French possessions.	Remarks.
Madder, root, green	5	Free	220 pounds	$0 93	$1 02	In Algiers and Corsica as in France; in Guiana, in foreign vessels, prohibited; in West Indies, free.	
dry	5	Free	do	1 86	2 24$\frac{7}{10}$		
ground	5	Free	do	5 55	6 11		
extract of	20	4	do	Prohibited.	Prohibited.	In Algiers, 25 per cent. ad valorem; in Corsica, prohibited in Guiana and West Indies. in foreign vessels, prohibited.	
Magnesia, carbonate of	30	24	do	37 03$\frac{1}{3}$	39 79$\frac{1}{2}$	In Algiers and Corsica as in France; in Guiana and West Indies, in foreign vessels, prohibited.	Chloride of magnesia enjoys a bounty of $12 22 per 220 pounds, if exported from France.
sulphate of	20	15	do	12 96	14 07		
Manganese	20	15	do	18$\frac{2}{5}$	20$\frac{1}{2}$		
Manilla grass, unmanufactured	25	19	do	18$\frac{3}{5}$	20$\frac{1}{2}$		
Manna	20	8	do	14 81	16 50		
Marrow	10	8	do	2 80	3 33	In Algiers and Corsica as in France; in Guiana, 5 per cent. ad valorem; in the West Indies, free.	
Marble, crude for statues, white, in blocks simply squared.	20	15	do	1 67$\frac{2}{5}$	2 04$\frac{3}{5}$	In Algiers and Corsica as in France; in Guiana and West Indies, in foreign vessels, prohibited.	
sculptured, moulded, polished, or otherwise worked, without distinction as to the kind of marble.	30	24	do	7 40	8 14		Antiques, as objects of collection, pay only 1 per cent. ad valorem. The works of French artists at Rome are free.

FRANCE AND HER POSSESSIONS—TARIFFS—Continued.

Denomination of merchandise.	Duties on imports. Into the United States from foreign nations, per cent. ad valorem, under the act of— 1846.	1857.	Into France from foreign nations. Number, weight, or measure.	In national vessels.	In foreign vessels.	Into French possessions.	Remarks.
Mats, straw, grass, &c., common	25	19	220 pounds	$0 37$\frac{1}{5}$	$0 41$\frac{1}{5}$	In Algiers and Corsica as in France; in Guiana and West Indies, in foreign vessels, prohibited.	
fine	25	19	2.20 pounds	93	1 02		
Medicinal drugs, prepared	30	24		Prohibited, with the exception of distilled alcoholic liquids and extract of Jesuits' bark.			
unprepared, as bark, not otherwise enumerated.	20	15	do	7 03$\frac{7}{10}$	10 95$\frac{1}{2}$	In Algiers and Corsica as in France; in Guiana, in foreign vessels, prohibited; in West Indies, free.	
Mill cranks of wrought iron	30	24	do	9 30	10 20$\frac{9}{10}$	In Algiers and in Corsica as in France; in Guiana and West Indies, in foreign vessels, prohibited.	Implements of husbandry, imported from France into Guiana in French vessels, free.
saws	30	24	do	25 92$\frac{1}{2}$	27 68		
irons	30	24	do	9 30	10 20$\frac{9}{10}$		
Mineralogy, specimens of	Free	Free		1 per cent ad valorem.		In Algiers and Corsica as in France; in Guiana, free; in the West Indies, in foreign vessels, prohibited.	Specimens of mineralogy for French national museums are free.
Molasses, from the French Colonies.	30	24		Free	Prohibited.	Prohibited	It allowed to French vessels of over 60 tons burden, only.
from foreign countries.	30	24	220 pounds	55$\frac{4}{5}$	2 40$\frac{7}{10}$		

FRANCE AND HER POSSESSIONS—TARIFFS—Continued.

Denomination of merchandise.	Duties on imports. Into the United States from foreign nations, per cent. ad valorem, under the act of— 1846.	1857.	Into France from foreign nations. Number, weight, or measure.	In national vessels.	In foreign vessels.	Into French possessions.	Remarks.
Molasses, from entrepots	30	24	220 pounds	\$1 48$\frac{4}{5}$ If of the sort used for the distillation of liquors; all other kinds prohibited.	\$2 40$\frac{7}{10}$	In Algiers and Corsica as in France; in Guiana and West Indies, in foreign vessels, prohibited.	
Mother of pearl shells, unwrought.	5	4	do	4 68	6 48	In Algiers and Corsica as in France; in Guiana and the West Indies, free.	
sawed or separated from the crust.	5	4	do	9 30	12 96		
Moulds, button	25	19	do	2 40$\frac{7}{10}$	2 64$\frac{4}{5}$	In Algiers and Corsica as in France; in Guiana and in the West Indies, in foreign vessels, prohibited.	
Mules, for breed	Free	Free	Each	2 80$\frac{4}{5}$	2 80$\frac{4}{5}$	In Algiers and Corsica as in France; in Guiana, free; in the West Indies, 10 per cent. ad valorem.	
otherwise	20	Free					
Muriatic acid	20	4	220 pounds	11 48	12 51	In Corsica and Algiers as in France; in Guiana and in the West Indies, in foreign vessels, prohibited.	Muriatic acid exported from France enjoys a bounty of 55$\frac{4}{5}$ cents per 220 pounds.
Musical instruments	20	15		See instruments, musical.			
Musk	30	24	do	18 51	20 13	In Corsica and Algiers as in France; in Guiana and West Indies, in foreign vessels, prohibited.	
Muskets, for soldiers	30	24		Prohibited		Prohibited.	

FRANCE AND HER POSSESSIONS—TARIFFS—Continued.

Denomination of merchandise.	Duties on imports. Into the United States from foreign nations, per cent. ad valorem, under the act of— 1846.	1857.	Into France from foreign nations. Number, weight, or measure.	In national vessels.	In foreign vessels.	Into French possessions.	Remarks.
Muskets, for commerce	30	24	220 pounds	$37 03	$39 79½	In Corsica and Algiers as in France; in Guiana and West Indies, in foreign vessels, prohibited.	
Mustard, grain	Free	Free	do	93	1 02		
flour	20	15	do	4 68	5 09		
Nails, all kinds, iron	30	24		Prohibited.		In Algiers, 25 per cent. ad valorem; in Guiana and the West Indies, in foreign vessels, prohibited.	
Nails, all kinds, copper	20	15					
Needles, all kinds, under 1½ inches long.	20	15	2.20 pounds	1 48⅘	1 62 9/10	In Algiers and Corsica as in France; in Guiana and West Indies, in foreign vessels, prohibited.	
under 1½ to 2 inches long	20	15	do	93	1 02		
over 2 inches long	20	15	do	37⅕	40 7/10		
Nicaragua wood, in sticks	5	Free	220 pounds	Free	1 11⅗	In Algiers and Corsica as in France; in Guiana, in foreign vessels, prohibited; in West Indies, free.	
ground	20	4	do	3 70 3/10	4 07⅖		
Nitre, not refined	5	4	do	1 38	4 68	In Algiers and Corsica as in France; in Guiana and the West Indies, in foreign vessels, prohibited.	
refined or partially	10	8					
Nuts, common	30	24	220 pounds	1 48⅘	1 62 9/10	In Algiers, free; in Corsica, one-half of the French duties; in Guiana, 5 per cent. ad valorem; in West Indies, 4 per cent. ad valorem.	
oil of	30	24	do	1 86	2 80⅘	In Algiers and Corsica as in France; in Guiana and the West Indies, in foreign vessels, prohibited.	
Nutmegs, from Bourbon and French Guiana.	40	4	do	18⅗	Prohibited.	In foreign vessels prohibited	Nutmegs from the French colonies can be admitted in Guiana into the entrepot fictif

FRANCE AND HER POSSESSIONS—TARIFFS—Continued.

Denomination of merchandise.	Duties on imports. Into the United States from foreign nations, per cent. ad valorem, under the act of— 1846.	1857.	Into France from foreign nations. Number, weight, or measure.	In national vessels.	In foreign vessels.	Into French possessions.	Remarks.
Nutmegs, from India	40	4	220 pounds	$0 27 9/10	$0 74 2/5	In Algiers as in France; in Corsica, one-half of the French duty; in Guiana, in foreign vessels, prohibited; in West Indies, free.	
from elsewhere	40	4	do	37 1/5	74 2/5		
Oakum or junk	Free	Free	do	2	2	In Algiers and Corsica as in France; in Guiana and the West Indies, in foreign vessels, prohibited.	Oakum pays by the French tariff the same duty as rags.
Oatmeal	20	15		See barley	(a)	See barley.	
Oats	20	15					
Oil, sweet	30	24	220 pounds	2 40 7/10	2 80 4/5	In Algiers and Corsica as in France; in Guiana and West Indies, in foreign vessels, prohibited.	*Sweet oil:* If imported into France in French vessels not from the countries of production, an additional duty of $0 55 3/5 is to be paid. If imported into France from Algiers, free. By the treaty of February 14, 1852, Sardinian olive oil is admitted in French and Sardinian vessels at a duty of $2 77 per 220 pounds.
palm and cocoa-nut	10	4	do	93	1 86		
of oleaginous seeds	20	15	do	1 86	2 80 4/5		
others not mentioned in the tariff.			2.20 pounds	4 3/5	4 3/5		
absynth or wormwood	30	24	do	13 4/5	14 1/2		
spermaceti, crude	20	15	220 pounds	3 70 1/3	4 07	In Algiers and Corsica as in France; in Guiana, 5 per cent. ad valorem; in West Indies, in foreign vessels, prohibited.	Crude spermaceti oil, as a product of the United States fishery, and not included in the treaty of 1822, is subject to the duty given under the head of foreign vessels, though the importation into France may have taken place direct from the United States. French fishery products enjoy a bounty.
refined	20	15	do	13 88	15 03		
French fishery.	20	15	do	3 7/10	Prohibited	In foreign vessels, prohibited.	

(a) When wheat is 28 francs or more in the first class markets of France, 26 or more in the second, 24 or more in the third, and 22 or more in the fourth, per hectolitre, (2.83 bushels,) then the duty on oats is 3¾ centimes ($0 00.70) per hectolitre in each of these markets, and the duty on oatmeal per 100 kilogrammes (220 pounds) is 27¼ centimes, ($0 05.14.) The duty goes on increasing in like manner as the price of wheat decreases, and when wheat is less than 22 francs in the standard markets respectively, then the duty increases by 52¼ centimes ($0 09.82) on each hectolitre of oats, by the *decrease* of each franc in the price of each hectolitre of wheat, and by 2.47½ francs per 100 kilogrammes of oatmeal. At the custom-houses of France the hectolitre of oats is estimated at 51 kilogrammes, or 112 2-5 pounds.—(See barley.)

FRANCE AND HER POSSESSIONS—TARIFFS—Continued.

DENOMINATION OF MERCHANDISE.	DUTIES ON IMPORTS. Into the United States from foreign nations, per cent. ad valorem, under the act of—		INTO FRANCE FROM FOREIGN NATIONS.			INTO FRENCH POSSESSIONS.	REMARKS.
	1846.	1857.	Number, weight, or measure.	In national vessels.	In foreign vessels.		
Oil, whale and other fish, from the French fisheries.	20	15	220 pounds	$0 2 4/5	Prohibited	Prohibited in foreign vessels.	
whale from foreign fisheries.	20	15	do	2 80 4/5	$5 55 1/2	In Algiers and Corsica as in France; in Guiana, 5 per cent. ad valorem; in West Indies, in foreign vessels, prohibited.	
castor or ricini	20	15	2.20 pounds	4 3/5	4 3/5	In Algiers and Corsica as in France; in Guiana and the West Indies, in foreign vessels, prohibited.	
Olives, fresh	30	24	220 pounds	93	1 11 3/5	In Algiers and Corsica as in France; in Guiana, 5 per cent. ad valorem; in the West Indies, 4 per cent. ad valorem.	
Onions, bulbous root	20	15	do	93	1 02	In Algiers, free; in Corsica as in France; in Guiana, 5 per cent. ad valorem, in the West Indies, free.	
Opium	20	15	do	37 03 1/3	39 79 1/2	In Algiers and Corsica as in France; in Guiana and the West Indies, in foreign vessels, prohibited.	
Oranges	20	8	do	1 86	2 04 3/5	In Algiers and orsica as in France; in Guiana, 5 per cent. ad valorem; in the West Indies, 4 per cent. ad valorem.	
Organs	20	15		See instruments, musical.			
Ornamental feathers	30	24		See feathers.			

FRANCE AND HER POSSESSIONS—TARIFFS—Continued.

Denomination of merchandise.	Into the United States from foreign nations, per cent. ad valorem, under the act of— 1846.	1857.	Into France from foreign nations. Number, weight, or measure.	In national vessels.	In foreign vessels.	Into French possessions.	Remarks.
Orris root	20	15	220 pounds	$7 $40\frac{7}{10}$	$8 50	In Algiers and Corsica as in France; in Guiana and the West Indies, in foreign vessels, prohibited.	
Oxen	20	Free	Each	$55\frac{4}{5}$	$55\frac{4}{5}$	In Algiers, free; in Corsica, $18\frac{3}{5}$ cents per 220 pounds; in Guiana, free; in the West Indies, 10 per cent. ad valorem.	
Ox-horns, raw	5	4	220 pounds	$1\frac{4}{5}$	$1\frac{4}{5}$	In Algiers and Corsica as in France; in Guiana, in foreign vessels, prohibited; in the West Indies, free.	
prepared	30	24	do	4 68	5 $09\frac{1}{5}$		
Pack-thread, of hemp	30	24	do	4 68	5 $09\frac{1}{5}$	In Algiers and Corsica as in France; in Guiana and the West Indies, in foreign vessels, prohibited.	
Palm oil	10	4	do	93	1 86		
Pans, warming, of copper	30	24		See copper			
Pantaloons	30	24		30 per cent. ad val.			Ready-made clothing is only admitted in Guiana into the entrepot fictif.
Paper, wrapping	30	24	do	14 81	16 01	In Algiers and Corsica as in France. In Guiana and the West Indies, in foreign vessels, prohibited.	Old paper and waste paper pay the same duty as rags.
white, or ruled for music, or for registers, or lists.	30	24	do	28 09	29 $69\frac{1}{4}$		
colored, in reams or quires, for binding, &c.	30	24	do	16 $66\frac{3}{5}$	17 96		Gilt or silver edged paper is assimilated to the colored paper given in the tariff.
painted, in rolls, for hanging.	30	24	do	23 14	24 75		
silk paper, in imitation of Chinese.	30	24	do	18 51	20 13		

FRANCE AND HER POSSESSIONS—TARIFFS—Continued.

Denomination of merchandise.	Duties on imports. Into the United States from foreign nations, per cent. ad valorem, under the act of—		Into France from foreign nations.			Into French possessions.	Remarks.
	1846.	1857.	Number, weight, or measure.	In national vessels.	In foreign vessels.		
Parasols and sunshades—							
Silk	30	24	Each	$0 37$\frac{1}{5}$	$0 37$\frac{1}{5}$	In Algiers and Corsica as in France. In Guiana and the West Indies, in foreign vessels, prohibited.	
Linen, waxed	30	24	do	13$\frac{4}{5}$	13$\frac{4}{5}$		
Cotton	30	24		Prohibited		In Algiers, 25 per cent. ad valorem. In Corsica as in France. In Guiana and West Indies, in foreign vessels, prohibited.	
Paste, almond	30	24	220 pounds.	4 62$\frac{9}{10}$	5 15$\frac{1}{2}$	In Algiers and Corsica as in France. In Guiana and the West Indies, in foreign vessels, prohibited.	
Pasteboard—							
To press cloth, in sheets	30	24	do	14 81	16 01		
In sheets, sized and pressed, and other pasteboards in sheets.	30	24	do	28 09	29 69$\frac{1}{4}$	In Algiers, in national vessels, $27 77; in foreign vessels, $29 62, per 220 lbs. In Corsica as in France. In Guiana and the West Indies, in foreign vessels, prohibited.	
Moulded, or papier maché	30	24	do	37 03$\frac{1}{3}$	39 79$\frac{1}{2}$	In Algiers and Corsica as in France. In Guiana and West Indies, in foreign vessels, prohibited.	
Cut and sewed together	30	24	do	28 51	20 13		
Paving stones	20	15	do	Free	0$\frac{1}{5}$	In Corsica as in France. In Algiers free. In Guiana and the West Indies, in foreign vessels, prohibited.	
Pearls—							
Mother of, shells unwrought	5	4	do	4 68	6 48	In Corsica and Algiers as in France. In Guiana, in foreign vessels, prohibited. In West Indies, free.	
sawed or separated from the crust.	5	4	do	9 30	12 96		

FRANCE AND HER POSSESSIONS—TARIFFS—Continued.

DENOMINATION OF MERCHANDISE.	DUTIES ON IMPORTS. Into the United States from foreign nations, per cent. ad valorem, under the act of— 1846.	1857.	INTO FRANCE FROM FOREIGN NATIONS. Number, weight, or measure.	In national vessels.	In foreign vessels.	INTO FRENCH POSSESSIONS.	REMARKS.
Pearls—fine, set	30	24	Hectogramme	$0 $09\frac{3}{10}$	$0 $09\frac{3}{10}$	In Corsica and Algiers as in France. In Guiana and the West Indies, in foreign vessels, prohibited.	
not set	10	4	0.220 pound				
Pebbles, Brazil, for spectacles	30	24	2.20 pounds	$7\frac{3}{5}$	$9\frac{3}{10}$		
Pencils, black lead—							
In pine wood	30	24	220 pounds	18 51	20 13		
In cedar wood	30	24	do	37 $03\frac{1}{3}$	39 $79\frac{1}{2}$		
From French Guiana	30	24	do	1 86	Prohibited.	Prohibited in foreign vessels.	
Pepper, all kinds—							
From East Indies	30	4	do	7 40	19 $66\frac{1}{3}$	In Algiers and Corsica as in France. In Guiana, in foreign vessels, prohibited. In West Indies, free.	Pepper from the French colonies, and in French vessels, can be admitted in Guiana into the entrepôt fictif.
From elsewhere	30	4	do	15 81	19 $66\frac{1}{3}$		
Perfumery—							Animal substances, used for medicines and perfumeries, may be imported free into the French West Indies.
Scented waters, alcoholic	30	24	do	28 09	29 $96\frac{1}{4}$	In Algiers and Corsica as in France. In Guiana and West Indies, in foreign vessels, prohibited.	The difference between alcoholic scented water and that without alcoholic parts, is, that the former are inflammable, and the latter not. Lavender and rosewater, and also eau de Cologne, belong to this class, (scented waters.)
without alcohol	30	24		18 51	20 13		
Vinegars perfumed and prepared.	30	24	do	18 51	20 13		
Pastes, liquid, or in cakes, of almonds or pine apples.	30	24	do	4 68	5 $09\frac{1}{5}$		
Soaps, liquid, in powder, cakes, or balls.	30	24	do	30 37	32 35		
Hair powder	30	24	do	4 68	5 $09\frac{1}{5}$		Alcoholic scented waters pay, if imported from foreign countries, for every 220 pounds, the same duty as 100 quarts of liquor, also imported from foreign countries.
Scented, or powder from Cyprus.	30	24	2.20 pounds	1 $66\frac{3}{5}$	1 $83\frac{1}{3}$		
All other perfumed powders.	30	24	220 pounds	34 07	36 24		
Pomatum of all sorts	30	24	do	22 77	24 37		

FRANCE AND HER POSSESSIONS—TARIFFS—Continued.

DENOMINATION OF MERCHANDISE.	DUTIES ON IMPORTS.						REMARKS.
	Into the United States from foreign nations, per cent. ad valorem, under the act of—		INTO FRANCE FROM FOREIGN NATIONS.			INTO FRENCH POSSESSIONS.	
	1846.	1857.	Number, weight, or measure.	In national vessels.	In foreign vessels.		
Perfumery, paints for the face or skin, white.	30	24	220 pounds	$18 14	$19 51	In Algiers and Corsica as in France. In Guiana and West Indies, in foreign vessels, prohibited.	
rouge (red)	30	24	2.20 pounds	31 48	34 62		
Personal baggage in actual use	Free	Free		Free	Free	See apparel, wearing.	
other	According to kind.			30 per ct. ad valorem			
Peruvian bark	15	Free	220 pounds	Free	5 58	In Algiers and Corsica as in France. In Guiana, in foreign vessels, prohibited. In West Indies, free.	
Piano-fortes, square	20	15	Each	55 $55\frac{1}{2}$	55 $55\frac{1}{2}$	In Algiers and Corsica as in France. In Guiana and West Indies, in foreign vessels, prohibited.	
long, or organ-shaped.	20	15	do	74 $07\frac{2}{5}$	74 $07\frac{2}{5}$		
Pickled fish of all kinds	20	15	220 pounds	18 51	20 13		See remarks on article Fish.
Pimento, from French Guiana	40	4	do	1 86	Prohibited.	In foreign vessels, prohibited.	
East Indies	40	4	do	8 33	21 29	In Algiers and Corsica as in France. In Guiana and the West Indies, in foreign vessels, prohibited.	
elsewhere	40	4	do	16 66	21 29		
Pine apples	20	8	do	74	1 $63\frac{1}{10}$	In Algiers, free. In Corsica, one-half of the duties in France. In Guiana, 5 per cent. ad valorem. In West Indies, 4 per cent. ad valorem.	
Pipes, lead	20	15	do	4 $44\frac{2}{5}$	4 $88\frac{4}{5}$	In Algiers and Corsica as in France. In Guiana and the West Indies, in foreign vessels, prohibited.	

FRANCE AND HER POSSESSIONS—TARIFFS—Continued.

DENOMINATION OF MERCHANDISE	DUTIES ON IMPORTS. Into the United States from foreign nations, per cent. ad valorem, under the act of— 1846.	1857.	INTO FRANCE FROM FOREIGN NATIONS. Number, weight, or measure.	In national vessels.	In foreign vessels.	INTO FRENCH POSSESSIONS.	REMARKS.
Plaitings of straw, common	30	24	220 pounds	$0 37$\frac{1}{5}$	$0 41$\frac{1}{5}$	In Algiers and Corsica as in France; in Guiana and in the West Indies, in foreign vessels, prohibited.	
fine	30	24	220 pounds	93	1 02		
Planks	20	15		See Wood.			
Plants, not otherwise provided for.	Free	Free		1 pr. ct. ad specimens	valorem, as of botany.	In Corsica and Algiers as in France; in Guiana and the West Indies, free.	
Plates, stereotype	20	15		15 per cent.	ad valorem.	In Corsica and Algiers as in France; in Guiana and West Indies, in foreign vessels, prohibited.	
Polished steel saddlery	30	24		Prohibited.		In Algiers, 25 per cent. ad valorem; in Corsica as in France; in Guiana and West Indies, in foreign vessels, prohibited.	
Porcelain, common	30	24	220 pounds	30 37	32 35	In Algiers and Corsica as in France; in Guiana and the West Indies, in foreign vessels, prohibited.	Porcelain garnished with gilt copper is prohibited; old porcelain, as object of curiosity, admitted at one per cent. ad valorem; porcelain showing traces of use, and the property of persons intending to settle in France, 15 per cent. ad valorem.
fine	30	24	do	60 55	63 79		
Pork	20	15	do	9$\frac{3}{10}$	9$\frac{3}{10}$	In Algiers the same as in France. In Corsica, in French vessels, $1 86; in foreign vessels, $2 05 per 220 pounds. In Guiana, 5 per cent. ad valorem. In West Indies, in foreign vessels, prohibited.	Pork, if salted with French salt, and exported from France, enjoys a bounty of 53$\frac{7}{10}$ cents per 220 pounds.

FRANCE AND HER POSSESSIONS—TARIFFS—Continued.

Denomination of merchandise.	Duties on imports. Into the United States from foreign nations, per cent. ad valorem, under the act of— 1846.	1857.	Into France from foreign nations. Number, weight, or measure.	In national vessels.	In foreign vessels.	Into French possessions.	Remarks.
Porter, in casks	30	24	Hectolitre, or 26 gallons.	\$1 $12\frac{1}{3}$	\$1 $12\frac{1}{3}$	In Algiers and Corsica as in France; in Guiana and the West Indies, in foreign vessels, prohibited; in Oceanica, per dozen bottles, $74\frac{2}{5}$ cents.	Ale, and all other liquids in bottles, pay an additional duty of $2\frac{4}{5}$ cents for each quart as duty on the bottles. Empty bottles are prohibited.
in bottles	30	24	do	3 $93\frac{1}{4}$	3 $93\frac{1}{4}$		
Potash, bichromate of	20	15	220 pounds	27 77	29 62	In Algiers and Corsica as in France; in Guiana and the West Indies, in foreign vessels, prohibited.	Chlorate of potassium, exported from France, enjoys a bounty of \$12 22 per 220 pounds.
chromate of	20	15	do	28 $08\frac{9}{10}$	29 $96\frac{1}{4}$		
hydriodate of	20	15	2.20 pounds	2 $80\frac{4}{5}$	3 $05\frac{1}{2}$		
prussiate of	20	15	220 pounds	38 88	41 29		
carbonate of	20	15	do	1 $11\frac{3}{5}$	2 $23\frac{1}{5}$		
Potatoes	30	24	do	$9\frac{3}{10}$	$9\frac{3}{10}$	In Algiers and Corsica as in France; in Guiana, 5 per cent. ad valorem; in West Indies, in foreign vessels, prohibited.	
Powder, hair	30	24	do	4 $68\frac{1}{5}$	5 15	In Algiers and Corsica as in France; in Guiana and the West Indies, in foreign vessels, prohibited.	
tooth and cosmetic	30	24	do	32 22	36 24		
gun	20	15		Prohibited.		Prohibited in foreign vessels	Gunpowder, however, can be admitted in Guiana into the entrepot fictif, even if imported from foreign countries, and in foreign vessels.
Prunes	40	8	do	2 $99\frac{3}{5}$	3 $25\frac{9}{10}$	In Algiers, free; in Corsica as in France; in Guiana, 5 per cent. ad valorem; in the West Indies, 4 per cent. ad valorem.	
Prussian blue	20	4	do	27 77	29 96	In Algiers and Corsica as in France; in Guiana and the West Indies, in foreign vessels, prohibited.	
Quicksilver	20	15	do	3 $70\frac{1}{3}$	4 07		
Quills	20	15	do	1 86	3 $70\frac{1}{3}$		
prepared	20	15	do	44 44	47 12		

FRANCE AND HER POSSESSIONS—TARIFFS—Continued.

Denomination of merchandise.	Duties on imports. Into the United States from foreign nations, per cent. ad valorem, under the act of— 1846.	1857.	Into France from foreign nations. Number, weight, or measure.	In national vessels.	In foreign vessels.	Into French possessions.	Remarks.
Quinine, sulphate of	20	15		Prohibited.		In Algiers, 25 per cent. ad valorem; in Corsica as in France; in Guiana and West Indies, in foreign vessels, prohibited.	
Raisins, of all kinds	40	8	220 pounds.	$0 04$\frac{3}{5}$	$0 37$\frac{1}{5}$	In Algiers, free; in Corsica, one-half of the duties in France; in Guiana, in foreign vessels, prohibited; in West Indies, 4 per cent. ad valorem.	
Rape seed oil	20	15	do	1 86	2 80$\frac{4}{5}$	In Algiers and Corsica as in France; in Guiana and the West Indies, in foreign vessels, prohibited.	
Rattans and reeds—							
Unmanufactured	10	Free	do	Free	7 40	In Algiers and Corsica as in France; in Guiana, in foreign vessels, prohibited; in West Indies, free.	
Split	20	15					
Raven's duck, hemp or flax	20	15		Submitted to the duty of the component material.			
Ready-made clothing	30	24		30 per cent. ad valorem.		In Algiers and Corsica as in France; in Guiana and the West Indies, in foreign vessels, prohibited.	Ready-made clothing can be imported in Guiana into the entrepot fictif. If exported from France in quantities of at least 55 pounds, (25 kilogrammes,) it will receive, as bounty, the same amount as the importation duty on the material of which the clothing is manufactured.
Reaping hooks	30	24	do	28 09	29 96$\frac{1}{4}$		Reaping hooks from France, in French vessels, free in Guiana.
Red lead	20	15	do	4 44$\frac{2}{5}$	4 88$\frac{4}{5}$		
Venetian, considered as ochre.	30	24	do	37$\frac{1}{5}$	40$\frac{7}{10}$		
wood, in sticks	5	Free	do	Free	1 11$\frac{3}{5}$		
Regulus of antimony	20	8	do	4 81	5 29		

FRANCE AND HER POSSESSIONS—TARIFFS—Continued.

Denomination of merchandise	Duties on imports: Into the United States, from foreign nations, per cent. ad valorem, under the act of— 1846.	1857.	Into France from foreign nations: Number, weight, or measure.	In national vessels.	In foreign vessels.	Into French possessions.	Remarks.
Rhubarb	20	15	220 lbs.	$18 51	$32 40	In Algiers and Corsica as in France. In Guiana, in foreign vessels, prohibited. In West Indies, free.	
Rice	20	15	do.	46½	1 67⅗	In Corsica, in French vessels, 18⅗ cents; in foreign, 20½ cents per 220 lbs. In Algiers the same as in France, except as regards the rice of Piedmont, which pays, in foreign vessels, $1 67⅗ per 220 lbs. In Guiana, 5 per cent. ad valorem. In the West Indies, $1 30⅕ per 220 lbs.	*Rice.*—The rice of Piedmont is short, thick, and rounded. The extremity of the grain opposite to the crease is flat. The rice of Carolina is longer, and transparent as alabaster. The extremity of the grain opposite to the crease is sharp-pointed. The rice of India consists of small fine grains. The rice of Brazil is less transparent, less thick, and much more broken than that of Carolina. The rice of Egypt is short, small, and flat, and less transparent than that of Carolina; the extremity opposite the crease is rounded. Rice from India pays, in French vessels, only $9\frac{3}{10}$ cents, and, from Sardinia, $41\frac{3}{10}$ cents per 220 lbs. The paddy pays only one-half the duties on the grain.
paddy	20	15	do.	23¼	83⅗		
Rifles, for soldiers	30	24		Prohibited.	Prohibited.	Prohibited.	The difference between arms for the army and for commerce consists in the ornamenting and calibre. Pocket pistols, which are also prohibited, can, however, be admitted into the entrepot.
for commerce	30	24	do.	37 03	39 79½	In Algiers and Corsica as in France. In Guiana and West Indies, in foreign vessels, prohibited.	
Rods, braziers	30	24	do.	9 25	10 28½		
Roman or blue vitriol	20	15	do.	5 74	6 38½		

FRANCE AND HER POSSESSIONS—TARIFFS—Continued.

Denomination of merchandise.	Duties on imports. Into the United States, from foreign nations, per cent. ad valorem, under the act of— 1846.	1857.	Into France from foreign nations. Number, weight, or measure.	In national vessels.	In foreign vessels.	Into French possessions.	Remarks.
Roofing slates	25	19		15 per cent.	ad valorem.	In Algiers, free. In Corsica as in France. In Guiana and West Indies, in foreign vessels, prohibited.	
Roots, arrow	20	15	220 lbs	$2 77	$4 62	In Corsica and Algiers as in France. In Guiana and West Indies, in foreign vessels, prohibited.	Arrow root, as a farinaceous substance, pays, in the French tariff, the same duty as sago.
colombo	20	15	do	2 77	4 62	In Guiana, in foreign vessels, prohibited. In West Indies, free. In Corsica and Algiers as in France.	
medicinal, not otherwise enumerated.	20	15	do	2 $80\frac{4}{5}$	4 68		
ginger	40	15	do	3 $70\frac{1}{3}$	4 74		
madder, green	5	Free	do	93	1 02		
dry	5	Free	do	1 86	2 $40\frac{7}{10}$		
ground	5	Free	do	5 55	6 11		
Rose, essential oil of	30	24	2. 20 lbs	7 40	8 15	In Algiers and Corsica as in France. In Guiana and the West Indies, in foreign vessels, prohibited.	
water	30	24	220 lbs	18 51	20 13		
Rosemary, essential oil of	30	24	2. 20 lbs	$13\frac{4}{5}$	$14\frac{4}{5}$		
Rosin (raw)	20	8	220 lbs	93	1 02	In Algiers and Corsica as in France. In Guiana, in foreign vessels, prohibited. In West Indies, in foreign vessels, 14 cents per 220 lbs.	

FRANCE AND HER POSSESSIONS—TARIFFS—Continued.

DENOMINATION OF MERCHANDISE.	Duties on imports: Into the United States from foreign nations, per cent. ad valorem, under the act of— 1846.	1857.	Into France from foreign nations: Number, weight, or measure.	In national vessels.	In foreign vessels.	Into French possessions.	REMARKS.
Rubber, India	10	4	220 lbs	Not from countries Free; From entrepots, $0 93	European $1 86; 1 86	In Algiers and Corsica as in France. In Guiana and the West Indies, in foreign vessels, prohibited.	India rubber, in the shape of boots, shoes, bottles, &c., is admitted on paying on raw unmanufactered India rubber, provided it will be sold in the custom-house itself; however, if imported in such a state that it can serve for other purposes, then, as raw India rubber, it is subject to the duty on manufactures of India rubber. The duty on manufactures of gutta percha is similar to that on articles of India rubber.
Rubber, India, manufactured, unmixed.	30	24	do	3 70⅓	4 07½		
Rubber, India, manufactured, mixed with other materials, except tissues.			do	37 03⅓	39 79½		
Rye and rye flour	20	15	See barley. (a)			See barley. (b)	
Saffron	20	15	2.20 pounds	93	1 02	In Algiers and Corsica as in France; in Guiana and West Indies, in foreign vessels, prohibited.	
Sago, from East Indies	20	15	220 pounds	1 86	7 40$\frac{7}{10}$	In Algiers as in France; in Guiana, 5 per cent. ad valorem; in the West Indies, in foreign vessels, prohibited.	
from countries out of Europe.	20	15	do	3 70⅓	7 40$\frac{7}{10}$		
from entrepots	20	15	do	5 55	7 40$\frac{7}{10}$		

(a) When wheat is 28 francs, or more, in the 1st class markets of France; 26, or more, in the 2d; 24, or more, in the 3d, and 22, or more, in the 4th, per hectolitre, (2.83 bushels,) then the duty on rye is 15 centimes, (2.81 cents,) per hectolitre, in each of the markets; and the duty on its flour, per 100 kilogrammes, (220 lbs.,) is 32¼ centim s, (6.02 cents.) The duty goes on increasing in like manner as the price of wheat decreases, and when wheat is less than 22 francs in the standard markets, respectively, then the duty increases by 90 centimes, (16 85 cents,) on each hectolitre of rye, by the *decrease* of each franc in the price of each hectolitre of wheat, and by francs 2.92 (54.29 cents) on every 100 kilogrammes of rye meal.—(See barley.)

At the custom-houses of France the hectolitre of rye is reckoned at 66 ki ogrammes, or 146¼ lbs.

(b) In Algiers and Corsica as in France. In Guiana, 5 per cent. ad valorem. In West Indies, in foreign vessels, prohibited.

FRANCE AND HER POSSESSIONS—TARIFFS—Continued.

DENOMINATION OF MERCHANDISE.	DUTIES ON IMPORTS. Into the United States from foreign nations, per cent. ad valorem, under the act of— 1846.	1857.	INTO FRANCE FROM FOREIGN NATIONS. Number, weight, or measure.	In national vessels.	In foreign vessels.	INTO FRENCH POSSESSIONS.	REMARKS.
Sail duck, including Holland, ravens, and Russia.	20	15	....	According	to material.	Sails on board of vessels necessary for the general use are free.	
Salad oil............	30	24	220 pounds.	$2 $40\frac{7}{10}$	$2 $80\frac{4}{5}$	In Algiers and Corsica as in France; in Guiana and West Indies, in foreign vessels, prohibited.	
Salmon, pickled............	20	15	....do......	18 51	20 13		In Guiana, salted fish imported direct from France, in French vessels, free.
smoked or dried....	20	15	....do......	7 $40\frac{2}{3}$	8 $14\frac{3}{4}$	In Corsica and Algiers as in France; in Guiana, 5 per cent. ad valorem; in West Indies, in foreign vessels, prohibited.	Raw products of fishery are not included in the treaty of 1822; though they may be imported direct into France, they are subject to the duties on foreign vessels
Salt, marine, saline, stone or rock.	20	15					
Salt, crude, on the canal and Atlantic ocean.	20	15	....do......	$32\frac{1}{4}$	$41\frac{3}{5}$	In Algiers, in French vessels, $55\frac{1}{4}$ cents, in foreign, 61 cts. per 220 pounds; in Corsica as in France; in Guiana, 5 per cent. ad val.; in the West Indies, 93 cents per 220 pounds.	Foreign, sea, and rock salts, or from Algiers and the French possessions, after having paid the regular custom-house duties, are subject to another additional consumption duty of $1 86 per 220 pounds, if they are not used in the manufacture of soda. There is no distinction made in the tariff between marine, saline, or rock salts. Nationalized salt, or of national origin, used for the French fisheries, are exempted from all duties. The products of the French fisheries, in order to be entitled to bounty, must be salted with French salts, (or foreign salt that has paid
Salt, crude, on the Mediterranean.	20	15	....do......	$9\frac{3}{10}$	$18\frac{3}{5}$		
Salt, crude, from the French colonies. (*a*)	20	15	....	Free.....	Prohibited.	In foreign vessels, prohibited.	
Salt, refined, on the canal and Atlantic ocean.	20	15	....do......	$50\frac{9}{10}$	$60\frac{1}{10}$	Same as crude salt.	
Salt refined, on the Mediterranean.	20	15	....do......	$9\frac{3}{10}$	$18\frac{3}{5}$		
Salt, refined, from the French colonies.	20	15	....	Free.....	Prohibited.	In foreign vessels, prohibited.	

(*a*) For the sake of convenience and conciseness, some of the French and French colonial distinctions and discriminations in the denominations of merchandise are inserted in the general nomenclature, while the corresponding rates of duty are noted in the appropriate columns.

FRANCE AND HER POSSESSIONS—TARIFFS—Continued.

DENOMINATION OF MERCHANDISE.	DUTIES ON IMPORTS.						REMARKS.
	Into the United States from foreign nations, per cent. ad valorem, under the act of—		INTO FRANCE FROM FOREIGN NATIONS.			INTO FRENCH POSSESSIONS.	
	1846.	1857.	Number, weight, or measure.	In national vessels.	In foreign vessels		
Salts, Glauber	20	15	220 pounds.	$55\frac{3}{5}$	$2 $42\frac{7}{10}$	In Algiers and Corsica as in France; in Guiana and West Indies, in foreign vessels, prohibited.	the importation duty.) French fishing vessels may even buy the salt abroad, but they must remit to the French custom-houses, for every 220 pounds, $9\frac{3}{10}$ cents. The French custom-house officers calculate that, for every 220 pounds of fresh cod fish, there are 200 pounds of salt necessary; and for every 220 pounds of dried cod fish, 266 lbs. of salt.
Epsom	20	15	do	12 96	14 07		
Sand, for manufacturing glass	20	15		Free	Free	Free.	
Sandal wood, powdered	20	15	do	3 $70\frac{1}{3}$	4 $07\frac{2}{5}$	In Algiers and Corsica as in France; in Guiana, in foreign vessels, prohibited; in West Indies, free.	
in sticks	30	8	do	Free	1 $11\frac{3}{5}$		
Saltpetre, from East Indies, crude.	5	4	do	$18\frac{3}{5}$	4 68	In Algiers and Corsica as in France; in Guiana and West Indies, in foreign vessels, prohibited.	
Saltpetre, from countries out of Europe, refined, or partially so.	10	8	do	1 $38\frac{4}{5}$	4 68		Glauber salts of 80 degrees, exported from France, enjoys a bounty of $2 04 per 220 pounds.
Saltpetre, from entrepots			do	3 $70\frac{1}{3}$	4 68		
Sardines, dry, salted, smoked	20	15	do	7 $40\frac{2}{3}$	8 $14\frac{3}{4}$	In Algiers and Corsica as in France; in Guiana and the West Indies, in foreign vessels, prohibited.	
in oil	40	30	do	18 51	20 13		
Sarsaparilla, from Senegal and French Guiana.	20	15	do	7 $40\frac{7}{10}$	Prohibited.	Prohibited in foreign vessels.	
Sarsaparilla, from countries out of Europe.	20	15	do	13 88	23 14	In Corsica and Algiers as in France; in Guiana and the West Indies, in foreign vessels, prohibited.	
Sarsaparilla, from entrepots	20	15	do	18 51	23 14		Agricultural implements and utensils of husbandry may be imported into Guiana from France, and in French vessels, free.
Saws, over 57 inches long	30	24	do	25 $92\frac{1}{2}$	27 68		
all under 57 inches long	30	24	do	37 $03\frac{1}{3}$	39 $79\frac{1}{2}$		
Scrap and old iron	30	24	do	2 $24\frac{7}{10}$	2 $44\frac{2}{5}$		

FRANCE AND HER POSSESSIONS—TARIFFS—Continued.

Denomination of merchandise.	Duties on imports. Into the United States from foreign nations, per cent. ad valorem, under the act of— 1846.	1857.	Into France from foreign nations. Number, weight, or measure.	In national vessels.	In foreign vessels.	Into French possessions.	Remarks.
Sculpture, especially imported	Free	Free	All articles of collect'n, if not destined for commercial purposes, admitted at 1 per ct. ad val. —(See Paintings.)			In Corsica and Algiers as in France; in Guiana and the West Indies, in foreign vessels, prohibited.	The works of French artists at Rome are also admitted at 1 per cent. ad val.
Scythes	30	24	220 pounds	$14 81	$16 01		Scythes, if imported into Guiana direct from France, and in French vessels, are free.
Sealing wax	30	24	do	18 51	20 13		
Seeds, linseed	10	Free	do	46¼	81⅔	In Algiers and Corsica as in France; in Guiana, in foreign vessels, prohibited; in West Indies, free.	Linseed, for seed, can be imported into France free of duty, if it comes from ports situated on the White sea or the Baltic.
hemp	10	8	do	46¼	81⅔		
aniseed	20	4	do	3 70¼		In Algiers and Corsica as in France; in Guiana and West Indies, in foreign vessels, prohibited.	
mustard	Free	Free	do	93	1 02		
Senna, leaves	20	15	do	Free	3 70⅓	In Algiers and Corsica as in France; in Guiana, in foreign vessels, prohibited; in West Indies, free.	
from entrepots	20	15	do	1 86	3 70⅓		
Senegal, gum, from Senegal	10	8	do	1 86	Prohibited	In foreign vessels, prohibited.	
Sewing silk	30	24	2.20 pounds	56⅔	61	In Corsica and Algiers as in France; in Guiana and West Indies, in foreign vessels, prohibited.	
cotton	25	24		Prohibited.	Prohibited.		
Sewing flax, unbleached, 6,000 metres to the kilogramme, more or less.	20	15	do	8 14	8 96		
Sheathing copper, for ships	Free	Free	220 pounds	9 25	10 29⅓	In Algiers and Corsica as in France. In Guiana and the West Indies, in foreign vessels, prohibited.	Copper beaten and laminated enjoys, if exported from France, a bounty equal to the amount paid as duty on the importation of the crude metal.

FRANCE AND HER POSSESSIONS—TARIFFS—Continued.

DENOMINATION OF MERCHANDISE.	DUTIES ON IMPORTS. Into the United States from foreign nations, per cent. ad valorem, under the act of—		INTO FRANCE FROM FOREIGN NATIONS.			INTO FRENCH POSSESSIONS.	REMARKS.
	1846.	1857.	Number, weight, or measure.	In national vessels.	In foreign vessels.		
Shell, cocoa	10	4	220 pounds	$10 $20\frac{9}{10}$	$19 $66\frac{1}{3}$	In Corsica and Algiers as in France. In Guiana, in foreign vessels, prohibited. In West Indies, free.	
turtle, from India	5	4	do	5 $55\frac{1}{2}$	28 09		
Shawls, cashmere	30	24	Apiece	18 51	18 51	In Algiers and Corsica as in France. In Guiana and the West Indies, in foreign vessels, prohibited.	In Guiana, tissues of silk, cotton, or wool are to be admitted into the entrepot fictif. Plain China crape shawls, of foreign origin, intended to be embroidered in France, may be temporarily admitted free of duty, on condition of being re-exported within six months, under the bonds and formalities prescribed by the 5th article of the law of July 5, 1836. These formalities include the declaration to the custom-house, the stamp on the package, and the direction which the shawls have to take in order to be admitted.
wool	30	24		See wool.			
cotton	30	24		Prohibited.		In Algiers, 25 per cent. ad valorem. In Corsica as in France. In Guiana and West Indies, in foreign vessels, prohibited.	
silk	30	24		See silk.			
hot, iron	30	24		Prohibited.		Prohibited.	
lead	20	15		Prohibited.		Prohibited.	
Shovels	30	24	220 pounds	9 30	10 29	In Algiers and Corsica as in France. In Guiana, free. In the West Indies, 75 cents per dozen.	
Sickles, of iron or steel	30	24	do	14 81	16 01	In Algiers and Corsica as in France. In Guiana, in foreign vessels, prohibited. In the West Indies, $55\frac{4}{5}$ cents per doz.	In Guiana, sickles imported from France, and in French vessels, are free.

FRANCE AND HER POSSESSIONS—TARIFFS—Continued.

Denomination of merchandise.	Duties on imports. Into the United States from foreign nations, per cent. ad valorem, under the act of— 1846.	1857.	Into France from foreign nations. Number, weight, or measure.	In national vessels.	In foreign vessels.	Into French possessions.	Remarks.
Sienna earth	30	24	220 pounds	$0 37$\frac{1}{5}$	$0 40$\frac{4}{10}$	In Algiers and Corsica as in France. In Guiana and the West Indies, in foreign vessels, prohibited.	
Side-arms of all descriptions for soldiers.	30	24		Prohibited		Prohibited.	Old side-arms, as objects of collection, 1 per cent. ad valorem.
Side-arms of all descriptions for commerce.	30	24	220 pounds	74 06	77 31	In Algiers and Corsica as in France. In Guiana and the West Indies, in foreign vessels, prohibited.	
Silk, in cocoons	15	Free	do	18$\frac{3}{5}$	20$\frac{2}{5}$		Cocoons from Sardinia are free.
raw, unfolded by merely hot water process.	15	12	2.20 pounds	1	1		
organzine	15	12	do	2	2		
sewing	30	24	do	56$\frac{3}{5}$	61		
spun, *fleuret*, raw	15	12	do	18$\frac{3}{5}$	20$\frac{2}{5}$		
spun, *fleuret*, dyed	15	12	do	55$\frac{4}{5}$	61		
tissues of pure silk, plain.	25	19	do	2 96	3 74		
tissues, glazed, watered, damasked, or figured.	25	19	do	3 51	3 87		Silk tissues, in Guiana, are admitted into the entrepot fictif.
tissues, figured or worked with pure gold and silver.	30	24	do	5 74	6 31		Silk tissues from India are prohibited, if imported indirect.
tissue, with imitation of gold and silver.	25	19		Prohibited			
carpets or tapestry, mix'd with linen thread, or not.	25	19	220 pounds	56 66	59 90		

FRANCE AND HER POSSESSIONS—TARIFFS—Continued.

DENOMINATION OF MERCHANDISE.	DUTIES ON IMPORTS.						REMARKS.
	Into the United States from foreign nations, per cent. ad valorem, under the act of—		INTO FRANCE FROM FOREIGN NATIONS.			INTO FRENCH POSSESSIONS.	
	1846.	1857.	Number, weight, or measure.	In national vessels.	In foreign vessels.		
Silk, tulle	25	19		Prohibited.		In Algiers and Corsica as in France. In Guiana and the West Indies, in foreign vessels, prohibited.	
gauze, of pure silk	25	19	2.20 pounds.	$5 74	$6 31		
gauze, mixed with thread.	25	19	do	3 14	3 46		
gauze, mixed with pure gold or silver.	25	24	do	11 48	12 51		
gauze, mixed with artificial gold or silver.	25	24		Prohibited.			
lace of silk, called blonde lace.	25	19		15 per ct.	ad valorem.		
lace of silk with fine gold.	25	24	do	37 03⅓	39 79½		
lace of silk with fine silver.	25	24	do	18 51	20 13		
lace of silk with artificial gold or silver.	25	24	do	4 68	5 09		
hosiery	25	24	220 pounds.	222 22	225 46		
small wares of pure silk.	25	24	2.20 pounds.	2 96	3 74		
mixed with gold and silver.	25	24	do	4 68	5 09		
mixed with artificial gold and silver.	25	24	do	1 48	1 62		
ribbons or velvet of silk.	25	19	220 pounds.	148 14	151 38		
Silver, coins	Free	Free	2.20 pounds.	0⅕	0⅕	In Algiers and Corsica as in France; in Guiana and the West Indies, free.	Old coins, as objects of collection, may be admitted at 1 per cent. ad valorem.

FRANCE AND HER POSSESSIONS—TARIFFS—Continued.

Denomination of merchandise.	Duties on imports. Into the United States from foreign nations, per cent. ad valorem, under the act of— 1846.	1857.	Into France from foreign nations. Number, weight, or measure.	In national vessels.	In foreign vessels.	Into French possessions.	Remarks.
Sirup of sugar cane	30	24		Pays the same duty as sugar of the first type, but of the best quality.—(See Sugar.)			
Skins, raw, salted	5	4		$13\frac{1}{3}$ per cent. ad valorem.		In Algiers and Corsica as in France; in Guiana, in foreign vessels, prohibited; in the West Indies, free.	Skins imported from countries west of Cape Horn pay only one-half of this duty.
Snuffs, for private orders	40	30		Prohibited		In foreign vessels, prohibited.	
for government orders	40	30	220 pounds	Free	$2 $80\frac{4}{5}$	In Algiers and Corsica as in France; in Guiana and the West Indies, in foreign vessels, prohibited.	
Soap, common	30	24		Prohibited		In Corsica as in France; in Algiers, 25 per cent. ad valorem; in Guiana and West Indies, in foreign vessels, prohibited.	Soap exported from France enjoys the following bounties: 1. Of palm or cocoa oil, mixed with animal fat, $74\frac{2}{3}$ cents per 220 pounds. 2. Mixed with olive or any other vegetable oil, (white or marble soap,) $1 51 per 220 pounds. 3. Of animal fats mixed or not with resins, $1 $11\frac{2}{3}$ per 220 pounds.
perfumed	30	24	do	$30 37	32 35	In Algiers and Corsica as in France; in Guiana and the West Indies, in foreign vessels, prohibited.	
Soda, of all kinds	10	8	do	4 90	5 38		Soda and several of its compositions enjoy, if exported from France, the following bounties: 1. Soda, crude, of at least 53 degrees, $80\frac{1}{2}$ cents per 220 pounds.
nitrate of	5	4	do	1 38	4 68		
Spades, of iron or steel	30	24	do	9 30	10 29		

FRANCE AND HER POSSESSIONS—TARIFFS—Continued.

Denomination of merchandise.	DUTIES ON IMPORTS. Into the United States from foreign nations, per cent. ad valorem, under the act of— 1846.	1857.	Into France from foreign nations. Number, weight, or measure.	In national vessels.	In foreign vessels.	Into French possessions.	Remarks.
							2. Soda in crystals, 80½ cents per 220 pounds. 3. Salt of soda, up to 80 degrees, \$2 04⅗ per 220 pounds. 4. Sulphate of soda, \$1 11⅗ per 220 pounds. Spades, if imported into Guiana from France, and in French vessels, are free.
Spermaceti, from French fisheries.	20	15	220 pounds	\$0 03$\frac{7}{10}$	Prohibited	In foreign vessels, prohibited	Raw and pressed spermaceti is excepted from the benefits of the treaty of 1822, and always has to pay the duty imposed on foreign vessels.
from foreign fisheries—							
raw	20	15	do	3 70⅓	\$4 07	In Algiers and Corsica as in France; in Guiana and West Indies, in foreign vessels, prohibited.	Into Guiana, all spirituous liquids, with the exception of brandy, French and Martinique cordials, kirschenwasser, and gin, can be admitted into the entrepot fictif, if from France, and in French vessels. If exported from Guiana, spirits of molasses will pay, besides the 2 per cent. ad valorem duty, an additional duty of 9$\frac{3}{10}$ cents per 264 gallons, (1,000 litres.)
pressed	20	15	do	5 55	6 11		
refined	20	15	do	13 88	15 00		
candles	20	15	do	40 74	43 24		
Spirits, of wine	100	30	Hectolitre, or 26 gallons.	2 80⅘	2 80⅘		
of cherries, (kirschenwasser.)	100	30	do	2 80⅘	2 80⅘		
of molasses from Fr. colonies.	100	30		Free	Free		
of molasses from elsewhere.	100	30	do	2 80⅘	2 80⅘		
rice, (arrack)	100	30	do	2 80⅘	2 80⅘	Into Oceanica, in casks, 11¼ cents per quart; in bottles, 74⅔ cents per dozen.	French and Tahitian vessels pay, in Oceanica, only one-half of the duty.
of all other sorts	100	30	do	2 80⅘	2 80⅘		
of turpentine	20	15	220 pounds	4 68	5 09		
Sponges, common	20	8	do	11 23½	12 26½	In Algiers and Corsica as in France; in Guiana and West Indies, in foreign vessels, prohibited.	
fine	20	8	do	37 03⅓	39 79½		

FRANCE AND HER POSSESSIONS—TARIFFS—Continued.

Denomination of merchandise.	Duties on imports. Into the United States from foreign nations, per cent. ad valorem, under the act of— 1846.	1857.	Into France from foreign nations. Number, weight, or measure.	In national vessels.	In foreign vessels.	Into French possessions.	Remarks.
Statuary, as objects of taste	Free	Free		As objects of taste, 1 per cent. ad valorem.		In Algiers and Corsica as in France; in Guiana and the West Indies, in foreign vessels, prohibited. (Statuary, of marble and of alabaster; Stones, precious, crude, unset and cut, set; flint; pumice)	Statuary, the work of French artists residing in Rome, is also 1 per cent. ad valorem.
of marble	30	Free	220 pounds	$7 40	$8 14		
of alabaster	40	Free		15 per cent. ad valorem.			
Stones, precious, crude, unset	10	4	0.22 lb. ($\frac{1}{4}$ lb.)	$4\frac{3}{5}$	$4\frac{3}{5}$		
Stones, precious, cut, set	30	24	do	$18\frac{3}{5}$	$20\frac{3}{5}$		
flint	5	4	220 pounds	$1\frac{4}{5}$	$1\frac{4}{5}$		
pumice	10	8	do	93	1 02		
for lithography	20	15	do	$37\frac{3}{5}$	$40\frac{7}{10}$		
whetstones, rough	20	15	do	$37\frac{3}{5}$	$40\frac{7}{10}$		
whetstones, cut	20	15	do	93	1 02		
Steel, in bars, hammered	20	15	do	11 $23\frac{1}{2}$	12 $26\frac{1}{2}$	In Algiers, in national vessels, $3 72, in foreign, $4 07 per 220 pounds. In Corsica as in France. In Guiana and West Indies, in foreign vessels, prohibited. (Steel, in bars, hammered and cast)	
Steel, in bars, cast	15	12	do	22 $47\frac{1}{4}$	23 79		
in sheets, of all kinds	20	15	do	14 81	16 01	In Algiers, in national vessels, $7 40, in foreign, $8 14 per 220 pounds. In Corsica as in France. In Guiana and the West Indies, in foreign vessels, prohibited.	
drawn, or wire	30	24	do	18 51	20 13	In Algiers, in national vessels, $9 30, in foreign, $10 18 per 220 pounds. In Corsica as in France. In Guiana and the West Indies, in foreign vessels, prohibited.	

FRANCE AND HER POSSESSIONS—TARIFFS—Continued.

Denomination of merchandise	Duties on imports. Into the United States from foreign nations, per cent. ad valorem, under the act of— 1846.	1857.	Into France from foreign nations. Number, weight, or measure.	In national vessels.	In foreign vessels.	Into French possessions.	Remarks.
Steel—tools, of pure steel	30	24	220 pounds	$37 03⅓	$39 79½	In Algiers and Corsica as in France. In Guiana and the West Indies, in foreign vessels, prohibited.	Some tools, as hatchets, &c., if imported from France, and in French vessels, into Guiana, are free.
all other manufactures	30	24		Prohibited.		Into Algiers, 25 per cent. ad valorem. In Corsica as in France. In Guiana and the West Indies, in foreign vessels, prohibited.	
Sugar, not refined	30	24					Sugar can be imported into Guiana from the French colonies, and in French vessels, for the entrepot fictif. The same can also be imported into Algiers for a duty of $9 30 per 220 pounds, if coming direct from the countries of production. Not refined sugar, but of better quality than that of the 1st type, pays, in Algiers, in every instance, 41⅔ cents more per 220 pounds.
from French colonies from beyond the Cape of Good Hope.	30	24	do	6 48	Prohibited.	In foreign vessels, prohibited.	
from America	30	24	do	7 03	Prohibited.	In foreign vessels, prohibited.	
from China, Cochin China, Philippines, and Siam.	30	24	do	8 88	12 59	In Algiers, in national vessels, $7 22 per 220 pounds. In foreign vessels, prohibited. In Corsica as in France. In Guiana and the West Indies, in foreign vessels, prohibited.	
from other south Asiatic countries.	30	24	do	9 30	12 59	In Algiers, in national vessels, $7 50 per 220 pounds. In foreign vessels, prohibited. In Corsica as in France. In Guiana and the West Indies, in foreign vessels, prohibited.	

FRANCE AND HER POSSESSIONS—TARIFFS—Continued.

Denomination of merchandise.	Duties on imports. Into the United States, from foreign nations, per cent. ad valorem, under the act of— 1846.	1857.	Into France from foreign nations. Number, weight, or measure.	In national vessels.	In foreign vessels.	Into French possessions.	Remarks.
Sugar, from other, not European countries.	30	24	220 pounds	$9 81	$12 59	In Algiers, in national vessels, $7 91 per 220 pounds, in foreign, if on direct voyage from the country of production, $9 30. In Corsica as in France. In Guiana and the West Indies, in foreign vessels, prohibited.	
from entrepots	30	24	...do...	11 68	12 59	In Algiers, in national vessels, $9 30 per 220 pounds. In foreign, prohibited. In Corsica as in France. In Guiana and the West Indies, in foreign vessels, prohibited.	
not refined, but of better quality than the above, pays, in every instance, 3 francs, or 55⅘ cents, more per 220 pounds.							
refined	30	24	...	...	...	...	Foreign raw sugar, if refined in France, enjoys, if exported, the following bounties: If imported from China, Cochin China, Siam, and the Philippines, $15 13 per 220 pounds. From other south Asiatic countries, $15 71 per 220 pounds. From countries out of Europe, $16 58 per 220 pounds. Refined sugar can be admitted in Guiana into the entrepot fictif, if imported in foreign vessels.
from French colonies beyond the Cape of Good Hope.	30	24	220 pounds	7 74	Prohibited.	In foreign vessels, prohibited	
from America	30	24	...do...	8 35	Prohibited.		
from elsewhere	30	24	...	Prohibited.	...	In Algiers and Corsica as in France. In Guiana and West Indies, in foreign vessels, prohibited.	
Sugar of lead	20	15	...do...	12 97	14 07		
Tallow, raw, of all kinds	10	8	...do...	93	1 48	In Algiers and Corsica as in France. In Guiana, 5 per cent. ad valorem. In West Indies, free.	

FRANCE AND HER POSSESSIONS—TARIFFS—Continued.

Denomination of merchandise.	Duties on imports. Into the United States from foreign nations, per cent. ad valorem, under the act of— 1846.	1857.	Into France from foreign nations. Number, weight, or measure.	In national vessels.	In foreign vessels.	Into French possessions.	Remarks.
Tallow candles	20	15	220 pounds	$1 86	$2 04	In Algiers and Corsica as in France. In Guiana, 5 per cent. ad valorem. In West Indies, in foreign vessels, prohibited.	
Tamarinds, preserved in sugar	40	30	do	11 48	12 51	In Algiers and Corsica as in France. In Guiana and the West Indies, in foreign vessels, prohibited.	
Tapioca	20	15	do	1 10	1 42½		
Tar and pitch	20	15	do	64⅘	1 01	In Algiers and Corsica as in France. In Guiana, 5 per cent. ad valorem. In West Indies, 13⅘ cents per 220 pounds.	
Tarred cables and cordage	25	19		See cables and cordage.			
Tartar, cream of	20	4	do	5 55½	6 11	In Algiers and Corsica as in France. In Guiana and the West Indies, in foreign vessels, prohibited.	
crude	5	Free	do	55⅘	2 24		
emetic	20	15	do	1 86	5 09		
Teas, of all kinds, from India	(a)20	(a)15	2. 20 pounds	28	1 11⅗		(a) Except when imported direct from place of production, in American or equalized vessels, when teas of all kinds are free.
from ports of the Baltic and Black sea.	20	15	do	46⅘	1 11⅗		
from elsewhere	20	15	do	93	1 11⅗		
Teeth of elephants, ivory, from Senegal.	5	Free	do	4 68	Prohibited.	In foreign vessels, prohibited.	
Teeth of elephants, from India	5	Free	do	4 68	12 96	In Algiers and Corsica as in France; in Guiana, in foreign vessels, prohibited; in West Indies, free.	
Teeth of elephants, from Africa, except Senegal.	5	Free	do	4 68	12 96		
Teeth of elephants, from all other places.	5	Free	do	10 20$\frac{9}{10}$	12 96		

FRANCE AND HER POSSESSIONS—TARIFFS—Continued.

Denomination of merchandise.	Duties on imports. Into the United States from foreign nations, per cent. ad valorem, under the act of— 1846.	1857.	Into France from foreign nations. Number, weight, or measure.	In national vessels.	In foreign vessels.	Into French possessions.	Remarks.
Terra, Japonica	10	Free	2.20 pounds	\$0 37⅕	\$0 40⅖	In Algiers and Corsica as in France; in Guiana and West Indies, in foreign vessels prohibited.	Terra Japonica and Terra de Sienna are considered in the French tariff as ochres, and pay similar duties.
Sienna	30	15	do	37⅕	40⅖		
Thibet, and other goats' hair	20	15		See Hair	See Hair		
manufactured Cashmere shawls.	30	24	Each	18 51	18 51		
Thread, cotton	25	24		Prohibited.	See Cotton.	In Algiers 25 per cent. ad valorem; in Corsica as in France; in Guiana and West Indies, in foreign vessels, prohibited.	
lace	20	15		5 pr. ct.	ad valorem.	In Algiers and Corsica as in France; in Guiana and the West Indies, in foreign vessels, prohibited.	
packthread, of hemp	30	24	220 pounds	4 68	5 09⅕		
Tiles, flat	20	15	1,000	74⅖	74⅖	In Algiers, free; in Corsica as in France; in Guiana and the West Indies, in foreign vessels, prohibited.	
ridged	20	15	do	4 68	4 68		
square	20	15	do	1 86	1 68		
Tin, ore	20	15	220 pounds	Free	18⅗	In Algiers and Corsica as in France; in Guiana, in foreign vessels, prohibited; In West Indies, free.	Raw tin is one of those articles not included in the treaty of June 24, 1822, therefore it has to pay the duty designated under the head of foreign vessels; even if the importation should be direct from the United States to France.
crude { from India	20	15	do	2	93	In Algiers, free; in Corsica as in France; in Guiana, in foreign vessels, prohibited; in West Indies, free.	
crude { from elsewhere	20	15	do	37⅘	93		
beaten or laminated	15	8	do	11 23½	12 26½		
tin pots, common	30	24	do	18 51	20 13	In Algiers and Corsica as in France; in Guiana and the West Indies, in foreign vessels, prohibited.	
fine	30	24	do	37 03⅓	39 79½		

FRANCE AND HER POSSESSIONS—TARIFFS—Continued.

Denomination of merchandise.	Duties on imports. Into the United States from foreign nations, per cent. ad valorem, under the act of— 1846.	1857.	Into France from foreign nations. Number, weight, or measure.	In national vessels.	In foreign vessels.	Into French possessions.	Remarks.
Tin, all other manufactures	30	24	220 pounds	Prohibited.	Prohibited.	In Algiers, 25 per cent. ad valorem; in Corsica as in France; in Guiana and West Indies, in foreign vessels, prohibited.	
oxide of	20	15	do	$0 37	$0 $40\frac{7}{10}$	In Algiers and Corsica as in France; in Guiana and the West Indies, in foreign vessels, prohibited.	Tobacco imported into France from Algiers is free of duty.
Tobacco, leaf, for the French government:							Manufactured tobacco can be imported into France only on account of the government. There is one exception by which private persons may import the same for sanitary purposes and habitual uses, the quantity of which, however, can never exceed 10 kilogrammes, (22 pounds.) In this case the duty is fixed on cigars at $4 44 per 2.20 pounds, and on tobacco in powder, carrottes, and other manufactures, at $1 86 per 2.20 pounds. The consumer cannot buy it through a third person, as the commerce is to be direct. Travellers can import for this duty a quantity of not more than one kilogramme (2.20 lbs.) of tobacco, and not more than 500 cigars. If surpassing these amounts the importation is prohibited.
from countries out of Europe. (a)			do	Free	1 86	Into Algiers as in France; in Corsica, in national vessels, $11 11, in foreign, $12 12 per 220 pounds; in Guiana, 5 per cent. ad valorem; in West Indies, $3 70 per 220 pounds.	
from entrepots			do	93	1 86		
for private account				Prohibited	Prohibited		
unmanufactured	30	24					
manufactured	40	30					
cigars, and other manufactured tobacco for the government.			Manufactured	tobacco is	a monopoly	of the government.	
cigars and other manufactured tobacco from countries out of Europe.			do	Free	2 $80\frac{4}{5}$	In Algiers as in France; in Corsica, in French vessels, $18 51, in foreign, $19 90 per 220 pounds; in Guiana, in foreign vessels, prohibited; in West Indies, $5 55 per 220 pounds.	

(a) The nomenclature, as already intimated, is, for convenience, adapted to the tariffs of France.

FRANCE AND HER POSSESSIONS—TARIFFS—Continued.

Denomination of merchandise.	Duties on imports. Into the United States from foreign nations, per cent. ad valorem, under the act of— 1846.	1857.	Into France from foreign nations. Number, weight, or measure.	In national vessels.	In foreign vessels.	Into French possessions.	Remarks.
Tobacco, cigars, and other manufactured tobacco from entrepots.			220 pounds	$1 30	$2 80$\frac{4}{5}$	In Algiers as in France; in Corsica, in French 51, in foreign, $19 90 per 220 pounds; in Guiana, in foreign vessels, prohibited; in West Indies, $5 55 per 220 pounds.	
cigars, and other manufactured tobacco for private account.				Prohibited.	Prohibited.		
Tools, of pure iron	30	24	220 pounds	9 30	10 20	In Algiers and Corsica as in France; in Guiana and the West Indies, in foreign vessels, prohibited.	In Guiana, tools, as shovels, hoes, hatchets, ploughs, harrows, and similar articles, are free, if direct from France in French vessels. In the West Indies, hoes and shovels are admissible at a duty of 74$\frac{2}{5}$ cents per dozen. Foreign vessels, however, may import into the West Indies pruning hooks and cutlasses at 55$\frac{4}{5}$ cents per dozen.
of steeled iron	30	24	do	37 03$\frac{1}{3}$	39 79$\frac{1}{2}$		
of copper or brass	30	24	do	28 09	29 96$\frac{1}{4}$		
files and rasps, coarse cut, called common.	30	24	do	14 81	16 01		
files and rasps to polish, called fine, of 6$\frac{2}{3}$ inches long, and over.	30	24	do	37 03$\frac{1}{3}$	39 79$\frac{1}{2}$		
files and rasps of less than 6$\frac{2}{3}$ inches long.	30	24	do	45 55	49 07		
saws	30	24	do	See Saws	See Saws		
Tortoise shell, from India			220 pounds	5 55$\frac{1}{2}$	28 09	In Algiers and Corsica as in France; in Guiana, in foreign vessels, prohibited; in the West Indies, free.	
from countries out of Europe.			do	12 96	28 09		

FRANCE AND HER POSSESSIONS—TARIFFS—Continued.

Denomination of merchandise.	Duties on imports. Into the United States from foreign nations, per cent. ad valorem, under the act of— 1846.	1857.	Into France from foreign nations. Number, weight, or measure.	In national vessels.	In foreign vessels.	Into French possessions.	Remarks.
Tortoise shell, from entrepots.			220 pounds	$18 51	$28 09	In Algiers and Corsica as in France; in Guiana, in foreign vessels, prohibited; in the West Indies, free.	
unmanufact'd	5	4					
manufact'd	30	24					
Tulle, of silk	25	24	220 pounds	Prohibited		In Algiers and Corsica as in France; in Guiana and the West Indies, in foreign vessels, prohibited.	
of linen	20	15	do	Prohibited			
Twines and packthread	30	24	do	4 68	5 09$\frac{1}{5}$		
Types, printing	20	15				In Algiers and Corsica as in France; in Guiana and West Indies, in foreign vessels, prohibited.	
new, in the French language.	20	15	do	37 03$\frac{1}{3}$	39 79$\frac{1}{2}$		Types in the French language are the same as in the English.
new, in German	20	15	do	9 30	10 20		
in all others	20	15	do	18 51	20 13		
old and out of use	20	15	do	27 77	29 96		
Umbrellas and parasols	30	24					
of silk	30	24	Each	37$\frac{1}{5}$	37$\frac{1}{5}$		Frames and sticks alone pay one-fifth of the duty on a silken umbrella or parasol.
of linen, waxed	30	24	do	13$\frac{4}{5}$	13$\frac{4}{5}$		
of cotton	30	24		Prohibited			
Vanilla beans, from Réunion	20	15		Free	Prohibited	Prohibited in foreign vessels.	
from countries west of Cape Horn.	20	15	2.20 pounds	4 68	1 02	In Algiers and Corsica as in France; in Guiana, in foreign vessels, prohibited; in West Indies, free.	
from elsewhere	20	15	do	93	1 02		

FRANCE AND HER POSSESSIONS—TARIFFS—Continued.

Denomination of merchandise.	Duties on imports. Into the United States from foreign nations, per cent. ad valorem, under the act of— 1846.	1857.	Into France from foreign nations. Number, weight, or measure.	In national vessels.	In foreign vessels.	Into French possessions.	Remarks.
Varnish, red	20	15	220 pounds	$7 59	$8 35	In Algiers and Corsica as in France; in Guiana and the West Indies, in foreign vessels, prohibited.	
other kinds	20	15	do	6 11	6 72		
Veils, of silk	25	24	2.20 pounds	5 74	6 31	In Algiers and Corsica as in France; in Guiana and the West Indies, in foreign vessels, prohibited.	
mixed with thread	25	24	do	3 14	3 46		
mixed with pure gold or silver.	25	24	do	11 48	12 51		
Veils, of linen	20	15		Prohibited.		In Algiers, 25 per cent. ad valorem; in Corsica as in France; in Guiana and West Indies, in foreign vessels, prohibited.	
of cotton	25	24		5 per cent.	ad val		
Venetian carpets	30	24	do	See Carpets.			
red, as ochre	30	24	220 pounds	$37\frac{1}{3}$	$40\frac{7}{10}$	In Algiers and Corsica as in France; in Guiana and the West Indies, in foreign vessels, prohibited.	
Verdigris, humid	20	15	do	2 40	2 64		
dry	20	15	do	5 74	6 31		
Vessels of copper, common	30	24	do	18 51	20 13		
fine	30	24	do	37 $03\frac{1}{3}$	39 $79\frac{1}{2}$		
of cast iron	30	24		Prohibited		In Algiers, 25 per ct. ad val.; in Corsica as in France; in Guiana and West Indies, in foreign vessels, prohibited.	
of tin, common	30	24	do	18 51	20 13	In Algiers and Corsica as in France; in Guiana and the West Indies, in foreign vessels, prohibited.	
fine	30	24	do	37 $03\frac{1}{3}$	39 $79\frac{1}{2}$		
of lead	30	24	do	4 44	4 88		
Vinegar, of wine	30	24	Hectolitre, 26 gallons.	1 86	1 86	In Algiers and Corsica as in France; in Guiana and the West Indies, in foreign vessels, prohibited.	
of beer	30	24	do	$37\frac{1}{3}$	$37\frac{1}{3}$		

FRANCE AND HER POSSESSIONS—TARIFFS—Continued.

Denomination of merchandise.	Duties on imports. Into the United States from foreign nations, per cent. ad valorem, under the act of— 1846.	1857.	Into France from foreign nations. Number, weight, or measure.	In national vessels.	In foreign vessels.	Into French possessions.	Remarks.
Vitriol, blue or Roman, copper	20	15	220 pounds	$5 74	$6 38½	In Algiers and Corsica as in France. In Guiana and West Indies, in foreign vessels, prohibited.	
green, iron	20	15	do	1 11⅗	1 22⅕		
white, zinc	20	15	do	5 74	6 38½		
oil of	10	4	do	7 59	8 35		
Ware, earthen, pottery, common.	30	24	do	1 11⅗	1 22⅕		Pottery bearing traces of use, and belonging to immigrants, pays 15 per cent. ad valorem.
earthen of Fayence, common.	30	24	do	9 07⅖	9 98		
stone, table & kitchen	30	24	do	2 80⅘	3 05½		
stone, fine	30	24	do	Prohibited		In Algiers, in foreign vessels, from $5 55 to $27 18 per 220 pounds. In Corsica as in France. In Guiana and the West Indies, in foreign vessels, prohibited.	
porcelain, common	30	24	do	30 37	32 35	In Algiers and Corsica as in France. In Guiana and the West Indies, in foreign vessels, prohibited. For remarks, *see Glass.*	By common porcelain, is understood such as is not gilt, painted, or otherwise ornamented, and having only one color. Porcelain garnished with gilt copper is prohibited. If old, and objects of curiosity, admitted at 1 per cent. ad valorem. Porcelain bearing traces of use, and the property of persons intending to settle in France, admitted at 15 per cent. ad valorem.
fine	30	24	do	60 55	63 79		
glass, crystals for watches, spectacles, cut and polished.	30	24	do	37 03⅓	39 79½		
glass, in masses, or in tubes, not cut.	30	24	2.20 pounds	55⅘	61$\frac{1}{10}$		
glass beads, pierced	30	24	do	18⅗	20½		
all other glassware	30	24		Prohibited.	See Glass.		
japanned	30	24		do		In Algiers, 25 per ct. ad valorem. In Corsica as in France. In Guiana and West Indies, in foreign vessels, prohibited.	

FRANCE AND HER POSSESSIONS—TARIFFS—Continued.

Denomination of merchandise.	Duties on imports. Into the United States from foreign nations, per cent. ad valorem, under the act of— 1846.	1857.	Into France from foreign nations. Number, weight, or measure.	In national vessels.	In foreign vessels.	Into [illegible] sessions.	Remarks.
Watches, gold, movements simple.	10	8	Each	$0 59	$0 59		
repeaters	10	8	do	84	84		
silver, or other inferior metal, movements simple.	10	8	do	$20\frac{2}{5}$	$20\frac{2}{5}$		
silver, or other inferior metal, repeaters.	10	8	do	$33\frac{1}{3}$	$33\frac{1}{2}$		
independent second watches, & pocket chronometers, gold.	10	8	do	1 $12\frac{1}{2}$	1 $12\frac{1}{2}$	In Algiers and Corsica as in France. In Guiana and the West Indies, in foreign vessels, prohibited.	
the same, without gold case.	10	8	do	10 per cent	ad valorem.		
musical boxes	20	15	2.20 pounds	93	1 02		
clocks, of wood, metal movements	30	24	Each	$37\frac{1}{5}$	$37\frac{1}{5}$		Clocks of wood, which pay $18\frac{3}{5}$ cents each, must have movements entirely of wood.
all other clocks of wood.	30	21	do	$18\frac{3}{5}$	$18\frac{3}{5}$		
movements of all sorts.	10	8		10 per cent	ad valorem.		
Wax, unmanufactured—							
yellow or brown	20	15					
from Senegal	20	15	220 pounds	$55\frac{4}{5}$	Prohibited.	In foreign vessels, prohibited.	

FRANCE AND HER POSSESSIONS—TARIFFS—Continued.

DENOMINATION OF MERCHANDISE.	DUTIES ON IMPORTS.						REMARKS.
	Into the United States from foreign nations, per cent. ad valorem, under the act of—		INTO FRANCE FROM FOREIGN NATIONS.			INTO FRENCH POSSESSIONS.	
	1846.	1857.	Number, weight, or measure.	In national vessels.	In foreign vessels.		
Wax—Continued—							
from India			220 lbs	$0 93	$2 $80\frac{4}{5}$	In Algiers and Corsica as in France. In Guiana and the West Indies, in foreign vessels, prohibited.	
from countries out of Europe.			do	1 48	2 $80\frac{4}{5}$		
from entrepots			do	1 86	2 $80\frac{4}{5}$		
white			do	11 $23\frac{1}{2}$	12 $26\frac{1}{2}$		
manufactured, yellow			do	9 30	10 $20\frac{9}{10}$		
white			do	15 74	16 98		
sealing			do	18 51	20 13		
Whale oil, of foreign fishing	20	15	do				Both whale oil and raw whalebone are not included in the treaty of June 24, 1822, and pay, therefore, the same duty as all other unequalized vessels, even if imported direct from the United States into France.
from countries out of Europe.			do	2 $80\frac{4}{5}$	5 $55\frac{1}{2}$	In Algiers and Corsica as in France. In Guiana, 5 per cent. ad valorem. In West Indies, in foreign vessels, prohibited.	
from entrepots			do	3 $70\frac{1}{3}$	5 $55\frac{1}{2}$		
of French fishing			do	$2\frac{4}{5}$	Prohibited.	In foreign vessels, prohibited.	
bone, of French fishing			do	$3\frac{7}{10}$	Prohibited.		
of foreign fishing			do	5 55	6 48	In Algiers and Corsica as in France. In Guiana, 5 per cent. ad valorem. In the West Indies, free.	
Wheat	(a)20	15		See Barley.			

(a) When wheat is 28 francs, or more, in the 1st class markets of France; 26, or more, in the 2d; 24, or more in the 3d and 22, or more, in the 5th, per hectolitre, then the duty on wheat is 25 centimes (4.68 cents,) per hectolitre in each of these markets; and the duty on its flour, per 100 kilogrammes, is 50 centimes, (9.86 cents) The duty goes on increasing in like manner as the price of wheat decreases, and when wheat is less than 22 francs in the standard markets, respectively, then the duty increases by francs 1.50 centimes, (28.08 cents,) on each hectolitre of wheat by the *decrease* of each franc in the price of each hectolitre of wheat; and by frs. 4.50 centimes on every 100 kilogrammes of wheat flour. By the French customs calculation, the hectolitre of wheat equals 76 kilogrammes, or $168\frac{3}{4}$ lbs.

Denomination of merchandise.	Duties on imports: Into the United States from foreign nations, per cent. ad valorem, under the act of— 1846.	1857.	Into France from foreign nations: Number, weight, or measure.	In national vessels.	In foreign vessels.	Into French possessions.	Remarks.
White arsenic	15	4	220 lbs	$0 $18\frac{3}{5}$	$0 $20\frac{1}{2}$	In Algiers and Corsica as in France. In Guiana and West Indies, in foreign vessels, prohibited.	The importers of white arsenic, after having discharged the tariff duty, have to take out a certificate from the custom-house. in which the quantity and the name of the receiver are put down.
lead	20	15	do	5 $55\frac{1}{2}$	6 11		
Windsor soap	30	24	do	32 35	32 35		
Window glass	20	15		Prohibited.	See Glass.	In Algiers, 25 per cent. ad valorem. In Corsica as in France. In Guiana and West Indies, in foreign vessels, prohibited.	
Wines, all kinds	40	30	Hectolitre, 26 gallons.	$4\frac{3}{5}$ If in bottles, $12\frac{1}{2}$ cents per gall., additional.	$4\frac{3}{4}$	In Algiers and Corsica as in France. In Guiana, in foreign vessels, prohibited. In the West Indies, in national vessels from France, $4\frac{3}{5}$ cts., and from foreign countries, in foreign vessels, 93 cents per 26 gallons. In Oceanica, $1 86 per barrel.	By the treaty of 1831, the red wines of France are admitted into the United States at 6 cents per gallon, in casks; the white wine, in casks, at 10 cents; and all sorts of wine, in bottles, at 22 cents. In Guiana, French colonial wines, imported in French vessels, may be admitted into the entrepot fictif. In the West Indies Madeira wines form an exception; they pay, if imported from foreign countries, $11 11 per 26 gallons. In Oceanica, Haytien and French vessels pay only one-half of this duty.
in bottles	40	30	Gallon	$12\frac{1}{2}$	$12\frac{1}{2}$		
bottles, if empty	30	24		Prohibited.	Prohibited.	In Algiers, 25 per cent. ad valorem. In Corsica as in France. In Guiana and West Indies, in foreign vessels, prohibited.	
Wire, iron, tinned or not	30	24	220 lbs	11 $23\frac{1}{2}$	12 $26\frac{1}{2}$	In Algiers and Corsica as in France. In Guiana and West Indies, in foreign vessels, prohibited.	
for instruments	30	24	do	12 96	14 07		
steel, of all kinds	30	24	do	12 96	14 07		

FRANCE AND HER POSSESSIONS—TARIFFS—Continued.

Denomination of merchandise.	Duties on imports. Into the United States from foreign nations, per cent. ad valorem, under the act of—		Into France from foreign nations.			Into French possessions.	Remarks.
	1846.	1857.	Number, weight, or measure.	In national vessels.	In foreign vessels.		
Wire, copper, gilded, to imitate gold.	30	24	220 lbs.	$52 96	$56 74	In Algiers and Corsica as in France. In Guiana and West Indies, in foreign vessels, prohibited.	
copper, not gilded or colored to imitate gold.	30	24	do	18 51	20 13		
brass, polished	30	24		Prohibited.	Prohibited.		
polished or not, for cords for musical instrum'ts.	30	24	220 lbs.	18 51	20 13		
brass, to be used in embroidery.	30	24	do	52 96	56 74		
brass, gilded, spun on thread.	30	24	do	60 55	63 79		
brass, gilded, spun on silk.	30	24	do	175 92	179 16		
brass, silvered, spun on thread.	30	24	do	60 55	63 79		
brass, silvered, spun on silk.	30	24	do	112 35	114 35		
Wood,(a) fire, in sticks	30	24	1 stère=$35\frac{1}{3}$ cubic feet.	1	1	In Algiers, free. In Corsica as in France. In Guiana, pitch pine 5 per cent. ad valorem. In the West Indies, 4 per cent. ad valorem.	
in faggots	30	24	100 pieces	1	1		

(a) See linens.

FRANCE AND HER POSSESSIONS—TARIFFS—Continued.

DENOMINATION OF MERCHANDISE.	DUTIES ON IMPORTS.						REMARKS.
	Into the United States from foreign nations, per cent. ad valorem, under the act of—		INTO FRANCE FROM FOREIGN NATIONS.			INTO FRENCH POSSESSIONS.	
	1846.	1857.	Number, weight, or measure.	In national vessels.	In foreign vessels.		
Wool, raw	30	24(a)					The common worsted yarn, though not prohibited, can only be imported through the ports of Calais, Boulogne, Dunkirk, and Havre, in order to be forwarded under leaden seal (sons plomb) and under bonds (acquit à caution) to the custom-house at Paris, in order to be there verified, marked, and the duty paid. Through all other frontiers this kind of yarn continues to be prohibited.
from India	30	24	2.20 pounds	$0 $9\frac{3}{10}$(b)		In Algiers and Corsica as in France: in Guiana and West Indies, in foreign vessels, prohibited.	
from elsewhere	30	24		20 per cent.	ad val.(b)		
combed	30	24		30 per cent.	ad val		
dyed	30	24	220 pounds	55 $55\frac{1}{2}$	$58 79		
refuse	30	24	do	$18\frac{3}{5}$	$20\frac{2}{5}$		
yarn merely divested of grease, combed or twisted into one or more threads.	25	19	2.20 pounds	1 30	1 42		
all other yarns	25	19		Prohibited		In Algiers, 25 per cent. ad valorem; in Corsica as in France; in Guiana and West Indies, in foreign vessels, prohibited.	
Woolen manufactures:							
Blankets	20	15	220 pounds	37 $03\frac{1}{3}$	39 $79\frac{1}{2}$	In Algiers, in French vessels, $44\frac{2}{5}$ cents, and in foreign, 48 cents per 2.20 pounds; in Corsica as in France; in Guiana and the West Indies, in foreign vessels, prohibited.	Both woolen yarn and tissues enjoy a bounty if exported from France. Woolen hosiery, &c., and carpets receive $18 51 per 220 pounds. Carpets belonging to persons immigrating into France, and exhibiting traces of use, pay 15 per cent. ad valorem.
Carpets, half wool and half linen.	30	24	do	46 $81\frac{2}{3}$	46 $81\frac{2}{3}$	In Algiers and Corsica as in France; in Guiana and the West Indies, in foreign vessels, prohibited.	

(a) By the tariff of 1857, wool unmanufactured, the value of 20 cents per pound, or less, at the port of exportation, is free, provided it is imported in ordinary condition.

(b) 20 per cent. ad valorem, and 55 4-5 cents additional for every 220 pounds.

FRANCE AND HER POSSESSIONS—TARIFFS—Continued.

DENOMINATION OF MERCHANDISE.	DUTIES ON IMPORTS. Into the United States from foreign nations, per cent. ad valorem, under the act of— 1846.	1857.	INTO FRANCE FROM FOREIGN NATIONS. Number, weight, or measure.	In national vessels.	In foreign vessels.	INTO FRENCH POSSESSIONS.	REMARKS.
Wool carpets, knotted, one side presenting a face of linen, as Brussels carpet.	30	24	220 pounds	$55 55$\frac{1}{2}$	$58 79	In Algiers and Corsica as in France; in Guiana and the West Indies, in foreign vessels, prohibited.	
All other carpets	30	24		Prohibited			
Zurich crape	30	24	220 pounds	37 03$\frac{1}{3}$	39 79$\frac{1}{2}$		
Cloth made for and to be used in paper mills.	30	24	do	37 03$\frac{1}{3}$	39 79$\frac{1}{2}$		
Hosiery of wool, of all kinds	30	24		Prohibited		Into Algiers, in French vessels, $1 24, in foreign, $1 38 per 220 pounds; in Corsica as in France; in Guiana and West Indies, in foreign vessels, prohibited.	Woolen tissues can be admitted in Guiana, in foreign vessels, into the entrepot fictif.
Lace work of pure wool, white.	30	24	220 pounds	35 18	37 40	In Algiers and Corsica as in France; in Guiana and the West Indies, in foreign vessels, prohibited.	All embroideries made with the hand on canvas are prohibited.
dyed	30	24	do	40 74	43 24		
mixed with thread, wool and hair.	30	24	do	40 74	43 24		
All woolen manufactures here not enumerated.	30	24		Prohibited		In Algiers, 25 per cent. ad valorem; in Corsica as in France; in Guiana and West Indies, in foreign vessels, prohibited.	
Yarns, cotton twist of No. 143 and under, simple.	25	24	2.20 pounds	1 30$\frac{3}{10}$	1 42	In Algiers and Corsica as in France; in Guiana and the West Indies, in foreign vessels, prohibited.	
threaded or twisted.	25	19	do	1 48$\frac{4}{5}$	1 62$\frac{9}{10}$		

FRANCE AND HER POSSESSIONS—TARIFFS—Continued.

Denomination of merchandise.	Duties on imports. Into the United States from foreign nations, per cent. ad valorem, under the act of— 1846.	1857.	Into France from foreign nations. Number, weight, or measure.	In national vessels.	In foreign vessels.	Into French possessions.	Remarks.
Yarns, all other cotton	25	24		Prohibited		In Algiers, 25 per cent. ad valorem; in Corsica as in France; in Guiana and West Indies, in foreign vessels, prohibited.	
linen	20	15		Note (a)		In Algiers and Corsica as in France; in Guiana and the West Indies, in foreign vessels, prohibited.	
threaded	20	15	2.20 pounds	$1 48 4/5	$1 69 9/10		
woolen	25	19		See Wool			
of goats' hair	25	19	220 pounds	3 70 1/3	4 07		
of cow and similar hair	25	19	do	1 67	1 83		
of Manila and Calcutta hemp, (phormium tenax,) raw.	20	15	do	11 23 1/2	12 26 1/2		
bleached	20	15	do	15 00	16 20		
dyed	20	15	do	14 81	16 01		
Zinc, calamine, stones	5	4	do	Free	18 3/5	In Algiers, zinc of the first fusion, either in masses, bars, or sheets, free; all other articles of, the same as in France; in Corsica, also, the same as in France; in Guiana and the West Indies, in foreign vessels, prohibited.	Zinc from China is known by the name of tutenag. In France, the admission of all zinc ore or pigs is free of duty, if to be laminated in France and afterwards exported.
ground	5	4	do	1 4/5	28		
fused into masses, ingots, sheets or bars.	15	12	do	1 4/5	28		
drawn and laminated	15	12	do	9 30	10 20		
manufactures of zinc	30	24		Prohibited			
sulphate of, (white vitriol.)	20	15	220 pounds	5 74	6 38 1/2		

(a) According to the number of threads, color, if twisted, or simply spun, &c., &c.

SPAIN

AND

HER POSSESSIONS.

SPAIN AND HER POSSESSIONS.

SPAIN AND THE BALEARIC ISLANDS.

The tariff is that of July 17, 1849, with changes and modifications down to June 5, 1853.(a)

Money.—100 centavos = 1 real

1 real plate = 10 cents, United States standard.

1 real vellon = 5 " "

Weights and measures.—1 arroba = 25.36 pounds, or 25 pounds 7 ounces, United States standard.

1 quintal = 4 arrobas = 101.44 pounds, United States standard.

1 arroba of wine = 4.43 gallons, "

1 fanega of grain = 1.60 bushels, "

1 tonelada = 20 quintals = 2,070½ pounds, avoirdupois.

1 pipe of wine = 30 arrobas. 1 vara = 33⅓ inches, English. 1 libra = 1 pound 3 drachms.

Articles not designated in the tariff pay a duty of 15 per cent. ad valorem in national vessels, and 18 per cent. ad valorem in oreign vessels and by land.

The value of goods paying an ad valorem duty is determined by the invoice. In event of dispute, the government may seize the goods by paying the importer 10 per cent. extra on the invoice valuation.

For the custom-house regulations respecting the importation of merchandise, the product of Spanish possessions in America; respecting importation from the depots of Havana and Porto Rico, of foreign produce; and respecting the importation of the produce of Spanish possessions in Asia, and of foreign countries of Asia, as well as details of custom-house regulations generally, and of moneys, weights, and measures; and the principles in accordance with which the tariff is formed, reference is directed to "Commercial Digests," vol. I, page 167.

(a) *Changes.*—For subsequent changes and modifications, reference is invited to Appendix and Annual Reports of the Secretary of State on Foreign Commerce.

TARIFF OF EXPORTATION.

DENOMINATION OF MERCHANDISE.	Number or weight, to which is affixed the duties in the next columns.	DUTIES.	
		In national vessels.	In foreign vessels, or by land.
	Quint.=101 lbs.		
Galena, (sulphuret of lead,) not argentiferous	do	$0 16	$0 21¼
Black copper, in the state of the first fusion	do	28¼	38
Iron girts or hoops, (*mena de hierro,*) from the province of Biscaya	do	5	5¼
Lead, in pigs	do	2¾	8
Litharge, containing less than 1 ounce of silver per quintal	do	31¾	42½
Silk, in cocoons	do	2 65	4 00
Timber for ship building (*a*)		5 per cent. ad valorem.	8 per ct. ad valorem.

(*a*) The exportation of woods for ship building is suspended, nntil the government shall otherwise direct, that the construction of merchantmen and men-of-war may not be interfered with, nor the interest of the owners of forests.

ARTICLES PROHIBITED TO BE EXPORTED.

1. Galena, (sulphuret of lead,) argentiferous.
2. Bark(*a*) of the cork, red and white oak, and all other trees used for tanning purposes.
3. Cork, in tablets, boards and pieces, from the province of Gerona.
4. Lead, having 24 adarmes, and over, of silver per quintal.
5. Litharge containing more than one ounce silver per 101 pounds.
6. Rags of cotton, hemp and linen, and things worn out of these materials.

ARTICLES THAT ARE PROHIBITED IMPORTATION INTO SPAIN.

1. Arms, projectiles and munitions, including every sort of gunpowder.
2. Boots and shoes, excepting those of travellers brought for their individual use.
3. Maps and plans, of Spanish authors, the copyright to which has not yet expired.
4. Books and prints in the Spanish language, by Spanish authors, when not introduced by the proprietors of the copyright; missals, breviaries, prayer books, and other books of the liturgy. Dictionaries and vocabularies are not to be understood as prohibited which do not infringe the copyright of Spanish authors as protected by the laws in force.
5. Cinnabar.
6. Common salt.
7. Charts published by the department of the marina and reprinted abroad.
8. Insignia, devices, and military ornaments
9. Grain, flour, biscuits, bread and pastries for soup, when not permitted to be introduced by the corn law.
10. Leaf tobacco from all countries.
11. Pharmaceutic preparations, such as are prohibited by sanitary laws.
12. Pictures, figures, and whatever is offensive to morality, or that ridicules the Catholic religion.
13. Ready-made clothing, that of travellers excepted, for their individual use.
14. Quicksilver.
15. Ships of wood of less than 400 tons burden, each ton being equal to 20 quintals.

ARTICLES OF WOOL, COTTON, LINEN, HEMP OR SILK, THAT ARE ALSO PROHIBITED.

1. Cotton yarn, up to number 59 inclusive.
2. Cotton spun in two or mo t reads, for sewing or embroidering, up to number 59 inclusive.

(*a*) The prohibition of this article is suspended until such time as legislation shall adjust the public charities and welfare with those of labor and commerce. In particular instances favorable to commerce or agriculture, her Majesty may direct the exportation from determinate quarters, when the act will not be consistent, as the petition therefor shall set forth, with the public interests and the preservation of the forests.

3. Unbleached or bleached cloths, dyed, striped, woven in color or printed, up to 25 threads inclusive, counted in the warp of a square inch, Spanish.

4. White handkerchiefs, colored or printed, up to 19 threads inclusive.

5. Scotch muslins and batistes, plain, white, striped or printed, up to 14 threads inclusive.

6. Lustrings and similar stuffs used in the making of artificial flowers, up to 19 threads inclusive.

7. Thick cloths, generally used for pantaloons, jackets, and other articles of men's clothing, twilled, checkered or otherwise, containing more than ⅛ of cotton, up to 19 threads inclusive.

8. Stuffs of silk, wool, linen, and hemp, being of more than one-third the weight of cotton, although they be of 2 threads.

9. Cotton cloths, having a mixture of silk, wool, linen and hemp, of twenty threads and over, should the cotton exceed the part of ⅛.

10. Knit stuffs, in stockings, drawers, shirts, &c., or other forms.

11. All manufactures by the hand, where cotton constitutes more than 50 per cent. of the weight.

TOBACCO.

The "High Junt" of the government of the province and city of Malaga has abolished the prohibition of manufactured and other tobacco, by a decree dated July 27, 1854, because, as it is asserted in the decree, "many citizens have been brought into prison for having, with a natural love of gain, tried to obtain, by smuggling this article, a subsistence for their families, whilst the real violators of the customs laws, the buyers, are becoming wealthy." The decree is as follows:

ART. 1. From and after the 6th August, 1854, the tobacco lying in the public warehouses shall be sold at prices fixed in a special tariff.

ART. 2. From and after the 8th August of the same year, the importation of raw and manufactured tobacco shall be permitted, after having previously paid the duties set down in the following tariff:

DENOMINATION OF THE DIFFERENT KINDS OF TOBACCO.	Number, weight, and measure.	Rate of duty in Spanish currency.	Rate of duty in American currency.
		Reals vellon.	
Cigars, from Havana, of all kinds	Per pound	18	$0 90
Cajetillas cigars, of all kinds	do	12	60
Do from the Philippines	do	6	30
Picadura	do	8	40
Snuff, (rappee,) of all kinds	do	10	50
Virginia cigars	do	5	25
Cigars from the Philippines	do	3	15
Raw Virginia tobacco, all kinds	do	3	15
Raw tobacco from the Philippines	do	2	10
Raw tobacco from Havana	do	5	25
Hazel colored snuff	do	8	40
Tusas(a) of Guatemala	do	18	90
Tusas of Spain	do	8	40

These rates are for Spanish vessels; foreign vessels pay rates one-third higher.

ART. 3. The importation of tobacco is permitted through the port of the city of Malaga alone, under the same formalities and rules as other colonial and foreign goods.

ART. 4. Should it be attempted to make a false custom-house declaration, in order to avoid the full amount of duty to be paid on tobacco, the penalty will be the same as in similar cases with other merchandise.

(a) A small cigar, covered with the finest husk of the corn.

APPENDIX.

Under date of September 29, 1855, an edition of a tariff, applicable to Spain and the Balearic Islands, framed in conformity to the bases of the law of July 17, 1849, was published in Madrid by royal authority, prepared under direction of the minister of the treasury, to take effect January 1, 1856, embodying all custom-house legislation subsequent to March 1, 1852, with notes and explanations, and presenting weights and measures, not only in accordance with the system now in force, but also in accordance with the decimal system, in adjacent parallel columns

A return from the United States consulate at Cadiz, dated October 3, 1855, an abstract of which is annexed, affords a resumé of interest relative to the tariff policy of Spain :

"Within the last twelve months, no variation has been made in the commercial system of Spain, its custom-house tariffs or regulations, as respects foreign commerce; and although during that period the Madrid Gazette—the official organ for dromulgating the laws and government dispositions—has published over twelve hundred decrees, royal orders, &c., not more than four of them have any reference to commercial matters. Spain is the last country in Europe to change her commercial system, or abolish long established monopolies. The reform of the custom-houses and tariffs in this country has always been a task before which every administration has retrograded; and, as if experience has not sufficed to afford conviction of the necessity of a change, no minister who has attained power has had the courage to complete the work commenced in 1849. The law of the 17th of July of that year authorized the government to revise the custom-house tariffs upon bases therein established, admitting certain classes of cotton fabrics; and the royal decree of 5th of October approved in all its parts the new custom-house regimen. In 1850 certain dispositions were made, some of them explanatory, and others reforming the custom-house instructions and tariffs; and in March, 1852, the government published an edition of both, which is the one at present in force. The Señor Bermudez de Castro, when minister of the treasury, endeavored to relieve the tariff of a number of trifling articles, of very small product to the public revenue, and by a royal decree of the 12th of May, 1853, they were declared of free entry; but by another decree of the 2d of June following, the duties previously levied on a part of these same articles were re-established.

Such may be said to be the brief history of the Spanish custom-houses, the complicated legislation of which, so prejudicial to commerce, still exists, and without teaching anything in a liberal sense to those who govern.

During the administration of Señor Collado, as minister of the treasury, there was no decree made relating to foreign commerce, except a royal order of 28th December, 1854, with direction to the *four* custom-houses of Corunna, Barcelona, Malaga, and Cadiz, for the admission of French scientific and literary works, in compliance with the convention between Spain and France respecting literary property, to go into effect the 1st of January, 1855. His successor, Señor Sevillano, made a slight reform in the nomenclature of certain classes of paper, called *continuo*, for papering habitations and writing—modifying the duties thereon one-fourth, and simplifying a few insignificant articles in the tariff; also, admitting the importation of sulphur, in a crude state, under foreign flags, at 8 reals 45 centimes, and the same article refined, or flour of sulphur, at 12 reals 35 centimes per quintal. Within the short period of one month this minister was succeeded by Señor Madoz; but in his time nothing was done nor any variation made, except one royal order changing what his predecessor had effected with respect to paper. This order has been criticized by the press, because neither the order nor the meaning thereof can be understood or obeyed. Señor Bruel, the present minister of the treasury, although he has not yet effected any change, appears to be endeavoring to establish a series of radical reforms in the various branches of the tariffs and custom-house regulations; moderating the duties on the introduction of *raw* materials, and enlarging the number of those articles not hitherto admitted to commerce. With the views and representations of this minister, to effect these objects, the Queen's decree of the 30th, and order thereon of the 31st of July of the present year, was issued, establishing a "*Junta consultina de aranceles*," or a board of consultation in relation to custom-house tariffs, regulations, and all matters relating to imports and exports, with extensive powers, and determining their attributions. The object of this board is declared to be to discuss and propose to the minister of the hacienda all reforms which they may conceive ought to be made in the custom-house tariffs, and to occupy themselves with, and direct all the proceedings which may be found with respect to the understanding of the same, their application and modification; as also, with respect to the reclamations of foreign powers, and those which ought to be made on the part of Spain, with respect to the agreements and treaties of navigation or commerce, and any other affair whatever relative to the mercantile legislation."

Changes.—By decrees of various dates, during the first half of 1857, the per centage decrease on previous rates on certain articles when imported in foreign vessels may be noted, approximately, as follows:(*a*)

On iron, in bits, padlocks, locks, stirrups, hinges, bolts, knees, &c., 65 per cent.; gilt or plated, vices, jacks, &c., 68; silk, floss, 87; spun or twisted, 62; cotton cloth, gummed, 75; oil, cocoa, and palm, 36.

On glass bottles, empty, for re-exportation; cobalt, enamel; canvas, white, silk twist; swords and sabres, all kinds; surgical instruments; razor cases with seven blades and one handle; whips with handles of tortoise shell, &c.; printing types of zinc; slates, polished, above eleven inches; handles of steel, and other fine metals, for sticks, parasols, &c.; and rings of tortoise shell or metal, gilt or plated, previously free, duties have been imposed, and the ad valorem rates on several articles have been raised.

(*a*) See note page 93.

CUBA.

The tariff is that of 1847, with changes and modifications up to February 1, 1853.(a)

Money.—1 dollar = 100 cents = $1 United States currency. Weights and measures generally the same as in Spain.

All articles not enumerated in the tariff are subject to the same duties as those to which they are analogous.

In virtue of the provisions and regulations of royal orders, Spanish flour, imported in Spanish bottoms, will pay the sole duty of $2 per barrel, and in foreign ships, $6. Foreign flour, imported in foreign ships, will pay $9 50, and in national ships, $8 50 per barrel; and in both cases there shall be paid an extraordinary duty of 2 per cent. on the value thereof, and 1 per cent. on the total amount of the duties.

In addition to the 33½, the 27½, and the 7½ per cent. designated by the tariff as the sole import duty, (in which rates are included the 1 per cent. consulado duty; the 2 per cent. extraordinary duty, by virtue of the royal orders of December 4, 1844; the ½ of 1 per cent. duty devoted to the redemption of the coupons of the Seville presetas,) there shall be collected at all the custom-houses on the island 1 per cent. balanza duty, that is, on the total amount of the duties paid, in accordance with the royal order of November 5, 1824, respecting imports and exports, with the exception only of those goods that have fixed rates, foreign flour not included.

By virtue of a royal order, dated November 3, 1850, there was declared on the 19th December of the same year an additional duty of 1½ per cent. on valuation of all foreign imports, and 1-7 to be charged over and above the amount up to that time paid on Spanish imports.

This increase was to cover certain necessities of the government, and was to be in force two years only. This additional per centage, is, however, still exacted. In the custom-houses of Havana and Matanzas, exclusively, are to be paid 50 cents on each pipe of wine, *aguardiente*, or liquors introduced; 25 cents on each half pipe; 12 cents on each demijohn; and 12 cents on the dozen flasks, bottles, or jugs; which amount is to cover the duty assigned for the *Casa de Beneficienc a.*

Several cloths in the tariff being assessed by the piece, according to the number of stated yards which they usually contain, no return of duty will be made for any deficiencies in such quantity, unless it exceeds 6 per cent. on the piece, and the fact be stated at the time of making the entry.

Cinnamon and *canelon* may be sold at public auction in the warehouse of damaged goods, though they may not have been injured, the duty being paid in accordance with the price they bring, unless it exceed the valuation of the tariff, when they will be subject to what it requires.

Ale, beer, porter, wines, cordials, spirituous liquors, Cologne water, olives, preserves, sweetmeats, &c., are subject to a deduction of 5 per cent.; bottles, pipes, crystals, demijohns, vials, and articles of china, earthen, and glass ware, &c., to a deduction of 6 per cent.; and jerked beef to a deduction of 14 per cent.

FREE LIST.

Asses, (jacks;) barks, for tanning purposes; boilers, of copper or iron; bottoms, of copper or iron; dice and chessmen, of iron; gold and silver, in bars, bullion, or coin; ice and snow; leeches; machines or centrifugal apparatus, for sugar fabrication; mills, for cleaning rice; molasses boilers, of copper or iron; mares; iron, pieces for the repair of machinery in steam engines and sugar mills; iron, to be placed as frame at the opening of ovens, both for baking and smelting purposes; iron crowns, for sugar mills; pans of copper or iron, for engines; pile engines, and cylinders or rollers, for sugar mills; purificative stuffs of copper or iron, for tanning purposes; plants, alive, and trees; pipes of iron, for engines; pieces of iron or steel, for paving purposes; paving stones; ploughs, of Roville; single or loose pieces, for repairing engines and sugar mills; silver, in bullion and coin; steam engines, with all apparatus, for refining syrup and sugar; skimmers of iron, for machines, &c.; stallions; square stones (flags for pavements) of the black stones of Antwerpen, and all similar, pay one-fourth less than marble of the respective dimensions; steam engines, for ingenious purposes; vats of copper or iron, for boiling down the sugar cane a second time.

(a) See "Consular Returns—Commerce," Vol. 3, pp. 126, 127.

TARIFF OF EXPORTATION.

Demomination of merchandise.	Number, weight, or measure.	Fixed value on the number, weight, or measure.	Per cent. ad valorem. For foreign ports. In foreign ships.	In national ships.	For national ports, in national ships.
Beeswax, yellow	Arroba, 25 lbs. 7 oz.	$3 00	7¼	4	3
white	Arroba	4 50	7¼	4	3
Cacao	Arroba	2 50	7¼	4	3
Cedar logs, squaring more than 24 inches	Vara, 33⅓ inches	3 00	7¼	4	3
from 15 to 24 inches	Vara	2 00	7¼	4	3
beams, under 15 inches	Vara	75	7¼	4	3
planks, the running	Vara	62	7¼	4	3
boards	Var	37	7¼	4	3
Copper ore, sole duty, 9 cents, (considered as equal to the cost of digging)	Quintal, 101 lbs				
Coffee	Quintal	4 00	5	3	3
Cigars, sole duty, 50 cents	Thousand				
paper, in paper boxes	Hundred	2 50	7¼	4	3
Gold, in bullion or coin	Ounce	16 00	2¼	2¼	
Hides, raw	One	1 50	7¼	4	3
Hogs, living, sole duty, $1 50	One				
Honey, the 100 gallons	Hogshead or bocoy	18 75	7¼	4	3
Horses and cattle, sole duty, $3 50	One				
Mahogany logs, and of all hard woods, of more than 24 inches	Vara	7 00	7¼	4	3
Mahogany logs, 15 to 24 inches	Vara	5 00	7¼	4	3
beams, up to 15 inches	Vara	2 50	7¼	4	3
plank	Vara	1 12	7¼	4	3
boards	Vara	75	7¼	4	3
Mules, sole duty, $4 50	One				
Preserves, of marmalade, or in syrup	Arroba	4 50	7¼	4	3
Silver, in bullion or coin	Pound	16 00	3¼	3¼	
Sugar of all kinds, sole duty, 37½ cents in foreign ships, 25 cents in national, the	Box				
Tobacco, leaf, sole duty, in foreign ships $1 50, in national 75 cents, the	Quintal				
Tobacco, in powder	Quintal	12 50	7¼	4	3
Tortoise shell	Pound	6 00	7¼	4	3
Woods, fustic, braziletto, lignum vitæ, and all other in stick, not mentioned in the tariff	Quintal	1 00	7¼	4	3

NOTE.—Logs and beams are measured by their widest parts.

Gold and silver, in bullion and coin, when registered in a foreign ship for a national port, are exempt from all duties.

Productions of the island not designated in this tariff are free of export duty.

PORTO RICO.

The tariff is that of August 2, 1849, with changes and modifications up to November 1, 185'.

MONEYS, WEIGHTS, AND MEASURES, the same as in Spain and Cuba.

The maquina piastre varies in value from 108 to 130 per hundred Spanish piastres.(*a*)

Duties may be paid at the rate of three-fourths in maquina to one-fourth Spanish.

Articles not included in the tariff are subject to rates levied on those to which they are analogous.

Imports, not produced in countries whence they come, will pay an additional duty of 2½ per cent. on the duties imposed by the tariff.(*b*)

Products of the island, timber excepted, are free from export duty.

For custom-house regulations in detail, and tonnage duties, see Digests, Vol. 1, p. 214.

FREE LIST.

Alembics, from Spain and in Spanish vessels ; asses, (jacks ;) boilers of iron or copper, for sugar works ; cylinders for sugar mills ; coggs of iron or steel, for sugar works ; curtains of iron or copper, for sugar works ; coal, (mineral ;) clarifiers of iron or copper, for sugar works ; flooring of iron or copper, for the ovens of sugar works ; gold in bars, bullion, and coin ; ice and snow ; iron mouth-pieces, for sugar engines ; iron chimneys, for sugar works ; jars of earthen, for sugar works ; leeches ; lime, (unslaked ;) mares ; manures, in Spanish vessels and from Spanish ports ; mills for hulling and cleaning rice, and for winnowing coffee, and shelling corn, and cleaning cotton, from Spain and in Spanish ships ; pieces (extra) of iron or steel, for repair of steam engines and sugar mills ; plants, (living,) from Spanish ports, and brought in Spanish bottoms ; Pumps, of iron ; ploughs, of Roville ; silver, in bullion and in coin ; seed, from Spain and in Spanish vessels ; skimmers, (of iron,) for sugar ; stallions ; steam engines, from Spain and in Spanish vessels ; stone coal ; trees, from Spain and in Spanish vessels ; vats, of copper or iron, for holding syrup.

REMARKS.

1. All machines for agricultural purposes, not mentioned in this tariff, provided they are Spanish products and are imp rted Spanish vessels, are free of duty ; whilst those of foreign make, or brought in foreign ships, according to the 4th section of the royal order of the 8th of August, 1851, pay 1 per cent.

2. Sacred vessels, ornaments, books of the choir, missals, church organs, and all other articles destined for the direct purpose worship in the churches, are free, if made in Spain and introduced in Spanish vessels, according to the royal order of the 29th of July, 1846 ; but in such cases the introduction is to be proceeded with by the steps pointed out by the *superintendencia*, according to its circular of the 28th April, 1851.

3. Military dress, and other like articles for the troops are free of duty, whenever it shall appear, in due form, that they have been manufactured in the kingdom from materials raised or made in it, according to the royal orders communicated to the *superintendencia* o the 27th March, 1845, 17th February, 1847, and 4th of February, 1848.

(*a*) The maquina or macuquina currency of the island is silver cut into various forms and shapes, and stamped to represent various fractions of a dollar. In its present mutilated state it takes from $20 to $24 to weigh as much as $16 round money; and the value varies according to the demand for round money to pay custom-house dues and to make remittances to foreign countries A similar currency exists in the Spanish colonies of South America, called *maquina de papalote y cruz*, or "windmill and cross money," the cross being not unlike the fan of a windmill. The coin was composed of lumps of bullion, gold or silver, flattened and impressed by a hammer, the edge presenting every variety of form except that of a circle, and affording ample scope for clipping. The device was a large cross of equal arms with loaded ends. The date of the coin is about a century since, but some of it bears date as late as 1770.

A royal order, dated May 5, 1857, published July 27 by the captain general of the island, provides for the entire extinction of the macuquina money, the government exchanging it for Spanish money at a discount of 12½ per cent. on the former. The amount in circulation at that date was estimated at $1,500,000, and the expenses of the exchange, recoining, &c., &c., was estimated at about 30 per cent. on that sum, for which loss the government indemnifies itself by an export duty on produce of the island, commencing August 4, and continuing until the amount is paid off, as follows: On sugar, 6¼ cents per 100 lbs.; on coffee, 25 cents per 100 lbs.; on tobacco, 87½ cents per 100 lbs.; on molasses, 50 cents per cask; on rum, $1 per cask.

(*b*) A circular from the superintendency general of Porto Rico, dated April 5, 1856, gives notice of the following important reductions in the duties on importations:

1. To favor the direct trade between the places of production and Porto Rico, a reduction of 6 per cent. in the duties imposed by t e tariff.

2d. That the fine of two per cent. additional duty, heretofore imposed on all goods coming from St. Thomas that by mistake were wrongly classed, be abolished.

3d. That the additional duty of 2½ per cent., heretofore charged on cargoes of vessels that called at any other port to try the market previous to coming to Porto Rico, be discontinued, provided the vessel does not discharge any part, but comes on with the full cargo, as originally shipped.

4th. That vessels which bring full cargoes for the deposit stores in this city shall be exempt from the payment of tonnage dues, which will be paid by the goods when they are entered for consumption, in addition to the import duties imposed by the tariff.

5th. That, to create funds for building new deposit stores, the deposit duty shall be raised to one per cent. every 6 months, payable in 24 hours after the deposit is made, and in the first 24 hours of the succeeding 6 months, instead of a half per cent., which has heretofore been paid.

TABLE OF TARES.

DENOMINATION OF MERCHANDISE.	RATES.
Hogsheads and casks (*tercios*) filled with sugar, coffee, hams, tallow, raw or purified, codfish, raw Virginia tobacco, rice, and North American cheese	10 per cent
Barrels of lard, similar to those containing salt pork	21 per cent
Firkins (*cuñetas*) filled with lard and butter	23 per cent
Barrels filled with hams, sugar, coffee, peas, onions, potatoes, and other dry vegetables, and fruits, subject to weight	20 pounds
Barrels and firkins filled with purgative salts, or cream of tartar	10 per cent
Barrels filled with cloves	6 per cent
Barrels similar to those in which ship bread (sea biscuit) is transported, according to size, if half or quarter barrels	20, 10, and 5 lbs.
Boxes filled with rhubarb, quinine, jalap, and other medicinal articles in powder, of only small weight, up to 12 pounds weight	4 pounds
Boxes filled with fine biscuit, tea, and similar articles, up to 25 net pounds	9 per cent
Boxes of cinnamon up to 140 pounds, net weight	18 per cent
Boxes of codfish	18 per cent
Boxes filled with spermaceti, composition, or tallow candles, or soap	20 per cent
Boxes of flour paste	26 per cent
Boxes and firkins with Manila tobacco	24 per cent
Boxes of sugar from Havanna	14 per cent
Baskets with flour paste or potatoes	4 pounds
Bags of all sizes with cinnamon	7 per cent
Bales, linen, filled with raw Virginia tobacco, of which 4 make a hogshead	4 pounds
Bales of twine, and of lines for fishing	1 pound
Hide or skin bales of cotton, up to 100 pounds, net weight	8 pounds
Sacks filled with potatoes and cabbages	1 pound
Sacks of coffee, rice, peas, and other pulse, up to 100 pounds, net weight	1 pound
The same, up to 150 to 200 pounds	2 pounds
Sacks filled with almonds, aniseed, canary seed, and filberts, up to 100 pounds, net weight	1 pound
Sacks filled with senna leaves, nuts, hops, and other similar articles, up to 150 to 200 pounds, net weight	3 pounds
Sacks filled with cocoa, up to 165 pounds, net weight	1½ pound
Sacks filled with black pepper, up to 100 pounds, net weight	1½ pound
Sacks filled with pimento, or ground pepper, up to 150 pounds, net weight	4 pounds
Hampers filled with raw St. Domingo tobacco	10 pounds
Hampers filled with lavender and rosemary	12 pounds
Hampers filled with potatoes, biscuits, or onions	22 pounds
Wax in cakes, wrapped up in nankeen or other cloth	1 pound
Bags filled with indigo, up to 100 pounds, net weight	16 pounds

TARIFF OF EXPORTATION.

DENOMINATION OF MERCHANDISE.	Number, weight, or measure.	Fixed value on the number, weight, or measure.	PER CENT. AD VALOREM.		
			For foreign ports.		For national ports in national ships.
			In foreign ships.	In national ships.	
Aguardiente	Pipe or hogshead	$25 00	Free		
Bricks and tiles	Thousand	8 00	Free		
Barrigone, (gorbellies,) of all sizes	One	35 00	20	13	5
Benches, of wood, for sugar mills	One	25 00	20	13	5
Boards, of carob, 4 yards long, and 1½ inches thick	One	1 50	20	13	5
of capá, tortugo, and yaiti, 4 yards long × 1½ inches thick	One	1 50	20	13	5
of cedar, 4 yards long × 1½ inches thick	One	2 00	20	13	5
Beams, large and crowns	One	10 00	20	13	5
middle	One	5 00	20	13	5
large, for houses	One	6 25	20	13	5
middling	One	4 00	20	1	5
small, of 5 to 6 yards	One	3 00	20	13	5
Cabezotas, 8 or 9 yards long	One	75 00	20	13	5
middle sized, 5 or 6 yards long	One	50 00	20	13	5
Cotton, in seed	Quintal = 101 lbs.	5 00	Free		
clean	Quintal	10 00	Free		
Clubs of wood, for sugar mills and other uses, 5 to 8 yards long, and 20 to 24 inches in diameter	One	1 00	20	13	5
Charcoal	Quintal	1 00	Fr e		
Cross-bars, of onca and anzuba wood	One	38 00	20	13	5
Coffee, all	Quintal	6 00	Free		
Crowns, (coronas)	One	20 00	Free		
Espinilla	Quintal	75	20	13	5
Fustics, braziletto, guayacan, and other kinds of wood in small trunks, not given in the tariff	Quintal	2 00	20	13	5
Gold, bullion, and in coin	Ounce	16 00	2	2	
Horns, cows', natural	Hundred	1 50	Free		
lesser, natural	Hundred	75	Free		
Hides, raw, of horses and cattle	Quintal	9 00	Free		
of sheep and goats	Quintal	50	Free		
Honey	100 gall. hogsheads.	18 77	Free		
Joists, of aceittillo and yaiti	One	1 50	20	13	5
of the algarroba	One	1 25	20	13	5
of the capá	One	75	20	13	5
of all other kinds of wood	One	50	20	13	5
Lignumvitæ	Ton	15 00	20	13	5
Mulberry timber, (palo mora)	Quintal	75	20	13	5
Mangrove bark	Quintal	1 00	Free		
Maize, shelled	Fanega = 1½ bush's	2 50	Free		

TARIFF OF EXPORTATION—Continued.

Denomination of merchandise.	Number, weight, or measure.	Fixed value on the number, weight, or measure.	Per cent. ad valorem. For foreign ports. In foreign ships.	In national ships.	For national ports in national ships.
Maize, on the ear	Quintal	$0 37½	Free		
Nudoz or nues, (knots and nuts)	One	30 00	20	13	5
Pepper, Tabasco	Quintal	6 00	Fr		
Plank, of cedar, 4 yards in length by 4 inches thick	One	5 00	20	13	5
of carob, 4 yards in length by 20 to 24 inches wide, and 4 inches thick	One	6 00	20	13	5
of capá	One	2 00	20	13	5
of anzuba	One	5 00	20	13	5
Posts or stakes, chopped in the centre, 3 yards long, of cajaoba, anzuba, and limoncillo wood	One	1 00	20	13	5
the same doubled	One	2 00	20	13	5
without being worked, of 3½ yards length, and 6 inches in diameter	One	75	20	13	5
of 6⅔ yards length, and 6 inches in diameter	One	1 50	20	13	5
of 9 yards length, and 10 to 12 inches in diameter	One	5 00	20	13	5
worked, of cajaoba and anzuba	Per foot	37½	20	13	5
Rabos, (in paper or other mills, the tail which supports the hammer that beats the pulp,) large ones	One	50 00	20	13	5
middle sized	One	35 00	20	13	5
Rice, in the hull	Fanega	2 00	Free		
Rollizas, single	One	8 00	20	13	5
double	One	16 00	20	13	5
triple	One	24 00	20	13	5
Silver, bullion and coin	Pound	16 00	3	2	
Shelves and props, of 8 to 10 cubic inches, and 6 yards long	One	8 00	20	13	5
Spindles and pendules	One	50 00	20	13	5
Springs of wood, for machines, &c	One	12 00	20	13	5
Starch	Quintal	5 00	Free		
Sugar, of all kinds	Quintal	3 00	Free		
Sugar-cane	Hundred	1 00	Free		
Trunks and logs, of cedar, algarroba, or capá, 3 to 4 yards long, and 10 to 12 inches square	One	12 00	20	13	5
Tortoise shell	Pound	8 00	Free		
Woods, in sticks, of the mahogany— 3 feet in length	One	1 00	20	13	5
6 feet in length	One	2 00	20	13	5
Same, not reduced 3⅓ varas in length, and 6 inches in diameter	One	75	20	13	5
Same, 6⅔ varas long, 6 inches in diameter	One	1 50	20	13	5

TARIFF OF EXPORTATION—Continued.

Denomination of merchandise.	Number, weight, or measure.	Fixed value on the number, weight, or measure.	Per cent. ad valorem.		
			For foreign ports.		For national ports in national ships.
			In foreign ships.	In national ships.	
Woods, in sticks, of the mahogany—Continued.					
Same, 9 varas in length, 10 to 12 inches in diameter	One	$5 00	20	13	5
Same, wrought	Per foot	37½	20	13	5
Joists, 6 varas in length, squaring from 8 to 10 inches	One	8 00	20	13	5
wood, in blocks, for mills, or other purposes, 5 to 8 varas in length, and 20 to 24 inches diameter	One	16 00	20	13	5
Wood	Horse load	50	Fr e		

COMPARATIVE

UNITED STATES AND SPAIN

DENOMINATION OF MERCHANDISE.	DUTIES ON IMPORTS.				
	Into the United States from foreign nations, per cent. ad valorem, under the act of—		TARIFF OF GENERAL IMPORTATION INTO SPAIN.		
	1846.	1857.	Number, weight, or measure.	In national vessels.	In foreign vessels.
Acetate of lead	20	15	1 libra, 1 lb. 3 drs.	$0 01	$0 01¼
morphia	30	24	Ounce	32	42½
potash	20	15	1 lb. 3 drs	25 per cent.	30 per cent.
Acid, boracic	20	4	do	1½	2
muriatic	20	4	do	4¼	5¼
sulphuric	10	4	1 quintal, 101 lbs.	53	63½
oxalic	20	4	1 lb. 3 drs	2¾	3¼
tartaric	20	4	do	4¾	5¾
All other acids(*a*)	20	4	do	8	9½
Adzes	30	24	do	3¼	4
Alba canella	20	15	do	3¾	5¼
Almonds, with shells	40	30	1 aroba, 25 lbs. 7 oz.	21¼	25½
Almonds, without	40	30	do	55¾	66¾
paste	30	24	1 lb. 3 drs	16	19
Aloes	20	4	do	6¼	7¾
Alum, common	20	15	25 lbs. 7 oz	10½	12¾
Amber, crude	20	4	1 lb. 3 drs	4¼	5¼
Ambergris	20	4	do	2 39	2 50
Anchors, or parts thereof	30	24	101 lbs	1 06	1 50
Angora, goat's hair	20	15	25 lbs. 7 oz	7¾	10
Animals for improving the breed—					
Horses	Free	Free	Each	4 25 to 6 35	$5 to 7 50
Asses	Free	do	do	1 27½	1 44
Goats of Thibet	Free	do	do	6¼	12
Sheep, German	Free	do	do	4¾	9½
Bulls and cows	Free	do	do	3 60	4 35
Animals, otherwise—					
Geldings	20	Free	do	85 00	106 00
Mules over 3 years	20	Free	do	10 60	12 70
Oxen and cows over 2 years	20	Free	do	3 20	3 80
Aniseed	20	4	1 lb. drs	5	6
oil of	30	24	do	5¼	6¼

(*a*) All other acids used for chemical or medicinal purposes, or for manufacturing, or in th fine arts, not otherwise provided for.

TARIFFS.

AND HER POSSESSIONS.

DUTIES ON IMPORTS.

TARIFF OF IMPORTATION INTO THE ISLAND OF CUBA.					TARIFF OF IMPORTATION INTO THE ISLAND OF PORTO RICO.				
		Per centage duty on the fixed value.					Per centage duty on the fixed value.		
Number, weight, or measure.	Fixed value on the number, weight, or measure.	Foreign productions under a foreign flag.	Foreign productions under the national flag, and those of Spain under a foreign flag.	Foreign productions under the national flag, imported from Spain proper.	Number, weight, or measure.	Fixed value on the number, weight, or measure.	Foreign productions under a foreign flag.	Foreign productions under the national flag, and those of Spain under a foreign flag.	Foreign productions under the national flag, imported from Spain proper.
101 lbs	$18 75	27½	19½	19½	101 lbs	$18 50	23	16	16
Ounce	3 00	27½	19½	19½	Ounce	3 00	23	16	16
1 lb. 3 drs	50	27½	19½	19½	1 lb. 3 drs	50	23	16	16
....do	75	27½	19½	19½	....do	75	23	16	16
25 lbs. 7 oz	1 50	27½	19½	19½	....do	1 50	23	16	16
....do	1 50	27½	19½	19½	101 lbs	6 00	23	16	16
1 lb. 3 drs	50	27½	19½	19½	1 lb. 3 drs	75	23	16	16
....do	50	27½	19½	19½	....do	50	23	16	16
....	Valuation.	27½	19½	19½	....	Valuation.	23	16	16
....	Valuation.	27½	19½	19½	....	Valuation.	23	16	16
1 lb. 3 drs	1 00	27½	19½	19½	1 lb. 3 drs	1 00	23	16	16
25 lbs. 7 oz	1 25	33½	23½	23½	101 lbs	5 00	29	20	20
....do	4 00	33½	23½	23½	....do	16 00	29	20	20
1 lb. 3 drs	25	27½	19½	19½	1 lb. 3 drs	25	23	16	16
....do	25	27½	19½	19½	....do	37½	23	16	16
25 lbs. 7 oz	1 25	27½	19½	19½	101 lbs	25 00	23	16	16
1 lb. 3 drs	50	27½	19½	19½	1 lb. 3 drs	50	23	16	16
Ounce	2 00	27½	19½	19½	Ounce	4 00	23	16	16
101 lbs	6 50	33½	23½	23½	101 lbs	8 00	29	20	20
25 lbs 7 oz	7 00	27½	19½	19½	....do	25 00	23	16	16
}	Stallions, mares, and jackasses free				....	Stallions, mares, jackasses, and asses, free.			
}	Valuation.	33½	23½	23½	....	Valuation.	23	16	16
25 lbs. 7 oz	1 50	33½	23½	23½	101 lbs	8 00	29	20	20
1 lb. 3 drs	2 00	27½	19½	19½	1 lb. 3 drs	2 00	23	16	16

TARIFFS—Continued.

Denomination of merchandise.	Duties on imports. Into the United States from foreign nations, per cent. ad valorem, under the act of—		Tariff of general importation into Spain.		
	1846.	1857.	Number, weight, or measure.	In national vessels.	In foreign vessels.
Antimony, crude	20	8	1 lb. 3 drs	$0 01½	$0 01¾
regulus of	20	8	do	2½	3
Anvils	30	24	101 lbs	3 18	3 80
Apparatus, philosophical	According to material.			15 per cent.	18 per cent.
Arabic, gum	10	8	1 lb. 3 drs	2	2¾
Argol or argal, crude tartar	5	Free	do	4¾	5¾
Arrack	100	30	1 arroba, or 4.245 gallons.	1 06	1 32¼
Arsenic	15	4	101 lbs	79½	95½
Articles of gold or silver	30	24		6 per cent	6
Artificial flowers	30	24	1 lb. 3 drs	3 18	3 80
Asafœtida	20	4	do	3	4
Bacon	20	15	25 lbs. 7 oz	63½	76¼
Baizes and bockings	25	19	1 lb. 3 drs	42½	50¾
Balsam, copaiba, in capsules	30	24	do	32	38
Band iron, slit, rolled, or hammered	30	24	101 lbs	1 60	2 65
Barilla	10	4	do	63½	77¼
Barley, hulled, pearl or other	20	15	25 lbs. 7 oz(a)	9½	11¾
Bark, Alcornoque, tanners'	5	4	101 lbs	6¼	8¼
Jesuits', or Peruvian	15	Free	1 lb. 3 drs	10½	12½
Bars, brass, in	5	Free	101 lbs	8 50	10 60
copper, in	5	Free	do	2 38½	3 20
iron	30	24	do	2 12	2 54¼
lead, in	20	15	do	95½	1 14½
tin, in	5	Free	do	1 59	1 90
Beads, purses, with metal clasps	30	24		30 per cent	36 per ct
wax	30	24	1 lb. 3 drs	63½	76¼
glass	30	24	do	3¼	4
Beans, vanilla	20	15	do	32	42½
tonka, or tonqua	20	15	do	32	42½
Beef	20	15	25 lbs. 7 oz	31¾	38¼
Beer, ale, and porter, in bottles	30	24			
in casks	30	24	4.245 gallons	55¾	66¾

(a) 200 lbs. = 3 bushels

TARIFFS—Continued.

DUTIES ON IMPORTS.

TARIFF OF IMPORTATION INTO THE ISLAND OF CUBA.					TARIFF OF IMPORTATION INTO THE ISLAND OF PORTO RICO.				
		Per centage duty on the fixed value.					Per centage duty on the fixed value.		
Number, weight, or measure.	Fixed value on the number, weight, or measure.	Foreign productions under a foreign flag.	Foreign productions under the national flag, and those of Spain under a foreign flag.	Foreign productions under the national flag, imported from Spain proper.	Number, weight, or measure.	Fixed value on the number, weight, or measure.	Foreign productions under a foreign flag.	Foreign productions under the national flag, and those of Spain under a foreign flag.	Foreign productions under the national flag, imported from Spain proper.
25 lbs. 7 oz......	$2 00	27½	19½	19½	101 lbs.........	$8 00	23	16	16
1 lb. 3 drs.......	25	27½	19½	19½	1 lb. 3 drs......	25	23	16	16
101 lbs..........	7 50	33½	23½	23½	101 lbs.........	10 00	29	20	20
....	Valuation.	27½	19½	19½	....	Valuation.	23	16	16
25 lbs. 7 oz......	6 00	27½	19½	19½	101 lbs.........	16 00	23	16	16
101 lbs..........	6 00	27½	19½	19½	....	6 00	23	16	16
4.245 gallons	5 00	33½	23½	23½	Dozen bottles ...	4 50	29	20	20
101 lbs	12 50	27½	19½	19½	101 lbs.........	12 50	23	16	16
Valuation	Valuation...	7½	5½	5½	....	Valuation ..	6	4	4
Dozen	3 75	27½	19½	19½	Dozen..........	3 75	23	16	16
1 lb. 3 drs	25	27½	19½	19½	1 lb. 3 drs......	25	23	16	16
25 lbs. 7 oz	2 00	33½	23½	23½	101 lbs.........	9 00	29	20	20
1.08 yard	25	33½	23½	23½	1.08 yard.......	50	29	20	20
....	Valuation...	27½	19½	19½	....	Valuation ..	23	16	16
101 lbs	6 00	33½	23½	23½	101 lbs.........	8 00	29	20	20
......do........	2 00	27½	19½	19½	......do........	2 00	23	16	16
25 lbs. 7 oz	1 50	27½	19½	19½	1½ bushel.......	6 00	23	16	16
......do........	1 25	33½	23½	23½	101 lbs.........	5 00	29	20	20
101 lbs , yellow..	12 50	27½	19½	19½	101 lbs., yellow .	12 50	23	16	16
101 lbs	25 00	33½	23½	23½	101 lbs.........	25 00	23	16	16
......do........	15 00	27½	19½	19½	......do........	16 00	23	16	16
......do........	3 25	33½	23½	23½	......do........	4 00	29	20	20
......do........	4 00	27½	19½	19½	......do........	4 00	23	16	16
......do........	20 00	27½	19½	19½	......do........	20 00	23	16	16
One	75	27½	19½	19½	One	Valuation ..	23	16	16
144 strings......	Valuation. $1 50 to $2.	27½	19½	19½	{ 12 strings ..... A gross	75 3 00 }	23	16	16
1 lb. 3 drs.......	25	27½	19½	19½	1 lb. 3 drs......	1 00	23	16	16
100............	5 50	2	2	2	......do........	5 00	23	16	16
100............	5 50	2	2	2	......do........	5 00	23	16	16
Barrel	9 00	33½	23½	23½	Barrel	9 00	23½	17¼	17¼
Dozen	3 00	33½	23½	23½	Dozen	2 00	29	20	20
4.245 gallons	1 50	33½	23½	23½	112 quarts......	6 25	29	20	20

TARIFFS—Continued.

DENOMINATION OF MERCHANDISE.	DUTIES ON IMPORTS.				
	Into the United States from foreign nations, per cent. ad valorem, under the act of—		TARIFF OF GENERAL IMPORTATION INTO SPAIN.		
	1846.	1857.	Number, weight, or measure.	In national vessels.	In foreign vessels.
Beeswax, yellow	20	15	25 lbs 7 oz	$1 06	$1 27¼
white	20	15	do	1 59	1 90¾
Bergamot, oil and essence	30	24	1 lb. 3 drs	16	19
Berries, juniper	20	15	25 lbs. 7 oz	16	19
Birds, intended for sale	20	Free	Each	79½	95½
Bismuth	20	Free		Free	Free
Blacksmiths' hammers and sledges	30	24	1 lb. 3 drs	3¼	4
Blank books, bound or unbound	20	15	25 lbs. 7 oz	5 30	6 35
Blankets, of wool	20	15	Each	Com'n, 1 27¼	1 52½
Bole, Armenian	20	15	1 lb. 3 drs	1½	1¾
Bolts, of iron	30	24	101 lbs	31 80	38 50
of copper	30	24	1 lb. 3 drs	25½	31¾
Bonnets for women, other than leghorn	30	24	do	Wool, 1 80	2 30
				Silk, 2 65	3 18
Books, blank, bound or unbound	20	15	25 lbs. 7 oz	5 30	6 35
Boots and bootees	30	24	Prohibited, except those of travellers		
Botany, specimens of	Free	Free		Free	
Boxes, paper	30	24	Dozen	19	22¾
Braces	30	24	Dozen	80	1 00
Bracelets, hair	30	24	1 lb. 3 drs	6 64½	9 95
Brads, of all sizes	30	24	101 lbs	3 20	4 20
Brandy	100	30	4.245 galls	1 07	1 32½
Brass, all manufactures of	30	24	1 lb. 3 drs	37	43¾
in bars, blocks, or pigs	5	Free	101 lbs	8 50	10 60
kettles	30	24	1 lb. 3 drs	17	21¼
wire	30	24	101 lbs	13 25	17 50
saddlery	30	24	1 lb. 3 drs	37	43¾
old, and unfit for use	5	Free	101 lbs.	8 50	10 60
Braziers' copper	20	15	1 lb. 3 drs	17	21¼
Brazil paste	15	12	1 lb. 3 drs	32	38
Braziletto	5	Free	101 lbs	6¼	8½

TARIFFS—Continued.

DUTIES ON IMPORTS.

TARIFF OF IMPORTATION INTO THE ISLAND OF CUBA.					TARIFF OF IMPORTATION INTO THE ISLAND OF PORTO RICO.				
		Per centage duty on the fixed value.					Per centage duty on the fixed value.		
Number, weight, or measure.	Fixed value on the number, weight, or measure.	Foreign productions under a foreign flag.	Foreign productions under the national flag, and those of Spain under a foreign flag.	Foreign productions under the national flag, imported from Spain proper.	Number, weight, or measure.	Fixed value on the number, weight, or measure.	Foreign productions under a foreign flag.	Foreign productions under the national flag, and those of Spain under a foreign flag.	Foreign productions under the national flag, imported from Spain proper.
Prohibited					101 lbs	$15 00	29	20	20
do					do	37 50	29	20	20
1 lb. 3 drs	$1 25	27½	19½	19½	1 lb. 3 drs	1 75	23	16	16
25 lbs. 7 oz	2 00	27½	19½	91½	101 lbs	8 00	23	16	16
Dozen	7 50	33½	23½	23½	Dozen	7 50	29	20	20
1 lb. 3 drs	75	27½	19½	19½	1 lb. 3 drs	75	23	16	16
Dozen	3 00	27½	19½	19½		Valuation	23	16	16
One	62½ cents to $12, according to size.	33½	23½	23½	62½ cents to $12, according to size.		29	20	20
	Valuation	27½	19½	19		Valuation	23	16	16
25 lbs. 7 oz	1 00	27½	19½	19½	101 lbs	4 00	23	16	16
Dozen	1 50	33½	23½	23½	Dozen	2 25	29	20	20
do	12 00	33½	23½	23½	do	12 00	29	20	20
One	2 25	27½	19½	19½	One	Valuation	23	16	16
25 lbs. 7 oz	6 25	33½	23½	23½	101 lbs	$25 to $50	23	16	16
For men and boys, pairs; for wo doz. pairs; for per doz. pairs.	$15 per doz men, $9 per children, $3	33½	23½	23½	For men and dozen pairs; $9 per dozen children, $4 50 pairs.	boys, $15 per for women, pairs; for per dozen	29	20	20
			Free				Free		
Dozen	2 25	27½	19½	19½	Dozen	3 00	23	16	16
do	1 00 to 2 00	27½	19½	19½	Dozen	1 00	23	16	16
	Valuation.	27½	19½	19½		Valuation.	23	16	16
101 lbs	37 50	27½	19½	19½	101 lbs	37 50	23	16	16
Dozen bottles	4 50	33½	23½	23½	Dozen bottles	6 00	29	20	20
101 lbs	37 50	33½	23½	23½	1 lb. 3 drs	50	23	16	16
25 lbs. 7 ozs	6 25	33½	23½	23½	101 lbs	25 00	23	16	16
101 lbs	37 50	33½	23½	23½	1 lb. 3 drs	50	23	16	16
do	37 50	33½	23½	23½	do	37½	23	16	16
	Valuation.	33½	22½	23½	do	50	23	16	16
101 lbs	10 00	27½	19½	19½	101 lbs	10 00	23	16	16
do	37 50	33½	23½	23½	1 lb. 3 drs	50	23	16	16
1 lb. 3 drs	1 00	27½	19½	19½	do	1 00	23	16	16
101 lbs	2 25	2	2	2	101 lbs.	2 00	1	1	1

TARIFFS—Continued.

DENOMINATION OF MERCHANDISE.	DUTIES ON IMPORTS.				
	Into the United States from foreign nations, per cent. ad valorem, under the act of—		TARIFF OF GENERAL IMPORTATION INTO SPAIN.		
	1846.	1857.	Number, weight, or measure.	In national vessels.	In foreign vessels.
Bricks	20	15	M.	$1 90	$2 54½
Bridles	30	24		30 per cent.	40 per cent.
Brimstone and sulphur, lac	15	4	101 lbs	1 19¼	1 43
Bristles	5	4		Free	Free
Brown sugar	30	24	25 lbs. 7 oz	85	1 06
Buckles, iron or tin, for braces	30	24	1 lb. 3 drs	8	9½
Bullion, of gold or silver	Free	Free			Free
Busts, according to material	Free	Free		25 per cent.	30 per cent
Butter	20	15	1 lb. 3 dr	8½	10½
Buttons, mother of pearl	25	19	do	20	24
Cables, tarred or untarred	25	19	101 pounds	3 18	3 81½
			tarre	Free	Free
iron chain	30	24	101 pounds	31¾	42½
Camlets of goat and camels' hair	25	19	1 lb. 3 drs	12	14¼
Cambrics	20	15	101 pounds	119 25	148 40
Camels' hair, in raw state	10	8	25 lbs. 7 oz	7¾	10
Camphor, gum	25	8	1 lb. 3 drs	16	19
Candles, spermaceti	20	15	do	8	9½
tallow	20	15	25 lbs. 7 oz		95½
wax	20	15	1 lb. 3 drs	9¼	11¼
Canella, alba	20	15	do	3¾	5¼
Cannon, brass or iron	30	24		rohibited	
Cantharides	20	8	do	16	19
Caps and hats, of fur, leather, &c	30	24	One	1 32½	1 59
of silk	30	24	1 lb. 3 drs	3 18	3 71½
Carbonate of soda	20	8		Free	Free
Cards, playing	30	24	Dozen	30 per ct.	36 per ct.
Carriages, all kinds and parts of	30	24		25 per ct.	30 per ct.
springs for	30	24	101 pounds	4 24	5 10
Cascarilla bark	20	8		Free	Free
Cashmere of Thibet	30	24	1 lb. 3 drs	12	14¼
shawls	30	24	do	12	14¼
Cassia	40	4	do	3¼	5¼
oil of	30	24	do	95½	1 27½

TARIFFS—Continued.

DUTIES ON IMPORTS.

TARIFF OF IMPORTATION INTO THE ISLAND OF CUBA.					TARIFF OF IMPORTATION INTO THE ISLAND OF PORTO RICO.				
Number, weight, or measure.	Fixed value on the number, weight, or measure.	Per centage duty on the fixed value.			Number, weight, or measure.	Fixed value on the number, weight, or measure.	Per centage duty on the fixed value.		
		Foreign productions under a foreign flag.	Foreign productions under the national flag, and those of Spain under a foreign flag.	Foreign productions under the national flag, imported from Spain proper.			Foreign productions under a foreign flag.	Foreign productions under the national flag, and those of Spain under a foreign flag.	Foreign productions under the national flag, imported from Spain proper.
M..............	$12 00	33½	23½	23½	M...with the fire common	mark $16 00	29	20	20
....	Valuation.	27½	19½	19½	....	Vl tion.	23	16	16
101 lbs..........	3 00	27$\frac{1}{1}$	19½	19½	101 lbs..........	3 00	23	16	16
....do..........	For brushes, 12 50	27½	19½	19½	..do..........	37 50	23	16	16
Prohibited	Prohibited.	....	....	....	..do..........	9 00	4	4	4
12 pairs	1 00	27½	19½	19½	12 pairs	1 00	23	16	16
....	Free......	....	....	....	....	Free......	....	....	....
....	Valuation.	27½	19½	19½	....	Valuation.	23	16	16
101 lbs..........	16 00	27½	19½	19½	101 lbs..........	16 00	23	16	16
Gross...........	75	27½	19½	19½	Gross..........	75	29	20	20
						to 3 00	23	16	16
101 pounds......	12 00	33½	23½	23½	101 lbs..........	12 00	29	20	20
......do........	7 00	33½	23½	23½	......do........	8 00	29	20	20
25 lbs. 7 oz......	6 30	27½	19½	19½	......do........	25 00	23	16	16
....	Valuation ..	27½	19½	19½	....	Valuation ..	23	16	16
25 lbs. 7 oz......	5 00	27½	19½	19½	1 lb. 3 drs......	25	23	16	16
1 lb. 3 drs......	50	27½	19½	19½	......do........	50	23	16	16
101 pounds......	32 00	27½	19½	19½	101 lbs..........	32 00	23	16	16
......do........	12 00	33½	23½	23½	......do........	12 00	29	20	20
......do........	62 50	33½	23½	23½	......do........	62 50	29	20	20
1 lb. 3 drs......	1 00	27½	19½	19½	1 lb. 3 drs......	1 00	23	16	16
101 lbs., iron....	4 50	33½	23½	23½	101 lbs..........	4 50	29	20	20
1 lb. 3 drs......	75	27½	19½	19½	1 lb. 3 drs......	1 25	23	16	16
....	Valuation ..	33½	23½	23½	....	Valuation ..	23	16	16
Dozen	4 50	33½	23½	23½	Dozen	4 50	29	20	20
25 lbs. 7 oz......	1 50	27½	19½	19½	101 lbs..........	6 00	23	16	16
Gross...........	12 00	33½	23½	23½	Gross..........	12 00	29	20	20
One	750 00	33½	23½	23½	One	750 00	29	20	20
For one carriage..	7 50	27½	19½	19½	For one carriage.	7 50	23	16	16
1 lb. 3 drs......	25	27½	19½	19½	1 lb. 3 drs......	25	23	16	16
25 lbs. 7 oz......	6 30	27½	19½	19½	101 lbs..........	25 00	23	16	16
......do........	6 30	27½	19½	19½	......do........	25 00	23	16	16
......do........	3 25	27½	19½	19½	......do........	12 00	23	16	16
1 lb. 3 drs......	3 00	27½	19½	19½	1 lb. 3 drs......	3 00	23	16	16

TARIFFS—Continued.

DENOMINATION OF MERCHANDISE.	DUTIES ON IMPORTS. Into the United States from foreign nations, per cent. ad valorem, under the act of—		TARIFF OF GENERAL IMPORTATION INTO SPAIN.		
	1846.	1857.	Number, weight, or measure.	In national vessels.	In foreign vessels.
Castings, iron, for vessels	30	24	2,020 lbs	....	$2 65
all other	30	24	101 pounds	$1 60	2 10
Castor, oil of	20	15	1 lb. 3 drs	5¼	6¼
Casts, of bronze or plaster	30	24	....	15 per ct	18 per ct
Catsup	30	24	1 lb. 3drs	5¾	7½
Chafing dishes, of copper	30	24	do	25½	31¾
Chamomile flowers	20	15	do	4¼	5¼
Cheese, common	30	24	25 lbs. 7 oz	90	95
other kinds	30	24	do	1 07	1 27
Cherry brandy, or rum	100	30	4.245 gallons	1 06	1 32½
Chesnuts, castanas	30	24	25 lbs. 7 oz	23¾	28½
China ware	30	24	piece	2 65	3 18
Chip hats, or bonnets	30	24	do	30 per cent.	36 per ct.
Chisels, socket and other	30	24	1 lb 3 drs	6¼	7¾
Chocolate	20	15	do	10½	12⅓
Chromate of potash	20	15	do	3¼	4
Cinnamon	30	4	do	26½	31¾
oil of	30	24	do	95½	1 27¼
Citron, fruit	20	8	25 lbs. 7 oz	8	9½
Clothing, ready made	30	24	....	....	Prohibited.
Cloves	40	4	1 lb. 3 drs	11¾	15
oil of	30	24	do	6¼	7¾
Coal, stone	30	24	101 pounds	8	10⅒
hods, of copper	30	24	1 lb. 3 drs	17	21¼
Cochineal	10	4	1 lb	16	19
Cocoa(a)	10	4			
from the Spanish colonies	....	....	101 pounds	1 01¼	2 65
from Caraccas, Campano, Cayenne, Castenno, Curaçoa, Magdalena, Maracaibo, and Trinidad.	....	....	(direct) 101 lbs	7 40	9 50
	....	....	(indirect) do	9 50	11 65
from all places west of Cape Horn, Maranon and other ports and places not designated.	....	....	(direct) do	3 18	5 30
	....	....	(indirect) do	4 77	6 90
Coculus Indicus	20	15	101 pounds	2½	3
Codfish	20	15	do	1 59	2 12

(a) For the sake of convenience and conciseness, the Spanish and Spanish colonial distinctions and discriminations in the denomination of merchandise are inserted in the general nomenclature, while the corresponding rates of duty are noted in the appropriate columns.

TARIFFS—Continued.

DUTIES ON IMPORTS.

TARIFF OF IMPORTATION INTO THE ISLAND OF CUBA.					TARIFF OF IMPORTATION INTO THE ISLAND OF PORTO RICO.				
		Per centage duty on the fixed value.					Per centage duty on the fixed value.		
Number, weight, or measure.	Fixed value on the number, weight, or measure.	Foreign productions under a foreign flag.	Foreign productions under the national flag, and those of Spain under a foreign flag.	Foreign productions under the national flag, imported from Spain proper.	Number, weight, or measure.	Fixed value on the number, weight, or measure.	Foreign productions under a foreign flag.	Foreign productions under the national flag, and those of Spain under a foreign flag.	Foreign productions under the national flag, imported from Spain proper.
....	Valuation ..	33½	23½	23½	....	Valuation ..	23	16	16
....	See machines.	....	....	....	....	....	....	....	....
25 lbs. 7 oz......	$4 00	33½	23½	23½	1 quart........	$0 25	23	16	16
....	Valuation ..	27½	19½	19½	....	Valuation ..	23	16	16
25 lbs. 7 oz......	2 50	27½	19½	19½	101 lbs........	10 00	23	16	16
101 lbs..........	37 50	33½	23½	23½	......do........	37 50	29	20	20
1 lb. 3 drs......	12½	27½	19½	19½	......do........	18 75	23	16	16
101 lbs..........	10 00(a)	27½	19½	19½	......do........	16 00(b)	23	16	16
......do........	12 50(b)	27½	19½	19½	......do........	10 00(c)	23	16	16
4. 245 gallons....	6 00	33½	23½	23½	quart..........	37½	29	20	20
101 pounds......	5 00	33½	23½	23½	101 pounds.....	5 00	29	20	20
piece..........	Valuation ..	27½	19½	19½	piece..........	Valuation...	23	16	16
....	Valuation ..	33½	23½	23½	....	Valuation...	29	20	20
dozen..........	$2 to $2 25	27½	19½	19½	dozen..........	2 25	23	20	20
1 lb. 3 drs......	50	33¼	23½	23½	1 lb. 3 drs......	50	29	20	20
......do........	60	27½	19½	19½	......do........	62½	23	16	16
......do........	1 50	27½	19½	19½	......do........	4 00	23	16	16
......do........	3 00	27½	19½	19½	......do........	3 00	23	16	16
barrel..........	3 00	27½	19½	19½	barrel..........	3 00	29	20	20
....	Valuation ..	27½	19½	19½	....	Valuation...	23	16	16
1 lb. 3 drs......	3 00	27½	19½	19½	1 lb. 3 drs......	3 00	23	16	16
101 pounds......	37 50	27½	19½	19½	101 pounds.....	37 50	23	16	16
404 pounds......	75	33½	23½	23½	......do........	37½	Free...	Free...	Free...
101 pounds......	37 50	33½	23½	23½	......do........	37 50	29	20	20
25 lbs. 3 drs.....	25 00	2 00	2 00	2 00	1 lb 3 drs......	2 00	2	2	2
} 101 pounds....	16 00	27½	19½	19½	101 pounds.....	16 00	23	16	16
} ......do......	7 00	27½	19½	19½	....	10 00	23	16	16
1 lb 3 drs.......	25	27½	19½	19½	1 lb. 3 drs......	25	23	16	16
101 pounds......	3 50	27½	19½	19½	101 pounds.....	3 00	23½	17¼	14¼

(a) From the United States. (b) From Europe. (c) From other parts.

TARIFFS—Continued

DENOMINATION OF MERCHANDISE.	DUTIES ON IMPORTS.				
	Into the United States from foreign nations, per cent. ad valorem, under the act of—		TARIFF OF GENERAL IMPORTATION INTO SPAIN.		
	1846.	1857.	Number, weight, or measure.	In national vessels.	In foreign vessels.
Coffee, on American and equalized vessels, free	Free	Free	101 lbs	From Spanish America, $1 69½ From Spanish Oceanica, 74¼ From other countries, 4 24	$3 30 2 95 6 35
on all other	20	15			
mills	30	24	one	16	19
Cologne water	30	24	1 lb. 3 drs	16	19
Copper, of first fusion, or old	5	Free	101 lbs	2 40	3 20
refined, or rose copper	30	24	do	3 20	4 26
in plates, black or blank	30	24	do	10 60	13 26
in utensils, partially wrought	30	24	1 lb. 3 drs	17	22
as common hardware, basins, &c	30	24	do	25	30½
nails	20	15	101 lbs	7 59	9 40
or steel engravings	30	24	1 lb 3 drs	80	95
Copperas	20	15	25 lbs. 7 oz	8	9½
Coral, crude	20	15	1 lb. 3 drs	10½	12¾
manufactured	30	24	do	2 40	2 85
Cordials, of all kinds, in casks	100	30	4. 245 gallons	3 31¼	4 00
in bottles	100	30			
Cork, unmanufactured	15	4	25 lbs. 7 oz	4	7½
Corks	30	24	1 lb. 3 drs	16	21¼
Cotton, raw	Free	Free	101 lbs		
from Spanish colonies			do	37	1 32½
from foreign countries producing cotton			do	79½	1 85
from foreign countries not producing cotton			do	2 12	3 20
all manufactures of, (common cloths)	25	24(a)	1 lb. 3 drs	29¾ to 55¾(b)	35½ to 66¾
twist, cotton yarn, cotton thread	25	24	do	21¼ to 42½	25½ to 51
Cranks, mill, wrought iron	30	24	do	3¼	4
Crystals, watch	30	24	do	21¼	25½
Currants	40	8	25 lbs. 7 oz	8	9½
Dates	40	8	1 lb. 3 drs	3¼	4
Demijohns, all sizes	30	24	25 lbs. 7 oz	53	63½
Down, of all kinds	25	19	1 lb. 3 drs	40	47½
Earthenware	30	24	25 lbs. 7 oz	1 59	1 90¾
Essences	30	24	1 lb 3 drs	11¾	15

(a) By treasury decisions under the act of 1857, cotton laces, insertings, trimming laces, and braid, are subject to a duty of 19 per cent.; and cotton hosiery, (all made on frames,) silk hatters' plush and silk velvet, (cotton chief value,) and cotton velvet, are subject to 15 per cent.

(b) See articles prohibited.

TARIFFS—Continued.

DUTIES ON IMPORTS.

TARIFF OF IMPORTATION INTO THE ISLAND OF CUBA.					TARIFF OF IMPORTATION INTO THE ISLAND OF PORTO RICO.				
		Per centage duty on the fixed value.					Per centage duty on the fixed value.		
Number, weight, or measure.	Fixed value on the number, weight, or measure.	Foreign productions under a foreign flag.	Foreign productions under the national flag, and those of Spain under a foreign flag.	Foreign productions under the national flag, imported from Spain proper.	Number, weight, or measure.	Fixed value on the number, weight, or measure.	Foreign productions under a foreign flag.	Foreign productions under the national flag, and those of Spain under a foreign flag.	Foreign productions under the national flag, imported from Spain proper.
......From Spanish possessions in Spanish ships.									
25 lbs. 7 oz......	$1 00	....	....	....	101 pounds.....	$6 00			
From foreign countries prohibited.									
Dozen	6 00	27½	19½	19½	dozen	6 00	23	16	16
24 flasks........	1 75	27½	19½	19½	dozen flasks.....	75	23	16	16
101 lbs.........	10 00	27½	19½	19½	101 lbs	10 00	23	16	16
......do.......	25 00	33½	23½	23½	......do.......	30 00	29	20	20
......do.......	25 00	33½	23½	23½	......do.......	30 00	29	20	20
......do.......	37 50	33½	23½	23½	......do.......	37 50	29	20	20
......do.......	37 50	33½	23½	23½	....	37 50	29	20	20
....	....	....	....	....	101 lbs.........	37 50	29	20	
101 pounds......	37 50	33½	23½	23½	......do.......	30 00	29	20	20
......do.......	3 00	27½	19½	19½	......do.......	3 00	23	16	16
....	Valuation ..	27½	19½	19½	....	Valuation...	23	16	16
1 lb. 3 drs.......	50 to 9 00	27½	19½	19½	1 lb. 3 drs	37½ to 9 00	23	16	16
4. 245 gallons....	5 00	33½	23½	23½	1 quart	37½	29	20	20
Dozen..........	2 00	33½	23½	23½	Dozen	4 50	29	20	20
25 lbs. 7 oz......	1 25	33½	23½	23½	101 lbs.........	5 00	29	20	20
1,000..........	50	33½	23½	23½	1,000..........	50	29	20	20
101 lbs.........	5 00	27½	19½	19½	101 lbs.........	5 00	23	16	16
....	....	....	....	....	....	....	....	....	....
....	....	....	....	....	....	....	....	....	....
....	....	....	....	....	....	....	....	....	....
....	Valuation ..	33½	23½	23½	....	Valuation ..	29	20	20
1 lb. 3 drs.......	75	33½	23½	23½	1 lb. 3 drs......	75	29	20	20
Dozen	7 00	33½	23½	23½	101 lbs.........	10 00	29	20	20
Gross..........	4 50	27½	19½	19½	Gross	4 50	23	16	16
Barrel	3 00	27½	19½	19½	Barrel	3 00	29	20	20
101 lbs	12 50	33½	23½	23½	101 lbs.........	12 50		20	20
Dozen	4 50	27½	19½	19½	Dozen	4 50	23	16	16
25 lbs. 7 oz......	6 25	27½	19½	19½	101 lbs.........	25 00	23	16	16
Piece	Valuation...	27½	19½	19½	Piece	Valuation...	23	16	16
....	...do......	27½	19½	19½	....	....do.....	23	16	16

TARIFFS—Continued.

DENOMINATION OF MERCHANDISE.	DUTIES ON IMPORTS. Into the United States from foreign nations, per cent. ad valorem, under the act of—		TARIFF OF GENERAL IMPORTATION INTO SPAIN.		
	46.	1857.	Number, weight, or measure.	In national vessels.	In foreign vessels.
Feathers for beds	25	19	1 lb. 3 drs	$0 40	$0 47½
Figs	40	8	25 lbs. 7 oz	(Dry) 23¾	28½
Filberts	30	24	....do	23¾	28½
Fish, dried or smoked, foreign caught	20	15	101 lbs	2 65	3 18
pickled, salmon	20	15	....do	2 65	3 18
mackerel	20	15	....do	2 65	3 18
codfish	20	15	....do	1 59	2 12
all other	20	15	....do	2 65	3 18
Flats, straw, for hats or bonnets	30	24	1 lb. 3 drs	40	47½
Flies, Spanish, (cantharides)	20	8	....do	16	19
Flints	5	4	25 lbs 7 oz	32	38
Floor cloth, printed or painted	30	24	1 lb. 3 drs	3¼	4
mattings of flags, jute, &c	25	19	....do	40	47½
Floss silks	25	19	....do	1 32½	1 60
Flour	20	15	Prohibited, if not permitted by special order of the government.		
Flowers, artificial, made up	30	24	1 lb. 3 drs	3 18	3 80
chamomile	20	15	....do	4¼	5¼
Folio and quarto post paper	30	24	25 lbs 7 oz	2 64	3 16
Frankincense	20	8	1 lb. 3 drs	16	19
Fruits, green	20	8	25 lbs. 7 oz	8	9½
Furniture, household	30	24		30 per cent.	36 per cent.
Furs, dressed	20	15 }		10 per cent.	12 per cent.
undressed	10	8 }			
hats and caps of	30	24	One	1 32½	1 59
Galls, nut	5	Free	1 lb. 3 drs	1 00	1 25
Gamboge, refined	20	15	....do	10½	12¾
Ginger and ginger root	40	15		30	40
Glass, cut	40	30	25 lbs. 7 oz	1 48½	1 78½
crystals for watches	30	24	1 lb. 3 drs	21¼	25½
demijohns, common	30	24	25 lbs. 7 oz	53	63½
bottles, common	30	24	....do	53	63½
window	20	15	....do	1 85½	2 12½

TARIFFS—Continued.

DUTIES ON IMPORTS.

TARIFF OF IMPORTATION INTO THE ISLAND OF CUBA.					TARIFF OF IMPORTATION INTO THE ISLAND OF PORTO RICO.				
		Per centage duty on the fixed value.					Per centage duty on the fixed value.		
Number, weight, or measure.	Fixed value on the number, weight, or measure.	Foreign productions under a foreign flag.	Foreign productions under the national flag, and those of Spain under a foreign flag.	Foreign productions under the national flag, imported from Spain proper.	Number, weight, or measure.	Fixed value on the number, weight, or measure.	Foreign productions under a foreign flag.	Foreign productions under the national flag, and those of Spain under a foreign flag.	Foreign productions under the nationa flag, imported from Spain proper.
25 lbs. 7 oz.	$6 25	27½	19½	19½	101 lbs.	$25 00	23	16	16
27 lbs. 7 oz.	1 00	33½	23½	23½	do.	4 00	29	20	20
do.	1 50	33½	23½	23½	do.	6 00	29	20	20
101 lbs	3 50	33½	23½	23½	do.	3 50	29	20	20
do.	25 00	27½	19½	19½	do.	25 00	23	16	16
do.	12 50	33½	23½	23½	do.	12 50	29	20	20
do.	3 50	27½	19½	19½	do.	3 00	23½	17¼	14¼
do.	12 50	33½	23½	23½	do.	12 50	29	20	20
	Valuation	27½	19½	19½		Valuation	23	16	16
1 lb. 3 drs.	75	27½	19½	19½	1 lb. 3 drs.	1 25	23	16	16
101 lbs	8 00	33½	23½	23½	101 lbs.	6 00	29	20	20
Vara	25	27½	19½	19½	Vara	25	23	16	16
do.	25	33½	23½	23½	do.	25	29	20	20
1 lb. 3 drs.	4 00	27½	19½	19½	1 lb. 3 drs.	4 50	23	16	16
Barrel	12 50	(a)			Barrel	12 50	43½	35½	23¼
Dozen	3 75	27½	19½	19½	Dozen	3 75	23	16	16
1 lb. 3 drs.	12½	27½	19½	19½	101 lbs.	18 75	23	16	16
Ream	3 00	27½	19½	19½	Ream	3 00	23	16	16
101 lbs	12 50	27½	19½	19½	101 lbs.	12 50	23	16	16
Barrel	3 00	27½	19½	19½	Barrel		29	20	20
	Valuation	33½	23½	23½		Valuation	29	20	20
	do.	33½	23½	23½		do.	29	20	20
	do.	33½	23½	23½		do.	29	20	20
25 lbs. 7 oz.	4 00	27½	19½	19½	101 lbs.	16 00	23	16	16
1 lb. 3 drs.	75	27½	19½	19½	1 lb. 3 drs.	75	23	16	16
101 lbs	18 75	27½	19½	19½	101 lbs.	12 50	23	16	16
	Valuation	27½	19½	19½		Valuation	23	16	16
Gross	4 50	27½	19½	19½	Gross	4 50	23	16	16
Dozen	4 50	27½	19½	19½	Dozen	4 50	23	16	16
Gross	4 50	27½	19½	19½	Gross	4 50	23	16	16
Per box containing 100 sq. feet.	7 50	27½	19½	19½	Per box containing 100 sq. feet	7 50	23	16	

(a) Spanish flour in Spanish ships, per barrel, $2; Spanish flour in foreign ships, per barrel, $6; foreign flour in foreign ships, per barrel, $9 50; foreign flour in Spanish ships, per barrel, $8 50.

TARIFFS—Continued.

DENOMINATION OF MERCHANDISE.	DUTIES ON IMPORTS.				
	Into the United States from foreign nations, per cent. ad valorem, under the act of—		TARIFF OF GENERAL IMPORTATION INTO SPAIN.		
	1846.	1857.	Number, weight, or measure.	In national vessels.	In foreign vessels.
Glauber salts	20	15	25 lbs. 7 oz	$0 16	$0 19
Gloves, cotton	20	15	Dozen	1 90	2 30
silk	30	24	1 lb. 3 drs	3 18	3 71½
leather	30	24	Dozen	1 90	2 30
fencing	30	24	....do	1 90	2 30
Glue	20	15	25 lbs. 7 oz	53	63½
Goats' hair, Angora	20	15	....do	7¼	10
skins, salted	20	15	101 lbs	53	63½
Gold, articles composed of	30	24	1 lb. 3 drs	6 per cent	6 per cent
epaulets	30	24		6 per cent	6 per cent
Gold, bars and coins	Free	Free		Free	Free
leaf	15	12	1 lb. 3 drs	53	63½
watches, and parts of	10	8		20 per cent	25 per cent.
Grass, matting or flags	25	19	1 lb. 3 drs	40	47½
Grindstones	5	4	101 lbs	13¼	16
Guitars	20	15	One	2 12	2 54½
Gum, Arabic	10	8	1 lb. 3 drs	2	2¾
elastic, unmanufactured	10	8		Free	Free
Gunpowder	20	15	Prohibited	Prohibited.	Prohibited.
Gutta percha	10	4	See Indian rubber.		
Hair, Angora goats', raw	20	15	25 lbs. 7 oz	7¼	10
manufactured	30	24	1 lb. 3 drs	12	14¼
bracelets	30	24	....do	Of human hair—	
				6 62½	7 95
camels	10	8		Free	Free
human, unmanufactured	30	24	1 lb. 3 drs	16	21¾
manufactured	30	24		Free	Free
head dresses of	30	24	1 lb. 3 drs	6 62½	7 95
pencils	30	24	....do	16	19
Hammers, all kinds	30	24	....do	3¼	4
Hams and bacon	20	15	25 lbs. 7 oz.	63½	76¼
Handkerchiefs, cotton	25	24	1 lb. 3 drs	36½ to 55¾	53½ to 66¾
linen	20	15	....do	15 per cent.	18 per cent.
silk	25	19	....do	95½ to 4 24	1 14½ to 5 08¾
Harness, leather	30	24		30 per cent	40 per cent.
Hatchets	30	24	1 lb. 3 drs	3¼	4
Hartshorn	30	24	25 lbs. 7 oz	12¾	17

TARIFFS—Continued.

DUTIES ON IMPORTS.

TARIFF OF IMPORTATION INTO THE ISLAND OF CUBA.					TARIFF OF IMPORTATION INTO THE ISLAND OF PORTO RICO.				
		Per centage duty on the fixed value.					Per centage duty on the fixed value.		
Number, weight, or measure.	Fixed value on the number, weight, or measure.	Foreign productions under a foreign flag.	Foreign productions under the national flag, and those of Spain under a foreign flag.	Foreign productions under the national flag, imported from Spain proper.	Number, weight, or measure.	Fixed value on the number, weight, or measure.	Foreign productions under a foreign flag.	Foreign productions under the national flag, and those of Spain under a foreign flag.	Foreign productions under the national flag, imported from Spain proper.
101 lbs	$2 00	27½	19½	19½	101 lbs	$3 00	23	16	16
12 pairs	1 50	27½	19½	19½	12 pairs	2 00	23	16	16
..do	3 00	27½	19½	19½	Dozen pairs	5 00	23	16	16
..do	4 50	27½	19½	19½	...do	4 50	23	16	16
..do	6 00	27½	19½	19½	...do	6 00	23	16	16
25 lbs. 7 oz	3 00	33½	23½	23½	101 lbs	12 00	23	16	16
..do	7 00	27½	19½	19½	...do	25 00	23	16	16
Dozen	4 50	33½	23½	23½	Dozen	4 50	29	20	20
	Valuation	7½	5½	5½		Valuation	6	4	4
Pair	18 75	33½	23½	23½	Pair	18 75	29	20	20
	Free	Free	Free	Free		Free	Free	Free	Free
Ream	12 00	23½	23½	23½	Ream	12 00	29	20	20
	Valuation.	7½	5½	5½		Valuation.	6	4	4
Vara, yard	25	33½	23½	23½	Vara	25	29	20	20
	Valuation.	27½	19½	19½		Valuation.	23	16	16
One	4 50	27½	19½	19½	One	6 00	23	16	16
25 lbs. 7 oz.	6 00	27½	19½	19½	101 lbs	16 00	23	16	16
1 lb. 3 drs.	50	27½	19½	19½	1 lb. 3 drs	50	23	16	16
101 lbs	18 00	27½	19½	19½	101 lbs	18 00	23	16	16
25 lbs. 7 oz	7 00	27½	19½	19½	..do	25 00	23	16	16
....do	6 30	27½	19½	19½	..do	25 00	23	16	16
	Valuation.	27½	19½	19½		Valuation.	23	16	16
25 lbs. 7 oz.	5 00	27½	19½	19½	1 lb. 3 drs	25	23	16	16
1 lb. 3 drs	5 00	27½	19½	19½	....do	5 00	23	16	16
	Valuation.	27½	19½	19½		Valuation.	23	16	16
	....do	27½	19½	19½		....do	23	16	16
Dozen	75 cts. to 2 00	27½	19½	19½	Dozen	$1 50 to 3 75	23	16	16
Dozen	3 00	27½	19½	19½	..do	3 00	23	16	16
25 lbs. 7 oz.	2 00	33½	23½	23½	101 lbs	9 00	29	20	20
2 dozens	$2 25 to 3 50	33½	23½	23½	Dozen	$1 12½ to 2 00	29	20	20
Dozen	$6 to $15	27½	19½	19½	..do	$3 to $12	23	16	16
Dozen	$3 to $6	27½	19½	19½	..do	$8 to $12	23	16	16
For 1 horse, fine	50 00	33½	23½	23½	Com'n, for 1 horse	6 00	29	20	
For 2 horses, fine	75 00	33½	23½	23½	Finer, for 1 horse	50 00	29	20	20
Com'n, for 1 horse	12 50	33½	23½	23½	Finer, for 2 horses	75 00	29	20	20
Dozen	6 00	33½	23½	23½	Dozen	6 00	29	20	20
1 lb. 3 drs	25	27½	19½	19½	1 lb. 3 drs	25	23	16	16

TARIFFS—Continued.

Denomination of merchandise.	Duties on imports. Into the United States from foreign nations, per cent. ad valorem, under the act of— 1846.	1857.	Tariff of general importation into Spain. Number, weight, or measure.	In national vessels.	In foreign vessels.
Hats, bodies or felts, wool	20	15		25 per cent	30 per cent.
Hemp, unmanufactured	30	24	101 lbs	$2 12	$2 65
Hempseed oil	20	15	1 lb. drs	5¼	6¼
Hemp or flax, all manufactures	20	15	101 lbs	2 75½	3 45
Hides, raw	5	4	do	From Spanish	possessions.
				43¾	1 56½
				From other p'	ts of America
				72½	1 86¼
				From Europe,	kins, of
				1 29¼	2 76¾
Hods, for coal, copper	30	24	1 lb. 3 drs	17	21¼
Hoop iron and hoops	30	24	101 lbs	1 60	2 65
Horn, ox, and horn tips	5	4	do	8	16
spoons	30	24	Gross	1 40	1 70
Hosiery, all kinds	30	24	According to ma	terial	
except woolen	30	24			
Ice	20	Free			
India-rubber, manufactured	10	4	1 lb. 3 drs	2	2¾
manufactures of	30	24	manufactured	Free	Free
Indigo	10	4	101 lbs	From Spanish	colonies
				42½	3 20
				From foreign	indigo pro-
				ducing coun	tries.
				3 18	6 35
				From Eu	rope.
				15 90	21 20
Indian corn, meal	20	15		Prohibited,	except by
grain	20	15		special or	der.
Instruments, musical, of brass	20	15		20 per cent.	24 per cent.
of ivory	20	15		do	do
of wood	20	15		do	do
strings for	20	15	Ounce	4¾	5¾
Inventions, models of	Free	Free		6 per cent	8 per cent.
Ipecacuanha	20	15		Free	Free

TARIFFS—Continued.

DUTIES ON IMPORTS.

TARIFF OF IMPORTATION INTO THE ISLAND OF CUBA.					TARIFF OF IMPORTATION INTO THE ISLAND OF PORTO RICO.				
Number, weight, or measure.	Fixed value on the number, weight, or measure.	Per centage duty on the fixed value.			Number, weight, or measure.	Fixed value on the number, weight, or measure.	Per centage duty on the fixed value.		
		Foreign productions under a foreign flag.	oreign productions under the national flag, and those of Spain under a foreign flag.	Foreign productions under the national flag, imported from Spain proper.			Foreign productions under a foreign flag.	Foreign productions under the national flag, and those of Spain under a foreign flag.	Foreign productions under the national flag, and those from Spain proper.
Dozen	$3 00	27½	19½	19½	Dozen	$3 00	23	16	16
101 lbs.	7 50	33½	23½	23½	101 lbs	5 00	29	20	20
4.245 galls	2 00	27½	19½	19½	1 quart	18¾	23	16	16
101 lbs.	7 50	33½	33½	23½	101 lbs	5 00	29	20	20
Of cattle and horses.					Of cattle or horses.				
One	1 50	33½	23½	23½	101 lbs	10 00	29	20	20
					Of goats or sheep.				
One	....	....	....	....	Dozen	4 50	29	20	20
goats and sheep.					Of deer, &c.				
Dozen	4 50	33½	23½	23½	Dozen	4 00	23	16	16
Of deer, &c.									
Dozen	6 00		19½	19½					
101 lbs	37 50	33½	23½	23½	101 lbs	37	29	20	20
....do	6 00	33½	23½	23½	....do	8 00	29	20	20
100	1 to 1 25	2	2	2	100	1 to 1 25	23	16	16
Dozen	1 00	27½	19½	19½	Dozen	1 00	23	16	16
....	Valuation ..	{ 27½	19½	19½	....	Valuation ..	23	16	16
		33½	23½	23½			29	20	20
....	....do	33½	23½	23½	....	....do	29	20	20
....	Free	....	....	....	....	....	ree ..	....	....
1 lb. 3 drs	50	27½	19½	19½	1 lb. 3 drs	50	23	16	16
...do. (in deposit)	1 00	2	2	2	....do	1 00	23	16	16
Barrel of 200 lb ..	5 00	33½	23½	23½	Barrel of 220 lbs.	4 00	29½	21¼	17¼
......do	4 00	33½	23½	23½	3 bushels	2 50	29	20	20
}	Valuation ..	27½	19½	19½	....	Valuation ..	23	16	16
1 bundle or roll ..	50	33½	23½	23½	Bundle or roll ..	50	29	20	20
....	Valuation ..	27½	19½	19½	....	Valuation ..	23	16	16
101 lbs	50 00	27½	19½	19½	101 lbs	62 50	23	16	16

TARIFFS—Continued.

DENOMINATION OF MERCHANDISE.	DUTIES ON IMPORTS. Into the United States from foreign nations, per cent. ad valorem, under the act of—		Tariff of general importation into Spain.		
	1846.	1857.	Number, weight, or measure.	In national vessels.	In foreign vessels.
Iron, all manufactures of, (a)	30	24	1 lb. 3 drs	Ordinary, 2 ct	$0 02¾
				Fine, 3¼ cts.	4
in bars and bolts	30	24	101 lbs	$2 12	2 54½
cables or chains, or parts of, (b)	30	24	do	31¾	42½
Iron, cannon	30	24		Prohibited	
castings for vessels	30	24	2, 020 lbs. (1 ton)		2 65
nails, cut or wrought	30	24	101 pounds	3 20	4 20
nail or spike rods, or nail plates	30	24	do	3 20	4 20
mills, and mill cranks, of wrought iron	30	24	1 pound 3 drs	3¼	4
screw, called wood screw	30	24	do	3¼	4
in pigs	30	24	101 pounds	42½	50¾
wire, annealed	30	24	do	2 40	3 30
or steel wire	30	24	do	3 20	4 20
in sheets	30	24	do	2 12	2 50½
spikes	30	24	do	3 20	4 20
Isinglass	20	15	1 pound 3 drs	6¼	8½
Ivory, manufactures of, not otherwise enumerated	30	24		15 per cent	18 per cent.
Jalap	20	15	1 pound 3 drs	3¼	4
Japanned saddlery, all kinds	20	15		30 per cent	40 per cent.
Jewelry, of all kinds	30	24		6 per cent	6 per cent
Juniper berries	20	15	25 pounds 7 oz	16	19
oil of	30	24	1 pound 3 drs	11¾	15
Kentledge	30	24	101 pounds	42½	50¾
Kettles, brass	30	24	1 pound 3 drs	17	21¼
cast iron (c)	30	24	do	3¼	4
Knitting needles	20	15	1 lb. 3 drs	19	23
Knives, cutting	30	24	Dozen	12 to 40	14¼ to 47¾
drawing	30	24	do	21¼	25½
Lac dye	5	4	1 lb. 3 drs	1½	1¾
Laces, of cotton	25	19			
of silk	25	19		25 per cent.	30 per cent.
Lamp black	20	15	101 pounds	1 19¼	1 43
Lapis calaminaris	20	15	1 lb. 3 drs	1½	1¾
Lard	20	15	25 lbs. 7 oz	99½	1 19¼

(a) Not otherwise specified, or of which iron is a component material.
(b) Manufactured, in whole or in part.
(c) With drop handles of wrought iron, tinned inside, japanned outside, sheet iron lid with brass knobs.

TARIFFS—Continued.

DUTIES ON IMPORTS.

TARIFF OF IMPORTATION INTO THE ISLAND OF CUBA.					TARIFF OF IMPORTATION INTO THE ISLAND OF PORTO RICO.				
Number, weight, or measure.	Fixed value on the number, weight, or measure.	Per centage duty on the fixed value.			Number, weight, or measure.	Fixed value on the number, weight, or measure.	Per centage duty on the fixed value.		
		Foreign productions under a foreign flag.	Foreign productions under the national flag, and those of Spain under a foreign flag.	Foreign productions under the national flag, imported from Spain proper.			Foreign productions under a foreign flag.	Foreign productions under the national flag, and those of Spain under a foreign flag.	Foreign productions under the national flag, imported from Spain proper.
....	Valuation ..	33½	23½	23½	....	Valuation ..	29	20	20
101 pounds......	$3 25	33½	23½	23½	101 pounds.....	$4 00	29	20	20
....do..........	7 00	33½	23½	23½	....do..........	8 00	29	20	20
....do..........	4 50	33½	23½	23½	....do..........	4 50	29	20	20
....	Valuation ..	33½	23½	23½	....	Valuation ..	29	20	20
101 pounds......	7 00	33½	23½	23½	101 pounds.....	8 00	29	20	20
......do........	3 25	33½	23½	23½	......do........	4 00	29	20	20
Dozen	7 00	33½	23½	23½	......do........	10 00	29	20	20
....	Valuation, or	27½	19½	19½	....	Valuation, or	23	16	16
Gross	50	27½	19½	19½	Gross..........	50	23	16	16
101 pounds......	2 00	33½	23½	23½	101 pounds.....	2 00	29	20	20
25 pounds 7 oz...	2 00	27½	19½	19½	1 pound 3 drs...	12½	29	20	20
......do........	2 00	33½	23½	23½	......do........	12½	29	20	20
101 pounds......	3 25	33½	23½	23½	101 pounds.....	4 00	29	20	20
......do........	7 00	33½	23½	23½	......do........	8 00	29	20	20
1 pound 3 drs....	1 00	27½	19½	19½	1 pound 3 drs...	1 00	23	16	16
....	Valuation ..	27½	19½	19½	....	Valuation ..	23	16	16
Ounce	2 00	27½	19½	19½	Ounce..........	1 50	23	16	15
....	Valuation ..	33½	23½	23½	....	Valuation ..	29	20	20
....	....do......	7½	5½	5½	....	....do......	6	4	4
25 pounds 7 oz....	2 00	27½	19½	19½	101 pounds.....	8 00	23	16	16
1 pound 3 drs....	25	27½	19½	19½	1 pound 3 drs...	25	23	16	16
101 pounds......	2 00	33½	23½	23½	101 pounds.....	2 00	29	20	20
......do........	37 50	33½	23½	23½	1 pound 3 drs...	50	29	20	20
....	Valuation ..	27½	19½	19½	....	Valuation ..	23	16	16
Dozen	25	27½	19¾	19½	Dozen..........	25	23	16	16
......do........	$1 50 to $9 00	27½	19½	19½	......do........	$1 25 to $9	23	16	16
......do........	4 50	27½	19½	19½	......do........	4 50	23	16	16
1 lb. 3 drs.......	25	27½	19½	19½	1 lb. 3 drs......	37½	23	16	16
2 varas..........	25	33½	23½	23½	Vara	12½	29	20	20
Vara............	25	27½	19½	19½	....	Valuation ..	23	16	16
25 lbs. 7 oz......	2 00	27½	19½	19½	101 pounds	8 00	23	16	16
101 pounds......	25 00	27½	19⅛	19½	......do........	25 00	23	16	16
25 lbs. 7 oz......	3 00	33½	23½	23½	......do........	10 00	23	16	16

TARIFFS—Continued.

DENOMINATION OF MERCHANDISE.	DUTIES ON IMPORTS. Into the United States from foreign nations, per cent. ad valorem, under the act of— 1846.	1857.	TARIFF OF GENERAL IMPORTATION INTO SPAIN. Number, weight, or measure.	In national vessels.	In foreign vessels.
Lavender, essential oil of	30	24	1 lb. 3 drs	$0 16	$0 19
Lead, nitrate of	20	15		Free	Free
old and scrap	20	15			
pencils.	30	24	Ounce	2½	3¼
in bars or sheets	20	15	101 lbs	95½	1 14½
red and white, dry or ground in oil	20	15			
manufactured into shot	20	15			
sugar of	20	15	1 lb. 3 drs	1	1¼
manufactured into pipes	20	15	101 pounds	1 59	1 90
other manufactures of (*a*)	30	24	do	1 59	1 90
Leaf, gold and silver	15	12	1 lb. 3 drs	53	63½
Leather, not manufactured	20	15	1 lb. 3 drs	12	14¼
manufactures of	30	24			
Leeches	20	15	1 lb. 3 drs	4¾	5¾
Leghorn hats or bonnets	30	24		30 per cent	36 per ct
Lemons	20	8	1 lb. 3 drs	8	9½
essential oil of	30	24	do	4	5
Lime	10	8	101 lbs	6¼	7¾
Linen, bleached or unbleached, under 8 threads	20	15	do	16 72½	21 20
from 9 to 12 threads			do	25 44	31 80
13 to 18 do			do	36 57	45 00
19 to 24 do			do	47 70	58 30
25 to 30 do			do	63 60	79 50
31 and upwards			do	119 25	148 40
cambrics	20	15	do	119 25	148 40
tapes	20	15	do	34 45	42 40
Linseed, oil of	20	15	4.245 gallons	40	47½
Liquors	100	30	do	3 31¼	4 00
Locks	30	24	According to size,	construction,	material of
Logwood	5	Free	101 lbs.	1	1½

(*a*) Not otherwise provided for, or of which lead is a component material.

TARIFFS—Continued.

DUTIES ON IMPORTS.

TARIFF OF IMPORTATION INTO THE ISLAND OF CUBA.					TARIFF OF IMPORTATION INTO THE ISLAND OF PORTO RICO.				
		Per centage duty on the fixed value.					Per centage duty on the fixed value.		
Number, weight, or measure.	Fixed value on the number, weight, or measure.	Foreign productions under a foreign flag.	Foreign productions under the national flag, and those of Spain under a foreign flag.	Foreign productions under the national flag, imported from Spain proper.	Number, weight, or measure.	Fixed value on the number, weight, or measure.	Foreign productions under a foreign flag.	Foreign productions under the national flag, and those of Spain under a foreign flag.	Foreign productions under the national flag, imported from Spain proper.
1 lb. 3 drs	$1 00	27½	19½	19½	1 lb. 3 drs	$1 00	23	16	16
......do......	25	27½	19½	19½	......do......	25	23	16	16
101 pounds	2 50	27½	19½	19½	101 pounds	2 50	23	16	16
25 lbs. 7 oz	7 00	27½	19½	19½	......do......	28 00	23	16	16
101 pounds	4 00	27½	19½	19½	......do......	4 00	23	16	16
25 lbs 7 oz	3 50	33½	23½	23½	......do......	10 00	23	16	16
101 pounds	6 25	27½	19½	19½	......do......	5 00	23	16	16
......do......	18 75	27½	19½	19½	......do......	18 50	23	16	16
......do......	7 50	27½	19½	19½	......do......	7 50	23	16	16
......do......	7 50	27½	19½	19½	......do......	7 50	23	16	16
ream	12 00	33½	23½	23½	ream	12 00	29	20	20
Side	3 00	33½	23½	23½	101 lbs	25 00	29	20	20
	Valuation	33½	23½	23½		Valuation	29	20	20
		Free	Free	Free			Free	Free	Free
One	Valuation	27½	19½	19½	Dozen	with garniture. 36 00	23	16	16
Barrel	3 00	27½	19½	19½	Barrel	3 00	23	16	16
1 lb. 3 drs	2 00	27½	19½	19½	1 lb. 3 drs	2 00	23	16	16
Barrel of 200 lbs.	1 00	33½	23	23½	Barrel, (200 lbs)	1 00	29	20	20
	Valuation	27½	19½	19½		Valuation	23	16	16
	Valuation	27½	19½	19½		Valuation	23	16	16
36 varas, (yards)	75	33½	23½	23½	12 pieces	37½	23	16	16
4.245 gallons	2 00	27½	19½	19½	1 quart	18¾	23	16	16
......do......	In casks, 5 00	33½	23½	23½	Quart	In casks, 31¼	29	20	20
Dozen	In bottles, 2 00	33½	23½	23½	Dozen	In bottles, 4 50	29	20	20
which they are manufactured, and the uses to which they are applied.(a)									
One horse's load	50	33½	23½	23½	one horse's load	50	29	20	20

(a) Such is the extent, variety, and minuteness of the nomenclature and the corresponding rates of duties set down under the heads of "looking-glasses," "locks," and of some other articles in the tariffs of Spain, Cuba, and Porto Rico, that anything like a summary view of those rates in comparison with the rate of the single item in the tariff of the United States, seems impracticable, in a condensed statement like the present.

TARIFFS—Continued.

DENOMINATION OF MERCHANDISE.	DUTIES ON IMPORTS.				
	Into the United States from foreign nations, per cent. ad valorem, under the act of—		TARIFF OF GENERAL IMPORTATION INTO SPAIN.		
	1846.	1857.	Number, weight, or measure.	In national vessels.	In foreign vessels.
Machines	30	24	Locomotives, boil	ers, &c., appa	ratus, with
			low pressure, pa	y 2 per cent.,	3 per cent.
			All complete spin	ning, weaving	, printing,
			paper-making m	achines, cylin	ders for the
			fabrication of tin	and fine iron	plates ; ma-
			chines for agricu	ltural and min	ing pur-
			poses, for perfora	tion of artesia	n wells, and
			hydraulic wheels	, pay 3 pr. ct.,	4 per cent.
			All other complet	e machines, o	f all classes,
			not enumerated	in this tariff,	pay—
				6 per cent.	8 per cent.
			Cauldrons, and al	l loose pieces	for every
			kind of machine	s, 10 per cent.	12 per ct.
Mackerel	20	15	101 lbs.	$2 65	$3 18
Madder or madder root	5	Free	25 lbs. 7 oz.	9	12
Magnesia, carbonate	30	24	1 lb	5	7
Manganese	20	15	100 lbs	13	17
Manna	20	15	1 lb. 3 drs	$4\frac{3}{4}$	$5\frac{3}{4}$
Manufactured and prepared quills	20	15	do	16	19
Marble, unmanufactured	20	15		40 per cent.	50 per cent.
busts of	30	24		25 per cent.	30 per cent.
Mathematical instruments	30	24		15 per cent.	18 per cent.

TARIFFS—Continued.

DUTIES ON IMPORTS.

Tariff of importation into the island of Cuba.					Tariff of importation into the island of Porto Rico.				
Number, weight, or measure.	Fixed value on the number, weight, or measure.	Per centage duty on the fixed value. Foreign productions under a foreign flag.	Foreign productions under the national flag, and those of Spain under a foreign flag.	Foreign productions under the national flag, imported from Spain proper.	Number, weight, or measure.	Fixed value on the number, weight, or measure.	Percentage duty on the fixed value. Foreign productions under a foreign flag.	Foreign productions under the national flag, and those of Spain under a foreign flag.	Foreign productions under the national flag, imported from Spain proper.
	Large steam engines for ships, and other uses,					Large steam engines for ships, and other uses,			
One	$2,000 00	27½	19½	19½	One	$2,000 00	23	16	16
	Electric machines of all sizes:					For making chocolate,			
One	50 00	27½	19½	19½	One	80 00	23	16	16
	Printing machines:					For making vermicelli,			
	Valuation	27½	19½	19½	One	50 00	23	16	16
	Machines for decorticating and cleaning coffee:					Electric machines of all dimensions,			
One	12 00	27½	19½	19½	One	50 00	23	16	16
	Butter-making machines:					For decorticating and cleaning coffee,			
One	2 00	27½	19½	19½	One	12 00	23	16	16
	Machines for making button-holes of metal:					For making butter,			
					One	2 00	23	16	16
One	50	27½	19½	19½		For making metal holes,			
					One	50	23	16	16
						Printing machines,			
					One	Valuation	23	16	16
	Free. Steam engines for ingenious purposes; machines and centrifugal apparatus for manufacturing sugar; steam engines, with all necessaries for refining molasses and sugar; pile engines and cylinders or rollers for sugar mills; single or loose pieces for repairing engines and sugar mills; iron dies and skimmers for sugar machines; iron crowns for sugar mills.					Free. Refiners of copper or iron for engines; iron crowns for sugar mills and engines; iron dies for engines; iron skimmers for sugar; pile engines, and cylinders or rollers for sugar mills; loose pieces for repairing steam engines and sugar mills. Machines for agricultural purposes are, if Spanish product, or in Spanish ships, free; but, as foreign fabrics, and in foreign ships, they pay 1 per cent.			
Barrel of 200 lbs	4 50	27½	19½	19½	Barrel of 200 lbs.	4 00	23	16	16
101 lbs	18 50	27½	19½	19½	101 lbs	18 50	23	16	16
25 lbs. 7 oz	1 50	27½	19½	19½	do	6 00	23	16	16
do	2 00	27½	19½	19½	do	8 00	23	16	16
do	7 50	27½	19½	19½	do	30 00	23	16	16
1,000	2 50	27½	19½	19½	1,000	2 50	23	16	16
	Valuation.	27½	19½	19½		Valuation.	23	16	16
	Valuation.	27½	19½	19½		Valuation.	23	16	16
	Valuation.	27½	19½	19		Valuation.	23	16	16

TARIFFS—Continued.

DENOMINATION OF MERCHANDISE.	DUTIES ON IMPORTS.				
	Into the United States from foreign nations, per cent. ad valorem, under the act of—		TARIFF OF GENERAL IMPORTATION INTO SPAIN.		
	1846.	1857.	Number, weight, or measure.	In national vessels.	In foreign vessels.
Matting, floor	25	19	1 lb. 3 drs	$0 40	$0 47½
Metal busts	30	24		25 per cent.	30 per cent.
Millinery, of all kinds	30	24			
Mill cranks, of wrought iron	30	24	1 lb. 3 drs	3¼	4
saws	30	24	do	6¼	7¾
stones	10	4	101 lbs	13¼	16
Mills, coffee	30	24	One	16	19
			One	To be fastened	to the wall,
				32½	42½
Mineralogy, specimens of	Free	Free		6 per cent.	8 per cent.
Music, printed in sheets	10	4	25 lbs. 7 oz	2 12	2 54½
Mules	20	Free	Each	1 to 3	years old,
				7 95	9 50
Musk	30	24	Ounce	53	63½
Muskets and bayonets	30	24		Prohibited	
Myrrh, gum, refined	20	15	1 lb	4¾	5½
Nails, brads	30	24	101 lbs	3 20	4 20
copper	20	15	do	7 59	9 40
iron, cut or wrought	30	24	do	3 20	4 20
Nail rods, of iron	30	24	do	3 20	4 20
Needles, knitting	20	15	1 lb. 3 drs	19	23
sewing	20	15	do	23¾	28½
Nitrate of lead	20	15		Free	Free
silver	30	24	Ounce	24	28½
Nitre, crude	5	4	101 lbs	2 06¾	3 10
Nutmegs	40	4	1 lb. 3 drs	10½	12½
Nux vomica	10	8		Free	Free
Oats	20	15		Prohibited	
Ochres, common, dry	30	15	1 lb. 3 drs	2½	3
Oil of Anise seed	30	24	do	5¼	6¼
essential, of bergamot	30	24	do	16	19
of cassia	30	24	do	95½	1 27½
of cinnamon	30	24	do	95½	1 27½
castor or ricini	20	15	do	5¼	6¼
cloves	30	24	do	11¾	15
hemp seed	20	15	do	5¼	6¼
juniper	30	24	do	11¾	15

TARIFFS—Continued.

DUTIES ON IMPORTS.

TARIFF OF IMPORTATION INTO THE ISLAND OF CUBA.					TARIFF OF IMPORTATION INTO THE ISLAND OF PORTO RICO.				
		Per centage duty on the fixed value.					Per centage duty on the fixed value.		
Number, weight, or measure.	Fixed value on the number, weight, or measure.	Foreign productions under a foreign flag.	Foreign productions under the national flag, and those of Spain under a foreign flag.	Foreign productions under the national flag, imported from Spain proper.	Number, weight, or measure.	Fixed value on the number, weight, or measure.	Foreign productions under a foreign flag.	Foreign productions under the national flag, and those of Spain under a foreign flag.	Foreign productions under the national flag imported from Spain proper.
Vara	$0 25	33½	23½	23½	Vara	$0 25	29	20	20
	Valuation.	27½	19½	19½		Valuation.	23	16	16
	Valuation.	33½	23½	23½		Valuation.	29	20	20
Dozen	7 00	33½	23½	23½	101 lbs	10 00	29	20	20
One	6 50	33½	23½	23½	One	6 50	29	20	20
One	10 00	27½	19½	19½	One	7 50	23	16	16
Dozen	6 00	27½	19½	19½	Dozen	6 00	23	16	16
	Valuation.	27½	19½	19½		Valuation.	23	16	16
Sheet	5	33½	23½	23½	Sheet	5	29	20	20
	Valuation.	33½	23½	23½		Valuation.	29	20	20
Ounce	3 00	27½	19½	19½	Ounce	5 00	23	16	16
	Prohibited					Prohibited			
2 lbs. 6 drs	75	27½	19½	19½	1 lb. 3 drs	37½	23	16	16
101 lbs	37 50	27½	19½	19¾	101 lbs	37 50	23	16	16
do	25 00	33½	23½	23½	do	30 00	29	20	20
do	7	33½	23½	23½	do	8 00	29	20	20
do	3 25	33½	23½	23½	do	4 00	29	20	20
Dozen	25	27½	19½	19½	Dozen	25	23	16	16
1,000	75	27½	19½	19½	1,000	75	23	16	16
1 lb. 3 drs	25	27½	19½	19½	1 lb. 3 drs	25	23	16	16
Ounce	1 25	27½	19½	19½	Ounce	1 25	23	16	16
101 lbs	8 00	27½	19½	19½	101 lbs	8 00	23	16	16
1 lb. 3 drs	1 50	27½	19½	19½	1 lb. 3 drs	1 50	23	16	16
101 lbs	18 75	27½	19½	19½	do	18¾	23	16	16
do	1 50	33½	23½	23½	101 lbs	1 50	29	20	20
do	2 50	27½	19½	19½	do	2 50	23	16	16
1 lb. 3 drs	2 00	27½	19½	19½	1 lb. 3 drs	2 00	23	16	16
do	1 25	27½	19½	19½	do	1 75	23	16	16
do	3 00	27½	19½	19½	do	3 00	23	16	16
do	3 00	27½	19½	19½	do	3 00	23	16	16
25 lbs. 7 oz	4 00	33½	23½	23½	1 quart	25	23	16	16
1 lb. 3 drs	3 00	27½	19½	19½	1 lb. 3 drs	3 00	23	16	16
4.245 galls	2 00	27½	19½	19½	1 quart	18¾	23	16	16
1 lb. 3 drs	25	27½	19½	19	1 lb. 3 drs	25	23	16	16

TARIFFS—Continued.

DENOMINATION OF MERCHANDISE.	DUTIES ON IMPORTS. Into the United States from foreign nations, per cent. ad valorem, under the act of—		TARIFF OF GENERAL IMPORTATION INTO SPAIN.		
	1846.	1857.	Number, weight, or measure.	In national vessels.	In foreign vessels.
Oil, lavender	30	24	1 lb. 3 drs	$0 95½	$1 27½
lemon	30	24	do	11¾	15
linseed	20	15	4.245 galls	40	47½
olive	30	24	do	79½	1 06
rape seed	20	15	1 lb. 3 drs	5¼	6¼
whale, or other fish oil of foreign fisheries	20	15	4.245 galls	26½	33
vitriol	10	4	101 lbs	53	63½
cloth, of every description	30	24	1 lb. 3 drs	Common, 3	4
				Fine, 16	19
				Silk, 40	53
Olives	30	24	25 lbs. 7 oz	42½	51
Old brass, copper, or pewter	5	Free	101 lbs	8 50	10 60
Onions	20	15			
Opium	20	15	1 lb. 3 drs	32	38
Oranges, dried, pressed, preserved, &c.	40	8	25 lbs. 7 oz	1 06	1 32½
Orchille, dye	5	Free	101 lbs	1 59	1 90
Orris, or iris, root	20	15	1 lb. 3 drs	1½	2
in powder	20	15			
Oxen	20	Free	Each, over 2 yrs.	3 20	3 80
Ox horns	5	4	101 lbs	8	16
Oxide of zinc	20	15	do	5¼	5¾
Packthread	30	24	do	13 25	15 90
Palm leaf, baskets, brooms, &c	30	24		30 per cent.	36 per cent.
Pans, warming, copper	30	24	1 lb. 3 drs	17 to 25½	21¼ to 31¾
Paper, of all kinds(a)	30	24	25 lbs. 7 oz	1 68	2 01¾
foolscap	30	24	do	2 64	3 16¾
boxes	30	24	Dozen	19	22¾
hangings	20	15		30 per cent.	36 per cent.
colored	30	24	1 lb. 3 drs	5¼	6¼
Parasols and sunshades, silk	30	24	One	85	1 02½
cotton	30	24	do	30	36
Parchment	30	24	1 lb. 3 drs	8	9½

(a) Not otherwise provided for.

TARIFFS—Continued.

DUTIES ON IMPORTS.

TARIFF OF IMPORTATION INTO THE ISLAND OF CUBA.					TARIFF OF IMPORTATION INTO THE ISLAND OF PORTO RICO.				
		Per centage duty on the fixed value.					Per centage duty on the fixed value.		
Number, weight, or measure.	Fixed value on the number, weight, or measure.	Foreign productions under a foreign flag.	Foreign productions under the national flag, and those of Spain under a foreign flag.	Foreign productions under the national flag, imported from Spain proper.	Number, weight, or measure.	Fixed value on the number, weight, or measure.	Foreign productions under a foreign flag.	Foreign productions under the national flag, and those of Spain under a foreign flag.	Foreign productions under the national flag, imported from Spain proper.
1 lb. 3 drs	$1 00	27½	19½	19½	1 lb. 3 drs	$1 00	23	16	16
do	2 00	27½	19½	19½	do	2 00	23	16	16
4.245 galls	2 00	27½	19½	19½	1 quart	18¾	23	16	16
do	2 00	33½	23½	23½	4.245 galls	2 50	29	20	20
do	2 00	27½	19½	19½	1 quart	18¾	23	16	16
do	2 50	27½	19½	19½	1 quart whale 2 quarts other	18¾ 25	23	16	16
25 lbs. 7 oz	1 50	27½	19½	19½	101 lbs	6 00	23	16	16
Vara	Common, 25 Fine, 50	27½	19½	19½	Vara	Common, 25 Fine, 75 Silk, 75	23	16	16
25 lbs. 7 oz	1 00	33½	23½	23½	25 lbs. 7 oz	1 25	29	20	20
101 lbs	10 00	27½	19½	19½	101 lbs	10 00	23	16	16
Barrel	2 00	33½	23½	23½	do	2 00	29	20	20
1 lb. 3 drs	3 00	27	19½	19½	1 lb. 3 drs	3 00	23	16	16
12 boxes	3 75	33½	25	23½	12 boxes	3 75	29	20	20
1 lb. 3 drs	9 00	27½	19½	19½	1 lb. 3 drs	9 00	23	16	16
101 lbs	12 50	½	19½	19½	101 lbs	12 50	23	16	16
do	25 00	27½	19½	19½	do	25 00	23	16	16
Each	62 50	33½	23½	23½	One	35 00	29	20	20
100	1 to 1 25	2	2	2	10	1 to 1 25	29	20	20
1 lb. 3 drs	75	27½	19½	19½	1 lb. 3 drs	75	23	16	16
101 lbs	17 50	33½	23½	23½	101 lbs	20 00	29	20	20
	Valuation	27½	19½	19½		Valuation	23	16	16
101 lbs	37 50	33½	23½	23½	101 lbs	37 50	29	20	20
	Valuation	33½	23½	23½		Valuation	29	20	20
Ream	3 00	33½	23½	23½	Ream	3 00	29	20	20
Dozen	2 25	27½	19½	19½	Dozen	3 00	23	16	16
Piece of 10 yards	75	33½	23½	23½	Piece of 10 yards	75	29	20	20
Ream	3 00	33½	23½	23½	Ream	3 00	29	20	20
One	According to	size,				According to	size,		
	1 50 to 2 00	27½	19½	19½		2 00 to 6 00	29	20	20
1 lb. 3 drs	Common, $1	27½	19½	19½	1 lb. 3 drs	Common, $1	23	16	16

TARIFFS—Continued.

DENOMINATION OF MERCHANDISE.	DUTIES ON IMPORTS.				
	Into the United States from foreign nations, per cent. ad valorem, under the act of—		TARIFF OF GENERAL IMPORTATION INTO SPAIN.		
	1846.	1857.	Number, weight, or measure.	In national vessels.	In foreign vessels.
Pasteboard	30	24	1 lb. 3 drs	$0 05¼	$0 06¼
Paving tiles	20	15	1,000	1 90	2 54½
Pencils, black lead	30	24	Ounce	2½	3¼
Penknives	30	24			
Pepper, black	30	4	101 lbs.	2 12	3 71
Cayenne, Chili, or African	30	4	do	2 12	3 71
Perfumes, of all kinds	30	24	1 lb. 3 drs	16	19
Perfumed or fancy, shaving and other soaps	30	24	do	16	19
Peruvian bark	15	Free	1 lb. 3 drs	10½	12½
Pewter, old	5	4	101 lbs	8 50	10 60
Piano-fortes	20	15	Each, under $200	53 00	63 60
			$200, and upwards	25 per cent.	30 per cent.
Pickled fish, other than mackerel and salmon	30	24	101 pounds	2 65	3 18
Pimento	40	4	do	2 12	3 71
Pins, of all kinds	30	24	1 pound 3 drs	12¾	15
Pipes, china and clay	30	24	25 lbs. 7 oz	40	53
Pitch, Burgundy	25	19	101 pounds	25½	34
common	20	15	do	12¾	17
Planks and boards, rough or dressed	20	15	From the colonies, or any other transmarine country, each, being 4 yds. long, 12½ inches wide, and 1½ inch thick,	1½	4
pine	20	15			
white pine	20	15			
maple	20	15			
cedar	20	15			
Plaster, busts of	30	24		25 per cent.	30 per cent.
casts of	30	24		15 per cent.	18 per cent.
of Paris, ground	20	15	101 pounds	5¼	6¼
Plated, or silver wire	30	24	1 pound 3 drs	10½	13¼
Platina, unmanufactured	Free	Free		Free	
in plates	30	24			
Plush, of silk and cotton	25	15	1 pound 3 drs	1 90¾	2 29
Porcelain	30	24	25 pounds 7 oz	2 65	63 50

TARIFFS—Continued.

DUTIES ON IMPORTS.

TARIFF OF IMPORTATION INTO THE ISLAND OF CUBA.					TARIFF OF IMPORTATION INTO THE ISLAND OF PORTO RICO.				
Number, weight, or measure.	Fixed value on the number, weight, or measure.	Per centage duty on the fixed value.			Number, weight, or measure.	Fixed value on the number, weight, or measure.	Per centage duty on the fixed value.		
		Foreign productions under a foreign flag.	Foreign productions under the national flag, and those of Spain under a foreign flag.	Foreign productions under the national flag, imported from Spain proper.			Foreign productions under a foreign flag.	Foreign productions under the national flag, and those of Spain under a foreign flag.	Foreign productions under the national flag, imported from Spain proper.
Ream	$3 00	27½	19½	19½	Ream	$3 00	23	16	16
1,000	12 00	33½	23½	23½	1,000, with the	fire mark, $16	29	20	20
					1,000	Common, $12	29	20	20
25 lbs 7 oz	7 00	27½	19½	19½	101 lbs	28 00	23	16	16
------	------	------	------	------	------	------	------	------	------
25 lbs. 7 oz	3 00	33½	23½	23½	101 lbs	12 00	29	20	20
do	2 00 }	27½	19½	19½	do	8 00 to 25 00	23	16	16
	to 6 25 }	33½	23½	23½					
	Valuation	27½	19½	19½		Valuation	23	16	16
Dozen cakes	75	27½	19½	19½	Dozen cakes	75	23	16	16
101 lbs	Yellow 12 50	27½	19½	19½	101 lbs	Yellow, $12 50	23	16	16
do	10 00	27½	19½	19½	do	10 00	23	16	16
One	300 00	27½	19½	19½		Valuation	23	16	16
101 pounds	12 50	33½	23½	23½	101 pounds	12 50	29	20	20
do	4 00	33½	23½	23½	do	4 00	29	20	20
1 pound 3 drs	50	27½	19½	19½	1 pound 3 drs	50	23	16	16
101 pounds	3 00	27½	19½	19½	101 pounds	3 00	23	16	16
Barrel	3 00	27½	19½	19½	do	6 00	23	16	16
do	3 00	27½	19½	19½	Barrel	3 00	23	16	16
M. feet	20 00	27½	19½	19½					
do					M. feet	15 00	23½	17¼	17¼
do	25 00	33½	23½	23½	do	25 00	23	16	16
do	25 00	33½	23½	23½	do	25 00	29	20	20
	Valuation	27½	19½	19½		Valuation	23	16	16
	Valuation	27½	19½	19½		Valuation	23	16	16
101 pounds	2 00	27½	19½	19½	101 pounds	2 00	23	16	16
Ounce	1 00	27½	19½	19½	1 pound 3 drs	16 00	23	16	16
------	------	------	------	------	------	------	------	------	------
Ounce	4 00	27½	19½	19½	Ounce	4 00	23	16	16
Vara (yd.) of silk	75	27½	19½	19½	Vara of silk	1 00	23	16	16
2 varas of cotton	75	33½	½	23½	Vara of cotton	37½	29	20	20
	Valuation	33	23	23½		Valuation	29	20	20

TARIFFS—Continued.

Denomination of merchandise.	Duties on imports.				
	Into the United States from foreign nations, per cent. ad valorem, under the act of—		Tariff of general importation into Spain.		
	1846.	1857.	Number, weight, or measure.	In national vessels.	In foreign vessels.
Pork	20	15	25 pounds 7 oz.	Sltd., $0 31¾ Smoked, 63½	$0 38¼ 76¼
Potash, chromate of	20	15	1 pound 3 drs	3¼	4
prussiate of	20	15	do	4¾	5¾
Potatoes	30	24	25 lbs. 7 oz. (about ½ bush.)	1½	2
Powder, hair, perfumed	30	24	1 lb. 3 drs	16	19
tooth, and cosmetics	30	24	do	16	19
Preserves in sugar, brandy, and molasses	40	30	25 lbs. 7 oz	1 06	1 32½
Prints and engravings	10	8	Piece	2 00	2 00
Printing paper	30	24	25 lbs. 7 oz	1 68	2 01¾
types, old or new	20	15	do	Of steel 1 27½	or lead, 1 52½
Prussian blue	20	4	1 lb. 3 drs	19	23
Prussiate of potash	20	15	do	4¾	5¾
Quassia wood	20	15	do	3¼	5¼
Quercitron bark	20	8	25 lbs. 7 oz	8	9½
Quicksilver	20	15		Prohibited	
Quills, manufactured	20	15	1 lb. 3 drs	16	19
Quinine, sulphate	20	15	Ounce	26½	32
Raisins of all kinds	40	8	25 lbs. 7 oz	23¾	28½
Rape seed, oil of	20	15	1 lb. 3 drs	5¼	6¼
Red, Venetian, as ochre in oil	30	24	do	16	19
Rice	20	15	101 lbs	1 69½	2 12
Rods, copper	20	15	do	10 60	13 25
Rose, essential oil of	30	24	Ounce	38¼	51¼
water	30	24	1 lb. 3 drs	16	19
wood	20	8	do	3¼	4
Rosemary, oil of	30	24	do	11¾	15
Rosin	20	15	101 lbs	79½	1 06
Saddlery, common, of all descriptions	20	15		30 per cent.	40 per cent.
Saddles and saddle trees	30	24		30 per cent.	40 per cent.
Saffron and saffron cakes	20	15	1 lb. 3 drs	47¾	57¼
Sago	20	15		Free	Free
Salt	20	15	All common salts	prohibited	

TARIFFS—Continued.

DUTIES ON IMPORTS.

TARIFF OF IMPORTATION INTO THE ISLAND OF CUBA.					TARIFF OF IMPORTATION INTO THE ISLAND OF PORTO RICO.				
		Per centage duty on the fixed value.					Per centage duty on the fixed value.		
Number, weight, or measure.	Fixed value on the number, weight, or measure.	Foreign productions under a foreign flag.	Foreign productions under the national flag, and those of Spain under a foreign flag.	Foreign productions under the national flag imported from Spain proper.	Number, weight, or measure.	Fixed value on the number, weight, or measure.	Foreign productions under a foreign flag.	Foreign productions under the national flag, and those of Spain under a foreign flag.	Foreign productions under the national flag imported from Spain proper.
Barrel, of 200 lbs.	Salt'd, 12 00	33½	23½	23½	Barrel, salted ...	$15 00	23½	17¼	14¼
25 pounds 7 oz...	Smk'd, 2 00	33½	23½	23½	101 lbs., smoked.	7 00	29	20	20
1 pound 3 drs....	60	27½	19½	19½	1 pound 3 drs...	62½	23	16	16
......do........	5 00	27½	19½	19½	......do........	6 00	23	16	16
Barrel	2 50	27½	19½	19½	101 lbs.........	1 50	23	16	16
25 lbs. 7 oz......	6 25	33½	23½	23½	1 lb. 3 drs......	25	29	20	20
12 boxes	50	27½	19½	19½	12 boxes, (cajitas)	1 00	23	16	16
12 boxes or bottles.	3 75	33½	23½	23½	12 bxs or bottles.	4 50	29	20	20
Piece	Valuation.	27½	19½	19½	....	Valuation.	23	16	16
Ream	$2 to 2 50	33½	23½	23½	Ream	$2 to 2 50	29	20	20
101 lbs..........	37 50	27½	19½	19½	101 lbs.........	37 50	23	16	16
....do..........	112 50	27½	19½	19½	....do..........	112 50	23	16	16
1 lb. 3 drs.......	5 00	27½	19½	19½	1 lb. 3 drs......	6 00	23	16	16
25 lbs 7 oz......	3 25	27½	19½	19½	101 lbs.........	12 00	23	16	16
....do..........	1 50	27½	19½	19½	....do..........	6 00	23	16	16
....do..........	15 00	2	2	2	....do..........	75 00	23	16	16
1,000...........	2 50	27½	19½	19½	1,000..........	2 50	23	16	16
Ounce	2 00	27½	19½	19½	Ounce	2 00	23	16	16
25 lbs. 7 oz......	1 00	33½	23½	23½	27 lbs. 7 oz.....	1 50	29	20	20
4.245 galls	2 00	27½	19½	19½	1 quart	18¾	23	16	16
25 lbs. 7 oz......	1 00	27½	19½	19½	101 lbs.........	4 00	23	16	16
....do..........	1 25	33½	23½	23½	....do..........	4 50	29	20	20
101 lbs..........	25 00	33½	23½	23½	....do..........	30 00	29	20	20
Ounce	4 00	27½	19½	19½	1 lb. 3 drs......	1 00	23	16	16
1 bottle..... ...	1 00	27½	19½	19½	1 bottle........	1 00	23	16	16
1 lb. 3 drs.......	50	27½	19½	19½	1 lb. 3 drs......	50	23	16	16
......do........	1 00	27½	19½	19½	......do........	4 00	23	16	16
101 lbs..........	Com., 12 50	27½	19½	19½	101 lbs.........	Com., 12 50	23	16	16
....	Valuation ...	33½	23½	23½	....	Valuation ...	29	20	20
....	$10 to 21 00	33½	23½	23½	....	$10 to 21 00	29	20	20
1 lb. 3 drs.......	5 00	33½	23½	23½	1 lb. 3 drs......	5 00	29	20	20
101 lbs..........	12 50	27½	19½	19½	101 lbs.........	12 50	23	16	16
....	As home (200 lbs.,) $1 87½.	product, under all	$1 25 per flags; for	3 bush., eign,	....	The same as	Cuba.		

TARIFFS—Continued.

Denomination of merchandise.	Duties on imports. Into the United States from foreign nations, per cent. ad valorem, under the act of— 1846.	1857.	Tariff of general importation into Spain. Number, weight, or measure.	In national vessels.	In foreign vessels.
Saltpetre, crude	5	4	101 lbs	$2 06¾	$3 10
refined	10	8	do	4 77	6 35
Salts, Glauber	20	15	25 lbs. 7 oz	16	19
Epsom	20	15	do	16	19
Rochelle	20	15			
Salad oil, olive	30	24	4.245 gallons	79½	1 06
Salmon, pickled, dried, or smoked	20	15	101 lbs	2 65	3 18
Sal soda, and all carbonates of soda, &c	20	8	1 lb. 3 drs	4¾	5¾
Sardines, pickled	20	15	101 lbs	2 65	3 18
in oil	40	30			
Saws, mill	30	24	1 lb. 3 drs	6¼	7¾
Scales, brass or copper	30	24	do	25½	31¾
Screws, iron, wood screws	30	24	do	3¼	4
Sculpture, especially imported	Free	Free		25 per cent.	30 per cent.
otherwise	According to material.			25 per cent.	30 per cent.
Scythes, of iron or steel	30	24	101 lbs	63½	85
Shawls, of silk	30	24	1 lb. 3 drs	2 65	3 18
of camel's or goat's hair	30	24	do	12	14¼
cotton	30	24	do	29¾ to 55¾	35½ to 66¾
Sheathing copper for ships	Free	Free	101 lbs	10 60	13 25
Shells, tortoise, and other, manufactured	5	4	1 lb. 3 drs	53	63½
Shoes and slippers	30	24		Prohibited	
Shot, lead	20	15		do	
Shovels, iron, of all kinds	30	24	One	21¼	25½
Sickles or reaping hooks	30	24	1 lb. 3 drs	3¼	4
Silk, raw	15	12	do	1 06	1 27¼
hats or caps of	30	24	do	3 18	3 71½
laces of	25	19		25 per cent.	30 per cent.
shawls	30	24	do	2 65	3 18
sewing	30	24	do	1 32½	1 60
and worsted shawls	30	24	do	2 65	3 18
Silver, bullion and coin	Free	Free			
lace	30	24		15 per cent.	18 per cent.
nitrate of	30	24	Ounce	24	28½
watches, and parts thereof	10	8		6 per cent.	8 per cent.

TARIFFS—Continued.

DUTIES ON IMPORTS.

TARIFF OF IMPORTATION INTO THE ISLAND OF CUBA.					TARIFF OF IMPORTATION INTO THE ISLAND OF PORTO RICO.				
		Per centage duty on the fixed value.					Per centage duty on the fixed value.		
Number, weight, or measure.	Fixed value on the number, weight, or measure.	Foreign productions under a foreign flag.	Foreign productions under the national flag, and those of Spain under a foreign flag.	Foreign productions under the national flag, imported from Spain proper.	Number, weight, or measure.	Fixed value on the number, weight, or measure.	Foreign productions under a foreign flag.	Foreign productions under the national flag, and those of Spain under a foreign flag.	Foreign productions under the national flag, imported from Spain proper.
101 lbs	$8 00	27½	19½	19½	101 lbs	$8 00	23	16	16
1 lb. 3 drs	25	27½	19½	19½	1 lb. 3 drs	25	23	16	16
101 lbs	2 00	27½	19½	19½	101 lbs	3 00	23	16	16
do	4 00	27½	19½	19½	do	4 00	23	16	16
do	25 00	27½	19½	19½	do	25 00	23	16	16
4.245 gallons	2 00	33½	23½	23½	4.245 gallons	2 50	29	20	20
101 lbs	25 00	27½	19½	19½	101 lbs	25 00	23	16	16
25 lbs. 7 oz	1 50	27½	19½	19½	do	6 00	23	16	16
101 lbs	4 00	33½	23½	23½	do	4 00	29½	21¼	71¼
do	25 00	33½	23½	½	1 lb. 3 drs	37½	23	16	16
One	6 50	33½	23½	23½	One	6 50	29	20	20
do	4 00	33½	23½	23½	One	4 00	29	20	20
Gross	50	27½	19½	19½	Gross	50	23	16	16
	Valuation	27½	19½	19½		Valuation	23	16	16
	Valuation	27½	19½	19½		Valuation	23	16	16
Dozen	6 00	27½	19½	19½	Dozen	6 00	23	16	16
	Valuation	27½	19½	19½		Valuation	23	16	16
25 lbs. 7 oz	6 30	27½	19½	19½	101 lbs	25 00	23	16	16
	Valuation	33½	23½	23½		Valuation	29	20	20
101 lbs	25 00	33½	23½	23½	101 lbs	30 00	29	20	20
1 lb. 3 drs	6 00	33½	23½	23½	1 lb. 3 drs	8 00	29	20	20
Dozen pairs	3 00	33½	23½	23½	Dozen	4 50	29	20	20
101 lbs	5 00	27½	19½	19½	101 lbs	5 00	23	16	16
Dozen	$3 to 9 00	33½	23½	23½	Dozen	$3 to 9 00	29	20	20
		27½	19½	19½			23	16	16
do	2 50	33½	23½	23½	Dozen	2 50	29	20	20
1 lb. 3 drs	3 00	27½	19½	19½	1 lb. 3 drs	3 75	23	16	16
Dozen	4 50	33½	23½	23½	Dozen	4 50	29	20	20
	Valuation	27½	19½	19½		Valuation	23	16	16
	Valuation	27½	19½	19½		Valuation	23	16	16
1 lb. 3 drs	4 00	27½	19½	19½	1 lb 3 drs	4 50	23	16	16
	Valuation	27½	19½	19½		Valuation	23	16	16
			Free				Free		
	Valuation	27½	19½	19½		Valuation	23	16	16
Ounce	1 25	27½	19½	19½	Ounce	1 25	23	16	16
One	12 00	7½	5½	5½	One	8 00	23	16	16

TARIFFS—Continued.

DENOMINATION OF MERCHANDISE.	DUTIES ON IMPORTS. Into the United States from foreign nations, per cent. ad valorem, under the act of—		TARIFF OF GENERAL IMPORTATION INTO SPAIN. Number, weight, or measure.	In national vessels.	In foreign vessels.
	1846.	1857.			
Silver, all manufactures (a)	30	24			
Skins, raw, salted	5	4	101 pounds	of sheep and	goats.
				$0 53	$0 63½
of sheep, with the wool on	20	15		1 59	1 90
Sledges and hammers, blacksmiths'	30	24	1 lb. 3 drs	3¼	4
Soap, common	30	24	101 pounds	3 40	4 25
Socket chisels	30	24	1 lb. 3 drs	6¼	7¼
Soda, carbonate of	20	8		Free	Free
Spades of iron or steel	30	24	do	3¼	4
Specimens of minerology	Free	Free	Each	6 per cent.	8 per cent.
Spectacles, set in copper, iron, or steel	30	24	Dozen	$0 19 to 1 51	$0 23 to 1 81¼
Spermaceti candles	20	15	1 lb. 3 drs	8	9½
oil, foreign fishing	20	15	4.245 gallons	26½	33
raw	20	15		3	4
Spikes, copper	20	15	101 pounds	7 59	9 40
iron	30	24	do	3 20	4 20
rods, or nail rods, iron	30	24	do	3 20	4 20
Spirits of turpentine	20	4			
Steel, cast, in bars	15	12	101 lbs	2 10	2 65
in sheets	20	15	do	2 10	2 65
all manufactures of (b)	30	24			
yards	30	24			
and iron wire	30	24	101 lbs	3 20	4 20
Stones, burr, wrought or unwrought	10	Free	do	13	16
precious, of all kinds, not set	10		One	3 per cent.	3 per cent.
wares	30		25 lbs. 7 oz	1 60	1 90¾
Sugar, of all kinds	30	24	do		
common white, from Spanish American possessions	30	24	do	42½	85
from other Spanish colonies	30	24	do	10½	53
from all other countries	30	24	do	85	1 06
in loaf or other form, refined	30	24	do		
from all Spanish colonies	30	24	do	63¾	1 06
from all other countries	30	24	do	1 59	2 01½
candy	30	24	do	1 59	2 01½

(a) Composed wholly or chiefly of silver.
(b) Not otherwise specified for, or of which steel is a component material.

TARIFFS—Continued.

DUTIES ON IMPORTS.

Tariff of importation into the island of Cuba.					Tariff of importation into the island of Porto Rico.				
		Per centage duty on the fixed value					Per centage duty on the fixed value.		
Number, weight, or measure.	Fixed value on the number, weight, or measure.	Foreign productions under a foreign flag.	Foreign productions under the national flag, and those of Spain under a foreign flag.	Foreign productions under the national flag, imported from Spain proper.	Number, weight, or measure.	Fixed value on the number, weight, or measure.	Foreign productions under a foreign flag.	Foreign productions under the national flag, and those of Spain under a foreign flag.	Foreign productions under the national flag, imported from Spain proper.
1 lb. 3 drs	$16 00	27½	19½	19½	1 lb 3 drs	$16 00	23	16	16
Dozen of goats	or sheep,	--------	--------	--------	Dozen of goats	and sheep,			
--------	4 50	33½	23½	23½	--------	50	29	20	20
Dozen	3 00, or valuation	27½	19½	19½	Dozen	3 00, or valuation.	23	16	16
25 lbs. 7 oz	2 00	33½	23½	23½	101 pounds	10 00	29	20	20
Dozen	2 to 2 25	27½	19½	19½	Dozen	2 25	23	16	16
25 lbs. 7 oz	1 50	27½	19½	19½	101 pounds	6 00	23	16	16
Dozen	3 00	27½	19½	19½	Dozen	2 00 to 3 00	23	16	16
--------	Valuation	27½	19½	19½	--------	Valuation	23	16	16
--------	Valuation	27½	19½	19½	--------	Valuation	23	16	16
101 pounds	32 00	27½	19½	19½	101 pounds	30 00	23	16	16
4.245 gallons	2 50	27½	19½	19½	1 quart	18¾	23	16	16
101 pounds	25 00	33½	23½	23½	101 pounds	30 00	29	20	20
do	7 00	33½	23½	23½	do	8 00	29	20	20
do	3 25	23½	23½	23½	do	4 00	29	20	20
do	12 50	27½	19½	19½	do	12 50	23	16	16
101 lbs	8 00	33½	23½	23½	101 lbs	9 00	29	20	20
do	8 00	33½	23½	23½	do	9 00	29	20	02
--------	Valuation	33½	23½	23½	--------	Valuation	29	20	20
25 lbs. 7 oz	75	33½	23½	23½	101 lbs	4 00	29	20	20
do	2 00	33½	23½	23½	1 lb. 3 drs	12½	29	20	20
Each	10 00	27½	19½	19½	Each	7 50	23	16	16
--------	Valuation	7½	5½	5½	--------	Valuation	6	4	4
--------	do	27½	19½	19½	--------	do	23	16	16
Sugar	of all kinds	prohibit	ed.		101 lbs. Common	white, $9 00	4	4	2
--------	--------	--------	--------	--------	--------	--------	--------	--------	--------
--------	--------	--------	--------	--------	--------	--------	--------	--------	--------
--------	--------	--------	--------	--------	--------	--------	--------	--------	--------
--------	--------	--------	--------	--------	101 lbs	18 00	8	8	4
--------	--------	--------	--------	--------	--------	--------	--------	--------	--------
--------	--------	--------	--------	--------	--------	--------	--------	--------	--------
--------	--------	--------	--------	--------	101 lbs	18 00	8	8	4

TARIFFS—Continued.

DENOMINATION OF MERCHANDISE.	DUTIES ON IMPORTS.				
	Into the United States from foreign nations, per cent. ad valorem, under the act of—		TARIFF OF GENERAL IMPORTATION INTO SPAIN.		
	1846.	1857.	Number, weight, or measure.	In national vessels.	In foreign vessels.
Sulphate of quinine	20	15	Ounce	$0 26½	$0 32
Sulphur, or brimstone	20	15	101 pounds	1 19½	1 43
Tacks, brads, and sprigs, of all kinds	30	24			
Tallow, leaf	10	8	101 pounds	38¼	51
candles	20	15	25 pounds 7 oz	79½	95½
Tapioca	20	15	1 pound 3 drs	1½	1¾
Tartar, cream of	20	4			
crude	5	Free	1 pound 3 drs	4¾	5¾
emetic	20	15			
Tar	20	15	101 pounds	12¾	17
Teas, of all kinds, from the Philippines or China	(a)20	(a)15	1 pound 3 drs	10½	13¼
from all other countries	20	15	do	21¼	26½
Tamarinds	20	8	do	1	1¼
Tarred cables and cordage	25	19	25 pounds 7 oz	3 18	3 81½
Terra de Sienna, in oil	30	24	1 pound 3 drs	16	19
Thread lace	20	15	If cotton, prohibited; others	15 per cent.	30 per cent.
Tiles, building	20	15	1,000	1 90	2 54½
Tin, in blocks, pigs, or bars	5	Free	101 pounds	1 59	1 90
direct from Asia	5	Free	do	47½	1 60
foil, plates and sheets	15	8	1 pound 3 drs	6¼	7¾
all manufactures of (b)	30	24	do	20	24
Tobacco, unmanufactured	30	24	All leaf tobacco	prohibited.	
Virginia					
St. Domingo	30	24			
Cuba	30	24			
manufactured	40	30	Prohibited.		
Virginia, (in Manillas)					
cigars from foreign countries	40	30			
Cuba	40	30			
pipes, clay, china, &c.	30	24	25 lbs. 7 oz	40	53
Tow of flax or hemp	15	12	101 lbs	2 75½	3 45
Twines and packthread	30	24	do	13 25	15 90
Umbrellas and parasols, of all kinds	30	24			
silk	30	24	One	50	60

(a) Teas imported direct from place of production, in American or equalized vessels, free.
(b) Not specified, or of which tin is a component part.

TARIFFS—Continued.

DUTIES ON IMPORTS.

TARIFF OF IMPORTATION INTO THE ISLAND OF CUBA.					TARIFF OF IMPORTATION INTO THE ISLAND OF PORTO RICO.				
		Per centage duty on the fixed value.					Per centage duty on the fixed value.		
Num , weight, or measure.	Fixed value on the number, weight, or measure.	Foreign productions under a foreign flag.	Foreign productions under the national flag, and those of Spain under a foreign flag.	Foreign productions under the national flag, imported from Spain proper.	Number, weight, or measure.	Fixed value on the number, weight, or measure.	Foreign productions under a foreign flag.	Foreign productions under the national flag, and those of Spain under a foreign flag.	Foreign productions under the national flag, imported from Spain proper.
Ounce	$2 00	27½	19½	19½	Ounce	$2 00	23	16	16
101 pounds	3 00	27½	19½	19½	101 pounds	3 00	23	16	16
1,000	12½	27	19½	19½	1,000	12½	23	16	16
101 pounds	7 50	27½	19½	19½	101 pounds	7 50	23	16	16
do	12 00	33½		19½	do	12 00	29	20	20
do	12 50	2	19	23½	do	12 50	23	16	16
do	50 00	27½	19½	19½	do	50 00	23	16	16
do	6 00	27	19½	19½	do	6 00	23	16	16
do	50 00	27½	19	19½	do	50 00	23	16	16
barrel of 200 lbs	3 00	27½	19½	19½	barrel of 200 lbs	3 00	23	16	16
2 pounds	1 75	27½	19½	19½	1 pound 3 drs	75	23	16	16
25 pounds 7 oz	3 00	33½	23½	23½	101 pounds	12 00	29	20	20
101 pounds	12 00	33½	23½	23½	do	12 00	29	20	20
do	6 25	27½	19½	19½	do	6 25	23	16	16
	Valuation	27½	19½	19½		Valuation	23	16	16
1,000	12 00	33½	23½	23½	1,000	12 00 to 16 00	29	20	20
101 pounds	In bars 20 00 In pigs 14 00	27½	19½	19½	101 pounds	In bars 20 00 In pigs 14 00	23	16	16
do	22 50	33½	23½	23½	do	22 50	29	20	20
do	22 50	33½	23½	23½	do	22 50	29	20	20
101 lbs	In deposit, $6	2	2	2					
					101 lbs	8 00	A direct	duty of	$4 00.
					do	12 00	do	do	5 00.
					do	20 00	do	do	3 00.
101 lbs	In carots, $25	33½	23½	23½					
					101 lbs	10 00	A direct	duty of	$5 00.
					Millar (1,000)	3 00	do	do	2 00.
					do	10 00	do	do	2 00.
101 lbs	3 00	27½	19½	19½	101 lbs	3 00	23	16	16
do	7 50	33½	23½	23½	do	5 00	29	20	20
do	17 50	33½	23½	23½	do	20 00	29	20	20
One	1 50 to 2 00	27½	19½	19½	One	Valuation	23	16	16

TARIFFS—Continued.

DENOMINATION OF MERCHANDISE.	DUTIES ON IMPORTS. Into the United States from foreign nations, per cent. ad valorem, under the act of—		TARIFF OF GENERAL IMPORTATION INTO SPAIN.		
	1846.	1857.	Number, weight, or measure.	In national vessels.	In foreign vessels.
Umbrellas and parasols, cotton	30	24	One	30	36
Vanilla beans	20	15	1 lb. 3 drs	32	42½
Veils and lace, of silk	25	24	do	4 24	5 08¾
Velvet, silk	25	19	do	1 90¾	2 29
Venetian red, as ochre, in oil	30	24	do	16	19
Vessels, of copper	30	24	do	17	21¼
of cast iron	30	24	101 lbs	3 18	3 80
Vices	30	24	1 lb. 3 drs	6¼	7¾
Vinegar	30	24	4. 245 gallons	21¼	25½
Violins	20	15	One	2 38	2 86¼
Vitriol, blue or Roman	20	15	----	----	----
oil of	10	4	101 lbs	53	63½
white	20	15	1 lb. 3 drs	1	1¼
Wafers, of flour	30	24	do	25	28
Walking sticks, or canes	30	24	Dozen	1 27¼	1 52¾
Warming pans, of brass or copper	30	24	1 lb. 3 drs	17 to 25½	21¼ to 31¾
Wares, China	30	24	Piece	2 65	3 18
Wares, earthen	30	24	25 lbs. 7 oz.	1 59	1 90¾
stone	30	24	do	1 60	1 90¾
iron	30	24	Common,		
			1 lb. 3 drs	2	2¾
			Fine,	3¼	4
japanned	30	24	----	----	----
cabinet	30	24	----	30 per cent	36 per cent
Wash balls	30	24	1 lb. 3 drs	16	19
Washes, cosmetic and perfumes	30	24	do	16	19
Water, Cologne	30	24	do	16	19
rose	30	24	do	16	19
Wax, bees	20	15	25 lbs. 7 oz.	Yellow,	
				1 06	1 27¼
				White,	
				1 59	1 90¾
Wax candles	20	15	1 lb. 3 drs	9¼	11¼
sealing	30	24	do	40	47½

TARIFFS—Continued.

DUTIES ON IMPORTS.

Tariff of importation into the island of Cuba.					Tariff of importation into the island of Porto Rico.				
Number, weight, or measure.	Fixed value on the number, weight, or measure.	Per centage duty on the fixed value.			Number, weight, or measure.	Fixed value on the number, weight, or measure.	Per centage duty on the fixed value.		
		Foreign productions under a foreign flag.	Foreign productions under the national flag, and those of Spain under a foreign flag.	Foreign productions under the national flag, imported from Spain proper.			Foreign productions under a foreign flag.	Foreign productions under the national flag, and those of Spain under a foreign flag.	Foreign productions under the national flag, imported from Spain proper.
Dozen	$6 00	27½	23½	23½	Dozen	$6 00	29	20	20
100	50	2	2	2	1 lb. 3 drs	5 00	23	16	16
	Valuation	27½	19½	19½		Valuation	23	16	16
Vara	75	27½	19½	19½	Vara	2 00 to 4 00	23	16	16
25 lbs. 7 oz	1 00	27½	19½	19½	101 lbs	4 00	23	16	16
101 lbs	37 50	33½	23½	23½	do	37 50	29	20	20
	Valuation	27½	19½	19½		Valuation	23	16	16
	Valuation	33½	23½	23½		do	29	20	20
Pipe of 32 arrobas, or 145. 840 galls.	17 00	33½	23½	23½	145. 840 gallons	25 00	29	20	20
Each	3 00	27½	19½	19½	Each	3 00	23	16	16
101 lbs	12 50	27½	19½	19½	101 lbs	12 50	23	16	16
25 lbs. 7 oz	1 50	27½	19½	19½	do	6 00	23	16	16
101 lbs	12 50	27½	19½	19½	do	12 50	23	16	16
Dozen boxes	50	27½	19½	19½	Dozen boxes	75	23	16	16
Dozen	1 50 to 12 00	27½	19½	19½	Dozen	6 00 to 24 00	23	16	16
101 lbs	37 50	33½	23½	23½	101 lbs	37 50	29	20	20
Piece	Valuation	27½	19½	19½	Piece	Valuation	27½	19½	19½
	Valuation	27½	19½	19½		Valuation.	23	16	16
	do	27½	19½	19½		do	23	16	16
	do	27½	19½	19½		do	23	16	16
	do	27½	19½	19½		do	23	16	16
	do	37½	23½	23½		do	29	20	20
	do	33½	23½	23½		do	29	20	20
Dozen lls	75	27½	19½	19½	Dozen balls	75	23	16	16
	Valuation.	27½	19½	19½		Valuation	23	16	16
24 flasks	1 75	27½	19½	19½	Dozen flasks	75	23	16	16
1 bottle	1 00	27½	19½	19½	1 bottle	1 00	23	16	16
	Prohibited.	Prohib.	Prohib.	Prohib.		15 00	29	20	20
	Prohibited.	Prohib.	Prohib.	Prohb.	do	37 00	29	20	20
101 lbs	62 50	33½	23½	23½	101 lbs	62 50	29	20	20
1 lb. 3 drs	Common, 50	27½	19½	19½	1 lb. 3 drs.	50	23	16	16
	Fine, 1 00	27½	19½	19½		1 00	23	16	16

TARIFFS—Continued.

DENOMINATION OF MERCHANDISE.	DUTIES ON IMPORTS.				
	Into the United States from foreign nations, per cent ad valorem, under the act of—		TARIFF OF GENERAL IMPORTATION INTO SPAIN.		
	1846.	1857.	Number, weight, or measure.	In national vessel	In foreign vessels.
Whale oil	g	n fishing,			
	20	15	4.245 galls	$0 26½	$0 33
bone	Of foreig	n fishing,			
	20	15	11 lb. 3 dsr	2	2¾
Wheat	20	15	Prohibited, if not	permitted by	special or-
			der of the gove	rnment.	
Whiskey	100	30	4.245 galls	1 C6	1 32½
Wigs, hair	30	24	1 lb. 3 drs	6 62½	7 95
Willow baskets	30	24		25 per cent	30 per cent.
Window glass	20	15	25 lbs. 7 oz	1 85½	2 12½
Wines, Burgundy	40	30	32 qts., (in casks)	4 77	6 35
			One bottle	24	32
Champagne	40	30	Bottle	13¼	17½
claret	40	30	32 qts , (in casks)	4 77	6 35
			One bottle	24	32
Madeira	40	30	....do	24	32
sherry	40	30			
of all other kinds	40	30			
Wire, brass	30	24	101 lbs	13 25	17 50
iron or steel	30	24	....do	3 20	4 20
silvered or plated	30	24	1 lb. 3 drs	10½	13¼
annealed iron wire	30	24	101 lbs	2 40	3 30
Woad or pastel	10	4			
Wood, Brazil	5	Free	101 lbs	6¼	8½
Braziletto	5	..do	....do	6¼	8½
log	5	..do	....do	1	1½
Nicaragua	5	..do	....do	6¼	8½
red	5	..do	....do	6¼	8½
quassia	20	15	1 lb. 3 drs	3½	5¼
all manufactures of (*a*)	30	24		30 per cent	36 per cent.
screws	30	24	1 lb. 3 drs	3¼	4
staves	20	15	Per M from Hamburg.	2 65	3 55
			Do. elsewhere	1 32½	2 65
shingles	20	15			

(*a*) Not otherwise provided for.

TARIFFS—Continued.

DUTIES ON IMPORTS.

TARIFF OF IMPORTATION INTO THE ISLAND OF CUBA.					TARIFF OF IMPORTATION INTO THE ISLAND OF PORTO RICO.				
		Per centage duty on the fixed value.					Per centage duty on the fixed value.		
Number, weight, or measure.	Fixed value on the number weight, or measure.	Foreign productions under a foreign flag.	Foreign productions under the national flag, and those of Spain under a foreign flag.	Foreign productions under the national flag, imported from Spain proper.	Number, weight, or measure.	Fixed value on the number, weight, or measure.	Foreign productions under a foreign flag.	Foreign productions under the national flag, and those of Spain under a foreign flag.	Foreign productions under the national flag, imported from Spain proper.
4.245 galls	$2 50	27½	19½	19½	1 quart.........	$0 18¾	23	16	16
101 lbs..........	62 50	27½	19½	19½	101 lbs.........	62 50	23	16	16
..do...........	5 00	33½	23½	23	....do..........	5 00	29	20	0
See liquors.									
....	Valuation.	27½	19¼	19½	....	Valuation.	23	16	16
Dozen...........	1 50	27½	19½	19½	Dozen..........	1 50	23	16	16
Box, containing 100 square feet.					Box, containing 100 square feet.				
	7 50	33½	19½	19	....	7 50	23	16	16
Basket of a dozen bottles.	3 00	33½	23½	23	Basket of a dozen bottles.	3 00	29	20	20
Basket of a dozen bottles.	8 00	33½	23½	23½	Dozen bottles...	8 00	29	20	20
Basket of a dozen bottles	3 50	33½	23½	23½	Basket of a dozen bottles.	3 50	29	20	20
12 bottles	6 50	33½	23½	23½	4.245 galls......	3 75	29	20	20
4.245 galls......	1 50	33½	23½	23½	....do..........	1 50	29	20	20
Dozen bottles....	3 50	33½	23½	23½	Dozen bottles...	3 50	29	20	20
101 lbs	37 50	27½	19½	19½	1 lb. 3 drs......	37½	23	16	16
25 lbs. 7 oz......	2 00	33½	23½	23½	....do..........	12½	29	20	20
Ounce	1 00	27½	19½	19½	....do..........	16 00	23	16	16
25 lbs. 7 oz......	2 00	33½	23½	23½	....do..........	12½	23	16	16
....do..........	3 12½	27½	19½	19½	....do..........	12½	23	16	16
101 lbs	2 25	2	2	2	101 lbs.........	2 00	1	1	1
....do..........	2 25	2	2	2	....do..........	2 00	1	1	1
One horse load...	50	33½	23½	23½	One horse load..	50	29	20	20
101 lbs	2 25	2	2	2	101 lbs	2 00	1	1	1
....do..........	2 25	2	2	2	....do..........	2 00	1	1	1
25 lbs. 7 oz......	3 25	27½	19½	19½	....do..........	12 00	23	16	16
....	Valuation...	33½	23½	23½	....	Valuation...	29	20	20
Gross	50	27½	19½	19½	Gross	50	23	16	16
1,000..........	25 00	27½	19½	19½	Per 1,000	12 00	23½	17¼	14¼
Per 1,000	2 75	27½	19½	19½	....do..........	3 00	23¼	17¼	14¼

TARIFFS—Continued.

DENOMINATION OF MERCHANDISE.	DUTIES ON IMPORTS.				
	Into the United States from foreign nations, per cent. ad valorem, under the act of—		TARIFF OF GENERAL IMPORTATION INTO SPAIN.		
	1846.	1857.	Number, weight, or measure.	In national vessels.	In foreign vessels.
Wool, unmanufactured	30	(a) 24	101 lbs	$6 35	$8 50
blankets	20	15	One, common	1 27¼	1 52½
felts, or hat bodies	20	15		25 per cent.	30 per cent.
cloths, cassimeres, cassinets, &c	30	24	Square yard	19½	23½
cloths, very fine	30	24	do	79½	95½
baizes, bockings	25	19	1 lb. 3 drs	42½	50¾
all other manufactures of, or of which wool is a component material.	30	24	Square yard	13¼ to 79½	16 to 95½
Worsted and silk shawls, and other manufactures of	30	24	1 lb. 3 drs	2 65	3 18
braces, hose, gloves, shirts, &c	30	24			
Wrapping paper	30	24	1 lb. 3 drs	5¼	6¼
Yarns, of flax or hemp	20	15	101 lbs	19 90	23 85
of cotton	25	24		Prohibited	
Yellow ochre, dry, common	30	15	1 lb. 3 drs	2½	3
fine	30	15	do	16	19
Zinc, in blocks	5	4	101 lbs	3 62½	4 90¼
in pigs	5	4			
in sheets	15	12	101 lbs	5 08¾	6 35
manufactured	30	24	1 lb. 3 drs	8½	10½
sulphate of	20	15			
oxide of	20	15	101 lbs	5½	5¾

(a) Costing 20 cents or less per pound, at the port of exportation, provided it is imported in ordinary condition, free.

TARIFFS—Continued.

DUTIES ON IMPORTS.

TARIFF OF IMPORTATION INTO THE ISLAND OF CUBA.					TARIFF OF IMPORTATION INTO THE ISLAND OF PORTO RICO.				
		Per centage duty on the fixed value.					Per centage duty on the fixed value.		
Number, weight, or measure.	Fixed value on the number, weight, or measure.	Foreign productions under a foreign flag.	Foreign productions under the national flag, and those of Spain under a foreign flag.	Foreign productions under the national flag, imported from Spain proper.	Number, weight, or measure.	Fixed value on the number, weight, or measure.	Foreign productions under a foreign flag.	Foreign productions under the national flag, and those of Spain under a foreign flag.	Foreign productions under the national flag, imported from Spain proper.
----------	----------	------	------	------	101 lbs..........	$5 00	29	20	20
----------	Valuation ..	27½	19½	19½	----------	Valuation ..	23	16	16
Dozen	$3 00	27½	19½	19½	----------	Valuation ..	23	16	16
----------	Valuation ..	33½	23½	23½	----------	Valuation ..	29	20	20
----------	----------	------	------	------	----------	----------	------	------	------
1, 08 yard	25	33½	23½	23½	1. 08 yard	50	29	20	20
----------	Valuation ..	33½	23½	23½	----------	Valuation ..	29	20	20
----------	Valuation ..	27½	19½	19½	----------	Valuation ..	23	16	16
----------	Valuation ..	33½	23½	23½	----------	Valuation ..	29	20	20
Ream, brown....	25	33½	23½	23½	Ream, brown ...	50	29	20	20
101 lbs	37 50	33½	23½	23½	101 lbs..........	37 50	29	20	20
1 lb. 3 drs.......	75	33½	23½	23½	1 lb. 3 drs......	75	29	20	20
101 lbs..........	2 50	27½	19½	19½	101 lbs..........	2 50	23	16	16
......do........	6 25				......do........	6 25			
......do........	----------	27½	19½	19½	......do........	----------	23	16	16
......do........	7 50				......do........	7 50			
......do........	10 00				......do........	10 00			
----------	Valuation ..				----------	Valuation ..			
101 lbs..........	12 50				101 lbs..........	12 50			
1 lb. 3 drs.......	75				1 lb. 3 drs......	75			

PORTUGAL.

31 □

PORTUGAL.

The tariff is that of December, 31 1852, modified by the royal decrees of August 5th and October 16, 1854, and October 1 1855, (a) and applies equally to the Azores, Madra, and Cape Verd islands.

Money, Weights, and Measures.

1 milreis = 1,000 reis = $1 12.	1 canado = 29⅝ inches.
100 arratels = 100 pounds = 101 pounds avoirdupois.	1 canada = 3 pints.
1 arroba = 32 pounds.	1 almude = 18 quartilhos = 4½ gallons.
1 quintal = 128 pounds.	1 alquiere = 2-5 bushel.
1 tonelada = 54 arrobas.	1 mayo = 3 English quarts.
1 vara = 43⅓ inches.	1 tonelada = 225½ gallons.

Manufactures of cotton, linen, and silk, and also tea, wine, and spirituous or malt liquors, vinegar, vegetables, olive and rape seed oil are admitted in Portugal only at the ports of Lisbon and Oporto; at Angra, only, on the Island Terceira; at Ponta Delegada, only, on the Island St. Miguel; at Horta, only, on the Island Fayal; and at Funchal, only, on the Island of Madeira.

For plumbago, stamps, &c., 3 per cent. of the amount of duty is levied, to which is added, for the amortization of the notes of the Bank of Lisbon, an additional duty of 3 per cent.

Duties are calculated on the invoices, attested on oath to be true. When invoices are found incorrect, the goods are appropriated by the government, 10 per cent. more than the price specified in the invoice being paid the importer.

Spirits and silks are admitted on declaration that they conform in quality and value with the manifest.

Goods arriving in a damaged state, and the damage itself amounting to more than three per cent. of their value, are entitled to a deduction proportionate to the loss.

Export duties.—Gold pays $1 12 and silver 11 1-5 cents per 8 ounces. Cork bark and the like, for tanning, $1 34 2-5 per 100 pounds. Tartar of wine, raw, and glass, in broken pieces, $1 12 per 100 pounds each. Wine, exclusive of port, (which is subject to a special legislation annexed to the tariff,) 1 cent per almude = 4½ gallons. All other articles, not named, imported, pay on re-exportat[illegible] pe[illegible] cent. ad valorem.

(a) For later modifications, see Annual Repo[illegible]ts.
See Vol. 3, "Returns," p. 166.

COMPARATIVE TARIFFS.

UNITED STATES AND PORTUGAL.

DENOMINATION OF MERCHANDISE.	DUTIES ON IMPORTS INTO—			
	The United States, per cent. ad valorem, under the act of—		PORTUGAL.	
	1846.	1857.	Number, weight, or measure.	Rate of duty.
Anchors, and parts thereof	30	24	100 arratels, or 101 pounds	$0 43
Ashes, pot and pearl	20	15	do do	28
Beef, salted	20	15	do do	3 36
smoked	20	15	do do	3 36
Beer	30	24	1 almude, or $4\frac{1}{2}$ gallons	1 68
Biscuits and ship bread	20	15	1 arratel, or 1 pound	$5\frac{3}{5}$
Boots for men	30	24	per pair	3 58
shoes for women or men	30	24	do	1 12
Butter	20	15	101 pounds	6 16
Cables and cordage	25	19	do	2 68 to 3 58
Candles, spermaceti	20	15	do	10 08
Cheese, common	30	24	do	3 36
fine	30	24	do	6 72
Coaches	30	24	One	2 24
Cotton, raw	Free	Free	101 pounds	$2\frac{1}{5}$
manufactured	25 to 30	19 to 24	1 pound	6 to 70
Dye wood, in sticks	5	Free	1 arroba, or 32 pounds	5 to 32
Fish, dried or smoked	20	15	101 pounds	1 50
Flour	20	15	(a) 101 pounds	(a) 1 12
Gold and silver coin	Free	Free		Free.
Hams and bacon	20	15	101 pounds	3 36
Hides, dry or wet	5	4	do	$33\frac{3}{5}$
tanned	20	15	1 pound	$44\frac{3}{4}$
Indigo	10	4	101 pounds	1 12
Lard	20	15	do	1 44
Mahogany wood	20	8	1 quintal, or 128 pounds	12
Nails, iron, of all kinds	30	24	101 pounds	4 34
Oak bark	20	8	128 pounds	24
Oil, whale and other fish	20	15	101 pounds	$36\frac{1}{3}$
or in bottles	20	15	32 bottles	72
Paints and varnish	20 to 30	15 to 24		5 per ct. ad val.
Pitch	20	15	128 pounds	24
Pork, fresh or salted	20	15	101 pounds	3 36
Potatoes	30	24	do	67
Rice	20	15	do	1 27
paddy	20	15	do	83

(a) Wheat and all other grain are admitted only in small quantities, for seed. The government has been lately empowered by the Cortez to admit Indian corn, on account of the scarcity of this article in the country.

TARIFFS—Continued.

Denomination of merchandise.	Duties on imports into— The United States, per cent. ad valorem, under the act of— 1846.	1857.	Portugal. Number, weight, or measure.	Rate of duty.
Sugar, raw	30	24	101 pounds	$3 36
refined	30	24	do	5 60
Spermaceti	20	15	do	66½
Tar	20	15	128 pounds	12
Teas	(a)20	(a)15	1 pound	(b)89½
Tobacco, manufactured	40	30	The importation of tobacco sively to the Royal Con	belongs exclu- tract Company.
unmanufactured	30	24		
Turpentine	20	15	32 pounds	22
Wax, white	20	15	101 pounds	4 11
yellow	20	15	do	2 02
Whalebone	20	15	o	3¼
Wood, log, in sticks	5	Free	32 pounds	6
extract of, and chipped	20	4		
masts and spars	20	15	Each	10 to 1 84½ Accord'g to size.
Staves and heading, 29 inches in length	20	15	Per 100 pieces	12
30 to 37 "	20	15	do	14½
38 to 46 "	20	15	do	26
47 to 57 "	20	15	do	31

(a) Imported direct from place of production, in American or equalized vessels, free. See note p 168.
(b) In Portuguese ships of at least 100 tons.

TARIFF OF EXPORTATION.(a)

All liquors, gin, rum, &c	(b)100	30	1 almude, or 4½ gallons	2
Port wine, a general duty	40	30	Per pipe	2 68½
extra duty, 7 per cent	40	30	do	19
do 5 do	40	30	do	14½
notes, 5 per cent	40	30	do	14¾
fees, 3 per cent	40	30	do	7¾
exchange	40	30	do	11½

(a) According to consular return.
(b) The United States has no tariff of exportation. This column is given, as in similar cases, for the sake of contrast, not comparisor

BELGIUM.

BELGIUM.

The tariff is that established by the royal decree of August 28, 1853, with modifications down to April, 1855.(a)

Moneys are the same as in France—1 franc = 100 centimes = 18 3-5 cents United States currency.

Weights and measures.—One hundred kilogrammes = 220 lbs.; 1 kilogramme = 2.204 lbs; 1 hectolitre (dry capacity) = $2\frac{3}{4}$ bushels; 1 hectolitre (liquid capacity) = 26 gallons; 1 tonneau = 52 9-10 square feet.

All goods imported for re-exportation are free, whether the entry for home consumption of the same goods is prohibited or not. The following are exceptions, and the transit of the same is prohibited, if not imported direct by the government railway, viz: cattle, distilled spirits and cordials, rags, and vinegar.

The transmit of the following is entirely prohibited: iron ore, raw iron, forged iron, iron plates, old iron, railings, anchors, gunpowder, salt, syrup and molasses, refined sugar, and some other minor articles.

OFFICIAL DEFINITION OF TRANSIT.

SECTION I.

Article 1. Transit is the conveyance of merchandise over the territories of the kingdom.

SECTION II.

Article 2. There are two modes of transit:

1. Direct transit.
2. Transit through the entrepots.

DIRECT TRANSIT.

Article 3, § 1. Direct transit is that which is effected without entering the merchandise in entrepot. It takes place—

a. Over the railroads of the state.

b. By any other mode of carriage.

§ 2. Direct transit over the railroads of the state is effected—

a. On entrance by railroad.

On clearance by railroad or by sea.

b. On entrance by sea.

On clearance by sea, or by sea or railroad.

§ 3. Entrance and clearance by the rivers of Holland, the same as if by sea.

§ 4. Direct transit by any other route is effected without any distinction as respects entrance and clearance.

TRANSIT BY ENTREPOT.

Transit by entrepot applies to the re-exportation of merchandise deposited in such establishments.

Article 5, § 1. The government designates the bureaus open for the transitage of merchandise and the routes to be followed.

§ No merchandise admitted to transit unless specially declared at one of the bureaus before discharging a verification whether it is intended for transit or entrepot.

(a) By an act of May, 1856, modifications of the tariff of Belgium were made to some extent, the act to take effect January 1, 1858, or sooner, by royal decree, if thought best by the king. The duties imposed by this act on rice, tobacco, and sugar, the only articles affecting the United States, are as follows: Rice, not hulled, or paddy, per 220 lbs., 18 3-5 cents; rice, hulled, per 220 lbs., 37 1-5 cents. Tobacco, unmanufactured, in leaves or rolls, per 220 lbs., $2 4 3-5; stems, per 220 lbs., $1 30 1-5. Tobacco, manufactured, cigars, per 220 lbs., $39 99; other kinds, per 220 lbs., $6 51.

Transit duties and restrictions on the principal articles of commerce between the United States and Belgium.

DENOMINATION OF MERCHANDISE.	Number, weight, or measure.	Rate of duty.
Coal, stone	1,000 kilogs., or 2,220 lbs.	$1 11⅜
if from or to the United States		Free.
Cordage of all kinds, in quantities less than 1,000 kilogrammes, or 2,220 lbs.		Prohibited.
Fishes, sea, similar to those of the Belgian fisheries		Prohibited.
Gunpowder		Prohibited.
Iron		Prohibited.
Molasses and syrup		Prohibited.
Rags, direct per railroad		Free.
otherwise		Prohibited.
Salt, sea		Prohibited.
Slates	1,000 pieces	29⅜
if coming from or going to the United States		Free.
Sugar, refined		Prohibited.
Vinegar, direct per railroad		Free.
otherwise		Prohibited.
Woolen goods, such as cloths, cassimeres, and similar tissues, direct per railroad.		Free.
The same, otherwise	220 pounds	1 48⅜

1. Articles free of both exportation and importation duties are also free of transit duty.

2. Articles not enumerated in the above list, although subject to importation or exportation duty, are free of transit duty if transported by government railroad.

3. All other articles, if transported by the government railway, are subject to a duty of 10 per cent. on the amount of the export or import duty.

4. Besides the fixed rates of import, export, transit, and stamp duties, 16 per cent. additional duty is levied on the aggregate amount of the rates.

Tare.—For casks and chests, 15 per cent. is deducted on every 220 lbs ; leather bags, &c., 8 per cent ; mattings, canvas, &c., 3 per cent, unless otherwise specified.

DIFFERENTIAL DUTIES.

The following explanatory remarks are prefixed to the official publication of the Belgian tariff, July, 1855.

Belgium has concluded treaties of commerce and navigation with several foreign nations, which modify the general regulations of the tariff of duties. These modifications are comprehended under three heads :

1. Assimilation of foreign flags to the Belgian flag in respect to the importation of merchandise subject to differential duties.

2. Special reduction of import, export, and transit duties, in respect to certain descriptions of merchandise.

3. Assimilation of foreign flags to the Belgian flag in respect to tonnage duties.

Special reduction of import, export, and transit duties, are specified in pages. * * * * * * [These reductions referred to here are regulated by treaty, and equalize the flag of the nations to which they apply, as respects certain descriptions of merchandise, with the Belgian flag.]

The assimilation of foreign flags to the Belgian, in respect to the importation of merchandise subject to differential duties, exists in the cases and in respect to the flags specified and designated as follows :

1. Direct importation, by sea, from the country to which the vessel belongs, without regard to the producing country.

Flags thus assimilated : Austrian, United States, French, British, Greek, Guatemalian, Ionian, Mexican, Dutch, Peruvian, Pontifical, Sardinian.

In respect to the British flag, this assimilation exists, whether the merchandise is imported from the United Kingdom or from the colonial possessions.

As regards the Netherlands, it applies to importations by canals and rivers ; and, in respect to importations by sea, the Dutch flag is entitled to the deduction of ten per cent. provided for in the article of the royal order of February 2, 1852.

NOTE.—Royal order of February 2, 1852.—Merchandise subject to differential duties by reason of origin, country, whence exported, or flag, enjoy a deduction of ten per cent. if imported by sea in Belgian vessels, unless otherwise provided for by treaty. Direct importation by sea from the country to which the vessel belongs, provided the merchandise is the produce of the same country.

Flags thus assimilated: Brazil, Chili, the Two Sicilies, Russia.

2. Importation by sea from any country, provided the merchandise comes under the designation *elsewhere*, or from other places, in the tariff of differential duties.

Flags thus assimilated: Austrian, United States, Pontifical States, French, British, Guatemalian, Ionian, Dutch, Peruvian, and Sardinian.

Salt and the produce of the fisheries in all cases, excluded from the assimilation of flags. Nevertheless, rock salt is excepted from this exclusion—1st. When it is imported from France in French or British bottoms, provided that, if it is not of French production, it shall be proved by a certificate from the French custom-house that the cargo had been landed at a French port. 2d. When it is imported from the Netherlands in Dutch bottoms, provided the importer shall prove, by a certificate from a Dutch custom-house, that the cargo was received on board in a Dutch port. 3d. When it is imported from the kingdom of Sardinia in Sardinian vessels.

In all cases, the admission of salt in foreign bottoms is subject to the general condition applicable to the Belgian flag, namely, that the importation must be made in vessels coming direct from sea and measuring at least 50 tons.

In all cases the custom-house officers will require the production of the necessary documents to prove the nationality of vessels, conformably to the requirements of section 80.

NOTE.—Section 80.—Besides, in all cases when the vessels of nations are favored by any treaty stipulation, this favor will not apply, unless such vessels are ascertained to belong to such nation, in conformity with the laws and regulations in force, and their nationality be attested by sea letters, in the form prescribed, and duly certified by the competent authority of the nation to which the vessel belongs.

COMPARATIVE TARIFFS.

UNITED STATES AND BELGIUM.

DENOMINATION OF MERCHANDISE.	DUTIES ON IMPORTS INTO—			
	The United States, per cent. ad valorem, under the act of—		BELGIUM.	
	1846.	1857.	Number, weight, or measure.	Rate of duty.
Ashes, pot and pearl	20	15		Free.
Books, unbound	10 to 20	8 to 15	100 kilogrammes, 220 lbs.	$5 88
bound	10 to 20	8 to 15	do	7 85
Brown sugar	30	24	do	32
Candles	20	15	do	Sper'ceti, 15 96 Tallow, 5 41
Cards, playing	30	24	Per 12 dozen	2 37¾
Cassia lignea	40	4	220 pounds	5 55
Cheese	30	24	do	1 98½
China, white or colored	30	24	do	1 53
porcelain	30	24	do	11 11
Cloth and cassimeres	30	24	do	46 82
Cocoa	10	4	do	2 85
Coffee	(a)20	15	do	2 15
Copper, in blocks, sheets, &c	30	24	do	1
in plates	30	24	do	2 34
kettles and basins	30	24	do	2 34
sheathing for ships	Free	Free	do	2 34
Cotton, raw, in Belgian and equalized vessels, (b) direct from the country of production.	Free	Free	do	Free.
Cotton, raw, in foreign (not equalized) vessels, of the country of exportation.	Free	Free	do	Free.
Cotton, manufactured, plain, not colored	25	24	do	33 37
colored or printed	25	24	do	60 18
drills	25	24	do	25 92
laces, common white	25	19		12 per ct. ad val.
colored and white, stitched	25	19		18 per ct. ad val.
Dye wood, ground	20	4		Prohibited
in stick, Pernambuco, under Belgian or equalized flags.	5	Free	220 pounds	37
other, under the same	5	Free	do	⅕
Flannels	25	19	do	29 96¼
Flax, manufactured, batiste, (cambric)	20	15	1 kilogramme, 2.20 lbs	93
others, according to the number of threads	20	15	220 pounds	$26 22 to 56 18

(a) See note, p. 114. (b) The nomenclature, for the sake of convenience and conciseness, is adapted to the tariff of Belgium. See note, p. 157

TARIFFS—Continued.

Denomination of merchandise.	Duties on imports into—			
	The United States, per cent. ad valorem, under the act of—		Belgium.	
	1846.	1857.	Number, weight, or measure.	Rate of duty.
Flour	20	15	220 pounds	$0 $56\frac{1}{4}$
Garden seeds	Free	Free	do	$99\frac{1}{4}$
Glass, plain window	20	15	do	2 77
ware, cut	40	30	do	18 51
bottles, common	30	24	Per 100	1 $11\frac{1}{2}$
Hams and bacon	20	15	220 pounds	4 $15\frac{1}{2}$
Hats	30	24		10 per ct. ad val.
Hemp, not hackled	30	24	220 pounds	$37\frac{1}{2}$
hackled	20	15	do	1 20
Hides and skins, fresh, salt, or not, direct from the trans-Atlantic countries of production, in Belgian or equalized vessels.	Raw, 5	4	do	$9\frac{3}{5}$
	Tanned, 20	15	do	$9\frac{3}{5}$
Hides and skins, fresh, salt, or not, direct from the trans-Atlantic countries of production, in vessels from the country of exportation.	Raw, 5	4		
	Tanned, 20	15	do	$9\frac{3}{5}$
Hops	20	15	do	2 81
Hosiery, cotton and linen, mixed or not	20 to 30	15 to 24	do	27 77
woolen	30	24	do	46 29
Household furniture, of all kinds	30	24		20 per ct. ad val.
Indigo, direct from the country of production, in Belgian or equalized vessels.	10	4		Free.
Indigo, direct from the country of production, in foreign vessels.	10	4	220 pounds	Free.
Iron, ore	20	24	do	$8\frac{1}{3}$
cast, in bars	30	24	do	$83\frac{1}{3}$
cast, wrought in stoves, balls, shot, &c	30	24	do	2 73
forged in hoops and bands	30	24	do	5 09
nails	30	24	do	2 75
wrought in kettles, plates, anvils	30	24	do	5 09
anchors	30	24	do	2 73
Lard, in Belgian and equalized vessels	20	15	do	93
Lead, crude or in sheets, or old, in Belgian vessels, by sea, from all places.	20	15	do	$9\frac{1}{3}$
Lead, wrought, and in pencils, without wood	30	24	do	$83\frac{1}{3}$
Leather	20	15	do	5 $76\frac{2}{3}$
Linseed oil	20	15	do	2 $30\frac{1}{3}$
Lumber, of all sorts, by sea, direct, in Belgian or equalized vessels.	20	15	1 tonneau, $52\frac{9}{10}$ sq. feet	1 $67\frac{1}{2}$
Manufactures of castings	30	24	220 pounds	2 73
Nutmegs	40	4		20 per ct. ad val.
Oak bark, for tanning purposes	20	8	1,000 kilo., 2,200 lbs	$11\frac{1}{4}$
ground	20	8		6 per ct. ad val.

TARIFFS—Continued.

DENOMINATION OF MERCHANDISE.	DUTIES ON IMPORTS INTO— The United States, per cent. ad valorem, under the act of—		BELGIUM.	
	1846.	1857.	Number, weight, or measure.	Rate of duty.
Oil, whale and other fish	20	15	1 hectolitre, 26 gallons	$2 27
Paints and varnish	20 to 30	15 to 24		1 per ct. ad val.
Paper	30	24		15 per ct. ad val.
hangings	20	15		10 per ct. ad val.
Pepper and pimento, under Belgian flags	30 and 4		220 pounds	2 23
under other flags	40 and 4		do.	2 79
Pitch	20	15	13 barrels, 44,000 pounds	71⅙
Pork	20	15	220 pounds	93
Quicksilver	20	15	do	53⅓
Rape seed oil	20	15	do	2 30⅓
Ready-made clothing	30	24		20 per ct. ad val.
Rosin, raw, by sea, in Belgian or equalized vessels	20	15	220 pounds	14⅔
in other vessels	20	15	do	24
Rice	20	15	do	1 52
in hull	20	15	do	47
Salt, dry, or not, direct from trans-Atlantic countries, in Belgian or equalized vessels.	20	15	do	0⅕
in other vessels	20	15	do	$0 11
Silk, manufactures of all sorts, as satin, taffetas, velvet, handkerchiefs, &c.	25	19	2.20 pounds	1 02⅛
ribbons excepted, unbleached or half bleached, bleached, dyed, or printed.	25	19	do	2 06
Skins, tanned and dressed	20	15	220 pounds	5 76⅔
Spermaceti	20	15		2 per ct. ad val.
Sugar cane, raw, by sea, direct from the country of production, in Belgian vessels.	30	24	220 pounds	0⅕
in other vessels	30	24	do	32
from trans-Atlantic countries not those of production, in Belgian vessels.	30	24	do	31⅔
in other vessels	30	24	do	79⅔
in any other way	30	24		Prohibited.
refined, or raw mixed with refined	30	24	220 pounds	15 83
molasses of all sorts	30	24		Prohibited.
Tar	20	15		Free.
Tea	(a)20	15	220 pounds	12 10
Tobacco, leaf or rolls, from Porto Rico, Havana, Columbia, and Varinas, direct, in Belgian or equalized vessels.	30	24	do	2 75
in other vessels	30	24	do	3 06
from elsewhere	30	24	do	1 86
manufactured in snuff, or cut	40	30	do	5 83

(a) See note, p. 168.

TARIFFS—Continued.

DENOMINATION OF MERCHANDISE.	The United States, per cent. ad valorem, under the act of—		DUTIES ON IMPORTS INTO— BELGIUM.	
	1846.	1857.	Number, weight, or measure.	Rate of duty.
Tobacco, cigars, direct from the countries of production, beyond Europe, in Belgian vessels (and equalized.)	40	30	220 pounds	\$39 00
cigars, in vessels of countries of production, not equalized.	40	30	do	41 80
cigars, in other foreign vessels	40	30	do	45 60
cigars, from elsewhere	40	30	do	45 60
Turpentine, spirits of	20	15	do	11¼
Wax, raw	20	15	do	37½
refined	20	15	do	2 37¾
Whalebone	20	15	do	Raw, free. Cut, 11 40
Wines, in casks	40	30	26 gallons	37⅕
in bottles	40	30	100 to 116 to the hectolitre	2 24½
Wood, in Belgian or equalized vessels	20	8	52 9/10 square feet	37⅕
for ship building, oak	20	8	do	18⅔
masts and spars	20	8		1 per ct. ad val.
hoops	30	24		6 per ct. ad val.
Wool, in general, of every sort, without distinction of origin.	Unmanufactured, 30	(a)24		Free.
combed or dyed	30	24	220 pounds	8 33
Woolen stuffs, India shawls, cashmeres, and other similar stuffs of which wool is a component part.	30	24	do	50 92
yarn, raw, not twisted	25	19	do	20 37
cleansed or bleached	30	24	do	24 55
twisted or dyed	30	24	do	28 51
manufactures of wool or hair, pure or mixed	30	24	do	32 59

(a) See note, p. 179.

TARIFFS—Continued.

DENOMINATION OF MERCHANDISE.	Imported(a) into the United States, per cent. ad valorem, under the act of—		DUTIES ON EXPORTS FROM— BELGIUM.	
	1846.	1857.	Number, weight, or measure.	Rate of duty.
Cloths, hempen, linen, and tick, bed furniture	20	15	220 pounds	$0 01
for dress, unbleached	20	15	do	1
other sorts	20	15	do	1
cambric	20	15	do	7½
Cloth, cashmere, and similar tissues in which wool predominates.	30	24	do	2
coating, bear skin, and other heavy and thick materials.	30	24	do	2
all other stuffs of wool or hair, pure or mixed, raw or bleached.	30	24	do	2
Dyed or printed	30	24	do	2
Glass, common, bottles	30	24	100 pieces	2
containing 7 litres or more	30	24	Each	0⅗
green, hollow glass vessels	30	24	For 100 francs, or $18 52 worth.	0⅗
white, hollow glass vessels	30	24	do do	1
flint glass, plate glass, or rolled or raw	30	24	do do	18⅗
mirror glass, polished or not	30	24	do do	1
window glass	20	15	220 pounds	1
crystal, not pressed, polished, figured, gilt or painted	30	24	do	1
Iron, old, consisting of nails, plates, implements, &c.	30	24	do	1
any other sorts	30	24	do	1
ore	20	15		Prohibited.
cast, in bars, purified or dust	30	24	2,200 pounds	0⅕
cast, wrought in chimney plates, stoves, weights, &c., bars, anchors, cast or forged.	30	24	220 pounds	1
Machines, in iron, for factories and manufactures, steam machines, not including boilers.	30	24	do	1
boilers, in beaten and cast iron	30	24	do	0⅕
of which iron forms the principal part	30	24	do	1
of which iron forms only a subordinate part	30	24	For 100 frs., or $18 52 worth	1
others, as works of the materials from which they are made.	30	24	do do	1
Oils, of spices	30	24	do do	9⅗
beech, mast, olive, poppy, and other edible oils, also seed oils.	20 to 30	15 to 24	26 gallons	1
olive	30	24	do	2
palm and cocoa	10	4	220 pounds	2
train oil, whale, seal, also spermaceti	20	15	26 gallons	2
cod liver	20	15	do	1
turpentine	20	15	do	1

(a) See note, p. 245.

TARIFFS—Continued.

DENOMINATION OF MERCHANDISE	Imported(a) into the United States, per cent. ad valorem, under the act of—		DUTIES ON EXPORTS FROM— BELGIUM.	
	1846.	1857.	Number, weight, or measure.	Rate of duty.
Seeds, Canary	Free	Free	Hectolitre, or 2¾ bushels	$0 03¾
aniseed, green	20	4	220 pounds	11¼
mustard	Free	Free	2¾ bushels	3¾
colza, hempseed, linseed, sesame, and other oleagenous seeds.	20	8	1 last of 30 hectolitres, 82½ bushels.	2 22
clover	Free	Free	do do	2 35
Sugar, refined	30	24	220 pounds	17 68
skins, lamb, badger, roe, goat, elk, and calf, dressed	20	15	do	11¾
the same, not dressed	20	15	do	2 22
hare and beaver, not dressed	20	15	do	2 22
the same, dressed	20	15	do	11¾
Wheat	20	25	2,200 pounds	18⅜

(a) See note p. 245.

HOLLAND

AND

HER POSSESSIONS.

HOLLAND AND HER POSSESSIONS.

The tariff is that of September 1, 1854.(*a*)

Money.—One florin, or guilder = 100 cents = 40 cents United States currency.

Weights and measures.—One ell = 3.28 feet; 1 mudde of zak = 2.84 bushels; 1 vat hectolitre = 26.42 gallons; 1 kan litre = 2.11 pints; 1 pond kilogramme = 2.21 lbs; 100 lbs. kilogramme = 2.21 lbs. English; 1 last, grain = 85.20 bushels; 1 ton = 1,000 Holland pounds, 2,210 lbs American; 1 fass = 26 3-5 gallons; 1 last = 2 tons. (ship.)

Free list.—The ballast of vessels and the equipage or luggage of travellers.

Export duties.—Ashes, bones, bristles, cattle, copper, fish, furs, hair, hides, horses, madder, rags, straw, and some other articles are subjected to duties on exportation.

Tare.—On all goods charged by weight, and where no tare is mentioned in the tariff, as follows: On all casks, chests, &c., of wood, 15 per cent. on gross weight; on all packages of leather, linen, and the like, 8 per cent. on the gross weight; on all liquids, which are free of the excise laws, imported by sea, for leakage, from various European ports specified, 6 per cent. From elsewhere, 12 per cent.

There are no transit duties; with the exception of horses, cattle, and fish, the importer can, at his option, pay a duty of 10 per cent. ad valorem, nstead of such duty as is specified in the tariff.

TARIFF OF EXPORTATION.

DUTCH EAST INDIES.

DENOMINATION OF MERCHANDISE.	Imported(*b*) into the United States, per cent. ad valorem, under the act of—		DUTY ON EXPORTS.	
			DUTCH EAST INDIES—JAVA AND MADURA.	
	1846.	1857.	Number, weight, or measure.	Rate of duties.
All unenumerated goods				4 per ct. ad val.
Arack	100	30		6 per ct. do.
under Dutch and equalized flags	100	30		Free
Camphor	40	30	1 picul, 136 pounds	$2 80
Cloves	40	4	do. do.	7 60
Coffee	20	15	do. do.	12 per ct. ad val.
in Dutch or equalized vessels direct to Holland	Free	Free	do. do.	6 do. do.
Copper, Japan	30	24	do. do.	2 80
Gold and silver coins	Free	Free		4 per ct. ad val.
Hides, raw	5	4	100	3 20
Horses	20	Free	Each	16 00
Indigo	10	4	1 lb., or 1.037 American lb.	4
Mace	40	4	136 pounds	8 00
Nutmegs	40	4	do.	7 60
Oil, poppy	30	24	do.	1 20
Pepper, black	30	4	do.	80
white	30	4	do.	1 20
Rum, Java	100	30	1 leager, about 500 gallons.	4 80
Rice	20	15	136 pounds	4
Salt	20	15	do.	Free
Wood, sandal	30	8	do.	40
sapan	20	Free	do.	8

(*a*) For later modifications see Annual Reports.

(*b*) See note, p. 245.

DUTCH EAST INDIES.

(JAVA,(a) MADURA AND THE WEST COAST OF SUMATRA.)

The tariff is that of October 16, 1837, with alterations to December, 1853.

Money.—The same as that of Holland.

Weights and measures, also the same, with the exception of the following: 1 boyang = 62.431 bushels. 1 picul = 136 lbs. 1 oxhoft = ½ Dutch pipe = 61½ gallons English; 1 old Amsterdam pound, 0.494 Dutch pound = 1.032 lb. English.

The valuation (basis of duty unless where a specific duty is levied) is according to invoice prices, with 30 per cent. additional In case of doubt, the officers have the power to rate the valuation according to the market prices of the day.

The coasting trade is prohibited to foreign vessels. With this exception, equalized vessels enjoy like privileges with those of Holland.

National and equalized vessels pay only one-half the rates of duty specified, whether of import or export.

Since 1851, the following states have concluded reciprocal commercial treaties with Holland, as regards the Dutch East Indies: Austria, Hamburg, Prussia, the Zoll-Verein, Lubeck, Bremen, Mecklenburg-Schwerin, Sardinia, Great Britain, Norway, Papal States, Greece, Ionian Islands, Sweden, United States of North America, (in 1853,) and Tuscany.

WEST COAST OF SUMATRA.

The tariff is the same as that of Java and Madura, with the exception of the duty on opium, which is as follows:

Opium, Levantine, per 136 lbs.	$80 00
" Patra and Benares, per box of about 125 lbs.	140 00
" Matra	100 00
" Persian	80 00

Goods having already paid entrance duty in Java are free.

The duties on exports are also the same as those of Java and Madura, with the exception of the following articles:

Benzoin, first quality, per picul, 136 lbs.	$3 20
" second " " "	2 40
" third " " "	1 60
Camphor, " " "	40 00
Cassia, " " "	6 80
Salt, Java, " " "	free.
Sulphur, " " "	40

All wares, being products of the Indian Archipelago, exported to Java in Netherlands or equalized vessels, free.

DUTCH GUIANA AND WEST INDIES, (SURINAM, ST. MARTIN, SOUTH PART, ST. EUSTATIUS, SABA, CURACOA.)

The tariff is that of March 26, 1849; *money, weignts, and measures,* are the same as those of Holland.

Foreign, not equalized vessels, pay 6 per cent. ad valorem on imports or double duty. Imported goods are not subjected to an exportation duty. All products of the colony, except wood, have to pay an ad valorem duty when exported, viz: in Dutch and equalized vessels to Holland, or its colonies, 5 per cent. ad valorem; in Dutch vessels to foreign places, 7½ per cent; in oreign vessels, 10 per cent. Ad valorem duties are calculated on the current prices; or, when unknown, on the invoice valuation; or, if this seems too low, the goods are seized, and the importer is paid 12 per cent. additional. There is no transit duty. Plants, vegetables, and all effects of immigrants, are free.

(a) For the tariff of duties for the Island of Java, in full, see Vol. 1, "Digests," p. 273.

COMPARATIVE TARIFFS.

UNITED STATES AND HOLLAND AND HER POSSESSIONS.

Denomination of merchandise.	The United States, per cent. ad valorem, under the act of—		Duties on imports into— Holland.		Dutch East Indies.		Dutch Guiana and West Indies.	
	1846.	1857.	Number, weight, or measure.	Rate of duty.	Number, weight, or measure.	Rate of duty.	Number, weight, or measure.	Rate of duty.
Ashes, pot and pearl	20	15		Free		6 per ct. ad val.		3 per cent. ad val.
wood ashes and soda	10	4		Free				
Bacon, smoked	20	15	221 pounds	$0 23		24 per ct. ad val.	221 pounds	$0 20
Beef, salted	20	15	do	1 05		do	do	15
smoked	20	15	do	1 52		do		
Beer, ale, and porter, in casks	30	24	1 fass or $26\frac{2}{5}$ gallons.	1 00	1 oxhoft or $61\frac{1}{2}$ gallons.	$9 60, after deducting 3 per cent. ad val. for leakage.	100 pints or $18\frac{1}{10}$ gallons.	32
in bottles	30	24	100 bottles	1 30		$4 80, after deducting 8 per cent. for breakage.	100 bottles	48
Cables and cordage	25	19	221 pounds	80		24 per ct. ad val.		3 per cent. ad val.
Cheese	30	24	do	2 00		do	221 pounds	20
Coals, stone	30	24		Free		Free		Free
Coffee	20	Free	221 pounds	Free		No importation		3 per cent. ad val.
Copper, in bars	5	Free	do	Free		24 per ct. ad val.		3 per cent. ad val.
beaten or flattened, round or square, likewise basins and kettles as they leave the mill, and wire.	30	24	do	1 60				

TARIFFS—Continued.

Denomination of merchandise.	The United States, per cent. ad valorem, under the act of—		Duties on imports into— Holland.		Dutch East Indies.		Dutch Guiana and West Indies.	
	1846.	1857.	Number, weight, or measure.	Rate of duty.	Number, weight, or measure.	Rate of duty.	Number, weight, or measure.	Rate of duty.
Copper, beaten or flattened, plates and sheaths of yellow or red copper for sheathing ships' bottoms—								
Bolts and nails	20	15	221 pounds			24 per ct. ad val.		3 per cent. ad val.
Sheathing	Free	Free	do	$0 40				
Cotton, raw	Free	Free		Free		12½ per ct. ad val.		3 per cent. ad val.
manufactures of	20 to 30	15 to 24		6 per ct. ad val.				
Dyes and colors	20	Free		6 per ct. ad val.		12½ per ct. ad val.		3 per cent. ad val.
Earthen and stone ware	30	24		6 per ct. ad val.		24 per ct. ad val.		3 per cent. ad val.
Fish, herrings	20	15	Prohibited				221 pounds	$0 08
cod, salted	20	15	150 lbs. Holland, or 331½ lbs.	60		24 per ct. ad val.	do	8
stock fish	20	15	221 pounds	6				
Flour, all kinds	20	15	do	1 64		12 per ct. ad val.	Of wheat, 221 lbs.	12
							Rye	8
							Indian meal	6
Furniture, household	30	24		8 per ct. val.		12 per ct. ad val.		3 per cent. ad val.
Glass, window	20	15	221 pounds	5 per ct. ad val.				
looking-glasses	30	24		6 per ct. ad val.				
wares, uncolored and uncut	30	24	221 pounds	1 20		24 per ct. ad val.		3 per cent. ad val.
colored and cut	40	30	do	2 40				
bottles	30	24	100	40				
Grains, wheat	20	15	1 last, or 85.20 bushels.	3 20		24 per ct. ad val.		3 per cent. ad val.

TARIFFS—Continued.

Denomination of merchandise.	The United States, per cent. ad valorem, under the act of— 1846.	1857.	Holland. Number, weight, or measure.	Holland. Rate of duty.	Dutch East Indies. Number, weight, or measure.	Dutch East Indies. Rate of duty.	Dutch Guiana and West Indies. Number, weight, or measure.	Dutch Guiana and West Indies. Rate of duty.
Grains, rye	20	15	1 last or 85.20 bushels.	$2 40		24 per ct. ad val.		3 per cent. ad val.
barley and malt	20	15	1 last or 85.20 bushels.	1 80				
Hams	20	15	221 pounds	26		24 per ct. ad val.	221 pounds	$0 16
Hops	20	15	do	Free		12 per ct. ad val.		3 per cent. ad val.
Indian corn	20	15	85 20 bushels	2 40		12 per ct. ad val.	221 pounds	4
Lard	20	15	221 pounds	20		12 per ct. ad val.	do	20
Leather, raw	20	15	do	2 84		24 per ct. ad val.		3 per cent. ad val.
manufactures of	30	24		6 per ct. ad val.				
Lumber	20	15	1 ton or 2,210 lbs	3 per cent		$4 50		3 per cent. ad val.
Mackerel	20	15	221 pounds	8		24 per ct. ad val.	221 pounds	12
Metals—								
Iron, crude	30	24		Free		12 per ct. ad val.		3 per cent. ad val.
manufactures of	30	24		6 per ct. ad val.		24 per ct. ad val.		
Lead, in pigs	20	15	221 pounds	8		24 per ct. ad val.		
manufactures of	30	24	do	80		For tea boxes 6 per ct. ad val.		
Nails, Iron	30	24	do	30		12 per ct. ad val.		3 per cent. ad val.
Nails, Copper	20	15	do	30		12 per ct. ad val.		3 per cent. ad val.
Oils, whale	20	15	1 fass or 26⅔ gallons.	Free		12 per ct. ad val.		3 per cent. ad val.
Pepper	30	4	221 pounds	60		No importation		3 per cent. ad val.
Pimento	40	4	do	40				
Pitch	20	15		Free		6 per ct ad val.		3 per cent. ad val.
Pork, salted	20	15	221 pounds	20		Free	221 pounds	20

34 □

TARIFFS—Continued.

Denomination of merchandise.	The United States, per cent. ad valorem, under the act of— 1846.	1857.	Holland. Number, weight, or measure.	Holland. Rate of duty.	Dutch East Indies. Number, weight, or measure.	Dutch East Indies. Rate of duty.	Dutch Guiana and West Indies. Number, weight, or measure.	Dutch Guiana and West Indies. Rate of duty.
Pork, smoked	20	15	221 pounds	$0 26		Free	221 pounds	$0 20
Rosin	20	15	do	Free		6 per ct. ad val	do	6
Rice	20	15	do	$1\frac{1}{5}$		No importation	do	10
Rum, in bottles	100	30	100 bottles	60	100 bottles	$16 00	100 bottles	2 40
in casks	100	30		Free	1 pipe, 123 gallons.	48 00	100 pintes, $18\frac{1}{10}$ gallons.	1 60
Soap, common	30	24	221 pounds	1 80		12 per ct. ad val	221 pounds	30
perfumed	30	24	do	3 00				
Spices—								
cassia lignea	40	4		1 per ct. ad val		No importation		3 per cent. ad val.
Spermaceti candles	20	15	221 pounds	10 00	1 pond or 1.037 pounds.	$8\frac{1}{2}$	221 pounds	40
Sugar, raw	30	24	do	8				
refined	30	24	do	12 00		No importation	do	6
molasses	30	24	do	1 20				
Tallow	10	8	do	20		6 per ct. ad val	do	3 per cent. ad val.
candles	20	15	do	4 00				40
Tar	20	15		Free		6 per ct. ad val	do	4
Tea, from place of production	Free	Free	221 pounds	8 00		No importation		3 per cent. ad val.
Tobacco, leaf	30	24	do	28	1.037 pounds	$6\frac{1}{4}$	221 pounds	12
cigars	40	30	do	16 00	do	$6\frac{1}{4}$		3 per cent. ad val.
other manufactures	40	30	do	4 80	do	$6\frac{1}{4}$		
Turpentine	20	15		1 per ct. ad val		12 per ct. ad val		3 per cent. ad val.
Whalebone, unmanufactured	20	15		Free		12 per ct. ad val		3 per cent. ad val

TARIFFS—Continued.

DENOMINATION OF MERCHANDISE.	The United States per cent. ad valorem, under the act of—		DUTIES ON IMPORTS INTO— HOLLAND.		DUTCH EAST INDIES.		DUTCH GUIANA AND WEST INDIES.	
	1846.	1857.	Number, weight, or measure.	Rate of duty.	Number, weight, or measure.	Rate of duty.	Number, weight, or measure.	Rate of duty.
Wheat	20	15	1 last or 85.20 bushels.	$0 04		12 per ct. ad val.		3 per cent. ad val.
Wine, in casks	40	30		Free	$61\frac{1}{2}$ gallons	Red and white, $8 00	$18\frac{1}{10}$ gallons	$1 60
in bottles	40	30	100 bottles	64	100 bottles	Red and white, 4 00	100 bottles	2 40
Wood, staves or heading	20	15	ton or 2,210 lbs.	40			Bundle of 25 pieces.	$0\frac{4}{5}$
masts and spars	20	15		12 per ct. ad val.		6 per ct. ad val.	Shingles, per M	12
dye woods, in sticks	20	15		Free				
dye woods, ground	20	15	221 pounds	96				3 per cent. ad val.
manufactures of	30	24		6 per ct. ad val.				
Wool, raw	30	24		Free		No importation		
combed and colored	30	24	221 pounds	95	1 ell or $3\frac{1}{4}$ feet	Cloth, 80 cts. to $3 20.		3 per cent. ad val.
manufactures of	30	24	do	Very fine, 18 00 Coarse, 13 60	do	Bombazine $14\frac{1}{2}$ to 40 cents.		

NORTHERN EUROPE.

NORTHERN EUROPE.

RUSSIA.

The tariff is that of October 28, 1850, with the alterations (chiefly affecting manufactures) of June 23, 1854.(a)

The Russian government has been compelled to issue two different tariffs by the great territorial extent and the geographical situation of the country. One tariff is in force in the whole Russian Empire north of the Black sea, including the kingdom of Poland, and especially in all the ports of the Baltic and White seas ; the other comprises the coasts of the Black sea, including Transcaucasia.

The importation into Kamtschatka is entirely free.

Money.—1 silver ruble = 100 copecs = 75 cents.
1 copec = ¾ cent.
Weights and measures.—1 pood = 36.067 lbs.
1 chertwert of grain 5.95 bushels.
1 oxhoft = 58.428 gallons = 6 ankers.
1 anker = 9.738 gallons = 18 wedros.
1 wedro 3.246 gallons.
1 berkowitz or berquet = 360⅔ lbs.
1 archine = 28 inches.

The tariff of exportation gives the duties on the principal articles of export from Russia to the United States, for the ports of the Baltic and White seas only ; there are no duties levied on exports from the ports of the Black sea.

The deduction for *Tare* varies with the character of the goods.

The duty is generally levied on net weight. The article on which the duty has been paid is marked in the custom-house before leaving it with stamps of lead, paper, brass, or sealing wax, according to the nature of the goods.

TARIFF OF EXPORTATION.

DENOMINATION OF MERCHANDISE.	Imported into the United States, per cent. ad valorem, under the act of—(b)		DUTIES ON EXPORTS. RUSSIA.	
	1846.	1857.	Number, weight, or measure.	Rate of duty.
Fish glue	20	15	1 pood, or 36 lbs	$0 93¾
Flax	15	Free	1 berkowitz, 360⅔ lbs	62¼
Grain—rye, oats, Indian corn	20	15	1 chertwert, 5.95 bushels	2¼
and barley	20	15		
wheat	20	15	do	5¼
Hemp	30	24	360⅔ lbs	41¼
Hemp seed	10	8	5.95 bushels	12¾
Caviar	20	15	36 lbs	15
Linseed	10	Free	5.95 bushels	21
Rags	5	Free	36 lbs	45
woolen	5	4		
Tallow of all kinds	10	8	360⅔ lbs	82½
Wax, yellow, unmanufactured	20	15	36 lbs	41¼
white or red, unmanufactured	20	15	do	28½

(a) See vol. 3, "Returns," pp. 75, et seq. For recent changes, see Appendix.   (b) See note, p. 245.

APPENDIX.

On the 9th of June,(a) 1857, the Emperor of Russia gave his sanction to a new tariff, the rates of which present material reductions on those of the old. By this tariff, lower duties are levied on merchandise imported by land, or into the Transcaucasian ports of the Black sea, than if imported by sea, or into Russia and Poland. The statement annexed presents the rates on a few articles usually received from the United States, the money, weights, and measures not being reduced to the Federal standard.

The silver ruble = 100 copecs = 75 cents; the pood = about 36 pounds; the chertwert = nearly 6 bushels; the archine = about 28 inches, as already stated.

TARIFF OF IMPORTATION.

DENOMINATION OF MERCHANDISE.	Number, weight, or measure.	Into Russia and Poland.		Into Trans-Caucasian ports of the Black sea.	
		Rbl.	*cop.*	*Rbl.*	*cop.*
Almonds	Per pood	1	50		50
Animals		Free		Free	
Artificial flowers	Per pound	6	00	3	00
Bacon, by sea	Per pood	1	20		60
Beef	...do	1	20		60
Books and maps		Free		Free	
Brandy, by sea, to 11 degrees	Per pood	7	75	7	75
Brass, in pigs and bars	...do		60		58
manufactures of	...do	4	00	4	00
Bricks		Free		Free	
Bristles	Per pood	4	00	4	00
Cables and cordage	...do		40		40
Candles, tallow	...do	1	00	1	00
Cheese, by sea	...do	5	00	2	50
Cigars	Per pound	2	00		25
Cocoa, by sea	Per pood	2	00	1	25
Dye-wood	...do		8		5
Figs	...do	1	00		30
Furniture, common, by sea	...do		40		20
Gunpowder		Prohibited		Prohibited	
Hams	Per pood	1	20		60
Indigo, by sea	...do	3	50	1	25
Indian corn, by sea	Per chertwert		60		20
Iron, by sea	Per pood		40		15
Lead	...do		5		2½
Linen, by sea	Ad valorem	25 per cent		23 per cent	
Molasses	Per pood	1	00		80
Nails, of iron	...do	1	00		60
Nutmegs, by sea	...do		4		3
Nuts	...do		60		20
Oil, whale	...do		30		20
Pepper	...do	2	50	1	50
Pork	...do	1	20		60
Potatoes, by sea	Per chertwert		20	Free	

(a) O. S. May 28.

TARIFFS—Continued.

DENOMINATION OF MERCHANDISE.	Number, weight, or measure.	Into Russia and Poland.	Into trans-Caucasian ports of Black sea.
		Rbl. cop.	*Rbl. cop.*
Printing presses		Free	Free
Rosin	Per pood	30	30
Rye, meal, by sea	Per chertwert	60	20
Ship bread		Free	Free
Silk, raw	Per pood	40	Free
Soap, common	do	1 50	1 50
Stearine candles	do	1 00	1 00
Sugar, by sea	do	3 00	2 00
Tallow	do	30	20
Tobacco, leaf, all kinds	do	6 00	1 25
Turpentine	do	30	30
Vinegar	do	1 20	1 20
Whalebone, raw	do	2 00	1 00

The comparative statement subjoined affords information as regards reductions in the new tariff on the rates of the old one. The rates are given in rubles and copecs, and are applicable to merchandise imported by land into Russia and Poland :

ARTICLES.	TARIFF. Old.	TARIFF. New.	ARTICLES.	TARIFF. Old.	TARIFF. New.
	r. c.	r. c.		r. c.	r. c.
Cochineal............per pood..	6 0	4 0	Cotton goods—Continued.		
Coffee..................do.....	3 0	2 50	White, up to 12½ sq. archines..	0 80	0 40
Rice....................do.....	0 60	free.	Colored, up to 10.....do......	0 75	0 40
Sugar..................do.....	3 0	3 0	Colored, up to 12½....do......	1 0	0 40
Wine...................do.....	2 90	2 10	More than 12½.......do......	1 60	1 40
Wine...............per bottle..	0 50	0 30	Tulle........................	6 0	4 0
Champagne............do.....	0 90	0 90	Millinery.....................	2 0	1 0
Beer and porter..........do.....	0 35	0 20	Silk stuffs, thick..............	5 0	4 0
Almonds.............per pood..	2 0	1 50	Flannel......................	1 0	0 70
Fruits.................per 300..	0 80	0 40	Silk stuffs—		
Vanilla..............per pound..	0 35	0 20	Thin.......................	10 0	6 0
Pepper...............per pood..	3 20	2 50	Worked with gold and silver..	12 50	7 50
Cinnamon..............do.....	5 0	4 0	Herrings, Dutch, (per cask)—		
Tobacco, all sorts...............	6 0	6 0	Weighing 9 poods..per pood..	2 85	1 80
Snuff...............per pound..	1 70	0 80	Scotch.....................	1 30	0 90
Twist................per pood..	5 0	2 50	Currants......................	0 70	0 40
Twist, colored...........do.....	6 0	5 0	Annatto.............per pood..	0 40	0 10
Turkish red.............do.....	11 0	5 0	Umber.................do.....	0 15	0 10
Gums..................do.....	1 80	0 40	Saffron............per pound..	0 40	0 30
Madder.................do.....	0 80	0 50	Arsenic.............per pood..	1 20	0 50
Sal ammoniac...........do.....	1 0	0 20	Silk, raw...............do.....	1 0	0 40
Spelter..................do.....	1 20	1 60	Organzine, frame silk.per pound..	0 20	0 15
Brimstone..............do.....	0 3	free.	Joinery (unpolished)...per pood..	0 80	0 20
Sewing silk..........per pound..	0 80	0 15	Leather.............per pound..	0 25	0 10
Cotton goods—			India rubber..................	1 0	0 20
White, up to 10 square archines..	0 48	0 43	Furniture, inlaid...............	10 0	6 0

TARIFFS—Continued.

ARTICLES.	TARIFF. Old.		TARIFF. New.		ARTICLES.	TARIFF. Old.		TARIFF. New.	
	r.	c.	r.	c.		r.	c.	r.	c.
Playthings ....per pound..	1	0	0	30	Guns and pistols....per pound..	1	20	0	40
Flutes...............per piece..	1	0	0	50	Filligree work................	8	0	6	0
Boots...............per pound..	1	0	0	50	Soap, common	3	0	1	50
Boots, (ladies', of silk,)....do.....	2	0	1	0	Soap, perfumed................	10	0	5	0
Linens.................do.....	0	60	....		Men's and children's cloths, per value......................	50 per cent.		35 per cent.	
Linens, ad valorem	....		25 per cent.		Ladies' clothing	75 per cent.		35 per cent.	
Table cloths.........per pound..	1	20	0	70	Braces......................	1	50	0	70
Bronze.................do.....	1	50	0	50	Earthenware, common, per pood.	2	0	1	60
Bronze, below size......per piece..	3	0	1	0	China, white	9	0	6	0
Gold, wrought........per pound..	100	0	30	0	China, painted	20	0	12	0
Silver, wrought..........do.....	6	0	2	0	China, painted, best quality....	40	0	24	0
Platina, wrought ....do.....	20	0	16	0	Stearine or tallow candles, per pood......................	2	0	1	0
Tin plate..............per pood..	2	0	1	50	Glass, window................	3	0	2	0
Tin plate, varnished......do.....	3	0	1	50	Glassware.	20	0	10	0
Tin plate, wrought........do.....	4	0	2	50	Strings for musical instruments, per pound..................	0	80	0	30
Tin plate, painted, and with ornaments ....per pood..	12	0	8	0	Silk scarfs and shawls..........	8	0	4	0
Forks and knives.....per pound..	0	70	0	40	Silk stockings and gloves......	8	0	4	0
Turnery, polished ....do.....	0	40	0	10	Watches, gold................	2	0	1	20
Locksmiths' work...............	0	15	0	10	Cloth of every color............	....		1	40
Locksmiths' work, polished.......	0	15	0	20					
Clocks.........................	2	0	0	60					
Clocks, wooden.................	0	50	0	25					

The per centage decrease in 1857 on the rates of 1856 on certain articles imported by sea has been noted, approximately, as follows :(*a*) On cotton twist, wadding, and wick, 30 to 75 per cent. ; cotton goods, 17 to 75 ; linen, table linen, napkins, and towels, 42 ; silk, raw, 60 to 95 ; wadding, 97 ; thread 75 ; wool, raw, dyed, 80 ; carded or spun, for embroidery, 67 ; woolen cloths, 25 to 41 ; flannel, plush, frieze, baize, &c., 30 ; sugar, raw, 17 ; coffee, 17 ; cochineal, 60 ; pepper, 11 ; porter, bottled, 43 ; herrings, smoked, all kinds, 43 ; English and Scotch, 31 ; Dutch, 50 ; lead, in pigs, rolls, sheets, and pipes, 33 ; tin, 33 ; copper, red and yellow, in pigs, sheets, rods, &c., 40 ; quicksilver, 58 ; zinc, in pieces and sheets, 50 ; rum, arrack, and French brandy, 18 ; vinegar, cider, and perry, in casks, 20 ; in bottles, 67 ; hardware, locks of iron, unpolished, and hinges, screws, &c., 60 ; earthenware and crockery, white, or of ore color, plain, 20 ; china, 33 to 40.

Prohibition removed from porter and beer in casks, and from iron, pig, unwrought, and sheet, and for boilers.

SWEDEN.

The tariff is that of December 4, 1854, which went into effect January 1, 1855. (*b*)

Money.—Mostly paper. The only gold coin is the ducat of the usual weight—976 thousandths fine—125 pieces from a pound of fine gold. The paper money is of two kinds, viz: *Banco* and *Riksgald;* the former issued by the national bank; the latter by the Riksgald, or government bank. The banco is reckoned 50 per cent. better than the other. Since 1829, the established rate has been 2⅔ riksdalers banco to one specie daler, which would make the former equal to about 40 cents American ; but it fluctuates in value. The riksdaler may be estimated at 25 cents generally.

1 riksdaler banco = 48 skillings = 576 rundstykes = 39¾ cents.

12 rundstykes = 1 skilling.

48 skillings = 1 riksdaler banco.

1 riksdaler banco = 39¾ cents. 1 specie dollar = $1 06.

(*a*) See note, page 93. (*b*) See Appendix.

Weights and measures.—1 skilpund = 0.937 pounds, (in the tariff, for convenience, reckoned at 1 pound.)
1 lispund, viktualie weight, 18.745 pounds.
1 " metal " = 14.75 pounds, (United States standard.)
1 skippund, viktualie " = 374.913 pounds.
1 " staple " = 302 $\frac{2}{9}$ pounds.
1 " metal weight, = 453.470 pounds.
1 last = 18 skippunds = 2 tons 8 cwt.
1 tunna, liquid capacity, = 33.1526 gallons.
1 kanna, " " = 0.6908 gallons = 5½ pints, (about.)

All goods imported in foreign bottoms pay a differential duty of 40 per cent. import duty, and 50 per cent. export duty, unless a reciprocal treaty exists to the contrary. The United States concluded such a treaty in 1783—renewed and enlarged in 1816 and 1827.

Ad valorem entries are calculated on the invoice value, with all charges, expenses, and insurances added.

The highest bidder for the goods, within three days, can take them by paying the importer 10 per cent. over the sum bid.

Goods damaged by sea are sold by public auction, and the duty on them is paid at the lowest rate realized under the market price.

Drawbacks are allowed on refined sugar, tobacco, snuff, cotton textiles of yarn, of No. 32 and above; paddy and leather, in quantities not less than 100 pounds.

Articles exempt from duty are numerous.

The transit tariff is light.

TARIFF OF EXPORTATION.

DENOMINATION OF MERCHANDISE.	Imported(*a*) into the United States, per cent. ad valorem, under the act of—		DUTIES ON EXPORTS. SWEDEN.	
	1846.	1857.	Number, weight, or measure.	Rate of duty.
Copper, refined	30	24	302$\frac{2}{9}$ pounds	$4 00
crude	5	Free	do	66⅔
Iron, in bars and pigs	30	24		Prohibited
in sheets, over 1½ inch thick, and weighing over 453.470 pounds.	30	24		do
in sheets, under 1½ inch, &c., and under 453.470 lbs.	30	24	302$\frac{2}{9}$ pounds.	40
forged or rolled, in rods or sheets, ⅜ inch and upwards thick, and under 12 inches broad, and ⅜ inch square.	30	24	do	3½
cast	30	24	do	10

(*a*) See note, p. 245.

APPENDIX.

By a royal order of September 26, 1855, extended subsequently to 1856, and again to 1857, permission was granted to import the following articles into Sweden duty free: Breadstuffs, ground or not ground, all kinds; bread, all kinds; grain, all kinds; maize; rice, in the husk, or paddy; potatoes and potato meal; butter; cheese; meat, all kinds; cattle, oxen, cows and young cattle, calves, and swine; pork; fish, salted, all kinds, except anchovies, sardines, and tunny; fish, dried or smoked, all kinds, except salmon and eels; tallow; oil, all kinds of fat oil; train oil; stearine; candles, tallow, stearine, and margarine.

The import duty for 1857 was lowered on the following articles: Grits, all kinds, excepting of grain; rice meal; oils, fat, all kinds, not included in apothecaries' wares; stearine; candles, tallow and palmetin; candles, stearine and margarine.

By a decree of December, 1855, it was declared that, on and after the beginning of the year 1856, pig and ballast iron may be imported under a duty of one rix-dollar banco for every ship-pound staple-stad's weight; and that the following kinds of cast iron may be exported on and after the same date, viz: pig and ballast iron; cannon, swivel guns, and mortars, unstamped and unbored; and plates over 1½ inch thick, and weighing over one ship-pound; all against a duty of one rix-dollar banco for every ship-pound staple-stad's weight; and that hammered or rolled bar and flat iron, ⅜ inch thick and thereover, under 12 inches broad, and over ⅜ inch square, may be exported duty free.

From January 1, 1856, the prohibition on various manufactures of silk, cotton, woolen, and linen, was removed.

NORWAY.

The tariff is that of July 1, 1854, to remain in force till July 1, 1857.(a)

Money.—1 specie thaler = 120 skillings = $1 06.

Weights and measures.—1 commercial last 4,500 pounds.
1 lispund = 17.$\frac{615}{}$ pounds.
1 skippund = 320 pounds Norwegian, or 352 pounds avoirdupois.
1 ton = 40 cubic feet of square timber.
1 last = 50 cubic feet of timber.

FREE LIST.

Principal articles: Amber; arsenic; asphalt; fresh oysters; trees and plants; steam engines and other machines; dates; printing presses, with the necessary material and appurtenances; guano; diamonds and other precious stones, unset; iron guns and mortars; iron manufactures for industrial purposes, with special permit from the government; elephants' and walrusses' teeth; raw ivory; crude metals; skins and hides measuring over 56 inches, without heads, horns, and tail; flints; fish; skins, raw; wood in blocks; fruits not otherwise enumerated; oats and rye; meal, if imported through the ports of Hammerfest, Vardoe, or Vadsor; the mechanical utensils and furniture of immigrants; gypsum; gold in bars and old; gumelastic, unmanufactured; raw hair of horses, beavers, camels, &c.; hemp unhackled; hemp seed; horn; scientific charts and maps; wearing apparel of travellers; rags; minerals; models; bones; coals; pictures and statues; coins; musical notes and publications; pearls, fine; mother of pearl; ploughs; platina, unmanufactured; bark for tanning; shipchandlery; ship stores of vessels arriving; silver, unmanufactured; spermaceti; staves, rough; stone coals, if imported at Hammerfest, Vardoe, or Vadsor; oakum; live animals; whale bone, unmanufactured.

TARE LIST.

For casks, etc,	with	dry goods,	for every	ton	a tare of	24	pounds.
"	"	"	"	½	"	18	"
"	"	"	"	¼	"	12	"
"	"	"	"	⅛	"	8	"

For other barrels or boxes, 12 per cent.; for goods contained in bottles, flasks, glasses, demijohns, &c., 30 per cent.; for merchandise imported in leaden, iron, tin, or copper boxes, 20 per cent.; for goods packed up in matting, each matting, 4 pounds; for matting made of straw or gum, 3 per cent.; for rush mats, a double one, 4 pounds; single, 2 pounds; for sacks, woolen, 8 per cent.; canvas, per cent.

Export duties are levied on oak bark, cordage, fish, rags, wood, and timber, and on a few other minor articles.

Timber pays, per commercial last, (4,500 pounds,) 54⅓ cents; rags, per pound, ¾ cent; oak bark, per 352 pounds, 13 1-5 cents.

(a) See note, p. 261.

DENMARK AND HER COLONIAL POSSESSIONS.

The tariff of Denmark is that of 1851.

The German Duchies, Sleswig and Holstein, previous to 1850, had a separate tariff; since that time, Sleswig has been separated from Holstien, and is subjected to the same duties as given in the Danish Tariff, as regards the most important articles of commerce.

The cities Wandsbeck and Altona, in Holstein, are free ports.

Money.—1 rigsbank daler = 6 mark = 96 skillings = 0.52½ ; 1 specie daler = $1 05.

Weights and measures.—1 centner of 100 lbs. = 110⅓ lbs.; 1 lb. = 17⅗ oz.; 1 viertel, liquid capacity, = 1.9128 gallon; 1 toende, liquid capacity, = 34.681 gallons; 1 toende, dry capacity, = 3.954 bushels; 1 last = 2 tons.

FREE LIST.

Ashes, bacon, bark for tanning, bricks, bristles, butter, charcoal, copper, corn, cotton, dye and other woods, effects of travellers, flax, hair of all sorts, hemp, hemp seed and oil, hides and skins, iron, lead, maize, meat (fresh and salt,) pitch, potatoes, salt, spermaceti and oil, tallow, tar, wool, and zinc, are among the principal articles.

Tare.—For casks, with dry goods, each ton, 24 lbs.; each half ton, 18 lbs.; each one-fourth ton, 12 lbs.; each one-eighth ton, 8 lbs. For other boxes, &c., 16 per cent.; bottles, &c., in boxes, 50 per cent.; bottles, without boxes, 40 per cent; straw mattings, each, 4 lbs.; sacks or bags, single, each 2 per cent.; sacks or bags, double, 4 per cent.; common pack linen, 3 per cent.; ropes, 1 per cent.; tea, in boxes, 24 per cent.

TARIFF OF EXPORTATION.

DENOMINATION OF MERCHANDISE.	Imported(a) into the United States, per cent. ad valorem, under the act of—		DUTIES ON EXPORTS. DENMARK.	
	1846.	1857.	Number, weight, or measure.	Rate of duty.
Bark, oak and other, for dyeing purposes	5	Free	1 centner, or 110⅓ pounds	$0 17¼
Rags, of any kind, except woolen	5	Free	do	1 50
woolen		4	do	54⅔
Tallow	10	8	do	
Wool	30	24	do	81⅔

(a)See note, p. 245.

ST. CROIX.

The tariff is that established by a law passed by the Diet of Denmark, and sanctioned by the King, June 30, 1850, of which a translation is subjoined:

A.—NAVIGATION.

§ 1. All vessels, native or foreign, both from native and foreign ports, may trade to St. Croix, and there discharge and load at the two ports of entry, Christiansted and Frederiksted.

§ 2. Vessels belongingto the Danish West India Islands, trading between Denmark and the colonies, shall enjoy in future the same rights and privileges as vessels belonging to the mother country. Colonial vessels shall, however, as hitherto, take out a sea-pass.

§ 3. Every vessel is to pay tonnage dues according to its tonnage, both on entering and on leaving, at the following rate: If the vessel discharge or load to the amount of one-half its tonnage and above, per commercial last, 30 cents; if it discharge or load from one-quarter to one-half its tonnage, per commercial last, 20 cents; if it discharge or load less than one-quarter of its tonnage, per commercial last, 10 cents.

All vessels not discharging or loading are exempt from tonnage dues, as well as vessels belonging to the Danish West India Islands, when trading between St. Croix and the two other islands.

If tonnage dues are paid at one of the custom-houses of this island, or at St. Thomas, additional tonnage dues are to be paid only in case the vessel should again discharge or load during the same voyage goods to such an amount that, together with the previous amount discharged or loaded, it shall reach a quantity on which a higher tonnage due is fixed.

At Christiansted, vessels are further to pay one-half the amount of tonnage dues, at the above rate, for keeping the harbor, with wharves and other appurtenances, in repairs.

B.—IMPORTS.

§ 4. All goods, without exception, may be imported as well from Danish as foreign ports. Fire-arms and ammunition can only be landed on special permisssion from the governor general, and subject to such control as he may deem proper.

§ 5. Within 24 hours after the vessel has been brought to an anchor, the whole cargo, whether intended to be discharged or not, shall be entered at the custom-house, specified and in writing. If the whole cargo is not to be discharged, the remainder shall, on the vessel's clearing out, be entered for export in the same manner.

§ 6. On imports, the following duties and exemptions are fixed:

1st. In general—

a. Free of duty are: sugar, rum, and molasses puncheons; staves, headings, hoops; agricultural implements; all implements used for the manufacture of sugar, the distilling of rum, and for cane mills; mill timber; fire-bricks and fire-stone; machinery and parts thereof; fresh fish and turtles; greens and vegetables; coals; mules and asses; manure; printed books and papers; and used furniture, when imported as the property of a person going to reside in the island.

b. A fixed duty to be paid on flour of wheat, per 100 lbs., 60 cents; flour of rye, barley, oats, maize, and all other kinds of flour, per 100 lbs., 25 cents; bread of wheat, per 100 lbs., 75 cents; bread of other corn, per 100 lbs., 35 cents; peas dried, of any kind, per barrel, 25 cents; beans, likewise per barrel, 25 cents; beef, tongues, hams, sausages, pickled, smoked, or dried, per 100 lbs., $1 25; pork, pickled or smoked, per 100 lbs., 80 cents; fish, dried or salted, per 100 lbs., 25 cents; fish, pickled or smoked, per 100 lbs., 40 cents; butter, per 100 lbs., $1 50; cheese, per 100 lbs., $1 50; lard, per 100 lbs., 40 cents.

c Five per cent duty to be paid on iron, steel, lead, copper, zinc in bars, rolls, or plates; sheet iron, spelter, rope, tar, pitch, rosin, chalk, lime, temperline, cement, gypsum, bricks and tiles, flagstones, earthern pipes, lumber of every kind, except those mentioned under letter *a*; nails, screws spikes; tools of every description; ship's anchors, chains, and blocks; mule harness, raw leather, wooden yokes; live cattle, except mules and asses, which are free of duty, and horses, which are to pay a higher duty; oats, Indian corn, bran, hay; charcoal, salt, tallow; carts, wheels, axles and boxes for carts and sugar wagons; canvas for sails.

d. Twelve and a half per cent. duty to be paid on all other goods of whatsoever name, origin, and description, which are not enumerated under letters *a*, *b*, and *c*.

2d. Exceptions—

a. Free of duty are: all productions of the mother country, and all goods on which duties have been paid in Denmark, imported into this island in Danish vessels, from a Danish port, not a free port. Such goods shall be accompanied with a clearance, proving they are of Danish product or manufacture, or that duties have been paid on them in Denmark.

b. One-half the duty above mentioned to be paid on all foreign goods on which duties have not been paid, imported in Danish vessels, provided such goods are shipped from a Danish port, not a free port, and accompanied with a clearance. The transit duty, proved to have been paid at such port on the goods, will be deducted in the half duty.

c. Deduction of duty will be made on all goods on which duties have been paid in St. Thomas, which duty will be here deducted, provided such goods be accompanied with a clearance from the custom-house at St. Thomas showing the duty there paid, and this clearance be produced within fourteen days from its date.

3d. With respect to the importation of cards, the directions given in the enactment of the 9th of February, 1849, remain in force, with the only difference that the duties are to be paid in conformity with § 6, 1st, *d*, and 2d, *a*, *b*, and *c* of this law, instead of in conformity with the ordinance of the 6th of June, 1833, § 5, *a*, *c*, *d*, and *e*.

C.—EXPORTS.

§ 7. All goods, without exception, may be exported at the two ports of entry.

§ 8. On the produce of this island being exported, the following duties are to be paid:

1. *Sugar.*—A. In Danish vessels to a Danish port, not a free port, 5 per cent.; to a foreign place, 10 per cent.
B. In foreign vessels, in all cases, 10 per cent.

2. *Rum and molasses.*—A. In Danish vessels to a Danish port, not a free port, 3 per cent.; to a foreign place, 6 per cent.
B. In foreign vessels, in all cases, 6 per cent.

§ 9. On sugar, rum, and molasses imported into this island from St. Thomas or St. John's, when exported from here, will be deducted the duty which the clearance from either of said islands shows to have been paid there.

§ 10. All other goods, whether the produce of this island or imported, may be exported free of duty. On coffee, tobacco, and on the articles specified in § 6, 1st, *b*, will be given a drawback of the import duty proved to have been paid, provided the drawback on the goods exported by one clearance amounts to at least $10.

D.—CONDITIONAL PRIVILEGES OF FOREIGN VESSELS.

§ 11. The same rights and privileges which under this law are granted to Danish vessels, shall also be enjoyed by vessels of those foreign states which are in possession of colonies, and grant the same rights and privileges to Danish vessels as to their own in the trade to and from their colonies.

E.—COMMON RULES.

§ 12. The duty stated in the preceding §§ includes all that is to be paid to the custom-house on imports or exports of goods. All other hitherto existing charges, viz: weigh money and ten per cent. fees on the duty, are hereby abolished.

§ 13. All persons, natives or foreigners, owning, despatching, or possessing goods to be imported or exported, are at liberty to enter them and make out the manifest themselves.

If required, a verbal entry at the custom-house shall be sufficient, and the collector of customs shall be bound, without remuneration, to make out the manifest in due form for the signature of the concerned.

§ 14. The custom-house offices shall be open for transaction of business every day, except Sundays and festival days of the church, from 7 o'clock a. m. to 3 o'clock p. m.; but discharging and loading can be carried on at all times of the day from 6 o'clock morning to 6 o'clock evening.

Before any loading or unloading can take place, special notice shall be given in writing, the same day or the day previous, to the inspector of customs, of what goods are to be landed or taken on board that day, whereon the inspector shall attest that such notification has been made. This certificate shall be given on the notification and clearance being produced at any time between 6 o'clock in the morning and 6 o'clock in the evening.

§ 15. Loading or unloading, taking place without a certificate from the inspector of customs, or at other hours than specified in the preceding paragraph, is illegal, and punished with the confiscation of the goods in question, or of their value, if they are not brought forward.

§ 16. This ordinance is in force from the day of its publication, and from the same day all prior ordinances regarding trade and navigation at St. Croix, not in comformity herewith, are hereby repealed.

COMPARATIVE

UNITED STATES AND

DENOMINATION OF MERCHANDISE.	DUTIES ON IMPORTS INTO— The United States, per cent. ad valorem, under the act of— 1846.	1857.	RUSSIA. Number, weight, or measure.	Russia and Poland. Rate of duty.	Trans-Caucasian ports of Black sea. Rate of duty.
Almonds	40	30	1 pood, or 36 lbs	$1 50	$0 56¼
Apples, bitter	20	Free	Cask of 1 anker of 9.73 gallons.	90	Free
Artificial flowers	30	24	1 pound	6 00	2 25
Bacon	20	15	36 pounds	1 50	45
Beer, ale, and porter	30	24	Porter, in casks. 1 oxhoft, or 58.428 gals.	33 75	27 00
			In bottles, each	26¼	18¾
Beef	20	15	36 pounds	1 50	45
Brandy	100	30	9.73 gallons	13 87½ from 10 to 15 deg's above 15 degrees	13 87½ over proof, 20 81; over proof, 27 75.
Brass, in pigs and bars	5	Free	36 pounds	43½	43½
manufactures of	30	24	do	3 75	3 75
Bricks	20	15		Free	Free
Brushes, all kinds	30	24	1 pound	30	30
Butter	20	15	36 pounds	1 50	30
Cassia	40	4	do	3 75	2 25
Cables and cordage	25	19	do	30	30
Candles, spermaceti	20	15	do	3 00	3 00
Cheese	30	24	do	3 75	1 87½
Cigars	40	30	1 pound	1 50	18¾

TARIFFS.

NORTHERN EUROPE.

DUTIES ON IMPORTS INTO—

SWEDEN.		NORWAY.		DENMARK.	
Number, weight, or measure.	Rate of duty.	Number, weight, or measure.	Rate of duty.	Number, weight, or measure.	Rate of duty.
1 pound	$0 02½	1 pound	$0 04½	1 centner, or 110⅓ lbs.	$1 64
Fresh, per tunna	30	Fresh, 4.157 bushels.	1 06	324 bushels, fresh	13 50
Dry, per lispund, or 18⅔ pounds	7½	Dried, 1 pound	2¼	110⅓ lbs. others	13½
1 pound	6 00	1 pound	6 36	1 pound, or 17⅗ oz.	$0 65½ to 2 62½
18⅔ pounds	20	do	2¼	110⅓ pounds	1 09¾
Beer, porter, 1 kanna, or 5½ pints.	10	in casks, porter,	1⅘	In casks of 34.681 gallons.	1 57½
Ale do	5	1 pottle, or quart, ale.	3½	In bottles, 100	2 17¾
18⅔ pounds	6⅔	Dried, 1 pound	1⅔	Smoked, 110⅓ lbs.	1 09¾
				Salt	56
5½ pints, under 10 degrees, from corn, potatoes, and succulents.	25	In casks, per bbl.	9	In casks, 30 viertel, or 59⅓ gallons.	9 45
Rum (from molasses)	25	In bottles, pr. qt.	15⅔	In bottles, per 100.	6 36
do every degree above 10 degrees.	1⅔ additional.	Of corn	Prohibited.		
1 skippund, or 302⅔ lbs. (staple weight.)	6 66⅔	1 pound	14		Free.
1 pound	From 13⅓ to 30 cts.	Polished, 1 lb.	13¼	Polished, 110⅓ lbs.	8 75
		Unpolished, 1 lb.	8⅔	Unpolished, do	45⅓
1,000	80	1,000	1 27¼	1,000	1 09⅓
1 pound	20	1 pound	$0 10½ to 52⅔	Common, 110⅓ lbs	2 18½
				Fine do	13 12½
18⅔ pounds	26⅔	In casks, 1 lb.	2⅓	Barrel, of 250 lbs.	3 15
Cassia fistula	By special permission	Lignea, pound	Free.		
Cassia lignea, 1 lb.	6⅔	1 pound	9	110⅓ pounds	2 74
18⅔ pounds	New 13⅓ Old (broken up) free	do	$0 01⅔ to 2½		Not defined.
1 pound	8⅓	do	10⅔	110⅓ pounds	6 56
18⅔ pounds	40	do	1¼	do	2 18½
1 pound	45	do	26½	do	17 45

TARIFFS—Continued.

DENOMINATION OF MERCHANDISE.	DUTIES ON IMPORTS INTO—				
	The United States, per cent. ad valorem, under the act of—		RUSSIA.		
	1846.	1857.	Number, weight, or measure.	Russia and Poland. Rate of duty.	Trans-Caucasian ports of Black sea. Rate of duty.
Coal, stone	30	24	36 pounds	Free	Free
Cocoa	10	4	do	$2 25	$1 50
Coffee	(a)20	(a)15	do	2 77 ½	1 87½
Combs	30	24	1 pound		30
Cotton, raw	Free	Free	36 pounds	18¾	Free
printed manufactures	25	24	1 pound	$0 56¼ to 1 20	$0 45 to 1 05
bleached and unbleached, ditto	25	24	do	$0 36 to 1 20	$0 26¼ to 1 05
American bolting cloth	According to material.	Free	do	$0 36 to 1 20	15½
Copper, crude	Free	Free	36 pounds	43½	43½
in plates or sheets	20	15	do	43½	43½
manufactures of	30	24	do	3 75	3 75
Dye-wood, in stick	5	Free	do	6	3¾
ground	20	Free	do	15	15
Earthen and stone ware		24	Common of Fayence, 36 pounds.	45	66¾
			Fine do	2 25	3 00
Figs	40	8	36 pounds	1 05	71¼
Fish, dried or smoked, unless otherwise specified.	20	15	do	75	75
herrings, salted	20	15	Cask, of 324 lbs	67½	30
Flour, wheat	20	15	Chertwert, 5.95 bus.	3 37½	33⅜
Furniture, household	30	24	36 pounds	$0 60 to 7 50	37½ to 90
Glass, window	20	15	do	2 25	1 50

(a) See note p. 114.

TARIFFS—Continued.

DUTIES ON IMPORTS INTO—

SWEDEN.		NORWAY.		DENMARK.	
Number, weight, or measure.	Rate of duty.	Number, weight or measure.	Rate of duty.	Number, weight, or measure.	Rate of duty.
....	At designated ports free.	....	Free............	100 toendes, or 400 bushels.	$3 26
1 pound..........	$0 02½	1 pound........	$0 2⅜	110⅓ pounds	1 22¼
........do........	2½	......do........	2⅜	........do........	1 64½
Of tortoise shell, 1 lb.	2 40	Wooden, 1 pound	32	....	Not defined.
Of horn	40	Bone, 1 pound..	57	....	
....	Free.............	1 pound........	(Nearly) 0½	....	Free.
1 pound..........	Not otherwise described, 26⅔	......do........	31⅜	110⅓ pounds......	17 45
........do........	20	......do........	Unbleached, 9		
			Bleached, 22	........do........	9 17½
........do........	20	......do........	4½	........do........	17½
302⅔ pounds......	40	Old and broken, for melting.	Free............	....	Free.
........do........	2 66⅔	......do........	2⅝	110⅓ pounds	1 48⅔
Nails or plates for ships. 1 pound.	66⅔				
	5	......do........	$0 7⅛ to 25	........do........	$4 37¼ to 17 45
Brazil, Pernambuco, sandal, 1 pound.	Free.............	Pernambuco, 1 lb.	0½	........do........	13
do. ground do.	8	Do. ground, 1 lb.	2¼	........do........	13
1 pound..........	Potters' wares, 2⅔ Stonewares, plain 4⅙	1 pound........	1⅜	........do........	54⅔
1 pound..........	1⅔	......do........	2¼	........do........	54⅔
Salted codfish, per barrel, or 4 bushels	45	Smoked, 1 lb.....	2½	1 toende, or 3.944 bushels.	43⅔
Dried codfish, per 18⅔ pounds.	10	Salt or dried, 1 lb.	5¼		
Salted herrings, per barrel.	13⅓	....	....	Salted herrings....	52½
4 bushels wheat, in grain.	60	Of wheat, 17.615 pounds.	14¼ 7$\frac{1}{18}$	Wheat, 3.944 bush.	78
If ground, 168 lbs.	60 and 10 per ct. additional.	Of rye, at designated ports, free		Rye, ...do....	34½
If old, and not too much for actual use.	10 pr. ct. ad val...	1 pound........	.67 to $0 08	110⅓ pounds	$1 21 to 3 50½
18⅔ pounds.......	33⅓	......do........	2½	........do........	2 18d

TARIFFS—Continued.

Denomination of merchandise.	Duties on imports into— The United States, per cent. ad valorem, under the act of— 1846.	1857.	Russia. Number, weight, or measure.	Russia and Poland. Rate of duty.	Trans-Caucasian ports of Black sea. Rate of duty.
Gunpowder	20	15		Prohibited	Prohibited
Hams	20	15	36 pounds	$1 50	$0 45
Hats and caps, of straw, leghorn, &c	30	24	1 pound	4 50	2 25
Hops	20	15	36 pounds	1 08¾	93¾
Indigo	10	4	do	1 68¾	2 62½
Indian corn	20	15	5 95 bushels	1 50	15
Iron, in bars	30	24	36 pounds	Prohibited	37½
castings	30	24	do	60	37½
nails	30	24	do	75	45
manufactures of	30	24		Prohibited	Prohibited
Lard	20	15	36 pounds	1 50	30
Lead, in pigs and bars	20	15	do	7½	(Nearly) 2
manufactures of, uncolored and unjapanned.	30	24	1 pound	3¾	3¾
manufactures of, colored and japanned.	30	24	do	3¾	3¾
Leather, unmanufactured	20	15	36 pounds	18¾	13¾
saddlery, and all articles thereof	30	24	1 pound	30	30
Linen, bleached and unbleached	20	15	do	90 cts. to 2 62½	60 cts. to 2 62½
Mace	40	4	36 pounds	5 62½	3 75
Medicinal drugs	20	15		Free, except those at 18¾ per lb.	already prepared,
Molasses	30	24	36 pounds	1 50	1 12½
Nails — Iron	30	24	do	75	45
Nails — Copper	20	15	do	75	45
Nutmegs	40	4	do	5 62½	3 75
Nuts	30	24	do	56¼	22½
Oil, whale	20	15	do	52½	45
Opium	20	15	1 pound	33¾	Free

TARIFFS—Continued.

DUTIES ON IMPORTS INTO—

SWEDEN.		NORWAY.		DENMARK.	
Number, weight, or measure.	Rate of duty.	Number, weight, or measure.	Rate of duty.	Number, weight, or measure.	Rate of duty.
....	Prohibited........	1 pound........	$0 03½	110⅓ pounds......	$2 18½
18⅔ pounds.......	$0 20	......do.......	2⅓	......do.........	1 14¼
One............	40	......do.......	42⅗	17⅗ ounces	1 05 to 1 74¾
18⅔ pounds.......	40	......do.......	2⅗	110⅓ pounds......	3 15
1 pound	1⅔	......do.......	18⅔	......do.........	6 57
1 tunna, or 4.157 bushels.	10	1 ton, or 300 bush	14	1 tøende, or 3.944 bushels.	22⅛
Raw and ballast, cast.	Prohibited........	1 skeppund, or 352 lbs.	1 30¾	Crude and old....	Free.
				In bars, 110⅓	20
1 pound..........	From 1 to 30 cts...	Pots, 1 pound.	1⅔	110⅓ pounds......	From 78 cts. to 6 56
2 in. and upwards long, 302⅔ lbs.	1 33⅓	.......do......	1⅓ to 3½	3 in. long and upwards, 110⅓ lbs.	69⅗
				Und. 3 in., 110 lbs.	1 09¼
1 pound..........	Not otherwise described, 10	.......do......	4½ to37½	110⅓ pounds......	1 62½ to 17 45
18⅔ pounds.......	20	.......do......	1⅔	......do.........	54⅗
302⅔ pounds......	20	.......do......	0⅕	....	Free.
1 pound	1⅘	.......do......	1	110⅓ pounds	6 56
....do..........	5	.......do......	1	......do.........	6 56
....do..........	10	.......do......	⅕ to 5 cts.	......do.........	8 74½
Fine, 1 pound ..	23¼	.......do......	14¼ to 26 cts.	......do.........	Ornamental, gilt, &c., 17 45
Common, 1 pound..	20	.......do......	14¼ to 26 cts.	......do.........	All other kinds, 6 82½
Drill, 1 pound..	16½	.......do......	Unbleached, 5⅓	......do.........	7 87½
Sail duck, 1 pound..	3	.......do......	Bleached, 12⅓	......do.........	7 87½
1 pound	10	.......do......	18½	......do.........	13 12½
which are admitted	With special persion, free.	Prepared.	10 per ct. ad val.	....	Not otherwise described, 1 10
1 pound	1⅔	1 pound.......	1⅓	110⅓ pounds	43⅕
302⅔ pounds	2 in. long, and over. 2 00	......do.......	1⅓ to 3½ cts.	3 in. long, and upwards, 110⅓ lbs	69⅗
1 pound	All others, 15	......do.......	1⅓ to 3½ cts.	Und. 3 in., 110⅓ lbs.	1 09¼
....do..........	6⅔	......do.......	17⅔	110⅓ pounds	8 74½
1 kanna, or 5½ pints	1⅔	......do.......	1¼	......do.........	38¾
18⅔ pounds	5	......do.......	0⅔	1 cask, of 30 galls.	1 18
For medicinal purposes by special permission.	Free............	......do.......	30⅔	....	Free............

TARIFFS—Continued.

DENOMINATION OF MERCHANDISE.	DUTIES ON IMPORTS INTO— The United States per cent. ad valorem, under the act of—		RUSSIA.		
	1846.	1857.	Number, weight, or measure.	Russia and Poland. Rate of duty.	Trans-Caucasian ports of Black sea. Rate of duty.
Paints (not otherwise described)	20	15	36 pounds	$1 20	$0 75
varnishes	20	15	In oil, 1 pound	11¼	11¼
Pepper, black	30	4	36 pounds	2 40	87½
Pimento	40	4	......do	1 50	75
Pork	20	15	Salted and smoked, 36 lbs.	1 50	45
Potatoes	30	24	5.95 bushels	15	Free
Printing presses	30	24		Free	Free
Rice	20	15	36 pounds	45	15
Rosin	20	15	......do	15	15
Rye meal	20	15	5.95 bushels	2 25	22½
Ship bread	20	15	36 pounds	30	30
Silk, dyed	30	24	1 pound	3 75	3 00
Soap, common	30	24	36 pounds	2 25	2 25
perfumed	30	24	......do	7 50	4 50
Spermaceti	20	15	......do	1 20	93¾
candles	20	15	......do	3 00	3 00
Sugar, refined	30	24	......do	Prohibited	2 25
Muscovado, brown, and white crushed.	30	24			
Tallow	10	8	36 pounds	22½	3¾
candles	20	15	......do	1 50	81
Tobacco, leaf	30	24	......do	4 50	93¾
manufactured for smoking	40	30	1 pound	45	7½
cigars	40	30	......do	1 50	18¾
snuff	40	30	......do	1 27½	22½
Turpentine	20	15	36 pounds	90	37½
Vinegar, of wine	30	24	10 oxhofts, of 58.428 gallons.	18 00	18 00
table, in bottles	30	24	Per bottle	22½	22½
Whalebone, the product of foreign fisheries, cleaned and uncleaned.	20	15	1 pound	7½	3¾
Wines, not otherwise specified	40	30	58.428 gallons	36 00	26 25

TARIFFS—Continued.

DUTIES ON IMPORTS INTO—

SWEDEN.		NORWAY.		DENMARK.	
Number, weight, or measure.	Rate of duty.	Number, weight, or measure.	Rate of duty.	Number, weight, or measure.	Rate of duty.
1 d.	White lead, from 1⅔ to 6⅓.	1 pound	$0 00½ to 2 46½	110⅓ pounds	$0 34½ to 4 36¼
do	$0 2½	do	3½	do	2 72¾
do	2½	do	2½	do	1 9¼
			Cayenne, 31⅔		
do	2½	do	2¼	do	87
18⅔ pounds	20	Salted or smok'd.	2¼	Salted, 110⅓ lbs.	54½
				Smoked, 110⅓ lbs.	1 09¾
1 tunna, dry meas., or 4.157 bushels.	13⅓	1 tunna, or 3 bushels.	5⅓	--------	Free
--------	25 per ct. ad val.	Of all sorts	Free	110⅓ pounds	54½
Paddy, 4.157 bush.	50	Paddy, tunna, or 3 bushels.	72	Paddy, 110⅓ lbs.	43⅔
		Rice flour, 1 lb.	1¼	Meal, 110⅓ lbs	96⅙
18⅔ pounds	6⅔	1 lb	0⅓	110⅓ pounds	13
225 pounds	40 cts., and 10 cts. additional.	By Hammerfest, Vardoe & Varsoe.	Free	do	34½
1 po nd	1⅔	pound	1¼	do	Free
do	53⅓	do	54¼	All kind , 110⅓ lbs.	78 75
do	2½	do	2⅓	do	1 31
do	13⅓	do	13⅓	do	10 93 1/10
--------	Free	--------	Free	--------	Free
1 pound	8⅓	1 pound	10½	110⅓ pounds	6 56
do	4⅙	do	4½	do	3 28
--------	2 1/24	Unrefined	2¼	--------	--------
18⅔ pounds	13⅓	1 pound	1⅔	110⅓ pounds	1 09¼
pound	2 6/7	do	3½	do	2 18½
do	5⅚	do	5½	do	89⅔
do	11⅔	do	8 9/10	do	3 15
do	45	do	22	do	18 50
do	13½	do	12¼	do	4 37½
do	1⅔	do	0¼	do	16¾
5½ pints	(All sorts,) 5	In casks, 1 lb.	1¼	1 hogshead of 57 gallons.	1 96¼
		In botls., 1 qt.	2½		
--------	--------	--------	--------	--------	--------
--------	Free	Split	5¼	Unsplit	Free
		Rough	Free	Split, per 110 lbs	6 56¼
In casks, 5½ pints.	20	In casks, 1 lb.	3 3/10	In casks, hogshead of 57 gallons.	7 87½
In bottles, do	40	In bottles, 1 qt.	17⅓	Bottles, per 100	6 56

TARIFFS—Continued.

DENOMINATION OF MERCHANDISE.	DUTIES ON IMPORTS INTO—				
	The United States, per cent. ad valorem, under the act of—		RUSSIA.		
	1846.	1857.	Number, weight, or measure.	Russia and Poland. Rate of duty.	Trans-Caucasian ports of Black sea. Rate of duty.
Wood, boards	20	15	Per archine (28 in.) in length.	$0 01½	
shingles	30	24		Free	Free
veneers	30	24	36 pounds	75	$0 75
masts and spars	20	15		Free	Free
all other manufactures of	30	24	do	$0 60 to 7 50(a)	$0 37½ to 1 12½

(a) This latter duty applies only to ornamental furniture.

TARIFFS—Continued.

DUTIES ON IMPORTS INTO—

SWEDEN.		NORWAY.		DENMARK.	
Number, weight, or measure.	Rate of duty.	Number, weight, or measure.	Rate of duty.	Number, weight, or measure.	Rate of duty.
....	Free........	....	Free........	Per cask, or 2 tons of ship's burden.	(a)$1 57½
....	....	1,000........	$0 52⅔	....	(a)1 57½
....	10 per ct. ad val...	Up to ¼ in. thick, 1 lb.	5¼	Mahogany, 100 cubic feet.	1 36¼
				Veneers, 110⅓ lbs..	3 50
One........	Free........	....	5 per ct. ad val....	Per cask, or 2 tons of ship's burden.	(a)1 57½
....	33⅓ per ct. ad val.	Not otherwise described, 1 lb.	$2 50 ad val......	110⅓ lbs........	1 31 to 3 49⅓

(a) These articles are described generally, and so rated. They may, however, be comprehended under "articles not otherwise described." If so, the duty is $1 64 per centner of 110¼ pounds.

CENTRAL EUROPE.

CENTRAL EUROPE.

INDIRECT TRADE OF THE UNITED STATES WITH FOREIGN NATIONS.

ZOLLVEREIN.

The tariff is that of January 1, 1854.(a)

Moneys.—In the north, 1 thaler = 30 silbergroschen = 12 pfennigen = $0 69.

In the south, 1 florin, or guilder, = 60 kreutzer = $0 40.

Weights and Measures.(b)—1 centner = 100 lbs. = 110¼ lbs. avoirdupois.

1 scheffel = 16 metzen.

100 scheffel 18.901 imperial quarters.

1 ship's last = 37½ centner.

The Zollverein rests on treaties of the several States named below.

The States levy the duties on their frontiers, and receive, with one exception, proportions of the amount collected in the ratio of population, after payment of expenses.

Goods under 1-100 centner are not chargeable with duty; and no duty under 6 pfennigen, or 1 groschen, is levied.

The system of export and transit tariffs is somewhat complicated. Duties are levied at the gross weight, or at the net weight, tare being allowed at fixed rates.

List of the States at present composing the German Zollverein, since its union with the Steuerverein.

The kingdom of Prussia,
Bavaria,
Hanover,
Saxony,
Wurtemberg.
The Grand Duchy of Baden,
Oldenburg,
Luxembourg,
Sachen Weimer-Eisenach,
Hessen Darmstadt.
The Electorate of Hessen Cassel.
The Duchy of Brunswick,
The Duchy of Nassau,
Sachsen Meiningen,
Sachsen Altenburg,
Sachsen Coburg-Gotha,
Anhalt-Bernburg, Cothen and Dessau.
The Principality of Hessen Homburg,
Schwartzburg Rudolstadt,
Schwartzburg Sondershausen,
Reuss Greiz,
Reuss Schleiz and Reuss Lobenstein Ebersdorf.
Waldeck.
Free town of Frankfort-on-the-Mayn.

(a) See note, p. 261. In October, 1856, a few modifications of the tariffs of the Zollverein were made, but in no respect interesting to the United States trade.

(b) By virtue of a law of May 17, 1856, the weights hitherto exclusively recognized in the tariff of the States of the Zollverein were adopted as the general standard of weights in the kingdom of Prussia.

AUSTRIA.

The tariff is that of 1852, with later changes of December 3, 1853.(a)

Moneys.—1 florin, or guilder, = 60 kreutzer = $0 48½.

Weights and Measures.—1 centner = 100 lbs. = 110¼ lbs. avoirdupois.(b)

The following tariff applies to the whole of the Austrian empire, with the exception of Styria, the district of the free port Trieste, of Venice, Fiume, Buccari, Porto Ré, Zengg, Carlopago, Brody in Galicia; Dalmatia, and the Quarnerian islands. The importation, exportation, and transit of kitchen-salt, gun-powder, tobacco, raw or manufactured, though specified in the tariff, can only be allowed to take place by special permission—the government retaining the monopoly of these articles. The import duty, if not otherwise stated, implies net weight; while the export and transit duties, if not otherwise stated, imply, on the contrary, gross weight.

In February and March, 1857, the duties on looms of any motive power for weaving, and on machines for spinning yarn, were removed.

SWITZERLAND.

The tariff is that of January 1, 1352.

Money.—1 franc = 100 rappen, or centimes, = $0 8.6.

Weights and measures.—1 centner = 101 lbs. = 110¼ avoirdupois

Whenever the duty is paid by *weight*, the gross is understood, without deduction for *tare.*

Export duty.—All articles not named in the nomenclature of the tariff pay 2 cents per 110¼ lbs.

Transit duty.—Most articles pay one cent per 110¼ lbs. for every distance not exceeding 32 English miles; beyond that distance about 6 cents per 110¼ lbs.

(a) See note, p. 261 By an ordinance of March 20, 1856, several important modifications of the general tariff of 1853 were made, part of which went into force April 1, and the other part July 1, 1856. By this ordinance, reductions were made in the import duties on cocoa, coffee, spices, sugar, molasses, fish, oils, wines, ead, iron, preserves of all kinds, and yarns of all kinds. The per centage decrease on previous rates, effected by this ordinance, may be noted, approximately, as follows: (a) On cocoa, 20 per cent. Coffee, raw, and substitutes of, 25; roasted, 20. Drugs, common, including pepper, 25; fine, as cinnamon, cassia lignea, 30; superfine, as nutmegs, mace, 70 Sugar, refined, 10; raw, and in liquid state, 18; for refining, 14; syrup of sugar, 40. Fish, prepared, salted, dried, smoked, pickled, and shellfish, 37. Oil, fat, in jars and bottles, 25. Wine, in bottles and jars, 17; in casks and skins, 20. Chocolate, confectionery, preserved meat, &c., 27. Lead, pig, and litharge, 17 and 20. Iron, bar and bolt, 28; cast, also iron and steel wire, 38. Yarns, linen and woolen, 17. Manufactures of lead, and in sheets, 33.

(b) The Prussian zoll centner was formerly estimated at 123⅙ lbs.; but in 1851, for sake of conformity with the rates of the Zollverein, the value of 110.27 English pounds was adopted.

(a) See note, p. 93.

COMPARATIVE TARIFFS.

UNITED STATES AND CENTRAL EUROPE.

DENOMINATION OF MERCHANDISE.	The United States, per cent. ad valorem, under the act of—		DUTIES ON IMPORTS INTO— ZOLLVEREIN.		AUSTRIA.		SWITZERLAND.	
	1846.	1857.	Number, weight, or measure.	Rate of duty.	Number, weight, or measure.	Rate of duty.	Number, weight, or measure.	Rate of duty.
Ale, in bottles	30	24	110¼ pounds	$5 52	110¼ pounds	$3 63	110¼ pounds	$2 78
in casks	30	24	do	1 72½	do	36⅜	do	27½
Alum	20	15	do	92	do	52¾	do	6
					(When imported	by sea,) $8\frac{1}{12}$		
Anise seed	20	4	do	69		4 85	do	37
Ashes, pot	20	15	do	11½	110¼ pounds	$4\frac{1}{24}$	do	6
Apples, bitter	20	Free		Free	do	$4\frac{4}{5}$	do	13½
Apparel, wearing	Free	Free		Free		Free		Free
Baggage, personal, in actual use	Free	Free		Free		Free		Free
Bark, Jesuits', or Peruvian	15	Free	110¼ pounds	2 30	110¼ pounds	36⅜	110¼ pounds	64
Cascarilla	20	8	do	2 30	do	36⅜		
all, for dyeing purposes	20	8		Free	do	$4\frac{4}{5}$	110¼ pounds	6
Beans, vanilla	20	15	110¼ pounds	4 48½	do	24 25	do	64
Beef, fresh	20	15	do	1 38	do	36⅜	do	65
smoked, salted, or dried	20	15	do	1 38	do	1 21¼	do	65
Beer, ale, porter, in bottles	30	24	do	5 52	do	3 63	do	2 78
in casks	30	24	do	1 72½	do	36⅜	do	27½
Beeswax	20	15	do	1 72½	do	1 94	do	65
Boards and plank, rough or dressed, pine	20	15	1 ship's last, or 4,125 lbs.	23	100 cubic feet	36⅜	1,100 pounds	11
oak	20	15	4,125 pounds	69				

TARIFFS—Continued.

DENOMINATION OF MERCHANDISE	The United States, per cent. ad valorem, under the act of— 1846.	1857.	DUTIES ON IMPORTS INTO— ZOLLVEREIN. Number, weight, or measure.	ZOLLVEREIN. Rate of duty.	AUSTRIA. Number, weight, or measure.	AUSTRIA. Rate of duty.	SWITZERLAND. Number, weight, or measure.	SWITZERLAND. Rate of duty.
Bone, whale	20	15		Free	110¼ pounds	$0 36⅜	110¼ pounds	$0 37
Brandy	100	30	110¼ pounds	$5 52	do	3 84¾	In bottles, 110¼ lbs.	2 78
			If in boxes, (bottles,) 24 lbs. will be deducted.				In bbls, 110¼ lbs.	27½
Brass, in sheets, rolled, &c	30	24	110¼ pounds	4 14			110¼ pounds	27½
manufactured into kettles and other utensils.	30	24	do	6 90	110¼ pounds	3 84	do	1 48
Brazil wood, in sticks	5	Free	do	Free	do	4$\frac{1}{24}$	do	6
ground in powder	20	12	do	11⅓	do	36⅜	do	14
Brushes, all kinds, common	30	24	do	2 07	do	6 06	do	64
fine	30	24	do	6 90	do	24 25	do	1 48
Butter	20	15	do	2 53	do	1 21¼	do	14
Candles, wax	20	15			do	3 84¾	do	2 78
tallow	20	15	110¼ pounds	4 14	do	1 21¼	do	37
sperm	20	15			do	1 94	do	2 78
stearine	20	15			do		do	2 78
Carpets	30	24	110¼ pounds	13 80	do	24 25	do	2 78
Chamomile flowers	20	15	do	2 30	do	2 42½	do	64
Cheese	30	24	do	2 53	do	2 42⅓	do	64
Chemical preparations	30	15	do	2 30		2 42¼	do	64
China ware, white	30	24	do	6 90	110¼ pounds	7 27½	do	
colored	30	24					do	48
and white with colored	30	24						
and porcelain stripes	30	24	110¼ pounds	17 25	110¼ pounds	19 40	110¼ pounds	1 48
Chocolate	20	15	do	7 59	do	9 70	do	2 78

TARIFFS—Continued.

Denomination of merchandise.	The United States, per cent. ad valorem, under the act of— 1846.	1857.	Zollverein. Number, weight, or measure.	Zollverein. Rate of duty.	Austria. Number, weight, or measure.	Austria. Rate of duty.	Switzerland. Number, weight, or measure.	Switzerland. Rate of duty.
Cigars	40	30	110¼ pounds	$13 80	110¼ pounds, with permission from government.	$12 12½	110¼ pounds	$2 78
Cinnamon	30	4	do	4 48½	110¼ pounds	12 12½	do	64
Citron	20	8	do	1 38	do	1 21¼	do	64
Cloth, oil, coarse, not printed, linen	30	24	do	1 38	do	24 25	do	From 1 48 to 2 78
all other kinds			do	3 45				
silk	25	19	do	7 59				
India rubber	30	24	do	3 45				
Clothing, ready-made	30	24	do	75 90	do (fine)	72 75	do	2 78
Cloves	40	4	do	4 48½	do	12 12½	do	64
Coal, stone	30	24	do	2 9/10		Free	1,100 pounds	9
Cochineal	10	4		Free	110¼ pounds	36⅜	110¼ pounds	37
Cocoa, in beans and shells	10	4	110¼ pounds	4 48½	do, raw	3 84¾	do., raw	27½
					do, ground	6 06¼	do., ground	64
Coffee, raw, and its substitutes	(a)20	(a)15	do	3 45	do	4 85	do	27½
Coins, of gold, silver, or copper	Free	Free		Free		Free		Free.
Copper, crude	Free	Free	110¼ pounds	34½	110¼ pounds	36⅜	110¼ pounds	14
in sheets, hammered, polished, and plated.	30	24	do	4 14	do	3 84¾	do	27½
in pans, kettles, &c., and all other goods of copper or brass, also japanned.	30	24	do	6 90			do	1 48
Cutlery	30	24	do	6 90	110¼ pounds	4 85	do	1 48
Cubebs	20	15	do	4 48½	do	4 85	do	64
Cotton, raw	Free	Free		Free		Free	do	6

(a) See note, p. 114.

TARIFFS—Continued.

Denomination of merchandise.	The United States, per cent. ad valorem, under the act of—		Duties on imports into— Zollverein.		Austria.		Switzerland.	
	1846.	1857.	Number, weight, or measure.	Rate of duty.	Number, weight, or measure.	Rate of duty.	Number, weight, or measure.	Rate of duty.
Cotton, unbleached, yarn, unmixed, or mixed with wool or linen, one or two threads.	25	19	110¼ pounds	$2 07	110¼ pounds	$2 91	110¼ pounds	$0 37
bleached, three threads and upwards	25	19	do	5 52			do	64
Drugs for dyes, not enumerated	20	Free	do	11½	110¼ pounds	$4\frac{1}{12}$	do	64
medicinal, not enumerated	20	15	do	2 30	do	2 42½		
Dyeing articles, not enumerated	20	Free	do	2 30	do	$4\frac{1}{12}$	do	64
woods, in blocks or sticks	20	Free		Free		Free	do	6
ground	20	Free	110¼ pounds	11½	110¼ pounds	34½	do	14
Earthenware, common	30	24	do	23	do	$4\frac{1}{24}$	do	27½
Fayence, white	30	24	do	3 45	do	2 42½	}	
gilt	30	24	do	6 90			} do	1 48
silvered and painted	30	24	do	6 90	110¼ pounds	4 85	}	
Figs	40	8	do	2 76	do	1 21	do	64
Fish, fresh	20	15		Free	do	1 21	1,100 pounds	55
Flax seed	20	15	110¼ pounds	$2\frac{9}{10}$		34½	110¼ pounds	3
Flour, wheat or other grain	20	15	do	1 38	110¼ pounds	36⅝	do	9
Furs, caps, gloves, and all furs covered with cloth, linen, &c.	30	24	do	15 18	do	48 50	do	2 78
Fur, without cloth covering	10	8	110¼ pounds	4 14	110¼ pounds	4 85	110¼ pounds	1 48
skins, for furs	10	8	do	46	do	21¼	do	6
Galls, nut	5	Free		Free		Free	do	14
Glauber salts	20	15	110¼ pounds	2 30	110¼ pounds	3 ⅜	do	64
Gold and silver, in bars, bullion, coin, and dusts	Free	Free		Free		Free		¼ Free.
Guano	Free	Free		Free		Free	1,100 pounds	3

TARIFFS—Continued.

Denomination of merchandise.	The United States, per cent. ad valorem, under the act of—		Duties on imports into— Zollverein.		Austria.		Switzerland.	
	1846.	1857.	Number, weight, or measure.	Rate of duty.	Number, weight, or measure.	Rate of duty.	Number, weight, or measure.	Rate of duty.
Grain, all kinds	20	15	1$\frac{13}{20}$ bushels	\$0 11$\frac{1}{2}$	110$\frac{1}{4}$ pounds	Wheat, \$0 16$\frac{1}{6}$; Rye, 12$\frac{1}{8}$	110$\frac{1}{4}$ pounds	\$0 03
Gum, Arabic	10	8		Free	do	36$\frac{3}{8}$	do	14
elastic, unmanufactured	10	8		Free			do	64
all medicinal, and for dyeing	20	8	110$\frac{1}{4}$ pounds	2 30	110$\frac{1}{4}$ pounds	4$\frac{1}{12}$	do	64
Gunpowder	20	15	do	1 38	For the government, free.			
Gutta percha, unmanufactured	20	4		Free	110$\frac{1}{4}$ pounds	3 84$\frac{3}{4}$	do	64
Hams	20	15	110$\frac{1}{4}$ pounds	1 38	do	1 21$\frac{1}{4}$	do	64
Herrings	20	15	1 barrel	69	do	1 94	do	64
Hides, green, salted, dry, raw	5	4		Free	do	21$\frac{1}{4}$	do	6
Hops	20	15	110$\frac{1}{4}$ pounds	1 72	do	1 21$\frac{1}{4}$	do	37
Horns	5	4		Free		Free	do	6
India rubber, unmanufactured	10	4		Free	110$\frac{1}{4}$ pounds	3 84$\frac{3}{4}$	do	64
Indigo	10			Free	do	36$\frac{3}{8}$	do	37
Instruments, astronomical, chirurgical, mathematical, mechanical, musical, optical, without regard to the materials of which made.	20 to 30	15 to 24	110$\frac{1}{4}$ pounds	4 14	do	4 85	do; Musical	1 48; 2 78
Ipecacuanha	20	15	do	2 30	do	2 42$\frac{1}{2}$	110$\frac{1}{4}$ pounds	64
Iron, crude or old	30	24	do	23	do	36$\frac{3}{8}$	do	6
pig, bar, and sheet	30	24	do	From 1 03$\frac{1}{2}$ to 1 72	do	1 21$\frac{1}{4}$	do	14
Ivory, unmanufactured	5	Free		Free		Free	do	37
Jesuits' bark	15	Free	110$\frac{1}{4}$ pounds	2 30	110$\frac{1}{4}$ pounds	2 42$\frac{1}{2}$	do	64
Jerked beef	20	15	do	1 38	do	1 21$\frac{1}{4}$	do	64
Kino gum	20	8		Free	do	2 42$\frac{1}{2}$	do	64

TARIFFS—Continued.

Denomination of merchandise.	The United States, per cent. ad valorem, under the act of— 1846	1857.	Duties on imports into— Zollverein. Number, weight, or measure.	Zollverein. Rate of duty.	Austria. Number, weight, or measure.	Austria. Rate of duty.	Switzerland. Number, weight, or measure.	Switzerland. Rate of duty.
Lac dye	5	4		Free	110¼ pounds	$0 36⅜	110¼ pounds	$0 64
Lard	20	15	110¼ pounds	$1 38	do	1 21¼	do	13½
Lead, crude, in blocks, bars, and old	20	15	do	17½	do	1 21¼	do	6
manufactures of, common, as shot, kettles, and rolled lead.	20 to 30	15 to 24	do	1 38	do	3 84¾	do	27½
manufactured, fine	30	24	do	6 90	do	7 27½	do	1 48
Leather, tanned	20	15	do	4 14	do	7 27½	do	37
Leather, common, saddlery, shoes, &c , bellows, carriages, with leather works.	20 to 30	15 to 24	do	6 90	do	7 27½	do	1 48
Leather wares, fine, of all kinds	30	24	do	15 18	do	19 40	do	2 78
Linen, raw yarn, spun by machines	20	15	do	38	do	1 21¼		
spun by hand	20	15	do	11½	do	36⅜	do	64
yarn, bleached, colored	20	15	do	2 07	do	4 85		
or wound	20	15	do	2 76	do	7 27½		
gray, for packing and sail duck	20	15	do	46	do	72¾	do	1 48
raw, tick and trellis	20	15	do	2 76	do	7 27½		
Linseed	10	Free	do	$2\frac{9}{10}$			do	3
Logwood	5	Free		Free		Free	do	6
Madeira wine, in bottles	40	30	110¼ pounds	5 52	110¼ pounds	7 27½	In jugs or bottles, 110¼ pounds.	2 78
Mahogany, unmanufactured	20	8		Free		Free	110¼ pounds	6
manufactured	40	30	110¼ pounds	2 07	110¼ pounds	7 27½	do	2 78
Manufactures of casting	30	24	do					
common	30	24	do	69	110¼ pounds	2 42½	do	64
and fine	30	24	do	4 14				

TARIFFS—Continued.

DENOMINATION OF MERCHANDISE.	The United States, per cent. ad valorem, under the act of—		DUTIES ON IMPORTS INTO— ZOLLVEREIN.		AUSTRIA.		SWITZERLAND.	
	1846.	1857.	Number, weight, or measure.	Rate of duty.	Number, weight, or measure.	Rate of duty.	Number, weight, or measure.	Rate of duty.
Marble, unmanufactured	20	15		Free		Free	110¼ pounds	$0 06
manufactured	30	24	110¼ pounds	$6 90	110¼ pounds	$0 72¾	do	27½
Medicinal drugs	20 to 30	15	do	2 30	do	2 42½	do	64
Musical instruments	20	15	do	4 14	do	4 85	do	2 78
Nails, iron	30	24	do	4 14	do	2 42½	do	37
Nutmegs	40	4	do	4 48½	do	24 25	do	64
Oil, spermaceti, in barrels	20	15	do	92	do	1 21¼	do	6
whale and other fish	20	15	do	34½	do	24¼	do	6
Paints and varnish	20	15	do	2 30			do	64
Paper, printing	30	24	do	69	110¼ pounds	1 45½	do	1 48
letter	30	24	do	3 45	do	3 84¾	} do	1 48
gold and silver	30	24	do	6 90	do	7 27½		
Pimento	40	4	do	4 48½	do	4 85	do	64
Pitch	20	15	do	11½		Free	do	6
Port wine	40	30	do	{ In bottles, 5 52 In casks, 4 14 }	110¼ pounds	7 27½	do	{ In bottles and casks, $2 78
Pot and pearl ash	20	15	do	11½		Free	do	6
Rice	20	15	do	69	110 pounds	36⅜	do	3
paddy	20	15	do	46	do	12⅛	do	3
Root, ginger	40	15	do	4 48½	do	4 85	do	64
medicinal, not provided for	20	15	do	2 30	do	2	do	64
Rosin	20	15		Free		Free	do	6
Saddlery, common	20	15	110¼ pounds	6 90	110¼ pounds	7 27½	do	1 48
fine	30	24	do	15 18	do	19 40	do	2 78
Skins and furs, salted and dry	5	4		Free		21⅓	do	6
designed for furs	10	8	110¼ pounds	46	110¼ pounds	1 21¼	do	6

TARIFFS—Continued.

DENOMINATION OF MERCHANDISE.	The United States, per cent. ad valorem, under the act of—		DUTIES ON IMPORTS INTO— ZOLLVEREIN.		AUSTRIA.		SWITZERLAND.	
	1846.	1857.	Number, weight, or measure.	Rate of duty.	Number, weight, or measure.	Rate of duty.	Number, weight, or measure.	Rate of duty.
Spirits of turpentine	20	15	110¼ pounds	$0 23	110¼ pounds	$0 36⅜	110¼ pounds	$0 14
Sugar, brown	30	24	do	5 52	do	5 33½	110¼ lbs., all sorts.	64
Tallow	10	8	do	2 07	do	36⅜	110¼ pounds	6
Tar	20	15	do	11½		Free	do	6
Teas	(a)20	(a)15	do	5 52	110¼ pounds	7 27½	do	2 78
Tobacco, leaf	30	24	do	2 76	110¼ lbs. Allowed to be imported only with permission of the government.	4 85(b)	do	64
smoking, in rolls	30	24	do	7 59		12 12½	do	1 48
cigars and snuffs	40	30	do	13 80		12 12½	do	2 8
Turpentine	20	15		Free	110¼ pounds	19	do	14
Wax	20	15	110¼ pounds	1 72½	do	1 94	do	27½
Wines	40	30	Bottles, 110¼ lbs.	5 52	do	7 27½	do	In casks, 27½
			Casks, 110¼ lbs.	4 14				In bottles, 2 78
Wearing apparel	Free	Free		Free		Free.		
Whalebone, unmanufactured	20	15		Free	110¼ pounds	36⅜	110¼ pounds	37
Wood, staves and heading	20	15	1 schiffs last = 4,125 pounds.	From 46 cents to 92 cents.	do	36⅜	1,100 pounds	11

(a) See note, p. 168. (b) Besides the import duty, an extra due for the grant of the license must be paid, amounting to 97 cents per pound for unmanufactured; $1 21½ per pound for manufactured.

SOUTHERN EUROPE.

SOUTHERN EUROPE.

SARDINIA.

The tariff is that of August, 1851, with alterations down to 1854(*a*.) The rates of duty are those levied on national and equalized vessels.

Unequalized vessels, that is, vessels belonging to nations not having reciprocal treaties with Sardinia, or not granting perfect reciprocity to the Sardinian flag, pay, of course, higher duties.

Money.—1 lira = 100 centesimi = 18.6 cents.

Weights and measures, are nearly the same as those in France, viz :

1 kilogramme = 2.204 lbs. avoirdupois ; 100 kilogrammes = 220.204 lbs. ; 1 hectolitre = 26.417 gallons.

The import tariff is divided into 20 generic classes, as is, also the export tariff. All duties on the import or export of grain and farinaceous food are repealed by the law of February 16, 1854.

Transit duties exist only on tobacco, playing cards, and salt.

The duties are generally levied upon gross weight.

TUSCANY.

The tariff is that of November 23, 1851.

Money.—1 lira = 20 soldi = 12 denari = 16 cents.

Weights and Measures.—1 cantaro = 100 libra = 74.86 pounds.
1 moggio = 16.59 pounds.
1 barile of wine = 12.04 gallons = 90 pounds avoirdupois.
1 barile of oil = 66 pounds.

Besides the duty specified in the tariff, there is also charged $8\frac{1}{3}$ per cent. of the value for the "*Tassa di beneficenza*," with the exception of nails and a few other articles.

Export and transit duties are levied generally on the same articles as the import. The export duty on oak timber was doubled August 1, 1854.

PAPAL STATES.

The tariff is that of December 26, 1850. (*a*)

Money.—1 scudi = 100 bajocchi = $1.

Weights and Measures.—1 centinajo 100 libra = 74.86 pounds.
1 rubbio of grain 8.36 bushels.
1 barile of wine = 15.81 gallons.

The export tariff has an extended nomenclature.

Transit duties are 3 cents on nearly all articles, per 50 miles, each package ; per 100 miles, 6 cents ; above 100 miles, 9 cents.

(*a*) See Appendix.

APPENDIX.

Partial modifications of the customs rates of the Papal States have repeatedly been made since 1850; but, in 1856, a quarto volume, embracing a new tariff, was issued, in which the modifications are general, the decrease or increase on former rates ranging from 10 to 100 per cent. Subjoined is a list of articles, with the corresponding rates of per centage decrease: (a)

On glass and glass ware, 16 to 50 per cent.; wares of terra cotta, porcelain, and alabaster, 25 to 50; wares of lead, iron, copper, and zinc, 50; manufactures of silk, linen, cotton and leather, 30 to 70; wearing apparel, 50; straw hats, 40; umbrellas, $33\frac{1}{3}$; files, $33\frac{1}{3}$; blankets, 70; tissues of cotton and flax, 25 to 50; linen or woolen thread, 33; skins, 40 to 50; oils, aromatic or medicinal, 50; quinine, 60; soap, common, 40; sponges, common, 50; acid, nitric, 30; acid, muriatic and sulphuric, $33\frac{1}{3}$; carbonate of amonia, 97; camphine, 95; borax, 50; copper, crude, 10; zinc, in sheets, 40; iron, pig, 50; iron, half refined, $11\frac{4}{5}$; gold, wire and sheets, 50; gold, leaf, $87\frac{1}{2}$; silver, wire and sheets, $30\frac{3}{5}$; silver, leaf, 50; meat, salted, smoked, or prepared, 40.

On exports, the duty on coarse silk is reduced two-thirds, and on wool and rags four-fifths, while on the export of wine the duty is doubled.

By virtue of a law of May 7, 1856, a per centage decrease on the rates of 1855, on certain articles, was effected, approximately, as follows: (a) On woolen fabrics, embroidered, 58 per cent.; linen cloth, dyed in the piece, 50; cotton, dyed in the piece, 50; cotton velvet and plush, 25; fabrics, bleached or unbleached, coarse, 33; tulle, 40; window glass, 50; mirrors, large, not silvered, 50; silvered, 40; small, silvered or not, 51; glass wares, polished, 17; ground or cut, 43; wood manufactures, common, 50; fine, and toys, 17. By the same law, on common cotton lace, an increase of 5.67 per cent. on previous rates was imposed.

By virtue of a law of March 26, 1857, a per centage decrease on the rates in force in 1856 was effected on certain articles, as follows: On manufactures of wool, also mixed with thread or cotton, in prunellas, velvets, &c., except alpaca, flannel, knitted works, &c., 2 per cent.; cottons of fustians, quilts, and the like, 50; muslins, white, plain, flowered, printed, knitted, and all manufactured goods of the kind not specified, and also embroidered goods, 33; linen goods, white or unbleached, plain, printed, and colored, or knitted, 17; articles of hair, pure or mixed with any material except silk, 50; furs, dressed or undressed, and manufactured, 17 to 70; soap of all sorts, 40; books, bound in cloth or colored cotton, 62. On wearing apparel, new, the duty in force in 1856 was double that of the stuffs of which the clothing was made; in 1857, the duty was reduced to the same as on the stuffs.

TWO SICILIES.

The tariff is that of 1824, with alterations and modifications down to 1850 (b)

Money.—1 ducat = 100 grani = 10 caralli = 80 cents.

Weights and Measures.(c)—1 cantaro grosso = 192.50 pounds.
1 cantaro sottile = 175 pounds.
1 cantaro = 100 rotoli.
1 rotolo = 1.964 pounds.
1 canna = 10 palmi = 2.306 yards.
1 botta = 128.878 gallons = $\frac{3}{4}$ pipe.
1 salma grossa of grain = 9.77 bushels.
1 salma generale = 7.85 bushels.
1 salma of wine = 23.06 gallons.

As the weights and measures of the Island of Sicily are larger than those of Naples, above given, a deduction is made for every palmo and canna of 2 per cent.; for the bottle, 21 per cent.; for every ounce or pound, 1 per cent.; for the rotolo and cantaro, 11 per cent.

The flag of the Two Sicilies has a deduction of 10 per cent. on imports, if a higher sum in the tariff has not been provided. The same deduction is granted, for a direct voyage, to the flags of those countries which have commercial treaties with the Two

(a) See note page 93.

(b) See note page 261. By virtue of the 11th article of a treaty concluded between the Two Sicilies and Spain, in 1856, the former grants to the latter, as a compensation for privileges abandoned enjoyed by the latter, in virtue of a treaty of 1817, important reductions in the customs rates on sugar, coffee, wax, honey, lead, wines, mercury, copper, and salted sardines. To these reductions the United States would seem entitled, under that clause of the treaty with the Two Sicilies of 1846, which provides, that "no higher duties shall be imposed on importations into either country, of articles from the other, than from any other country," and that "favors granted by either party to other nations shall be common to the other."

(c) See vol. 3, "Returns," p. 300.

Sicilies. These are the United States,(a) England, Russia, Sardinia, Denmark, Austria, Prussia, the Zollverein, Netherlands, and Belgium.

Transit duty.—On every package, 19 cents; on loose goods, (not packed,) 8¼ cents per 192 pounds.

Prohibited list.—Cocoons, (silk;) soda; timber for buildings, except specially permitted.

Export duty.—Animals, corn, grain, biscuit, tartar, maccaroni, madder, and a few other articles, only in national vessels, are exempt from duty on exportation.

(a) In July, 1851, a convention was agreed upon between the Two Sicilies and the United States, proposed by the latter, and embracing the following points: 1st. The reduction of 10 per cent. on the tariff on American produce and mannfactures, on *indirect* voyages. 2d. Liberty to United States vessels to touch at intermediate ports on their voyages to the ports of the Two Sicilies, without incurring extra duties of import on tonnage. 3d. The abolition of the 40 grains (less than 40 cents) duty on indirect voyages, and the subjection of direct and indirect voyages to an equal duty of 4 grains per ton. The discriminations, therefore, against foreign vessels does not apply to those of the United States.

COMPARATIVE TARIFFS.

UNITED STATES AND SOUTHERN EUROPE.

Denomination of merchandise.	The United States, per cent. ad valorem, under the act of—		Duties on imports into— Sardinia.		Tuscany.		Papal States.		Two Sicilies.	
	1846.	1857.	Number, weight, or measure.	Rate of duty.	Number, weight, or measure.	Rate of duty.	Number, weight, or measure.	Rate of duty.	Number, weight, or measure.	Rate of duty.
Beef, fresh	20	15	100 kilogram's, (220 lbs.)	$0 92½	1 cantaro = 74.86 lbs.	$0 50¼	Prohibited	Prohibited		Free.
salted or smoked	20	15	220 pounds	1 80½	74.86 lbs	1 20	1 centinajo = 74.86 lbs.	$2 50	192.50 lbs	$8 60
Beer, in casks	30	24	26.417 gallons.	1 08	1 barrel	1 35	74.86 lbs	2 00	1 ton	74⅘
in bottles	30	24	1 bottle	1						
Candles, tallow	20	15	220 lbs	92	74 86 lbs	1 20	74.86 lbs	3 00	1 cantaro = 192.50 lbs.	8 00
stearine	20	15	220 lbs	1 86			74.86 lbs	20 00		Not defined.
spermaceti	20	15	220 lbs	7 40	74.86 lbs	(Wax,) 2 00	74.86 lbs	20 00	1.964 lbs	33⅓
Cassia, (lignea)	40	4	220 lbs	7 20	74.86 lbs	1 60	74.86 lbs	5 00	1 ton	263 84
Castings, (iron)	30	24	220 lbs	2 70 to 10 80	74.86 lbs	From 16 to 80	74.86 lbs. (small articles.)	15 00	192.50 lbs	3 60
Cheese	30	24	220 lbs	3 60	74.86 lbs	From 16 to 80	74.86 lbs	3 75	192.50 lbs	6 40
Cigars, Havana, and such like.	40	30	2.204 pounds	3 70	74 86 lbs	1 60	74.86 lbs	30 00	192.50 lbs	14 40
Coaches	30	24	Each	1 87½ or 5 p. ct. ad val.		12½ per ct. ad valorem.	One	50 00	One	By sea, 91 42
Coal	30	24					74.86 lbs	2		Free.
Cocoa	10	4	220 pounds	6 47	74.86 lbs	1 12	74.86 lbs	1 00	1 ton Nuts, 1 ton	76 11 8 80

TARIFFS—Continued.

DENOMINATION OF MERCHANDISE.	DUTIES ON IMPORTS INTO— The United States, per cent. ad valorem, under the act of— 1846.	1857.	SARDINIA. Number, weight, or measure.	SARDINIA. Rate of duty.	TUSCANY. Number, weight, or measure.	TUSCANY. Rate of duty.	PAPAL STATES. Number, weight, or measure.	PAPAL STATES. Rate of duty.	TWO SICILIES. Number, weight, or measure.	TWO SICILIES. Rate of duty.
Coffee	20(a)	15(a)	220 pounds	$6 47	74.86 lbs	$1 60	74.86 lbs	$2 75	1 ton	$105 60
Cotton, raw	Free	Free		Free		Free	74.86 lbs	10	192.050	8 00
					74.86 lbs. simply spun.	20	74.86 lbs. spun, not colored.	1 00		
unbleached	25	19	1 pound	$8\frac{1}{2}$	74.86 lbs. colored and threaded	40	74.86 lbs. threaded and colored.	3 00	Canna = 2.306 yards.	F'm 47 to 64
bleached	25	24	1 pound	$10\frac{2}{3}$			74.86 lbs., all articles of.	12 00		
colored or dyed	25	24	do	$12\frac{4}{5}$					2.306 yards.	64
printed	25	24	do	17						
Dyewood, in sticks	5	Free	220 pounds	6		8	74.86 lbs	5	192.50 lbs	80
ground	5	Free	do	$18\frac{1}{2}$			do	50	do	80
Fish, dried or smoked, not described.	20	15	do	1 53			74.86 pounds	2 00	Codfish, per ton	28 36
codfish	20	15	do	1 39	74.86 pounds	80	do	40	Salted fish, not otherwise described, 192 50 pounds.	4 80
stock-fish	20	15	do	1 39	do	3	do	40	Stock-fish, not otherwise described, 192.50 pounds.	2 40

(a) See note, p. 114.

TARIFFS—Continued.

Denomination of merchandise.	DUTIES ON IMPORTS INTO— The United States, per cent. ad valorem, under the act of— 1846.	1857.	Sardinia. Number, weight, or measure.	Sardinia. Rate of duty.	Tuscany. Number, weight, or measure.	Tuscany. Rate of duty.	Papal States. Number, weight, or measure.	Papal States. Rate of duty.	Two Sicilies. Number, weight, or measure.	Two Sicilies. Rate of duty.
Flour	20	15	220 pounds	84	74.86 pounds	80	Regulated by market price, or prohibited.		In national and equalized vessels, per 192.50 lbs.	$0 80
									192.50 lbs. in foreign vessels.	1 60
Glass, mirrors, not framed	30	24	100 pounds	2 40	do	2 40	74.86 lbs. over 20 inches in size.	$10 00	According to size, from $12 to $118 per 192.50 pounds.	
sheet	20	15	do	1 44	do	1 20	Mirrors–74.86 lbs., over 34 inch. in size.	4 00	192.50 lbs	11 20
wrought, of all kinds	40	30	do	1 44	do	90	74.86 pounds	7 00		
Gold and silver coin	Free	Free	Free	Free	Free	Free	Free	Free	Free	Free.
Indigo	10	4	100 pounds	1 11	74.86 pounds	1 33	74.86 pounds	1 20	92.50 lbs	12 80
Liquors, in casks	100	30	26.417 galls	3 33 to 5 55	do	80	do	2 50	Rum, 192.50 lbs.	4 80
in bottles	100	30	1 bottle	6					1 bottle	4
Mahogany wood	20	8			do	8	do	50	Veneers, 192.50 lbs.	4 00
									Mahog'y wood	80
Nails	30	24	220 pounds	2 80	do	8	74.86	5 00	192.50 lbs	3 60
Oak bark	20	8		Free		Free	74.86 pounds	10	do	5
ground	20	8	220 pounds	4		Free	do	20	Not defined.	
Oil, whale, and other fish	20	15	do	92½	74.86 pounds	16⅔	do	50	192.50 lbs	3 20

TARIFFS—Continued.

DENOMINATION OF MERCHANDISE.	The United States, per cent. ad valorem, under the act of—		DUTIES ON IMPORTS INTO— SARDINIA.		TUSCANY.		PAPAL STATES.		TWO SICILIES.	
	1846.	1857.	Number, weight, or measure.	Rate of duty.	Number, weight, or measure.	Rate of duty.	Number, weight, or measure.	Rate of duty.	Number, weight, or measure.	Rate of duty.
Paints	20	15	220 pounds	$2 77½					192.50 pounds	$24 00
									1 ton.	
varnishes	20	15	do	3 70	74.86 pounds.	$1 06½	74.86 pounds.	$15 00	192.50 pounds	2 04
Pimento	40	4	do	6 47½	do	1 12	do	5 00	do	5 60
Pitch	20	15	do	18¾	do	5	do	2	do	68
Rice	20	15	do	55½	do	16	do	(a)60	do	1 60
Rosin	20	8	do	74⅗	do	47	Prepared,			
							74.86 pounds.	30	do	1 76
Spermaceti	20	15	do	3 70	1 pound	86½	do	1 20	In cakes or lumps	
									1.964 pounds.	16
Sugar, refined	30	24	do	4 62½	74.86 pounds.	1 60	do	7 00	Loaf, 192.50 lbs.	12 00
									Other kinds, do	8 00
Tar	20	15	do	18½	do	5	do	2	192.50 pounds	68
Teas	20	15(b)	2.204 pounds	27¾	do	4 96	do	8 00	1 964 pounds	36
Tobacco	30	24	Prohibited	Gov't monopoly	Leaf, 74 86 lbs	1 10½	Leaf, 74.86 lbs.	8 10	(Monopoly,) leaf	Prohibited.
							In rolls, do	10 00		
cigars	40	30	One.	1	All kinds, do	1 60	Cigars, do	30 00	{ Manufactu'd,	14 40
cigars	40	30	2.204 pounds	3 70			Snuff, do	20 00	{ 192.50 lbs.	
Turpentine	20	15	220 pounds	92½	74.86 pounds.	5	Oil of, do	30	192.50 pounds	1 60
Wearing apparel	Free	Free		Free		Free		Free	According to kind and quality.	
Whalebone	20	15	Not defined	Not defined	1 pound	1	74.88 pounds.	60	1 ton, 192.50.	3 20
Wines, French, in casks	40	30	26.417 galls	1 85 to 2 59	1 barrel	1 33	(Ordinary wine,) casks, with special permiss'n.	2 00	128.878 galls.	28 80
all kinds in bottles	40	30	1 bottle	6			Others, do	40	Each bottle	9⅗

(a) Duty is regulated by the market price.

(b) See note p. 168.

TARIFFS—Continued.

DENOMINATION OF MERCHANDISE.	DUTIES ON IMPORTS INTO—										
	The United States, per cent. ad valorem, under the act of—		SARDINIA.		TUSCANY.		PAPAL STATES.		TWO SICILIES.	
	1846.	1857.	Number, weight, or measure.	Rate of duty.	Number, weight, or measure.	Rate of duty.	Number, weight, or measure.	Rate of duty	Number, weight, or measure.	Rate of duty.
Wood, lumber	20	15		1 p. ct. ad val.	74.86 pounds.	$0 02	Sawn, 2 in. thick	100 ps. $2 33	The duty on tim-	ber is the same
							2 to 3	4 66	as the export	duty, with 20 p.
							3 to 6	12 43	ct. additional.	Thus, timber for
							Above 6	24 88	building, per	load of 45 palmi
masts and spars	20	15		1 p. ct. ad val.	do	5	Masts, &c., 100	ps., from $7 77 to 93 33.	in length, and	$1\frac{1}{4}$ palmi in
									breadth would	be $1 76, and 20
									per cent.	
staves and heading	20	15	Each	$0 0$\frac{1}{3}$	One last	19	100 ps und. 6 in.	23	Staves (oak) 5 p	almi, and head-
									ings $3\frac{1}{2}$ palmi	per 100 = 22.40
									and 20 per ct.	
							100 ps. over 6 in.	46	Timber for ship-	building strictly
									prohibited.	

TURKEY.

40 □

TURKEY

1. The tariff is the la est settled between Great Britain and Turkey, (as given by a British publication on Customs Tariffs of July, 1855,) and applies to the United States by virtue of the treaty with the Ottoman Porte of May 7, 1830, the first article of which declares that "American merchants, who shall come to the well-defended countries and ports of the Sublime Porte, shall pay the same duties and other imposts that are paid by merchants of the most favored friendly powers."

2. The duty on imports is ad valorem, 3 per cent. on the article landed, which is the actual tariff duty, and 2 per cent. additional when sold, or sent into the interior to be sold; making, in all cases, an aggregate of 5 per cent. ad valorem on all imports, which has, in most instances, been converted into a specific duty by stipulation.

3. The duty on exports, ad valorem, in lieu of, or in commutation of all other internal duties or taxes, is 9 per cent. internal duty on the article for exportation, and 3 per cent. additional, actually exported; making, in all cases, an aggregate of 12 per cent. ad valorem on all exports.

4. These duties are levied according to rates of valuation settled by treaty. The rates which were fixed by the British treaty of 1850 were adopted liberally by France, Austria, the Zollverein and other commercial nations. Russia had a distinct treaty, and is understood not to have entered into any stipulation for the abolition of the internal duties, in lieu of which England and other nations have agreed to pay 9 per cent. on exports.

5. Articles not enumerated are valued at the current prices of the day, 16 per cent. being deducted from such current price for articles of export, and 20 per cent. for articles of import; and if the current price cannot be agreed on, then the duty is levied in *kind*, 5 per cent. or 12 per cent. of the amount of the article itself being taken for duty. The deductions of 20 and 16 per cent. are applicable to all articles not rated, whether enumerated in the tariff or not.

Money.—3 aspers make 1 para; 40 paras, or 120 aspers, make 1 piastre = 4 cents; 30 aspers = 1 cent.

Weights and measures.—1 cantar = 100 rotoli = 127 lbs. English; 44 okes = 1 cantar; 1 oke = 2¾ lbs., or 2.83 lbs.; 1 oke (liquid measure) = 0.345 gallons,(a); 1 kilo (dry measure) = 1.455 bushels; 1 quintal of grain = 1.46 bushels; 1 quintal of wine = 13.50 gallons.

(a) See Vol. 3, "Returns," pp. 311 *et seq.*

COMPARATIVE TARIFFS.

UNITED STATES AND TURKEY.

DENOMINATION OF MERCHANDISE.	DUTIES ON IMPORTS INTO—			
	The United States, per cent. ad valorem, under the act of—		TURKEY.	
	1846.	1857.	Number, weight, or measure.	Rate of duty.
Bacon	20	15	Cantar, or 127 lbs	$0 34
Barley	20	15	Kilo., or $1\frac{1}{2}$ bushels	3 per cent. ad val.
Beef, salt	20	15	127 pounds	$7\frac{1}{5}$
Candles, tallow	20	15	do	$23\frac{1}{5}$
spermaceti	20	15	Oke, $2\frac{4}{5}$ pounds	$4\frac{1}{5}$
Carpeting, Brussels, Turkey, and other	30	24		3 per cent. ad val.
Cheese, English	30	24		do
Chocolate	20	15	$2\frac{4}{5}$ pounds	$2\frac{1}{4}$
Cigars	40	30	Per 1,000	15
Codfish	20	15	127 pounds	12
Coffee, West Indies and Brazil	(*a*)20	(*a*)15	100 okes, or 281 lbs	76
Mocha, brought from Europe	20	15	do	1 23
Cotton, manufactures of, calicoes, gray	25	24	$2\frac{4}{5}$ pounds	$2\frac{3}{5}$
twist, yarn, thread, white	25	24	do	3
dyed	25	24	do	3
drill, American	25	24	do	3 per cent. ad val.
fustian, $\frac{22}{27}$ inches wide	25	24	Yard	do
Currants, Zante	40	8	$2\frac{4}{5}$ pounds	$0\frac{1}{4}$
Sicilian	40	8	127 pounds	$26\frac{3}{5}$
Demijohns, containing about $1\frac{1}{3}$ gallon or more	30	34	100	36
Flour, American				3 per cent. ad val.
Furniture, household	30	24		do
Garden seeds, trees, &c	Free	Free		do
Gems, diamonds, precious stones, &c., not set	10	4		do
Glass, bottles	30	24	Containing under $\frac{1}{3}$ of a gal., per 100,	$8\frac{4}{5}$
			Containing under 1 gal., per 100,	18
manufactures of	30	24		3 per cent. ad val.
Gunny bags	20	15		do
cloth	20	15		do
Hair cloth and seating	25	19		do
Hams	20	15	127 pounds	34
Hemp, unmanufactured	30	24	do	$10\frac{3}{10}$
Hides, raw, ox and cow	5	4	Each	6
buffalo	5	4	do	12
American			do	$13\frac{1}{5}$

(*a*) See note p. 114.

TARIFFS—Continued.

DENOMINATION OF MERCHANDISE.	DUTIES ON IMPORTS INTO—			
	The United States, per cent. ad valorem, under the act of—		TURKEY.	
	1846.	1857.	Number, weight, or measure.	Rate of duty.
Iron castings	30	24		3 per cent. ad val.
Medicinal drugs, not otherwise described	20	15		do
Molasses	30	24		do
Nuts, pistachio	30	24	$2\frac{4}{5}$ pounds	$0 00$\frac{2}{3}$
Opium	20	15		3 per cent. ad val
Osnaburgs, &c	20	15		do
Paintings and statuary	20	Free		do
Paper	30	24		do
Pepper, black	30	4	$2\frac{4}{5}$ pounds	0$\frac{2}{3}$
Pimento	40	4	do	0$\frac{1}{2}$
Pitch	20	15		3 per cent. ad val.
Plums	30	8		do
Pork, salt	20	15		do
Prunes	40	8		do
Rags	5	Free(*a*)		do
Raisins	40	8	127 pounds	10$\frac{1}{3}$
Rosin	20	15		3 per ct. ad val
Rum, American	100	30	$\frac{1}{2}$ gallon	0$\frac{1}{2}$
English	100	30	do	0$\frac{1}{2}$
Shipbread	20	15		3 per ct. ad val
Silk, raw	15	Free		do
manufactures not specified	25	24		do
Skins, tanned and dressed	20	15		do
beaver	20	15	Each	4$\frac{1}{3}$
Spirits, from grain	100	30		3 per ct. ad val
of turpentine	20	15		do
Stationery	30	24		do
Stock-fish	20	15	127 pounds	12
Sugar, refined, in loaf	30	24	do	27$\frac{1}{10}$
crushed	30	24	do	20$\frac{2}{3}$
Tar	20	15		3 per ct. ad val
Tea, English	(*b*)20	(*b*)15	$2\frac{4}{5}$ pounds	3$\frac{3}{5}$
Russian	20	15	do	18
Tobacco, in leaf	30	24		3 per ct. ad val. for Virginia leaf.
Turpentine	20	15	$2\frac{4}{5}$ pounds	0$\frac{1}{2}$
Wares, China, and other	30	24		3 per ct. ad val
Whale oil	20	15		do
Whalebone	20	15		do
Wearing apparel	Free	Free		do
Wood, manufactures of	30	24		do

(*a*) Except woolen rags, and they pay 4 per cent.

(*b*) see note, p. 168.

TARIFFS—Continued.

DENOMINATION OF MERCHANDISE.	DUTIES ON IMPORTS INTO—			
	The United States per cent. ad valorem, under the act of—		TURKEY.	
	1846.	1857.	Number, weight, or measure.	Rate of duty.
Wood, unmanufactured, cedar and rose	20	8		3 per ct. ad val
ebony	20	8	127 pounds	18
mahogany	20	8		3 per ct. ad val
lignum vitæ	30	8		do
logwood	5	Free	do	$3\frac{1}{3}$
Wool, manufactures of	30	24		3 per ct. ad val
unmanufactured, merinos	30	24	$2\frac{4}{5}$ pounds	$3\frac{4}{5}$

NOTE.—All articles not enumerated in this tariff pay 3 per cent. ad valorem, and when sold, or sent into the interior for sale, 2 per cent. additional. The rate calculated in the tariff is based on the 3 per cent. ad valorem, import duty, to which is to be added the 2 per cent. internal duty.

TARIFF OF EXPORTATION.

DENOMINATION OF MERCHANDISE.	Imported(a) into the United States, per cent. ad valorem, under the act of— 1846.	1857.	DUTIES ON EXPORTS FROM— TURKEY. Number, weight, or measure.	Rate of duty.
Anise seed, from Cæsarea(b)	20	4	Oke, or $2\frac{4}{5}$ pounds	\$0 $00\frac{1}{5}$
Romelia	20	4	do	$0\frac{8}{15}$
Coffee, Mocha	(c)20	(c)15	do	$1\frac{2}{5}$
Cumin seed	Free	Free	do	$0\frac{7}{30}$
Drugs: colocynth	20	15	do	$1\frac{2}{5}$
salop, from Anatolia	20	15	do	$1\frac{2}{5}$
Romelia	20	15		3 per ct. ad valorem.
senna	20	15	do	$1\frac{1}{15}$
scamony	20	15		3 per ct. ad valorem
opium, from Anatolia	20	15	do	$20\frac{2}{5}$
Dyes: berries, yellow, from Cæsarea	20	Free	do	$3\frac{1}{10}$
Iskilib	20	Free	do	$3\frac{1}{10}$
Romelia	20	Free		$0\frac{13}{30}$
galls, all sorts	5 to 20	Free	Cantar, or 127 lbs	$43\frac{1}{5}$
madder roots from Cyprus, Syria, and Tripoli	5	Free	do	12
Anatolia	5	Free	do	70
saffron, from Anatolia	20	Free		$16\frac{1}{5}$
Romelia	20	Free		$4\frac{1}{5}$
Fruit: figs	40	8	127 pounds	3 per ct. ad valorem.
Carabournu raisins, called sultana	40	8	do	18
Vourla raisins, called sultana	40	8	do	$16\frac{4}{5}$
Beglerge raisins	40	8	do	$4\frac{4}{5}$
currants, called kush usumi	40	8	do	18
raisins	40	8	do	$4\frac{1}{15}$
Gums: arabic	10	8	$2\frac{4}{5}$ pounds	$0\frac{9}{10}$
incense, picked, best quality	20	8	127 pounds	$21\frac{3}{5}$
in powder	20	8	do	$10\frac{4}{5}$
mastic	10	8	bbl. of 70 okes, 196 lbs.	2 40
picked	10	8	$2\frac{4}{5}$ pounds	$16\frac{2}{5}$
myrrh	20	8	do	$0\frac{8}{15}$
Hides, dry, ox and buffalo, all sizes	5	4		3 per ct. ad valorem.
Licorice paste	20	15	127 pounds	$44\frac{2}{5}$
Manufactures of cotton, linen, silk, and woollen: boghassi, white, colored, and striped, from Denisli and Hamid.	20 to 30	15 to 24	$2\frac{4}{5}$ pounds	6
carpets, Turcoman	30	24	Each	$13\frac{1}{5}$
from Ushack	30	24	$2\frac{4}{5}$ pounds	$2\frac{2}{5}$
cloth, horse-hair, and horse-hair thread, called harrar and cazil, from Romelia.	10	8	do	$1\frac{2}{15}$
mohair yarn, from Angora	25	19	$2\frac{4}{5}$ pounds	$8\frac{2}{5}$
shawls, from Tunis, white	30	24	Each	$2\frac{3}{5}$
colored	30	24	do	$7\frac{1}{5}$

(a) See note, p. 245. (b) The nomenclature, for sake of convenience and conciseness, is adapted to the tariff of Turkey. (c) See note, p. 114.

TARIFFS—Continued.

DENOMINATION OF MERCHANDISE.	The United States, per cent. ad valorem, under the act of—		DUTIES ON EXPORTS FROM— TURKEY.	
	1846.	1857.	Number, weight, or measure.	Rate of duty.
Manufactures of stuff, silk, from Broussa, called—				
kutni and moreh	25	19		3 per cent. ad val.
merzifun beldy	25	19		do
tuff, woolen, from Tunis, called—				
shali or donluk shal	30	24	Piece	6
towels, linen, from Broussa	20	15	Pair	$4\frac{4}{5}$
Nuts: hazle nuts and filberts	30	24	127 pounds	$8\frac{3}{5}$
walnuts	30	24	100 okes or 280 lbs	$7\frac{2}{3}$
Saltpetre, from Egypt	5 to 10	8		3 per cent. ad val.
Sesamum seed	Free	Free	Kilo. of 20 okes, or 56 lbs.	$3\frac{1}{3}$
Silks: silk cocoons and silk pods	15	Free		3 per cent. ad val.
silk, Cyprus	25	19	$2\frac{4}{5}$ pounds	$14\frac{2}{5}$
from Broussa, Smyrna, and other places	25	19	do	24
Skins: Angora goat skins, white and colored	20	15	Each	$4\frac{1}{5}$
hare skins, from Anatolia	10 to 20	8 to 15	100 skins	$19\frac{4}{15}$
Timber	20	15		3 per cent. ad val.
Tobacco, gubeck baghtcha	30 to 40	24 to 30	$2\frac{4}{5}$ pounds	1
all other	30 to 40	24 to 30		3 per cent. ad val.
Wax: yellow beeswax	20	15	$2\frac{4}{5}$ pounds	$2\frac{7}{30}$
Wine, all sorts of Turkey, except Cyprus comandaria	40	30	Per liquid oke, or $2\frac{2}{3}$ pints.	$0\frac{1}{6}$
Cyprus comandaria	40	30	do	$0\frac{3}{5}$
Wool: sheeps' wool, of Romelia and Anatolia	30	24	127 pounds	$24\frac{2}{5}$
of Bagdad, Tripoli, and Africa	30	24	do	3 per cent. ad val.
goats' wool, (white,) called finik	20	15(a)	$2\frac{4}{5}$ pounds	$1\frac{3}{4}$

(a) Wool, unmanufactured, the value of 20 per cent. or less, at the port of exportation, free, provided it is imported in ordinary condition.

NOTE.—All articles not enumerated in this tariff pay 9 per cent. internal duty and 3 per cent. export duty. The rate calculated in the tariff is ba ıed on the 3 per cent. ad valorem export duty, to which is to be added the 9 per cent. internal duty.

MOROCCO.

MOROCCO.

The latest tariff regulations of Morocco are presented in a despatch from the United States consul at Tangier, bearing date April 10, 1857, as follows: (*a*)

"I am in the receipt of a note from the Moorish Minister of Foreign Affairs, announcing the gratifying fact that the Sultan of Morocco, with the view of inviting commerce to his dominions, has, from this day, (April 10,) abolished all monopolies or prohibitions on imported goods, except tobacco, pipes of all kinds used for smoking, opium, sulphur, powder, saltpetre, lead, arms of all kinds, and ammunition of war; and, further, that he has abolished, from same period, all monopolies or prohibitions on agricultural produce, or of any other article of export whatsoever in the empire of Morocco, except leeches, bark, tobacco, and other herbs used for smoking in pipes.

"His Majesty the Sultan of Morocco agrees that the duties to be levied on all articles imported into his territories shall not exceed in amount 10 per cent. on their value at the port of their disembarkation, and that the duties to be levied on all articles exported from his territories shall not exceed in amount the duties marked in the accompanying tariff.

"The Sultan of Morocco reserves to himself the right to prohibit any article of exportation, on his giving six months' notice of such contemplated prohibition.

"No tax, toll, duty, or charge whatever, except the export duty already mentioned, shall, under any pretext or on any account, be imposed on articles purchased for exportation; and absolute freedom shall, in all cases, be given to the buyer and seller to bargain together. No interference on the part of the Sultan's officers shall be permitted.

"His Majesty the Sultan of Morocco agrees that no anchorage, tonnage, import or other duty or charge, except the following, shall be levied on American or other vessels coming to this country to trade, viz: 7½ cents per ton on every vessel (except steam vessels) that does not exceed 200 tons in measurement. For sailing vessels over 200 tons, 7½ cents per ton for 200 of her tons, and 2½ cents per ton for the remainder.

"The same charges to be made in all the ports of Morocco, except Rabat and Larache, at which ports 5 cents per ton must be paid for pilotage into the river, should the vessel enter the river. At Mogadore, 5 cents per ton for pilotage on entering the port, and 7½ cents per ton for anchorage. Should the master of a vessel require at any other port a pilot, he must pay at the rate of 2½ cents per ton. This charge, however, is not to be exacted except when the master of a vessel requires a pilot. The sum of $16 must be paid on account of anchorage on a steam vessel entering any port in the Moorish dominions for the purpose of discharging or embarking a cargo. The masters of all vessels must pay, in addition to the aforesaid charges, the following sums to officers of the ports, but no other payment to be demanded of them, viz: A vessel exceeding 100 and not over 200 tons, $4; over 200 tons, $5. No charge for anchorage will be levied on steam or sail vessels which may enter the ports of Morocco for the purpose of seeking shelter from the weather, and which do not embark or discharge cargo.

"I take the liberty of enclosing a comparative table showing the difference between the duties on exports formerly paid at the Moorish ports, and those to be paid now that the new stipulations are in force.

"I also enclose a table showing to what extent the duties on imports have been reduced at the Moorish ports by the new stipulations.

"I also enclose a table showing, more or less, the difference between the amount of anchorage dues levied upon vessels that entered the ports of Morocco in 1855, and the amount those vessels would have paid according to the new tariff.

"Americans have, heretofore, been prevented from embarking extensively in the Moorish trade in consequence of the existence of monopolies or prohibitions, and the instability of the Moorish tariff."

(*a*) See vol. 1, "Digests," p 467; also, vol. 8, "Returns," pp. 856, *et seq.*

Table showing the difference between the duties on exports formerly paid at the Moorish ports, and those to be paid now that the new stipulations are in force.

ARTICLES OF EXPORT.	Per weight or measure.	Duties formerly levied.	Duties to be levied according to the new stipulations.
Wheat	Strike fanega. (a)		$1 00
Maize and dra	Full fanega. (b)	$0 75	50
Barley	Strike fanega. (c)		50
All other grain	Cwt		50
Flour	do	2 00	1 50
Bird seed	do	90	60
Dates	do	2 55	2 00
Almonds	do	2 55	1 75
Oranges, lemons, and limes	1,000	60	60
Wild marjoram	Cwt	90	50
Cumin seed	do	90	1 00
Oil	do	3 00	2 50
Gums	do	1 25	1 00
Henna	do	1 00	75
Wax	do	6 00	6 00
Rice	do	1 00	80
Wool, (washed)	do	4 50	4 00
Wool, (grease)	do	3 00	2 75
Hides, sheep and goat skins	do	1 80	1 80
Tanned skins, filaly, zawany, and cochineal leather	do		5 00
Horns	1,000	1 80	1 00
Tallow	Cwt		2 50
Mules	Head		25 00
Donkeys	do		5 00
Sheep	do	1 00	1 00
Goats	do		75
Fowls	Dozen	1 10	1 10
Eggs	1,000	2 55	2 55
Slippers	100	4 50	3 50
Porcupine quills	1,000		25
Gasool	Cwt	1 00	75
Ostrich feathers	Lb	1 80	1 80
Baskets	100	2 50	1 50
Caraway seed	Cwt	1 00	1 00
Combs of wood	100	25	25
Hair	Cwt	1 80	1 50
Raisins	do	1 00	1 00
Woolen sashes	100	7 50	5 00
Tackawt, (a dye)	Cwt	1 00	1 00
Tanned fleeces	do		1 80
Hemp and flax	do	2 50	2 00

(a) A strike fanega of wheat is equivalent to 90 American pounds.
(b) A full do. do. do. 118 do.
(c) A strike fanega of barley do. 60 do.

MOORISH TARIFF OF EXPORTS.

ARTICLES OF EXPORT.	Per weight or measure.	Amount.	ARTICLES OF EXPORT.	Per weight or measure.	Amount.
Wheat	Strike fanega (a)	$1 00	Horns	1,000	$1 00
Maize and dra	Full do. (b)	50	Tallow	Cwt.	2 50
Barley	Strike do. (c)	50	Mules	Head	25 00
All other grain	Cwt	50	Donkeys	do	5 00
Flour	do	1 50	Sheep	do	1 00
Bird seed	do	60	Goats	do	75
Dates	do	2 00	Fowls	Dozen	1 10
Almonds	do	1 75	Eggs	1,000	2 55
Oranges, lemons, and limes	1,000	60	Slippers	100	3 50
Wild marjoram	Cwt	50	Porcupine quills	1,000	25
Cumin seed	do	1 00	Gasool	Cwt.	75
Oil	do	2 50	Ostrich feathers	Lb.	1 80
Gums	do	1 00	Baskets	100	1 50
Henna	do	75	Caraway seed	Cwt	1 00
Wax	do	6 00	Combs of wood	100	25
Rice	do	80	Hair	Cwt	1 50
Wool, (washed)	do	4 00	Raisins	do	1 00
Wool, (grease)	do	2 75	Woolen sashes	100	5 00
Hides, sheep and goat skins	do	1 80	Tackawt, (a dye)	Cwt	1 00
Tanned skins, filaly, zawany, cochineal	do	5 50	Tanned fleeces	do	1 80
			Hemp and flax	do	2 00

(a) A strike fanega of wheat is equivalent to 90 American pounds.
(b) A full do. do. do. 118 do.
(c) A strike fanega of barley do. 60 do.

Table showing to what extent the duties on imports have been reduced at the Moorish ports by the new stipulations.

ON ARTICLES OF IMPORT.	Reduction, per cent.
On Brazil wood	20 per cent.
cochineal	90 do
coffee	20 do
raw cotton (a)	10 do
cotton thread	5 do
iron	90 do
raw silk	10 do
brown sugar	20 do
crushed sugar	15 do
loaf sugar	20 do
steel	80 do
tea	15 do

(a) Six thousand bales of United States cotton are annually consumed in Morocco. Now that the duty is reduced 10 per cent., the consumption will be largely augmented.

Table showing, more or less, the difference between the amount of anchorage dues levied upon vessels that entered the ports of Morocco in 1855, and the amount those vessels would have paid according to the tariff of the new convention.

PORT.	Number of vessels in 1855.	Amount of tonnage.	Average number of tons per vessel.	By old tariff, including all expenses, would have paid—	By new tariff, including all expenses, will pay—	Reduction per vessel.
Tangier	243	15,610	64	$8 00	$7 80	$0 20
Tetuan	111	4,101	37	5 65	4 65	1 00
Larache	18	1,420	79	12 00	9 75	2 25
Rabat	24	1,935	80	14 55	10 00	4 55
Casa Blanca	79	10,071	127	21 00	13 50	7 50
Mazagan	189	21,561	114	23 05	12 55	10 50
Saffi	84	10,457	124	42 00	13 30	28 70
Mogadore	88	9,524	108	36 40	12 00	24 40

CHINA.

CHINA.

The tariff is that fixed on, and made a part of the treaty of July 3, 1844, between China and the United States, liable to modification at the expiration of twelve years, and is identical with that established between Great Britain and China by the treaty of August 29, 1842, and in both cases applies only to the five ports—Canton, Amoy, Foochow, Ningpo, and Shanghai—which alone are open to foreign trade.(*a*)

Weights and Measures.—1 tael = $1\frac{1}{3}$ ounces (American.)

16 taels = 1 catty, or $1\frac{1}{3}$ pounds.

100 catties = 1 picul = $133\frac{1}{3}$ American pounds.

1 chih 11.77 American inches, or 0.358 metre.

Money.—1 tael of 10 mace of 10 condorin of 10 caesh of 10 chow = $1 48, United States currency.

1 mace = $14\frac{4}{5}$ cents.

1 condorin = 1 12-25, or nearly $1\frac{1}{2}$ cent.

Coined gold or silver, properly speaking, China has not. The duties are paid in silver, (sycee ;) and the foreign coins which aro not entirely of pure silver are reduced to pure silver ; and 100 taels of pure sycee silver are accepted in Amoy.

Rupees,	at the weight of	108 taels,	9 mace,	1 condorin,	5 caesh.
Peruvian dollars,	"	110 "	2 "	7 "	7 "
Mexican dollars,	"	100 "	6 "	2 "	9 "
Spanish dollars,	"	110 "	8 "	3 "	3 "

1 tael 2 mace is, besides this, calculated for melting and refining.

According to the Chinese Commercial Guide for 1844, the customs' authorities accept—

5 Spanish piasters (cut) at	3 taels,	1 mace,	8 condorin.
5 Mexican piasters "	3 "	1 "	9 "
5 Bolivian piasters "	3 "	2 "	1 "
20 Company's rupees "	3 "	6 "	5 "

The circulating medium at Canton is broken or defaced Spanish dollars, by weight, the proportion of which to a tael varies in different transactions, being, in calculations of prices or accounts between foreigners and native merchants, at the rate of 720 taels = $1,000 ; but in weighing money for payment, 717 taels = $1,000 ; except to the Company's treasury, or for Bengal opium, when it is weighed, 718 taels = $1,000 ; or to native merchants not of the colony, who receive, unless otherwise agreed, 715 taels for $1,000.

1 tael = 10 mace = 100 condorins = 1,000 cash = 1.208 ounce troy.

500 taels = 604 ounces troy ; 3,000 taels = 302 lbs. troy.

Usage has established a difference between the tael of commerce weight, at the rate of $133\frac{1}{3}$ lbs. avoirdupois, to the picul weight, $583\frac{1}{3}$ grains troy, and the tael of money weights, of which the old standard is 579.84 grains troy.

If there be any difference of opinion about the duty upon articles ad valorem, the importer and the customs officers will call upon two or three merchants, and the highest prices offered by them will be considered as the value.

The importation of opium is prohibited.

(*a*) An official circular was addressed to the leading British merchants at the five ports from the office of the British consulate at Canton, under date of August 8, 1857, on the subject of the tariff of China, the object of which will be inferred from the subjoined extract: "I have the honor to inform you that his excellency the earl of Elgin is desirous of obtaining as much information as possible with reference to the operation of the tariff of duties on exports and imports now established in the ports of China. He is led to believe that it admits, among other improvements, of modifications favorable to the development of the import trade in British manufactures, and that by reason of the diminution in the cost of production of some articles, and from the want of more specific denominations as applied to others, some important classes of British manufactured goods are charged with higher rates of duty than were in contemplation at the period when the present tariff was agreed on. His excellency accordingly instructs me to put myself in communication with the leading members of the British mercantile firms within this consular district, with a view of obtaining from them the information on these and similar points of detail which they are so well qualified to give; and his excellency authorizes me to add that he will receive with pleasure any suggestions of a more general nature bearing on the important subject of our commercial relations with China."

COMPARATIVE TARIFFS.

UNITED STATES AND CHINA.

DENOMINATION OF MERCHANDISE.	DUTIES ON IMPORTS INTO—			
	The United States, per cent. ad valorem, under the act of—		CHINA.	
	1846.	1857.	Number, weight, or measure.	Rate of duty.
Asafœtida	20	4	133¼ pounds	$1 48
Beeswax	20	15	do	1 48
Betel-nut(a)	30	24	do	21⅕
Bicho de mar,(b) 1st quality, black	20	15	do	1 18⅖
2d quality, white	20	15	do	29⅗
Birds' nests,(c) 1st quality, cleaned	20	15	do	7 40
2d quality, good, middling	20	15	do	3 70
3d quality, uncleaned	20	15	do	74
Camphor, (Malay,) 1st quality, crude	25	8	1⅓ pound	1 48
2d quality, refined	40	30	do	74
Cloves, 1st quality, picked	40	4	133¼ pounds	2 22
2d quality (mother)	40	4	do	74
Clocks,(d) watches, spy-glasses, all kinds of writing desks, dressing boxes, cutlery, perfumery, &c., &c.	30	24		5 per cent. ad val.
Canvas, 30 to 40 yards long, 24 to 31 in wide, hemp or flax	20	15	Piece	74
cotton	25	24		
Cochineal	10	4	133¼ pounds	7 40
Cornelians, unset	10	4	100 stones	74
set	20	15		
beads	10	4	133¼ pounds	14 80
Cotton, raw	Free	Free	do	59⅕
manufactures of: long cloths, white, 30 to 40 yards long, 30 to 36 inches wide.	25	24	Piece	22⅕
cambrics and muslins, 20 to 24 yards long, 40 to 46 inches wide.	25	24	Piece	22⅕
gray or unbleached, viz: long cloths, domestics, &c., &c., 30 to 40 yards long, 28 to 40 inches wide.	25	24	Piece	14⅘
gray, twilled, same dimensions	25	24	Piece	14⅘
chintz and prints of all kinds, 20 to 30 yards long, 27 to 30 inches wide.	25	24	Piece	29⅗

(a) The betel-nut is a fruit of the palm, imported into China from Java, Singapore, Sumatra, and Penang, and very popular throughout the east for chewing.

(b) Bicho de mar, or biche de mer, or tripang, a species of sea-slug, used for food. See note, vol. 3, "Returns," p. 395.

(c) Birds' nests, an article of luxury, a mucilaginous substance, white or pink, resembling isinglass, used for jellies, imported from Java and Sumatra—the habitation of a small swallow.

(d) *Into the United States*—Watches, 10 per cent. ad valorem by the tariffs of 1846, and 8 per cent. by that of 1857.

TARIFFS—Continued.

Denomination of merchandise.	Duties on imports into— The United States, per cent. ad valorem, under the act of— 1846.	1857.	China. Number, weight, or measure.	Rate of duty.
Cotton handkerchiefs, under 1 yard square	25	24	Each	$0 01½
above 1 yard square	25	24	Each	2¼
ginghams, dyed cotton, velveteens, silk and cotton mixtures, and all kinds of fancy goods not in current consumption.	25	24		5 per cent ad val.
yarn and thread	25	24	133¼ pounds	1 48
Cow bezoar(a)	20	15	1⅓ pound	1 48
Cutch(b)	10	Free	133¼ pounds	44⅖
Elephants' teeth, 1st quality, whole	5	Free	do	5 92
2d quality, broken	5	Free	do	2 96
Fish maws(c)	20	15	do	2 22
Flints	5	4	do	7⅖
Glass, glassware, and crystal ware of all kinds	30 to 40	24 to 30		5 per cent. ad val.
Gambier(d)	10	Free	133¼ pounds	22⅕
Ginseng,(e) first quality	20	15	do	56 24
second quality, or refuse	20	15	do	5 18
Gold and silver thread, first quality, or real	30	24	1⅓ pound	19⅖
second quality, or imitation	30	24	do	4⅗
Gums, Benjamin	30	24	do	1 48
olibanum(f)	20		do	74
myrrh(g)	20	15	do	74
not enumerated	10 to 30	8 to 24		10 per cent. ad val.
Horns, bullocks' and buffaloes'	5	Free	1⅓ pound	2 96
unicorns' or rhinoceros'	5	Free	do	4 44
Linen, fine, as Irish or Scotch	20	15	Piece	74
coarse, as linen and cotton mixtures, silk and linen mixtures, &c., &c.	25	19		5 per cent. ad val.
Mace, or flour of nutmeg	40	4	133¼ pounds	1 48
Mother-of-pearl	5	4	do	29⅗
Metals, copper, unmanufactured, as in pigs	5	Free	do	1 48
manufactured, as in sheets, rods, &c	20	15	do	2 22
iron, unmanufactured, as in pigs	30	24	do	14⅘
manufactured, as in bars, rods, &c	30	24	do	22⅕
lead, in pigs, or manufactured	20	15	do	59⅕
quicksilver	20	15	do	4 44
steel, unmanufactured	20	12	do	59⅕
tin	5	Free	do	1 48

(a) Cow bezoar, a resinous concretion found in the stomach of the goat of Persia, and valued by the Chinese as a medicine.

(b) Cutch, or terra japonica, a resin exuding from a tree growing in Persia, near the Gulf of Cutch; used as a dye, and sometimes chewed with the betel-nut.

(c) Fish maws, the stomachs of fishes, an article of luxury for food with the Chinese.

(d) Gambier, a resin, resembling cutch, imported from Java and Singapore in great quantities; used for dyeing cotton and silk yellow or brown, and or tanning hides.

(e) Ginseng, a dried root, imported from Tartary, but chiefly America, esteemed in China for supposed medicinal qualities.

(f) Olibanum, a gum resin, burned for incense in religious worship.

(g) Myrrh, a gum used by the Chinese for incense and perfumes, imported from Arabia and Abyssinia, as also bdellium.

TARIFFS—Continued.

DENOMINATION OF MERCHANDISE.	DUTIES ON IMPORTS INTO—			
	The United States, per cent. ad valorem, under the act of—		CHINA.	
	1846.	1857.	Number, weight, or measure.	Rate of duty.
Metals, tin plates	15	8	133$\frac{1}{4}$ pounds	\$0 59$\frac{1}{5}$
unenumerated	20	15		10 per cent. ad val.
Nutmegs, first quality, or cleaned	40	4	133$\frac{1}{4}$ pounds	2 96
second quality, or uncleaned	40	4	do	1 00
Opium	20	15		Prohibited.
Pepper	30	4	133$\frac{1}{4}$ pounds	59$\frac{1}{5}$
Putchuck(*a*)	20	15	do	1 11
Rattans	10 to 20	Free to 15	do	59$\frac{1}{5}$
Rice, paddy, grain of all kinds	20	15		Free
Rose maloes(*b*)	20		133$\frac{1}{4}$ pounds	1 48
Saltpetre, sold in China to government agents only, crude	5	4	do	44$\frac{2}{5}$
refined	10	8		
Sharks' fins,(*c*) first quality, white	20	15	do	1 48
second quality, black	20	15	do	74
Skins and furs, cow and ox hides, tanned	20	15	do	74
untanned	5	4		
sea otter skins	5	4	Each	22$\frac{1}{5}$
fox skins, large	5	4	do	22$\frac{1}{5}$
small	5	4	do	11$\frac{1}{4}$
tiger, leopard, and marten skins	5	4	do	22$\frac{1}{5}$
land otter, racoon, and shark skins	5	4	100	2 96
beaver skins	5	4	100	7 40
hare, rabbit, and ermine skins	5	4	100	74
Smaltz(*d*)	20	15	133$\frac{1}{4}$ pounds	5 92
Soap	30	24	do	74
Stock fish, &c	20	15	do	59$\frac{1}{5}$
Sea-horse teeth(*e*)	5	Free	do	2 96
Treasure and money of all kinds	Free	Free		Free.
Wine, beer, spirits, &c. wine	40	30		
in quart bottles beer	30	24	100 bottles	1 48
in pint bottles	100	30	do	74
in casks	100	30	133$\frac{1}{4}$ pounds	74
Woods: ebony, unmanufactured	20	8	do	22$\frac{1}{5}$
manufactured	40	30		
sandal wood	30	24	do	74
sapan wood	30	24	do	14$\frac{4}{5}$
unmanufactured woods	30	24		10 per cent. ad val.
Woolen manufactures, broad cloths, Spanish stripes	30	24	Chang, of 14 inc[illegible]	22$\frac{5}{7}$
habit cloth, &c., 51 to 64 inches wide	30	24		

(*a*) Putchuck, a fragrant root brought from Scinde; used for incense.
(*b*) Rose maloes, a scented, thick oil, imported from Persia.
(*c*) Sharks' fins, an article of food, imported from the Sandwich Islands.
(*d*) Smaltz, a blue powder, used in painting on porcelain and copper.
(*e*) Sea-horse teeth, used as ivory.

TARIFFS—Continued.

Denomination of merchandise.	Duties on imports into—			
	The United States, per cent. ad valorem, under the act of—		China.	
	1846.	1857.	Number, weight, or measure.	Rate of duty.
Woolen, long ells, cassimeres, flannel, and narrow cloths of this description.	25 to 30	19 to 24	Chang, of 141 inches.	\$0 10½
blankets, of all kinds	20	15	Each	14⅘
Dutch camlets	30	24	141 inches	22⅕
camlets	30	24	do	10½
imitation bombazettes, &c	30	24	do	5¼
bunting, narrow	30	24	do	2¼
unenumerated woolen goods, or silk and woolen, and cotton and woolen mixtures.	30	24		5 per cent. ad val.
yarn	25	19	133⅓ pounds	4 44

NOTE.—All articles not enumerated in this tariff pay 5 per cent. ad valorem.

TARIFF—Continued.

DENOMINATION OF MERCHANDISE.	Imported(a) into the United States, per cent. ad valorem, under the act of—		DUTIES ON EXPORTS FROM— CHINA.	
	1846.	1857.	Number, weight, or measure.	Rate of duty.
Alum	20	15	133¼ pounds	$0 14⅘
Anise seed, star	20	15	do	74
oil of	30	24	do	7 40
Arsenic	15	4	do	1 11
Bangles, or glass amulets(b)	30	24	do	74
Bamboo screens and bamboo ware of all kinds	30	24	do	29⅗
Brass, leaf	30	24	do	2 22
Building materials	20	15		Free.
Bone and horn ware	30	24	133¼ pounds	1 48
Camphor, crude	25	8	do	2 22
Camphor, refined	40	30	do	2 22
Canes, of all kinds	30	24	1,000	74
Capoor cutchery(c)	20		133¼ pounds	44⅖
Cassia(d)	40	4	do	1 11
buds	20	15	do	1 48
oil	30	24	do	7 40
China root(e)	20	15	do	29⅗
China ware, all kinds	30	24	do	74
Clothes, ready-made	30	24	do	74
Copper ware, pewter ware, &c	30	24	do	74
Corals, or false corals	30	24	do	74
Crackers and fire-works, of all kinds	30	24	do	1 11
Cubebs	20	15	do	2 22
Fans, as feather fans, &c	30	24	do	1 48
Furniture, of all kinds	30	24	do	29⅗
Gallengal, root(f)	20	15	do	14⅘
Gamboge	20	15	do	2 22
Glass and glassware, of all kinds	20 to 40	15 to 30	do	74
beads	30	24	do	74
Glue, as fish glue, &c	20	15	do	74
Grass cloth, all kinds(g)	25	19	do	1 48
Hartall(h)	20		do	74
Ivory ware, all kinds	20 to 30	15 to 24	do	7 40
Kittysols(i)	30	24	do	74
Lacquered ware, all kinds	30	24	do	1 48
Lead, white	20	15	do	37
red	20	15	do	74
Marble slabs	30	24	do	29⅗
Mats, straw, rattan, bamboo, &c	25	19	do	29⅗

(a) See note p. 245

(b) Bangles, wrist or ankle rings, made of vitreous substances.

(c) Capoor cutchery, the root of a Chinese plant, used for medicinal purposes and perfumery.

(d) Cassia, the bark of a Chinese tree, resembling cinnamon.

(e) China root, a medicinal root.

(f) Gallengal, the aromatic root of a plant, used principally in cooking and exported chiefly to India.

(g) Grass cloth, the linen of China, woven from the fibres of the *Sida* into handkerchiefs, &c., and exported chiefly to India and the United States.

(h) Hartall, a coloring drug; the native sulphuret of arsenic.

(i) Kittysols, cheap umbrellas, of bamboo frames and oiled paper or cheap silk.

TARIFFS—Continued.

DENOMINATION OF MERCHANDISE.	Imported into the United States, per cent. ad valorem, under the act of—		DUTIES ON EXPORTS FROM— CHINA.	
	1846.	1857.	Number, weight, or measure.	Rate of duty.
Mother-of-pearl ware	30	24	$133\frac{1}{3}$ pound	$1 48
Musk	30	24	$1\frac{1}{3}$ pounds	74
Nankeen and cotton cloth of all kinds	25	24	$133\frac{1}{3}$ pounds	1 48
Pictures, viz: large paintings	As objects of taste and not merchandise, free; otherwise— 20	15	Each	$14\frac{4}{5}$
of rice paper			100	$14\frac{4}{5}$
Paper fans	30	24	$133\frac{1}{3}$ pounds	74
Paper, of all kinds	30	24	do	74
Pearls, false(*a*)	Set 30 Not set 10	24 8	do	74
Preserves and sweetmeats, of all kinds	40	30	do	74
Rattan wood, of all kinds	10 to 20	Free & 15	do	$29\frac{3}{5}$
Rhubarb	20	15	do	1 48
Silk, raw, whether from Chekiang, Canton, or elsewhere, all kinds.	25	19	do	14 80
coarse, or refuse of silk	25	19	do	3 70
organzine, all kinds	25	19	do	14 80
ribbons, thread, &c., &c	25	19	do	14 80
silk piece goods of all kinds, as silks, satins, pongees, velvets, crapes, lutestrings, &c., &c.(*b*)	25	19	do	17 76
silk and cotton mixtures, silk and woolen mixtures, and goods of such classes.	25	19	do	4 4
Shoes and boots, of all kinds	30	24		
Sandal wood ware	30	24	$133\frac{1}{3}$ pounds	14 80
Soy(*c*)	30	24	do	$59\frac{1}{5}$
Silver and gold ware	30	24	do	14 80
Sugar, white and brown	30	24	do	37
Sugar candy, all kinds	30	24	do	$51\frac{4}{5}$
Tin foil	15	12	do	74
Tea	(*d*)20	(*d*)15	do	3 70
Tobacco, of all kinds	40 20	30 24	do	$29\frac{3}{5}$
Turmeric(*e*)	5	4	do	$29\frac{3}{5}$
Tortoise shell ware	30	24	do	14 80
Trunks(*f*)	30	24	do	$29\frac{3}{5}$
Treasure, *i. e.*, coin of all kinds	Free	Free		Free.

NOTE.—All articles not enumerated in this tariff pay 5 per cent. ad valorem.

(*a*) False pearls largely manufactured of fish glue, and exported to India.

(*b*) The additional duty of so much per piece, hitherto levied, to be henceforth abolished.

(*c*) Soy, a condiment made from a bean growing in China and Japan.

(*d*) See note, p. 168.

(*e*) Turmeric, a root useful for its aromatic and coloring properties.

(*f*) Trunks—boxes made of camphor wood, five in a nest, exported chiefly to India, South America, Sydney, &c. An inferior description are covered with leather.

WEST INDIAN STATES.

43 □

WEST INDIAN STATES.

HAYTI.

The tariff is that of November 13, 1854.

1. Every vessel (steam vessels excepted) entering a harbor of the empire has to pay, as wharf duties, 10 per cent., and as a consignation duty, 6 per cent. additional, if her freight be consigned to foreign commercial houses, and but 2 per cent. if to Haytian houses.

2. Tonnage duty one dollar in specie per ton, to be paid on clearance.

3. American vessels pay tonnage duty as per register; vessels of other nations as per measurement. Vessels leaving without discharging cargo pay $25 as anchorage dues; leaving for freights at other ports, from $10 to $15, according to tonnage.

4. Cotton and coffee are monopolies of the government, which prescribes the price to planters.

5. There are no *Measures* established by law.

Money.—1 silver gourde = 100 cents = $1. The Haytian (paper) gourde = 5 cents United States currency, (average.)

Import duties must be paid in foreign coin.

The French five franc piece is estimated at 93¾ cents.

Weight.—1 millier = 10 quintals; 1 quintal = 100 pounds = 108.1-25, avoirdupois.

Measure.—1 aune, or ell = 1½ yards English. Gallons and barrels are as the English. 1 tierce = 60 gallons.

Export and territorial duties are levied on cocoa, coffee, cotton, hides, Campeachy wood, and mahogany.

DOMINICAN REPUBLIC.

The tariff is that of July 7, 1847, with modifications down to June 4, 1853.(*a*) The general duty on all articles comprised in this tariff is 25 per cent. on a fixed value; the following, however, are excepted, and pay only 5 per cent.: All jewels and ornaments of gold and silver, all articles composed in part or entirely of said metals, as watches, &c., precious stones, zinc, and all thread laces. The following articles are exempt from duty:

1. Fire-arms, balls for rifles and cannons, swords, cartridge boxes, drums, trumpets, cartridges, steel helmets, epaulets, lances, uniforms, and all articles generally intended for military purposes and uses.

2. All machines for agricultural and industrial purposes; horses, mules, asses, and all other animals for breeding.

3. All machines and instruments for military and scientific purposes, books of all classes, (except those prohibited,) and the wearing apparel of travellers.

The duties are to be paid in specie, or in current State notes of the Republic, of which, according to the old issue, $10 in paper is equal to $1 in specie; and according to the new issue by the Treasury Department, $2 50 in paper to $1 in specie.

APPENDIX.

By a law of June 30, 1855, and another of July 8, of the same year, the customs regulations of the Dominican Republic were subjected to material alterations. Passages from the law of July 8, which presents new tariff rates, are translated and annexed:

LAW RESPECTING THE TARIFFS OF IMPORTATION AND EXPORTATION.

Santo Domingo, *July* 8, 1857.

The senate considering that it is necessary to amend the tariffs of importation and exportation of the 7th July, 1847, in order to render them harmonious, as well with the price currents of goods as with the new names of articles, has passed the following law:

(*a*) For subsequent changes see Appendix.

ART. 1. The tariffs of importation and of exportation, sanctioned by the senate, shall serve as a basis for the collection of duties, two months after the promulgation of the present law, for ships coming from Europe, thirty days for those coming from the United States, and fifteen days for those coming from the West Indies. The ships which shall have entered previous to the publication of the present law, or which may enter within the periods above fixed, shall pay the duties expressed in the previous tariff.

ART. 2. The account of import duties collected shall be drawn up in conformity to the valuations which are expressed in the present tariff, in hard money. The duties shall be collected at the rate of 25 per cent. on the valuation, payable in gold or silver money, or in paper money at its current value, which is to be fixed by the customs office, at regular periods, according to the information it may have received.

ART. 3. Importers or exporters must state, in writing, at the bottom of their manifests, whether they intend to pay in hard money or paper. In the latter case, they will indicate correctly the value of such paper for the time being.

ART. 4. The goods on which ad valorem duties shall be collected, those non-enumerated in the present tariff, and those on which the collection is to be made by appraisal, will each pay 25 per cent. on the invoice price or on the appraised value. The following goods are excepted, and will pay 5 per cent.:

1. Jewelry, trinkets, and articles of gold or silver, of which the material forms the principal value.
2. Watches.
3. Precious stones.

ART. 5. The following are, and shall remain, free from all import duties:

1. Sabres and cavalry swords, big drums, drums, clarions, cartridge-boxes, military caps, lances, soldier clothing, and epaulets.
2. Machines of every kind for agriculture and manufacturing, horses and other animals imported for the improvement of the breeds.
3. Machines and implements of all kinds for the arts and sciences; printed books of every kind, except those prohibited; luggage of travellers; and, finally, all articles which are set down in the tariff as exempt from duty.
4. Minerals of every kind, proceeding from mines worked on the soil of the republic.
5. Articles and ornaments, intended for the service of churches, on the declaration of the ecclesiastical authority.
6. Tiles, broken tiles, and bricks.

ART. 6. The account of export duties will be drawn up in conformity to the rates established in the tariff of exportation, in hard money, and the payment will be made according to the terms of Article 3.

ART. 7. The exportation of horses in a troop is and shall be prohibited.

ART. 8. Articles not enumerated in the tariff of exportation are exempt from all duties.

ART. 9. The manifests of importation and of exportation, and other kindred documents, shall state the value or the price, in hard money, of all articles, including specie imported or exported, paying or not paying the duties, in order to facilitate the national statistics.

ART. 10. The price adopted by the customs office shall serve as a basis for the formation of the account, and no change can be made in it.

ART. 11. The present law repeals the customs law of the 7th of July, 1847, as well as every other law, regulation, or order which may be contrary to it.

TARIFF OF EXPORTATION.

ART. 1. The export duties on the products of the soil of the republic are established as follows:

MERCHANDISE.	Number, weight, or measure.	Rate.
Animals, beeves	Head	$2 00
sheep and goats	do	50
hogs	do	50
Wood, mahogany, cedar, calla, abeyes, and espinilla	1,000 feet	5 00
Campeachy, Gaiac, and Mora	Ton	1 00
Wax, white	Quintal	1 50
yellow	do	1 00
Honey	Gallon	1
Hides	Each	6
Skins, of goats, sheep, and hogs	Dozen	25
Resin, of Gaiac, and other	Quintal	50
Leaf tobacco	do	50

ART. 2. Articles not enumerated in the present tariff are exempt from duty.

ART. 3. Export duties, according to the foregoing rates, in hard money, as well as import duties, will, in paper money, be paid at the current value of such money.

ART 4. They will continue to be collected by cash payment, and before the sailing of the vessel in which the exportation is effected.

ART. 5. This tariff shall be put in force within sixty days after its publication for vessels coming from Europe ; within thirty days for those coming from the United States ; and within fifteen days for those coming from the West Indies.

LIST OF TARES.

In imports and exports the following tares will be deducted : merchandise of every kind, in casks or tierces, 10 per cent.; in barrels, 20 pounds ; coffee, rice, corn, &c., in bags, 1 per cent.; butter and lard, in kegs, 1 per cent.; soap, wax and tallow candles, cheese, vermicelli, tobacco, and codfish, in boxes, 20 per cent.; tobacco, in seroons or packages, 8 pounds, the seroon or package, 8 per cent ; nails, in barrels, 8 per cent.; cinnamon, in boxes or bales, 10 per cent.

MONEYS, WEIGHTS AND MEASURES.

The money, weights and measures, employed in the tariffs of importation and exportation of the Dominican Republic, bear the following proportions to the money, weights, and measures of the United States :

1 piastre = \$1 = 100 cents, United States currency.
1 arroba = 25 pounds.
1 quintal = 4 arrobas = 101 lbs. (about.)
1 gallon = 4 quarts.
1 pound = 16 ounces.
1 foot = 12 inches.
3 feet = 1 yard.

TARIFF OF IMPORTATION.

The annexed statement presents the fixed values of most of the articles which are imported into the Dominican Republic, from the United States. The rates of duty are 25 per cent. on these fixed values.

DENOMINATION OF MERCHANDISE.	Number, weight, or measure.	Fixed value.	
Anise seed	101 pounds		$10 00
Anchors, and all parts	do		8 00
Apples	Barrel		3 00
Beer, ale, and porter, in bottles	Dozen		1 50
Biscuit (ship)	101 pounds		3 00
Books, all not prohibited		Free.	
Brandy	Gallon		1 00
Bricks		Free.	
Boots, for men	Dozen pairs		28 00
Butter	101 pounds		16 00
Cables and cordage	do		10 00
Candles, tallow	do		12 00
Carpets	Yard		75
Cheese, from the United States	101 pounds		10 00
Chocolate	Pound		50
Cider	Dozen bottles		3 00
Cigars	1,000		20 00
Cinnamon	Pound		30
Coaches		Free.	
Copper, in sheets	101 pounds		25 00

TARIFFS—Continued.

DENOMINATION OF MERCHANDISE.	Number, weight, or measure.	Fixed value.
Cotton, raw	101 pounds	$16 00
Demijohns, one to four gallons	Dozen	1 00 to 6 00
Earthenware	Dozen pieces	5 00 to 8 00
Flannels	Yard	30
Flour	Bbl of 175 to 200 lbs	8 00
Flowers, artificial	Dozen	3 00
Fruits, dry	101 pounds	8 00
Gin, in pipes and demijohns	Gallon	40
Gunpowder, coarse and fine	Pound	6 and 12 cents.
Hams	101 pounds	12 00
Hides and skins	Dozen	1 00 to 12 00
Hats, cotton, beaver, silk	do	12 00 to 48 00
Hemp	101 pounds	10 00
Herrings	do	3 00
Horses		Free.
Indian corn	Barrel	2 00
Indigo	Pound	1 00
Iron hoops	101 pounds	4 00
Jewelry		5 per cent. ad val.
Lard	101 pounds	10 00
Lead, raw	Pound	6
Leather		On valuation.
Mackerel	Barrel	7 00
Marble		Free.
Musical instruments		On valuation.
Mules		Free.
Nails, iron	101 pounds	5 00
Needles	1,000	75
Nutmegs	Pound	2 00
Oats	Barrel	3 00
Oil, whale	Gallon	40
Paper, common white writing	Ream	1 00
Pepper	Pound	10
Pitch	Barrel	4 00
Potatoes	do	2 50
Printing paper		On valuation.
Prunes	101 pounds	8 00
Raisins	do	8 00
Rosin	Barrel	4 00
Rum	Gallon	1 00
Rye	101 pounds	4 00
Saddles	Each	12 00
Sheep		Free.
Shoes, for men, common	Dozen	18 00
Snuff	101 pounds	8 00 to 12 00
Soap, common	do	6 00
Sugar	do	4 00 to 8 00

TARIFFS—Continued.

DENOMINATION OF MERCHANDISE.	Number, weight, or measure.	Fixed value.
Tallow	101 pounds	$8 00
Tar	Barrel	4 00
Tea	Pound	2 00
Tobacco, leaf of all kinds	101 pounds	10 00
Trunks	Each	2 00
Types, printing		Free.
Umbrellas, cotton, silk	Dozen	6 00 to 48 00
Vinegar, common	Gallon	25
Wearing apparel, common, for men	Each	12 00
Watches		On valuation.
Wines in casks, red and white	Gallon	37 to 40 cents.
Wool, raw	Pound	1 00

COMPARATIVE TARIFFS.

UNITED STATES AND WEST INDIAN STATES.

DENOMINATION OF MERCHANDISE.	DUTIES ON IMPORTS INTO— The United States, per cent. ad valorem, under the act of— 1846.	1857.	HAYTI. Number, weight, or measure.	Rate of duty.	DOMINICAN REPUBLIC. Number, weight, or measure.	Fixed value. (a)
Absynth, in baskets of 12 bottles	100	30	Dozen bottles	$0 75	Dozen bottles	$5 00
Aniseed, cordials	100	30	a on	25	do	4 00
Anchors, and all parts of	30	24	108 pounds	50	101 pounds	8
Apples	20	8	1 lb. 3 drs	2	(Dried) 1 lb. 3 drs.	10
Bagging, cotton and linen	25	15	100 pieces	2 50	Yard	From 4 to 15
Beef, salted	20	15	1 barrel	1 50	Barrel	12 00
smoked	20	15	108 pounds	1 50	101 pounds	18 00
Beer, ale, and porter, in bottles	30	24	Dozen	25	Dozen	1 00
Biscuit, common	20	15	108 pounds	37½	101 pounds	2 00
white	20	15	do	75	do	3 00
Brandy, in casks	100	30	Gallon	50	Gallon	1 00
in boxes	100	30	Dozen bottles	1 00	Dozen bottles	3 00
Bricks	20	15	1,000	1 00	1,000	6 00
Boots, common	30	24	Pair	25	Dozen	4 00
shoes for men	30	24	Dozen	1 50	do	10 00
Butter	20	15	108 pounds	1 00	101 pounds	5 00
Buttons, metal, for soldiers	25	19	12 dozen	18	}	Actual value.
officers	25	19	do	50		
of mother of pearl, silk	25	19	do	15		
linen or glass	25	19	do	15		
Cables and cordage	25	19	108 pounds	1 50	101 pounds	5 00 to 14 00
Candles, wax	20	15	1 lb. 3 drs	7	1 lb. 3 drs	50
tallow	20	15	do	2	do	9
Castings	30	24		According to value.		According to value.
Cheese, all kinds	30	24	1 lb. 3 drs	2	1 lb. 3 drs	10
Cider, in bottles	30	24	Dozen	25	Dozen	1 00
Cigars	40	30	100	25	1,000	10 00
Cloves	40	4	1 lb. 3 drs	9		Not defined.
Coaches	30	24	One	10 00	}	Ad val. on assessed value.
Cabriolets	30	24	do	5 00		
in pieces	30	24		12 per ct. ad valorem.		

(a) The rate of duty is 25 per cent. on the fixed value assigned to each article.

TARIFFS—Continued.

Denomination of merchandise.	Duties on imports into— The United States, per cent. ad valorem, under the act of— 1846.	1857.	Hayti. Number, weight, or measure.	Hayti. Rate of duty.	Dominican Republic. Number, weight, or measure.	Dominican Republic. Fixed value.
Cotton, manufactured, bleached or unbleached.	25	24	1½ yard	2 to 8 cts.	Yard	From 4 cents to 10 cts.
calico, fine	25	24	do	6		
common	25	24	do	4		
Combs, of shell, for women	30	24	Dozen	4 00	Dozen	From 50 cts. to $2, according to material & quality.
of horn, for women	30	24	do	2 00		
small, of ivory or shell	30	24	do	50		
of horn, common	30	24	do	25		
Coal, stone	30	24	Boucants(a)	1 00	Ton	4 00
Fish, codfish and other, dry or salted	20	15	Barrel	50	101 pounds	2 75
Flour, wheat	20	15	do	2 00	Barrel, of 175 to 200 pounds.	5 00
Indian corn	20	15	do	1 00	Barrel	2 00
rye or barley	20	15	do	1 00	do	2 00
Fruits, dry	20	8	1 lb. 3 drachms	2		
in brandy	40	30	12 bottles	50		
in vinegar	30	24	do	30		
Gin, in casks	100	30	Gallon	25	Gallon	25
Gold and silver coin	Free	Free		Free		Free
Gunpowder, fine	20	15	1 lb. 3 drachms	12	1 lb. 3 drachms	12
for cannons	20	15	do	5	do	8
Hams and bacon: hams	20	15	do	2	do	15
bacon	20	15	do	2	Barrel	12 00
Hides and skins, buffalo, raw	5	4	Dozen	12 00		On assessed value.
calf and other, raw	5	4	Piece	64		
patent	20	19	Dozen	3 00		
sheep skins, tanned	20	15	do	1 00		
Indian corn	20	15	Barrel	1 00	Barrel	1 00
Indigo	10	4	1 lb. 3 drachms	15	1 lb. 3 drachms	1 00
Iron hoops	30	24	108 pounds	75	101 pounds	3 00
Lard	20	15	do	1 50	do	3 50
Lead, in bars	20	15	1 lb. 3 drachms	1	do	4 00
in sheets	20	15	do	2	do	8 00
shot	20	15	do	4	do	8 00
Leather, tanned	20	15	Dozen hides	3 00		On valuation.
Morocco	20	15	do	1 00		
imitation	20	15	do	50		
horse, blackened	20	15	Per hide	30		
Linen, with or without cotton mixture	20	15	1½ yard	15		
the same, very coarse	20	15	do	6		
gray, fine and common	20	15	do	5		

(a) Large barrels used for flour, lime, &c.

TARIFFS—Continued.

Denomination of merchandise.	Duties on imports into— The United States, per cent. ad valorem, under the act of— 1846.	1857.	Hayti. Number, weight, or measure.	Rate of duty.	Dominican Republic. Number, weight, or measure.	Fixed value.
Mackerel	20	15	Barrel	$0 50	101 pounds	$2 75
Musical instruments, military	20	15	For full band	20 00		Free.
Nails, iron	30	24	108 pounds	1 00	101 pounds	5 00
copper	20	15	do	4 00	do	30 00
small, of copper and plated	20	15	do	4 00	1,000	1 50
small, of iron	30	24	do	1 00	1,000	40
Nutmegs	40	4	1 lb. 3 drachms	8	1 lb. 3 drachms	50
Oil, linseed	20	15	In casks, per gal.	12	1 gallon	50
olive, in baskets of 12 bottles	30	24	12 bottles	50	12 bottles	2 00
in boxes do	30	24	30 bottles	60	12 flasks	90
fish	20	15	Whale	5 pr. ct. ad val.	1 gallon	16
Paints and varnish, in small boxes	20	15	One	50	All kinds, 1 lb. 3 drachms.	10
for painters, (of all kinds,) in barrels.	20	15	1 lb. 3 drachms	1½		
Paper, drawing	30	24	100 sheets	1 00		Free.
vellum, fine gold-edged	30	24	24 do	1 00	White, common, per ream.	5
foolscap, under 15 inches	30	24	do	12	1 ream	1 50
Pepper, black	30	4	1 lb. 3 drachms	2	1 lb. 3 drachms	10
Pimento	40	4	do	2		
Pitch	20	15	Barrel	50	Barrel	2 00
Potatoes	30	24	do	40	do	1 50
Printing presses	30	24	One	4 00		On valuation.
Raisins	40	8	1 lb. 3 drachms	2	1 lb. 3 drachms	12½
Rice	20	15	108 pounds	75	101 pounds	3 00
Snuff	40	30	1 lb. 3 drachms	20	1 lb. 3 drachms	3 00
Soap, of all kinds	30	24	108 pounds	1 25	101 pounds	4 50
perfumed, wash balls	30	24	Dozen	16	1 lb. 3 drachms	1 00
Sugar, refined	30	24	1 lb. 3 drachms	3	101 pounds	6 00
Tallow, raw	10	8	do	1	do	8 00
Tin, in bars	5	Free	108 pounds	3 00	1 lb. 3 drachms	5
Teas	20(a)	15(a)		5 pr. ct. ad val.	do	50
Tobacco, leaf	30	24	1 lb. 3 drachms	4	Virginia, 101 lbs.	16 00
					Other do	20 00
chewing	40	30	do	4	1 lb. 3 drachms	15
in cigars	40	30	Per 100	25	Virginia, 1,000	5 00
					Other do	10 00
Twine	30	24	1 lb. 3 drachms	20	1 lb. 3 drachms	25
Types, for printing	20	15	do	1		Free.
Umbrellas, silk, fine	30	24	Each	1 50	Each	3 00

(a) See note, p. 169.

TARIFFS—Continued.

DENOMINATION OF MERCHANDISE.	DUTIES ON IMPORTS INTO—					
	The United States, per cent. ad valorem, under the act of—		HAYTI.		DOMINICAN REPUBLIC.	
	1846.	1857.	Number, weight, or measure.	Rate of duty.	Number, weight, or measure.	Fixed value.
Umbrellas, parasols, &c., of same quality.	30	24	Each	$0 80	Each	$1 50
Vinegar, in bottles	30	24	12 bottles	8	1 dozen	1 00
in barrels	30	24	1 gallon	2	1 gallon	25
Wearing apparel	Free	Free		Free		Free
Watches, gold	10	8	One	1 50		5 per cent. on assessed value.
silver, fine	10	8	One	75		
common	10	8	One	75		
Wines, red, in casks	40	30	60 gallons	3 00	Gallon	25
white, in casks	40	30	Gallon	12	do	75
Madeira and Oporto, in bottles	40	30	Case, of 12 bottles	50	Dozen	6 00
in casks	40	30	Gallon	12	Gallon	2 00
Wood: boards, common pine	20	15	1,080 pounds	1 75	1,000 feet	10 00
pitch pine	20	15	do	2 50	do	12 00
Yarn, cotton, bleached, assorted	25	24	1 lb. 3 drachms	14	White or colored, 1 lb. 3 drachms.	20 to 30
dyed	25	24	do	12	Black do	30

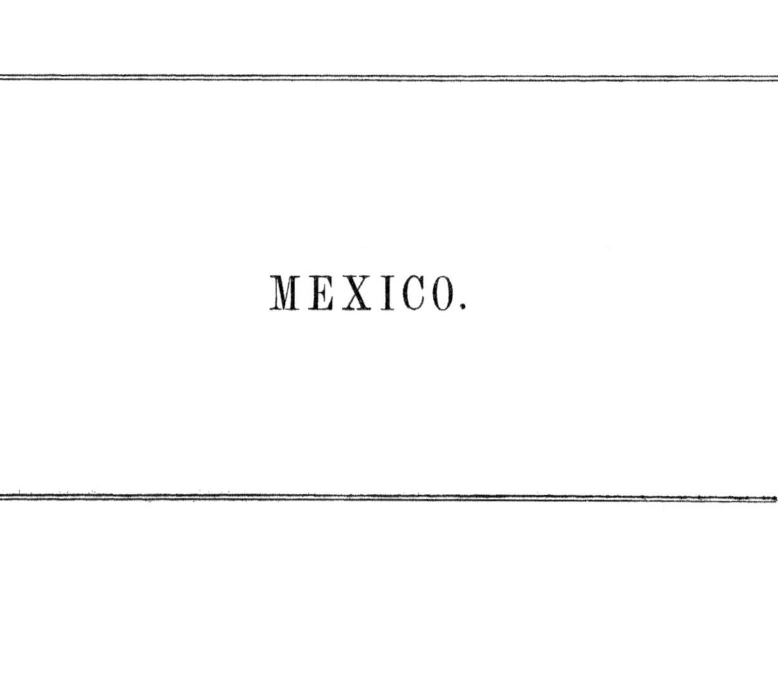

MEXICO.

MEXICO.

Three tariffs are given in corresponding columns—that of June 1, 1853, and that of August 12, 1845—which latter tariff, as modified by the decree of November 24, 1849, was revived and put in force by decree of Augus (a)

Money.—1 peso fuerte = 8 reals = 100 cents = $1.

Weights.—1 quintal = 4 arrobas = 101.44 lbs. ; 1 lb. = 1.014 lb.

Measures.—1 arroba = 25.402 lbs, (or 25 pounds 7 ounces ;) 1 vara = 0.927 yard = 33⅓ inches.

The following ports, by the tariff of 1853, are open to foreign trade, presenting a few changes from the tariff of 1845 :

In the Gulf of Mexico.—Sisal, Campechy, Vera Cruz, San Juan Bautista de Tabasco, Tampico de Tamaulipas, Matamoras.

In the Pacific ocean—Acapulco, Manzanilla, San Blas, Mazatlan.

In the Gulf of California.—Guaymas.

By land :—Northern frontiers.—Matamoras, Presidio del Norte, Pasa del Norte.

Southern frontiers.—Comitan, Tuxtla Chico.

For the coasting trade.—In the Gulf of Mexico : Isla del Carmen, Goatzacoalco, Alvarado, Tecotula, Tuxpam, Santecomapan, Soto la Maxina.

Eastern coast of Yucatan—Bacalar.

Pacific ocean—Tonalá.

Gulf of Tehuantepec—Santa Maria.

Gulf of California—San José del Cabo, La Paz, Navachiste, Altata.

Invoices must, under a fine of from $200 to $1,500, be certified by the Mexican consul resident at the foreign port whence the goods are exported to Mexico ; or, in his absence, by the consul of some nation friendly to Mexico, or by two well known merchants.

Beside the import duties stated in the tariff of 1853, an additional duty of 18 per cent. (viz : 1 per cent. import duty, 2 per cent. average, and 15 per cent. international import) is levied on the value of all goods imported, except jewelry.

Under the tariff of August 12, 1845, modified by the decree of November 24, 1849, the register of cargo of each vessel must contain—

1st. A copy of the general manifest.

2d. A special invoice for each article of cargo.

3d. A certificate of tonnage, signed by the captain of the port whence the vessel cleared.

4th. The sheets of his despatches, free from erasures, interlineations, &c., and properly arranged.

APPENDIX.

Since the preceding prefatory remarks were written, a new general tariff, under date 31st January, 1856, has reached the department.(b) It is much more liberal than either of the tariffs which preceded it, and as it is the only tariff now in force in Mexico, it is given in juxtaposition with those of 1845 (revived by decree of 1855) and 1853, so that a comparison can be instituted, by merely casting the eye across the sheet, between the rates of the old tariff and the new one.

Section 2d, article 21st, of the new tariff requires the captains of all vessels having merchandise on board, arriving at a Mexican port, to exhibit a general manifest in the following form :

" General manifest of merchandize destined for the port of ———, in the Republic of Mexico, in charge of Captain N, whose

(a) See Appendix.

The uncertain character of the customs rates of Mexico may be inferred from the following extract from a return from the consulate of Vera Cruz, under date of October 10, 1855: "There are now no less than four distinct tariffs in operation and counter operation here, not to mention concessions and special privileges granted to certain places and favored individuals. The tariffs to which I allude are sent herewith, viz: Those of 'Ceballos,' (January 24, 1853,) 'Gamboa,' (March 1, 1853,) 'Santa Anna,' (June 1, 1853,) and that of October 4, 1845. It will be seen that three of these tariffs were originally promulgated all within the space of less than five months. Besides these, Commonfort has lately published *his* tariff in Guadalaxara, and Vidaurri another one at Monterey. How many more there may be in different sections of the country I shall not attempt to record."

(b) See Vol. 1 " Digests," pp. 589 *et seq.*

name is subscribed hereto, a citizen of ———, in the ship N, [insert nationality, class, name, and tonnage,] consigned to the house of N. Established at the said port, [or to the aforesaid captain or supercargo.]

Marks and countermarks.	Numbers.	Gross weight of each package.	Number of packages.	Description of packages.	Gen'l character of merchandise.	Consignors.	Consignees.
J. A.	1 to 10	1–100 lbs.	10 (ten)	Barrels.	White wine.	N. N.	N. N.
P. M.	1 to 10	1–100 lbs.	10 (ten)	Tierces of gen'l merchandise.	Textures of cotton.	N. N.	N. N.

Done at the port of ———.

Signed by the captain, who also made oath that he would not receive on board other merchandise, and that he proceeds to Mexico for the purpose of lawful commerce."

The consignor must also forward a particular invoice, specifying each description or package of merchandise, for which a form is also prescribed.(*a*)

The 3d section of the same article requires as well the general manifest as the particular invoices, referred to in section 2d, to be presented to the Mexican consul, or vice consul, at the port where the merchandise is received on board; or, if no such official is accredited at such port, then to such consul or vice consul at the nearest port or place, and, in either case, requesting a receipt from such official, which must be presented at the custom-house of the first port where the vessel may call for the purpose of discharging her cargo.

The 4th section dispensed with this formality in respect of vessels arriving at Pacific ports from the East Indies or the Sandwich Islands.

The 5th section of the same article allows foreign vessels to impo merchandise destined for two or three Mexican ports, the documents specified in section two being separately made out for each port at the port of departure, the officers at the first port of arrival giving the requisite notice to the officers of the other ports to which the vessel may be destined.

The 6th section relates to the conveyance of passengers.

The 7th section allows 12 hours from the time of casting anchor for correcting and adding to the general manifest and invoice, the reasons for such alterations to be expressed, under oath, that the party acted lawfully and in good faith.

Changes.—The per centage increase or decrease in the rates of duty imposed on the principal articles of merchandise by the tariff of January 31, 1856, compared with those imposed on the same articles by that in force in 1855, has been noted as follows—fractions disregarded :(*b*)

On manufactures of cotton, a decrease of from 10 to 60 per cent.; of linen, 10 to 40: of silk, 10 to 33; of wove, 4 to 40: of iron and ironmongery, and hardware of all kinds, 33 to 40: nails, 58 to 68: steel and steel pens, 17: cutlery of all kinds, 33 to 40: jewelry, 40: fire-arms, 73; not for military purposes, 40: fruits, 50: ham, pork, &c., 16: cheese, 25: harness, common, for wagons, 10: carriages, 4-wheeled, for more than two persons, 20: staves and headings, all sizes, 40: wine and spirits, 11 to 33: window glass, 17: mirrors, with or without frames, 40: bottles, usual size, 10: crystal and wrought glass, 55; cut glass, beads, and rosaries, 40: beer and cider in bottles, 33; in casks, 50: biscuits, 20: blacking, 33: books, printed, bound, 67; blank, 10: bricks, glazed, 14: bristles for shoemakers, 40: butter, 20: buttons, common, of all sorts, 40: candles, stearine, 33: cinnamon, 33: clocks, all kinds, except gold and silver, 40: cloves, 40: cordage of hemp, 4: corks for bottles, 20: fish, codfish, and other sorts, dried or smoked, 50; sardines, salmon, &c., salted or pickled, 25: gloves, cotton or linen, 10; large, plain, leather, for men or women, 40: hair, beaver, rabbit, &c., for hats, 40: ink of all kinds, 40: mustard, 4: oil-cloth for tables and flooring, 40: paper, brown, 25; hangings, 50; letter, ruled, and copying, 20: pencils of all sorts, 33: pepper and pimento, 20: pipes, tobacco, common, 40: perfumery and pomatum, 10: prints and engravings, 40: shoes of India rubber, 40: soap, toilet, fine, 20: tea, 30: tiles for roofing, 81: umbrellas, cotton, 37; silk, 25: vinegar, 33: wax, bleached or not, 12; virgin, 8; sealing, 40.

Prohibition removed from lead, and a duty of 20 per cent. ad valorem imposed; also from apparel and dresses of all sorts, and 60 per cent. ad valorem imposed; also from molasses and sulphur, and 50 per cent. ad valorem imposed on each.

On pianos, organs, and all sorts of musical instruments, the specific duty is changed into an ad valorem duty of 30 per cent.; the same on furniture of all sorts of wood, to 25 per cent.; the same on plain white or colored muslins, 21 per cent

On a few articles of linen and woolen manufactures, there is a per centage increase of duty of from 3 to 25 per cent.; on fine gunpowder, 400 per cent.; on silver, wrought, and on cork wood, raw, 20 per cent; on slates, 100 per cent.

(*a*) See vol. 1 "Digests," p. 592.

(*b*) See note, p. 93.

COMPARATIVE TARIFFS.

UNITED STATES AND MEXICO.

Denomination of merchandise. (a)	The United States, per cent. ad valorem, under the act of— 1846.	1857.	Mexico. Number, weight, or measure.	Tariff of 1845. (b) Rate of duty.	Tariff of 1855. Rate of duty.	Tariff of 1856. Rate of duty.
Almonds, sweet and bitter	40	30	Quintal = 101 lbs.	$5 00	$6 00	$4 00
in the shell	40	30	do	3 00	00	2 00
Apples, bitter	20	Free	do	1 00	3 00	1 00
Arrack, in bottles or casks, (for which bottles and casks a separate duty is to be paid.)	100	30	do	12 00	18 00	12 00
Artificial flowers	30	24	Libra, or 1.014 lb	2 00	1 00	60
Beer, ale, porter, and cider, in bottles	30	24	101 pounds	6 00	8 00	4 00
in casks	30	24	do	4 00	4 00	2 00
Biscuit, or shipbread	20	15	do	3 00	4 00	2 40
Books, printed	10 to 20	8 to 15	do	6 00	8 00	2 00
maps	10	Free		Free	Free	Free.
Boots and shoes, of India rubber	30	24	101 pounds	15 00		9 00
of leather	30	24		Prohibited	Prohibited	Prohibited.
Bottles, of glass, common	30	24	Dozen	50	75 (common and smaller)	45
smaller	30	24	do	30		30
Brass, in sheets	30	24	101 pounds	9 00	10 00	6 00
Bricks, common	20	15	1,000	2 00	3 00	1 00
glazed	20	15	do	3 50	5 00	3 00

(a) This nomenclature, for sake of convenience and conciseness, has been adapted to the tariff of Mexico.

(b) This tariff was modified by a decree, November, 1849.

TARIFFS—Continued.

Denomination of merchandise.	Duties on imports into— The United States, per cent. ad valorem, under the act of— 1846.	1857.	Mexico. Number, weight, or measure.	Tariff of 1845. Rate of duty.	Tariff of 1855. Rate of duty.	Tariff of 1856. Rate of duty.
Broadcloth, if not of the first quality	30	24	Sq. vara, or yard	Prohibited		$0 50 (all descriptions.)
Brushes, horse and shoe	30	24	101 pounds.	$6 00	$6 00	From $6 to $18.
clothes and tooth	30	24	do	10 00	10 00	
very fine	30	24	do	30 00	30 00	
Butter, gross weight	20	15	do	6 00	8 00	4 80
Buttons, metal, horn, and whalebone, common	25	19	do	10 00		6 00
fine, silvered, and gilt	25	19	do	30 00	30 00	18 00
Cables and cordage	25	19	do	2 50		2 40
Camphor, refined	40	30			40 per cent.	40 per cent. ad valorem.
Candles, stearine	20	15	101 pounds	6 00		4 00
spermaceti	20	15	do	15 00	25 00	12 00
Cassia	40	4	1. 014 pound	75	1 00	50
Cards, playing	30	24		Prohibited	Prohibited	Prohibited.
Cheese of all kinds, gross weight	30	24	101 pounds	4 00	4 00	3 00
Cinnamon	30	4	1. 014 pound	75	1 00	50
Clocks	30	24	101 pounds	30 00		From $6 to $18.
Clothing, ready-made, all kinds	30	24		Prohibited	Prohibited	60 per cent. ad valorem.
Cloves	40	4	1. 014 pound	50	50	30
Coaches and other carriages, common, with only 2 wheels	30	24	Each	15 00	25 00	15 00
4 wheels	30	24	do	60 00	200 00	30 00
fine, open, 2 wheels, for 2 persons	30	24	do	30 00	50 00	30 00
for more than 2 persons	30	24	do	40 00	60 00	40 00
fine, covered, for more than 2 persons	30	24	do	55 00	200 00	60 00
not covered, 4 wheels, for 2 persons	30	24	do	60 00	300 00	60 00
for more than 2 persons	30	24	do	100 00	300 00	80 00

TARIFFS—Continued.

Denomination of merchandise.	The United States, per cent. ad valorem, under the act of— 1846.	1857.	Mexico. Number, weight, or measure.	Tariff of 1845. Rate of duty.	Tariff of 1855. Rate of duty.	Tariff of 1856. Rate of duty.
Coaches, fine, 4 wheels, for two persons, covered	30	24	Each	$130 00	$300 00	$80 00
for more than two, covered	30	24	do	200 00	300 00	180 00
omnibuses	30	24	do	60 00	100 00	80 00
Coals, stone, if imported to a place where they are scarce	30	24		Free	Free	Free, (unconditionally.)
Cocoa, from Guayaquil, Para, and islands	10	4	101 pounds	3 00	4 00	2 40
from all other places	10	4	do	6 00	8 00	5 00
Coffee	(a)20	(a)15		Prohibited	Prohibited	Prohibited.
Combs, of ivory	30	24	101 pounds	40 00	40 00	1 80 (common and boxwood.) 24 00 (tortoise shell.)
of wood	30	24	do	2 00	3 00	24 00
of china, cane, &c.	30	24	do	5 00	8 00	4 80 (of all descriptions.)
Copper, in pigs, and manufactured into utensils for domestic use — pigs	5	Free		Prohibited	Prohibited	40 per cent. ad val., (in sheets.)
— manuf's.	30	24				
weights	30	24	101 pounds	9 00		
Cork bark, raw, and in sheets	15	4	do	1 00	2 00	1 20
manufactured into corks	30	24	do	5 00	8 00	1 20
Cotton, raw, free of internal duties	Raw, free	Free	do	3 00	Prohibited	1 50
bleached and unbleached cloths, ribbed and plain, not exceeding 30 threads, weft and warp, on the quarter inch, at and under 1 vara wide.	25	24	Vara	5	10	3
the same, exceeding 30 threads, weft and warp, on the quarter inch, at and under 1 vara wide.	25	24	Vara	6	15	5
stockings of all kinds, for grown persons	20	15	Dozen	1 00	1 50	45

(a) See note, page 114.

TARIFFS—Continued.

Denomination of merchandise.	Duties on imports into— The United States, per cent. ad valorem, under the act of— 1846.	1857.	Mexico. Number, weight, or measure.	Tariff of 1845. Rate of duty.	Tariff of 1855. Rate of duty.	Tariff of 1856. Rate of duty.
Cotton stockings, for children	20	15	Dozen	$0 50	$0 50	$0 30
handkerchiefs, printed, striped, or checked, at and under 1.59 yard wide.	25	24	Each	4	10 to 12½ cts.	4
handkerchiefs, plain white, with white or colored borders, at and under 1.59 yard wide.	25	24	Each	6	10 to 12½ cts.	5
laces of all kinds	25	19	1.014 pound	1 50		1 20
Cutlery	30	24	101 pounds	15 00	(Com'n) $15, (fine) $30	9 00
Demijohns	30	24	Dozen	60	1 00	60
Earthen and stone ware, of all kinds	30	24	101 pounds	4 00	6 00	3 00
porcelain of all kinds	30	24	do	8 00		3 00
Figs	40	8	do	2 00	3 00	1 00
Fire-arms, guns and rifles	30	24	do	20 00	Prohibited	$12 to $18.
Fish, cod, and all other kinds, dried, smoked, or salted	20	15	do	4 00	4 00	2 00
sardines, salmon, and all other kinds, in oil, pickled or salted, gross weight	40	30	do	4 00	4 00	3 00
Flour, wheat, except for Yucatan	20	15		Prohibited	Prohibited, except for Yucatan.	Prohibited, except for Yucatan, Tampico, Matamoras, and the north'n frontier custom-houses.
Flowers, artificial	30	24		Prohibited	1 00 per pound	60
Gin, in bottles and casks; (the bottles and casks pay separate duties.)	100	30	101 pounds	10 00	16 00	10 00
Glass wares, of all kinds, without allowance for breakage	25 to 40	19 to 30	do	8 00	6 00	3 60
window, of all kinds, without any allowance for breakage.	20	15	do	6 00	10 00	5 00
Gold leaf, or tinsel	15	12	do	Prohibited		9 00

TARIFFS—Continued.

DENOMINATION OF MERCHANDISE.	The United States, per cent. ad valorem, under the act of— 1846.	1857.	MEXICO. Number, weight, or measure.	Tariff of 1845. Rate of duty.	Tariff of 1855. Rate of duty.	Tariff of 1856. Rate of duty.
Gunpowder, (except for sporting)	(all) 20	(all) 15	1.014 pound	Prohibited	Prohibited	$0 50
Hams and sausages	20	15	do	$6 00	$8 00	5 00
Hats, gentlemen's, of all kinds	30	24	Each		3 00	2 00 (made up.)
Household furniture	30	24				25 per cent. ad valorem.
Ice	20	Free	101 pounds	15	25	3
Iron—						
In sheets, wrought, or cast	30	24	do	2 00	3 00	2 00
Cast nails, of all sizes	30	24	do	Prohibited	Prohibited	2 50
Hatchets, wire, chains	30	24	do	2 00	3 00	2 00
Lard	20	15		Prohibited	Prohibited	Prohibited. (See Flour.)
Lead, crude, and in shot	20	15		Prohibited		20 per cent. ad valorem.
Linen, carpeting, or of hemp or tow alone, at and under a vara wide.	20	15	Square vara	7	12½	5
sheetings, of flax or hemp, or imitations of them, at and under a vara wide.	20	15	do	4	7	3⅓
tapes, of all kinds and colors	20	15	1.014 pound	36	60	40
gloves, of all classes and colors	30	24	Dozen	50	75	45
thread, of all kinds, numbers, and colors	20	15	1.014 pound	45	75	45
bleached and unbleached plain cloths, of 36 threads to the quarter inch, and at and under a vara wide.	20	15	Vara	5	6	5
The same, more than 36 threads to the quarter inch	20	15	do	7	9	7
plain cloths, made of the last mentioned materials, printed, striped, or shaded, at and under a vara wide.	20	15	do	7	9	

TARIFFS—Continued.

Denomination of merchandise.	Duties on imports into— The United States, per cent. ad valorem, under the act of— 1846.	1857.	Mexico. Number, weight, or measure.	Tariff of 1845. Rate of duty.	Tariff of 1855. Rate of duty.	Tariff of 1856. Rate of duty.
Linen, bleached, unbleached, or colored cloths, figured, twilled or damasked, at and under a vara wide.	20	15	Vara	$0 09	$0 11	$0 07
stockings, of all kinds, for grown persons	30	24	Dozen	1 00	1 50	45
for children	30	24	do	50	50	30
handkerchiefs, striped or colored, of one square yard	20	15	do	60	1 50	50
white, or with a colored border	20	15	do	1 00	1 50	
white or colored, embroidered	20	15	do	2 00	Not defined	2 00
Liquors, of all kinds	100	30	101 pounds	12 00	Not prohibited or otherwise described, 12 00	Prohibited, unless specially defined in tariff. Stout, in bottles, $4 80.
Marble, manufactures of	30	24	do	8 00	8 00	Different duties.
Medicinal drugs	20	15		40 per ct. ad val.	Specified duties on each article thereof, per tariff of 1845, modified by decree of 1849.	40 per cent. ad valorem.
Molasses	30	24		Prohibited	Prohibited	50 per cent. ad valorem.
Musical instruments, all kinds, except pianos and organs	(all)20	(all)15	101 pounds	15 00	15 00	9 00
Nutmegs	40	4				40 per cent. ad valorem.
Nuts	20 to 30	15 to 24	101 pounds	2 00	4 00	Not defined.
Oil, spermaceti	20	15	do	6 00	Not defined	12 00
Paper, brown, net weight	30	24	do	2 00	3 00	1 50
letter, net weight	30	24	do	10 00	16 00	From $8 to $9.
ruled for account, and other uses, gilt	30	24	do	12 00	24 00	9 00

TARIFFS—Continued.

DENOMINATION OF MERCHANDISE.	The United States, per cent. ad valorem, under the act of—		DUTIES ON IMPORTS INTO— MEXICO.			
	1846.	1857.	Number, weight, or measure.	Tariff of 1845. Rate of duty.	Tariff of 1855. Rate of duty.	Tariff of 1856. Rate of duty.
Paper hangings	20	15	101 pounds	$8 00	$6 00	$3 00
printing	30	24	do	3 00	6 00	2 50
Pepper, of all kinds	30	4	do	6 00		4 80
Pianos, square	20	15	Each	60 00	100 00	Of all kinds, 30 per ct. ad val.
vertical	20	15	do	90 00	150 00	
grand piano	20	15	do	120 00	200 00	
Pimento	40	4	101 pounds	6 00	Not specially defined.	4 80
Ploughshares, of the same form as those used in the country.	30	24		Prohibited	Prohibited	Ploughs and ploughshares, free
Pork, salt, cured or pressed, with the offal of pigs, (hams and sausages excepted.)	20	15	101 pounds	do	do	5 00
Prunes and plums { prunes / plums	40 / 30	8	do	2 00	3 00	1 00
Raisins	40	8	do	2 00	3 00	1 00
Rye, and all other grain	20	15		Prohibited	Prohibited	Prohibited. (See Flour.)
Ready-made clothes	30	24		do	do	60 per cent. ad valorem.
Rice	20	15		do	do	Prohibited.
Rum, in bottles and casks, (bottles and casks pay separate duty.)	100	30	101 pounds	12 00	18 00	12 00
Saltpetre { crude / refined	5 / 10	4 / 8		Prohibited	Prohibited	40 per cent. ad valorem.
Silk, blonde, and other lace, and netting of all kinds and colors, plain and embroidered.	25 to 30	19 to 24	1.014 pound	8 00	12 00	7 20
untwisted silk, or "quiña," of all qualities and colors.	30	24	do	1 20	2 00	1 20
sewing silk	30	24	do	2 00	3 00	1 80

TARIFFS—Continued.

Denomination of merchandise.	Duties on imports into— The United States, per cent. ad valorem, under the act of— 1846.	1857.	Mexico. Number, weight, or measure.	Tariff of 1845. Rate of duty.	Tariff of 1855. Rate of duty.	Tariff of 1856. Rate of duty.
Silk, all, mixed with other stuffs, will pay the following duties:						
cotton and silk	25	19	1.014 pound	$1 00	$1 50	Not separately defined.
linen and silk	25	19	do	1 30	1 80	
wool and silk	25	19	do	1 50	2 00	
mixed with two different stuffs, (metals excepted)	25	19	do	1 50	2 00	
mixed with metals	25	19		20 per ct ad val.		
Skins and furs, beaver, of all classes	20	15	1 014 pound	1 00	2 00	
rabbit and others, for hats	10	8	do	50	75	
Soap, of all kinds	30	24	101 pounds	Prohibited	Prohibited	(Fine,) $24.
Spermaceti, raw	20	15	do	6 00	12 00	7 50
manufactured	20	15	do	15 00	25 00	12 00
Steel	15 to 30	12 to 24	do	1 50	2 00	1 25
Tallow, raw and refined	10	8		Prohibited	Prohibited	50 per cent. ad val.
Teas, of all kinds	(a)20	(a)15	1.014 pound	50	Black, 50 cts.; green, 75 cents.	35
Tin, in blocks	5	Free		Prohibited	Prohibited	Not defined.
in plates, of all kinds and sizes	15	8	101 pounds	4 00	4 50	20 per cent. ad val.
Tiles	20	15	1,000	4 00	6 00	75
Tobacco	30 to 40	24 to 30	Of all kinds can	only be imported	on demand of the gov	ernment, as it is a monopoly.
Umbrellas, cotton	30	24	Each	40		25
silk	30	24	do	1 00	1 25	75
Vinegar, in barrels, net weight	30	24	101 pounds	1 50	2 00	1 00

(a) See note, p. 168.

TARIFFS—Continued.

Denomination of merchandise.	The United States, per cent. ad valorem, under the act of—		Duties on imports into— Mexico. Tariff of 1845.		Tariff of 1855.	Tariff of 1856.
	1846.	1857.	Number, weight, or measure.	Rate of duty.	Rate of duty.	Rate of duty.
Vinegar, in bottles, net weight	30	24	101 pounds	$2 00		
Wax, bleached and unbleached	20	15	do	15 00	$22 00	$13 25
virgin	20	15	do	13 00	20 00	12 00
manufactures of	20	15		Prohibited	Prohibited	Prohibited.
Whalebone, unmanufactured	20	15	101 pounds	6 00	6 00	4 00
Wheat and all other grain	20	15		Prohibited	Prohibited	Prohibited, (see Flour.)
Wood, timber for building	20	15		Free	Prohibited, except at Tampico and Matamoras.	Free.
masts and spars	20	15		Free	Free	Free.
boxes of	30	24		25 per ct. ad val.		25 per cent. ad val.
staves and heading, gross weight	20	15	101 pounds	50	50	30
fine wood, in veneers	30	24	1,000 square feet	5 00	8 00	4 80
for building, already worked	30	24		25 per ct. ad val.		Free.
shingles	20	15	1,000	1 20	2 00	Free.
Wool, raw, net weight	(a)30	(a)24	101 pounds	2 50	00	2 40
carpeting, Brussels, of all kinds, at and under a vara wide.	30	24	Square vara	50	75	20 cents to 45 cents.
socks and half stockings, of all colors, for adults	30	24	Dozen	50	75	48
same, for children	30	24	do	30	75	48
twilled cassimeres, of all kinds and colors, at and under a vara wide.	30	24	Vara	40	75	45

(a) See note, p. 320.

TARIFFS—Continued.

DENOMINATION OF MERCHANDISE.	DUTIES ON IMPORTS INTO—					
	The United States, per cent. ad valorem, under the act of—		MEXICO.			
			Tariff of 1845.		Tariff of 1855.	Tariff of 1856.
	1846.	1857.	Number, weight, or measure.	Rate of duty.	Rate of duty.	Rate of duty.
Wool stockings, of all sizes and colors, for adults	30	24	Dozen	$1 00	$1 50	(See Cotton and linen gloves, &c.)
white and colored plain cloths, at and under one vara wide.	30	24	Vara	7½	12½	$50
cloths of all colors, worked, damasked, crossed, striped, and twilled, at and under a vara wide.	30	24	do	9	15	12

CENTRAL AMERICAN STATES.

CENTRAL AMERICAN STATES.

GUATEMALA.

The tariff is that of 1855.

Moneys.—The same as in all other Spanish American countries—1 Peso = 100 centavos = $1.

Weights.—1 quintal = 100 libras = 1 1.44 lbs.

1 arroba = 25 lbs. 7 oz.

1 libra, 1.014 lb.

Prohibited list.—Guns, muskets, and all other arms for military purposes; munitions of war, as lead, balls, and gunpowder, and rifles; prints, cuts, pictures, &c., bearing against religion and morals; books, manuscripts, &c., specially interdicted.

Free list.—Anchors, cables, rigging, and all other articles belonging to ships' material not comprehended in the following tariff; quicksilver, barometers, fire engines, staves, and heading of all kinds; scientific instruments and agricultural implements, books, music, maps, and geographical charts; machines and steam engines; gold and silver coins; barrels, hogsheads, &c., for exporting the productions of the country.

All articles not comprehended in the tariff pay 24 per cent. on the invoice value, with an addition of 20 per cent. on the aggregate amount of such duty.

Articles not clearly described in invoices are subject to the same duty as those to which they have the nearest correspondence.

Duties are payable one-half at least in silver, the remainder in gold coin.

COMPARATIVE TARIFFS.

UNITED STATES AND GUATEMALA.

DENOMINATION OF MERCHANDISE.	DUTIES ON IMPORTS INTO—			
	The United States, per cent. ad valorem, under the act of—		GUATEMALA.	
	1846.	1857.	Number, weight, or measure.	Rate of duty.
Apples, fresh	20	8		Free.
dried	20	8	Arroba, (25 lbs. 7 oz)	$0 60
Beef, dried or salted	20	15	do	48
cured or pickled	20	15	1.014 pound	6
Beer of all kinds	30	24	Dozen bottles	50
Biscuit or ship bread, fine	20	15	25 pounds	50
Books, printed	10	8		Free.
blank	20	15	24 per cent. on the invoice value, with an addition of 20 per cent. on the aggregate amount.	
Boots and shoes, of calf skin, for men	30	24	Pair	4
of all kinds, for women	30	24	Dozen pair	3 45
of silk, for children	30	24	do	1 72
Brandy of all kinds—				
in boxes containing one dozen bottles			Box	72
in demijohns of 1 to 1½ arrobas of 16 to 18 bottles.	100	30	Demijohn	86
in casks or barrels of from 15 to 18 gallons.			Barrel	3 44
Butter	20	15	25 lbs. 7 oz	84
Cables	25	19		Free.
Cassia lignea	40	4	1.014 pound	25
Cheese of all sorts	30	24	101 pounds	2 88
Cinnamon	30	4	1.014 pound	25
common kind, called canelon	30	4	do	4½
Clothing, ready made—				
pantaloons, of cloth or cassimere	30	24	Dozen	17 28
common, of cotton	30	24	do	7 20
coats, of cloth or cassimere	30	24	Each	4 80
shirts, cotton	30	24	Dozen	1 20
woolen, for sailors	30	24	do	1 40
for common use	30	24	do	1 92
flannel	30	24	do	1 44
linen	30	24	do	3 60
Irish linen	30	24	do	7 20
of batiste, (lawn)	30	24	do	12 00
Cloths and cassimeres, common	30	24	Yard	54

TARIFFS—Continued.

DENOMINATION OF MERCHANDISE.	DUTIES ON IMPORTS INTO—			
	The United States, per cent. ad valorem, under the act of—		GUATEMALA.	
	1846.	1857.	Number, weight, or measure.	Rate of duty.
Cloths and cassimeres, fine	30	24	Yard	$0 78
Cloves	40	4	1.014 pound	8
Coaches and other carriages	30	24	24 per cent. on the invoice value, per cent on the aggregate.	with an addition of 20
Coal, stone	30	24		Free.
Cocoa, from Tabasco(*a*)	10	4	A quantity of 60 pounds	1 25
from Guayaquil	10	4	25 lbs. 7 oz.	36
Combs, of boxwood	30	24	Gross	1 00
bone	30	24	do	3 00
ivory	30	24	Dozen	48
Coffee, from Central American States	20(*b*)	15(*b*)	101 pounds	50
from other countries			do	1 00
Copper, manufactured into cooking utensils and similar objects.	30	24	1.014 pound	12½
Cotton handkerchiefs, common	25	24	Dozen	1 00
fine	25	24	do	2 00
stockings, for men, common	20	15	do	42
fine	20	15	do	72
for women, common	20	15	do	30
fine	20	15	do	48
drill, up to 32 inches broad	25	24	Yard	2½
colored	25	24	do	3
Demijohns	30	24	Dozen	96
bottles	30	24	do	15
Earthen and stone ware, in boxes	30	24	Box of 137 to 150 pounds	3 36
imitation of porcelain, in small pieces.	30	24	Dozen pieces	18
Fish, in oil	40	30	1.014 pound	4½
Flour	20	15	25 lbs. 7 oz.	25
Grain spirits—				
in boxes containing a dozen bottles	100	30	One box	72
in demijohns of 4 to 6 gallons	100	30	One	86
in casks or barrels of about 20 gallons	100	30	One barrel	3 44
Glass, window, in boxes of from 100 to 125 lbs. weight.	20	15	Box	1 92
in glasses and other smaller household articles.	30	24	Box from 137 to 150 pounds	3 60
Do......do....fine cut	40	30	do	7 20
bottles of common glass	30	24	Dozen	15
Gunpowder	20	15		Prohibited.
Hams	20	15	1.014 pound	4

(*a*) The nomenclature is adapted to the tariff of Guatemala. (*b*) See note, p. 114.

TARIFFS—Continued.

DENOMINATION OF MERCHANDISE.	DUTIES ON IMPORTS INTO—			
	The United States, per cent. ad valorem, under the act of—		GUATEMALA.	
	1846.	1857.	Number, weight, or measure.	Rate of duty.
Hats, of cotton felt, for men	30	24	Dozen	$4 80
for children	30	24	do	2 16
of fur, beaver, for men, fine	30	24	do	11 52
of silk felt, for men	30	24	do	5 76
of chip, common	30	24	do	1 44
middling	30	24	do	4 80
very fine	30	24	do	17 28
Hops	20	15	24 per cent. on the invoice value, with an addition of 20 per cent. on the aggregate.	
Horned cattle	20	Free		Free.
Hosiery, cotton stockings for men, common	20	15	Dozen	42
for men, fine	20	15	do	72
for women, com'n	20	15	do	30
for women, fine	20	15	do	48
woolen stockings, common	30	24	do	72
fine	30	24	do	1 00
silk stockings, for women	30	24	do	2 40
for men	30	24	do	2 16
Household furniture, wooden	30	24		40 per cent. ad val.
Indian corn	20	15	24 per cent. on the invoice value, with an addition of 20 per cent. on the aggregate.	
Iron, in bars or sheets	30	24	101 pounds	1 68
cast in pieces, as smoothing irons, pots.	30	24	do	3 00
cast, in hoes, shovels, &c	30	24	do	5 00
manufactured into carpenters' tools, as hatchets, hammers, tongs, and similar things.	30	24	do	4 80
rails, of all sizes	30	24	do	3 00
cables and chains for vessels	30	24		Free.
machines	30	24		Free.
steel, in bars and sheets	15	12	101 pounds	1 92
cast, in bars of all sizes	15	12	do	1 92
old steel	20	15	do	1 70
Jewelry, of gold and silver, and fine precious stones.	30	24	2 per cent. on the invoice value, with an addition of 100 per cent. on the aggregate.	
Lard	20	15	25 pounds 7 oz	60
Linen, Irish, common and middling	20	15	Yard	3
fine	20	15	do	12
mixed, common	20	15	do	3½
fine	20	15	do	7
drills, colored or white, up to 1 yard wide, common.	20	15	do	5

TARIFFS—Continued.

Denomination of merchandise.	Duties on imports into— The United States, per cent. ad valorem, under the act of— 1846.	1857.	Guatemala. Number, weight, or measure.	Rate of duty.
Linen drills, colored or white, up to 1 yard wide, fine	20	15	Yard	$0 08
drills mixed, common	20	15	..do	4½
fine	20	15	..do	6½
bagging	20	15		Free
Linseed oil	20	15	1 014 pound	84
Liquors, of all sorts, (not otherwise described,) in boxes of one dozen bottles.	100	30	Box of 12 bottles	1 02
Liquors, brandies of all kinds, in barrels of 12 to 15 gallons.	100	30	Barrel	3 44
Marble slabs, for tables and other uses	30	24	24 per cent. on the invoice value, with an increase of 20 per cent. on the aggregate.	
Muskets and rifles, single barreled, common	30	24	Each	2 40
fine	30	24	..do	4 32
double barreled, common	30	24	..do	3 36
fine	30	24	..do	5 76
for military purposes	30	24		Prohibited.
pistols, one or two barreled, common	30	24	Pair	1 92
pocket pistols, one or two barreled, fine	30	24	..do	3 84
pistols, five or six shooting	30	24	One	4 80
Nutmegs	40	4	1.014 pound	50
Nux vomica	10	8	......do	12
Oil, spermaceti	20	15	......do	7
Paints, in powder	20	15	25 pounds 7 oz	48
in oil	20	15	......do	84
Paper, writing, common	30	24	Ream	25
half white	30	24	..do	50
white	30	24	..do	75
printing in large sheets	30	24	..do	1 00
vellum, common sheets	30	24	..do	2 00
larger sheets	30	24	..do	4 00
ruled, for music	30	24	..do	84
colored, for artificial flowers, &c	30	24	..do	1 25
gilt and silvered	30	24	..do	7 50
brown	30	24	..do	18
Playing cards, of common paper	30	24	Gross	3 50
of middling paper	30	24	..do	4 50
of fine paper	30	24	..do	5 00
Pitch	20	15	25 pounds 7 oz	50
Pork, salt	20	15	......do	48
cured or pickled	20	15	1.014 pound	6
Printing presses	30	24	Each	Free.

TARIFFS—Continued.

DENOMINATION OF MERCHANDISE.	DUTIES ON IMPORTS INTO—			
	The United States, per cent. ad valorem, under the act of—		GUATEMALA.	
	1846.	1857.	Number, weight, or measure.	Rate of duty.
Raisins	40	8	25 pounds 7 oz	$0 37
Rice	20	15	do	24
Rosin	20	15	do	50
Rye, oats, and other small grain	20	15	24 per cent. on the invoice value, per cent. on the aggregate.	and an addition of 20
Saddlery, saddles for men or women	30	24	Each	6 72
bridles, complete, common	20	15	Dozen	6 00
Soap, common	30	24	25 pounds 7 oz	72
fine, perfumed, in cakes	30	24	Dozen	12
Spermaceti, unmanufactured, or in candles	20	15	1.014 pound	7
Spirits of molasses, in boxes containing 12 bottles.	100	30	Box	72
Spirits of molasses, in barrels of about 12 to 15 gallons.	100	30	Barrel	3 44
Tallow candles, common	20	15	1.014 pound	3
purified or stearine	20	15	do	5
Tar	20	15	25 pounds 7 oz	50
Teas of China, black or green	Free(a)	Free(a)	1.014 pound	18
Tin, in pigs and bars	5	Free	101 pounds	5 00
worked into cooking and other utensils	30	24	1.014 pound	12½
Tobacco { unmanufactured	30	24 }	24 per cent. on the invoice value, per cent. on the aggregate.	with an addition of 20
Tobacco { manufactured	40	30 }		
Umbrellas, silk	30	24	Dozen	5 00
silk, double, very fine	30	24	do	7 50
parasols, silk	30	24	do	2 88
silk, embroidered	30	24	do	4 80
of cotton, all sizes	30	24	do	1 92
Vinegar, in demijohns	30	24	One	50
in barrels	30	24	One	2 00
Wax, white, unmanufactured	20	15	25 pounds 7 oz	2 40
candles	20	15	1.014 pound	12
in flowers	20	15	do	24
Wines, sweet, of all kinds	40	30	Dozen bottles	72
in casks of 8 to 12 gallons	40	30	Cask	1 20
claret, in bottles	40	30	Dozen	60
in casks of 8 to 12 gallons	40	30	Cask	1 08
in barrels of 20 to 25 gallons	40	30	Barrel	2 16
champagne, in bottles	40	30	Dozen	2 40
Wooden manufactures, as furniture	30	24		40 per cent. ad val.
Woolen manufactures, cassimeres, common	30	24	Yard	54
fine	30	24	do	78
shirts, for sailors	30	24	Dozen	1 40
for common use	30	24	do	1 92

(a) See note, page 168.

SAN SALVADOR.

The tariff is that of 1837, with subsequent alterations and modifications down to July, 1855.(a)

Moneys, weights and measures are the same as in the other Spanish American Republics:

1 peso = 100 cents $1 American currency.
1 quintal = 101.44 lbs. avoirdupois.
1 arroba = 25 lbs. 7 oz.
1 lb. = 1.014 lb. avoirdupois.

Gallons and yards the same as those of the United States.

Goods, wares and merchandise imported, no matter whence they come or where produced, pay 24 per cent. in discharge of all duties on the valuation given in the following tariff of prices. Until recently this ad valorem duty was only 20 per cent.; but the actual value of most of the articles enumerated in the tariff of 1837 being now much higher than the permanent value assigned to each at that period, it was deemed the simplest way to protect the treasury from diminution of revenue, which must result from under valuation of the principal articles of commerce to raise the ad valorem duty to 24 per cent. While, however, the import duty is apparently raised 4 per cent., it is in reality lower than the duty of 1837, owing to the cause assigned above.

Free list.—Books, instruments of arts and science; paper; instruments and machines for agricultural and mining purposes; seeds and plants not cultivated in the republic; gold and silver in bullion and coin; quicksilver.

Living cochineal, and the seed of the indigo plant are prohibited to be exported. Gold, if exported in sums of upwards of 16 dollars, pays 1 per cent. ad valorem. Precious stones and jewels pay the same export duty. Silver pays 3 per cent. ad valorem.

(a) By a decree of March 10, 1856, import duties were reduced from 24 to 20 per cent. ad valorem, showing a decrease of nearly 17 per cent. on previous rates.

COMPARATIVE TARIFFS.

UNITED STATES AND SAN SALVADOR.

Denomination of merchandise.	Duties on imports into— The United States, per cent. ad valorem, under the act of— 1846.	1857.	San Salvador. Number, weight, or measure.	Fixed value (a)
Apples, fresh	20	8		Free.
Beef, in barrels	20	15	Quintal=101 lbs.	$5 00
Beer, in common bottles	30	24	Dozen	2 50
Biscuit or ship bread	20	15	101 pounds	3 00
Books, printed	10	8		Free.
Boots and shoes of all kinds	30	24	Dozen	From $6 00 to 18 00
Brandy of all kinds, in bottles	100	30	do	2 50
in casks	100	30	Gallon	1 00
gin in bottles	100	30	Dozen	2 00
Bricks, common	20	15	1,000	15 00
Butter	20	15	1.014 pound	12
Cables, iron	30	24	101 pounds	6 00
Cassia	40	4	1.014 pound	25
Cheese, of all sorts	30	24	25 pounds 7 oz	4 00
Cider, in common bottles	20	15	Dozen	2 00
Cinnamon	30	4	1.014 pound	25
Clothing, ready made, pantaloons, (wool)	30	24	Dozen pieces	48 00
Cloths and cassimeres, up to 33 inches broad	30	24	Yard	1 00
Cloves	40	4	1.014 pound	25
Coaches with four wheels, and all the necessaries	30	24	Each	200 00
Coals, stone	30	24		Free.
Cocoa, from Guayaquil	10	4	101 pounds	6 00
from Tabasco, Trinidad, Venezuela, &c	10	4	do	9 00
Coffee	(b)20	(b)15	do	7 00
Combs, of wood, horn, or brass	30	24	Gross	6 00
of ivory, of all sizes	30	24	Dozen	1 00
of mother-of-pearl	30	24	Gross	9 00
Copper, in sheets, for sheathing vessels	Free	Free	1.014 pound	30
in bars, or crude	5	Free	101 pounds	25
manufactured into utensils, as cooking, &c.	30	24	1.014 pound	37
in boilers, kettles, for agriculture				25
Cotton, raw	Free	Free		No importation.
drill, white or colored	25	24	Yard	12
laces, 1 inch broad, and in pieces of 12 yards	25	19	Dozen pieces	2 00
stockings, for men	20	15	Dozen pairs	1 75
for women	20	15	do	1 00
for children	20	15	do	75
shirts, white or colored	20	15	Dozen	6 00

(a) Rate of duty 24 per cent. on fixed value assigned to each article.

(b) See note page 114.

TARIFFS—Continued.

DENOMINATION OF MERCHANDISE.	DUTIES ON IMPORTS INTO—			
	The United States, per cent. ad valorem, under the act of—		SAN SALVADOR.	
	1846.	1857.	Number, weight, or measure.	Fixed value.
Cotton gloves, white or colored	20	15	Dozen	$1 00
Demijohns	30	24	......do	50
Earthen and stone ware, common	30	24	......do	50
middling, fine	30	24	Dozen pieces	3 00
imitation of china, in small pieces	30	24	Dozen	1 00
porcelain, small pieces, as plates, cups, &c	30	24	......do	2 00
do. in large pieces	30	24	......do	12 00
Fish, herrings, codfish, and all other kinds	20	15	101 pounds	6 00
Flour, of all kinds	20	15	......do	4 00
Grain spirits, in bottles	100	30	Dozen	2 50
in casks	100	30	Gallon	1 00
Gunpowder, in barrels or casks, of all sorts	20	15	25 pounds 7 oz	4 00
Hams and bacon, smoked	20	15	......do	3 00
salted, in barrels	20	15	101 pounds	5 00
Hats, straw, Italian or Chinese, for men	30	24	Dozen	18 00
from Guayaquil	30	24	......do	4 50 to 6 00
caps, made of cloth, for men	30	24	......do	18 00
for children	30	24	......do	10 00
Hosiery, cotton stockings for men	20	15	Dozen pairs	1 75
for women	20	15	......do	1 00
for children	20	15	......do	75
silk stockings for men and women	30	24	......do	10 00
embroidered	30	24	......do	12 00
wool stockings, white or colored	30	24	......do	3 00
Household furniture, chairs, common, wood	30	24	Dozen	20 00
the seating of junk	30	24	......do	30 00
made of fine woods	30	24	} ......do	} 50 00
the seating of hair, &c	30	24		
Iron, crude, of all kinds	30	24	101 pounds	4 00
cast, in pieces for domestic use, as cooking, &c	30	24	......do	6 00
do do the inside tinned	30	24	......do	10 00
cast, in boilers, for boiling the indigo	30	24	}	} Free.
in machines for sugar factories and others	30	24		
cast, in shovels, hoes, &c	30	24	101 pounds	6 00
steel	20	15	......do	7 00
Lard	20	15	......do	5 00
Linen, Irish	20	15	Yard	25
drills, middling	20	15	......do	15
fine	20	15	......do	30
bagging	20	15		Free.
laces, up to 1 inch broad	20	15	Yard	6
" 2 inches broad	20	15	......do	12
" 4 " "	20	15	......do	25
" 6 " "	20	15	......do	50

TARIFFS—Continued.

Denomination of merchandise.	Duties on imports into—			
	The United States, per cent. ad valorem, under the act of—		San Salvador.	
	1846.	1857.	Number, weight, or measure.	Fixed value.
Linen, stockings for men and women	20	15	Dozen pairs	$4 00
Linseed oil	20	15	Gallon	1 00
Liquors, gin, in bottles	100	30	Dozen	2 00
all other kinds, in bottles	100	30	do	2 50
in casks	100	30	Gallon	1 00
Marble, white or colored, in slabs for tables, and other uses, up to 20 inches wide.	30	24	Superficial foot	1 50
Ditto, up to 25 inches wide	30	24	do	2 00
more than 25 inches wide	30	24	do	3 00
Muskets and rifles	30	24		Prohibited.
Nutmegs	40	4	1 014 pound	50
Oil, spermaceti, whale, and all other fish	20	15	Gallon	1 00
Paints, in powder	20	15	25 pounds 7 oz	2 00
in oil	20	15	do	3 00
Paper, printing	30	24	Ream	1 50
letter	30	24	do	2 00
pasteboard	30	24	101 pounds	8 00
colored, gilt, silvered, marbled, &c., for artificial flowers, and other uses	30	24	Ream	4 00
painted and varnished, as paper hangings	20	15	Piece of 12 yards	1 50
Playing cards, of common paper	30	24	Gross	4 00
fine paper	30	24	do	8 00
Pitch	20	15	101 pounds	4 00
Pork, salt	20	15	do	5 00
Printing presses	30	24		Free.
Raisins	40	8	25 pounds 7 oz	2 00
Rice	20	15	do	3 00
Soap, common	30	24	101 pounds	8 00
fine, scented, in cakes	30	24	Dozen	30
Sugar of all kinds	30	24	101 pounds	30 00
Tar	20	15	do	4 00
Teas of all kinds	(a)20	(a)15	1 014 pound	50
Tin, crude, in bars	5	Free	101 pounds	18 00
worked, in pieces for domestic use	30	24	1.014 pound	40
Tobacco	30 to 40	24 to 30	Government	monopoly.
Trunks of wood, large	30	24	Pair	20 00
middling	30	24	do	15 00
small	30	24	do	8 00
Umbrellas, of silk	30	20	Dozen	36 00
of cotton	30	24	do	2 00
parasols, of silk	30	24	do	24 00

(a) See note, p. 168.

TARIFFS—Continued

DENOMINATION OF MERCHANDISE.	DUTIES ON IMPORTS INTO—			
	The United States, per cent. ad valorem, under the act of—		SAN SALVADOR.	
	1846.	1857.	Number, weight, or measure.	Fixed value.
Umbrellas and parasols, embroidered	30	24	Dozen	$30 00
Vinegar	20	15	Gallon	50
Wax, white, unmanufactured	20	15	101 pounds	45 00
Whale oil	20	15	Gallon	1 00
Wines, white, French, in bottles	40	30	Dozen	2 00
Champagne, in bottles	40	30	....do	6 00
Madeira and port, in bottles	40	30	....do	3 00
red, Spanish and French, in casks	40	30	Gallon	50
in bottles	40	30	Dozen	2 00
Woolen blankets, white or colored	20	15	....do	18 00
carpets, striped or with flowers, mixed with other stuffs or not, 1 to 3 yards long, and 1 to 2 yards broad.	30	24	One piece	15 00
stockings, white or colored	30	24	Dozen	3 00

COSTA RICA.

The tariff is that of August 31, 1854, with later modifications to take effect July 1, 1855.(a)

Money.—The same as in Mexico.

1 peso = 100 cents = $1.

Weights and measures.—1 quintal = 101.44 pounds.

1 libra = 1.014 pound.

1 arroba = 25 pounds 7 ounces.

1 vara = 33⅓ inches.

All manufacturers of tobacco, including cigars, gunpowder, and saltpetre, are government monopolies.

FREE LIST.

1. All printed books for instruction or entertainment, if they are not in opposition to religion and morals; also, all periodicals and every sort of printed publication.
2. Music and musical instruments, which are not manufactured at home.
3. Seeds and plants not cultivated in Costa Rica.
4. Gold and silver, in coins or dust.
5. All kinds of complete machines and iron wheels with teeth.
6. Quicksilver, stone coal, packthread, empty sacks, or materials of which to make them.
7. Instruments of art and science.
8. All kinds of carriages, coaches, cars, &c.

PROHIBITED LIST.

1. Tobacco, in leaf or manufactured.
2. All spirits of molasses or rum, such as is manufactured in Costa Rica; obscene pictures, books, and all other things offending the public morals; eatables spoiled or of bad quality, as dangerous to public health; fire-arms of all classes, and also munitions of war, if not ordered by the government itself.

Articles prohibited to be exported, are tobacco in leaves and stems, unless by special permit from the government.

Gold in coins pays at exportation two per cent. ad valorem; in ingots, powder, or jewels, four per cent. ad valorem; and silver in coins eight per cent. ad valorem.(b)

Coffee pays an exportation duty of 12½ cents per 101 pounds.

The money thus obtained is used for establishing new, and keeping in order the already existing turnpikes. All other goods are free of exportation duty. The duties may be paid after three, six, or nine months, according to the amount to be paid.

Punta Arenas, on the Pacific ocean, is a port entirely free of duties on importation, exportation, and deposit, as well as on loading and discharging cargoes; nor are anchorage or tonnage duties charged; but there are certain other duties to be paid, both by national and by foreign vessels, as follows:

1. Quarantine fees, when the vessel anchors in the bay, or in the interior harbor, for each foot of depth, 75 cents.
2. Clearance duty, three dollars.
3. Hospital(c) dues, fifty cents per head.
4. Light-house dues, six and one-quarter cents per ton.

Golfo Dulce, also situated on the Pacific, is, like Punta Arenas, a free port; but the roads thence into the interior are so rough that no importation can be effected.

Merchandise imported through the port of San Juan del Norte, (Greytown,) or on the river Sarapequi, at San José, pay the general tariff duties, with a deduction of ten per cent. ad valorem.

Merchandise imported through the port of Martina, on the Atlantic, pays at Cortago the duties established in the general tariff, with a deduction of 10 per cent. ad valorem. In Martina, foreign vessels are subject to 25 cents per ton tonnage duty; national vessels to only 12½ cents. If they come from Central American ports, they have to pay only one-half of the said tonnage duties.

Besides the importation and maritime duties, there are the following:

1. Storage, or warehouse rent, 6¼ cents for every 25 pounds gross weight per month.
2. Municipal and bridge tolls, (intended for turnpikes,) 37½ cents for each quintal, (101 lbs.)

(a) See Appendix.
For the tariff of Nicaragua of July 21, 1856, see Volume I "Digests," p. 599 *et seq.*

(b) An official publication of recent date says: "It is presumed that these duties are abolished."

(c) Founded for the benefit of foreigners as well as natives.

APPENDIX.

By a law which came into force August 1, 1857, the duties on certain articles imported into Costa Rica were reduced, and the rates now stand as follows:

Cottons—in blankets, unbleached, plain, serge, and canvas	5 cents per pound.
Japanned calf	20 "
Blacking	3 "
Matches	7 "
Wool, without being manufactured	2 "
Wick	6 "
Sandpaper	3 "
Perfumery, in oils and scented waters, small soaps, pastilles, powders, pomades, or any other such articles	10 "
Calf skins or tanned leather, of all colors, dressed skeep skins, and morocco leather	14 "
Powder, manufactured into crackers and artificial fire-works	16 "
Writing ink, in earthern or glass inkstands	5 "

By a decree of the president of the republic of Costa Rica, bearing date September 21, 1857, all foreign spirits are placed on the same footing as gunpowder, rum, and tobacco, which are contraband articles, except when imported on account of the government; and, according to article 22, chapter 11, of the tariff and custom-house ordinances, all vessels arriving at the port of Punta Arenas having on board any of these articles, are required to deposit them in the public stores, at the cost of $2 per month for each hundred weight, (although they may be destined for other ports,) or to leave the port within twelve hours. A translation of the decree is annexed:

"Considering, 1st. That the introduction into the republic of foreign liquors by private individuals is obviously prejudicial to the public revenue derived from those of domestic manufacture; 2d. That the frauds arising from their free introduction oblige the authorities to prosecute and punish those who sell liquor, clandestinely, and without previous permission; and 3d. That, on this account, reason, morality, and justice advise the prevention of the wrong, in order to escape the hard necessity of punishing it, I decree—

"ARTICLE 1. Ten months from this date the importation of every kind of foreign spirits, on account of private individuals, is prohibited; and those having these articles on hand at the termination of the period specified, are required to export them.

"ART. 2. The government will cause to be procured, on account of the state, all the various kinds of foreign spirits in common use, in order that the same may be expended in such public places as shall be instituted for this purpose; and the proprietors of hotels and restaurants will purchase at wholesale in those places for the supply of their establishments.

"ART. 3. The minister of finance is charged with the execution of the present decree, and with submitting the same for the approbation of the most excellent congress."

COMPARATIVE TARIFFS.

UNITED STATES AND COSTA RICA.

DENOMINATION OF MERCHANDISE.	DUTIES ON IMPORTS INTO— The United States, per cent. ad valorem, under the act of— 1846.	1857.	COSTA RICA. Number, weight, or measure.	Rate of duty.
Apples, fresh	20	8		Free.
Beef, salted	20	15	Quintal, or 101 lbs	$0 62½
Beer, ale, porter, and cider, in casks or bottles	30	24	do	1 00
Biscuit or ship bread	20	15	1.014 pound	3
Books, printed	10	8		Free.
Boots and shoes of all kinds	30	24	1.014 pound	25
Brandy, of sugar cane	100	30		Prohibited.
in bottles	100	30	1.014 pound	9
in barrels and demijohns	100	30	do	11
Bricks	20	15		Free.
Butter	20	15	101 pounds	3 00
Cables, iron	30	24	do	3 00
Cassia	40	4	1.014 pound	6¼
Cheese of all sorts	30	24	do	4
Cinnamon	30	4	do	6¼
Clothing, ready-made, for men and women—				
of cotton	30	24	do	15
linen	30	24	do	18
woolen	30	24	do	30
Cloths and cassimeres	30	24	do	25
Cloves	40	4	do	6¼
Coaches and other carriages	30	24		Free.
Coal, stone	30	24		Free.
Cocoa, in beans of all kinds	10	4	101 pounds	3 00
from Central America	10	4	do	1 50
ground, from all countries	10	4	1.014 pound	6
Combs	30	24	do	20
Coffee, foreign	(a)20	(a)15	do	25
Copper, in bars and pigs	5	Free	101 pounds	1 00
manufactured, in sheets	20	15		
kettles, stills, and similar articles, of more than two pounds weight.	30	24	101 pounds	10 00

(a)See note, page 114.

TARIFFS—Continued.

DENOMINATION OF MERCHANDISE.	DUTIES ON IMPORTS INTO—			
	The United States, per cent. ad volorem, under the act of—		COSTA RICA.	
	1846.	1857.	Number, weight, or measure.	Rate of duty.
Cotton, bleached	25	24	1.014 pound	$0 7
unbleached	25	24	do	5
drills, white	25	24	do	8
striped and printed	25	24	do	8
ready-made clothing	30	24	do	15
lace	25	19	do	25
Demijohns and bottles	30	24	101 pounds	2 50
Earthen and stone ware	30	24	do	1 50
porcelain, or imitation of	30	24	do	4 00
Fish, dry	20	15	do	2 00
Flour of all kinds	20	15		Free.
Grain spirits, in bottles	100	30	1.014 pound	9
in barrels and demijohns	100	30	do	11
Glass, all kinds, in bottles, vases, cups, &c	30	24	101 pounds	2 00
window	20	15	do	1 50
Gunpowder	20	15	Government monopoly	Governm't monopoly.
Hams and bacon	20	15	101 pounds	2 00
Hats, of beaver, fur, wool, felt	30	24	1.014 pound	15
straw, of jipijapa, and all other kinds	30	24	do	60
Hops	20	15		Free.
Horned cattle	20	Free		Free.
Hosiery, cotton	20	15	1.014 pound	12
woolen	30	24	do	8
silk	30	24	do	30
Household furniture	30	24	101 pounds	5 00
Indian corn	20	15		Free.
meal	20	15		Free.
Iron, in bars	30	24	101 pounds	37½
forged or beaten in square bars and sheets, round, or in any other shape.	30	24	do	50
castings, for balconies, windows, and similar objects.	30	24	do	1 00
cast, in pots, kettles, boilers, pans, and similar articles.	30	24	do	2 50
nails and screws, with or without heads, of other metal.	30	24	1.014 pound	2½
ploughs and harrows	30	24		Free.
locks, screws, keys, &c	30	24	1.014 pound	10
chains, of all sizes	30	24	101 pounds	3 00
hatchets, adzes, &c., over 2 lbs	30	24	do	2 50
steel, manufactured	30	24	1.014 pound	1
carpenters' tools of	30	24	do	6

TARIFFS—Continued.

DENOMINATION OF MERCHANDISE.	DUTIES ON IMPORTS INTO—			
	The United States, per cent. ad valorem, under the act of—		COSTA RICA.	
	1846.	1857.	Number, weight, or measure.	Rate of duty.
Jewelry	30	24	Ounce	$0 50
Lard	20	15	101 pounds	3 00
Linen, Irish	20	15	1.014 pound	15
drills	20	15	do	10
bagging	20	15		Free.
Linseed oil	20	15	1 014 pound	4
Liquors, as gin and spirituous liquors	100	30	do	11
of sugar cane, as rum	100	30		Prohibited.
Marble, manufactures of	30	24	101 pounds	5 00
unmanufactured, squared	20	15	do	1 00
Medicinal drugs	20	15	1.014 pound	12
Muskets, and all other fire-arms	30	24	101 pounds	(With permis'n) 10 00
Nutmegs	40	4	1.014 pound	6¼
Oil, spermaceti, of all kinds	20	15	Gallon	4
Paints	20	15	do	2
Paper, printing	30	24	101 pounds	2 00
writing	30	24	do	3 00
brown, wrapping	30	24	do	2 00
ruled, for music	30	24		Free.
Playing cards, common and fine	30	24	101 pounds	6 00
Pitch	20	15	do	1 00
Pork, salt	20	15	do	62½
Printing presses	30	24		Free.
Raisins	40	8	1.014 pound	2
Rosin	20	15	101 pounds	1 00
Rye, oats, and other small grain	20	15		Free.
Saddlery	30	24	1.014 pound	20
Soap, common, from foreign countries	30	24	do	2
perfumed, or not	30	24	do	4
common, from Central America and New Granada.	30	24	101 pounds	1 00
Spermaceti, unmanufactured	20	15	do	5 00
candles, and otherwise manufactured.	20	15	do	6 25
Spirits, of molasses	100	30		Prohibited.
Sugar, refined	30	24	101 pounds	1 00
Tallow, raw	10	8	do	1 00
candles	20	15	1.014 pound	2
composition	20	15	do	3
Tar	20	15	101 pounds	1 00
Teas, of all kinds	(a)20	(a)15	1.014 pound	6

(a) See note, p. 168.

TARIFFS—Continued.

DENOMINATION OF MERCHANDISE.	DUTIES ON IMPORTS INTO—			
	The United States, per cent. ad valorem, under the act of—		COSTA RICA.	
	1846.	1857.	Number, weight, or measure.	Rate of duty.
Tin, in bars and pigs	5	Free	101 pounds	$2 00
Tobacco	30 to 40	24 to 30	Government monopoly	Governm't monopoly.
Trunks, all kinds	30	24	1.014 pound	5
Turpentine, gum	20	15	101 pounds	3 00
Umbrellas and parasols, of silk	30	24	1.014 pound	20
of cotton	30	24	do	5
Vinegar, common	30	24	do	3
Wax, white and yellow	20	15	do	9
candles	20	15	do	12
Whale oil	20	15	do	4
Wines, of all classes, in casks, demijohns, or bottles.	40	30	101 pounds	2 00
Wood, manufactures, furniture	30	24	do	5 00
Woolen textiles, of all kinds, not otherwise described.	30	24	1.014 pound	20

SOUTH AMERICAN STATES.

SOUTH AMERICAN STATES.

NEW GRANADA.

The tariff is that established by the special decrees of October 18 and 31, 1854. It went into effect May 1, 1855. (a)

Moneys.—The same as in Mexico, viz: 1 peso = 8 reals = 100 cents $1.

Weights and measures.—1 pound = 1.014.
100 pounds = 4 arrobas.
100 pounds = 101½ pounds avoirdupois.
1 vara = 33⅓ inches English
1 quintal = 101.44 pounds.
1 kilogramme = 2.1.5 pounds.
1 miriagramo (or myriagramme) = 26 pounds, 9 ounces, 10 pennyweights.

Goods imported into the Isthmus of Panama, although a part of the New Granadian Republic, are exempt from duty; but, if imported from the Isthmus into New Granada, they are charged the regular duties as if coming from foreign countries.

FREE LIST.

Animals for breed; beaver and other skins; beehives and bees; books, printed; carts; casks; coal; gold, silver, and platina, in dust; implements for agriculture and mining; scientific and surgical instruments; medals; mills; paintings and engravings; paper for printing; plants; seeds; statues and busts; steam engines; wool; effects of ambassadors, and equipage of travellers.

PROHIBITED LIST.

Arms; obscene books and prints; coin, defaced or clipped; rum; tobacco, raw.

Coasting trade free to foreign vessels.

APPENDIX.

By virtue of the tariff act which came into force in New Granada, June 25, 1856, an increase of duty from 25 to 100 per cent was imposed on nearly every article of import, presenting an exception to the tariff modifications of almost every other commercial country for years past. The per centage increase of rates on the principal articles of merchandise, by virtue of this act, on the rates previously levied, has been noted as follows, fractions being disregarded: (b)

On the following articles the increase is 25 per cent.: steel, not manufactured; needles and fish hooks of certain descriptions; indigo; sugar candy; phials; cocoa, manufactured; cocoa nuts; padlocks of iron or brass; candlesticks of glass or chrystal; brushes for the teeth; nails, &c.; locks; beer; copper in sheets; glasses, small, for liquors, cut or not; knives for shoemakers, &c.; spurs, cast iron; chisels; bottles; large forge bellows; carbine hooks; buckles of metal; watchmakers' tools; common lead pencils; china ware, small articles; mirrors of certain sizes; hammers of all kinds; mills, small, and coffee mills, &c.; razors; brown paper; Jamaica pepper; pipes of clay, for smoking; dishes of glass or crystal; lead in pigs, plates, balls, and shot; metallic pens; reins for bridles; castors for tables, &c.; tallow or stearine; ink in powder, paste, or liquid; glasses, watch, magnifying, &c.

On the following articles the increase is 26 per cent.: spirits from cane and its compounds, in those provinces in which this article is not a monopoly; spirits of turpentine; scented waters of all kinds; iron wire; white lead in powder or oil; raw cotton in bulk and in seed; trunks with merchandise; bottles and demijohns; brooches for clasps, &c.; shoe brushes, &c.;

(a) The rates of this tariff were modified by an act of June 25, 1856, in conformity with which a new tariff was put forth under date of August 1 the same year. See Appendix.

See vol. 1, "Digests," p. 615, and vol. 3, "Returns," p. 482.

(b) See note, p. 98.

copper in bars or cakes ; compasses ; fine penknives ; spoons of tin, iron, copper, &c. ; large knives, and knives of ivory, &c., and balance handle knives with forks ; thimbles ; snuffers ; screwdrivers ; fowling pieces ; mirrors with gilt frames ; tin, pewter, &c., in bars or cakes ; felts for hats ; nails, brads, &c. ; liquor cases ; saddletrees ; toilet soap ; sealing wax ; files ; linen manufactures, common ; mustard ; mainsprings for clocks and watches ; paper, writing, hanging, &c. ; umbrellas of silk of all sizes ; pincers of all sorts ; pistols, common ; earthen pitchers, jars, &c. ; saltcellars of glass or crystal ; saws, pit and frame ; scissors, small, &c. ; turpentine ; zinc, manufactures of.

On the following articles the increase is 27 per cent. : cruet stands ; needles of wire, bone, &c. ; silver, brass, and piano wire ; door bolts, small ; carpeting in pieces ; cotton manufactures ; currycombs of iron ; plate holders ; pin cases ; chandeliers of glass or metal ; harness for two beasts ; trunks without merchandise ; scales ; bridle bits ; copper pumps for engines ; silk brocade ; wax candles ; bedsteads ; sofas ; sieves of wire, silk, &c. ; clothes brushes, &c. ; cranks of iron ; clothes presses ; watch guards ; swords ; small looking glasses ; iron pickaxes ; stirrups ; pianos ; flasks ; decanters ; small buckles for braces, &c. ; whips ; lawn ; lace ; fringes, &c., of linen ; porcelain ; manufactures of German silver ; saddles ; dial plates ; razors in cases ; organs ; gilt paper hangings ; cotton umbrellas ; pistols ; powder flasks ; bottle stands ; watches ; manufactures of silk of all kinds ; fine scissors ; gold braid ; window glass.

On a certain description of needles, packing, sailmakers', &c., the increase is 100 per cent. ; on irons for carpenters' planes, &c., and small hand bellows, 150 ; on fine gold wire, 154 ; and on sperm oil, manufactured, 160 per cent.

There is a decrease of duty on buttons of from 40 to 80 per cent. ; on chairs, of 68 ; augers, 36 ; common glass bottles, 40 ; gloves of buckskin, &c., 54 and 52 ; stirrup leathers, 37 ; and on a few other unimportant articles.

COMPARATIVE TARIFFS.

UNITED STATES AND NEW GRANADA.

DENOMINATION OF MERCHANDISE.	DUTIES ON IMPORTS INTO—			
	The United States, per cent. ad valorem, under the act of—		NEW GRANADA.	
	1846.	1857.	Number, weight, or measure.	Rate of duty.
Apples	20	8	Barrel	$0 80
Artificial flowers	30	24	Dozen	80
Beef	20	15		Free.
Beer	30	24	1. 014 pounds	0⅔
Biscuit and shipbread	20	15	2. 20 pounds	1
Brandy, of 20 degrees	100	30	...do	16
Brass, in pigs	5	Free	...do	4
in sheets	30	24	...do	10
otherwise manufactured	30	24	...do	15
Bricks and tiles	20	15		Free.
Brushes, horse	30	24	Dozen	40
cloth	30	24	...do	1 20
common, for shoes	30	24	...do	60
Butter	20	15		Free.
Cards, playing	30	24	Gross	4 80
Cassia	40	4	2. 20 pounds	60
Cheese	30	24	...do	2
Cloves	40	4	...do	20
Cinnamon	30	4	...do	60
Coal, stone	30	24		Free.
Coffee	(a)20	(a)15	2. 20 pounds	1
Combs	30	24	Dozen	40
Cotton, raw	Free	Free	2. 20 pounds	5
manufactured into shawls, stockings, gloves, bonnets, caps, &c	20 to 25	15 to 24	...do	40
muslins, gauzes, shawls, braids, and similar kinds	25	24	...do	55
all other manufactures	25	15 to 24	Miriágramo, (26 lbs 9 oz.	2 24
Earthen and stone ware, of all kinds	30	24	Dozen	20
Fish, pickled, salted, dry	20	15		Free.
Flour, wheat, maize, barley, or oats	20	15		Free.

(a) See note p. 114

TARIFFS—Continued.

DENOMINATION OF MERCHANDISE.	DUTIES ON IMPORTS INTO— The United States, per cent. ad valorem, under the act of— 1846.	1857.	NEW GRANADA. Number, weight, or measure.	Rate of duty.
Glass, window	20	15	Box of 100 to 125 pounds.	$2 40
watch crystals	30	24	Dozen	20
bottles, common	30	24	....do	5
Gunpowder, in barrels	20	15	1. 014 pounds	$2\frac{1}{2}$
Hams and bacon	20	15		Free.
Hats, straw, jipijapa	30	24	Dozen	3 60
other kinds	30	24	....do	60
of fur, of all sorts, trimmed	30	24	....do	4 80
not trimmed	30	24	....do	3 60
Household furniture, mahogany chairs, painted or varnished	30	24	....do	6 00
lounges	30	24	Each	12 50
tables	30	24	....do	5 00
Indian corn	20	15		Free.
Iron in bars	30	24		Free.
castings	30	24	Kilogramme, $2\frac{1}{5}$ lbs.	1
manufactures of	30	24	26 pounds 9 oz	24
nails, spikes, &c	30	24	....do	48
Lard	20	15		Free.
Lead in bars, sheets, balls, shot	20	15	26 pounds 9 oz	32
in pipes, and all other manufactures of	20 to 30	15 to 24	$2\frac{1}{5}$ pounds	5
Leather, tanned, horse, cow, and that of any other animal	20	15	....do	4
Lime	10	8	26 pounds 9 oz	1
Linen, unmanufactured	20	15	$2\frac{1}{5}$ pounds	4
manufactured into common cloths, drills, &c	20	15	....do	40
Irish linen	20	15	....do	60
laces	20	15	....do	6 00
Linseed oil	20	15	1. 014 pound	$3\frac{3}{5}$
Medicinal drugs	20	15		25 per cent. ad val.
Molasses	30	24	$2\frac{1}{5}$ pounds	1
Musical instruments, pianos	20	15	Each	20 00
flutes	20	15	....do	20
violins	20	15	....do	1 20
guitars	20	15	....do	80
Nuts	30	24	26 pounds 9 oz	0
Oil, whale and other fish	20	15	1. 014 pound	$6\frac{1}{4}$
Paints of all kinds	20	15	$2\frac{1}{5}$ pounds	12
Paper, writing	30	24	1 ream	40
brown	30	24	....do	20
Pepper	30	4	1. 014 pound	$3\frac{3}{5}$
Pitch	20	15	....do	$\frac{1}{2}$
Pork	20	15		Free.

TARIFFS—Continued.

DENOMINATION OF MERCHANDISE.	DUTIES ON IMPORTS INTO—			
	The United States, per cent. ad valorem, under the act of—		NEW GRANADA.	
	1846.	1857.	Number, weight, or measure.	Rate of duty.
Potatoes	30	24	26 pounds 9 oz	$0 02
Press, copying, for letters	30	24	do	80
Rice	20	15		Free.
Rye	20	15		Free.
Raisins	40	8	1. 014 pound	1¼
Saddlery, complete harness, fine, for two horses	30	24	Each	16 00
for one horse			do	7 00
common, for two horses			do	2 40
for one horse			do	1 60
Salt	20	15	26 pounds 9 oz	16
Silk, not manufactured	15	12	2⅓ pounds	1 60
manufactured into cloths	25	19	do	2 40
blondes, shawls, mantillas	25	24	do	4 80
Spermaceti, raw	20	15	do	10
candles	20	15	do	20
Sugar of all kinds	30	24		Free.
candy	30	24	2⅓ pounds	10
Tallow, raw, in paste or ste rine	10	8	do	2
Tar	20	15	26 pounds 9 oz	8
Teas	(a)20	(a)15	2⅓ pounds	20
Tin, manufactures of	30	24	do	25
Tobacco, cigars	40	30	do	80
cigarettos, (small cigars)	40	30	do	1 00
unmanufactured, leaf	30	24	do	20
Umbrellas and parasols, silk, of all sizes	30	24	Each	60
cotton, of all sizes	30	24	Dozen	2 00
Vinegar	30	24	2⅓ pounds	8
Wax, white or yellow	20	15	do	20
candles	20	15	do	40
Wines, red	40	30	do	6
all other	40	30	do	10
Wood, for construction, as lumber, boards, &c	20	15		Free.

(a) See note, p. 168.

VENEZUELA.

The tariff is that of May 7, 1841, with alterations down to 1852.(a) Weights, measures, and coins, the same as in Mexico; the Venezuelan dollar, however, differing in value. By a law of May 30, 1848, the dollar of the United States is made equal to $1 34⅜ Venezuelan currency.

In addition to the duties specified in the tariff, is an additional one of 10 per cent. ad valorem; and since July 1, 1851, by an act of Congress, a subsequent duty of 20 per cent. on the whole amount paid. In virtue of that act, articles put down in the tariff as free of duty have to pay 15 per cent. ad valorem. The whole duties, besides that given in the tariff, may be summed up as follows: 10 per cent. additional duty on the amount of the duty specified in the tariff; 3 per cent. road tax on the additional duty and the duty per tariff; 2 per cent. wharf dues on the same amount; 20 per cent. extra contribution, ditto; ¼ per cent. for the church, ditto.

All articles not enumerated in the tariff are subjected to a duty of 30 per cent. ad valorem. The importation of salt, cacao, molasses, sugar, and rum, is prohibited.

Duties are estimated upon the importer's valuation of the goods, without a custom-house oath, and are paid in the currency of Venezuela. Goods which are thought to be undervalued may be seized, on payment of 10 per cent. in addition to the valuation presented by the importer.

APPENDIX.

By a decree of the president of Venezuela, dated November 8, 1856, a new tariff of imports was established, to take effect, in virtue of a decree of subsequent date in regard to the United States, from and after April 1, of the same year. Under the former tariff, about one hundred and sixty enumerated articles paid duties ad valorem, while, under the recent decree, specific duties, with a few exceptions, are applied. The difference between the first or ordinary duty levied under the old Tariff and that levied under the new, on the principal articles imported into Venezuela from the United States, may be perceived at a glance from the comparative statement subjoined.

ARTICLES.	Old Tariff.	New Tariff.
Apples	15 per cent. ad valorem	50 cents per 100 pounds
Axes and hatchets	$1 50 per dozen	$1 60 per dozen
Beeswax, white	8 cents per pound	10 cents per pound
Beeswax, yellow	4 cents....do	5....do......do
Carriages	30 per cent. ad valorem	$50 each
Corn meal	15 per cent...do	25 cents per barrel
Cotton gins	.....do......do	$3 each
Corn shelling mills	.....do......do	$75 each
Candles, sperm	10 cents per pound	11 cents per pound
Candles, tallow	$4 per 101 pounds	$4 40 per 101 pounds
Candles, adamantine	30 per cent. ad valorem	7 cents per pound
Cotton, white, unbleached domestic	1¾ cent per yard	2 cents per yard
Gunpowder	12 cents per pound	15 cents per pound
Muskets	$1 50 each	$2 each
Matches, common	12 cents per dozen boxes	15 cents per M. matches
Nails, iron	$3 per 101 pounds	$3 30 per 101 pounds
Ox carts	15 per cent. ad valorem	$12 each
Potatoes	.....do......do	25 cents per barrel
Rye meal	1 cent per pound	1¼ cent per pound
Shot	$2 50 per 101 pounds	$2 75 per 101 pounds
Sealing-wax	37 cents per pound	40 cents per pound
Soap, common	4 cents per pound	3½ cents per pound
Tobacco, Virginia, leaf	$6 per 101 pounds	$6 60 per 101 pounds
Do.....do...manufactured	5 cents per pound	5½ cents per pound
Wheelbarrows	15 per cent. ad valorem	$1 each
Boards, white pine	$4 per M. feet	$4 40 per M. feet
Boards, pitch pine	$6 per M. feet	$6 60....do

(a) For subsequent changes and for additional duties or contributions imposed on duties collected, see Appendix and "Annual Reports on Foreign Commerce;" also, vol. iii, "Returns," pp. 437, *et seq.*

Butter, codfish, cheese, white bleached cotton domestics, flour, hams, herrings, and lard, bear the same ordinary or first duty in both tariffs.

Upon the above rates, additional duties or contributions, for various purposes, are levied. The method of estimating the duties on imports, in accordance with the tariff rates, and the additional duties, is exemplified in the Consular Returns from which these facts are derived, as follows:

According to the old tariff the duty on a barrel of flour was	$4 00
10 per cent. additional duty on $4	40
4 per cent. additional duty on $4 40	18
20 per cent. additional duty on $4 40	88
½ per cent. additional duty on $4 40	2
Total amount of duty	5 48

According to the new tariff the duty on a barrel of flour is	$4 00
4 per cent. additional duty on $4	16
20 per cent. additional duty on $4	80
½ per cent. additional duty on $4	2
Total amount of duty	4 98

"Thus it will appear (continues the Return) that the new tariff abandons the extra contribution of 10 per cent. upon flour; so, also, on butter, cheese, codfish; cotton, bleached domestics; hams, herrings, lard, soap, &c.; while it is merged into the first or ordinary duty upon many other articles; consequently, the latter will be admitted with but a slight charge. The new tariff imposes a duty upon merchandise or effects heretofore admitted free, with the exception of rice; trees for planting; beans; peas; mineral coal; vetches; luggage; herbage; corn; gold or silver in bars; samples of cloths, &c., of no value; gold in coin, in bars, or dust; platina in bars, &c.; cloth for chalice; live plants; seeds and wheat in grain; and prohibits absolutely the importation of salt, coffee, cocoa, sugar, molasses, and rum made from the sugar cane, unless imported in bottles. A decree, dated November 5, 1856, taking effect simultaneously with the new tariff, so far as the United States are concerned, prescribes regulations for the government of the officers of customs, tribunals, consuls, merchants, masters of vessels, &c., &c., in relation to imports from foreign countries at the ports of Venezuela, a translation of a portion of which, more immediately connected with the duties required to be performed by masters of vesels trading with Venezuela, and by merchants who may ship merchandise to the ports thereof, is annexed:

"ARTICLE 1. Immediately after a vessel anchors at any port of entry for external commerce in the republic, the collector of the customs, or any other person he may designate, and the commander of the revenue guard, where such officer is stationed, shall make the visit of entrance, accompanied by one or more watchmen.

"ARTICLE 2. If the vessel proceeds from a foreign port, and with cargo on board, the master will be required to deliver: 1st, the vessel's register; 2d, the manifest of the cargo, specifying the class and name of the vessel, the nation to which she belongs, her tonnage, the name of the master, the name of the port or place from whence proceeding, the number of packages of which the cargo consists, mentioning whether boxes, bales, barrels, trunks, hogsheads, &c., &c., and expressing, likewise, the numbers and marks, the name of the port to which the merchandise is destined, and the name of the consignees of the same, in conformity to the bills of lading signed by the master; and, at the port of the manifest, shall be made to appear a list of the ship's provisions or stores, and of the other articles on board, consisting of spare sails, rigging, &c., &c., belonging to and for the vessels use; 3d, a sealed package containing the original invoices of the merchandise shipped on board, *viséd* by the Venzuelan consul, or, in the absence of such consul, by that of a friendly or neutral nation; and if there be none such, then by the chief civil magistrate of the place from whence the shipment is made, it being necessary in this case to specify the fact of the absence of such Venzuelan or neutral consul. In order to comply with these requirements the merchants making the shipment will present to the respective functionary two copies of the invoice of merchandise shipped, expressing therein the quantity of goods, class, number, weight and measure, and the price. These two copies, which are required to be *viséd* by the consul, will be placed by the latter within sealed envelopes, one of which shall be delivered to the merchant, and the other forwarded by the consul to the collector of the customs of the port of the vessel's destination.

"ARTICLE 3 prescribes the penalties in the event of the infringement by the masters of vessels of the foregoing regulation. The failure to deliver the register subjects the vessel and cargo to embargo, and to be surrendered to the courts for adjudication according to the laws. The non-delivery of the manifest renders the master liable to a fine of $200; and when both the manifest and the bills of lading are missing, the decree imposes a penalty of $500. Should a master neglect, no matter for what cause, to deliver the sealed package containing the invoices, he subjects himself to a fine of $1,000; and, in the event of the seal of said package being broken, or the invoices being altered, or in any manner changed, the said master becomes liable to prosecution for a crime before the competent tribunal."

Under date of April 12, 1856, a decree was put forth by the Senate and House of Representatives of Venezuela in Congress assembled, as follows:

ARTICLE I. From the 1st day of July of the present year an extraordinary contribution shall be collected in the custom-houses of the republic upon the articles hereinafter designated and in the manner to be specified.

ART. 2. On all merchandise and effects subject to import duty, and which may be entered at any custom-house of the republic, there shall be levied an additional contribution of 20 per cent. upon the amount of said duties; and of 15 per cent. ad valorem upon free articles, excepting gold and silver in coin, in bars, bullion, or dust; printing presses and printed books; machinery, and other articles which were exempted from all duty for the benefit of public works by the legislative decree of February 22, 1851.

1st. The amount of these duties shall be paid in cash, if not exceeding $400; or within 30 days, should the amount exceed said sum.

2d. In liquidating these extraordinary duties, the rules and regulations established by law for the government of custom-houses shall be observed.

ART. 3. The national productions and manufactures hereinafter mentioned, and which may be exported at any of the ports of the republic, shall be subject to the following duty:

Cotton	$0 35	per quintal.
Starch	50	do.
Indigo	4	per pound.
Cocoa	50	per fanega.
Coffee	31¼	per quintal.
Horses	3 00	each.
Hides, raw, (ox and cow)	12½	each.
Hides of other animals	3	each.
Cattle	1 00	per head.
Hats (palm-leaf)	75	per dozen.
Mules	4 00	each.
Quina	1	per pound.
Tobacco (leaf)	1	do.
Sarsaparilla	2	do.
Mares	3 00	each.
Larrapia (Tonquin beans)	2	per pound.
Dye-wood	50	per ton.

ART. 4. Upon the national productions and manufactures not specified in the preceding article a duty of 4 per cent. ad valorem shall be levied and collected.

ART. 5. Gold and silver in coin shall be subject on exportation to a duty—the first mentioned of 1 per cent., and the latter of 2 per cent.

ART. 6. On the last day of every month a list shall be affixed to the doors of the custom-houses, containing the current prices of the national productions and manufactures at the respective ports, which, on being exported, are subject to the duty of 4 per cent., according to article 4.

ART. 7. The list of the prices-current designated in the preceding article shall be made, signed, and sworn to on the same day by a "junta," composed of the collector, deputy collector, the chief civil magistrate, a merchant, and an agriculturist appointed by the civil authority.

Lastly, the "junta," referred to in this article, shall be presided over by the chief civil magistrate.

ART. 8. The collector shall forward by the first mail to the tribunal of accounts a copy of said list, authenticated by himself and by the others who made it.

ART. 9. The legislative decrees of May 2, 1849, and April 23, 1851, are hereby repealed.

Under date of May 25, 1857, a decree was approved by the President of Venezuela, which provides as follows:

ART. 1. From the 1st of July of the present year there shall be levied throughout all the custom-houses of the republic a subsidiary contribution of 10 per cent. upon all the national duties which may be therein collected. This contribution shall be paid within 30 days after the liquidation of the duties.

ART. 2. The 2 per cent. established by article 3 of the law of April 29, 1856, in relation to port dues, are included in the 10 per cent. directed to be levied by the foregoing article.

* * * * * * * * * * * * *

ART. 4. The proceeds of this contribution shall be applied to objects and works of general utility and to the improvement of the towns.

* * * * * * * * * * * * *

ART. 8. The laws of May 10, 1847, April 23, 1853, and April 28, 1854, are hereby repealed.

By an act which took effect June 1, 1857, per centage increase of duty was imposed on certain articles, as follows:(a) On

(a) See note p. 98.

cotton damask, 12 per cent.; Britannias, 20; quiltings, 12; quilts, printed, 10; linen damask, 11; ticking, 20; bombazines, 12; flannel, 20; wove, in hanks, or worsted, 48; stockings, silk, linen, or woolen, 33; copper, in sheets, 17; unwrought, 10; nails, of copper or of mixed metal, 317; of iron, 100; tin sheets, in boxes, 10; lead, in pigs, 33; steel, in bars, large or small, 56; packing needles, 10; sewing or embroidery needles, 25. On cotton bombazette the per centage decrease is 16 per cent.; and on agricultural machines and those for cleaning cotton, free in 1856, a specific duty is imposed of $2 40, each, for the latter, and $1 20, each, for the former.

COMPARATIVE TARIFFS.

UNITED STATES AND VENEZUELA.

DENOMINATION OF MERCHANDISE.	DUTIES ON IMPORTS INTO—			
	The United States, per cent. ad valorem, under the act of—		VENEZUELA.	
	1846.	1857.	Number, weight, or measure.	Rate of duty.
Apples	20	8		15 per cent. ad val.
Beef, salted	20	15	1 pound 3 drs	$0 02
Beer, in bottles	30	24	12 bottles	80
in casks	30	24	4.245 gallons	50
Biscuit or ship bread	20	15	1 pound 3 drs	4
Books, printed	10 to 20	8 to 15		Free.
blank	20	15		30 per cent. ad val.
Boots, of leather, for men	30	24	Pair	1 50
shoes for men	30	24	....do	30
for women	30	24	....do	20
for children	30	24	....do	6
Brandy, in bottles	100	30	Dozen	4 00
in casks	100	30	25 pounds 7 oz	3 50
Bricks	20	15		Free.
Brushes, clothes	30	24	Dozen	2 00
shoe	30	24	... do	75
tooth	30	24	....do	50
Cables and cordage	25	19	101 pounds	2 00
Candles, tallow	20	15	....do	4 00
spermaceti	20	15	1 pound 3 drs	10
wax	20	15	....do	16
Castings, if for industrial or agricultural use	30	24		Free.
other	30	24		30 per cent. ad val.
Cigars, Havana	40	30	1,000	3 00
Virginia, San Domingo, and Porto Rico(a)	40	30	....do	2 00
Cider, in bottles	30	24	Dozen	80
in casks, &c	30	24	4.245 gallons	50
Cheese of all kinds	30	24	1 pound 3 drs	5
Cloves	40	4	....do	25
Coal, stone	30	24		Free.

(a) See note, page 319.

TARIFFS—Continued.

DENOMINATION OF MERCHANDISE.	DUTIES ON IMPORTS INTO—			
	The United States, per cent. ad valorem, under the act of—		VENEZUELA.	
	1846.	1857.	Number, weight, or measure.	Rate of duty.
Coaches and other carriages	30	24		30 per cent. ad val.
Copper, in sheets	20	15	101 pounds.	$3 00
manufactured, not otherwise enumerated	30	24		30 per cent. ad val.
Cotton for lamps, wicks	25	24	1 pound 3 drs.	18
yarn	25	24	do	18
batiste, (lawn)	25	24	Yard	3
Demijohns	30	24	Dozen	1 00
Earthen and stone ware	30	24		30 per cent. ad val.
Fish, salted, not otherwise enumerated	20	15	1 pound 3 drs.	4
salmon, salted	20	15	do	3
fresh	20	15	do	5
codfish	20	15	do	2½
Flour, wheat	20	15	1 barrel of 150 to 200 pounds.	4 00
Indian corn	20	15		Free.
rye or barley	20	15		Free.
Flowers, artificial	30	24	Dozen	30 per cent.
Fruits, dry, not specified	20	8	1 pound 3 drs	4
in brandy, &c	40	30	do	6
Glass, plain	20	15		30 per cent. ad val.
watch, spectacles, &c	30	24	Dozen	25
cylinders, large, for lamps	20	15	do	50
Gold and silver coins	Free	Free		Free.
Gunpowder	20	15	1 pound 3 drs	12
Hams and bacon	20	15	do	5
Hats, of beaver, wool	30	24	Each	1 00
of cotton or silk	30	24	do	50
fine, military	30	24	do	2 00
of jipijapa straw	30	24	do	50
Herrings	20	15	1 pound 3 drs	3
Indian corn, grain	20	15		Free.
Iron hoops	30	24	101 pounds.	1 60
Jewelry	30	24		3 per cent. ad val.
Lard	20	15	1 pound 3 drs	4
Lead, unmanufactured	20	15	101 pounds.	1 50
manufactured, and not enumerated	30	24		30 per cent. ad val.
shot	20	15	101 pounds.	2 50
Machines for agricultural and industrial purposes	30	24		Free.
Mackerel	20	15	1 pound 3 drs	4
Nails, iron	30	24	101 pounds.	3
copper, gilt or not	20	15	do	25
Nutmegs	40	4	1 pound 3 drs	50
Oil, whale and other fish	20	15	do	3
linseed	20	15	4.245 gallons	90

TARIFFS—Continued.

DENOMINATION OF MERCHANDISE.	DUTIES ON IMPORTS INTO— The United States, per cent. ad valorem, under the act of— 1846.	1857.	VENEZUELA. Number, weight, or measure.	Rate of duty
Oil, olive	30	24	Dozen bottles	$0 75
Pitch	20	15		Free.
Paper, music	30	24		Free.
letter	30	24	Ream, of 450 sheets	60
printing	30	24		Free.
Paints and varnish, prepared in oil	20	15	25 pounds 7 oz	1 00
Pepper, black	30	4	101 pounds	5 00
Pimento	40	4	do	3 00
Pork, salted or smoked	20	15	1 pound 3 drs	2½
Potatoes	30	24		15 per cent. ad val.
Printing presses	30	24		Free.
Rice	20	15		Free.
Rosin	20	15		Free.
Soap, common	30	24	1 pound 3 drs	4
perfumed and fancy	30	24	do	25
Spermaceti	20	15	do	10
Tallow, raw	10	8	101 pounds	2 00
manufactured	20	15	do	4 00
Tar, barrel of 8 arrobas	20	15	16 gallons	1 00
Teas	20(a)	15(a)	1 pound 3 drs	50
Tin, in powder	20	15	do	60
in bars and pigs	5	Free	101 pounds	6 00
Twine	30	24	1 pound 3 drs	5
Tobacco, from Havana, cigars	40	30	1,000	3 00
raw	30	24	1 pound 3 drs	10
from Virginia, San Domingo, Porto Rico, in cigars	40	30	1,000	2 00
Do do do do unmanuf'd	30	24	101 pounds	6 00
Umbrellas, silk, from 25 to 40 inches	30	24	One do	75
parasols, silk, up to 24 inches	30	24	do	50
cotton	30	24	do	25
Vinegar, in bottles	30	24	Dozen	1 00
in casks	30	24	4.245 gallons	50
Watches	10	8		3 per cent. ad val.
clocks	30	24		30 per cent. ad val.
Wax, white	20	15	1 pound 3 drs	8
yellow	20	15	do	4
Wood, boards, pine	20	15	M feet	6 00
shingles	20	15	M	1 00
Wines, Burgundy, Champagne, Madeira, and Oporto, in bottles	40	30	Dozen	3 00
the same in casks	40	30	4 245 gallons	2 00
red, Catalan, Marseilles, and all others not enumerated, in bottles	40	30	Dozen	1 00
the same in casks	40	30	4.245 gallons	75
white, in bottles	40	30	Dozen	1 00
in casks	40	30	4 245 gallons	75

(a) See note, page 168.

EQUADOR.

The tariff is that of November 4, 1849, ordered to be observed by the legislature of 1855.(a)

Money.—The same as in Mexico. 1 peso = 100 cents = $1.

Weight.—1 quintal = 4 arrobas (of 25 lbs. 7 ounces) = ⅝ avoirdupois.

Measure.—1 vara = 33⅓ inches English.

Goods re-exported pay 2 per cent. ad valorem, gold, silver, and jewels excepted.

The following ports are open to importation and exportation: Guayaquil, Manta, and San Lorenzo; and for exportation only, Santa Elena, Callao, and Bahia de Caracas. Loga and Ibarra, from the land side, are considered ports.

The duties are to be paid within ten days, when they amount to 100 pesos; within thirty days, when they amount to from 100 to 500 pesos; within forty-five days, when they amount to from 500 to 2,000 pesos; within seventy-five days, when they amount to from 2,000 to 6,000 pesos; within one hundred days, when they amount to from 6,000 to 12,000 pesos; and when more than 12,000 pesos, in one hundred and fifty days.

Besides the duties, there are levied small sums as toll tax, (*derecho depeso.*)

Export Duties.—Gold, ½ per cent. ad valorem; silver, 1 per cent.; mangelwurzel, 50 cents per 100 lbs.

Straw, for hats, 10 per cent. ad valorem.

Free List.—Printed books and music, maps, ships' materials, fresh fruit, vegetables, fire engines, surgical and mathematical instruments, agricultural implements, tools of immigrants, useful machines and inventions, &c.

(a) See vol. 1 "Digests," p. 688.

By a law of November, 1856, an export duty of 50 cents per 100 lbs. on Peruvian bark, sarsaparilla, and India rubber, imposed by a law of 1855, was repealed; and by the same law the duties on certain articles were modified so as to stand as follows:

Brandy and other ardent spirits, (except gin,) in bottles, per dozen	$2 00
Brandy and other ardent spirits, in barrels, per gallon	50
Alcohol, per gallon	1 50
Wooden painted trunks, each	25
Sieves, per dozen	50
Iron stoves and furnaces, per pound	4
Flour, per barrel, or sack of 200 pounds	6 00

COMPARATIVE TARIFFS.

UNITED STATES AND EQUADOR.

DENOMINATION OF MERCHANDISE.	DUTIES ON IMPORTS INTO— The United States, per cent. ad valorem, under the act of—		EQUADOR.	
	1846.	1857.	Number, weight, or measure.	Rate of duty.
Apples	20	8		Free.
Beef	20	15	101 pounds	$2 00
Beer, in bottles	30	24	Dozen	75
in casks	30	24	Gallon	25
Biscuit or ship bread, fine	20	15	101 pounds	4 00
common	20	15	do	3 00
Books, printed	10 to 20	8 to 15		Free.
blank	20	15	1 pound 3 drs	6¼
Boots and half boots, for men	30	24	Pair	1 50
shoes of calfskin, for men	30	24	do	6 00
for mariners and soldiers	30	24	do	1 50
Brandy, in bottles	100	30	Dozen	2 00
in casks	100	30	Gallon	75
Brushes, clothes	30	24	Dozen	75
common, for shoes	30	24	do	25
tooth	30	24	do	12½
Cables and cordage	25	19	101 pounds	37½
Camphor	25 to 40	8 to 30	1 pound 3 drs	30
Candles, wax	20	15	do	18¾
tallow	20	15	do	3
spermaceti	20	15	do	6¼
composition	20	15	do	6¼
Cigars	40	30	1,000	5 00
Cider, in bottles	30	24	Dozen	1 00
in casks, &c.	30	24	Gallon	25
Cheese of all kinds	30	24	101 pounds	2 00
Cloves	40	4	1 pound 3 drs	6¼
Coal, stone	30	24	101 pounds	4
Coaches and other carriages	30	24	One	5 00
Copper, in bars	5	Free	101 pounds	2 50
manufactured in utensils, &c	30	24	1 pound 3 drs	6¼

TARIFFS—Continued.

Denomination of merchandise.	Duties on imports into— The United States per cent. ad valorem, under the act of— 1846.	1857.	Equador. Number, weight, or measure.	Rate of duty.
Cotton, raw	Free	Free	101 pounds	$0 50
drills	25	24	Yard	2½
shirtings	25	24	do	2
osnaburgs	20	15	do	2
Earthen and stone ware	30	24	Crate	5 00
Fire engines	30	24		Free.
Fish, stock	20	15	101 pounds	3 00
salmon, salted	20	15	do	3 00
fresh	20	15	1 pound 3 drs	12½
all other salted	20	15	101 pounds	2 00
Flour, wheat, in barrels, or sacks of 190 to 200 pounds	20	15	One	7 50
rye	20	15	101 pounds	2 00
Indian corn	20	15	do	2 00
barley	20	15	do	3 00
Flowers, artificial	30	24	Dozen	1 00
Fruits, dry	20	8	1 pound 3 drs	3
fresh, of all kinds	20	8		Free.
in brandy, &c.	40	30	1 pound 3 drs	6¼
Glass, plain, boxes of 100 feet square	20	15	Box	1 00
watch	30	24	Gross	1 25
Gold and silver coins	Free	Free		Free.
Gunpowder	20	15	101 pounds	2 00
Hams and bacon of Chili	20	15	Each	12½
from other parts	20	15	do	50
Hats of cotton, wool, or silk	30	24	do	1 00
for soldiers and priests	30	24	do	1 25
manilla	30	24	Dozen	12 00
of Italian straw, for ladies	30	24	Each	2 00
Herrings	20	15	101 pounds	3 00
Hides and skins, of oxen	raw 5	4	Each	25
of goats			Dozen	36
of the vicuña of Chili(a)	tann'd 20	15	Each	36
Household furniture, tables	30	24	do	4 50
Indian corn	20	15	101 pounds	1 00
Indigo	10	4	1 pound 3 drs	12½
Lard	20	15	101 pounds	4 50
Lead, in bars	20	15	do	1 00
in sheets	20	15	do	1 25
all manufactures of	30	24	do	1 50
shot	20	15	do	2 00
Machines for sugar manufacturing	30	24		Free.
Mackerel	20	15	101 pounds	2 00

(a) See note, p. 31

TARIFFS—Continued.

DENOMINATION OF MERCHANDISE.	DUTIES ON IMPORTS INTO—			
	The United States, per cent. ad valorem, under the act of—		EQUADOR.	
	1846.	1857.	Number, weight, or measure.	Rate of duty.
Marble, manufactured, in pieces	30	24	101 pounds	$1 00
Nails, iron	30	24	do	1 00
copper	20	15	do	1 44
tacks, of gilt metal	30	24	1 pound 3 drs	6¼
Nutmegs	40	4	do	25
Oil, whale and other fish	20	15	Gallon	5
spermaceti	20	15	do	8
linseed	20	15	do	12½
olive, in bottles	30	24	Dozen	62½
in casks	30	24	Gallon	15
Pitch	20	15	101 pounds	30
Paints and varnish	20	15	do	2 00
Pork, salted	20	15	do	2 00
Paper, letter	30	24	Ream	25
ruled, for music	30	24		Free.
printing, large sheets	30	24	Ream	75
Pepper, black	30	4	101 pounds	2 00
Pimento	40	4	do	3 00
Rice	20	15	do	3 00
Rosin	20	15	do	20
Soap, common	30	24	do	1 50
perfumed, in cakes	30	24	Dozen	12½ to 25
Sugar, refined	30	24	101 pounds	4 00
Tallow	10	8	do	2 00
Tar	20	15	do	25
Teas	20(a)	15(a)	1 lb 3 drs	18¾
Tin, in bars	5	Free	101 pounds	2 50
Tobacco—Bracamoro, Brazilian, Central American, Paraguayan, Laña, Virginia, Macassar, or from other parts	Unmanufactured, 30; Manufactured, 40	Unmanufactured, 24; Manufactured, 30	101 pounds	10 00
Cuban cigars	40	30	1,000	5 00
Trunks	According to material.		Two	4 00
Chinese			do	3 00
Umbrellas, of silk	30	24	Each	1 00
cotton	30	24	Dozen	2 00
parasols	30	24	Each	50 to 1 00
Vinegar	30	24	Gallon	15
Watches, of gold	10	8	Each	12 50
silver	10	8	do	5 00
clocks	30	24	do	5 00

(a) See note, p. 168.

TARIFFS—Continued.

DENOMINATION OF MERCHANDISE.	DUTIES ON IMPORTS INTO—			
	The United States, per cent. ad valorem, under the act of—		EQUADOR.	
	1846.	1857.	Number, weight, or measure.	Rate of duty.
Wax, white, raw	20	15	101 pounds	$9 00
manufactured	20	15	do	14 50
Wood, boards one inch thick	20	15	Foot	2
shingles	20	15	M	3 36
Whiskey and gin, in bottles	100	30	Dozen	1 50
in casks	100	30	Gallon	50
Wines, Burgundy, in bottles	40	30	Dozen	2 00
Oporto, in bottles	40	30	do	2 00
Champagne and Rhenish	40	30	do	2 00
all other, in bottles	40	30	do	1 00
red and white, and all other, in barrels	40	30	Gallon	15

BRAZIL.

The tariff is that of August 12, 1844.(a)

For the despatch of goods subject to ad valorem duties, the merchant or consignee is obliged to show a declaration stating the prices of his goods, and the original invoices duly certified.

In the absence of the original invoice, there may be presented two certificates by two brokers, or by two merchants of the place, showing the current prices of the goods.

Transit duty, 1 per cent. ad valorem.

Money.—1 milrei = 1,000 reis, and varies in value. It is estimated in the tariff of 1844 at 55 cents.

Weights and Measures.—Generally the same as in Portugal. 1 arroba = $32\frac{1}{2}$ lbs.; 1 quintal = 4 arrobas = 128 arratels, or about $129\frac{1}{2}$ lbs. English; 1 arratel = 1 lb.; 1 alqueire of Rio Janeiro = 1.135 bushel; 1 alqueire of Bahia = 0.863 bushel; 1 canada of Bahia = 1.87 gallon; 1 canada of Rio Janeiro = 0.364 gallon.

The weights and measures of Brazil, as compared with those of the United States, may be stated as follows:

98.8 Brazilian libras = 100 United States pounds.
133 ...do....varas = 100......do..... yards.
141.6...do....canadas = 100......do..... gallons.
97 ...do....alqueires = 100......do..... bushels.

APPENDIX.

The tariff of August 12, 1844, has been superseded by a new one, bearing date March 28, 1857, to take effect July 1, of the same year. By this tariff, important reductions are made on raw materials and articles of food, while to a large number of articles are assigned fixed duties, on which, under the old tariff, were levied ad valorem rates of from 20 to 30 per cent. The subjoined statement has been received from United States consuls at Brazilian ports:

Duties on the principal articles of merchandise imported from the United States by the new Brazilian tariff, to take effect on and after the 1st July, 1857, the value of the milrei being calculated at fifty-five cents federal currency.

ARTICLES.		Duty by the new tariff, in dollars and cents.	Duty by the old tariff, in dollars and cents.
Flour	per barrel	$1 32	$1 65
Beef	do	1 84	2 76
Pork	do	2 08	3 57
Rosin	do	15	1 06
Pitch	do	58	58
Tar	do	1 34	48
Blue drills, 30-inch	per yard	$3\frac{3}{4}$	Very nearly the same.
Striped drills, 27-inch	do	$3\frac{1}{2}$	
Plain stripes, 27-inch	do	$2\frac{7}{8}$	
Gray drills, 27-inch	do	$2\frac{7}{8}$	
White drills, 27-inch	do	$3\frac{1}{2}$	
Domestics, 30-inch	do	$2\frac{1}{3}$	
Gray osnaburgs, if under 40 reed, 25 inch	do	$2\frac{3}{8}$	
if over 40 reed, 25-inch	do	$1\frac{7}{8}$	

(a) See Appendix. See Vol. 3 "Returns," p. 456.

TARIFFS—Continued.

ARTICLES.	Duty by the new tariff, in dollars and cents.	Duty by the old tariff, in dollars and cents.
Pilot bread and crackers.........per arroba, 32⅜ lbs. English..	$0 22	$0 55
Navy bread, ordinary.........do.........do.........	9	22
Lard.........do.........do.........	82	82
Hams.........do.........do.........	1 23	1 06
Cheese.........do.........do.........	2 11	2 11
Tea (of any quality).........per pound....	24¾	33
Pepper (India).........do.........	3⅝	2¾
Cinnamon, China, or white.........do.........	8	8
Ceylon.........do.........	27½	....
Wax, white.........do.........	12	11½
yellow.........do.........	11	11½
Spirits of turpentine.........do.........	0⅝	2½
Sperm candles.........do.........	11½	10
Whale oil.........per gallon....	14	14
Codfish, drum.........4 arrobas, per quintal, 129½ pounds English..	82	1 38
Pine boards, inch.........per 1,000....	5 31	6 32
Clocks, all of wood.........each.........	66 }	30 per ct. ad val.
metal mountings.........do.........	1 32 }	
Agricultural instruments.........5 per cent. ad val.	....	....
Machinery for the use of manufactories, steamships, and railroads.......do.	....	....
Wooden buckets with iron hoops.........each.........	6⅗	6⅗
Whale boats of 4 oars.........do.........	24 75	30 per cent.
of more than 4 oars.........do.........	33 00	....do.
Boats of 2 oars.........do.........	16 50	....do.
Launches.........do.........	33 00	....do.
Floor matting of straw.........per yard....	13⅕	13⅕
Sail twine.........per arroba...	66	1 32
Ice.........per ton......	11	99
Paste blacking.........per pound...	9 9/10	21½
Iron nails, up to 2 inches in length.........per arroba...	88	1 32
American arm chairs, painted or varnished.........each.........	56	Not provided for.
Chairs, ordinary, painted or varnished.........do.........	35⅕	....do......do.
American rocking chairs, painted or varnished.........do.........	2 64	....do......do.
Stuffed rocking chairs, all kinds.........do.........	6 60	3 30
Plain rocking chairs.........do.........	5 50	3 30

The annexed statement affords a comparison of the rates of duty on the principal articles of importation into Brazil, under the tariffs of 1844 *and* 1857, *in milreis, the value of the milrei being about* 55 *cents federal currency.*

DUTIES ON IMPORTS INTO BRAZIL.

UNDER THE TARIFF OF 1844.

Articles.	Reis.	Per—	Tare.	Remarks.
			Per cent.	
Ale and porter	300	Canada		In casks.
	400			In bottles or jugs.
Bran	300	Arroba	2	In bags.
Brandy, 20° proof, Cartier	500	Canada		In casks.
Butter	120	Pound	30	In barrels.
Candles—				
Sperm	180	do	Net.	
Composition	200	do	Net.	
Cigars	1‖500	100		
Cheese—				
Dutch	240	Each	16	In single cases.
English	180	Pound	22	In cases with partitions.
Other sorts	120	do		
Coals	600	Ton		
Codfish	2‖500	Quintal	14	In barrels or cases.
Coffee bagging	61½	Vara		
Copper	120	Pound	4	In barrels.
Cordage—				
Russian and English	6‖000	Quintal	Net.	
Manilla	75‖00	do	Net.	
Coir	4‖500	do	Net.	
Deals, 3 by 9 inches, and 14 feet	4‖355	Dozen		
Demijohns—				
One gallon	120	Each		
Three gallons	180	do		
Five gallons	240	do		
Duck—				
English	3‖000	Piece		
German	3‖000	do		
Russian	3‖000	do		
Flour	3‖000	Barrel		6 arrobas.
Gin—				
In casks	300	Canada		
In demijohns	540	do		
In jugs	400	do		
In cases	400	do		
Glass—				
Bottles	2‖500	100		
Window	1‖800	Box		

DUTIES ON IMPORTS INTO BRAZIL—Continued.

UNDER THE TARIFF OF 1844.

Articles.	Reis.	Per—	Tare.	Remarks.
			Per cent.	
Grease	1‖200	Arroba	10	In barrels or pipes.
Gunpowder	180	Pound	Net.	
Hams—				
Covered	1‖920	Arroba		
Salt			40	In barerls.
Hides—				
Ox, dry	40	Pound		
Salted	30	do		
Iron, bar—				
Swedish	1‖750	Quintal	Net.	
British	1‖250	do		
Jerked beef	500	Arroba	Net.	
Lard	1‖500	do	22	In barrels.
Lead—				
Bar and sheet	3‖000	Quintal	Net.	
Shot	4‖500	do	10	In barrels.
Linseed oil	54	Pound	16	In barrels or casks.
Lumber	11½	Foot		
Mess beef	750	Arroba	30	In barrels.
Mess pork	1‖000	do	30	In barrels.
Olive oil—				
In casks	360	Canada		
In bottles	750	do		
Paper, wrapping, up to 14 inches	210	Ream		
Pepper	50	Pound	2	In bags.
Pitch—				
Swedish	3‖000	Barrel		
American	1‖050	do		
Raisins	1‖200	Arroba	10	In boxes.
Rice	120	do	10	In barrels.
In husk	100	do	2	In bags.
Rosin	960	Quintal	10	In barrels.
Sail cloth—				
Russian	6‖000	Piece		
English	4‖800	do		
Narrow	3‖600	do		
German	6‖000	do		
Sail twine	120	Pound	18	In barrels.
Salt	160	Alqueire		
Saltpetre	1‖250	Arroba	10	In barrels.
Sewing silk	1‖000	Pound		
Soap—				
Mediterranean	70	do	18	In boxes.
Other sorts	40	do		
Spirit	300	do	Net.	

DUTIES ON IMPORTS INTO BRAZIL—Continued.

UNDER THE TARIFF OF 1844.

Articles.	Reis.	Per—	Tare.	Remarks.
			Per cent.	
Steel	4‖000	Quintal	8	In boxes.
Tallow—				
In barrels	1‖080	Arroba	14	
In bladders	1‖500	do	10	
In candles	2‖800	do	10	
Tar—				
Swedish	2‖000	Barrel		
American	875	do		
Tea	600	Pound	30 24 22 20	
Tin plates	4‖000	Box		
Tobacco—				
Roll	6‖000	Arroba	10 2 12	In boxes. In bales. In barrels.
Leaf	6‖000	do		
Turpentine	85	Pound	20 10	In barrels. In tins.
Vermicelli	1‖200	Arroba	10	In boxes.
Vinegar	80	Canada		
Wax—				
White or yellow	210	Pound	Gross.	
In candles or roll	225	do	Net.	
White lead	4‖800	Quintal	8	In barrels.
Wines—				
Red or white, Lisbon, in casks	240	Canada		
Port, Feitoria, in casks	500	do		
Port, common, in casks	220	do		
Champagne, in casks	750	do		
in bottles	2‖400	do		
Sherry, in casks	600	do		
in bottles	1‖500	do		
Madeira, superior, in casks	600	do		
ordinary, in casks	200	do		
in bottles	1‖500	do		
Bordeaux, superior, in casks	280	do		
ordinary, in casks	200	do		
fine, in bottles	1‖500	do		
ordinary, in bottles	600	do		
Figueira, in casks	200	do		
Burgundy, in bottles	1‖500	do		
in casks	200	do		
Rhenish, white or red, in bottles	1‖500	do		

By the old tariff all sorts of Portuguese, Spanish, French, and other sorts of wines from the Mediterranean, used to pay 200 rs. per canada.

All other sorts not specified, in bottles, 1‖200 per canada.

In the above duties were included those of the common bottles; if the wines were imported in flasks or other sort of vessels, these had then to be paid for according to the tariff.

DUTIES ON IMPORTS INTO BRAZIL—Continued.

UNDER THE TARIFF OF 1857.

Articles.	Reis.	Per—	Tare.	Remarks.
			Per cent.	
Ale and porter—				
In casks	300	Canada		5 p.ct. abatem'nt breakage.
In bottles	450	do		
In jugs	360	do		
Bran	150	Arroba	10	In barrels or cases.
Brandy, 20° proof, Cartier	750	Canada		5 p.ct. abatem'nt breakage.
Butter	120	Pound	26	
Candles—				
Sperm	210	do	12	In boxes.
Composition	200	do	10	In boxes.
Cigars	900	do	8	In boxes.
Cheese—				
Dutch	120	do	15	In boxes.
English	180	do	20	In boxes with partitions.
Other sorts	120	do		
Coals	600	Ton	Net.	
Codfish	1‖500	Quintal	12	In barrels, tubs, cases, &c.
Coffee bagging	80	Pound	5	In cases.
Copper	100	do	5	In barrels or cases.
Cordage—				
Russian and English	4‖800	Quintal		
Manilla	6‖000	do	Net.	
Coir	3‖600	do		
Deals, 9 inches and 14 feet	7‖258	Dozen		2½ to 3 inches.
	4‖838	do		2 to 2½ inches.
	3‖629	do		½ to 2 inches.
	2‖419	do		1 to 1½ inch.
	1‖205	do		1 inch.
Demijohns	20	Pound	20	In barrels or cases.
	20	do	20	In barrels or cases.
	20	do	20	In barrels or cases.
Duck—				
English	120	do	Net.	
German				
Russian				
Flour	2‖400	Barrel	10	In barrels.
			2	In sacks.
Gin—				
In casks	300	Canada		
In demijohns	360	do		
In jugs	360	do		
In cases	450	do		

DUTIES ON IMPORTS INTO BRAZIL—Continued.

UNDER THE TARIFF OF 1857.

Articles	Reis.	Per—	Tare.	Remarks.
			Per cent.	
Glass—				
Bottles	20	Pound	10	In crates.
Window	20	do	20	In barrels.
Grease	750	Arroba	12	In barrels and cases.
Gunpowder	200	Pound	10	In barrels.
			2	In tins.
Hams—				
Covered	2||240	Arroba	2	
Salt	1||280	do	45	
Hides –				
Ox, dry	40	Pound	Net.	
Salted	40	do	Net.	
Iron bar—				
Swedish	400	Quintal	Net.	
British	400	do	Net.	
Jerked beef	400	Arroba		
Lard	1||500	do	25	In barrels or tubs.
Lead—				
Bar and sheet	3||000	Quintal	5	In barrels or boxes.
Shot	4||500	do	5	Idem.
Linseed oil	10	Pound	16	In barrels and ½ casks.
			5	In tins.
Lumber	19½	Foot		
Mess beef	480	Arroba	35	In barrels or tubs.
pork	540	do		
Olive oil—				
In casks	360	Canada		
In bottles	540	do		
		do		In bottles.
Paper, wrapping	30	Pound	2	In bales.
			10	In cases.
Pepper	70	do	2	In bags.
Pitch—				
Swedish	200	Arroba	20	In wooden casks.
American	150	do	20	Idem.
Raisins	1||200	do	8	In boxes.
Rice	120	do	14	In barrels or cases.
in husk	100	do	14	Idem.
Rosin	150	Quintal	17	Idem.
Sail cloth—				
Russian, English, Narrow, German	120	Pound	Net.	
Sail twine	37½	do	Net.	

DUTIES ON IMPORTS INTO BRAZIL—Continued.

UNDER THE TARIFF OF 1857.

Articles.	Reis.	Per—	Tare.	Remarks.
			Per cent.	
Salt	50	Alqueire		
Saltpetre—				
Refined	320	Arroba	10	In barrels.
Raw	250	do	10	Idem.
Sewing silk	1‖200	Pound	Gross.	
Soap—				
Mediterranean	50	do	10	In boxes.
Other sorts	30	do	10	Idem.
Spirit	750	Canada		20° proof.
Steel	800	Quintal	5	In barrels or boxes.
Tallow—				
In barrels	540	Arroba		
In bladders	750	do	12	In barrels or cases.
In candles	1‖800	do		
Tar—				
Swedish	500	do	20	In barrels.
American	400	do	20	Idem.
Tea	450	Pound	32	Wooden boxes, up to 20 lbs.
			25	Idem, 40 pounds.
			23	Idem, 70 pounds.
			22	Idem, 100 pounds.
			40	In double wooden chests.
			18	In tins.
Tin plates	900	Arroba	5	In barrels or boxes.
Tobacco—			8	In boxes.
Roll	3‖000	do	10	In barrels.
Leaf	3‖600	do	2	In bags or bales.
			5	In roll.
Turpentine	10	Pound	2	In tins.
			10	In jugs.
Vermicelli	600	Arroba	10	In barrels or boxes.
Vinegar	80	Canada		
Wax—				
White or yellow	200	Pound	Gross.	
In candles or roll	300	do	Net.	
White lead	1‖200	Quintal	10	In barrels or boxes.
Wines—				
Red or white Lisbon	240	Canada		
Port, Feitoria	600	do		
Port, common	240	do		
Champagne	2‖400	do		
Champagne	2‖400	do		
Sherry	600	do		
Sherry	900	do		

DUTIES ON IMPORTS INTO BRAZIL—Continued.

UNDER THE TARIFF OF 1857.

Articles.	Reis.	Per—	Tare.	Remarks.
			Per cent.	
Wines—Continued.				
Madeira, superior	600	Canada		
Madeira, ordinary	240	do		
Madeira	900	do		
Bordeaux, superior	280	do		
Bordeaux, ordinary	200	do		
Bordeaux, fine	420	do		
Bordeaux, ordinary	300	do		
Figueira	240	o		
Burgundy	420	do		
Burgundy	280	do		
Rhenish, white or red	2||400	do		

By the new tariff the party is allowed 5 per cent. abatement for breakage, having at the same time the right of paying, if it suits him, for the quantity in a perfect condition, after a verification of the real amount of breakage.

The above applies to all liquids in whatsoever vessels they may be imported.

All liquors imported in demijohns or jugs must pay 20 per cent., and in bottles, 50 per cent. over the duty they pay when coming in casks; we must, however, observe, that in the above table the duties for ale, porter, and gin already comprehend this per centage.

Brazil and English weights and measures compared.—Libra, 1.012 pound. Arroba, 32.379 pounds. Quintal, 127.517 pounds. Alqueire, .998 bushel. Canada, .703 old gallon. Pipe, 126.587 old gallon.

COMPARATIVE TARIFFS.

UNITED STATES AND BRAZIL.

DENOMINATION OF MERCHANDISE.	DUTIES ON IMPORTS INTO—			
	The United States, per cent. ad valorem, under the act of—		BRAZIL.	
	1846.	1857.	Number, weight, or measure.	Rate of duty.
Bacon	20	15	Pound	$0 03
Beef, dried	20	15	Arroba, (32½ lbs.)	27½
salted	20	15	do	41¾
Beer, in casks	30	24	Canada of Bahia, (1. 87 gallon.)	16½
in bottles	30	24		22
Boots for men	30	24	Pair	51⅗
for soldiers	30	24	do	17⅗
for boys	30	24	do	26⅖
and shoes for women, of leather	30	24	do	17⅗
Brandy, whiskey, rum	100	30	1. 87 gallon	27½
Brass, in plates	30	24	Pound	6½
Bricks	20	15	,000	2 43⅗
Brushes, clothes, common	30	24	Dozen	41¾
fine	30	24	do	1 65
hair, common	30	24	do	51⅘
fine	30	24	do	1 05⅗
tooth, common	30	24	do	13⅕
fine	30	24	do	33
shoe	30	24	do	39⅗
Butter	20	15	Pound	6½
Cables and cordage of flax	25	19	100 arratels, 129½ lbs.	3 30
Camphor, crude	25	8	Pound	27¾
refined	40	30	do	27¾
Candles, spermaceti	20	15	do	10
tallow	20	15	32½ pounds	1 42
wax	20	15	Pound	11
Cattle, horned, for breed	Free	Free		5 to 10 per cent. ad valorem.
otherwise	20	Free		
Cheese, English	30	24	Pound	10
other kinds	30	24	do	6½
Cocoa	10	4	32½ pounds	66

TARIFFS—Continued.

Denomination of merchandise.	Duties on imports into— The United States, per cent. ad valorem, under the act of— 1846.	185	Brazil. Number, weight, or measure.	Rate of duty.
Copper for sheathing ships	Free	Free	Pound	$0 06½
Coal, stone	30	24	Ton, (2,200 lbs.)	33
Coaches and other carriages	30	24		
Cars with two wheels	30	24	Each	13 20
with four wheels	30	24	do	(a)26 40
Coaches with four wheels, with cushions	30	24	do	462 00
without cushions	30	24		396 00
Cotton cloths, unbleached	25	19	Square yard	4
colored and striped	25	24	do	5
bleached	25	24	do	6½
embroidered and printed	25	24	do	6½
Fish, dried or salted	20	15	32½ pounds	44
Flax, manufactures of, linen, common	20	15	Square yard	18⅛
middling	20	15	do	27¼
fine	20	15	do	36⅓
mixed with cotton	20	15	do	23$\frac{1}{10}$
Flour	20	15	Barrel of, 6 arrobas, 195 pounds.	1
Glass, window	20	15	Square foot	
Gunny bags	20	15	Each	8¼
Gunpowder of all kinds	20	15	Pound	10
Hams	20	15	32½ pounds	1 05⅗
Hats, of felt, common	30	24	Each	33
fine	30	24	do	66
very fine	30	24	do	1 32
Hides, oxen, dried	5	4	Pound	2
salted	5	4	do	2⅓
Ice	20	Free	2,200 pounds	99
Iron nails and spikes, under 1½ inch	30	24	32½ pounds	1 32
1½ to 3½ inches	30	24	do	66
over 3½ inches	30	24	do	41¼
in bars	30	24	129½ pounds	68¾
Lard	20	15	32½ pounds	82½
Lead in bars and pigs	20	15	129½ pounds	1 65
Leather, calf skin	20	19	Pound	13¾
Lime	10	8	Alqueire of Rio, 1.135 bushel.	6⅗
Marble, polished, squared, &c., or not, manufactured	30	24	100 square inches	3⅗
unmanufactured	20	15	do	3⅗
Nuts	30	(b)24	32½ pounds	52⅘
Oil, spermaceti	20	15	1.87 gallon	15⅗
whale	20	15	do	9$\frac{9}{10}$

(a) With springs, 50 per cent additional on respective values.

(b) Nuts used in dyeing, free.

TARIFFS—Continued.

DENOMINATION OF MERCHANDISE.	DUTIES ON IMPORTS INTO—			
	The United States, per cent. ad valorem, under the act of—		BRAZIL.	
	1846.	1857.	Number, weight, or measure.	Rate of duty.
Oil, linseed	20	15	1.87 gallon	$0 14
Paints, oil	20	15	Pound	2¼
Paper, blue writing	30	24	Ream	39⅔
white writing	30	24	....do	28
letter, quarto	30	24	....do	49½
printing	30	24	....do	55
Pepper	30	4	Pound	27½
Pitch, American(a)	20	15	Barrel	48
from other countries	20	15	....do	1 10
Pork, salt	20	15	32½ pounds	55
Saddlery, harness, common	20	15	Pound	2 64
fine	30	24	....do	(b)11 00
Sail duck, up to 25 inches wide, and 30 yards long	20	15	Piece	1 65
over 25 inches wide, and 30 yards long	20	15	....do	1 76
Salt	20	15	1.135 pound	8⅓
Ship-bread, common	20	15	32½ pounds	22
fine	20	15	....do	55
Silk, ribbons ½ inch wide	25	19	100 yards	33
1 inch wide	25	19	....do	82½
damask	25	19	Square yard	82½
Soap, castile	30	24		40 per cent. ad val.
Steel of all kinds	15 & 30	12 & 24	129½ pounds	2 20
Tallow, raw	10	8	32½ pounds	59⅔
Tar, Swedish	20	15	Barrel	1 10
American	20	15	....do	48
Teas of all kinds	(c)20	(c)15	Pound	33
Tin in bars	5	Free	....do	4
Tobacco, smoking, in rolls or leaves	30	24	32½ pounds	3 30
Twine, linen	30	24	1,000 yards	6½
Wax, white and yellow	20	15	Pound	10½
candles	20	15	....do	11
Wool cloths, common	30	24	Square yard	25
middling	30	24	....do	66
fine	30	24	....do	1 32
Wood, boards, fern, up to ½ inch thick	20	15	1,000 sq. palmas(e)	(d)3 30
Wine, Madeira, in casks	40	30	1.87 gallon	38½
in bottles	40	30	....do	82½
port, in casks	40	30	....do	27½
in bottles	40	30	....do	66

(a) See note, p. 319. (b) With white or yellow ornaments, 50 per cent. ad valorem additional on value. (c) See note, p. 168.
(d) For every half inch thicker, one half of the above duty added; if less than half inch, no addition made. Oak and other boards used in ship building charged, according to the thickness, twice as much as fern boards. (e) One palma, 8½ inches.

PERU.

The tariff is that of November 25, 1854, modified by a decree of May 1, 1855.(a)

Money.—Same as in Mexico: 1 peso = 100 cents = $1.

Weights and measures.—1 quintal = 4 arrobas (of 25 lbs. 7 oz.) = 100 libras 101.44 lbs.; 1 lb. = 1.014 lb.

All merchandise not enumerated in the official tariff pays 20 per cent. ad valorem.

Free list.—*Principal articles.*—Tar ; live animals ; quicksilver ; iron chains and cables ; salted pork and beef, in barrels ; stone coal ; geographical charts ; lumber for house building ; cooking apparatus for vessels ; scientific collections and objects of curiosity ; staves and headings of all kinds ; oakum ; fresh fruits ; printing presses ; scientific instruments of all kinds ; cordage and tow ; bricks ; iron bars ; timber for ship building ; hops ; machines for agricultural and mining purposes ; printed music ; sheathing copper in sheets ; seeds of all sorts.

The following articles are also free, if imported through the ports of Iquique, Arica, or Islay: fresh or salted meat ; barley ; beans ; lard ; lentils ; and Indian corn.

In the port of Iquique, foreign goods in national vessels, if consisting of steel, iron nails, wood, tallow, and articles of food, (flour excepted,) pay only one-half the ordinary duties ; empty sacks, gunny cloth, yarn for making bagging, wood and stone coals, are free under all flags.

Prohibited list.—Gunpowder, all kinds ; fire-arms and munitions of war ; books offending the public morals ; and eatables of a bad quality injurious to health.

All merchandise imported direct from Europe, Asia, or North America, through the larger ports of the republic, are permitted to pay 10 per cent. of the total amount of duties levied in "consolidation bonds," (government's bonds.)

Gold and silver, in bullion or coin, are exempt from export duty.

(a) See vol. 3 "Returns," p. 460.

Changes.—On the 8th of March, 1857, all duties on sugar, rice, butter, cheese, lard, and tallow were removed, for a period of eighteen months from that date ; and the duty on flour entered at the ports of Arica, Iquique, and Payta was reduced 50 per cent.

COMPARATIVE TARIFFS.

UNITED STATES AND PERU.

DENOMINATION OF MERCHANDISE.	DUTIES ON IMPORTS INTO—				
	The United States, per cent. ad valorem, under the act of—		PERU.		
	1846.	1857.	Number, weight, or measure.	Fixed value on the number, weight, or measure.	Per centage duty on the fixed value.
Ale, in casks	30	24	Gallon	Specific duty	$0 25
in bottles	30	24	Dozen	do	1 50
Brandy, in casks	100	30	Gallon { over 30 degrees	do	1 50
			Gallon { under 30 degrees	do	1 00
in bottles	100	30	Dozen { over 30 degrees	do	3 00
			Dozen { under 30 degrees	do	3 00
Bacon	20	15			Free.
Bullion, silver	Free	Free			Free.
Brass, manufactures of	30	24		Valuation	25
Books, printed	10 & 20	8 & 15	101 pounds	$60 00	3
blank	20	15	do	30 00	25
Beer, in bottles	30	24	Dozen	Specific duty	1 50
in casks	30	24	Gallon	do	25
Beef, salted	20	15	101 pounds	6 50	3
Butter	20	15	1.014 pound	Specific duty	12½
Brushes, clothes	30	24	Dozen	3 00	25
tooth	30	24	do	75	25
shoe	30	24	do	1 00	25
horse	30	24	do	2 50	25
scrubbing	30	24	do	5 00	25
Boots and shoes	30	24		Valuation	40
Coffee	(a)20	(a)15	101 pounds	Specific duty	5 00
Copper ore	Free	Free	do	18 00	1
Cheese	30	24	do	Specific duty	4 00
Cordials, in bottles	100	30	Dozen	do	2 50
Cider, in casks	30	24	Gallon	do	25
in bottles	30	24	Dozen	do	1 50
Cables, of hemp	25	19	101 pounds		Free.
Champagne, in bottles	40	30	Dozen	Specific duty	4 00
Cordage, tarred or untarred	25	19			Free.
Cotton, raw	Free	Free	101 pounds	Valuation	20

(a) See note, page 114.

TARIFFS—Continued.

DENOMINATION OF MERCHANDISE.	DUTIES ON IMPORTS INTO—				
	The United States, per cent. ad valorem, under the act of—		PERU.		
	1846.	1857.	Number, weight, or measure.	Fixed value on the number, weight, or measure.	Per centage duty on the fixed value.
Cotton, manufactures of, fustians up to 4 yard wide.	25	19	Dozen yards	$6 00	$0 15
Copper, manufactures of	30	24	1. 014 pound	37	15
Candles, spermaceti	20	15	....do	Specific duty..	12½
tallow	20	15	....do	......do......	12½
Cigars	40	30	....do	......do......	62½
Furs, undressed	10	8		Valuation	20
Fish, dried	20	15	101 pounds	5 00	3
codfish, dried	20	15	....do	5 00	10
Flour, in barrels or sacks of 190 to 200 lbs.	20	15	....do	Specific duty..	2 00
Furniture, household	30	24		Valuation	30
Flax, maunfactures of	20	15		......do......	28
Grain spirits, in bottles	100	80	Dozen	Specific duty..	3 00
Gold, coin	Free...	Free...			Free.
Gunny bags	20	15			Free.
Glue	20	15	101 pounds	12 00	25
Hides, raw, of oxen	5	4	One	5 00	20
Hams	20	15	1. 014 pound	20	3
Hats	30	24		Valuation	30
straw	30	24			Free.
Ice	20	Free...			Free.
Indian corn	20	15	101 pounds	1 50	20
Iron castings	30	24		Valuation	25
manufactures of	30	24		....do........	25
for agricultural and mechanical purposes.	30	24			Free.
Linens	20	15		Valuation	20
Lead, red, in powder	20	15	101 pounds	4 00	20
Lime	10	8	......do	2 00	20
Lead, white	20	15	......do	3 00	20
Lard	20	15	......do	Specific duty..	1 00
Lead, manufactures of	30	24	......do	7 00	20
Marble, manufactures of	30	24		Valuation	20
Medicinal drugs	20	15		....do........	20
Molasses	30	24		....do........	20
Musical instruments	20	15		....do........	30
Nails, iron	30	24	101 pounds	5 50	6
copper	20	15	......do	30 00	15
Oil, linseed	20	15	Gallon	90	10
Pewter, manufactures of	30	24		Valuation	6
Paints, common	20	15	101 pounds	7 00	20
fine, in pots	20	15	Dozen pots	75	20

TARIFFS—Continued.

DENOMINATION OF MERCHANDISE.	DUTIES ON IMPORTS INTO—				
	The United States, per cent. ad valorem, under the act of—		PERU.		
	1846.	1857.	Number, weight, or measure.	Fixed value on the number, weight, or measure.	Rate of duty on the fixed value.
Paper	30	24		Valuation	20
for music	30	24		do	10
Pitch	20	15			Free.
Pork	20	15			Free.
Pepper, black, in grain	30	4	101 pounds	$10 00	20
ground	30	4	1. 014 pound	15	20
Rosin in barrels	20	15			Free.
Rice	20	15	101 pounds	Specific duty	$2 00
Soap, common	30	24		do	4 00
fine	30	24		Valuation	20 and 30
Saddlery	20 to 30	15 to 24		do	30
Spirits of turpentine	20	15		do	20
Sugar, refined	30	24	Arroba, 25 pounds 7 oz	Specific duty	1 50
Ship bread	20	15	101 pounds	10 00	30
Snuff	40	30	1. 014 pound	1 00	$20 per 101 lbs.
Salt	20	15	101 pounds	10 00	20
Silver coin	Free	Free			Free.
Silk, piece goods	25	19		Valuation	20
Steel, cast	15	12	101 pounds	8 00	Free.
Tobacco, manufactured, twisted	40	30	do	20 00	$20 per 101 lbs.
chewing	40	30	do	15 00	Free.
unmanufactured	30	24	do	20 00	$20 per 101 lbs.
Teas	(a)20	(a)15	1. 014 pound	Specific duty	18¾
Vinegar	30	24	Gallon	30	20
Varnish	20	15	do	37	20
for vessels	20	15		Valuation	Free.
Wood, manufactures of	30	24		do	30
Worsted stuff, piece goods	25	19		do	20
Wine, in bottles, Burgundy, Madeira, Xeres, and Port.	40	30	Dozen	Specific duty	2 50
Champagne	40	30	do	do	4 00
all other kinds	40	30	do	do	1 50

(a) See note, p. 168.

BOLIVIA.

The tariff is that of November 2, 1844, modified June 8, 1850.(a)

Money.—The same as in Mexico and Peru, viz : 1 peso = 100 cents = $1

Weights and measures.—1 quintal = 101.44 lbs.; 1 libra = 1.014 lb.; 1 arroba = 25.6 lbs. 7 oz.

Peruvian bark can be exported only throught the port of Cobija. Gold, in dust or bars, pays an export duty of 3 per cent. ad valorem, while dollars pay 6 per cent. ad valorem.

Besides the rates of import duties specified in the tariff, an extra ½ per cent. is levied on all imports, for the benefit of the "Chamber of Commerce."

(a) See vol. 1, "Digests," p. 716, *et seq.*

COMPARATIVE TARIFFS.

UNITED STATES AND BOLIVIA.

DENOMINATION OF MERCHANDISE.	DUTIES ON IMPORTS INTO— The United States, per cent. ad valorem, under the act of— 1846.	1857.	BOLIVIA. Per centage ad valorem.
Articles not enumerated	20	15	28
Beverages, brought by sea	According to the	nature of.	36
Bedsteads of iron and brass	30	24	28
Books, imported by land	According	to kind.	6
Cocoa	10	4	36
Caps	30	24	28
Cards, playing	30	24	20
Candlesticks, lanterns, chandeliers	According to	material.	28
Cigars	40	30	28
Earthenware	30	24	8
Furniture, toilet looking-glasses	30	24	28
Glass and crystals	Glass 20 to 40	15 to 30	8
	Crystal 30	24	
Gold and silverware	30	24	6
Hosiery	According to	material.	28
Indian corn	20	15	Free.
Iron, manufactures	30	24	6
Leaf, gold	15	12	28
Linen, also embroidered	Linens 20	15	18
	Embroidered 30	24	
Paper, writing	30	24	8
Perfumery	30	24	28
Powder and matches	Powder 20	15	Prohibited.
	Matches, wax 20	15	
	Matches, other 30	24	
Shirting, gray, ("tocuyos")	According to	material.	28
Shoes for women	30	24	28
Silk goods	25 to 30	19 to 24	18
Watches and clocks	Watches 10	8	28
	Clocks 30	24	
Woolen manufactures	30	24	18

CHILI.

The tariff is that of 1854.(a)

Money.—1 peso = 8 reals = $1

Weights and measures.—The gallon, yard, foot, and inch, are the same as in the United States. The pound is the Castilian, 1 lb. = 1.014 lb. English. The quintal = 101.44 lbs. One quintal = 4 arrobas (of 25 lbs. 7 oz.) = 101½ lbs. avoirdupois. One vara = 33⅓ inches English. One fanega = 2½ bushels.

Copper in bars pays an export duty of 5 per cent. ad valorem.

APPENDIX.

An edition of the Customs Tariff, applicable to each year, is annually put forth by the government of Chili, as is done by the governments of some other countries. In these annual editions, although the rate of duty per cent. on the rates of fixed values may remain unchanged, these rates of valuation themselves often sustain material modification. Thus, the rates of duty per cent. in 1853, as well as in 1855, were 25 per cent. and 30 per cent., respectively, on the fixed values; but there was a marked change in those values themselves in the tariff for 1855 compared with those for 1853. The per centage decrease in the rates of duty levied on certain articles of import in 1855 on those levied in 1853, effected by this change in the fixed values, has been noted as follows:(b)

On manufactures of cotton, a per centage decrease of from 5 to 36 per cent., according to the character and quality of the articles specified; on those of linen, from 10 to 25; on those of silk, from 7 to 21; on those of wool, from 8 to 25; on hardware, from 12 to 20; on spermaceti candles, 11; on porcelain cups and saucers, 12; on leather, kid, shoe, cut, or prepared, 12; on Morocco leather, 20; on salt, refined, in barrels or bags, 33.

On a few articles of hardware and linen there appears an increase of duty; also on sheep's wool, unwashed, 25 per cent.; on tallow candles, 6; on earthenware, 11 to 12; on oil, whale, linseed, rapeseed, &c., 7; on rice, 17; on coffee, 25; on soap, common, in bars, 20; and on better qualities of soaps, in any form, 28.

(a) See Appendix.

(b) See note p. 98.

COMPARATIVE TARIFFS.

UNITED STATES AND CHILI.

Denomination of merchandise.	Duties on imports into— The United States, per cent. ad valorem, under the act of— 1846.	1857.	Chili. Number, weight, or measure.	Fixed value on the number, weight, and measure.	Per centage duty on the fixed value.
Ashes, pot and pearl	20	15	Quintal, (101 lbs.)	$5 00	25
Beer, ale, and porter, in bottles	30	24	Dozen	Specific duty	$1 00
in casks	30	24	Gallon	do	25
Beef, salted	20	15	101 pounds	7 00	Free.
Biscuit or ship bread, common	20	15	do	3 00	25
Books and maps: books	10 to 20	8 to 15			Free.
Books and maps: maps	10	Free			
Boots and shoes, of calf skin, for men	30	24	Dozen	18 00	15
common, for soldiers	30	24	do	9 00	15
for women	30	24	do	6 00	15
of gum elastic, for men	30	24	do	12 00	15
of gum elastic, for women	30	24	do	9 00	15
Brandy and all other liquors, in bottles	100	30	do	Specific duty	3 00
in casks	100	30	Gallon	do	1 00
Brushes, for boots	30	24	Dozen	100 00	25
for horses	30	24	do	2 50	25
for clothes	30	24	do	5 00	25
for teeth	30	24	Gross	12 00	25
Butter	30	15	1.014 pound	20	25
Cables and cordage	25	19		Valuation	25
Cassia	40	4	101 pounds	16 00	25
Cheese	30	24	Libra, (1.014 lb)	18¾	25
Cinnamon	30	4	do	80	25
Cloves	40	4	do	20	25
Coal, stone	30	24			Free.
Coaches and other carriages	30	24		Valuation	25
Coffee	20	15	101 pounds	10 00	25
Copper, manufactures of	30	24	1.014 pound	40	25
for sheathing ships	Free	Free	101 pounds	13 00	25
Cotton, raw, not picked	Free	Free	do	4 00	25

TARIFFS—Continued.

DENOMINATION OF MERCHANDISE.	DUTIES ON IMPORTS INTO—				
	The United States, per cent. ad valorem, under the act of—		CHILI.		
	1846.	1857.	mber, weight, or measure.	Fixed value on the number, weight, and measure.	Per centage duty on the fixed value.
Cotton, raw, picked	Free	Free	101 pounds	$8 00	25
manufactures of	25	24	1.014 pound	37½	25
Earthen and stone wares	30	24		Valuation	25
Fire engines	30	24			Free.
Fish, dry or smoked, small, as anchovies, herrings, sardines, &c.; dried	20	15			
smoked, or salted, in earthen, lead, or glass vessels, in oil	40	30	1.014 pound	10	25
Fish, large, as codfish, mackerel, &c	20	15	101 pounds	6 00	25
salmon	20	15	do	10 00	25
Flour	20	15	do	If under $4 per 101 pounds, If over $4 per 101 pounds, free.	25
Glass, window	20	15	100 superficial feet	3 00	25
skylights for ships	30	24	Dozen	6 00	25
for watches	30	24	do	1 00	25
Gunny bags	20	15	1.014 pound	14	25
Hams and bacon	20	15	do	14	25
Hats, of fur, round, common, and trimmed	30	24	Dozen	48 00	30
Hats, of fur, round, fine, and not trimmed	30	24	do	36 00	30
Hats, of felt, of silk, or mixture, round	30	24	do	30 00	30
straw	30	24		Valuation	25
Hops	20	15		do	25
Household furniture	30	24		do	25
Indian corn	20	15	Fanega, (2.57 bush's)	If under $3 per fanaga If over $3 per fanaga	25 Free.
Iron, in bars	30	24			Free.
castings	30	24		Valuation	25
nails	30	24	1. 014 pound	8 to 12½ cents	25
manufactures of	30	24		Valuation	25
Lard	20	15	1. 0 pound	12½	25
Lead, in bars	20	15			Free.
in sheets	20	15			Free.
manufactured, in pieces under 10 pounds	30	24	101 pounds	6 00	25
Linen, bleached and unbleached	20	15		Valuation	25
Linseed oil	20	15	Gallon	80	25
Marble, manufactured into slabs	30	24	Superficial foot	81¼	25
round	30	24	Every inch in diam	40	25
other manufactures	30	24		Valuation	25
Medicinal drugs	20	15		do	25

TARIFFS—Continued.

DENOMINATION OF MERCHANDISE.	DUTIE ON IMPORTS INTO—				
	The United States, per cent. ad valorem, under the act of—		CHILI.		
	1846.	1857.	Number, weight, or measure	Fixed value on the number, eight, and measure.	Per centage duty on the fixed value.
Molasses	30	24	Gallon	$0 25	25
Paints and varnish, in oil	20	15	101 pounds	6 00	25
dry	20	15		Valuation	25
Paper	30	24		do	25
Pepper, black	30	4	1.014 pound	9	25
Pimento	40	4	101 pounds	5 00	25
Pork, salted	20	15	do	8 00	Free
Printing presses	30	24			Free
Prunes and plums, net wt. plums	30	8	1.014 pound	10	6
prunes	40	8			
Raisins	40	8	101 pounds	10 00	6
Rice, Carolina	20	15	do	5 50	25
from other places	20	15	do	3 50	25
ground, in jars or packages, gross weight.	20	15	1.014 pound	12½	25
Rosin	20	15	101 pounds	2 00	Free.
Saddlery, harness for one horse	30	24	Each	25 00	25
other articles	30	24		Valuation	25
Salt, common	20	15	101 pounds	40	25
refined, ground, in barrels and bags.	20	15	do	1 00	25
Silk manufactures	25	19		Valuation	15
Silver, in specie	Free	Free			Free.
Spermaceti, raw	20	15	1.014 pound	37½	Free.
refined	20	15	do	75	Free.
candles	20	15	do	40	25
Soap, common	30	24	101 pounds	6 00	25
fine	30	24	do	9 00	25
perfumed, common	30	24	1.014 pound	40	25
finer	30	24	Dozen cakes	1 00	25
Stearine candles	20	15	1.014 pound	26	25
Sugar, refined	30	24	Arroba, (25 lbs. 7 oz)	2 00	25
not refined	30	24	do do	1 75	25
Tallow, purified	10	8	101 pounds	11 00	6
not purified	10	8	do	7 00	6
candles	20	15	do	16 00	25
Tar	20	15	do	2 00	Free.
Teas	(a)20	(a)15	1.014 pound	25	(Specific duty.)
Tin, in bars	5	Free			Free.
Twine, hemp, for sails	30	24	1.014 pound	25	25
Tobacco, raw, unmanufactured	30	24	Governm't monopoly.		
paper cigars	40	30	1.014 pound	31¼	25

(a) See note, p. 168.

TARIFFS—Continued.

DENOMINATION OF MERCHANDISE.	DUTIES ON IMPORTS INTO—				
	The United States, per cent. ad valorem, under the act of—		CHILI.		
	1846.	1857.	Number, weight, or measure.	Fixed value on the number, weight, and measure.	Per centage duty on the fixed value.
Tobacco, chewing	40	30	1.014 pound	$0 20	25
cigars	40	30	....do	75	(Specific.)
Vinegar, in common bottles	30	24	Dozen	2 00	25
in casks	30	24	Gallon	40	25
Wax, yellow or white	20	15	101 pounds	50 00	25
candles	20	15	1. 014 pound	50	25
Wines, white, in bottles	40	30	Dozen	1 25	(Specific.)
in casks	40	30	Gallon	37	(Specific.)
red, in bottles	40	30	Dozen	1 00	(Specific.)
in casks	40	30	Gallon	25	(Specific.)
Wood, unmanufactured, as mahogany, cedar, ebony, sandal, and jàcarandá.	20	8	Square foot	1 50	Free.
Wood, in trunks, white, as pine, oak, &c.	20	8	....do	25	Free.
Wood, same kinds, in planks, boards, &c.	20	15	Miller, (1,000 feet)	35 00	Free.

ARGENTINE REPUBLIC.

THE tariff is that of January 1, 1854.(a)

Money.—1 dollar silver = 8 reals silver = 96 cents American.

1 dollar paper = 8 reals paper = 5 cents American currency.

Weights and Measures.—The same as in the other South American republics:

1 arroba = 25 pounds 7 ounces.

1 quintal = 101 pounds.

1 fanega = 2¼ bushels, English.

The duties are calculated upon the wholesale market prices, by inspectors, assisted by appraisers. Should any article consist of two or more materials which have different duties assigned to them by this tariff, the highest duty is levied.

The inspectors are assisted by appraisers for the valuation of such articles as are intended for consumption; the inspectors of liquids and provisions, by one appraiser who is conversant with these articles; the three inspectors of manufactured articles are each accompanied by two appraisers, one of whom must be conversant with the price of manufactured goods in general, and the other with the value of hardware.

The appraisers attend daily to despatch the articles, and conjointly with the inspector, and in presence of the interested party, fix the valuation, which is noted by the inspector. The appraisers attend on the following day, at the office of the inspector, to revise the valuation made on the preceding day, at which the interested party may attend; and the manifest being signed by the inspector and the appraisers, and the date having been appended, the inspector submits it to the collector general for his immediate inspection.

Should any difference, exceeding 10 per cent. on the valuation, arise between the inspector and the interested party, three import merchants decide thereon before the collector of customs.

The merchant arbitrators, when once met, must decide before separating, and their decision is carried into effect without appeal.

When the amount of duty exceeds one thousand dollars, the merchants accept bills for the payment of equal instalments at the peremptory terms of three and six months. No one indebted to the custom-house after the expiration of the latter term is admitted to transact business in the office.

The alterations made by the present tariff, in the import and export duties, came into effect from and after the 1st of January, 1854.

The government has raised the duties on manufactured silks to 12 per cent., and those on woollen and cotton cloths to 12 per cent.

TARIFF OF EXPORTATION.

DENOMINATION OF MERCHANDISE.	Number, weight, or measure.	Rates of duty.
Animals—horses	Each	$0 20
Beef dried or salted, in barrels	Quintal (101 lbs.)	15
Bones	4 per cent. ad val.	
Cattle, bullocks, cows, &c.	Each	3
Swine and sheep	..do	10
Feathers, (ostrich)	4 per cent. ad val.	
Hair and wool, worked or not	Arroba (25 lbs. 7 oz.)	10
Hides and skins, bull, ox, cow, and calf	Each	10
mule, or wild horse	..do	5
sheep	D zen	15
slunk, and other not described	4 per cent. ad val.	
Horns and tips of horns	......do........do..	....
Oil, animal	25 lbs. 7 oz	7½
Tallow and grease, raw or melted	......do	7½
Tongues, salted in barrels	Dozen	2½
Articles not otherwise described, generally the produce of the republic		Free.

(a) See vol. 3, "Returns," p. 478.

COMPARATIVE TARIFFS.

UNITED STATES AND ARGENTINE REPUBLIC.

Denomination of merchandise.	Duties on imports into— The United States, per cent. ad valorem, under the act of— 1846.	1857.	Argentine Republic. Per cent. duty ad valorem.
Barilla	10	4	15
Beer	30	24	25
Biscuit or ship bread	20	15	15
Books, printed	10 & 20	8 & 1	Free.
music	10	8	Free.
blank	20	15	15
Boots and shoes	30	24	20
for use in the field	30	24	20
shoes of India rubber	30	24	20
Brandy	100	30	25
Bricks	20	15	5
Cables and cordage	25	19	15
Camphor, crude	25	8	15
refined	40	30	15
Candles, wax, sperm, stearine	20	15	15
tallow	20	15	15
Castings	30	24	5
Cigars	40	30	20
Cider	30	24	25
Cheese	30	24	20
Cloves	40	4	15
Coal, stone	30	24	5
Coaches and other carriages	30	24	15
Copper in pigs	5	Free	5
in sheets	20	15	5
Cotton, fustians	25	19	15
raw	Free	Free	5
Demijohns	30	24	15
Earthen and stoneware	30	24	15
Fish stock	20	15	20
Flour, foreign	20	15	Pr. quintal, (101 lbs.,) $1.44, specific duty.
Flowers, artificial	30	24	15
Fruits, in vinegar	30	24	20
in brandy, &c.	40	30	20
Glass of all classes	20 to 40	15 to 30	15
Gold and silver coins	Free	Free	Free.
Gunpowder	20	15	15
Hams and bacon	20	15	20
Hats, straw	30	24	15
for ladies, ornamented	30	24	15
of felt, wool, silk, or beaver.	30	24	15
Herrings	20	15	20
Household furniture, tables	30	24	15
Indian corn	20	15	Pr. fanega, ($2\frac{1}{2}$ bush.) 96c. specific duty.
Indigo	10	4	15
Iron hoops	30	24	15
Lard	20	15	20
Lead, in bars, rolls, or pigs and sheets.	20	15	5
shot	20	15	15
Machines of all classes	30	24	5
Mackerel	20	15	20
Marble, manufactured	30	24	15

TARIFFS—Continued.

DENOMINATION OF MERCHANDISE.	DUTIES ON IMPORTS INTO— The United States, per cent. ad valorem, under the act of— 1846.	1857.	ARGENTINE REPUBLIC. Per cent. duty ad valorem.	DENOMINATION OF MERCHANDISE.	DUTIES ON IMPORTS INTO— The United States, per cent. ad valorem, under the act of— 184 .	1857.	ARGENTINE REPUBLIC. Per cent. duty ad valorem.
Marble, not manufactured	20	15	15	Spirituous liquors	100	30	25
Nails, iron	30	24	15	Tallow, raw unmanufactured	10	8	15
copper	20	15	15	Tar	20	15	15
Nutmegs	40	4	15	Teas	(a)20	(a)15	20
Oil, whale	20	15	15	Tin, in bars	5	Free	5
olive	0	24	20	in sheets	15	8	5
linseed	20	15	15	Twine	30	24	15
Paper, music	10	4	15	Types, printing	20	15	15
all other not enumerated.	30	24	15	for marking and stamping.	20	15	15
Paints and varnish	20	15	15	Tobacco	30	24	20
Pepper, black	30	4	15	Trunks	Accord'g	to mat'l.	15
Pitch	20	15	15	Umbrellas, parasols, &c., silk or cotton.	30	24	15
Potatoes	30	24	20	Vinegar	30	24	15
Printing presses	30	24	5	Watches of silver or gold	10	8	5
Pork, salted	20	15	20	and clocks	30	24	15
Rice	20	15	20	Wax, white or yellow	20	15	15
Rosin	20	15	15	Wood, boards, planks	20	15	5
Soap	30	24	15	shingles	20	15	5
Sugar	30	24	20	Wines, red and white	40	30	25
Shoes	30	24	20				

(a) See note, page 168.

URUGUAY.

The tariff is that of October 11, 1853.(*a*)

All articles not enumerated in the tariff are subject to a duty of 20 per cent ad valorem, which valuation, however, is regulated at ten per cent. under the wholesale prices, as per invoice of despatch.

The open ports are Montevideo, Maldonado, Colonia, Soriano, San Salvador, Carmelo, Mercedes, Higueritas, Paisandie, Salto, Santa Rosa, Constitucion, Rosario, Villa de Artigas y Cebollati, and the inland ports of Tacuarembo, Cuareim, and Santa Teresa. Warehouses are established at the ports of Montevideo, Maldonado, Colonia, Higueritas, Paisandie, Salto, Santa Rosa, and Constitucion.

The period for depositing in warehouses is indefinite, so long as the articles continue uninjured.

Storage is paid as follows: ⅛ per cent. per month on the value of dry goods; 31 cents per month on every pipe of the bulk of 6 barrels; 7½ cents per month on every barrel of flour; and 7½ cents per month n every 200 pounds of any other bulkv article.

Money.—Peso = 8 reals = 800 reis = 100 cents =$1 United States currency

NOTE.—The par of United States silver coin is lower than that of other nations—*e. g.*, the Spanish silver dollar (*patacon*) equals 1,000 reis; five franc piece (French) equals 900 reis; some other foreign coins equal 960 reis, whilst the United States dollar is not current at more than 800 reis, which is less than its intrinsic value.

Weights and measures.—1 quintal = 4 arrobas (of 25 pounds 7 ounces) = 100 pounds = 101½ = pounds avoirdupois.
20 quintals = 1 ton = 2,000 pounds = 2,030 pounds avoirdupois.
106.27 varas = 100 yards, United States.
1 fanega = 3 4-5 bushels, United States.
1 ppie = 180.76 frascos = 128 gallons, United States.
1 ton of salt = 7½ fanegas = 2,100 to 2,175 pounds, United States.
1 fanega of wheat = 225 to 230 pounds, United States.
1 fanega of barley = 7 arrobas = 177 pounds, United States.
1 pesada of dry hides = 40 pounds, United States
1 pesada of salted hides 75 pounds, United State

Goods for re-exportation, from deposit, are free of all duty.

Eslingage, or wharfage regulated at one-half of what each package pays for one month's storage.

Duties on imports.—When the amount is under $500 payment, to be cash; otherwise, h lf the amount to be paid cash, one-fourth in bill at two months, and one-fourth in bill at three months.

Duties on exports.—All the products of the country, and foreign goods which have paid duty or are free of import duty, are exempt from export duty.

The transit, by transhipment or reshipment in the ports of deposit of all merchandise or produce destined to any of those ports, or to foreign markets, is allowed free of all duty

The transit by land between Salto and Constitucion, and Santa Rosa, to be on the same terms as if effected by transhipment or reshipment.

All produce imported from ports inside Capes Sta. Maria and San Antonio is exempt from export duty.

Port charges.—Custom-house officers, one dollar per day, while the register for discharging and loading is open; expenses opening register for dischaging, about $20; expenses for loading and clearing out, $35; bill of health, pilotage, anchorage, &c., $24; tonnage dues, per register ton, three rials (31 c.)

APPENDIX.

The per centage decrease in the duties levied on certain articles by virtue of the tariff of Uruguay, which came into force July 17, 1856, as compared with those levied by that of October 11, 1853, are stated as follows:(*b*)

A decrease of 25 per cent. on bombazine; silk; blankets; buckles of iron and steel; bunting; baizes; iron chains; carpeting; mixed damask; common earthenware; flannel; cotton fringe; fire grates; common galloons; gunpowder; common guns; hatchets; iron hammers; cotton, wool, and linen hose; cotton and linen handkerchiefs; common and ivory knives and forks; lamps; cotton lace; lustres; madopollams; muslins; nails, wrought and cut, nankeens; cotton net; oilcloth for covers; planes; cotton prints; pistols; cotton and linen plush; parasols; horse rugs; razors; common snuffers, swords; stew pans; cotton, and wool, and silk shawls; sashes, cotton and wool; shot, white shirtings; cotton ticks; teapots; towels; silk umbrellas; velveteen; of 33 per cent. on boots and shoes, and ponches, ready made; of 20 per cent. on cinnamon, rice, sugars, tea; of 16 per cent. on brandies, beer ale, or porter, snuffs, vinegar, wines; of 75 per cent. on copper sheathing and zinc; of 30 per cent. on linen cambrics, silk felt, silk handkerchiefs, plain silk, satin; of 65 per cent on silk galloons; of 27 per cent. on gin; of 40 per cent. on pine planks; of 50 per cent. on sulphur and tiles; while the increase on linen and silk lace, and wheat starch, is 50 per cent.; and on wheat 17 per cent.

(*a*) See vol. 1 "Digests," p. 774, for tariffs of July 17, 1856; als Appendix.
(*b*) See note, page 93.

COMPARATIVE TARIFFS.

UNITED STATES AND URUGUAY.

Denomination of merchandise.	Duties on imports into— The United States, per cent. ad valorem, under the act of— 1846.	1857.	Uruguay. Per cent. duty, ad valorem.
Animals, living, for breed	Free	Free	Free.
Ashes	20	15	Free.
Bark for tanning	20	Free	Free.
Beef	20	15	30
Beer, porter, and ale	30	24	30
Biscuit	20	15	30
Books, printed	10 to 20	8 to 15	Free.
Boots and shoes	30	24	30
Brandy	100	30	30
Butter	20	15	30
Cables and cordage	25	19	5
Cambrics, thread, cotton	25	24	10
linen	20	15	10
Candles, tallow	20	15	30
Caps and bonnets	30	24	30
Cards, playing	30	24	35
Cheese	30	24	30
Chewing tobacco	40	30	30
Cider	30	24	30
Cigars	40	30	35
Cinnamon	30	4	25
Coaches and other carriages	30	24	30
Coal	30	24	Free.
Coffee	20	15	25
Combs, feathers, and artificial flowers.	30	24	30
Cotton, raw	Free	Free	30
Clothes, ready-made	30	24	30
Drugs	20	15	25
Eatables in general	20	15	25

Denomination of merchandise.	Duties on imports into— The United States, per cent. ad valorem, under the act of— 1846.	1857.	Uruguay. Per cent. duty, ad valorem.
Fish, dried or smoked	20	15	25
Flour	20	15	35
Furniture, household	30	24	30
Glass, looking	30	24	30
window	20	15	30
ware	20 to 40	15 to 30	30
crystals	30	24	30
Gold and silver coin	Free	Free	Free.
Grain, wheat	20	15	30
Gypsum, unground	Free	Free	5
Hams	20	15	30
Harness	30	24	30
Hats	30	24	30
Hides, oxen, cow, or horse, salted or dry, raw.	5	4	Free.
tanned	20	15	Free.
Hoops, wooden	30	24	Free.
Indian corn	20	15	30
Instruments for science, mathematical and surgical.	30	24	Free.
Instruments, philosophical	Accord'g	to mat'l.	Free.
Iron, bars, sheet, wire	30	24	5
Jewelry, false	30	24	30
Lard	20	15	30
Liquors and all other spirits	100	30	30
Machines for agricultural and industrial purposes.		24	Free.
Maps	10	Free	Free.
Oil, sweet	30	24	25
whale and other fish	(a)20	(a)15	30

(a) Produce of American fisheries, free.

TARIFFS—Continued.

Denomination of merchandise.	Duties on imports into— The United States, per cent. ad valorem, under the act of— 1846.	1857.	Uruguay. Per cent duty, ad valorem.	Denomination of merchandise.	Duties on imports into— The United States, per cent. ad valorem, under the act of— 1846.	1857.	Uruguay. Per cent. duty, ad valorem.
Perfumery	30	24	30	Staves and heading	20	15	Free.
Pork, salt	20	15	30	Sugar	30	24	25
Printing presses	30	24	Free.	Tar and pitch	(a)20	(a)15	5
paper	30	24	Free.	Teas	20	15	25
Roman cement	20	15	5	Tobacco, leaf	30	24	25
Salt, common	20	15	Free.	snuff, and other manufactures of.	40	30	30
Silk, manufactures of	25	19	10				
Skins, sheep and other, raw	5	4	Free.	Wood, shingles	20	15	5
Soap	30	24	30	timber, rough	20	15	5
Spices, all	30 to 40	4	25	planed and boards	20	15	5

(a) See note, page 168.

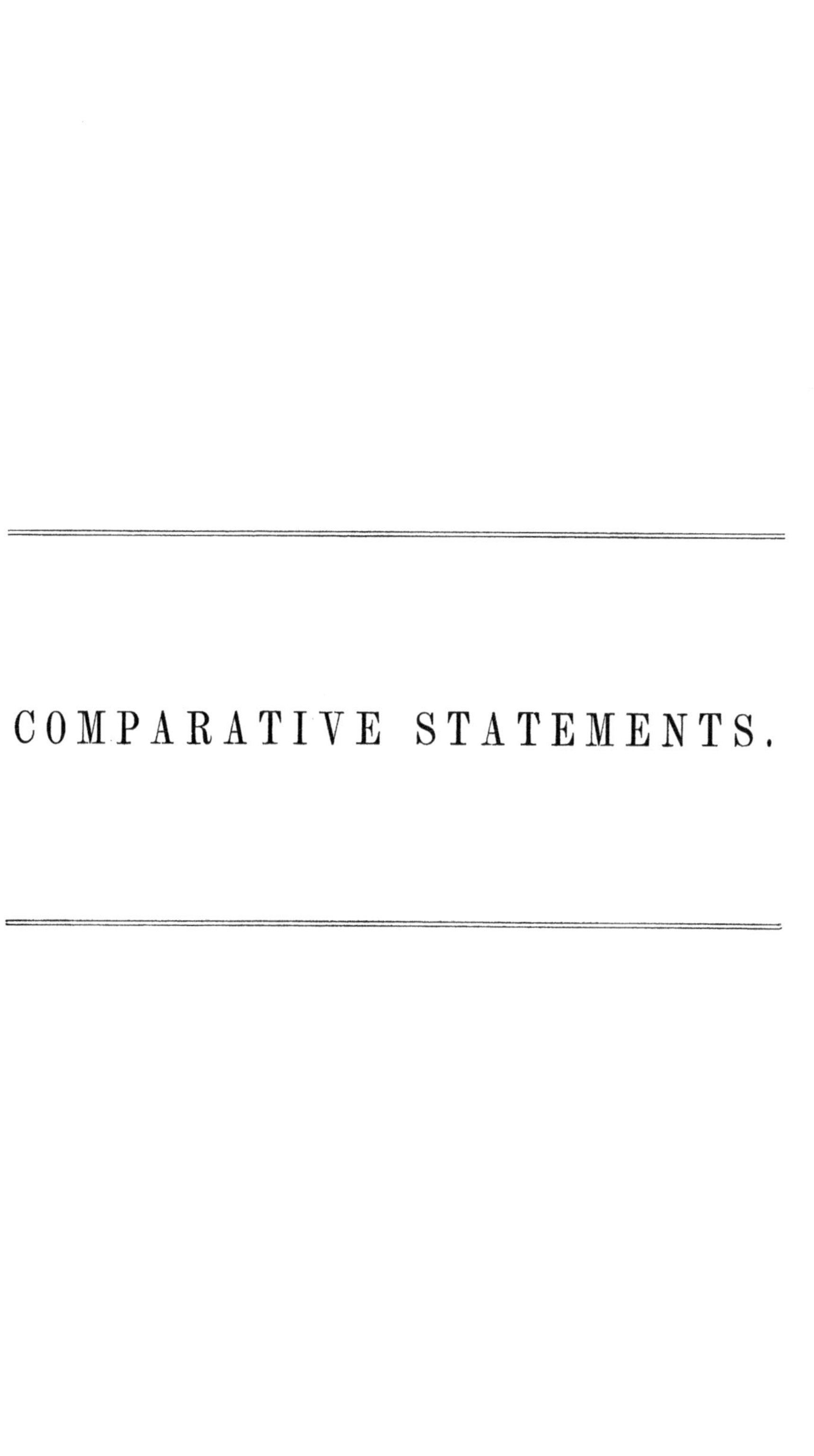

COMPARATIVE STATEMENTS.

Comparative statement exhibiting import duties levied by principal commercial nations, respectively, on staple products of the United States. (a)

STAPLE PRODUCTS.	DUTIES ON IMPORTS INTO—				
	The United States, per cent. ad valorem, under the act of—		GREAT BRITAIN.	FRANCE.	SPAIN.
	1846.	1857.	Tariff, 1853.	Tariff, 1844–1855.	Tariff, 1852–1853.
Oil, spermaceti	20	15	Free	\$3 $70\frac{1}{3}$ per 100 kilogrammes, = 220 pounds.	33 cts. per arroba, = 4.245 gallons.
Oil, whale and other fish.	20	15	...do	\$7 $40\frac{2}{3}$ per 220 pounds	33 cts. per arroba, = 4.245 gallons.
Whalebone	20	15	...do	\$5 $55\frac{1}{2}$ per 220 pounds	$2\frac{3}{4}$ cts. per 1 lb. 3 drachms.
Dried fish	20	15	...do	\$7 $40\frac{2}{3}$ per 220 pounds	\$2 $91\frac{1}{2}$ per quintal, = 101 lbs. If direct from fisheries, \$2 12.
Staves	20	15	Free; \$2 16 per load, = 50 cubic feet, when exceeding 72 inches long, by 7 inches wide.	$37\frac{1}{2}$ cents per M	\$2 65 per M
Shingles	20	15	\$2 40 per load	$9\frac{3}{10}$ cents per M	Not defined
Lumber	20	15	...do	$2\frac{7}{10}$ cents per 100 metres long, = 110 yards.	For ship building, 3 per cent.
Timber	20	15	\$1 80 per load	2 cents per stere, = 35.31 square feet.	Joists and beams, $7\frac{1}{4}$ cts. per cubic foot.
Tar	20	15	Free	$64\frac{4}{5}$ cents per 220 pounds	17 cts. per quintal
Pitch	20	15	...do	93 cents per 220 pounds	34 cts. per quintal
Rosin and turpentine.	20	15	...do	93 cts. per 220 lbs. (rosin.)	\$1 06 per quintal; rosin, $42\frac{1}{2}$ per quintal.
Ashes	20	15	...do	$18\frac{3}{10}$ cts. per 220 pounds	$63\frac{1}{2}$ cts. per quintal
Skins and furs	20	19 & 15	...do	$3\frac{7}{10}$ to $8\frac{1}{3}$ cents each	No importation
Beef	20	15	...do	\$6 20 per 220 lbs. (salted.)	$38\frac{1}{4}$ cts. per arroba, = 25 lbs. 7 oz., salted; $78\frac{1}{4}$ cts., smoked.
Tallow	10	8	36 cts. per cwt., = 112 lbs.	\$2 77 per 220 pounds	51 cts. per quintal, in leaf.
Butter	20	15	\$1 20 per cwt	...do ...do	$10\frac{1}{2}$ cts. per 1 lb. 3 drs
Cheese	30	24	60 cents per cwt	\$2 $80\frac{4}{5}$ per 220 pounds	\$1 $27\frac{1}{2}$ per arroba
Pork	20	15	Free	$9\frac{3}{10}$ cts. per 220 lbs. (salted.)	$38\frac{1}{4}$ cts. per arroba, salted; $78\frac{1}{4}$ cts., smoked.
Bacon	20	15	...do	$9\frac{3}{10}$ cents per 220 pounds	$76\frac{1}{4}$ cts per arroba
Lard	20	15	...do	...do ...do	\$1 $19\frac{1}{4}$ cts. per arroba

(a) This statement gives import duties on the staple products of the United States generally in a crude form, exported in United States vessels directly to the foreign countries specified, and is designed to embrace no country the aggregate value of whose annual trade with the United States does not exceed five millions of dollars. The Hanse Towns, whose trade with the United States amounts to some twenty-two millions annually, have been omitted, because the duties at the two principal places, Bremen and Hamburg—which are also the principal ports of entry for the Zollverein—are invariably and respectively $\frac{2}{3}$ and $\frac{1}{3}$ of one per cent. on the value of each article; and China, whose annual trade with the United States exceeds fourteen millions, because of a like uniformity of duty; cured fish, whale oil, whalebone, wheat, flour, staves, shingles, tar, pitch, ashes, beef, and pork, paying, respectively, a duty of 5 per cent. ad valorem; timber and lumber a duty of 10 per cent., and Indian corn and rice being free; while cotton goods pay 22 1-5 cents per piece of 24 yards for cambrics, and 14 4-5 cents per 40 yards for domestics, 29 3-5 cents per picul of $133\frac{1}{3}$ lbs. for tobacco, and 59 1-5 cents per picul for cotton.

The column devoted to Great Britain embraces England, Scotland, and Ireland only.

For changes and modifications, reference is invited to the tariff of each country specified, to be found elsewhere in the volume.

COMPARATIVE STATEMENT—Continued.

STAPLE PRODUCTS.	DUTIES ON IMPORTS INTO— The United States, per cent. ad valorem, under the act of—		GREAT BRITAIN.	FRANCE.	SPAIN.
	1846.	1857.	Tariff, 1853.	Tariff, 1844-1855.	Tariff, 1852-1853.
Wheat	20	15	24 cents per quarter, = 8 bushels.	$4\frac{3}{5}$ to $87\frac{9}{10}$ cents per hectolitre of 2. 84 bushels, according to price in the markets.	Prohibited, unless by special license.
Flour	20	15	9 cents per cwt	$9\frac{3}{10}$ cts. to $2 59 per 220 pounds, according to price in the markets.	Prohibited, unless by special license.
Indian corn	20	15	24 cents per quarter, = 8 bushels.	$2\frac{3}{5}$ to $48\frac{3}{10}$ cts. per hectolitre, according to price.	Prohibited, unless by special license.
Indian meal	20	15	9 cents per cwt	$5\frac{1}{2}$ cts. to $1 55 per 220 pounds, according to price in the markets.	Prohibited, unless by special license.
Ship bread	20	15	do	No importation	No importation
Rice	20	15	9 cents per cwt.; in the husk, 18 cts. per quarter.	$46\frac{1}{2}$ cents per 220 lbs.; in the husk, $23\frac{1}{4}$ cents per 220 pounds.	$2 12 per quintal
Cotton	Free	Free	Free	$3 72 per 220 pounds	$1 85 per quintal
Tobacco	30	24	72 cents per pound, and 5 per cent. additional.	Government monopoly.	15 cts. per 1 lb. 3 drs., in Malaga; elsewhere, prohibited.
Candles, tallow	20	15	56 cents per cwt	$4 $62\frac{1}{2}$ per 220 pounds	$95\frac{1}{2}$ cts. per arroba
Soap	30	24	16 cents per cwt	Prohibited	$2 65 per quintal; $4 25 per quintal, (hard.)
Tobacco, manufactured.	40	30	$2 16 per pound, and 5 per cent. additional.	Government monopoly	Prohibited. In Malaga, Virginia cigars, 25 cts. per 1 lb. 7 oz.
Iron, manufactures of.	30	24	30 cents per cwt	Prohibited, except wire, $11 11 per 220 pounds.	2 to 4 cts. per lb., according to quality.
Wood, manufactures of.	30	24	Generally 10 per cent. ad valorem.	Household and other wares 15 per cent. ad valorem.	36 per cent. ad valorem
Cotton goods, white	20	19	5 per cent. ad valorem	Prohibited	$35\frac{1}{2}$ cts. per 1 lb. 3 drs
Cotton goods, colored.	25	24	Free	do	$35\frac{1}{2}$ to $66\frac{3}{4}$ cts. per 1 lb. 3 drs., according to quality.

COMPARATIVE STATEMENT—Continued.

STAPLE PRODUCTS.	DUTIES ON IMPORTS INTO— The United States, per cent. ad valorem, under the act of— 1846.	1857.	CUBA. Tariff, 1854.	ZOLLVEREIN. Tariff, 1854.	BELGIUM. Tariff, 1853-1855.
Oil, spermaceti	20	15	27½ per cent. on valuation of $2 50 per arroba, = 25 lbs. 7 oz.	34½ cts. per centner, = 110¼ lbs.	$2 27 per hectolitre, = 26½ gallons.
Oil, whale and other fish.	20	15	27½ per cent. on valuation of $2 50 per arroba, = 25 lbs. 7 oz.	34½ cts. per centner, = 110¼ lbs.	$2 27 per hectolitre, = 26½ gallons.
Whalebone	20	15	27½ per cent. on valuation of $62 50 per quintal.	Free	$11 40 per 100 kilogrammes, = 220 lbs.; raw, free.
Dried fish	20	15	33½ per cent. on valuation of $3 50 per quintal.	69 cts per ton	$4 75 per 340 lbs
Staves	20	15	27½ per cent. on valuation of $25 per M. of cedar or maple, and $20 per M. of pine.	46 cts. per shcifflast, = 4,124 lbs., for pine, beach, &c.; 92 cts. for oak; 24 cts. by land.	$1 67½ per 100 for hhds.; for common, 40 cts.
Shingles	20	15	27½ per cent. on valuation of $3 75 per M.	46 cts. per schifflast, = 4,124 lbs., for pine, beach, &c.; 92 cts. for oak; 24 cts. by land.	40 cts. per 100
Lumber	20	15	27½ per cent. on valuation of $25 per M. of cedar or maple, and $20 per M. of pine.	23 cts. per 100 square feet for pine.	$1 67½ per tonneau, = 52$\frac{8}{10}$ square feet.
Timber	20	15	33½ per cent. ad valorem	69 cts. per 75 cubic feet for oak, 23 cts. for pine.	37½ cts. per tonneau
Tar	20	15	27½ per cent. on valuation of $3 per bbl. of 200 lbs.	11½ cts. per centner	Free
Pitch	20	15	27½ per cent. on valuation of $3 per bbl. of 200 lbs.	do do	71⅛ cts. per 44,000 lbs
Rosin and turpentine.	20	15	27½ per cent. on valuation of $12 50 per quintal.	Free. Turpentine 1 per cent. ad valorem.	14⅜ cts. per 220 lbs., (rosin.)
Ashes	20	15	27½ per cent. on valuation of 37½ cts. per lb., (potash.)	11½ cts. per centner, (potash) Wood, free.	Free
Skins and furs	20	19 & 15	No importation	46 cts. per centner	1 to 6 per cent. ad valorem, raw or dressed.
Beef	20	15	33½ per cent. on valuation of $9 per bbl., (salted.)	$1 38 per centner, (salted)	93 cts. per 220 lbs
Tallow	10	8	27½ per cent. on valuation of $7 50 per quintal.	$2 07 per centner	47 cts. per 220 lbs
Butter	20	15	27½ per cent. on valuation of $16 per quintal.	$2 53 per centner	No importation

COMPARATIVE STATEMENT—Continued.

STAPLE PRODUCTS.	DUTIES ON IMPORTS INTO—				
	The United States, per cent. ad valorem, under the act of—		CUBA.	ZOLLVEREIN.	BELGIUM.
	1846.	1857.	Tariff, 1854.	Tariff, 1854.	Tariff, 1853-1855.
Cheese	30	24	27½ per cent. on valuation of $10 per quintal.	$2 53 per centner	$1 98½ per 220 lbs
Pork	20	15	33⅓ per cent. on valuation of $12 per bbl., (salted)	$1 38 per centner, (salted.)	93 cts. per 220 lbs
Bacon	20	15	33⅓ per cent. on valuation of $2 per arroba.	$1 38 per centner	$2 77 per 220 lbs
Lard	20	15	33⅓ per cent. on valuation of $3 per arroba.	do	93 cts per 220 lbs
Wheat	20	15	33⅓ per cent. on valuation of $5 per quintal.	11½ cts. per scheffel, = 1½ bushel. On the left side of the Elbe, 2⅔ cts. per scheffel.	18¾ cts. per 220 lbs
Flour	20	15	$9 50 per barrel	$1 38 per centner	57 cts. per 220 lbs., when not free by royal order.
Indian corn	20	15	33⅓ per cent. on valuation of $4 per barrel.	11½ cts. per scheffel	13 cts. per 220 lbs
Indian meal	20	15	33⅓ per cent. on valuation of $5 per barrel.	$1 38 per centner	No importation
Ship bread	20	15	33⅓ per cent. on valuation of $2 per arroba.	No importation	57 cts per 220 lbs
Rice	20	15	33⅓ per cent. on valuation of $1 25 per arroba.	69 cts. per centner; 45 cts. in the husk.	$1 52 per 220 lbs; 47 cts. in husk.
Cotton	Free	Free	27½ per cent. on valuation of $10 per quintal, picked; not picked, $5.	Free	Free
Tobacco	30	24	2 per cent. on valuation of $5 per quintal, in deposit.	$2 76 per centner	$1 86 per 220 lbs
Candles, tallow	20	15	33⅓ per cent. on valuation of $12 per quintal.	$4 14 per centner	$5 41 per 220 lbs
Soap	30	24	33⅓ per cent. on valuation of $2 per arroba.	$2 30 per centner, (common white.)	No importation
Tobacco, manufactured.	40	30	33⅓ per cent. on valuation of $25 per quintal.	$7 59 per centner; cigars and snuff, $13 80.	$39 per 220 lbs. cigars
Iron, manufactures of.	30	24	33⅓ per cent. ad valorem	No importation	$5 09 per 220 lbs.; $2 75 per 220 lbs. nails.
Wood, manufactures of	30	24	do do	do	6 per cent. ad valorem. (This applies only to hoops.)
Cotton goods, white	20	19	do do	$5 52 per centner	$33 37 per 220 lbs
Cotton goods, colored.	25	24	do do	do	$60 18 per 220 lbs

COMPARATIVE STATEMENT—Continued.

STAPLE PRODUCTS.	DUTIES ON IMPORTS INTO—				
	The United States, per cent. ad valorem, under the act of—		HOLLAND.	BRAZIL.	MEXICO.
	1846.	1857.	Tariff, 1854.	Tariff, 1844.	Tariff, 1856.
Oil, spermaceti	20	15	Free	(a) 15⅗ cts. per canada, = 1. 87 gallon.	$12 per 101 lbs
Oil, whale and other fish.	20	15	do	$9\frac{9}{10}$ cts. per 1. 87 gallon	Free; (of Pacific fishery)
Whalebone	20	15	do		$4 per 101 lbs
Dried fish	20	15	60 cts. per 331½ lbs	44 cts. per arroba, = 32½ lbs.	$2 per 101 lbs
Staves	20	15	40 cts. per ton, = 2, 210 lbs.		30 cts. per 101 lbs
Shingles	20	15	Not defined		Free
Lumber	20	15	30 cts. per ton		Free; (for building)
Timber	20	15	For ship building, bark on, 10 cts. per ton.		do do
Tar	20	15	Free	48 cts. per barrel	Not defined
Pitch	20	15	do	do	do
Rosin and turpentine.	20	15	Rosin, free; turpentine, 1 per cent. ad valorem.		do
Ashes	20	15	Free		do
Skins and furs	20	19 & 15	1 to 6 per cent. ad valorem, raw or dressed.		60 cts. (beaver) per 1. 014 lb.; 30 cts. (hare, &c., for hats,) per 1. 014 lb.
Beef	20	15	$2 40 per 221 lbs., (salted;) $3 20 per 221 lbs., (smoked.)	Dried, 27½ cts. per arroba; salted, 41¾ cts. per arroba.	$5 per 101 lbs
Tallow	10	8	20 cts. per 221 lbs	59⅗ cts. per arroba	50 per cent. ad valorem
Butter	20	15	$1 20 per 221 lbs		$4 80 per 101 lbs
Cheese	30	24	$2 per 221 lbs	6½ cts. per arroba	$3 per 101 lbs
Pork	20	15	20 cts. per 221 lbs, (salted.)	55 cts. per arroba	$5 per 101 lbs
Bacon	20	15	26 cts. per 221 lbs	3 cts. per lb	do
Lard	20	15	20 cts. per 221 lbs	82½ cts per arroba	Prohibited, except at Yucatan, Tampico, Matamoras, and the custom-houses of the northern frontiers.
Wheat	20	15	$3 20 per last, = $85\frac{20}{100}$ bushels.		Prohibited, except for consumption and through the custom-houses of the northern frontiers.
Flour	20	15	$1 80 per 221 lbs	$1 65 per barrel of 195 lbs.	Prohibited. (See Lard)
Indian corn	20	15	$2 40 per last		Prohibited. (See Wheat)
Indian meal	20	15	$1 80 per 221 lbs		do do

(a) The milrei is estimated at 55 cents.

COMPARATIVE STATEMENT—Continued.

STAPLE PRODUCTS.	DUTIES ON IMPORTS INTO—				
	The United States, per cent. ad valorem, under the act of—		HOLLAND.	BRAZIL.	MEXICO.
	1846.	1857.	Tariff, 1854.	Tariff, 1844.	Tariff, 1856.
Ship bread	20	15	$1 80 per 221 lbs		$2 40 cts. per 101 lbs
Rice	20	15	12 cts. per 221 lbs		Prohibited
Cotton	Free	Free	Free		$1 50 per 101 lbs
Tobacco	30	24	28 cts. per 221 lbs	$3 30 per arroba	Government monopoly
Candles, tallow	20	15	$4 per 221 lbs	$1 42 per arroba	50 per cent. ad valorem
Soap	30	24	$1 80 per 221 lbs	Castile soap, 40 per cent. ad valorem.	$24 per 101 lbs., (fine)
Tobacco, manufactured.	40	30	$4 80 per 221 lbs.; cigars, $16.		See Tobacco
Iron, manufactures of.	30	24	6 per cent. ad valorem; nails, 60 cts. per 221 lbs.	Nails and spikes, 41½ cts. to $1 32 per 129½ lbs.	$2 per 101 lbs. hatchets, wire chains; $2 50 per 101 lbs. cut nails.
Wood, manufactures of.	30	24	6 per cent. ad valorem		
Cotton goods, white	20	19	do do	4 to 6½ cts. per square yard.	3 to 5 cts. per vara
Cotton goods, colored.	25	24	do do		do do

COMPARATIVE STATEMENT—Continued.

STAPLE PRODUCTS.	DUTIES ON IMPORTS INTO—				
	The United States, per cent. ad valorem, under the act of—		CHILI.	VENEZUELA.	HAYTI.
	1846.	1857.	Tariff, 1854.	Tariff, 1841-1852.	Tariff, 1854.
Oil, spermaceti	20	15	Free	3 cts. per lb., = 1 lb. 3 drachms.	5 cts. per gallon
Oil, whale and other fish.	20	15	25 per cent. on valuation of 80 cts. per gallon.	3 cts. per lb., = 1 lb. 3 drachms	5 per cent. ad valorem
Whalebone	20	15	Raw, free	2 cts. per lb	5 cts. per lb, = 1 lb. 3 drachms.
Dried fish	20	15	25 per cent. on valuation of $6 per quintal, = 101 lbs.	2½ cts. per lb	42 cts. per 100 lbs., = 108 lbs.; 50 cts. per barrel.
Staves	20	15	Free	Free	75 cts. per M
Shingles	20	15	25 per cent. on valuation of $14 per M.	$1 per M	Not defined
Lumber	20	15	Free, on valuation of $35 per M. feet	$6 per M., (pine boards)	$1 75 per M., boards; oak, $3 50.
Timber	20	15	Free, on valuation of 25 cts. per square foot.	$9 per M., (pine beams)	$2 for hard, and $3 for soft, per 1,080 lbs.
Tar	20	15	Free	$1 per bbl., = 8 arrobas, or 16 gallons.	75 cts. per barrel
Pitch	20	15	do	Free	50 cts. per barrel
Rosin and turpentine.	20	15	do	Rosin, free; turpentine, 90 cts. per arroba.	Not defined
Ashes	20	15	25 per cent. on valuation of $5 per quintal.	Not defined	do
Skins and furs	20	19 & 15	No importation	do	Buffalo, $12 per dozen
Beef	20	15	Salted, free	2 cts. per lb	$1 50 per barrel, (salted;) $1 50 per bbl., (smoked.)
Tallow	10	8	6 per cent. on valuation of $11 per quintal, purified; $7 crude.	$2 per quintal, = 101 lbs	1 cent per lb
Butter	20	15	25 per cent. on valuation of 20 cts. per lb., = 1.014 lb.	6 cts. per lb	$1 50 per 100 lbs
Cheese	30	24	25 per cent. on valuation of 18¾ per lb.	5 cts. per lb	2 cts. per lb
Pork	20	15	25 per cent on valuation of $5 per quintal; salted, free.	2½ cts. per lb	$1 per bbl., (salted;) $1 50 per barrel, (smoked.)
Bacon	20	15	25 per cent. on valuation of 14 cts. per lb.	5 cts. per lb	2 cts. per lb
Lard	20	15	25 per cent. on valuation of 12½ cts. per lb.	4 cts. per lb	$1 50 per 100 lbs

COMPARATIVE STATEMENT—Continued.

STAPLE PRODUCTS.	DUTIES ON IMPORTS INTO—				
	The United States, per cent. ad valorem, under the act of—		CHILI.	VENEZUELA.	HAYTI.
	1846.	1857.	Tariff, 1854.	Tariff, 1841-1852.	Tariff, 1854.
Wheat	20	15	25 per cent. ad valorem, the price per fanega (2½ bushels) being under $3; over, free.	Seed, free; otherwise not defined.	Not defined
Flour	20	15	25 per cent. ad valorem, the price per quintal being under $4; over, free.	$4 per barrel of 200 lbs	$2 per barrel
Indian corn	20	15	See Wheat	Free	$1 per barrel
Indian meal	20	15	do	do	do
Ship bread	20	15	25 per cent. on valuation of $3 per quintal.	4 cts. per lb	37½ cts. per 100 lbs
Rice	20	15	25 per cent. on valuation of $5 50 per quintal from Carolina; elsewhere on valuation of $3 50.	Free	75 cts. per 100 lbs
Cotton	Free	Free	25 per cent. on valuation of $4 per quintal, (not picked;) picked, $8.	Not defined	No importation
Tobacco	30	24	Government monopoly	$6 per quintal	4 cts. per 1 lb. 3 drachms.
Candles, tallow	20	15	25 per cent. on valuation of $16 per quintal	$4 per quintal	2 cts. per lb
Soap	30	24	25 per cent. on valuation of $6 per quintal, common; $9 fine.	4 cts. per lb	$1 25 per 100 lbs
Tobacco, manufactured.	40	30	25 per cent. on valuation of 20 cts. per lb.; cigars, 75 cts. per lb.	Cigars, $2 per 1,000	4 cts. per lb.; snuff, 20 cts. per lb.; cigars, 25 cts. per 100.
Iron, manufactures of.	30	24	25 per cent. ad valorem	Nails, 6 cts. per 1,000; hoops, $1 60 per quintal.	Nails, $1 50 per 100 lbs.; hoops, $9 75 per 100 lbs.
Wood, manufactures of.	30	24	do do	Furniture, 6 cts. per foot	Not defined
Cotton goods, white	20	19	do do	18 cts. per lb., (yarn)	2 to 8 cts. per yard
Cotton goods, colored.	25	24	do do	3 cts. per vara, = 33⅓ inches.	do do

Comparative statement exhibiting import duties levied by the States of South America, respectively, on articles received from the United States.(a)

DENOMINATION OF MERCHANDISE.	DUTIES ON IMPORTS INTO—					
	The United States, per cent. ad valorem, under the act of—		NEW GRENADA.—Tariff of 1855.		VENEZUELA.—Tariff of 1841–1852.	
	1846.	1857.	Number, weight, or measure.	Rate of duty.	Number, weight, or measure.	Rate of duty.
Beef	20	15		Free	1 lb 3 drs., salte	$0 02
Beer, ale, porter—in bottles	30	24	1.014 pound	$0 0⅔	12 bottles	80
in casks	30	24	do	0⅔	4.245 gallons	50
Brandy, in bottles	100	30	1 kilo., or 2⅕ lbs.	16	Dozen	4 00
in casks	100	30	do	16		3 50
Cables and cordage	25	19			101 pounds	2 00
Candles, wax	20	15	2⅕ pounds	40	1.014 pound	16
tallow	20	15			101 pounds	4 00
spermaceti	20	15	2⅕ pounds	20	1.014 poun	10
Cheese of all kinds	30	24	do	2	do	5
Cider, in bottles	30	24	Same as beer		Dozen	80
in casks	30	24	do		4.245 gallons	50
Copper, manufactures of	30	24	2⅕ pounds	15		30 per ct. ad val.
in bars	5	Free			101 pounds	3 00
Cotton, raw	Free	Free	No importation		Wicks, 1.014 lb.	18
manufactures of	25 to 30	19 to 24	2⅕ pounds	40	Yard	3
Fish, cod	20	15		Free	1.014 pound	2½
Flour, wheat	20	15		Free	Bbl 150 to 200 lb.	4 00
Glass, window	20	15	Box, 100 to 125 lbs.	2 40		30 per ct. ad val.
Hams and bacon	20	15		Free	1 pound 3 drs	5
Hats, straw	30	24	Dozen	60	Each	50
Household furniture	30	24	Chairs, dozen	6 00	1 foot	6
Do. do	30	24	1 lounge	12 50	do	6
Do. do	30	24	1 table	5 00	do	6
Indian corn	20	15		Free		Free.
Lard	20	15		Free	1.014 pound	4
Lead, in bars and sheets	20	15	1 miriagramo = 26 lbs. 9 oz.	32	101 pounds	1 50
manufactures of	30	24	2⅕ pounds	5		30 per ct. ad val.
Nails, iron	30	24	26 pounds 9 oz.	48	1,000	6
Oil, whale and other fish	20	15	1.014 pound	6¼	1.014 pound	3
Pitch	20	15	do	0½		Free.
Paper, writing	30	24	Ream	40	Ream	60
printing	30	24				Free.
Paints	20	15	2⅕ pounds	12	25 lb. 7 oz., in oil.	1 00
Pork	20	15		Free	1.014 pound	2½
Rice	20	15		Free		30 per ct. ad val.
Rosin	20	15	2⅕ pounds	0½		Free.

(a) For changes, see tariff of each country, elsewhere in the volume.

COMPARATIVE STATEMENT—Continued.

DENOMINATION OF MERCHANDISE.	DUTIES ON IMPORTS INTO—					
	The United States, per cent. ad valorem, under the act of—		NEW GRENADA.—Tariff of 1855.		VENEZUELA.—Tariff of 1841–1852.	
	1846.	1857.	Number, weight, or measure.	Rate of duty.	Number, weight, or measure.	Rate of duty.
Soap, common	30	24	26 pounds 9 oz	$0 72	1. 014 pound	$0 04
perfumed	30	24	2⅓ pounds	50	do	25
Shoes and boots, leather	30	24	10 per cent. additional to the duty on leather.		1 pair	1 50
Sugar, refined	30	24	1. 014 pound	2¾	Prohibited	
Tallow	10	8	101 pounds	2 00	Raw, 101 pounds	2 00
Tar	20	15	26 pounds 9 oz	8	Barrel of 16 gals.	1 00
Teas	(a)20	(a)15	2⅓ pounds	20	1. 014 pound	50
Tobacco, unmanufactured	30	24	do	20	101 pounds	6 00
cigars, Havana	40	30	do	80	1,000	3 00
others	40	30	do	80	do	2 00
Umbrellas, silk	30	24	Each	60	Each	75
cotton	30	24	Dozen	2 00	do	25
Wax, raw, white	20	15	2⅓ pounds	20	1. 014 pound	8
yellow	20	15	do	20	do	4
Wood, boards, pine	20	15		Free	1,000 feet	6 00
shingles	20	15		Free	do	1 00
Wines, red	40	30	2⅓ pounds	6	4. 245 gallons	(In casks,) 75
white	40	30	do	10	do	75

(a) See note, p. 168.

COMPARATIVE STATEMENT—Continued.

DENOMINATION OF MERCHANDISE.	DUTIES ON IMPORTS INTO—					
	The United States, per cent. ad valorem, under the act of—		EQUADOR.—Tariff of 1847.		BRAZIL.—Tariff of 1844.	
	1846.	1857.	Number, weight, or measure.	Rate of duty.	Number, weight, or measure.	Rate of duty.(a)
Beef	20	15	Quintal, or 101 lbs.	$2 00	Arroba of 32⅓ lbs.	(Dried,) $0 27½ (Salted,) 41¾
Beer, ale, porter—in bottles	30	24	Dozen	75	----------	16
in casks	30	24	1 gallon	25	1 canada of Bahia = 1.87 gallon.	22
Brandy, in bottles	100	30	Dozen	2 00	do	27½
in casks	100	30	Gallon	75	do	27½
Cables and cordage	25	19	101 pounds	37½	Of flax, 100 arratels, 129½ lbs.	3 30
Candles, wax	20	15	1.014 pound	18¾	1 pound	11
tallow	20	15	do	3	Arroba, 32⅓ lbs	1 42
spermaceti	20	15	do	6¼	1 pound	10
Cheese of all kinds	30	24	101 pounds	2 00	English, 1 lb. Other, 1 pound	10 6½
Cider, in bottles	30	24	Doze	1 00	Same as beer	----------
in casks	30	24	Gallon	25	do	----------
Copper, manufactures of	30	24	1.014 pound	6¼	For sheathing ships, 1 lb.	6½
in bars	5	Free	101 pounds	2 50	do	6½
Cotton, raw	Free	Free	do	50	----------	----------
manufactures of	25 to 30	19 to 24	Yard	(Drills,) 2½	Square yard	From 4 to 6½
Fish, cod	20	15	101 pounds	3 00	Dried or salted, arroba, cod or other.	44
Flour, wheat	20	15	Barrel of about 200 pounds.	7 50	Barrel of 6 arrobas, 195 lbs.	1 65
Glass, window	20	15	Box of 100 feet sq	1 00	1 square foot	1
Hams and bacon	20	15	101 pounds	50	Hams, arroba	1 05⅔
Hats, straw	30	24	Each, for ladies	2 00	----------	----------
Household furniture	30	24	1 table	4 50	----------	----------
Indian corn	20	15	101 pounds	1 00	----------	----------
Lard	20	15	do	4 50	Arroba	82½
Lead, in bars and sheets	20	15	do	1 00	In bars and pigs, 129½ pounds.	1 65
manufactures of	30	24	do	1 50	do	1 65
Nails, iron	30	24	do	1 00	----------	----------
Oil, whale and other fish	20	15	Gallon	5	Whale, per canada of Bahia, 1.87 gallon. Spermaceti, do.	$9\frac{9}{10}$ 15⅗
Pitch	20	15	101 pounds	30	American, per bbl. Other, per barrel	48 1 10

(a) The milrei is estimated at 55 cents.

COMPARATIVE STATEMENT—Continued.

DENOMINATION OF MERCHANDISE.	DUTIES ON IMPORTS INTO—					
	The United States, per cent. ad valorem, under the act of—		EQUADOR.—Tariff of 1847.		BRAZIL.—Tariff of 1844.	
	1846.	1857.	Number, weight, or measure.	Rate of duty.	Number, weight, or measure.	Rate of duty.
Paper, writing	30	24	Ream	$0 25	Blue, per ream	$0 39⅗
					White, per ream	28
printing	30	24	do	75	Ream	55
Paints	20	15	101 pounds	2 00	Oil paints, 1 lb	2¼
Pork	20	15	do	2 00	Salt, arroba	55
Rice	20	15	do	3 00		
Rosin	20	15	do	20		
Soap, common	30	24	do	1 50	Castile	40 per ct. ad val.
perfumed	30	24	Dozen cakes	12½ to 25		
Shoes and boots, leather	30	24	1 pair	1 50	Pair	8¼ to 51⅘
Sugar, refined	30	24	101 pounds	4 00		
Tallow	10	8	d	2 00	Raw, arroba	59⅗
Tar	20	15	do	25	Swedish, per bbl	1 10
					American, do	48
Teas	(a)20	(a)15	1.014 pound	18¾	1 pound	33
Tobacco, unmanufactured	30	24	101 pounds	10 00	Smok'g, in leaves, arroba.	3 30
cigars, Havana	40	30	1,000	5 00		
Umbrellas, silk	30	24	One	1 00		
cotton	30	24	Dozen	2 00		
Wax, raw, white	20	15	101 pounds	9 00	1 pound	10⅓
yellow	20	15				
Wood—boards, pine	20	15	1 foot	2	Fern boards, up to ½ inch thick, per 1,000 square palmos, (1 palmo = 8½ in.)	3 30
Shingles	20	15	1,000	3 36		3 30
Wines, red	40	30	Gallon	15	Per canada, 1.87 gallon.	27½ to 66
white	40	30				

(a) See note, p. 186.

COMPARATIVE STATEMENT—Continued.

DENOMINATION OF MERCHANDISE.	DUTIES ON IMPORTS INTO—						
	The United States, per cent. ad valorem, under the act of—		URUGUAY.	ARGENTINE REPUBLIC.	CHILI.		
			Tariff of 1853.	Tariff of 1854.	Tariff of 1854.		
	1846.	1857.	Per centage duty ad valorem.	Per centage duty ad valorem.	Number, weight, or measure.	Fixed value on the number, weight, or measure.	Per centage duty on the fixed value.
Beef	20	15	30	No importation	Quintal, or 101 lbs.	$7 00	Free
Beer, ale, porter—in bottles	30	24	30	25	Dozen; specific	duty of 1 00	
in casks	30	24	30	25	Gallon; specific	duty of 25	
Brandy, in bottles	100	30	30	25	Dozen; specific	duty of 3 00	
in casks	100	30	30	25	Gallon; specific	duty of 1 00	
Cables and cordage	25	19	5	15		Valuation	25
Candles, wax	20	15	30	15	1.014 pound	50	25
tallow	20	15	30	15	101 pounds	16 00	25
spermaceti	20	15	30	15	1.014 pound	40	25
Cheese of all kinds	30	24	30	20	do	18¾	25
Cider, in bottle	30	24	30	25	Same as beer		
in casks	30	24	30	25	do		
Copper, manufactures of	30	24		15	1.014 pound	40	25
in bars	5	Free		5	101 pounds	13 00	25
Cotton, raw	Free	Free	30	5	do	(Picked,) 8 00	25
manufactures of	25 to 30	19 to 24	30	Fustian, 15	20	1 pound	37½	25
Fish, cod	20	15	25	20	101 pounds	6 00	25
Flour, wheat	20	15	35	Per 101 lbs. $1 44	If the price is un	der $4 the quintal.	25
Glass, window	20	15	30	15	100 superficial feet	3 00	25
Hams and bacon	20	15	30	20	1.014 pound	14	25
Hats, straw	30	24	30	15		Valuation	25
Household furniture	30	24	30	15		do	25
Indian corn	20	15	30	Per fanega = 2½ bushels 96 cts.	If the price is un = 2.57 bushels.	der $3 per fanega,	25
					If the price is over	$3 per fanega	Free
Lard	20	15	30	20	1.014 pound	12½	25
Lead, in bars and sheets	20	15	30	5			Free
manufactures of	30	24	30	15	101 pounds	6 00	25
Nails, iron	30	24	30	15	1.014 pound	8 to 12½	25
Oil, whale and other fish	20	15	30	15			
Pitch	20	15	5	15	101 pounds	2 00	Free
Paper, writing	30	24	30	15		Valuation	25
printing	30	24	30	15			25
Paints	20	15	30	15	101 pounds	6 00	25
Pork	20	15	30	20	do	8 00	Free
Rice	20	15		20	Carolina, 101 lbs.	5 50	25
Rosin	20	15	5	15	101 pounds	2 00	Free
Soap, common	30	24	30	15	do	6 00	25
perfumed	30	24	30	15	1.014 pound	40	25
Shoes and boots, leather	30	24	30	20	Dozen, for men, of	calfskin, 18 00	15

COMPARATIVE STATEMENT—Continued.

DENOMINATION OF MERCHANDISE.	DUTIES ON IMPORTS INTO—						
	The United States, per cent. ad valorem, under the act of—		URUGUAY.	ARGENTINE REPUBLIC.	CHILI.		
			Tariff of 1853.	Tariff of 1854.	Tariff of 1854.		
	1846.	1857.	Per centage duty ad valorem.	Per centage duty ad valorem.	Number, weight, or measure.	Fixed value on the number, weight, or measure.	Per centage duty on the fixed value.
Sugar, refined	30	24	25	20	Arroba, or 25 lbs. 7 ounces.	$2 00	$0 25
Tallow	10	8	--------	(Raw,) 15	101 pounds	(Raw.) 7 00	6
Tar	20	15	5	15	------do	2 00	Free
Teas	(a)20	(a)15	25	20	Pound; specific	duty of 25	--------
Tobacco, unmanufactured	30	24	25	20	Monopoly	--------	--------
cigars, Havana	40	30	35	20	--------	--------	--------
others	40	30	35	20	Per pound	75	--------
Umbrellas, silk	30	24	--------	15	Each	2 50	25
cotton	30	24	--------	15	Dozen	6 50	25
Wax—raw, white	20	15	--------	15	101 pounds	50	25
yellow	20	15	--------	15	------do	50	25
Wood—boards, pine	20	15	25	5	1,000 feet	35 00	Free
shingles	20	15	5	5	--------	--------	--------
Wines, red	40	30	30	25	Gallon; specific	duty. 25	--------
white	40	30	30	25	----do------do	37½	--------

(a) See note, p. 168.

COMPARATIVE STATEMENT—Continued.

DENOMINATION OF MERCHANDISE.	DUTIES ON IMPORTS INTO—					
	The United States, per cent. ad valorem, under the act of—		BOLIVIA. Tariff of 1844–1850.	PERU. Tariff of 1855.		
	1846.	1857.	Per centage duty ad valorem.	Number, weight, or measure	Fixed value on the number, weight, or measure.	Per centage duty on the fixed value.
Beef	20	15	No importation	101 pounds	$6 50	$0 03
Beer, ale, porter—in bottles	30	24	36	Dozen	Specific duty	1 50
in casks	30	24	36	Gallon	do	25
Brandy, in bottles	100	30	36	Dozen—over 30 degrees	do	1 50
in casks	100	30	36	Gallon—over 30 degrees	do	1 50
				Do under 30 degrs.	do	1 00
Cables and cordage	25	19	28			Free.
Candles, wax	20	15				
tallow	20	15	28	1.014 pound	Specific duty	12½
spermaceti	20	15	28	do	do	12½
Cheese of all kinds	30	24	28	101 pounds	do	4 00
Cider, in bottles	30	24	36	Dozen	do	1 50
in casks	30	24	36	Gallon	do	25
Copper, manufactures of	30	24	28	1.014 pound	37	15
in bars	5	Free	28	In sheets		Free.
Cotton, raw	Free	Free	28	101 pounds	4 00	1
manufactures of	25 to 30	19 to 24	28	Fustian—dozen	6 00	15
Fish, cod	20	15	28	101 pounds	5 00	10
Flour, wheat	20	15	28	do	Specific duty	2 00
Glass, window	20	15	8		Valuation	25
Hams and bacon	20	15		1.014 pound	20	3
Hats, straw	30	24	28			Free.
				Other kinds	Valuation	30
Household furniture	30	24	28		do	30
Indian corn	20	15	Free	101 pounds	1 50	20
Lard	20	15	Free	do	Specific duty	1 00
Lead, in bars and sheets	20	15	28	do		Free.
manufactures of	30	24	28	do	7 00	20
Nails, iron	30	24	6	do	5 50	6
Oil, whale and other fish	20	15	28	Gallon	35	20
Pitch	20	15	28			Free.
Paper, writing	30	24	28		Valuation	20
printing	30	24		For music	do	10
Paints	20	15	28	Common—101 pounds	7 00	20
				Fine, in pots—dozen	75	20
Pork	20	15	Free	Salted		Free.
Rice	20	15	Free		Specific duty	2 00
Rosin	20	15	28	Barrel	4 00	Free.
Soap, common	30	24	28	101 pounds		
perfumed	30	24	28	do	25 00	20

COMPARATIVE STATEMENT—Continued.

EENOMINATION OF MERCHANDISE.	DUTIES ON IMPORTS INTO— The United States, per cent. ad valorem, under the act of— 1846.	1857.	BOLIVIA. Tariff of 1844–1850. Per centage duty ad valorem.	PERU. Tariff of 1855. Number, weight, or measure.	Fixed value on the number, weight, or measure.	Per centage duty on the fixed value.
Shoes and boots, leather	30	24	28	Dozen	$8 00	$0 30
Sugar, refined	30	24	28	Arroba, 25 pounds 7 oz	Specific duty	1 50
Tallow	10	8	28	101 pounds	do	2 00
Tar	20	15	28	Barrel	4 00	Free.
Teas	(a)20	(a)15	28	1.014 pound	Specific duty	18¾
Tobacco, unmanufactured	30	24	28	101 pounds	do	20 00
cigars, Havana	40	30	28	1.014 pound	do	62½
others	40	30	28	do	do	62½
Umbrellas, silk	30	24	28	Dozen	40 00	20
cotton	30	24	28	do	10 00	20
Wax—raw, white	20	15	28	101 pound	50 00	20
yellow"	20	15	28		30 00	20
Wood—boards, pine	20	15	28	do		Free.
shingles	20	15	28			Free.
Wines, red	40	30	36	Dozen bottles	Specific duty	1 50
white	40	30	36	do	do	1 50

(a) See note, p. 168.

Comparative statement exhibiting import duties levied by the States of Central America, respectively, on articles received from the United States.

DENOMINATION OF MERCHANDISE.	The United States, per cent. ad valorem, under the act of—		DUTIES ON IMPORTS INTO— GUATEMALA.		SAN SALVADOR.		COSTA RICA.(a)	
	1846.	1857.	Number, weight, or measure.	Rate of duty.	Number, weight, or measure.	Fixed value.(b)	Number, weight, or measure.	Rate of duty.
Bread, ship	20	15	Arroba, 25 lbs. 7 oz.	$0 50	Quintal, 101 pounds	$3 00	1. 014 pound	$0 03
Brandy, in bottles	100	30	Dozen	72	Dozen	2 50	Of sugar cane	Prohibited.
in barrels	100	30	15 to 18 gallons	3 44	Gallon	1 00	1. 014 gallon	11
Candles, tallow	20	15	1. 014 pound	3		Prohibited	1. 014 pound	2
stearine	20	15	do	5	1. 014 pound	30	do	3
Cider	30	24	Dozen bottles	5	Dozen bottles	2 00	In barrels of 101 lbs.	1 00
Copper, manufactures of	30	24	1. 014 pound	$12\frac{1}{2}$	101 pounds	25 to 37	101 pounds	(Stills) 10 00
Cotton goods, white	25	24	Yard	$2\frac{1}{2}$	Yard	12	1. 014 pound	7
colored	30	24	do	3	do	12	do	8
Cheese	30	24	101 pound	2 88	25 pounds 7 ounces	4 00	do	4
Cloths and casimeres, fine	30	24	Yard	78	Yard	1 00	do	25
Fish, in oil	20	15	1. 014 pound	$4\frac{1}{2}$	101 pounds	4 00	101 pounds	2 00
Flour	20	15	25 pounds 7 ounces	25	do	4 00		Free.
Gold and silver coin	Free	Free		Free		Free		Free.
Glass, window	20	15	Box of 137 to 150 lbs.	3 60	Dozen panes	38 to 100	101 pounds	1 50
Hides and skins	5	4	1. 014 pound	12	Dozen	12 00 to 24 00		Not defined.
Indigo	10	4	do	2 00		Not defined	1. 014 pound	$3\frac{1}{2}$
Pork, salt	20	15	25 pounds 7 ounces	48	101 pounds	5 00	101 pounds	$62\frac{1}{2}$
Printing presses	30	24		Free		Free		Free.
Paper, writing	30	24	Ream	25	Ream	2 00	101 pounds	3 00
Rice	20	15	25 pounds 7 ounces	24	25 pounds 7 ounces	3 00		Not defined.
Soap, common	30	24	do do	72	101 pounds	8 00	1. 014 pound	2
Silk, raw	15	12	1. 014 pound	72		Not defined	do	20
Shoes, calf skin, for men	30	24	Pair	4	Dozen	6 00 to 18 00	do	25
patent leather	30	24	Pair	57	do	do	do	25

(a) For tariff of Nicaragua, see volume 1 "Digests," page 599, *et seq.*

(b) Rate of duty 24 per cent. on the fixed value assigned to each article. March 10, 1856, the rate was reduced from 24 to 20 per cent.

COMPARATIVE STATEMENT—Continued.

DENOMINATION OF MERCHANDISE.	DUTIES ON IMPORTS INTO—							
	The United States, per cent. ad valorem, under the act of—		GUATEMALA.		SAN SALVADOR.		COSTA RICA.(a)	
	1846.	1857.	Number, weight, or measure.	Rate of duty.	Number, weight, or measure.	Fixed value.(b)	Number, weight, or measure.	Rate of duty.
Sheathing metal	Free	Free	1. 014 pound	$0 08	1. 014 pound	$0 30	1. 014 pound	$0 06
Spirits, in casks	100	30	12 to 15 gallons	3 44	Gallon	1 00	See brandy	
Teas	(c)20	(c)15	1. 014 pound	18	1. 014 pound	50	101 pounds	2 00
Tobacco, unmanufactured	30	24	24 per cent. on the invoice value, with an addition of 20 per cent. on the aggregate amount.		Government monopoly.		Prohibited	
manufactured	40	30						
Tin, crude	5	Free	101 pounds	5 00	101 pounds	18 00	101 pounds	2 00
Wines, in casks	40	30	12 to 15 gallons	2 16	Gallon	50	do	2 00
Wood, manufactured as furniture	30	24	40 per cent. ad val.		101 pounds	5 00	do	5 00

(a) For tariff of Nicaragua, see volume 1 "Digests," page 599, *et seq.*
(b) Rate of duty 24 per cent. on the fixed value assigned to each article. March 10, 1856, the rate was reduced from 24 to 20 per cent.
(c See note, page 168.

Comparative statement exhibiting the per centage increase or decrease of duties levied on certain articles in the countries specified, from 1846 *to* 1853, *inclusive;(a) showing the changes within that period, during which no change occurred in the tariff of the United States.*

DENOMINATION OF MERCHANDISE.	DUTIES ON IMPORTS INTO—				
	ENGLAND.	RUSSIA.	SWEDEN.	NORWAY.	DENMARK.
	Decrease.	Decrease.	Decrease.	Decrease.	Decrease.
Ale, beer, and porter	Same	Porter, in bot'ls, 30			
Coal	Same			50	64½
Coffee and cocoa	50 per cent.		Cocoa, 25.		
Copper	100 per cent	Manufactures of, 24¾.			Plates, bolts, nails, wire, 52¾
Cotton, yarn	Same	Twist, 20 to 48(b).			69 to 88½
manufactures of	Not made up, same	43 to 83⅓		22½	43 to 71⅓
Earthenware and porcelain	Common, same.	12½ to 34			Earthenware, 48; porcelain, 178 to 427¾ increase.
Fish	100 per cent.		Cod, 10; herrings, 278¾ inc.		
Glass	57½ per cent.	Plain, 83; cut, 33⅓ to 79.			
Hardware and cutlery	Common, 50 p. ct.	32½ to 87			50 to 66¾; fine, 100 increase.
Iron	Same	Manufactures of, 22 to 86⅓.	Anchors, 16¾; scissors, 54⅓; bar, prohibited.	Bar, 21½	
Lead	100 per cent	Manufactures, 83⅓			Pigs, free; rolls, 31.
Linen, yarn	Same	35⅓ to 57		28⅓	16¾ to 96¾
manufactures of	Same	48 to 89¼			6 to 96¼
Leather	Same	Prohib'n removed.			
manufactures of	Same	66¾			12½ to 26
Rum	2⅓ per cent.	42¾			25
Salt	Same				58¾ increase.
Silk, manufactures of	Same	1½ to 56¼.			
Steel	Same	38	33¾		
Sugar, refined	90½ per cent.				Prohib'n removed.
Tin	Same	Raw, 53¾; manufactured, 22 to 50.			Unwrought, free.
Wool	Same	Raw, and yarn, 28 to 90.			Yarn, 28⅓ increase.
manufactures of	Same	11½ to 60¾	50 to 100 increase	36½	18 to 33⅓ increase.

(a) See Appendix.
(b) According to character, quality, or value.

TARIFF CHANGES—Continued.

Denomination of merchandise.	Duties on imports into—				
	Zollverein.	Holland.	Belgium.(a)	Portugal.	
	Increase.	Decrease.	Decrease.	Increase.	Decrease.
Coal		Free	10¼ increase.		
Coffee and cocoa	54½ dec.			Coffee, 41 to 42½.	
Copper		Plates, bolts, nails, 75.	Cakes, blocks, 95.		
Cotton, yarn	50			1¾ to 9¼	Twisted, for sewing, 22¼.
manufactures of				7¼ to 15¾	Bobbinets, 25 to 86.
Fish			Herrings, 20.		
Hardware and cutlery				Fine, 20	Tools and knives, 4 to 70.
Iron		Anchors and machinery, 83¼; pig, bar, sheet, and railway, 50.		Wire, 21	Anchors, 14; pig and bar, 74½; sheet, 48.
Lead			Raw, free.		
Linen, yarn	200			7½ to 11	
manufactures of	9½ to 100	40 to 66¾	35¾ to 181½ increase.	11 to 34¼	Bleached, 7½ to 86¼.
Rum					72¼
Salt		Free	66⅔		
Silk, manufactures of			50		
Steel					Unwrought, 68.
Sugar, refined		Raw and clay, 80		Raw, 62.	
Tin			Raw, free.		
Wool			Yarn, 50 to 122 increase.		
manufactures of			Coarse, 164 inc.; fine, 37 decrease.	Carpets, 3¼ to 14¼	Damasks, 31¼ to 62½.

(a) In 1852 a discriminating duty of 10 per cent. in favor of Belgian vessels was abolished; this duty amounted to 20 per cent. on imports from places beyond the Cape of Good Hope and Cape Horn.

TARIFF CHANGES—Continued.

Denomination of merchandise.	Duties on imports into—				
	Spain.	Sardinia.	Austria.	Turkey.	Mexico.
	Decrease.	Decrease.	Decrease.	Decrease.	Decrease.
Ale, beer, and porter	Beer, in bottles, 71¼ in casks, 37½	....	Beer and ale, in bottles and jars, 50 increase.	Beer, in bottles, 20¼.	Ale in bottles, 25.
Coal	30	....	Free............	37½	
Coffee and cocoa	Coffee, 114 increase	....	Coffee, 12; cocoa, 25.	Coffee, 37½....	Cocoa, 25.
Copper	Sheets, 55½; bars, 59.	Cakes, sheets, 50; wrought, 50.			
Cotton, yarn	Prohib'n removed	....	17½ to 22½	42¼ to 47¼	Prohib'n removed
manufactures of	Prohib'n removed	50 to 50½; bobbinets, 20 to 71½.	68¾ to 83⅓	25 to 66	33¼ to 66¾
Earthenware and porcelain	....	24½ to 40½	....	....	Prohib'n removed
Fish	Cod, 35 increase..	Cod, 60; pilchards, 50.	Herrings, 25.....	Cod, 40.......	Cod, 20.
Glass	Window, 9½; glassware, 16¾.	Sheet, wrought, 15¾ to 58½.	Plate, 62½......	....	Wind'w, 40; glassware, 33¼ inc.
Hardware and cutlery	Knives and forks, 25; knives, fine, 20.	....	58¼ to 91½		
Iron	Bar, 14¾; pig, 27½ increase.	Anchors, 50; railway, 83¼; manufactures, 50.	Pig, 82; bar, 58½.	Bar, 28; wire, 20 to 29½.	Pig, 33¼; bar, 50.
Lead	....	....	Raw, 60.........	Pigs, 17¼; sheet, 8½.	
Linen, yarn	....	....	Thread, 12; 11 to 37½ increase.	....	40
manufactures of	12½ to 38¾	49 to 53¼	84½ to 85	....	28¾
Leather, manufactures of	Prohib'n removed	26¾ to 56	9½ to 11½ increase	....	33¼ increase.
Rum	....	....	44½	27½	33½
Silk, manufactures of	31 to 47½ increase	....	40 to 75	....	33¼; embroidery, 40.
Steel	....	....	....	....	25
Sugar, refined	17¾	46¾	22¼	25¾ to 30¾	
Tin	....	....	Raw, 82.........	Plates, 8¾; bars, 20¾.	
Wool,	Raw, prohibition removed.	Yarn, 50 to 50½	Raw, 83½; yarn, 20 to 66½ increase.		
manufactures of	30¼ to 80 increase	33¾ to 40; carpets, 50 to 66¾.	50½	36¼ to 58½	40 to 50

APPENDIX.

Marked as the changes in foreign tariffs will, by the preceding statement, be perceived to have been during the period of eight years which it embraces, they were hardly less noticeable during the two years immediately ensuing, as will be observed by the following statement, exhibiting the per centage decrease of duties levied on certain articles in the same countries in 1855, compared with the duties on those articles in 1853, which period of two years, added to the prior period of eight years, gives ten years, during all which period no change occurred in the tariff of the United States :(a)

Sweden.—On metals, from 25 to 80 per cent.; hardwares, 25 to 67; steam engines, 50; boilers, 75; tin wares, 25 and 33; glass bottles, 25 and 29; buttons, 50; candles, 50 to 67; cordage, 33; ships, steam, 60; sailing, 80; fish, 40 to 53; salt, 50; cheese, 20; butter, 50; sugar, 20; yarns, 37 to 56; threads, cotton and linen, 25 and 50; umbrellas, 50; silk, and manufactures of silk, 20 to 33; manufactures of cotton, 25 to 31; of linen, 14 to 50; of wool, 50; raw, wove, which in 1853 paid 5 cents per pound, in 1855 was admitted free.

Norway.—On cotton yarn, 20 to 25 per cent.; manufactures of cotton, 11 to 36; window glass, 25; iron, and certain manufactures of, 11 to 43; steel wares, unpolished, 9; coals, which in 1853 paid 18 cents per ton, in 1855 were admitted free.

Denmark.—On sugar, refined, 25 per cent.; manufactures, woollen, unmixed, 25; mixed with cotton, 20.

Zollverein.—On tea, 26 per cent.; zinc, raw, 50.

Holland.—On earthenware, 50 per cent.; beer, in bottles, 67; rum, arrack, and cordials, in bottles, 50; glassware, 32; bottles, 50; leather, tanned and prepared, 40; iron, nails, 50; certain iron wares, 67; manufactures of linen, 67; of wool, 12 to 33; of silk, 50; threads, sewing, of hemp, flax, tow, 33. Free in 1855, rum, arrack, and cordials, in casks, which in 1853 paid $2 42 per 22 gallons; also iron, cast in rough blocks, which paid ½ per cent. ad valorem also copper, red, raw, in cakes, pigs, and sheets, which paid 4 and 8 cents per cwt.; also lead, raw and old, which paid 4 cents per cwt.; also steel, in sheets, plates, &c., which paid 4 cents per cwt ; also tin, raw, which paid 30 cents.

Belgium.—Coals, which paid in 1853 $2 86 per ton, in 1855 were admitted free; also rice, which paid from 17 to 47 cents per cwt

France.—On iron, in pigs, 37 per cent.; in bars, according to dimensions, from 25 to 33 per cent.; in plates, 50 per cent.; steel, cast and wrought, from 50 to 75.

Portugal.—On cotton thread, plain, No. 41 to 80, 33 per cent.; No. 120 and more, 58 per cent.; china and porcelain, 25 per cent.; iron nails, 20 per cent.

Spain.—Tools of iron which, in 1853, paid 8 cents per pound, in 1855 were admitted free ; also copper ore, which paid 6 cents per cwt.; also zinc, which paid 16 cents per cwt.

Sardinia.—On rum, in casks, 34 per cent.; sugar, not refined, 12 per cent ; rice, 41 per cent ; fish, salted, smoked, or dried, 50 per cent.; saddlery and harness, plain, 25 per cent.; ornamented, 27 per cent ; yarns, linen, 9 to 40 per cent ; cotton, 19 to 24 per cent ; manufactures of cotton, 17 to 40 per cent.; of linen, 11 to 47 per cent.; paper, all sorts, 33 per cent.; colored and gilt, 25 per cent.; for hangings, 20 per cent.; iron, certain manufactures of, 25 to 75 per cent.; tin, in plates, not wrought, 33 per cent.; wrought, 50 per cent.; in rods, 20 per cent.; pottery, porcelain, white, &c., 36 per cent.; gilt, painted, &c., 17 per cent.; glass, sheet and wrought, all kinds, 46 per cent.; iron, cast, old and in pigs, which, in 1853, paid 5 cents per cwt., in 1855 admitted free ; on beer, in casks and bottles, there was an increase of 67 per cent. in 1855 on the rates of 1853 ; as, also, on rum, in bottles, of 98 per cent.

Austria.—On iron, pig and scrap, bar, railway, castings, and on steel, spring and cast, 15 to 37 per cent.; yarns, cotton and linen, 15 to 25 per cent.; manufactures, common, of cotton, 20 per cent.; of linen, 25 and 33 per cent.; of woolen, 40 per cent.; leather, fine, 25 per cent.; gloves of, 20 per cent.; glass, middle fine, 20 per cent.; fine, 25 per cent.; instruments, astronomical, optical, musical, &c., 33 per cent.; wool, sheep's, raw, which, in 1853, paid 4 cents per cwt., in 1855 was admitted free.

United States.—It may not prove unprofitable in concluding this general view of the per centage changes which took place in the tariffs of some of the principal foreign commercial countries during the period of ten years embraced between 1846 and 1856, during which period no change occured in the customs rates of the United States, to note those per centage changes which, a year later, by virtue of the act of March 3, 1857, actually did occur in the tariffs of the latter country as regards the articles of import named in the preceding comparative statement. Articles on which the decrease of rates by the act of 1857, on those levied by the act of 1846, is 20 per cent., are as follows : ale, beer, and porter ; coal ; earthenware and porcelain ; glass, plain ; hardware and cutlery ; iron, and manufactures of ; sugar of all kinds ; manufactures of silk, not otherwise specified ; manufactures of leather ; manufactures of wool ; wool, unmanufactured, not otherwise provided for.

Articles on which the per centage decrease is 25 per cent. are : coffee, not otherwise provided for ; fish, salted, smoked, dried, and pickled ; lead, manufactures of; linen yarn and manufactures of linen ; cut glass ; salt. On cocoa the per centage decrease is 60 per cent.; on rum and spirits, of all kinds, 70 per cent.; on manufactures of cotton, 24 per cent.; on cotton yarn, 4 per cent.

(a) See note, page 98.

Tin and copper, in pigs, bars, or old, which, under the act of 1846, paid 5 per cent., under that of 1857 are free; as, also, wool, costing 20 cents or less per pound, which paid 30 per cent.

Most articles which, under the tariff of 1846, paid 40 per cent. ad valorem, under that of 1857 pay but 30, presenting a per centage decrease of 25 per cent.; those which paid 30 per cent., pay 24, decrease 20 per cent.; those which paid 25, pay 19, decrease 24 per cent.; those which paid 20, pay 15, decrease 25; those which paid 15, pay 12; those which paid 10, pay 8; and those which paid 5, pay 4, presenting a per centage decrease in each instance of 20 per cent., while brandy and other spirits, distilled from grain and other materials, cordials, absynthe, arrack, curaçoa, kirschenwasser, liqueurs, maraschino, ratafia, and all other spirituous beverages of a similar character which paid 100 per cent. pay 30, presenting a per centage decrease of 70 per cent.

The exceptions to these rates are presented in the second section of the act of 1857, by virtue of which all manufactures composed wholly of cotton, which are bleached, printed, painted, or dyed, and de laines, pay 30 per cent.; japanned leather, or skins of all kinds, pay 25; ginger, green, ripe, dried, preserved, or pickled; ochres, and ochrey earths; medicinal roots, leaves, gums and resins, in a crude state, not otherwise provided for; wares, chemical, earthen or pottery, of a capacity exceeding ten gallons, pay 20; borate of lime and codilla, or tow of hemp or flax, pay 5; antimony, crude or regulus of; barks of all kinds not otherwise provided for; camphor, crude; cantharides; carbonate of soda; emery, in lump or pulverized; fruits, green, ripe, or dried; gums, Arabic, Barbary, copal, East India, Jeddo, Senegal, substitute, tragacanth, and all other gums and resins, in a crude state; machinery, exclusively designed, and expressly imported for the manufacture of flax and linen goods; sponges; tin, in plates or sheets, galvanized or ungalvanized; woods, namely, cedar, lignumvitæ, ebony, box, granadilla, mahogany, rose-wood, satin-wood, and all cabinet woods, pay 10; and acids, acetic, benzoic, boracic, citric, muriatic, white and yellow, oxalic, pyroligenous and tartaric, and all other acids of every description used for chemical or manufacturing purposes not otherwise provided; aloes; amber; ambergris; anniseed; annato, roucon or orleans; arsenic; articles not in a crude state used in dyeing or tanning not otherwise provided for; assafœtida; asphaltum; barilla; bleaching powder, or chloride of lime; borax, crude; boucho leaves; brimstone, crude, in bulk; cameos, mosaics, diamonds, gems, pearls, rubies, and other precious stones (not set;) chalk; clay, cochineal; cocoa, cocoanuts, and cocoa-shells; cork-tree bark; cream of tartar; extract of indigo; extracts and decoctions of logwood and other dyewoods not otherwise provided for; extract of madder; flint, ground; grindstones; gutta percha, unmanufactured; India rubber, in bottles, slabs or sheets, unmanufactured; India rubber, milk of; indigo; lac spirits; lac sulphur; lastings cut in strips or patterns of the size and shape for shoes, slippers, boots, bootees, gaiters, or buttons, exclusively, not combined with India rubber; manufactures of mohair cloth, silk twist, or other manufactures of cloth, suitable for the manufacture of shoes, cut in strips or patterns of the size and shape for shoes, slippers, boots, bootees, gaiters or buttons, exclusively, not combined with India rubber; music printed with lines, bound or unbound; oils, palm, seal and cocoanut; Prussian blue; soda ash; spices of all kinds; watch materials and unfinished parts of watches, and woad, or pastel, pay 5 per cent; presenting a per centage decrease on previous rates on many articles of from 45 to 95 per cent.

Among the large number of articles declared exempt from duty by the act of 1857, the rates paid by a few under the act of 1846 are subjoined, those paying a duty of 20 per cent. ad valorem being as follows: Animal carbon, animals not for breeding, bismuth, bitter apples, bolting cloths; cutch; ice; shingles and staves; bolts; substances expressly used for manures.

Articles which paid 15 per cent. are: Peruvian bark; dragon's blood; flax, unmanufactured; silk, raw, or as reeled from the cocoon, not being doubled, twisted, or advanced in manufacture in any way.

Articles which paid 10 per cent. are: Catechu, or terra japonica; burr stones, wrought or unwrought, but unmanufactured; linseed, but not including flaxseed; maps and charts; palm leaf, unmanufactured; rattans and reeds, unmanufactured.

Articles which paid 5 per cent. are: Argol, or wine lees; articles in a crude state used in dyeing or tanning, not otherwise provided for; bells, when old, and bell metal; berries, nuts, flowers, plants, and vegetables used exclusively in dyeing, or in composing dyes, not manufactured; brass, in bars, pigs and old; Brazil wood, brazilletto, and all other dye woods in sticks; copper in bars, pigs, and old; ivory, manufactured; madder root, madder ground or prepared; nutgalls; rags of whatever material, except wool; tin, in bars, pigs, or blocks; weld, or dyer's weed.

Wool, unmanufactured, of the value of 20 cents per pound or less at the port of exportation, provided it is imported in ordinary condition, which, under the act of 1857, is admitted free, paid a duty of 30 per cent. ad valorem under that of 1846.

Comparative statement exhibiting the rates of duty on principal imports payable under the several tariffs of the United States from 1789 to 1846, inclusive.(a)

DENOMINATION OF MERCHANDISE.	RATES OF DUTY PAYABLE UNDER THE ACTS OF—													
	Rates, &c.	July 4, 1789.	August 10, 1790.	May 2, 1792.	June 7, 1794.	January 29, 1795.	March 3, 1797.	May 13, 1800.	March 27, 1804.	July 1, 1812.	April 27, 1816.	May 22, 1824.	May 19, 1828.	July 14, 1832.	1832 and 1833.
Ale, beer, and porter, in casks	Per gal.	$0 05	$0 05	$0 08	$0 08	$0 08	$0 08	$0 08	$0 08	$0 16	$0 10	$0 15	$0 15	$0 15	$0 15
in bottles	do	$0 20 per doz.	$0 25 per doz.	$0 08	$0 08	$0 08	$0 08	$0 08	$0 08	$0 16	$0 15	$0 20	$0 20	$0 20	$0 20
Almonds	Per ct.	5	10	10	15	15	15	15	$0 02 per lb.	$0 04 per lb.	$0 03 per lb.	$0 03 per lb.	$0 03 per lb.	Free	Free.
Bonnets, of silk	do	7½	7½	10	15	15	15	15	17½	32½	30	30	30	25	25
Boots	Per pair.	$0 50	$0 50	$0 50	$0 75	$ 75	$0 75	$0 75	$0 75	$1 50	30 per ct.	30 per ct.	30 per ct.	30 per ct.	$1 50
Brandy	Per gal.	--------	$0 12–25	$0 28–50	$0 28–50	$0 28–50	$0 28–50	$0 28–50	$0 28–50	$0 56-100	$0 42–75	$0 42–75	$0 57–90	$0 57–90	$0 57–90
Brass, all manufactures of	Per ct.	5	5	10	10	15	15	15	17½	32½	20	25	25	25	25
Bristles	do	5	5	7½	10	12½	12½	12½	Free	Free	$0 03 per lb.	$0 03 per lb.	$0 03 per lb.	$0 03 per lb.	$0 03 per lb
Brushes, of all kinds	do	7½	7½	10	15	15	15	15	17½	32½	30	30	30	30	25

(a) For which is added a column giving the rates imposed by the act of March 3, 1857. The character and date of each of the several tariffs, special as well as general, enacted by Congress from 1789 to 1857, inclusive, may be stated as follows:

General.... Tariff .... July 4, 1789
Do........do .... Aug. 10, 1790
Do........do .... March 3, 1791
Do........do .... May 2, 1792
Special.......do.."sugar, snuff, internal duties" .... June 5, 1794
General......do .... June 7, 1794
Do........do .... Jan. 29, 1795
Do........do .... March 3, 1797
Special.......do..on salt, additional .... July 8, 1797
Do........do..on sugar and wines .... May 13, 1800
Do........do..Mediterranean fund .... March 26, 1804
Do........do..light money, &c .... March 27, 1804
Do........do..(war,) double duties .... July 1, 1812
Do........do..on salt .... July 29, 1813
Do........do..double duties continued .... Feb. 5, 1816
General......do..minimum system begun .... April 27, 1816
Special....Tariff, iron and alum, supplementary to act of 1816 .... April 20, 1818
Do........do..on wines .... March 3, 1819
General......do..revised, woollens, cottons, &c .... May 22, 1824
Do........do..minimums, extended .... May 19, 1828
Special.......do..on wines .... May 24, 1828
Do........do..on coffee, tea, &c .... May 20, 1830
Do........do..on molasses .... May 29, 1830
Do........do..on salt .... May 29, 1830
Do........do..on French wines .... July 13, 1832
General......do..modification of other acts, and did not go fully into operation .... July 14, 1832
Special.......do..on hardware, copper, &c .... March 2, 1833
Compromise..do..gradual reduction towards 20 per cent .... March 2, 1833
General......do..the one year .... Sept. 11, 1841
Do........do..ad valorem .... July 30, 1846
Do........do.....do.. ...(reduction) .... March 3, 1857

58 □

COMPARATIVE STATEMENT—Continued.

DENOMINATION OF MERCHANDISE.	Rates, &c.	RATES OF DUTY PAYABLE UNDER THE ACTS OF— July 4, 1789.	August 10, 1790.	May 2, 1792.	June 7, 1794.	January 29, 1795.	March 3, 1797.	May 13, 1800.	March 27, 1804.	July 1, 1812.	April 27, 1816.	May 22, 1824.	May 19, 1828.	July 14, 1832.	1832 and 1833.
Brussels carpeting	Per ct.	5	7½	10	15	15	15	15	17½	32½	25	$0 50 sq. yd.	$0 70 sq. yd.	$0 63 sq. yd.	$0 63 sq. yd.
Buttons, metal	do.	7½	7½	10	15	15	15	15	17½	32½	20	25	25	25	25
Candles, spermaceti	Per lb.	$0 06	$0 06	$0 06	$0 06	$0 06	$0 06	$0 06	$0 06	$0 12	$0 06	$0 06	$0 06	$0 06	$0 08
Carpeting	Per ct.	5	7½	10	15	15	15	15	17½	32½	$0 15–25 sq. yd.	$0 25–50 sq. yd.	$0 40–70 sq. yd.	$0 35–63 sq. yd.	$0 35–63 sq. yd.
Carriages and coaches	do.	15	15½	15½	20	20	20	20	22½	42½	30	30	30	30	30
Cassia	do.	5	10	10	15	15	15	15	$0 04 per lb.	$0 08 per lb.	$0 06 per lb.	$0 06 per lb.	$0 06 per lb.	Free	Free.
Cheese	Per lb.	$0 04	$0 04	$0 04	$0 07	$0 07	$0 07	$0 07	$0 07	$0 14	$0 09	$0 09	$0 09	$0 09	$0 09
China ware	Per ct.	10	12½	15	15	15	15	15	17½	32½	20	20	20	20	20
Clocks and watches	do.	5	10	10	15	15	15	15	17½	32½	Watches, 7½	Watches, 12½	12½	12½	12½
Cocoa	Per lb.	$0 01	$0 01	$0 02	$0 04	$0 04	$0 02	$0 02	$0 02	$0 04	$0 02	$0 02	$0 02	Free	Free.
Copper, manufactures of	Per ct.	5	7½	10	15	15	15	15	17½	32½	20	25	25	25	25
Cotton, manufactures of	do.	5	7½	7½	12½	12½	12½	12½	15	27	25	25	25	25	25
Currants	do.	5	10	10	15	15	15	15	$0 02 per lb.	$0 04 per lb.	$0 03 per lb.	$0 03 per lb.	$0 03 per lb.	Free	Free.
Earthenware and stoneware	do.	10	10	10	15	15	15	15	17½	32½	20	20	20	20	20
Figs	do.	10	10	10	15	15	15	15	$0 02 per lb.	$0 04 per lb.	$0 03 per lb.	$0 03 per lb.	$0 03 per lb.	Free	Free.
Floor cloths and mats	do.			10	15	15	15	15	17½	32½	30	30	50	43	42
Fringes, laces, tassels, &c., &c.	do.	5	7½	15	15	15	15	15	17½	32½	20	25	35	35	25
Fur hats, caps, &c.	do.			10	15	15	15	15	17½	32½	30	30	30	30	30
Gilt and plated ware	do.	7½	10	10	15	15	15	15	17½	32½	20	25	25	25	25
Ginger, in root	do.	5	10	10	10	15	15	15	17½	32½	15	15	15	Free	Free.
Glass, manufactures of	do.	10	12½	15	20	20	20	20	22½	42½	20	20	20	20	20

COMPARATIVE STATEMENT—Continued.

Denomination of merchandise.	Rates, &c.	July 4, 1789.	August 10, 1790.	May 2, 1792.	June 7, 1794.	January 29, 1795.	March 3, 1797.	May 13, 1800.	March 27, 1804.	July 1, 1812.	April 27, 1816.	May 22, 1824.	May 19, 1828	July 14, 1832.	1832 and 1833.
		Rates of duty payable under the acts of—													
Gloves, leather	Per ct.	7½	7½	10	15	15	15	15	17½	32½	30	30	30	30	30
Glue	do	5	5	15	15	15	15	15	$0 04 per lb.	$0 08 per lb.	$0 05 per lb.	$0 05 per lb.	$0 05 per lb.	$0 05 per lb.	$0 05 per lb
Gold, jewelry	do	7½	10	10	15	15	15	15	17½	32½	7½	12½	12½	12½	12½
laces, tresses, &c.	do	10	10	10	15	15	15	15	17½	32½	7½	12½	12½	12½	12½
Hoop iron	do	7½	7½	7½	10	10	10	12½	$0 01 per lb.	$0 02 per lb.	$2 50 per cwt.	$0 03 per lb.	$0 03½ per lb.	$0 03 per lb.	$0 03 per lb.
Indigo	Per lb.	$0 16	$0 25	$0 25	$0 25	$0 25	$0 25	$0 25	$0 25	$0 50	$0 15	$0 15	$0 15	20 to .50	15 per ct.
Iron castings	Per ct.	5	7½	10	15	15	15	15	17½	32½	20	$0 75 per cwt.	$0 01 per lb.	$0 01 per lb.	$0 01 per lb.
slit and rolled	do	5	7½	10	15	15	15	15	17½	32½	20	$0 03 per b.	$0 03½ per lb.	$0 03 per lb.	$0 03 per lb
locks, hoes, anvils, and vices	do	5	7½	10	10	10	10	12½	15	27½	20	$0 02 per lb.	$0 02 per lb.	$0 02 per lb.	$0 02 per lb
nails	Per lb	$0 01	$0 01	$0 02	$0 02	$0 02	$0 02	$0 02	$0 02	$0 04	$0 03	$0 04	$0 05	$0 05	$0 05
spikes	do	$0 01	$0 01	$0 01	$0 01	$0 01	$0 01	$0 01	$0 01	$0 02	$0 02	$0 03	$0 04	$0 04	$0 04
all manufactures of, not enumerated.	Per ct.	5	7½	10	15	15	15	15	17½	32½	20	25	25	25	25
bar and bolt	do	5	5	7½	10	10	12½	15	17½	32½	$1 50 per cwt.	$1 50 per cwt.	$1 85 per cwt.	$1 50 per cwt.	$1 50 per cwt.
anchors	do	7½	7½	7½	10	10	10	12½	$0 01½ per lb.	$0 03 per lb.	$1 50 per cwt.	$0 02 per lb.	$0 02 per lb.	$0 02 per lb.	$0 02 per lb.
Kid gloves	do	7½	7½	10	15	15	15	15	17½	32½	30	30	30	30	30
shoes	Per pr.	$0 07	$0 07	$0 10	$0 15	$0 15	$0 15	$0 15	$0 15	$0 30	$0 25	$0 25	$0 25	$0 25	$0 25
Laces, gold or silver	Per ct.	10	10	10	15	15	15	15	17½	32½	7½	12½	12½	12½	12½
and lawns	do	5	7½	7½	10	12½	12½	12½	15	27½	7½	12½	12½	12½	12½

COMPARATIVE STATEMENT—Continued.

DENOMINATION OF MERCHANDISE.	RATES OF DUTY PAYABLE UNDER THE ACTS OF—														
	Rates, &c.	July 4, 1789.	August 10, 1790.	May 2, 1792.	June 7, 1794.	January 29, 1795.	March 3, 1797.	May 13, 1800.	March 2, 1804.	July 1, 1812.	April 27, 1816.	May 22, 1824.	May 19, 1828.	July 14, 1832.	1832 and 1833.
Lead, manufactures of, not enumerated.	Per lb	....	$0 01	$0 01	$0 01	$0 01	$0 01	$0 01	$0 01	$0 02	20 per ct.	25 per ct.	25 per ct.	15 per ct.	15 per ct.
red and white	Per ct.	10	10	15	15	15	15	15	$0 02	$0 04	$0 03	$0 04	$0 05	$0 05	$0 05
									per lb.	per lb.	per lb.	per lb.	per lb.	per lb.	per lb.
Leather, tanned and tawed	do	7½	7½	10	15	15	15	15	17½	32½	30	30	30	30	30
manufactures of	do	7½	7½	10	15	15	15	15	17½	32½	30	30	30	30	30
Linen manufactures, plain	do	5	5	7½	10	10	12½	12½	15	27½	15	22	25	15	Free.
printed, stained, or colored	do	5	7½	7½	10	12½	12½	12½	15	27½	15	25	25	25	2[illegible]
Mace	do	5	10	15	15	15	15	15	$1 25	$2 50	$1 00	$1 00	$1 00	Free	Free.
									per lb.	per lb.	per lb.	per lb.	per lb.		
Marble and marble tables, &c	do	5	10	10	15	15	15	15	17½	32½	15 & 30	30 & 30	30 & 30	Free & 30	Free & 30
Molasses	Per gal.	$0 02½	$0 03	$0 03	$0 03	$0 03	$0 04	$0 05	$0 05	$0 10	$0 05	$0 05	$0 05	$0 05	$0 05
Nutmegs	Per cent.	5	10	10	15	15	15	15	$0 50	$1 00	$0 60	$0 60	$0 60	Free	Free.
									per lb.	per lb.	per lb.	per lb.	per lb.		
Ochre, in oil	do	10	10	15	15	15	15	15	$0 01	$0 02	$0 01	$0 01	$0 01	$0 01	$0 01
									per lb.	per lb.	per lb.	per lb.	per lb.	per lb.	per lb.
Paper and stationery	do	7½	10	10	10	10	10	12½	15	27½	30	$0 17	$0 17	$0 17	$0 17
												per lb.	per lb.	per lb.	per lb.
Pewter, manufactures of	Per cwt	$0 07½	$0 07½	$0 10	$0 15	$0 15	$0 15	$0 15	$0 17½	$0 32½	$0 20	$0 25	$0 25	$0 25	$0 25
Pimento	Per cent	5	5	$0 04	$0 04	$0 04	$0 04	$0 04	$0 04	$0 08	$0 06	$0 06	$0 06	Free	Free.
				per lb.	per lb.	per lb.	per lb.	per lb.	per lb	per lb.	per lb.	per lb.	per lb.		
Plums and prunes	do	5	10	10	15	15	15	15	$0 02	$0 04	$0 03	$0 04	$0 04	Free	Free.
									per lb.	per lb.	per lb.	per lb.	per lb.		
Raisins	do	5	10	10	15	15	15	15	$0 02	$0 04	$0 02	$0 03	$0 03	$0 03	Free.
									per lb.	per lb.	per lb.	per lb.	per lb.	per lb.	
Salt	Pr. bush.	$0 06	$0 12	$0 12	$0 12	$0 12	$0 20	$0 20	$0 20	Free	$0 20	$0 20	$0 20	Free	$0 10

COMPARATIVE STATEMENT—Continued.

DENOMINATION OF MERCHANDISE.	Rates, &c.	RATES OF DUTY PAYABLE UNDER THE ACTS OF— July 4, 1789.	August 10, 1790.	May 2, 1792.	June , 94.	January 29, 1795.	March 3, 1797.	May 13, 1800.	M ch 27, 1804.	July 1, 1812.	April 27, 1816.	May 22, 1824.	May 19, 1828.	July 14, 1832.	1882 and 1883.
Slates, ciphering	Per cent.	10	10	10	15	15	15	15	17½	32½	15	15	32½	25	25
Spirits, from grain, first proof	Per gal.	--------	$0 12	$0 28	$0 28	$0 28	$0 28	$0 28	$0 28	$0 56	$0 42	$0 42	$0 57	$0 57	57–90cts.
Sugar, brown	Per lb.	$0 01	1½	1½	1½	1½	2	2½	2½	5	3	3	3	2½	2½
white clayed	do	1½	2½	2½	3½	3	3	3	3	6	4	4	4	3½	3½
loaf	do	3	5	5	9	9	9	9	9	18	12	12	12	12	12
lump and other refined	do	1½	2	2½	6½	6½	6½	6½	6½	13	10	10	10	10	10
Teas, from places of their production—															
Bohea	do	6	10	10	10	10	12	12	12	24	12	12	12	Free	Free.
Souchong and other black	do	10	18	18	18	18	18	18	18	36	25	25	25	Free	Free.
Hyson, imperial, &c.	do	20	32	32	32	32	32	32	32	64	50	50	50	Free	Free.
from other places, Bohea	do	8	12	12	12	12	14	14	14	28	14	14	14	Free	10
Souchong and other black	do	13	21	21	21	21	21	21	21	42	34	34	34	Free	Free.
Tin, in pigs and bars	--------	Free	Free	Free	Free	Free	Free	Free	Free	Free	Free	Free	Free	Free	Free.
manufactures of	Per cent.	7½	7½	10	15	15	15	15	17½	32½	20	25	25	25	25
Wool, unmanufactured	do	Free	Free	Free	Free	Free	Free	Free	Free	Free	15	15 to 30	40 to 50	40	40
All goods, wares, and merchandise not otherwise enumerated or specified in the several tariffs.	do	5	5	7¼	10	10	10	12½	15	27½	15	15	15	15	15

COMPARATIVE STATEMENT—Continued.

Denomination of merchandise.	Rates of duty.	Reductions under the act of 1833. (a) Rate of duty. 1834 and 1835, 1-10 or 10 per cent.	1836 and 1837, 2-10 or 20 per cent.	1838 and 1839, 3-10 or 30 per cent.	1840 and 1841, 4-10 or 40 per cent.	Payable under the act of 1841; reduction under the act of 1833. Tariff of September 11, 1841, from October 1.	To June 30, 1842.	Duty imposed by the act of August, 1842.	Duty imposed by the act of July 30, 1846, per cent. ad valorem.	Per centage increase from 1789 to 1846.	Duty imposed by the act of March 3, 1857, per cent. ad valorem.
Ale, beer, and porter, in casks	Per gal	$0 14.65	$0 14.12	$0 14.46	$0 13.98	$0 13.98	$0 10.76	$0 15	30	5	24
in bottles	do	$0 20	$0 20	$0 19.97	$0 19.71	$0 19.54	$0 19.54	$0 20	30	Decrease, 3⅓	24
Almonds	Per cent	Free	Free	Free	Free	20	20	$0 03	40	35	30
								per pound.			
Bonnets, of silk	do	24½	24	23½	23	23	21½	$2 each	30	22½	24
Boots	Per pair	$1 40	$1 12	$1 22	$1 16	$1 16	$0 87.52	$1 25	30	13⅓	24
Brandy	Per gal	$0 52.97	$0 48.02	$0 43.19	$0 41	$0 41	$0 23.53	$1 00	100	90	30
Brass, all manufactures of	Per cent	24½	24	23½	23	23	21½	30	30	25	24
Bristles	do	3	3	3	3	Free	Free	$1 per lb	5	Same	4
		per pound.	per pound.	per pound	per pound.						
Brushes, of all kinds	do	24½	24	23½	23	23	21½	30	30	22½	24
Brussels carpeting	Per sq. yd.	$0 59.51	$0 56.78	$0 52.98	$0 49.32	$0 49.32	$0 37	$0 55	30	25	24
Buttons, metal	Per cent	24½	24	23½	23	23	21½	30	25	17½	19
Candles, spermaceti	Per pound	$0 08	$0 08	$0 08	$0 08	$0 08	$0 08	$0 08	20	Same	15
Carpeting	Per cent	59.51	56.78	52.98	49.32	49.32	37	30—65	30	25	24
		sq. yard.	sq. yard	sq. yard.	sq. yard.	sq. yard.	sq. yard.	sq. yard.			
Carriages and coaches	do	29	28	27	26	26	23	30	30	15	24
Cassia	do	Free	Free	Free	Free	20	20	$0 05	40	35	4
								per pound			

(a) By the act of March 2, 1833, it was provided that after December 31, 1833, all duties exceeding 20 per cent. should be reduced by biennially striking off one-tenth of the excess, until December 31, 1839; and that from and after December 31, 1841, one-half of the residue of such excess should be deducted; and from and after June 30, 1842, the other half should be deducted.

COMPARATIVE STATEMENT—Continued.

Denomination of merchandise.	Rates of duty.	Reductions under the act of 1833. Rate of duty. 1834 and 1835, 1-10 or 10 per cent.	1836 and 1837, 2-10 or 20 per cent.	1838 and 1839, 3-10 or 30 per cent.	1840 and 1841, 4-10 or 40 per cent.	Payable under the act of 1831; reduction under the act of 1833. Tariff of September 11, 1841, from October 1.	To June 30, 1842.	Duty imposed by the act of August, 1842.	Duty imposed by the act of July 30, 1846, per cent. ad valorem.	Per centage increase from 1789 to 1846.	Duty imposed by the act of March 3, 1857, per cent. ad valorem.
Cheese	Per pound.	$0 8.33	$0 7.68	$0 7.07	$0 6.38	$0 6.38	$0 4.34	$0 09 per pound.	30	Decrease, 3⅓	24
China ware	Per cent.	20	20	20	20	20	20	30	30	20	24
Clocks and watches	do	12½	12½	12½	12	20	20	Clocks, 25 Watches, 7½	30	25	Clocks, 24 Watches, 8
Cocoa	Per pound.	Free	Free	Free	Free	20 per cent.	20 per cent.	$0 01	10	5	4
Copper, manufactures of	Per cent.	24½	24	23½	23	23	21½	30	30	25	24
Cotton, manufactures of	do	24½	24	23½	23	23	21½	30	25	20	19 to 24
Currants	do	Free	Free	Free	Free	20	20	$0 03 per pound.	40	35	8
Earthenware and stoneware	do	20	20	20	20	20	20	30	30	20	24
Figs	do	Free	Free	Free	Free	20	20	$0 02 per pound.	40	30	8
Floor cloths and mats	Per sq. yd.	$0 40.83	$0 38.55	$0 31.15	$0 33.94	$0 33.94	$0 24.35	25	25	----	19
Fringes, laces, tassels, &c.	Per cent.	24½	24	23½	23	23	21½	20	25	20	15 to 19
Fur hats, caps, &c.	do	29	28	27	26	26	23	35	30	----	24
Gilt and plated ware	do	24½	24	23½	23	23	21½	30	30	----	24
Ginger, in root	do	Free	Free	Free	Free	20	20	$0 02 per pound.	40	22½	15
Glass, manufactures of	do	20	20	20	20	20	20	25	30	30	24
Gloves, leather	do	29	28	27	26	26	23	$1 25 per dozen.	30	22½	24

COMPARATIVE STATEMENT—Continued.

Denomination of merchandise.	Rates, &c.	Reductions under the act of 1833. Rate of duty.				Payable under the act of 1841; reduction under the act of 1833.		Duty imposed by the act of August, 1842.	Duty imposed by the act of July 30, 1846, per cent. ad valorem.	Per centage increase from 1789 to 1846.	Duty imposed by the act of March 3, 1857, per cent. ad valorem.
		1834 and 1835, 1-10 or 10 per cent.	1836 and 1837, 2-10 or 20 per cent.	1838 and 1839, 3-10 or 30 per cent.	1840 and 1841, 4-10 or 40 per cent.	Tariff of September 11, 1841, from October 1.	To June 30, 1842.				
Glue	Per cent	$0 04. 69 per pound.	$0 04. 41 per pound.	$0 04. 23 per pound.	$0 03. 99 per pound.	$0 03. 99 per pound.	$0 03. 16 per pound.	$0 05 per pound.	20	15	15
Gold, jewelry	do	12½	12½	12½	12½	20	20	20	30	22½	24
laces, tresses, &c	do	12½	12½	12½	12½	20	20	15	30	20	34
Hoop iron	Per pound	$0 02. 77 per pound.	$0 01. 57 per pound.	$0 02. 35 per pound.	$0 02. 15 per pound.	$0 02. 15 per pound.	$0 01. 41 per pound.	$0 02 per pound.	30	22½	24
Indigo	do	$0 15	$0 15	$0 15	$0 12	$0 20	$0 20	$0 05	10	Decrease, 10	4
Iron castings	do	$0 00. 95	$0 00. 87	$0 00. 88	$0 00. 86	$0 00. 86	$0 00. 67	$0 01½	30	25	24
slit and rolled	do	$0 02. 79	$0 02. 63	$0 02. 28	$0 02. 05	$0 02. 05	$0 01. 19	$0 02½	30	25	24
locks, hoes, anvils, and vices	do	$0 01. 92	$0 01. 87	$0 01. 83	$0 01. 74	$0 01. 74	$0 01. 49	30 per cent.	30	25	24
nails	do	$0 04. 66	$0 04. 38	$0 04. 00	$0 03. 75	$0 03. 75	$0 02. 69	30 per cent.	30	----------	24
spikes	do	$0 03. 69	$0 03. 41	$0 03. 12	$0 02. 80	$0 02. 80	$0 01. 74	30 per cent.	30	10	24
all manufactures of, not enumerated.	Per cent	24½	24	23½	23	23	21½	30	30	25	24
bar and bolt	Per cwt	$1 50	$1 30	$1 20	$1 07	$1 07	$0 68	$17 00 per ton.	30	25	24
anchors	Per pound	$0 1. 94	$0 1. 83	$0 1. 75	$0 1. 64	$0 1. 64	$0 1. 31	30 per cent.	30	22½	24
Kid gloves	Per cent	29	28	27	26	26	23	35	30	22½	24
shoes	Per pair	23. 65 cts.	22. 42 cts.	22. 47 cts.	20—57 cts.	20. 57 cts.	17. 33 cts.	35 per cent.	30	25	24
Laces, gold or silver	Per cent	12½	12½	12½	12½	20	20	15	30	20	24
and lawns	do	12½	12½	12½	12½	20	20	15	25	20	15, 19, & 24
Lead, manufactures of, not enume'd	do	15	45	15	15	20	20	30	30	20	24
red and white	Per pound	$0 04. 61	$0 04. 29	$0 03. 92	$0 03. 49	$0 03. 49	$0 02. 33	$0 00. 04	20	10	15

COMPARATIVE STATEMENT—Continued.

Denomination of merchandise	Rates, &c.	Reductions under the act of 1833. Rate of duty. 1834 and 1835, 1-10 or 10 per cent.	1836 and 1837, 2-10 or 20 per cent.	1838 and 1839, 3-10 or 30 per cent.	1840 and 1841, 4-10 or 40 per cent.	Payable under the act of 1841; reduction under the act of 1833. Tariff of September 11, 1841, from October 1.	To June 30, 1842.	Duty imposed by the act of August, 1842.	Duty imposed by the act of July 30, 1846, per cent. ad valorem.	Per centage increase from 1789 to 1846.	Duty imposed by the act of March 3, 1857, per cent. ad valorem.
Leather, tanned and tawed	Per cent	29	28	27	26	26	23	$0 06 per pound.	20	12½	5
manufactures of	do	29	28	27	26	26	23	35	30	22½	24
Linen manufactures, plain	do	Free	Free	Free	Free	20	20	25	20	15	5
printed, stained, or colored	do	24½	24	23½	23	23	21½	25	20	15	5
Mace	Per pound	Free	Free	Free	Free	20 per cent.	20 per cent.	$0 50	40	35	4
Marble and marble tables, &c	Per cent	Free & 29	Free & 28	Free & 27	Free & 26	20 & 26	20 & 23	25 & 30	20 & 30	15 & 25	15 to 24
Molasses	Per gallon	$0 4.84	$0 48.7	$0 4.61	$0 4.13	$0 4.13	$0 3.03	$0 04½	30	$15 65	24
Nutmegs	Per cent	Free	Free	Free	Free	20	20	30c. per lb.	40	35	4
Ochre, in oil	do	.93c. pr. lb.	.86c. pr. lb.	.77c. pr. lb.	.73c. pr. lb.	.73c. per lb.	.50c. per lb.	1c. per lb.	30	20	24
Paper and stationery	Per lb.	$0 15.32	$0 14.24	$0 12.73	$0 11.21	$0 11.21	$0 06.90	$0 15	30	22½	24
Pewter, manufactures of	Per cwt.	$0 24½	$0 24	$0 23½	$0 23	$0 23	$0 21½	$0 30	30	22½	24
Pimento	Per cent	Free	Free	Free	Free	20	20	5c. per lb.	40	35	4
Plums and prunes	do	do	do	do	do	20	20	3c. per lb.	30 and 40	25 and 35	8
Raisins	do	do	do	do	do	20	20	2c. per lb.	40		8
Salt	Per bush.	$0 9.25	$0 8.56	$0 7.88	$0 6.98	$0 6.98	$0 4.91	8c. per lb.	20	Decrease 30	15
Slates, ciphering	Per cent.	24½	24	23½	23	23	23½	25	25	15	19
Spirits, from grain, first proof	Per gallon	$0 52.97	$0 48.02	$0 43.19	$0 .41	$0 41	$0 23.53	$0 60	100	----------	30
Sugar, brown	Per lb.	2.34	2.23	2.04	1.86	1.86	1.07	2½	30	10	24
white clayed	do	2.97	2.80	2.79	2.52	2.52	1.19	6	30	10	24
loaf	do	11.06	10.07	7.53	7.96	7.96	4.59	6	30	5	24
lump, and other refined	do	9.22	8.61	7.63	6.84	6 84	3.92	6	30	10	24

COMPARATIVE STATEMENT—Continued.

Denomination of merchandise.	Rates, &c.	Reductions under act of 1833. Rate of duty. 1834-'35, 1-10, or 10 per cent.	1836-'37, 2-10, or 20 per cent.	1838-'39, 3-10, or 30 per cent.	1840-'41, 4-10, or 40 per cent.	Payable under the act of 1841; reduction under the act of 1833. Tariff of 1841 from Oct. 1.	To June 30, 1842.	Duty imposed by the act of August 30, 1842.	Duty imposed by the act of July 30, 1846, per cent. ad valorem.	Per centage increase from 1789 to 1846.	Duty imposed by the act of March 3, 1857.
Teas, from places of their production—											
Bohea	Per lb.	Free	Free	Free	Free	Free	Free	Free	Free	Decrease, 10	Free.
Souchong and other black	do	do	do	do	do	do	do	do	do	do 12½	Free.
Hyson, imperial, &c.	do	do	do	do	do	do	do	do	do	do 20	Free.
from other places, Bohea	do	$0 9.55	$0 9.32	$0 9.65	$0 8.82	$0 8.82	do	20 per cent.	20	12	15
Souchong and other black	do	Free	Free	Free	Free	Free	do	20 per cent.	20	3½	15
Tin, in pigs and bars		do	do	do	do	do	do	1 per cent.	5	5	Free.
manufactures of	Per cent.	24½	24	23½	23	23	21½	30	30	22½	
Wool, unmanufactured	do	38	36	34	32	32	26		30	30	(a)24
All goods, wares, and merchandise not otherwise enumerated or specified in the several tariffs.	do	15	15	15	15	20	20	20	20	15	15

(a) See note page 320.

Comparative statements, exhibiting the quantities and values of staple products exported from the United States into the principal commercial countries, together with the amounts of duties paid thereon, during the commercial years 1851, 1852, and 1853.

Approximation to statistical accuracy can alone be expected in statements like these. They partake, indeed, of the character of estimates rather than of statistics. The data on which they are based, consisting of quantities and values contained in the annual reports of the Treasury Department on commerce and navigation, cannot be deemed, in all cases, reliable, or rather, in many cases, they are not available as a basis for exhibiting, with anything like accuracy, the export trade in our leading staples, so as to estimate the duties charged thereon in foreign countries.

In many instances quantities of articles exported are given without corresponding values; in others, values are given without corresponding quantities, and the values attached to the same description of articles, in the same column, are observed frequently to vary, and often to a remarkable degree.

Thus, under the general caption "wood," we find given in distinct columns the quantity of each of the specific articles—"Staves and heading," "shingles," "boards, plank and scantling and hewn timber"—though the values are aggregated into one, while, under the same caption, the individual value of each of the articles, "other lumber"—"masts and spars," "oak bark and other dye," and all manufactures of wood—is given in separate columns, unaccompanied by the quantity of either. So, the separate quantities of "tar and pitch," "rosin and turpentine," are given while the values are combined; so of "beef," "tallow," "hides," and "horned cattle;" so of "butter and cheese;" so of "pork," "hams and other bacon;" "lard," and "hogs;" so (as to numbers) of "horses and mules;" so of "tallow candles and soap;" so of "snuff" and "tobacco manufactured;" so of "leather," and "boots and shoes," the pounds of leather and the number of pairs of boots and shoes being given, while the values of all are aggregated; so of "iron, and manufactures of," the quantities of "pig" and "bar" iron, and of "nails," being given distinct and in separate columns, while the values are given in the aggregate in one. The articles of "beer, ale, porter, and cider," occupy two columns, one for quantity, the other for value, when it would seem that each liquor should have two for itself. Among articles of which the value is given without quantity, quality, or number, by which alone, in many instances, the duties paid foreign countries on the articles respectively could be estimated, may be instanced, molasses, vinegar, linseed oil, coaches and carriages, hats, all manufactures of cotton, flax and hemp; and, generally, all manufactured articles whatsoever.

As regards the last named articles, it might not, in all instances, be important to know, or practicable to discover and state the exact numbers or quantities; but it would seem otherwise, as regards the article of the "manufactures of cotton," while the quantity, as well as the value of cottons, "printed or colored," "uncolored," "twist yarn and thread," and "other manufactures of," would afford data, often indispensable, in commercial estimates and calculations, especially those relating to the duties paid upon them under foreign tariffs. (*a*)

A single example will demonstrate the importance of having the quantity as well as the value of each article of export returned by the collectors of customs to the Treasury Department: in the table of exports to Venezuela for 1853, rosin and turpentine are found at the head of a column over the quantity 1,550 barrels. It is impossible to determine how many barrels of the one and how many barrels of the other article entered into this aggregate. And yet, in estimating the duties paid, the knowledge is very material; for, if the aggregate were all rosin, it would have entered the ports of Venezuela *free*, whereas if it were all turpentine, the duty would have been $967 50.

Two examples which meet the eye on opening "Commerce and Navigation," for two different years, will illustrate the assertion that the values attached to the same description of articles in the same column are often observed to vary to a remarkable extent.

Thus, in 1854, we find cotton exported to Cuba at less than three cents per pound, whilst we have the very same description of cotton, and in the very same column, sent to Mexico at 10¼ cents per pound!

In 1852, we find 29,301,928 pounds of cotton exported to Spain at an aggregate value of $570,195, giving less than two cents per pound; and yet, we learn from the Report on the Finances for the same year that the average price of cotton exported in 1852 was 8.05 cents per pound, and the fact is substantiated by calculations based on the quantities and values of the article exported to other countries named in the same column of "Commerce and Navigation" for the same year.

Once more: articles are sometimes enumerated in "Commerce and Navigation" as exported to countries into which, by their tariff regulations, they are forbidden entrance. For instance, in 1851, we find 273 barrels of beef, valued at $2,180, exported to Mexico, and 503,534 pounds of lard, the value of which latter article is unknown—the value of lard being merged into the aggregate value of pork, hams and other bacon, and hogs, in "Commerce and Navigation." In 1852 there were exported 35 barrels of beef, valued at $604, and 4,448 pounds of lard; in 1853, 139,117 pounds of lard. Yet, by the tariffs of Mexico, each of these years those articles were absolutely prohibited entrance into her ports. (*b*) These facts, though they may seem practi-

(*a*) Since this was written "Commerce and Navigation" for 1855 has appeared, and nearly every correction indicated in the text is found to have been made. Other changes and improvements have also been introduced, which, had they been found in the reports of 1851, 1852, and 1853, would have materially facilitated the preparation of these Statements, and have rendered the Statements themselves far more reliable.

(*b*) It is remarked in another part of this Report that special privileges and dispensations have frequently been granted by Mexican officials, reducing tariff rates of duty and admitting articles otherwise prohibited. Such may have been the case in regard to the articles mentioned in the text.

cally unimportant, yet serve to indicate an bsence of accuracy in custom-house returns, deserving, perhaps, the slight notice here bestowed.

It is not within the scope of these remarks, which are designed only to present facts to account for the absence of statistical exactness in the tabular statements which they introduce, to submit a cause for the inconsistencies, inaccuracies, and discrepancies thus noticed in the official Reports on Commerce and Navigation for the years specified, and much less to suggest a remedy.

The act of Congress which requires the Register of the Treasury annually to prepare statistical accounts of the commerce of he United States with foreign countries is that approved February 10, 1820, entitled "An act to provide for obtaining accurate statements of the commerce of the United States." By the third section of this act it is required, "that the kinds, quantities, and values of all articles imported, shall be distinctly stated in such accounts." If the section stopped here, there could certainly arise no complaint as to "quantites without values, and values without quantities." But it proceeds, "*except* in cases in which it may appear to the Secretary of the Treasury, that separate statements of the species, quantities, or values, of any particular articles, would swell the annual statements without utility; and, in such cases, the kinds and total values of such articles shall be stated together, or in such classes as the Secretary of the Treasury may think fit." That there are "cases" such as are thus provided for is unquestionable; but it is submitted whether a schedule of merchandise adopted for the object in question some thirty or forty years ago may not be deemed susceptible of modification and improvement.(*a*)

As for the absence of uniformity, consistency, or correctness in the statements of the values, quantities, or destination of articles exported from the United States, it is by no means easy to determine a probable cause.

The eleventh section of the act of 1820, already referred to, provides for these matters fully and distinctly. It declares "that before a clearance shall be granted for any vessel bound to a foreign place, the owners, shippers, or consignors of the cargo on board of such vessel, shall deliver to the collector manifests of the cargo, or the parts thereof, shipped by them, respectively, and shall verify the same by oath or affimation; and such manifests shall specify the kinds and quantites of the articles shipped by them, respectively, and the value of the total quantity of each kind of articles; and such oath or affirmation shall state that such manifest contains a full, just, and true account of all articles laden on board of such vessel by the owners, shippers, or consignors, respectively, and that the values of such are truly stated according to their actual cost, or the values which they truly bear at the port and time of exportion; and before a clearance shall be granted for any such vessel, the master of every such vessel, and the owners, shippers, and consignors of the cargo shall state, upon oath or affirmation to the collector, the foreign place or country in which such cargo is truly intended to be landed; and the said oaths or affirmation shall be taken and subscribed in writing."

How requirements so stringent as these could be eluded, except through gross delinquency or negligence on the part of those in office, or of fraud and perjury on the part of shippers, seems difficult to imagine. That they have been infringed, however, is unquestionably the fact. The attention of the Treasury Department has more than once been drawn to a disregard of the law in many particulars; and special circulars have been addressed to collectors of customs with a view to remedy the evil and arrest the wrong. In 1847, for example, Mr. Secretary Walker, perceiving the palpable disparity between the quantities and values of staple products exported to one particular country, (Mexico,) addressed such a circular to collectors of customs, in which, after assuming a probable cause for the omission, to wit: that the articles had been exported for the use of the United States army, then in that country, adds: "It is desirable that this omission be supplied, as it (the item of export omitted) properly forms a part of the industry of the country, and should find a place in the tables of commerce and navigation."

The valuations, especially, seem not, therefore, fixed even by the vacillating prices-current of the day in the different markets, but vary with the estimates of the consignors or shippers. To this fact, in connexion with others, is attributable, probably, that remarkable discrepancy which is detected between United States official reports of the values of articles, especially of our staples, exported to foreign countries, and the official statements of these countries themselves of the values of the same articles received at their ports from the United States.(*b*)

Similar discrepancies in *quantities* stated are, also, frequently observable.

Thus, in 1851, according to official statements of Cuba, 2,102½ barrels of United States flour were imported into that island; whereas, by the United States statement, the quantity is given at 5,511 barrels.(*c*)

The following table will more fully illustrate these discrepancies as respects the island of Cuba:

(*a*) As already stated such modification and improvement was being made in the Treasury Department, unknown to the Department of State, at the very time the above was penned; as appears by "Commerce and Navigation for 1855."

(*b*) The very light penalty prescribed for failing to deliver manifests at the ports of departure in the United States, together with the absence of the rigid scrutiny to which imports are subjected, may suggest some explanation of these discrepancies.

(*c*) It may be, however, that the exports of one year, as they appear in Commerce and Navigation, are not inserted in the Cuban "Balanza" until the following year; or that, instead of proceeding to the port of original destination captains, in obedience to private orders, sail thence, or even directly, for "a market." These suppositions, however, even if well founded, afford but little aid in arriving at accurate comparisons.

Comparative statement, exhibiting the values of certain staple products exported from the United States and imported into Cuba in 1851 *and* 1852, *as shown by official authorities of Cuba and the United States, respectively.*

CERTAIN STAPLE PRODUCTS.	VALUES IN DOLLARS.			
	1851.		1852.	
	United States statement.	Cuban statement.	United States statement.	Cuban statement.
Dried fish	84,935	158,778	88,222	131,457
Butter and cheese	72,958	110,478	77,862	86,032
Flour	27,260	(a)26,281	73,855	91,714
Indian corn	129,734	309,682	91,944	71,882
Indian meal	10,313	12,217	21,640	5,948
Ship bread	7,907	10,720	15,530	12,870
Rice	560,094	818,213	772,603	811,741

(a) 2,102½ barrels.

The variance in the values placed on these articles and others by the official estimates of the United States and Cuba, respectively, does not, however, affect the calculations of duties paid on the same, inasmuch as the rates of the Cuban tariff are almost invariably per cent. on a fixed valuation. The duty on rice, for example, imported under a foreign flag, is 33⅓ per cent. on a fixed valuation of $1 25 per arroba of 25 pounds 7 ounces, and 23½ per cent. on the same valuation and quantity when introduced under the national flag. This staple, however, as well as all others of United States production, is almost invariably imported in United States vessels, rendering a consideration of the lesser duty in the differential scale of that island unnecessary in the calculation of duties.

In ascertaining the amount of duties levied under the tariffs of other nations that have adopted the ad valorem principle, as applicable either to general or special imports, the valuation not being fixed, but fluctuating with invoices and prices current, discrepancies between the amounts thus obtained and those obtained under the United States valuation are strikingly manifest; and even when the value is fixed the discrepancy is often extraordinary and unaccountable, as may be seen in the following statement:

Comparative statement, exhibiting the amounts of duties paid on certain staple products exported from the United States and imported into Cuba in 1851, *as shown by official authorities of Cuba, and as calculated upon the quantities and values given by those of the United States.*

CERTAIN STAPLE PRODUCTS.	DUTIES PAID IN DOLLARS.	
	United States statement.	Cuban statement.
Dried fish	47,070	56,930
Butter and cheese	25,312	32,916
Flour(a)	52,989	20,704
Indian corn	109.526	111,036
Indian meal	6,090	4,380
Ship bread	12,782	3,843
Rice	273,418	292,370
(a)Flour in 1852	167,867	73,657

In further illustration of the discrepancies often observable between the United States official reports of the values and quantities of staples exported to foreign countries and the official reports of those countries themselves, exhibiting the values and quantities of the same articles imported from the United States, the following statement is given respecting Peru:

Statement exhibiting the quantities and values of certain exports from the United States to Peru, in 1852, as shown by the official reports of Peru and of the United States.

DESCRIPTION OF MERCHANDISE.	Values, Peruvian statement.	Values, United States statement.	Quantities, pounds.	Discrepancy.
Cotton piece goods	$257,987 87½	$198,983 00		(a)$59,004 87½
Ready made clothing	5,506 00	50 00		5,456 00
Household furniture	49,778 00	22,468 00		27,310 00
Flour	26,228 00	26,602 00		374 00
Whale oil	8,107 87½			(b)8,107 87½
Wax	7,893 75	3,014 00	Peru 15,327; United States 7,066.	4,879 75
Cigars	6,555 00	5,535 00	Peru 2,622; United States 279 M.	1,020 00

Total value of exports from the United States to Peru in 1852, as per Peruvian custom-house reports.......... $496,684 37½
Total value of exports from the United States to Peru the same year, as per United States treasury report.... 355,842 00

Total discrepancy........ 140,842 37½

It will be seen from the preceeding table that in the article *flour* the export entry in the United States and the import entry in Peru varied but slightly. For the preceding year, however, the discrepancy was enormous, thus:

Quantity and value of flour imported into Peru from the United States in 1851, as per Peruvian custom-house report, barrels 5,622; value........ $44,976 00

Quantity and value of flour exported from the United States to Peru in 1851, as per report of the United States Treasury Department, barrels 1,650; value........ 10,075 00

Discrepancy, barrels 3,972; value........ 34,901 00

Peru has been selected for the purpose of illustrating the difficulty, if not the utter impossibility, of arriving at statistical accuracy in those statements of duties paid, for the reason that the annual "*Balanza*" of that republic is made up with great care, and under the supervision of the treasury, and the figures are, therefore, less liable to mislead.

The same may be said relative to the commercial statistics of Chili, a decree having been passed by the Chilian government in 1843, providing for the establishment of a statistical board, since which period full returns have been regularly published, under the title of *Estadistic a Comercial de la Republica de Chile;* and yet, figures copied from these publications(c) and from the United States Treasury reports on commerce and navigation, when arranged in comparison with each other, present astounding results, as follows:

(a) From this should be deducted $1,699, the amount of cotton manufctures exported from the United States to Peru during this year, reducing the discrepancy to $57,305 87½.

(b) Although this article is registered in the official Balanza of Peru, direct from the United States, it is proper to remark, that it may have been deposited or sold by whalers on a cruise, and not have come direct from the United States. But this is mere conjecture. The great distance between the United States and Peru and the voyage around the cape to the ports of that republic, usually taking from 4 to 6 months, would afford a more satisfactory explanation of these discrepancies, if they were not found to run thorough a series of several consecutive years without much variation either as to aggregate or average results.

(c) See vol. 1 "Digests," pp. 732, *et seq.*

Commerce of the United States withi Chili the years specified.

YEARS.	United States report.		Chili report.		Discrepancies.	
	United States to Chili.	Chili to United States.	United States to Chili.	Chili to United States.	United States to Chili.	Chili to United States.
1845	$1,548,191	$1,123,690	$674,246	$1,280,042	$873,945	$156,352
1846	1,768,570	1,275,960	932,716	1,453,278	835,854	177,318
1847	1,671,610	1,716,903	819,445	1,596,154	852,165	120,749
1848	1,924,511	1,310,451	1,124,171	1,634,749	800,340	324,298
1849	2,017,100	1,817,723	1,100,345	3,589,888	916,755	1,772,165
1850	1,422,721	1,796,877	1,911,479	4,012,612	488,758	2,215,735
1851	1,895,305	2,734,746	4,594,211	3,515,235	2,698,906	780,489

If the official reports of the trade and navigation of France are compared with the official reports of the United States, similar discrepancies are frequently perceived.

The official " *Tableau General du Commerce de la France* for 1855 is at hand. On turning to the article tobacco, the quantity imported into France that year from the United States is found to be considerably over 29,368,400 pounds, at an actual value of $2,678,397, (the official value is more than double this sum,) whilst the United States official report for the same year gives only 18,672,000 pounds, at a value of $1,240,872, showing a difference between the two authorities, in quantity, of 10,696,400 pounds, and in value, of 1,437,525! The discrepancy in the article of rice is, in the quantity, upwards of 900,000 pounds, and in the value, $98,432! It would seem, also, that the discrepancies between the official reports of France and the United States, for any given year, are even more palpable and extraordinary, as regards the imports from France into the United States, than those which are observed in the exports from the United States to France.

From an official report recently published in that country, the value of imports into the United States from France are stated to exceed by 80,000,000 francs that given by the United States official report for the same year.

It is possible that products of Switzerland, Belgium, and other countries bordering on France, which pass through its territories in transit for the United States, may be included in the French official tables of export to this country; but this is barely possible, inasmuch as separate tables and distinct columns are invariably devoted to this branch of trade in the French reports. Besides, we find in "Commerce and Navigation," for several years, separate tables giving the "indirect trade," and designating the ports through which such products reach the United States. A comparison between the enormous discrepancy just noticed and the quantities or values reaching the United States or the countries above named, *via* France, would render this possibility even more remote.

A comparison of the official returns of trade between the United States and Great Britain, as given in the official reports of the two governments, respectively, exhibits, with respect to many important articles, a similar state of facts.

Thus, the British returns of trade for 1853 show 1,870,592 bushels of Indian corn imported from the United States that year, whilst the Treasury Report of the latter country states the quantity at 1,653,840 bushels. In the article of flour, the discrepancy amounts to 326,075 barrels, and in the article of cotton, to 110,144,690 pounds, (the excess appearing in the United States Treasury Report,) whilst the discrepancy in the total value of exports to Great Britain from the United States for the same year, as appears on a comparison of the official returns of the two nations, amounts to the enormous sum of $15,991,339!

An examination of the official returns of the trade of Belgium, Spain,(*a*) and other countries in Europe, leads to the same results; but it is deemed unnecessary to multiply examples, those already cited being deemed sufficient to explain and account

(*a*) Returns of trade between Spain and the United States for 1846, as per Spanish official reports, exhibit the following figures:

Imports from United States	$245,351
Exports to United States	982,962
Total trade	1,228,313

United States returns of trade between Spain and United States during the same year thus state the figures:

Imports from United States	$475,595
Exports to United States	1,011,879
Total trade	1,487,474
Discrepancy	259,161

Of this discrepancy the amount for imports into Spain from the United States is $238,244.

for any variations from the exact returns of trade with any particular country, should this ever be ascertained, which may be discovered in the statements given.

It is impossible to hazard even a conjecture, beyond that already suggested, as to the real cause of these numerous and manifest discrepancies between the official statements, both as respects quantities and values, of the exporting and importing countries. And, in addition to the suggestions just alluded to, it may be further observed that the facts have not been overlooked or lost sight of, that foreign imports to the United States bear their home values in our estimates; whilst United States imports, into most foreign countries, bear the values which they there sustain in their official reports ; nor, that the commercial years of different countries do not always coincide in point of time, commencing and closing at the same period. But, these facts duly considered, the discrepancies in estimated value still remain quite inexplicable, whilst those in quantity are wholly unaffected.

The circular of Mr. Secretary Walker relative to under valuation of exports has already been referred to. The following extract from a circular issued by the same gentleman, (December 18, 1849,) in reference to the palpable under-valuation(*a*) of *imports*, may throw some light on the subject of these discrepancies, if it does not suggest the proper remedy. "The department is apprized, from authentic sources, of a system, or practice, pursued by foreign shipers of merchandise, leading to impositions and frauds upon the revenue in the assessment of duties in our ports.

"The system or practice referred to consists in the preparation and transmission of double invoices of the identical goods embraced in the importation, with a material variation between the two invoices as to the cost or foreign market value of the same goods."

The "*double invoices*," designed to defraud the United States revenue by under-valuing imports at the United States custom-houses, exhibits a degree of dishonest ingenuity on the part of importers that may cast some slight suspicion on the genuineness of the documents w ich accompany their merchandise when they become exporters.

In a later report from the Treasury Department, namely: the Report on the Finances for 1854, page 20, the Secretary of the Treasury says: "There seems to be no express provision in any act of Congress * * * making it a felony to make false entries in the collector's books, or return false accounts to the treasury. * * * There has been no revision of the revenue laws since the enactment of 1789. The necessity of a revision is respectfully urged upon the consideration of Congress."

Several cases of fraud on the part of collectors, amounting in the aggregate to nearly $200,000, have of late been detected by the Treasury Department, the particulars of which have been communicated to Congress by the head of that department.(*b*)

But the only object these remarks have in view is to explain the difficulties, from what cause soever they may arise, in arriving at anything more in these comparative s'atements than well considered estimates, from the data to which access can be had. Whether the system under which this data is obtained is susceptible of improvement is not a question properly coming within the sphere of duties assigned to this office. A few suggestions, however, are respectfully submitted.

In order to arrive at substantial agreement between the tables of different countries, there should be a conformity between them as to the following particulars:

1. A more exact ascertainment of quantities and values of exports from each.

2. The article exported by one should be taken into account of the other, as of the date of export in which case corrections would result from losses at sea.

3. There should be a uniform mode of reporting the indirect trade—that is to say, no country should export, as exports of its own, the products of other countries merely passing through its territories for export. So, also, of imports, none should be entered as of the country in which received when merely for transit through to other countries. To these may be added a more exact observance, at the custom-houses, of existing laws, as well as the adoption by Congress of such general reforms in the revenue laws of the country as have already been submitted for its consideration by the head of the Treasury Department.

The general subject of the valuation of exports and imports in annual official statements of foreign trade has recently receiveo attention from the government of Great Britain. Prior to 1854,(*c*) and down to that year, the annual returns of the foreign

(*a*) The following statement of imports of guano from Peru, as given in Reports on Commerce and Navigation for the years designated, presents a most extraordinary case of this under valuation:

Imports of guano into the United States from Peru.

YEARS.	Quantity.	V .
	Tons.	
1853................	88,840	$96,563
1854................	175,849	692,072
1855............ ...	178,961	459,947

Average price less than $3 25 per ton, whilst its cost at the Chinchas, on boεrd ship, is well known to be, at the very lowest figure, from $20 to $25 per ton.

(*b*) These frauds were detected in the abstracts sent to the Treasury of *duties collected*, whereby the collectors were charged by that department with less than they had received; but it is evident that if these abstracts were false in respect of duties, they must have been equally so in regard to quantities and values, from which alone duties can result.

(*c*) In October, 1854, a Treasury minute directed the commissioners of customs to introduce a system by which the real values, hitherto wanted, should be computed upon the basis of actual prices, these prices for imports including all charges of freight and landing, but exclusive of duties.

trade of the United Kingdom had been made upon an estimate of value established by law in 1694, one hundred and fifty years previous.

The only exception to this rule was the domestic exports, or exports of the produce of the United Kingdom, of which, for many years, both the "official" or legal value, and the "real," declared, or estimated value, had been returned, the official value having been retained for the only purpose for which it can be viewed as at all valuable, comparison with the statements of prior and subsequent years. The "real value" now returned is based on actual current prices, and the estimates are made by an officer appointed for the special purpose at London and at Liverpool—the average annual prices fixed for the valuations being principally those of the markets of those cities—who are aided in their task by merchants, brokers, and chambers of commerce. The "official value," by the ancient standard, is also returned. The disparity between the values thus stated is striking, though less so in the aggregate value returned than in that of individual articles, or particular classes of articles, as may be perceived by the following statements:

The new computed real value of the total imports into the United Kingdom in 1854 was	£152,591,513
The old official value	124,338,478
Showing an excess of real value, or an increase of value, between 1694 and 1854 of nearly 23 per cent., or	28,253,035

While it has been estimated that the average increase in the value of wool, wine, brandy, flaxseed, butter, and tallow, each, is about 300 per cent.; in wood, timber, deals, and staves 510 per cent.; and in corn and flour 114 per cent. The official value of coffee, on the contrary, imported into the United Kingdom, in 1854, exceeds the actual value 164 per cent.; tea exceeds the value 55 per cent.; cotton manufactures exceed the actual value 50 per cent.; and raw cotton exceeds the actual value 42 per cent. Thus, articles of wood are worth more than five times as much now as they were a century and a half ago; wool, wine, brandy, butter, and tallow about three times as much; breadstuffs more than as much again; while coffee, in 1694, was worth nearly twice as much as in 1854; tea more than one-half as much again; cotton manufactures half as much again; and raw cotton nearly half as much again.

Of the imports from foreign countries and British possessions, respectively, a comparison exhibits results as follows:

From foreign countries.

Real value	£118,439,488	
Official value	93,940,967	
Excess of real value	24,498,521	or 26 per cent.

From British possessions.

Real value	£34,152,025	
Official value	30,397,511	
Excess of real value	3,754,514	or over $12\frac{1}{3}$ per cent.

The total value of exports of foreign and colonial produce, by the old and new systems, shows the subjoined comparison:

Old official value	£29,821,656	
New real value	18,648,978	
Excess of official value	11,172,678	or 38 per cent.

The staple products of the United States exported have alone been considered in these Comparative Statements. How large a proportion of the aggregate exports of domestic products these staples constitute may be inferred from the following recapitulation.

The average value of the staple products enumerated in the tables exported to thirteen of the principal commercial countries during the fiscal years 1851, 1852 and 1853 was $130,871,677.

The average value of domestic exports *not* enumerated in the tables, exported to the same countries, during the same years, was $42,030,311.

The average value of *all* domestic products exported to the same countries the same year was $172,901,988.

The average value of *all* domestic products exported to *all* foreign countries for the same three years was $200,825,466, leaving the average value of all domestic products exported to all countries, except the thirteen enumerated as the principal commercial countries, $27,923,481.

The average amount of duties paid on the $130,871,677 of staple products enumerated exported to the thirteen commercial countries being $30,474,279, that paid on the $172,901,988 (the average value of *all* domestic products exported to said countries) may be estimated at $40,261,296.

The same premises give the amount of duties paid on the $127,923,481 exported to the residue of the world at $6,509,796; and the amount paid on the $200,825,466 of *all* the domestic products exported to *all* countries at $46,763,390.

But this estimate is evidently too large, inasmuch as the duties levied by foreign tariffs on the articles enumerated in the tables are, generally, far higher than those which are not enumerated. The revenue derived from Great Britain for tobacco, for example, exceeds that derived from all other exports of the United States to that nation; while tobacco and breadstuffs, two of our heaviest domestic exports, are subjected by the tariffs of each of the countries specified to higher duties than are almost any of our minor domestic exports.

No country has been admitted into these Comparative Statements the aggregate of whose annual trade with the United States is less than five millions of dollars.

The only countries to which the export of other domestic products exceeds that of the staples enumerated in the tables are Cuba, China, Mexico, Chili, and Venezuela; while in Venezuela, in 1852 and 1853, the staples were in excess, and in Mexico in 1852. The average excess in the value of the articles *not* enumerated in the tables over those enumerated exported to those countries, the commercial years 1851, 1852, and 1853, was as follows:

Cuba, $294,946; China, $2,485,532; Mexico, $353,329; Chili, $658,952; Venezuela, $123,965.

In all the other countries named in the tables the average value of the enumerated articles for the same three years is greatly in excess over those not enumerated; in Belgium amounting to $2,577,753, and in Holland to $1,819,115; while the excess of the total average value of the staple exports over that of the other domestic exports for the three years specified amounts to $88,841,366.

There are some articles which, though found in the list of staple products of the United States, yet sometimes enter our ports as the produce of foreign countries. This anomaly is illustrated by the following statement, which gives the values of such articles, together with the duties accruing to the United States on the same as, also, the aggregate value of articles the produce of the United States brought back.

Comparative statement exhibiting the values of certain articles, staple products of the United States, the produce of foreign countries imported into the United States; together with the amount of duties paid thereon during the commercial years 1851, 1852, *and* 1853, *respectively.*

STAPLE PRODUCTS.	1851.		1852.		1853.	
	Values.	Duties paid.	Values.	Duties paid.	Values.	Duties paid.
Oil, spermaceti	$10	$2 00			$7	$1 40
whale, and other fish	1,281	256 20	$3,847	$769 40	255,781	51,156 20
Whalebone	1,033	206 60	1	20	696	139 20
Dried fish	27,769	5,553 80	55,171	11,034 20	214,116	42,823 20
Staves						
Shingles						
Lumber						
Timber						
Tar and pitch						
Rosin and turpentine						
Ashes						
Beef and pork	1,667	333 40	31,778	6,355 60	26,766	5,353 20
Tallow	12,306	1,230 60	1,320	132 00	64,114	6,411 40
Butter	37,536	7,507 20	79,883	15,976 60	330,326	66,065 20
Cheese	54,852	16,455 60	44,859	13,457 70	70,528	21,158 40
Pork—see Beef and Pork						
Bacon	13,456	2,691 20	13,358	2,671 60	7,455	1,491 00
Lard	131	26 20	5,987	1,197 40	946	189 20
Wheat	609,681	121,936 20	558,958	111,791 60	821.815	164,363 00
Flour	1,008,929	201,785 80	1,010,540	202,108 00	974,736	194,947 20
Indian corn						
meal						
Ship bread						
Rice						
Cotton	11,281	Free	12,521	Free	40,447	Free
Tobacco	555,608	166,682 40	587,395	176,218 50	855,803	256,740 90
Candles, tallow	28	5 60	283	56 60	3,017	603 40
Soap	62,616	18,784 80	51,502	15,450 60	80,424	24,127 20
Tobacco, manufactured	2,533,715	1,013,486 00	2,991,469	1,196,587 60	3,319,435	1,327,774 00
Total	4,931,899	1,556,943 60	5,448,872	1,753,807 60	7,066,412	2,163,344 10
Articles, the produce of the United States, brought back	186,386	Free	143,764	Free	194,096	Free

Some articles embraced in these statements, which now deserve to rank as staples of export, did not so rank prior to the dates of the Commercial Reports emanating from this department in 1839 and in 1842, whilst other articles have very materially decreased in importance as exports; both of which facts, together with others of much importance and interest, are fully exhibited by the following comparative statement.

Comparative statement of the value of the exports of the growth, produce, and manufacture of the United States during the commercial years 1830, 1835, 1840, 1845, 1850, *and* 1855, *with a column showing the increase or decrease in the exportation of each article during the intervening period of twenty-five years.*

DOMESTIC EXPORTS.	1830.	1835.	1840.	1845. (a)	1850.	1855.	Increase or decrease from 1830 to 1855.
Product of the sea.							
Fisheries—							
Oil, spermaceti	$38,618	$52,531	$430,490	$975,195	$788,794	$1,593,832	$1,555,214
Oil, whale and other fish	568,326	773,486	1,404,984	1,520,363	672,640	485,505	82,821
Whalebone	112,357	55,954	310,379	762,642	646,483	781,680	669,323
Spermaceti						45,411	45,411
Spermaceti candles	249,292	284,019	332,353	236,917	260,107	136,463	112,829
Fish, dried and smoked	530,690	783,895	541,058	803,353	365,349	379,892	150,798
Fish, pickled	225,987	224,639	179,106	208,654	91,445	94,111	131,876
Total product of the sea	1,725,270	2,174,524	3,198,370	4,507,124	2,824,818	3,516,894	1,791,624
Product of the forest.							
Wood—							
Masts and spars	13,327	29,437	29,049	28,692	52,109		13,327
Staves and heading						1,922,238	
Shingles	1,501,658	2,635,056	1,801,049	1,953,222	2,437,079	143,362	3,414,650
Boards, plank, and scantling						2,544,065	
Hewn timber						306,643	
Other lumber	148,257	247,032	270,933	369,505	107,827	677 659	529,402
Oak bark and other dye	220,275	73,877	229,510	70,616	205,771	99,168	121,107
All manufactures of wood	172,772	417,532	596,305	677,420	1,948,752	3,683,420	3,510,648
Naval stores—							
Tar and pitch	321,019	567,566	602,529	814,969	1,142,813	288,028	1,728,437
Rosin and turpentine						1,761,428	
Ashes, pot and pearl	1,105,127	571,591	533,193	1,210,496	572,870	448,499	656,628
Ginseng	67,852	94,960	22,728	177,146	122,916	19,796	48,056
Skins and furs	641,760	759,953	1,237,789	1,248,355	852,466	709,531	67,771
Total product of the forest	4,192,047	5,397,004	5,323,085	6,550,421	7,442,503	12,603,837	8,411,790

(a) In 1843 the fiscal year was made to close June 30 instead of September 30, as hitherto.

COMPARATIVE STATEMENT—Continued.

DOMESTIC EXPORTS.	1830.	1835.	1840.	1845. (a)	1850.	1855.	Increase or decrease from 1830 to 1855.
Product of agriculture.							
Of animals—							
Beef	$717,683	$638,761	$623,373	$1,926,809	$1,605,608	$2,600,547	$3,681,932
Tallow						1,352,406	
Hides						361,982	
Horned cattle						84,680	
Butter	142,370	164,809	210,749	878,865	1,215,463	418,723	790,387
Cheese						514,034	
Pork, pickled	(b)1,315,245	(b)1,776,732	(b)1,894,894	(b)2,991,284	(b)7,550,287	4,390,979	(b)10,289,729
Hams and bacon						3,195,978	
Lard						4,018,016	
Wool					22,778	27,802	27,802
Hogs	Vide supra	Vide supra	Vide supra	Vide supra	Vide supra	2,192	Vide supra.
Horses	182,244	285,028	246,320	385,488	139,494	108,484	9,660
Mules						83,420	
Sheep	22,110	36,566	30,698	23,948	15,753	18,837	3,273
Total product of animals	2,379,652	2,901,896	3,006,034	6,206,394	10,549,383	17,178,080	14,798,428
Vegetable food—							
Wheat	46,176	51,405	1,635,483	336,779	643,745	1,329,246	1,283,070
Flour	6,085,953	4,394,777	10,143,615	5,398,593	7,098,570	10,896,908	4,810,955
Indian corn	224,823	588,276	338,333	411,741	3,892,193	6,961,571	6,736,748
Indian meal	372,296	629,389	705,183	641,552	760,611	1,237,122	864,826
Rye meal	87,796	129,140	170,931	112,908	216,076	236,248	148,452
Rye, oats, and other small grain and pulse	66,249	96,478	113,393	177,953	121,191	238,976	172,727
Biscuit or ship bread	188,474	221,699	428,988	366,294	334,123	657,783	469,309
Potatoes	39,027	41,543	54,524	122,926	99,333	203,416	164,389
Apples	23,727	20,959	55,131	81,306	24,974	107,643	83,916

(a) In 1843 the fiscal year was made to close June 30 instead of September 30, as hitherto.

(b) And live hogs.

COMPARATIVE STATEMENT—Continued.

DOMESTIC EXPORTS.	1830.	1835.	1840.	1845.	1850.	1855.	Increase or decrease from 1830 to 1855.
Vegetable food—Continued.							
Onions						$64,496	$64,496
Rice	$1,986,824	$2,210,331	$1,942,076	$2,160,456	$2,631,557	1,717,953	268,871
Total vegetable food	9,121,345	8,383,997	15,587,657	9,810,508	15,822,373	23,651,362	14,530,017
Cotton	29,674,883	64,961,302	63,870,307	51,739,643	71,984,616	88,143,844	58,468,961
Tobacco	5,586,365	8,250,577	9,883,957	7,469,819	9,951,023	14,712,468	9,126,103
Hemp					5,633	121,320	121,320
Other agricultural products—							
Flaxseed	180,973	451,886	120,000	81,978	4,040	6,016	174,957
Clover seed						13,570	13,570
Brown sugar	2,975	8,526	45,940	11,107	23,037	286,408	283,433
Hops	30,312	90,720	11,235	90,341	142,692	1,310,720	1,280,408
Indigo	827	1,060	209	70			827
Total other agricultural productions	215,087	552,192	177,384	183,496	169,769	1,616,714	1,401,627
Manufactures.							
Refined sugar	193,084	62,293	1,214,658	164,662	285,056	526,463	333,379
Wax	153,666	93,919	59,685	234,794	118,055	69,905	83,761
Chocolate	893	2,605	2,048	1,461	2,260	2,771	1,878
Spirits, from grain	225,357	134,823	128,330	75,108	48,314	384,144	158,787
from molasses	49,798	158,544	283,707	216,118	268,290	1,448,280	1,398,482
from other materials						101,836	101,836
Molasses	3,968	1,963	9,775	20,771	14,137	189,830	185,862
Vinegar	6,690	4,540	6,401	14,375	11,182	17,281	10,591
Beer, ale, porter, and cider, in casks }					52,251	18,603	45,069
in bottles }						26,466	
Linseed oil }	35,039	47,728	63,348	92,614	229,741	49,580	1,151,693
Spirits of turpentine }						1,137,152	
Household furniture	239,463	264,790	295,844	277,488	278,025	803,960	564,497
Coaches and parts, and railroad cars and parts	51,190	83,525	74,416	55,821	95,722	290,525	239,33

COMPARATIVE STATEMENT—Continued.

DOMESTIC EXPORTS.	1830.	1835.	1840.	1845.	1850.	1855.	Increase or decrease from 1830 to 1855.
Manufactures—Continued.							
Hats, of fur or silk } of palm leaf }	$309,362	$171,531	$103,398	$70,597	$68,671	$140,692	$131,448
						37,222	
Saddlery	36,651	52,233	59,517	20,847	20,893	64,886	28,235
Trunks and valises	6,654	5,584	6,607	3,336	10,370	35,203	28,549
Adamantine and other candles } **Soap** }	619,238	534,467	451,995	623,946	664,963	699,141	492,111
						412,208	
Snuff } **Tobacco**, manufactured }	246,747	357,611	813,671	538,498	648,832	14,038	1,253,366
						1,486,075	
Gunpowder	128,625	227,961	117,347	122,599	190,352	356,051	227,426
Leather } **Boots and shoes** }	338,603	224,722	214,360	328,091	193,598	288,867	713,803
						763,539	
Cables and cordage	4,135	11,686	43,510	55,016	51,357	315,267	311,132
Salt	22,978	46,483	42,246	45,151	75,103	156,879	133,901
Lead	4,831	2,741	39,687	342,646	12,797	14,298	9,467
Iron—							
Pig } Bar } Nails }	96,189	90,266	147,397	77,669	154,210	23,060	192,248
						10,189	
						255,188	
Castings of	35,408	70,922	115,664	118,248	79,318	306,439	271,031
All other manufactures of	177,876	134,687	841,394	649,100	1,677,792	3,158,596	2,980,720
Copper and brass, and manufactures of	36,601	69,791	86,954	94,736	105,060	690,766	654,165
Drugs and medicines	92,154	148,560	122,387	212,837	334,789	788,114	695,960
Total certain manufactures	3,074,910	2,945,405	5,279,317	4,099,832	5,680,768	15,083,514	12,008,604
Cotton piece goods—							
Nankeens	1,093	400	1,200	1,174,038			
Other	61,800	397,412	398,977	516,243			
Printed or colored	62,893	397,812	400,177	1,690,281	606,631	2,613,655	2,550,762
White, other than duck	964,196	2,355,202	2,925,257	2,343,104	3,774,407	2,793,910	1,829,714
Duck } All other manufactures of }	266,350	105,667	224,173	294,543	353,386	113,366	183,266
						336,250	
Total cotton piece goods, and non-enumerated	1,318,183	2,858,681	3,549,607	4,327,928	4,734,424	5,857,181	4,538,998

COMPARATIVE STATEMENT—Continued.

DOMESTIC EXPORTS.	1830.	1835.	1840.	1845.	1850.	1855.	Increase or decrease from 1830 to 1855.
Manufactures—Continued.							
Hemp, cloth and thread	$2,152	$795	$7,114	$14,762	$1,183	$2,256	$354
bags, other manufactures of	1,769	1,575	1,128		10,593	34,002	32,223
Wearing apparel	101,277	106,786	152,055	59,653	207,632	223,801	121,524
Earthen and stone ware	2,773	16,427	10,959	7,393	15,644	32,119	29,346
Combs and buttons	124,589	101,367	40,299	23,794	23,987	32,049	92,540
Brushes of all kinds	6,116	3,377	12,263	2,206	2,827	10,856	4,740
Billiard tables and apparatus	316	5,316	2,471	1,551	2,295	4,916	4,600
Umbrellas and parasols	25,796	17,278	9,654	2,583	3,395	8,441	17,355
Morocco and leather not sold by the pound	70,968	11,847	19,557	16,363	3,800	36,045	34,923
Fire-engines		1,482	6,317	12,660	9,800	14,829	14,829
Printing presses and type	13,274	16,758	17,105	26,774	3,140	36,405	23,131
Musical instruments	10,261	8,627	12,199	18,309	39,242	106,857	96,596
Books and maps	32,004	59,991	29,632	43,298	21,634	207,218	175,214
Paper and stationery	40,994	69,700	76,957	106,190	119,475	185,637	144,643
Paints and varnish	13,716	22,976	34,631	50,165	99,696	163,096	149,380
Jewelry, real and mock		Vide infra.	Vide infra.	Vide infra.	Vide infra.	17,883	Vide infra.
Gold and silver, and gold leaf, (manufactures of.)	3,561	5,253	1,965	3,229	4,583	9,051	5,490
Glass	60,280	79,808	56,688	98,760	136,682	204,679	144,399
Tin	4,497	2,545	7,501	10,114	13,590	14,279	9,782
Pewter and lead	4,172	433	15,296	14,404	22,682	5,233	1,061
Marble and stone	4,655	8,687	35,794	17,626	34,510	168,546	163,891
Artificial flowers	(a)13,707	(a)16,973	(a)9,479	(a)10,435	(a)45,283	4,160	(a)8,336
Bricks and lime	2,482	4,133	16,949	8,701	16,348	57,393	54,911
India rubber boots and shoes						686,769	686,769
India rubber, all other manufactures of						722,338	722,338
Lard oil						82,945	82,945
Oil cake						739,580	739,589
Total certain manufact's, and non-enumerated	2,835,993	4,208,986	6,425,722	5,804,977	13,474,059	9,668,823	6,832,830

(a) And jewelry.

COMPARATIVE STATEMENT—Continued.

DOMESTIC EXPORTS.	1830.	1835.	1840.	1845.	1850.	1855.	Increase or decrease from 1830 to 1855.
Coal					$167,090	$637,006	$637,006
Ice					107,018	190,793	190,793
Gold and silver coin	$937,151	$729,610	$2,235,073	$844,446	2,046,679	19,842,423	18,905,272
bullion						34,114,995	34,114,995
Quicksilver						806,119	806,119
Articles not enumerated—							
Manufactured	347,228	869,283	403,496	1,269,338	3,869,071	3,274,843	2,927,615
Raw produce	309,249	543,916	740,305	1,315,578	679,556	1,545,518	1,236,269
Total exports of the produce of the United States, including articles not enumerated in the columns	59,462,029	101,189,082	113,895,634	99,299,776	136,946,912	246,708,553	187,246,524

By the preceding comparative statement it will be perceived that spermaceti, in 1830, does not appear in the list of exports in the United States treasury returns, while in 1855 the exports of this article amount to $45,411. It was, however, probably embraced under the general title *spermaceti oil*, which from $38,618, at that od, has now increased to $1,593,832.

Cotton duck does not appear as a staple manufacture until within the past few years. The value of this article exported in 1855 was $113,336.(*a*)

Bags and other manufactures of hemp, in 1830 an article of inconsiderable importance even for home consumption, has become quite important as a staple export, the value exported in 1855 being $34,002.

Earthen and stone ware may now be classed among our prominent exports, having risen from $2,773 in 1830, to upwards o; $30,000 in 1855, or nearly 1,500 per cent.

Articles made of India rubber have been added to our staple manufactures within the past few years. For the first time they appear in "Commerce and Navigation" for 1855; the exports of this class of goods during that year amount, in the aggregate, to $1,409,107.

Ice, coal, and quicksilver have also been added to our domestic exports, and will, doubtless, ere long rank in the class to which they respectively belong as leading export staples.

Flax seed has dwindled down from $180,973 in 1830, t $6,000 in 1855, and even to $4,000 five years before; whilst linseed oil, appearing within a few years, amounted to nearly ,000 in 1855.

Clover seed appears for the first time in 1855, and at the respectable figure of $13,570; whilst indigo totally disappears from our export tables, and is not found in our Treasury Reports even as an article of domestic produce.(*b*)

Molasses and vinegar have grown up, from mere experimental essays at production for home consumption, to staples that promise soon to occupy a prominent rank among our domestic exports, the former article having risen from less than $4,000 in 1830, to nearly $190,000 in 1855; whilst salt, salted provisions, lard, butter, cheese, leather, and the various manufactures thereof, have already taken rank among our prominent staple manufactured exports.

The article onions appears for the first time in 1855 as an export, and to the large amount of $64,496; lard oil to that of $82,945; while the article "oil cake" appears, also, for the first time, and at the enormous figure of $739,589.(*c*)

It will be observed that the appearence of this staple in the official report is simultaneous with the increase in the exportation of linseed oil, and the gradual disappearance of flax seed from the tables.

If we compare the value of the domestic exports of the United States in 1830 with that of the same in 1855 as arranged in *classes*, we find results of a similar character as when they are considered individually and in detail, as is exhibited by the following table:

Classes of domestic exports.	1830.	1855.	Increase.
Total value of products of the sea	$1,725,270	$3,516,894	$1,791,624
Total value of products of the forest	4,192,047	12,603,837	8,411,790
Total value of product of animals	2,379,652	17,178,080	14,798,428
Total value of vegetable food	9,121,345	23,651,362	14,530,017
Total value of other agricultural products	215,087	1,616,714	1,401,627
Total value of certain manufactures	3,074,910	15,083,514	12,008,604
Total value of cotton piece goods	1,318,183	5,857,181	4,538,998
Total value of certain manufactures, &c	2,835,993	9,668,823	6,832,830
Total value of exports of United States produce	59,462,029	246,708,553	187,246,524

This, however, is but a very brief synopsis of the changes, both in raw and manufactured products, which have marked our commercial progress during the past quarter of a century, but it is deemed sufficient for the purpose for which it is introduced.

Some articles, the product, and most articles, the manufactures of the United States, which are exported in large quantities are not embraced in these comparative statemants of exports and duties, for two reasons: 1st. Because they can scarcely be classed as staple products; and 2d. Because the rates of duties levied upon these articles under the tariffs of most foreign nations vary with the specific character of the manufactures to such an extent that it would be impossible to calculate the aggregates of duties on each, unless the quantities and values of each particular species of merchandise were specified, which is not the case. Yet, were these quantities and values known, each species of manufacture might properly demand a table for itself of considerable extent, far too extended, at any rate, to be reduced into the succinct form required by a tabular summary like the present.:

The following comparative statement exhibits the values of certain articles, chiefly of manufactures of the United States, exported the years specified, on which, for the reasons named, it was found impracticable to calculate the duties paid:

(*a*) Heretofore, this article has been supplied not only to the East India and North American colonies by the mother country, but to Cuba and most of the South American republics. In all these markets American cotton duck is now finding considerable favor; and it is a significant fact that the largest sales have been effected in the very markets in which England has heretofore enjoyed a complete monopoly. Thus, in 1855, the exports of duck to British North American possessions amounted to $81,119; to Australia, $25,887; to Cuba, $6,351; and to the South American republics, including China and the Sandwich Islands, $30,000.

(*b*) It is not, perhaps, generally known that indigo is a native of America, and is found, at this day, in its wild state, profusely scattered over all the southern States. Prior to the revolution, the British government gave the colonists a bounty of 24 cents per pound for cultivating it; and at the commencement of the present century, it is stated that considerable quantities of the article, some 130,000 pounds, had been exported from the southern States. Prior to the emancipation of slaves in Hayti it was the leading staple of that port of St. Domingo; but, since that period, the cultivation of, and the almost exclusive trade, in this article have been transferred to the East Indies. The sales in Calcutta now almost every year amount to about $15,000,000.

(*c*) This article may have been embraced in prior reports under the title "articles not enumerated."

Comparative statement exhibiting the values of certain articles, the produce and manufacture of the United States, exported to the principal commercial countries during the commercial years 1851, 1852, *and* 1853.

PRINCIPAL COMMERCIAL COUNTRIES.	VALUES IN DOLLARS.							
	1851.					1852.		
	Skins and furs.	Manufactures of iron.	Manufactures of wood.	Cotton goods, white.	Cotton goods, colored.	Skins and furs.	Manufactures of iron.	Manufactures of wood.
Great Britain	$752,786	$8,458	$136,252	....	....	$665,430	$13,751	$150,175
France	13,602	5,800	4,132	$3,346	....	9,566	370	7,906
Spain	....	....	1,075	....	....	....	....	4,780
Cuba	....	518,603	1,353,616	9,762	$5,873	....	664,628	1,433,706
Belgium	100	6	273	....	....	....	....	1,015
Holland	....	24	1,388	47	....	200	1,017	2,793
Hanse Towns	188,129	5,950	13,592	505	....	....	2,744	17,200
China	9,500	3,861	7,048	1,894,418	....	22,375	6,595	11,519
Brazil	....	1,957	19,278	350,344	263,059	....	29,014	19,402
Mexico	422	185,230	16,828	75,622	35,450	....	194,735	13,707
Chili	....	130,599	23,818	675,242	75,461	....	141,399	17,347
Venezuela	865	21,414	8,480	61,716	33,694	828	24,328	14,814
Hayti	....	11,592	4,380	78,115	217,936	....	13,784	6,080

COMPARATIVE STATEMENT—Continued.

PRINCIPAL COMMERCIAL COUNTRIES.	VALUES IN DOLLARS.						
	1852.		1853.				
	Cotton goods, white.	Cotton goods, colored.	Skins and furs.	Manufactures of iron.	Manufactures of wood.	Cotton goods, white.	Cotton goods, colored.
Great Britain	$3,114		$670,946	$45,185	$106,952	$706	$1,212
France	863	$1,393	12,489	16,751	15,996		
Spain	470	523			495		
Cuba	10,095	4,725		666,491	1,415,304	3.475	2,327
Belgium			168	1,860	1,087		
Holland			1,500	669	1,310		
Hanse Towns			59,822	3,883	31,275	2,000	
China	2,201,496		40,000	13,823	6,988	2,801,031	30,246
Brazil	395,550	240,725		53,536	29,366	195,915	230,945
Mexico	94,536	26,285	438	166,994	9,268	905,534	90,639
Chili	1,092,293			103,297	16,091	765,856	59,753
Venezuela	141,578	19,239	1,283	28,733	10,219	37,092	7,688
Hayti	205,103	28,925	232	29,894	5,437	135,341	37.766

Changes in the tariffs of foreign nations are also of frequent occurrence, even within a period so brief as that embraced in the statements, (although, with the exception of Belgium, Mexico, Chili, Holland, and Cuba, the rates of duty on the staple exports of the United States have been found quite the same under the tariffs in force in 1855, as under those in force in 1851, 1852, and 1853,) and minute discriminations of duty on the same articles, differing from each other only by shades of character, quality and value, as already mentioned, constantly occur. The rates of duty on the staple products are, moreover, not always clearly defined in the respective tariffs of foreign nations, even although the importations of the articles may be of considerable value and amount.

It is also to be taken into consideration, in making up statements or estimates like these, as already intimated in treating of Cuba, that the tariffs of some nations levy heavier duties on goods imported in foreign than in national vessels, or in vessels equalized by the effect of reciprocal treaties; also, that some states, under distinct and separate sovereignties, or united for govermental purposes only, yet grouped in the statements of the annual reports of the Treasury Department on commerce and navigation, under a single name, levy, under their respective tariffs, different rates of duty on the same description of merchandise, although the quantities and values of such merchandise are aggregated and placed to the general name. Thus, the empire of Hayti and the Dominican republic, both on the island of St. Domingo, have commercial laws and tariffs totally different; and the Hanse Towns, embracing Hamburg, Bremen, and Lubeck, have each different rates of duty on imports; yet the quantities and values of these imports are grouped in the official reports of exports of the United States, and placed to Hayti(a) only, in the one instance, and to the Hanse Towns in the other; so that it is impossible, from these reports, to gather the amount and value which went to each of the states respectively, and which should bear particular rates.

The Zollverein, or customs union of the German states, has not been considered in these statements, although receiving, no doubt, a sufficient amount of the staple products of the United States to be ranked among the principal commercial couutries, owing to the impossibility of learning the quantities and values of the same for the years specified. It is only since the year 1851 that the name of this customs union has appeared at all in the annual report of the Treasury Department on commerce and navigation, and even then, and since then, only the imports from that commercial confederation are given in a statement of "indirect trade" of the United States—the Zollverein, Austria, and Switzerland being grouped. In the Treasury Report for 1854 this statement did not appear. There may exist insurmountable obstacles to obtaining the exact amount of domestic exports of the United States to this commereial union; but the importance of its trade to this country, and its rapid increase, may be inferred from the facts that the value of imports into New York, the produce and manufacture of the Zollverein, through the ports of Bremen, Hamburg, Belgium, Holland, England, and France, were as follows, the years specified: in 1851, $3,575,405; in 1852, $9,357,194; in 1853, $9,848,108; in 1854, no statement; in 1855, $12,835,530.

Many of the suggestions relative to the Zollverein are not inapplicable to Switzerland.

Prussia appears in the catalogue of countries found in the report, and has always appeared there; but the exhibits of the trade with that state could, of course, furnish no adequate data from which to estimate the values of exports from the United States to the German commercial confederation.

The calculations required in making up these comparative statements have been, generally, intricate and numerous, the process necessary in obtaining each result involving little less than the solution of a problem; although, like the data from which they are wrought, and upon which they are based, the results of these calculations, from the nature of the case, partake, as observed at the commencement of these remarks, as much the character of well considered estimates as of exact and reliable statistics.

(a) The proper separation as respects these two states, Hayti and the Dominican republic, as well as of the Hanse Towns and other countries, has, it is perceived, been made in the Treasury Report on commerce and navigation for 1855, and constitutes one of the prominent improvements in that report over all its predecessors.

Comparative statement exhibiting the quantities and values of staple products of the United States imported into Great Britain, (a) together with the amounts of duties paid thereon, during the commercial years 1851, 1852, *and* 1853, *respectively.*

STAPLE PRODUCTS.	1851.			1852.			1853.		
	Quantities.	Values.	Duties paid.	Quantities.	Values.	Duties paid.	Quantities.	Values.	Duties paid.
Oil, spermaceti	843,826 gallons	$986,586		601,854 gallons	$761,597		1,082,969 galls	$1,358,608	
Oil, whale and other fish	615,016 gallons	262,016		225,636 gallons	112,068		18,177 gallons	10,192	
Whalebone	476,770 pounds	71,925		219,403 pounds	90,645		826,132 pounds	311,975	
Staves(b)	1,598 M			1,725 M			2,306 M		
Shingles	104 M	106,786			162,041			227,981	
Lumber	317 M feet			223 M feet			538 M feet		
Timber	5,047 tons		$9,690 24	12,008 tons		$23,055 36	28,990 tons		$55,660 80
Tar and pitch	57,743 barrels	761,408		27,775 barrels	945,224		25,046 barrels	1,099,532	
Rosin and turpentine	227,992 barrels			317,642 barrels			316,472 barrels		
Ashes	689 tons	79,286		168 tons	16,346		269 tons	27,135	
Beef	54,750 barrels	895,783		81,828 barrels	764,843		80,570 barrels	1,348,565	
Tallow	4,195,866 lbs.		13,486 66	2,421 436 lbs.		7,782 84	1,481,876 lbs.		4,763 16
Butter	1,396,277 lbs.	641,774	14,960 00	216,832 lbs.	349,912	2,323 00	251,868 lbs.	225,904	2,697 00
Cheese	8,641,617 lbs.		46,294 80	4,807,828 lbs.		25,756 20	2,038,935 lbs.		10,922 40
Pork	9,258 barrels			1,632 barrels			17,156 barrels		
Bacon	15,729,169 lbs.	1,587,351		3,207,993 lbs.	1,075,299		13,297,379 lbs.	2,239,094	
Lard	6,623,783 lbs.			8,976,124 lbs.			9,725,186 lbs.		
Wheat	592,583 bushels	644,722	17,777 49	2,049,557 bush.	2,056,686	61,486 71	3,574,248 bush.	4,040,378	107,227 44
Flour	1,004,783 bbls.	4,573,009	158,253 30	1,531,994 bbls.	6,308,378	241,289 05	1,378,065 bbls.	6,795,313	217,045 17
Indian corn	2,760,329 bush.	1,354,879	82,809 84	1,894,700 bush.	1,110,622	56,841 00	1,653,840 bush.	983,690	49,615 00
Indian meal	4,558 barrels	13,635	717,93	2,687 barrels	7,992	423 18	602 barrels	1,874	94 77
Ship bread		1,893	119 25		3,026	201 87		68	86 40
Rice	15,722 tierces	308,238	7,580 25	15,436 tierces	310,886	7,460 37	12,544 tierces	294,793	6,048 00
Cotton	670,645,122 lbs.	79,720,854		752,573,780 lbs.	59,666,209		768,596,498 lbs.	74,523,210	
Tobacco	23,698 hhds	3,458,885	21,048,602 00	17,696 hhds	2,512,225	12,866,731 25	32,236 hhds	3,438,423	23,381,841 00
Tobacco, manfactured	1,378,715 lbs.	258,723	2,990,960 55	1,778,193 lbs.	343,331	3,858,062 88	3,127,491 lbs.	569,213	6,783,840 56
		95,727,753	24,391,252 31		76,597,330	17,151,413 71		97,495,948	30,619,841 70

(a) England, Scotland, and Ireland.
(b) The duties paid on staves, shingles, and lumber cannot well be calculated, as they are levied on the load. The duties on timber have been estimated at the rate of $1 92 per ton of 40 cubic feet.

Comparative statement exhibiting the quantities and values of staple products of the United States imported into France, (a) together with the amounts of duties paid thereon, during the commercial years 1851, 1852, *and* 1853, *respectively.*

Staple products.	1851.			1852.			1853.		
	Quantities.	Values.	Duties paid.	Quantities.	Values.	Duties paid.	Quantities.	Values.	Duties paid.
Oil, spermaceti	989 gallons	$1,240	$133 32	1,101 gallons	$1,605	$148 30	16,049 gallons	$21,683	$993 04
whale and other fish	1,002 gallons	455	273 80	719 gallons	520	244 20			
Whalebone	743,990 pounds	268,440	18,780 90	448,788 lbs	171,981	11,326 64	1,061,624 lbs	418,495	26,803 37
Dried fish				84 cwt	420	288 60			
Staves	7,329 M		2,724 38	9,469 M		3,516 46	6,084 M		2,261 24
Shingles									
Lumber	720 M feet	351,733	58 88	460 M feet	457,351	37 61	495 M feet	312,355	40 50
Timber	990 tons		22 22	3,490 tons		88 55	2,070 tons		46 54
Tar and pitch	4,789 barrels	50,986	2,777 62	4,080 barrels	24,240	2,366 40		21,175	
Rosin and turpentine	26,856 barrels		24,972 16	13,115 barrels		12,176 95	14,183 barrels		13,190 19
Ashes	1,438 tons	167,283	2,631 54	1,819 tons	182,538	3,328 77	1,140 tons	112,781	2,106 20
Beef	1,021 barrels	30,510	5,753 00	1,086 barrels	8,922	6,125 00	305 barrels	3,290	1,717 00
Tallow	592,143 pounds		7,454 00	5,200 pounds		63 70	5,800 pounds		72 00
Pork	251 barrels		424 08	133 barrels		224 76	366 barrels		619 33
Bacon	20,408 pounds	46,320	172 00	4,367 pounds	3,443	35 34	4,904 pounds	23,765	40 92
Lard	787,273 pounds		6,655 08	8,108 pounds		68 82	160,444 pounds		1,356 94
Wheat (b)							6,100 bushels	7,200	976 00
Flour				2,700 brrels	12,404	405 00	8,784 barrels	40,600	1,317 60
Indian corn	110 bushels	68	7 70				100 bushels	50	7 00
Shipbread				1 barrel	5				
Rice	6,784 tierces	156,736	8,603 43	8,495 tierces	181,752	10,773 12	4,885 tierces	129,632	6,195 20
Cotton	139,164,571 lbs	18,124,512	2,353,145 00	186,214,270 lbs	15,438,586	3,148,712 16	189,226,913 lbs	19,248,076	3,216,857 52
Tobacco (c)	9,601 hhds	728,831		18,672 hhds	1,240,872		15,796 hhds	1,070,588	
Tobacco, manufactured	1,009 pounds	150		12,317 pounds	1,570		39,155 pounds	4,159	
		19,927,264	2,434,589 11		17,726,209	3,199,930 38		21,413,849	3,274,600 59

(a) France includes only dominions on the Atlantic and the Mediterranean, without other possessions.

(b) The duties on wheat, flour, corn, &c., varies with the price of wheat in the standard markets of France, from 22 to 28 francs per hectolitre of 2.75 bushels. The amount is here calculated on the rate when the price of the hectolitre of wheat is about 26 francs.

(c) Tobacco imported into France direct from the United States, and in French or United States vessels, pays, if for the government, no duty; otherwise, generally prohibited.

Comparative statement exhibiting the quantities and values of staple products of the United States imported into Spain,(a) together with the amounts of duties paid thereon, during the commercial years 1851, 1852, *and* 1853, *respectively.*

STAPLE PRODUCTS.	1851.			1852.			1853.		
	Quantities.	Values.	Duties paid.	Quantities.	Values.	Duties paid.	Quantities.	Values.	Duties paid.
Oil, spermaceti				600 gallons	$840	$46 59			
Whalebone	1,188 pounds	$439	$32 67						
Dried fish				13 cwt	38	37 89			
Staves	6,119 M		16, 215 35	3,248 M		8, 607 20	2,763 M		$7, 921 95
Shingles		329, 532		175 M	193, 270	263 75		$140, 270	
Lumber	3,495 M feet			2,482 M feet			959 M feet		
Timber	579 tons		1, 679 10	1,377 tons		3, 993 30	1,423 tons		4, 126 70
Tar and pitch	789 barrels	2, 099	(b)536 52	572 barrels	2, 064	388 96	200 barrels	375	136 00
Rosin and turpentine	757 barrels		1, 604 84	624 barrels		1, 322 88			
Beef	115 barrels	3, 669	351 90	136 barrels	1, 289	416 16	95 barrels	711	290 20
Tallow	49,464 pounds		252 26						
Butter									
Cheese				967 pounds	85	49 31			
Pork	140 barrels		428 40	27 barrels		82 62	145 barrels		443 70
Bacon		2, 210		1,000 pounds	500	30 50		2, 068	
Lard	6,499 pounds		310 65	340 pounds		16 25			
Flour				116 barrels	565				
Indian corn				125 bushels	93				
Rice				12 tierces	225	153 00			
Cotton	34,272,625 lbs	4, 387, 262	634, 043, 10	29,301,928 lbs	(c)2, 490, 663	542, 085 00	36,851,042 lbs	3, 932, 095	681, 743 50
Tobacco(d)	8,953 hogsheads	682, 352		6,843 hogsheads	417, 906		6,745 hogsheads	472, 757	
Candles, tallow				5,000 pounds	585	191 00			
Soap									
Tobacco, manufactured				61,016 pounds	6, 838		205 pounds	18	
		5, 407, 563	655, 454 79		3, 114, 961	557, 684 41		4, 548, 294	694, 662 05

(a) Spain includes only dominions on the Atlantic and the Mediterranean, without other possessions. (b) The duties are calculated on pitch, viz: 34 cts. per quintal. The duty on tar is only 17 cents per quintal.

(c) The value of cotton exported to Spain in 1852 is given by "Commerce and Navigation" for that year at $570,195. This is probably an error. The average cost of cotton per pound in 1852 is estimated at 8.05 cents; and, at this rate, the 29,301,928 pounds exported would amount in value to $2,358,805, as given in the table. The average cost of cotton per pound in 1851 was 12.11 cents.

(d) Government monopoly.

Comparative statement exhibiting the quantities and values of staple products of the United States imported into Cuba, together with the amounts of duties paid thereon, during the commercial years 1851, 1852, *and* 1853, *respectively.*

STAPLE PRODUCTS.	1851.			1852.			1853.		
	Quantities.	Values.	Duties paid.	Quantities.	Values.	Duties paid.	Quantities.	Values.	Duties paid.
Oil, spermaceti	17,087 gallons	$18,134	$3,759 25	3,689 gallons	$3,764	$811 25	4,320 gallons	$5,120	$950 13
whale, and other fish	184,094 gallons	105,142	40,500 63	138,084 gallons	84,814	30,377 87	202,264 gallons	139,589	44,497 75
Whalebone				510 pounds	301	85 93	940 pounds	382	154 48
Dried fish	37,509 quintals	84,935	47,070 00	38,691 cwt	88,222	48,553 75	30,726 cwt	73,869	38,558 00
Staves	3,713 M		25,505 40	521 M		3,584 50	3,392 M		23,303 04
Shingles	616 M	410,498	634 48	737 M	410,492	759 11	524 M	418,043	539 72
Lumber	54,491 M feet		299,600 00	31,156 M feet		171,358 00	28,700 M feet		144,935 00
Timber	573 tons			752 tons			837 tons		
Tar and pitch	2,764 barrels	5,047	2,280 30	1,504 barrels	2,988	1,240 80	1,983 barrels	5,127	1,635 97
Rosin and turpentine	5 barrels		4 12	153 barrels		126 63	203 barrels		167 47
Beef	1,652 barrels	59,201	4,956 00	2,671 barrels	67,000	8,013 00	1,419 barrels	107,226	4,257 80
Tallow	546,767 pounds		11,263 40	473,916 pounds		9,862 56	941,632 pounds		19,397 61
Butter	412,902 pounds	72,958	18,267 60	420,597 pounds	77,862	18,506 26	366,158 pounds	75,857	16,110 95
Cheese	256,162 pounds		7,044 45	339,162 pounds		9,326 95	156,021 pounds		4,291 57
Pork	3,364 barrels		13,456 00	3,162 barrels		12,648 00	4,323 barrels		17,292 00
Bacon	1,237,919 pounds	798,619	33,176 00	1,059,749 pounds	951 560	28,293 30	1,057,520 pounds	1,134,749	28,293 30
Lard	7,836,153 pounds		310,311 65	8,396,187 pounds		335,847 48	9,306,083 pounds		374,104 53
Wheat							36 bushels	41	33 50
Flour	5,511 barrels	27,260	52,989 00	17,200 barrels	73,855	167,867 00	1,537 barrels	7,730	15,134 00
Indian corn	229,105 bushels	129,734	109,526 00	167,621 bushels	91,944	80,130 00	30,417 bushels	16,165	14,539 40
Indian meal	3,398 barrels	10,313	6,090 00	6,577 barrels	21,640	11,790 00	1,369 barrels	4,559	2,395 75
Ship bread		7,907	12,782 00		15,530	25,264 80		10,429	17,436 00
Rice	27,618 tierces	560,094	273,418 20	35,386 tierces	722,603	355,629 30	25,058 tierces	630,912	251,832 90
Cotton	113,572 pounds	15,075	3,123 43	294,853 pounds	22,544	8,108 45	196,392 pounds	40,374	5,400 78
Tobacco	18 hogsheads	2,258	(a)21 60	97 hogsheads	11 590	(a)116 40	68 hogsheads	7,028	(a)81 68
Candles, tallow	715,674 pounds	105,422	28,767 12	544,118 pounds	92,000	21,872 82	287,211 pounds	68,563	11,545 00
Soap	380,748 pounds		10,153 28	721,460 pounds		19,046 50	606,168 pounds		16,002 69
Tobacco, manufactured	191,255 pounds	33,414	16,017 36	180,730 pounds	23,454	15,133 62	188,265 pounds	21,640	15,530 46
		2,446,011	1,330,717 27		2,762,163	1,384,354 28		2,767,403	1,067,420 68

(a) In the deposit.

Comparative statement exhibiting the quantities and values of staple products of the United States imported into Belgium, together with the amounts of duties paid thereon, during the commercial years 1851, 1852, *and* 1853, *respectively.*

STAPLE PRODUCTS.	1851.			1852.			1853.		
	Quantities.	Values.	Duties paid.	Quantities.	Values.	Duties paid.	Quantities.	Values.	Duties paid.
62 Oil, spermaceti	717 gallons	$806	$62 59	644 gallons	$806	$56 22	834 gallons	$1,068	$72 81
whale, and other fish	157,884 gallons	69,361	13.784 48	14,832 gallons	6,263	1,294 94	2,190 gallons	1,230	191 20
Whalebone	224,706 pounds	74,071	2,157 17	33,966 pounds	9,454	326 07	127,578 pounds	38,775	1,224 74
Staves	98 M		380 24	126 M		488 88	94 M		364 72
Shingles									
Lumber	219 M feet	9,778	6,913 83	237 M feet	9,186	7,482 09		4,014	
Timber									
Tar and pitch	103 barrels		3 66						
Rosin and turpentine	15,311 barrels	26,170	3,742 00	24,094 barrels	34,963	5,888 00	26,915 barrels	47,506	7,134 00
Ashes	1,594 tons	168,914	Free of duty	1,725 tons	170,338	Free of duty	1,015 tons	98,186	Free of duty.
Beef				371 barrels	6,500	313 41			
Tallow									
Pork	10 barrels		9 30				40 barrels		37 20
Bacon		4,429			5,370		28,186 pounds	10,679	357 12
Lard	74,660 pounds		312 88	61,965 pounds		261 94	72,092 pounds		304 70
Wheat				2,712 bushels	2,543	140 41	34,814 bushels	38,763	1,804 82
Flour				3,757 barrels	16,496	1,878 25	500 barrels	2,187	250 25
Indian corn				42 bushels	20	1 26	75 bushels	50	2 25
Rice	5,301 tierces	106,280	21,974 64	9,877 tierces	181,702	40,944 24	2,060 tierces	41,870	8,539 36
Cotton	16,335,018 lbs	2,145,270	742 50	27,157,809 lbs	2,227,826	1,234 44	15,494,442 lbs	1,476,104	704 29
Tobacco	523 hogsheads	45,226	4,423 08	7,016 hogsheads	451,958	58,317 26	6,933 hogsheads	443,651	58,616 04
Tobacco, manufactured	7,234 pounds	736	178 00	28,285 pounds	4,362	717 00	2,600 pounds	316	64 00
		2,651,041	54,684 37		3,117,787	119,344 41		2,204,399	79,667 50

Comparative statement exhibiting the quantities and values of staple products of the United States imported into Holland,(a) together with the amounts of duties paid thereon, during the commercial years 1851, 1852, and 1853, respectively.

STAPLE PRODUCTS.	1851.			1852.			1853.		
	Quantities.	Values.	Duties paid.	Quantities.	Values.	Duties paid.	Quantities.	Values.	Duties paid.
Oil, spermaceti	211 gallons	$262	$3 24	196 gallons	$247	$3 01			
whale, and other fish	540, 923 gallons	217, 617	8, 321 89	114, 605 gallons	51, 138	1, 763 15	10, 350 gallons	$4, 016	$159 23
Whalebone	7, 836 pounds	1, 705	308 97	5, 701 pounds	2, 464	74 66	24, 781 pounds	10, 196	53 00
Staves	1, 146 M			1, 005 M			689 M		
Shingles		53, 049			57, 463			35, 885	
Lumber	221 M feet		3, 120 53	179 M feet		3, 380 17	494 M feet		2, 110 88
Timber	797 tons		298 87	826 tons		309 55	335 tons		125 62
Tar and pitch	460 barrels	26, 359	23 00	2, 598 barrels	28, 737	129 90	2, 175 barrels	32, 109	108 75
Rosin and turpentine	14, 403 barrels		432 09	14, 784 barrels		443 52	17, 774 barrels		533 32
Ashes	1, 273 tons	133, 633	133 66	819 tons	84, 697	85 99	261 tons	25, 482	27 40
Beef	118 barrels	1, 000	339 84	100 barrels	2, 548	288 00			
Tallow				24, 723 pounds		22 47			
Pork	60 barrels		172 80				6 barrels		17 28
Bacon	8, 000 pounds	2, 573	145 45				693 pounds	997	14 30
Lard	3, 041 pounds		2 71	5, 834 pounds	515	5 60	8, 971 pounds		8 15
Wheat				19, 555 bushels	18, 851	736 18			
Flour	594 barrels	3, 045	962 28	10, 903 barrels	45, 121	17, 662 86	425 barrels	1, 958	688 50
Rice	4, 156 tierces	91, 340	906 80	4, 611 tierces	97, 558	969 68	199 tierces	4, 674	43 44
Cotton	5, 508, 670 lbs	589, 523	Free	10, 259, 042 lbs	815, 188	Free	7, 038, 994 lbs	668, 132	Free
Tobacco	11, 871 hhds	633, 834	15, 108 50	20, 720 hhds	939, 898	26, 370 08	23, 389 hhds	1, 119, 808	29, 767 92
Tobacco, manufactured	13, 651 pounds	3, 540	497 38	65, 429 pounds	10, 253	1, 427 08	45, 898 pounds	7, 121	1, 001 41
		1, 757, 480	30, 757 01		2, 154, 678	53, 671 90		1, 910, 378	34, 659 40

(a) Holland does not embrace colonies or dependencies.

Comparative statement exhibiting the quantities and values of staple products of the United States imported into Hanse Towns, together with the amounts of duties paid thereon, during the commercial years 1851, 1852, *and* 1853, *respectively.*

Staple products.	1851.			1852.			1853.		
	Quantities.	Values.	Duties paid.	Quantities.	Values.	Duties paid.	Quantities.	Values.	Duties paid.
Oil, spermaceti				40 gallons	$57	(a)$0 33	488 gallons	$637	$3 71
whale and other fish	307,023 gallons	$126,832	$739 85	244,045 gallons	101,118	598 18	1,007 gallons	500	2 92
Whalebone	770,575 lbs	253,082	1,476 31	472,093 lbs	160,594	936 57	746,278 lbs	268,436	1,565 88
Dried fish							10 cwt	27	15
Staves	158 M			239 M			448 M		
Shingles									
Lumber	613 M feet	22,084	128 84	958 M feet	28,385	165 58	461 M. feet	26,219	152 94
Timber	718 tons			3,767 tons			242 tons		
Tar and pitch	6,950 bbls	51,784	302 07				1,975 bbls	63,172	418 50
Rosin and turpentine	53,485 bbls			33,895 bbls	51,135	298 29	38,523 bbls		
Ashes(b)	811 tons	86,483	504 15	482 tons	49,521	288 87	623 tons	58,897	343 56
Beef	1,202 bbls	11,200	59 93	1,283 barrels	11,969	69 62	875 bbls	10,000	65 13
Tallow							3,001 lbs		
Butter							7,150 lbs	970	5 66
Cheese	7,503 lbs	230	1 34						
Pork	150 bbls			34 bbls			1,214 bbls		
Bacon		1,502	8 76		412	2 40	3,000 lbs	18,682	108 88
Lard	1,114 lbs			50 lbs			200 lbs		
Wheat				34,287 bushels	34,917	203 68	5,485 bushels	5,534	32 28
Flour	3,838 bbls	18,612	10,794 00	38,635 bbls	156,152	910 88	1,735 bbls	8,624	50 30
Indian corn	2,356 bushels	1,742	10 16	2,072 bushels	1,668	9 73	12,804 bushels	9,419	54 94
Indian meal				20 bbls	70	40			
Ship bread		38	22	30 bbls	85	49			
Rice	17,867 tierces	381,863	2,227 53	14,998 tierces	316,781	1,847 89	1,057 tierces	25,922	151 21
Cotton	16,716,571 lbs	2,060,979	12,022 37	22,138,228 lbs	1,890,807	11,029 72	22,671,782 lbs	2,259,909	13,182 80
Tobacco	22,506 hhds	1,558,304	9,090 10	40,056 hhds	2,121,934	12,377 95	53,351 hhds	2,822,348	16,463 69
Candles, tallow	50 lbs	412	2 40						
Soap	8,000 lbs								
Tobacco, manufactured	273,426 lbs	51,000	297 50	126,734 lbs	25,150	146 71	275,151 lbs	37,975	221 52
		4,626,147	37,655 53		4,950,755	28,887 29		5,617,271	32,824 07

(a)The duties paid are calculated upon a rate of 7-12 of one per cent., being the average of the Bremen rate of ⅔ of one per cent., and the Hamburg rate of ½ of one per cent., the quantities and values of the staple products of the United States imported into the two ports being deemed nearly enough equal to warrant the average. The importation into Lubec is too small for consideration in this calculation.

(b)This duty is calculated for Hamburg only, as ashes are free in the port of Bremen.

Comparative statement exhibiting the quantities and values of staple products of the United States imported into China, together with the amounts of duties paid thereon, during the commercial years 1851, 1852, and 1853, respectively.

STAPLE PRODUCTS.	1851.			1852.			1853.		
	Quantities.	Values.	Duties paid.	Quantities.	Values.	Duties paid.	Quantities.	Values.	Duties paid.
Oil, spermaceti	163 gallons	$163	$8 15						
whale and other fish	104 do	83	4 15						
Staves	8 M	6,204	620 00	3 M	$4,221	$420 00	50 M feet	$1,406	$140 00
Lumber	220 M feet			165 M feet					
Tar and pitch	325 barrels	690	34 50	395 barrels	655	32 75	430 barrels	1,020	51 00
Rosin and turpentine				15 do			6 do		
Beef	546 barrels	5,163	258 15	194 do	2,369	118 45	2,076 do	25,574	1,278 70
Butter	19,016 pounds	3,167	190 16	16,505 pounds	3,562	165 00	22,460 pounds	19,209	224 60
Cheese	890 do		5 34	250 do		1 50	840 do		5 04
Pork	275 barrels			303 barrels			1,531 barrels		
Bacon	6,702 pounds	3,200	160 00	4,200 pounds	5,284	264 20	1,800 pounds	23,845	1,192 25
Lard							500 do		
Flour	1,853 barrels	12,649	632 45	4,452 barrels	24,966	1,248 30	3,518 barrels	23,020	1,151 50
Indian meal	20 do	71	3 55				35 do	109	5 45
Ship bread		2,833	141 65		2,709	135 45		3,432	171 60
Tobacco				2 hogsheads	155	4 20			
Candles, tallow		1,179	137 52	800 pounds	1,145	99 36	3,250 pounds	981	37 44
Soap	25,516 pounds			18,381 do			6,990 do		
Tobacco, manufactured	16,988 do	3,291	35 56	59,675 do	7,777	125 44	44,395 do	5,951	93 24
		38,693	2,231 18		52,843	2,614 65		104,549	4,347 82

Comparative statement exhibiting the quantities and values of staple products of the United States imported into Brazil, together with the amounts of duties paid thereon, during the commercial years 1851, 1852, *and* 1853, *respectively.*

STAPLE PRODUCTS.	1851.			1852.			1853.		
	Quantities.	Values.	Duties paid.	Quantities.	Values.	Duties paid.	Quantities.	Values.	Duties paid.
Oil, spermaceti	5 gallons	$8	(a)$0 43				161 gallons	$170	$27 90
whale, and other fish	2,849 gallons	1,752	197 80	484 gallons	$255	33 10	177 gallons	122	12 29
Dried fish	1,054 quintals	2,575	1,317 60	145 cwt	484	181 20	1,631 cwt	1,554	2,038 00
Staves				6 M			142 M		
Shingles	35 M						47 M		
Lumber	2,214 M feet	28,778	9,365 22	964 M feet	13,978	4,193 40	2,569 M feet	40,445	10,966 87
Timber									
Tar and pitch	1,869 barrels	31,020	710 22	188 barrels	14,421	71 44	135 barrels	13,417	51 30
Rosin and turpentine	21,018 barrels		5,464 88	10,217 barrels		2,656 42	8,828 barrels		2,295 28
Ashes				2 tons	172				
Beef	991 barrels	7,028	2,095 96	248 barrels	2,400	524 52	329 barrels	4,700	2,783 34
Tallow									
Butter	6,388 pounds	4,189	415 22		853		598 pounds	539	38 87
Cheese	29,323 pounds		1,905 99	9,700 pounds		630 50	3,886 pounds		252 59
Pork	492 barrels		1,387 44	2 barrels		5 64	31 barrels		87 42
Bacon	116,105 pounds	43,376	3,483 15	20,936 pounds	20,046	628 06	31,350 pounds	36,622	940 50
Lard	316,664 pounds		8,038 39	163,558 pounds		4,151 85	266,769 pounds		6,771 82
Wheat				6,239 bushels	5,096	1,019 20			
Flour	369,975 barrels	2,021,631	610,458 00	345,025 barrels	1,639,285	569,291 25	433,843 barrels	2,434,187	715,840 95
Indian meal	214 barrels	701	175 25	50 barrels	161	40 25	38 barrels	131	33 00
Ship bread	4,805 barrels	15,695	6,606 82	3,148 barrels	3,997	4,328 50	4,139 barrels	15,609	5,691 20
Rice	20 tierces	407	122 00	79 tierces	1,934	580 00	56 tierces	1,404	421 00
Tobacco	161 hogsheads	22,398	13,438 80	223 hogsheads	21,217	12,730 20	183 hogsheads	17,953	10,771 80
Candles, tallow	27,545 pounds	16,868	1,203 50	112,059 pounds	36,002	4,973 04	4,330 pounds	21,344	187 64
Soap	209,422 pounds		4,711 99	231,596 pounds		5,210 91	371,649 pounds		8,362 10
Tobacco, manufactured	61,716 pounds	10,564	6,171 60	88,595 pounds	13,841	8,859 50	49,958 pounds	6,642	4,995 80
		2,206,990	677,270 26		1,779,142	620,108 98		2,594,839	772,569 67

(a) The duties are calculated upon the rates of the tariff of 1844. The *milrei* of Brazil varies in value. It is here estimated at the average between a minimum of 47 cents and a maximum of 55 cents.

Comparative statement exhibiting the quantities and values of staple products of the United States imported into Mexico, together with the amounts of duties paid thereon,(a) during the commercial years 1851, 1852, *and* 1853, *respectively.*

STAPLE PRODUCTS.	1851.			1852.			1853.		
	Quantities.	Values.	Duties paid.	Quantities.	Values.	Duties paid.	Quantities.	Values.	Duties paid.
Oil, spermaceti	113 gallons	$113	$39 88	1,912 gallons	$2,623	$674 82	1,870 gallons	$2,166	$660 00
whale and other fish	4,400 gallons	2,243	1,552 94	2,914 do	1,740	1,028 47	2,788 do	2,093	984 00
Whalebone							200 pounds	93	12 00
Dried fish	796 quintals	2,174	3,184 00	2,943 cwt	2,661	11,772 00	358 cwt	1,223	1,432 00
Staves	8 M			2 M					
Shingles	467 M	9,378	560 40	277 M	12,276	332 40	266 M	8,697	372 40
Lumber	704 M feet			725 M. feet			535 M feet		
Tar and pitch	1,545 barrels	4,638	778 77	1,598 barrels	3,642	791 01	886 barrels	3,083	428 47
Rosin and turpentine	552 do		375 36	44 do		29 92	178 do		121 04
Beef	273 do	2,180	Prohibited	35 do	604	Prohibited			Prohibited
Tallow			do			do			do
Butter	60,325 pounds	9,256	3,619 50	49,908 pounds	8,203	2,994 48	48,261 pounds	9,962	2,895 66
Cheese	18,038 do		721 52	16,485 do		659 40	17,140 do		685 60
Pork	850 barrels		2,040 00			Prohibited			Prohibited
Bacon	21,017 pounds	48,494	1,261 02	19,507 pounds	2,687	930 42	26,351 pounds	17,486	1,581 06
Lard	503,534 do		Prohibited	4,448 pounds		Prohibited	139,117 do		Prohibited
Wheat			do			do			do
Flour	14,964 barrels	71,545	14,964 00	25,081 bushels	115,242	25,071 00	17,039 barrels	85,198	17,039 00
Indian corn	21,731 bushels	14,939							
Indian meal	21 barrels	63							
Ship bread		4,882			2,098			1,168	
Rice	145 tierces	3,470	326 25	13 tierces	227	29 25			Prohibited
Cotton	845,960 pounds	101,945	25,378 80	6,700,091 lbs	551,942	201,002 73	7,463,851 lbs	813,501	223,915 53
Tobacco				12 hogsheads	1,597		10 hogsheads	1,033	
Candles, tallow	5,420 pounds	1,362	408 60	10,050 pounds	2,839	851 70	33,057 pounds	6,285	1,885 50
Soap	13,600 do			9,167 do			1,988 do		
Tobacco, manufactured	24,057 do	5,675		38,709 do	9,087		38,246 do	3,610	
		282,357	55,211 04		717,468	246,167 60		955,598	252,012 26

(a) The duties given in this table, owing to the frequent changes in the Mexican tariff, are merely approximative. Indeed, during the years designated, the payment of duties on foreign imports into Mexico seems to have been graduated rather by the terms and conditions of special privileges, than by the fixed rates of the different tariffs enacted and partially enforced.

Comparative statement exhibiting the quantities and values of staple products of the United States imported into Chili, together with the amounts of duties paid thereon, during the commercial years 1851, 1852, *and* 1853, *respectively.*

Staple products.	1851. Quantities.	1851. Values.	1851. Duties paid.	1852. Quantities.	1852. Values.	1852. Duties paid.	1853. Quantities.	1853. Values.	1853. Duties paid.
Oil, spermaceti			Free			Free			Free
whale and other fish	2,041 gallons	$1,500	$408 20						
Dried fish	7 quintals	20	10 50				140 cwt	$465	$210 00
Staves	143 M		Free	90 M		Free	80 M		Free
Shingles		12,366		54 M	$30,963	$189 00	50 M	45,933	175 00
Lumber	99 M feet		Free	1,392 M feet		Free	2,029 M feet		Free
Tar and pitch	557 barrels	2,394	Free	602 barrels	2,323	Free	3,134 barrels	7,603	Free
Rosin and turpentine	780 do		Free	887 do		Free	576 do		Free
Ashes	3 tons	375					1 ton	148	
Beef	2,459 barrels	26,436	Free	2,083 barrels	19,275	Free	4,279 barrels	51,199	Free
Tallow	91,143 pounds		382 80				90,578 pounds		382 46
Butter	51,187 do	12,309	2,559 35	16,486 pounds	3,621	824 30	8,544 do	1,933	427 20
Cheese	34,327 do		1,609 00	10,608 do		497 25	1,353 do		63 37½
Pork	1,754 barrels		Free	20 barrels		Free	2,509 barrels		Free
Bacon	249,194 pounds	83,864	8,722 00	89,552 pounds	37,378	3,134 32	349,355 pounds	153,350	12,227 42
Lard	491,652 do		15,364 00	233,668 do		7,302 00	534,898 do		16,715 00
Flour (a)	4,327 barrels	29,769	See note	6,836 barrels	32,764	See note	10,870 barrels	60,480	See note
Indian meal							35 do	129	Undefi'd in t'iff.
Ship bread		2,926	967 50		1,509	2,688 00		4,777	2,119 50
Rice	2,825 tierces	54,279	18,306 25	1,434 tierces	28,763	11,805 50	1,965 tierces	51,670	16,211 25
Cotton				18,000 pounds	1,175	Free	30,000 pounds	3,000	Free
Tobacco	13 hogsheads	1,043		158 hogsheads	17,527		196 hogsheads	20,515	
Candles, tallow	12,900 pounds	6,665	516 00	26,875 pounds	17,411	1,075 00	77,000 pounds	27,190	3,080 00
Soap	129,873 do		1,948 09	290,997 do		4,364 95	323,308 do		4,849 62
Tobacco, manufactured	113,926 do	7,815	5,696 30	260,802 do	29,225	13,040 10	93,010 do	14,502	4,650 50
		241,761	56,489 99		221,934	44,920 42		442,894	61,111 32

(a) When flour in Chili is under four dollars per quintal, 25 per cent. on value; when over that price, free.

Comparative statement exhibiting the quantities and values of staple products of the United States imported into Venezuela, together with the amounts of duties paid thereon, during the commercial years 1851, 1852, *and* 1853, *respectively.*

STAPLE PRODUCTS.	1851. Quantities.	1851. Values.	1851. Duties paid.	1852. Quantities.	1852. Values.	1852. Duties paid.	1853. Quantities.	1853. Values.	1853. Duties paid.
Oil, spermaceti	43 gallons	$59	$10 32				394 gallons	$510	$94 56
whale and other fish	1,361 gallons	812	326 64				1,897 gallons	777	455 28
Dried fish	334 quintals	1,097	835 00	633 cwt	$2,353	$1,582 50	408 cwt	1,804	1,020 00
Staves	2 M		Free			Free			Free
Shingles							18 M	6,255	
Lumber	243 M feet	5,286	1,588 80	417 M feet	7,624	2,287 20	320 M feet		1,876 00
Timber									
Tar and pitch	399 barrels	2,039	Tar, 399 00(*c*)	204 barrels	2,260	Tar, 204 00(*c*)	231 barrels	3,225	Tar, 231 00(*c*)
Rosin and turpentine(*a*)	751 barrels			1,016 barrels			1,550 barrels		
Ashes	1 ton	70							
Beef	206 barrels	2,575	824 00	59 barrels	1,441	236 00	120 barrels	2,267	480 00
Tallow	6,567 pounds		130 04	6,793 pounds		134 54	7,34[illegible] pounds		145 3[illegible]
Butter	102,811 pounds	11,831	6,168 66	98,673 pounds	15,315	5,920 38	94,859 pounds	16,199	5,691 5[illegible]
Cheese	17,672 pounds		883 60	21,241 pounds		1,062 05	5,715 pounds		235 75
Pork	143 barrels		715 00	31 barrels		155 00	265 barrels		1,325 00
Bacon	79,206 pounds	19,728	3,960 30	84,115 pounds	27,690	4,205 75	57,769 pounds	17,136	2,888 45
Lard	132,691 pounds		5,307 00	181,119 pounds		7,244 76	55,163 pounds		2,206 52
Flour	40,383 barrels	198,800	161,532 00	43,679 barrels	190,773	174,716 00	43,881 barrels	218,578	175,524 00
Indian corn	596 bushels	390	Free of duty	8,886 bushels	5,732	Free of duty	1,128 bushels	798	Free of duty.
Indian meal	1,132 barrels	3,538	Free of duty	943 barrels	2,796	Free of duty	1,122 barrels	3,603	Free of duty.
Ship bread	453 barrels	1,626	3,624 00	298 barrels	1,057	2,384 00	549 barrels	1,411	4,392 00
Rice	547 tierces	11,211	Free of duty	520 tierces	11,422	Free of duty	425 tierces	11,740	Free of duty.
Tobacco	125 hogsheads	15,450	7,500 00	210 hogsheads	19,505	12,474 00	160 hogsheads	15,690	9,504 00
Candles, tallow	133,506 pounds	22,684	5,340 24	112,862 pounds	15,395	4,514 48	53,861 pounds	8,663	2,154 44
Soap	114,323 pounds		4,572 92	30,428 pounds		1,217 12	7,016 pounds		280 64
Tobacco, manufactured(*b*)	38,225 pounds	5,702		21,342 pounds	3,357		17,774 pounds	1,109	
		302,898	202,717 52		306,720	218,337 78		309,765	208,504 55

(*a*) The quantities are not given separately; the duties cannot be calculated, as rosin is free and turpentine 90 cents per arroba. (*b*) Not defined, except as cigars and snuff. (*c*) Pitch, free.

Comparative statement, exhibiting the quantities and values of staple products of the United States imported into Hayti,(a) together with the amounts of duties paid thereon, during the commercial years 1851, 1852, *and* 1853, *respectively.*

STAPLE PRODUCTS.	1851.			1852.			1853.		
	Quantities.	Values.	Duties paid.	Quantities.	Values.	Duties paid.	Quantities.	Values.	Duties paid.
Oil, spermaceti	89 gallons	$112	$4 45	40 gallons	$40	$2 00	273 gallons	$331	$13 65
Oil, whale and other fish	5,937 gallons	3,169	296 85	3,485 gallons	2,490	174 25	5,921 gallons	4,217	296 05
Dried fish	56,263 quintals	162,201	23,630 46	49,790 cwt	162,073	20,911 80	45,718 cwt	155,677	192 01
Staves	96 M		72 00	73 M		54 75	41 M		30 75
Shingles	2,603 M	66,645		4,876 M	89,620		2,409 M	70,798	
Lumber	4,038 M. feet		10,095 00	5,105 M. feet		12,762 50	4,079 M. feet		10,197 50
Tar and pitch	771 bbls	1,425	(b)616 50	668 bbls	1,225	506 25	526 bbls	1,494	517 50
Rosin and turpentine	51 bbls			7 bbls			164 bbls		
Ashes	1 ton	70							
Beef	2,013 bbls	17,219	3,019 50	2,404 bbls	20,873	3,606 00	1,472 bbls	16,561	2,208 00
Tallow				623 lbs		6 23	1,685 lbs		16 85
Butter	118,850 lbs	24,753	1,100 00	121,694 lbs	29,719	1,027 00	148,393 lbs	45,275	1,374 00
Cheese	101,791 lbs		2,035 82	140,642 lbs		2,812 84	178,326 lbs		3,566 52
Pork	19,706 bbls		19,706 00	13,683 bbls		13,683 00	15,252 bbls		15,252 00
Bacon	155,549 lbs	297,904	3,110 98	98,924 lbs	283,029	1,978 48	212,213 lbs	352,468	4,244 26
Lard	483,845 lbs		7,257 67	426,790 lbs		6,401 85	510,499 lbs		7,657 48
Flour	43,867 bbls	219,170	87,734 00	42,902 bbls	181,030	85,804 00	50,421 bbls	263,009	100,842 00
Indian corn				30 bushels	26	10 00	125 bushels	75	42 00
Indian meal	163 bbls	650	163 00	662 bbls	2,203	662 00	591 bbls	2,157	591 00
Ship bread	3,678 bbls	11,277	1,379 15	2,285 bbls	7,144	855 21	2,564 bbls	8,446	961 50
Rice	953 tierces	18,851	3,970 60	1,605 tierces	32,188	6,687 00	1,834 tierces	38,484	7,641 75
Tobacco	307 hhds	41,629	122 80	402 hhds	47,879	160 80	379 hhds	37,227	151 60
Candles, tallow	62,342 lbs	114,166	1,246 84	89,988 lbs	109,651	1,799 76	82,570 lbs	167,714	1,651 40
Soap	1,925,692 lbs		222,287 00	1,755,044 lbs		20,313 00	2,753,050 lbs		31,863 00
Tobacco, manufactured	59,468 lbs	8,065	2,378 00	33,128 lbs	4.019	1,325 00	76,748 lbs	7,638	3,069 00
		987,206	390,226 52		973,209	181,543 72		1,181,571	192,379 82

(a) Hayti includes the Dominican Republic.

(b) This may be rather above the actual amount, as the duty has been calculated according to the rate marked in the tariff for tar, (75 cents per barrel,) and not by the rate assigned to pitch, (50 cents per barrel.)

Summary statement, exhibiting the aggregate value of the staple and other domestic products of the United States, exported to the principal commercial countries, during the commercial years 1851, 1852, *and* 1853; *together with the aggregate amount of duties paid on the staple products exported.*

No.	PRINCIPAL COMMERCIAL COUNTRIES.	Aggregate value of staple products enumerated in the tables.			Aggregate value of domestic exports not enumerated in the tables.			No.
		1851.	1852.	1853.	1851.	1852.	1833.	
1	Great Britain	$95,727,753	$76,597,330	$97,495,948	$13,804,559	$44,105,725	$20,583,058	1
2	France	19,927,264	17,726,209	21,413,849	5,374,816	4,463,871	3,706,957	2
3	Spain	5,407,563	3,114,961	4,548,294	908,481	101,857	6,856	3
4	Cuba	2,446,011	2,762,163	2,767,403	2,793,265	3,061,033	3,006,116	4
5	Belgium	2,651,041	3,117,787	2,204,399	58,352	84,976	96,639	5
6	Holland	1,757,480	2,154,678	1,910,378	153,635	138,170	73,385	6
7	Hanse Towns	4,626,147	4,950,755	5,617,271	779,809	1,245,172	1,892,144	7
8	China	38,693	52,843	104,459	2,117,352	2,427,223	3,108,115	8
9	Brazil	2,206,990	1,779,142	2,594,839	921,966	1,002,924	1,139,351	9
10	Mexico	282,357	707,468	955,598	732,333	698,904	1,574,172	10
11	Chili	241,761	221,934	442,894	347,116	821,902	1,714,426	11
12	Venezuela	302,898	306,720	309,765	551,881	299,304	440,094	12
13	Hayti	987,206	973,209	1,181,571	692,136	506,117	556,842	13
	Total	136,603,164	114,465,199	141,546,668	29,235,601	58,957,178	37,898,155	

SUMMARY STATEMENT—Continued.

No.	PRINCIPAL COMMERCIAL COUNTRIES.	Aggregate value of all domestic products exported.			Aggregate amount of duties paid, as calculated on staple products enumerated in the tables.			No.
		1851.	1852.	1853.	1851.	1852.	1853.	
1	Great Britain	$109,532,312	$120,703,055	$118,079,006	$24,391,252 31	$17,151,413 71	$30,619,841 70	1
2	France	25,302,080	22,190,080	25,120,806	2,434,589 11	3,199,930 38	3,274,600 59	2
3	Spain	6,316,044	3,216,818	4,555,150	655,454 79	557,684 41	694,662 05	3
4	Cuba	5,239,276	5,823,196	5,773,519	1,330,717 27	1,384,354 28	1,067,420 68	4
5	Belgium	2,709,393	3,202,763	2,301,038	54,684 37	119,344 41	79,667 50	5
6	Holland	1,911,115	2,292,848	1,983,763	30,757 01	53,671 90	34,659 40	6
7	Hanse Towns	5,405,956	6,195,927	7,509,415	37,655 53	28,887 29	32,824 07	7
8	China	2,155,945	2,480,066	3,212,574	2,231 18	2,614 65	4,347 82	8
9	Brazil	3,128,956	2,782,066	3,734,190	677,270 26	620,108 98	772,569 67	9
10	Mexico	1,014,690	1,406,372	2,529,770	55,211 04	246,167 60	252,012 26	10
11	Chili	588,877	1,043,836	2,157,320	56,489 99	44,920 42	61,111 32	11
12	Venezuela	854,779	606,024	749,859	202,717 52	218,337 78	208,504 55	12
13	Hayti	1,679,342	1,479,326	1,738,413	390,226 52	181,543,72	192,379 82	13
	Total	165,838,765	173,422,377	179,444,823	30,319,256 90	23,808,979 53	37,294,601 43	

Summary statement, exhibiting the average value of the staple and other domestic products of the United States, exported to the principal commercial countries, during the commercial years 1851, 1852, *and* 1853, *together with the average amount of duties paid on the staple products exported.*

PRINCIPAL COMMERCIAL COUNTRIES.	Average value of staple products enumerated.	Average value of domestic exports not enumerated.	Average value of all domestic products exported.	Average amount of duties paid on staple products enumerated.
Great Britain	$89,940,343⅔	$26,164,447⅓	$116,104,791	$24,054,169 24
France	19,689,107⅓	4,515,214⅔	24,204,322	2,969,706 69⅓
Spain	4,356,939⅓	339,064⅔	4,696,004	635,933 75
Cuba	2,658,525⅔	2,953,471⅓	5,611,997	1,260,830 74⅓
Belgium	2,657,742⅓	79,989	2,737,731⅓	84,565 42⅔
Holland	1,940,845⅓	121,730	2,062,575⅓	39,696 10⅓
Hanse Towns	5,064,724⅓	1,305,708⅓	6,370,432⅔	33,122 29⅔
China	65,331⅔	2,550,863⅓	2,616,195	3,064 55
Brazil	2,193,657	1,021,413⅔	3,215,070⅔	689,982 97
Mexico	648,474⅓	1,001,803	1,650,277⅓	184,463 63⅓
Chili	302,196⅓	961,148	1,263,344⅓	54,173 91
Venezuela	306,461	430,426⅓	736,887⅓	209,853 28⅓
Hayti	1,047,328⅔	585,031⅔	1,632,360⅓	254,716 68⅔
Total	130,871,677	42,030,311⅓	172,901,988⅓	30,474,279 28⅔

DUTIES

ON

THE STAPLE PRODUCTS

OF THE

UNITED STATES IN ALL FOREIGN COUNTRIES.

DUTIES

ON THE

STAPLE PRODUCTS OF THE UNITED STATES

IN

ALL FOREIGN COUNTRIES.

COUNTRIES.	PRODUCTS OF THE SEA.		
	CURED FISH.(a)		
	United States fishery.	National fishery.	Discrimination.
Argentine Republic	Stock fish, 20 per cent. ad valorem	Same	None
Austria	Codfish and other, dried, smoked, or salted, per gross centner = 110 pounds, $1 94.	Same	None
Belgium	Codfish, per ton of 150 to 160 kilogrammes, or 330 to 340 pounds, $4 75.	P 220 pounds, 18½ cents.	28 cents per barrel
Bolivia	28 per cent. ad valorem	Same	None
Brazil	Dried or smoked, 1 arroba, or 25.6 pounds, 33⅜ cts. (By latest tariff, 5 to 15 per cent. ad val.)	Same	None
Central America	*Costa Rica:* Dried, salted, or in oil, $2 per quintal, (101 lbs.)		None
	Guatemala: Not defined in the tariff. Except as to fish cured in oil, 4½ cents per 1.014 lb.		
	San Salvador: 24 per cent on a fixed value of $6 per quintal.		
Chili	Dry or smoked, small, as anchovies, herrings, sardines, 25 per cent. on a valuation of 10 cts. per 1 014 pound.		
	Larger ones, dried, smoked, &c., as codfish, mackerel, &c., 25 per cent. on the valuation of $6 per quintal, (101 pounds.)	Same	None
	Do., salmon, 25 per cent. on a valuation of $10 per quintal.		
China	5 per cent. ad valorem. Stock fish, per pikcul, (133⅓ pounds,) 59⅓ cents.	Same	All countries having treaties, same.

(a) The nomenclature of these statements is, for the sake of uniformity and comparison, adopted from that of the similar reports of 1839 and 1842 although some articles which were prominent as staple exports then can scarcely be so considered now, and *vice versa*. For changes in rates of duty see tariffs of each country, respectively.

DUTIES—Continued.

COUNTRIES.	PRODUCTS OF THE SEA. CURED FISH. United States fishery.	National fishery.	Discrimination.
Denmark and colonies	1 toende, or 3.944 buhels, 42⅝ to 25 cents. St. Croix, dried, salted, per 110⅜ lbs., 25 cents. Smoked, per 110⅝ pounds, 40 cents.	Same	None
Dominican Republic	Codfish, 25 per cent. on a fixed value of $ 75 per quintal, (101 pounds.)	Same	None
Equador	Stock fish, per quintal, $3; salmon, salted, per quintal, $3; salmon, fresh, 1 lb. 3 drs., 12½ cents; salmon, all other salted, per quintal, $2.	Same	None
France and possessions	Dried, salted, or smoked codfish, on French vessels from foreign countries, $7 40⅝ per 220 pounds; foreign vessels, $8 14¾ per 220 lbs. Corsica, foreign fishing in foreign ships, $3 [illegible]5 Corsica, foreign fishing in French ships, $[illegible] 77½ per 220 pounds. Martinique, 220 pounds, $1 30$\frac{3}{10}$.	French fishery, free. French fishery, free.	This article not being included in the commercial treaty between France and the United States, has to pay the duty on foreign vessels.
Great Britain and possessions	Free North American possessions, free West Indies, from 48 cents to $2 per barrel Australian possessions, from 24 to 48 per cent East Indies, from 36 cts. per cwt. to 5 per cent. ad val	Free Free Same Same Same	None None None None None
Hayti	Mackerel, per barrel, 50 cents; stockfish, per 100 pounds, = 108 pounds English, 42 cents.	Same	10 per cent. wharfage duty additional, and $1 per ton tonnage duty.
Hanse Towns	Hamburg, ½ of 1 per cent. ad valorem. Bremen, ⅝ of 1 per cent. ad valorem Lubeck, 1 tonne, or 200 pounds, 3½ cents.	Same	None
Holland and colonies	Codfish, salted, 60 cents per 150 Hollandish, or 331½ English pounds. Dutch East Indies, 24 per cent. ad valorem. Dutch Guiana and West Indies, 8 cts. per 221 lbs.	Free.	If not the produce of United States, subject to discriminating duties.
Mexico	Codfish, and all other kinds, dried, smoked, or salted, $2 per quintal, (101 pounds.)	Same	None
New Granada	Pickled, salted, dry, free	Same	None
Norway	Smoked, per pound, 2½ cents; dried or salt, per pound, 5¼ cents.	Same	None
Papal States	Dried or smoked, 1 centinajo, (74.86 lbs.,) $2; stockfish, per 1 centinajo, (74.86 lbs.,) 40 cts.	Same	None
Peru	Dried, 3 per cent. on a valuation of $5 per quintal, (101 lbs.;) codfish, 10 per cent. on a valuation of $5 per quintal, (101 pounds.)	Same	None
Portugal	Dried or smoked, (101 pounds,) $1 50	Same	In the direct trade none.
Russia	Per pood, (36 pounds,) 75 cents, unless otherwise described; herrings, 67 cts per cask of 324 lbs.	Stockfish free, if brought by the inhabitants of the government of Archangel.	

DUTIES—Continued.

COUNTRIES.	PRODUCT OF THE SEA.		
	CURED FISH.		
	United States fishery.	National fishery.	Discrimination.
Sandwich Islands	5 per cent. ad valorem	Same	None
Sardinia	Dried or smoked, 100 kilogrammes or 220 pounds, $1 53; stockfish, per 220 pounds, $1 38½.	ame	None
Spain and possessions	Codfish, direct from the fisheries in Europe or America, under the national flag, per quintal, $1 59; under a foreign flag, $2 12. From other foreign countries, or indirect, under the national flag, $2 38½; and under a foreign flag, $2 91½ per quintal.		A discrimination in favor of the Spanish flag against that of the United States, of 53 cents per quintal if imported direct from the country of production, and of 47 cents per quintal if from other countries.
	Cuba— Codfish, on a valuation of $3 50 per quintal, (101 lbs.;) other fish, pickled, on a valuation of $12 50 per quintal, (101 lbs.):— Foreign produce, direct from the fisheries in Spanish vessels, 19½ per cent.; in foreign vessels, 33½ per ct.; from Spain, in Spanish vessels, 19½ per cent. Spanish produce, from Spain, in Spanish vessels, 7½ per cent.; in foreign vessels, 14 per cent.		Spanish productions on Spanish vessels are in favor 20 per cent. against those of the United States in U. States ships.
	Porto Rico— Codfish, and all other kinds, on a valuation of $3 per quintal:— Foreign produce, direct from the country of production, in Spanish vessels, 17¼ per ct.; in foreign vessels, 23½ per ct.; from Spain, in Spanish vessels, 14¼ per cent. Spanish produce, from Spain, the country of production, in Spanish vessels, 6¾ per cent.; in foreign vessels, 15 per cent.		Spanish productions on Spanish vessels in favor, by 16¾ per cent. on the fixed value, against those of the United States in U. States vessels.
	Philippine Islands: No definition given in the tariff.		
Sweden	Codfish, per barrel, (4 bushels,) 45 cents; herring, per barrel, 13⅓ cents.	Same	None
Switzerland	Smoked, in oil, or salted, per 110¼ pounds, 64 cts	Same	None
Turkey	Codfish, per cantar, (127 pounds,) 12 cents, with an addition of 2 per cent. ad val. internal duty.	Same	None
Tuscany	Per 74.86 lbs., dried or smoked, from 3 to 80 cts.	Same	None

DUTIES—Continued.

COUNTRIES.	PRODUCT OF THE SEA.		
	CURED FISH.		
	United States fishery.	National fishery.	Discrimination.
Two Sicilies	Dried or smoked, per 192½ pounds, $4 80; stockfish, per 192½ pounds, $2 40.	Same	If direct from the U. States, a deduction of 10 per cent. ad val.; but if product of other countries, discrimination, as well as tonnage duties, are to be paid.
Uruguay	Dried or smoked, 25 per cent. ad valorem	Same	None
Venezuela	Salmon, salted, 1.014 pound, 3 cents; salmon, fresh, 1.014 pound, 5 cents; stockfish, 1.014 lb., 2½ cents; not otherwise enumerated, 4 cts.	Same	None
Zollverein	Stockfish, and other dried, smoked, in oil, or salted, per ton, 69 cents.	Same	None

DUTIES—Continued.

COUNTRIES.	PRODUCT OF THE SEA.		
	WHALE OIL.		
	United States fishery.	National fishery.	Discrimination.
Argentine Republic	15 per cent. ad valorem	Same	None.
Austria	Whale and other fish oil, 110 lbs., 24¼ cents	Same	None.
Belgium	Per 1 hectolitre or 26½ gallons, $2 27	Free	$2 27 per hectolitre, against U. S. fishery.
Bolivia	28 per cent ad valorem	Same	None.
Brazil	1 canada or 1.872 gallon, 12½ cents. (By latest tariff, 15 per cent. ad valorem.)	Same	None.
Central America	*Costa Rica*—per 101 lbs., $5	Same	None.
	Guatemala—1.014 pound, 7 cents.		
Chili	25 per cent. per gallon of 80 cents valuation	Same	None.
China	5 per cent. ad valorem	Same	None.
Denmark and colonies	1 cask of 30 gallons, $1 18	Same	None.
Dominican Republic	25 per cent. on fixed valuation of, per gallon, 16 cents.	Same	None.
Equador	Whale and other fish, per gallon, 5 cents; spermaceti, per gallon, 8 cents.	Same	None.
France and possessions	In French vessels from other than European countries, $7 40⅗ per 220 lbs; in French vessels from entrepots, $8 88⅗ per 220 lbs; in foreign vessels, $10 37 per 220 lbs.	From French fishery, 3 cents per 220 lbs.	This article not being included in the commercial treaty between France and the United States, has to pay the duty on foreign vessels, under all circumstances, and therefore the French shipping is in favor against that of the United States.
	Martinique—prohibited importation in other than French vessels.		
Great Britain and possessions.	Free	Free	None.
	North American possessions—from 3½ to 12½ per cent. ad valorem prior to reciprocity treaty, now free.	Same	None.
	West Indies—from 1 to 5 per cent. ad valorem.	Same	None.
	Australian possessions—generally free; in some of the colonies, 6 cents per gallon.	Same	None.
	East Indies—5 per cent. ad valorem.	Same	None.
Hayti	5 per cent. ad valorem; spermaceti, 1.014 lb., 5 cents.	Same	Wharfage duty 10 per cent. ad valorem, and tonnage duty $1 per ton, of which duty Haytian vessels are free.

DUTIES—Continued.

COUNTRIES.	PRODUCT OF THE SEA.		
	WHALE OIL.		
	United States fishery.	National fishery.	Discrimination.
Hanse Towns	Hamburg—½ of 1 per cent. ad valorem	Same	None.
	Bremen—⅔ of 1 per cent. ad valorem	Same	None.
	Lubeck—½ of 1 per cent. ad valorem	Same	None.
Holland and colonies	Free Dutch East Indies.—American, as equalized vessels, 6 per cent. ad valorem, whilst foreign, not equalized, vessels pay 12 per cent. ad valorem. Dutch Guiana and West Indies.—American vessels 3 per cent. ad valorem, other foreign, not equalized, 6 per cent. ad valorem.	Free	If not the produce of the United States, subject to discriminating duties.
Mexico	Free, if from the Pacific fishery	Same	None.
New Grenada	Per 1.014 lb., 6¼ cents	Same	None.
Norway	Per lb., ⅔ of a cent	Same	None.
Papal States	1 centinajo, (74.86 lbs.,) 50 cents	Same	None.
Peru	20 per cent. on a valuation of 35 cts. per gallon	Same	None.
Portugal	101 lbs., 36½ cents	Same	As product of United States fisheries none, if imported direct.
Russia	Per pood, (36 lbs.,) 52½ cents	Same	None.
Sandwich Islands	5 per cent ad valorem	Same	None.
Sardinia	Per 100 kilogrammes, 92½ cents	Same	None.
Spain and possessions	In national vessels, per arroba, (4. 245 gallons,) 26½ cents.; in foreign vessels, per arroba, (4. 245 gallons,) 33 cents.		In favor of Spanish vessels by 6½ cts. per ar. against Amer'n.
	Cuba— On a valuation of $2 50 per arroba, (4. 245 gallons) Foreign produce, direct from the country of production, in Spanish vessels, 19½ per cent.; in foreign vessels, 27½ per cent.; from Spain, in Spanish vessels, 19½ per cent. Spanish produce, in foreign vessels, 14½ per cent.; in Spanish vessels, 7½ per cent.		Spanish productions, on Spanish vessels, are in favor by 20 per cent. on the fixed value, against those of the United States, in United States vessels.
	Porto Rico— On a valuation of 18¾ cents per quart Foreign produce, direct from the country of production, in Spanish vessels, 16 per cent.; in foreign vessels, 23 per cent.; from Spain, in Spanish vessels, 16 per cent. Spanish produce, in foreign vessels, 12 per cent.; in Spanish vessels, 7 per cent.		Spanish productions, on Spanish vessels, are in favor by 16¾ per cent. on the fixed value, against those of the United States, in United States vessels.

DUTIES—Continued.

COUNTRIES.	PRODUCT OF THE SEA.		
	WHALE OIL.		
	United States fishery.	National fishery.	Discrimination.
Spain and possessions—Cont'd	*Philippine islands*— Under Spanish flag, Spanish products, 3 per cent. ad valorem; foreign products, 8 per cent. ad valorem. Under foreign flag, Spanish products, 40 per cent. ad valorem; foreign products, 50 per cent. ad valorem.	....	Spanish products, under the Spanish flag, 47 per cent. ad valorem in favor, against those of the United States, in United States vessels.
Sweden	Per lispund, (18¾ pounds,) 5 cents	Same	None
Switzerland	110¼ pounds, 64 cents	Same	None
Turkey	5 per cent. ad valorem, (including the 2 per cent. internal duty.)	Same	None
Tuscany	Per 74.86 pounds, 16⅔ cents	Same	None
Two Sicilies	Per 192½ pounds, $3 20	Same	On American vessels direct from United States fisheries a deduction of 10 per cent. ad valorem; but if from other places, subject to discrimination and tonnage duties
Uruguay	20 per cent. ad valorem	Same	None
Venezuela	Per 1.014 pound, 3 cents	Same	None
Zollverein	Per 110¼ pounds, 34½ cents	Same	None

DUTIES—Continued.

COUNTRIES.	PRODUCT OF THE SEA.		
	WHALEBONE.		
	United States fishery.	National fishery.	Discrimination.
Argentine Republic	20 per cent ad valorem	Same	None
Austria	Per centner, 110 pounds, 36⅝ cents	Same	None
Belgium	Raw, free; cut, $11 40, per 220 pounds	Same	None
Bolivia	28 per cent. ad valorem	Same	None
Brazil	1 quintal, (130.06 pounds,) $7 05. (By latest tariff, 15 to 30 per cent. ad valorem.)	Same	None
Central America	*Costa Rica:* Worked into all articles, 1.014 pound, 16 cents. *Guatemala:* For umbrellas, 1 dozen, 24 cents; unmanufactured, no definition given.	Same	None
Chili	Raw, free; manufactures of, 25 per cent. on a valuation of $1 per pound.	Same	None
China	5 per cent. ad valorem	Same	None
Denmark and colonies	Rough, free; split, $6 56¼ per 110 pounds; St. Croix, 12½ per cent. ad valorem.	Same	None
Dominican Republic	25 per cent. ad valorem	Same	None
Equador	Unmanufactured, per quintal, (101 pounds,) $6	Same	None
France and possessions	In French vessels from foreign countries, $5 55½ per 220 pounds. Foreign vessels from foreign countries, $6 48 per 220 pounds. Martinique, per 220 pounds, 1 cent.	French fishery, 4 cts. per 220 pounds.	This article, not being included in the commercial treaty between France and the United States, has to pay duty on foreign vessels under all circumstances, and, therefore, French shipping is in favor against that of the United States.
Great Britain and possessions	Free	Free	None
	North American possessions, from 3½ to 12½ per cent. prior to reciprocity treaty—now free.	Same	None
	West Indies, generally 5 per cent	Same	None
	Australian possessions, generally free	Same	None
	East Indies, from 5 to 10 per cent	Same	None
Hayti	1.014 pound, 5 cents	Same	10 per cent. wharfage duty; $1 per ton, tonnage duty; 6 per cent. ad valorem, consignment duty; of which duties, except 2 per cent. consignment duty, Haytian vessels are free.

DUTIES—Continued.

COUNTRIES.	PRODUCT OF THE SEA.		
	WHALEBONE.		
	United States fishery.	National fishery.	Descrimination.
Hanse Towns	Hamburg, ½ of 1 per cent. ad valorem. Bremen, ⅔ of 1 per cent. ad valorem Lubeck, ½ of 1 per cent. ad valorem.	Same	None
Holland and colonies.	Free Dutch East Indies, 12 per cent. ad valorem; equalized, 6 per cent. ad valorem. Dutch Guiana and West Indies, 6 per cent. ad valorem; equalized, 3 per cent. ad valorem.	Free	If not the produce of the United States, subject to discriminating duties.
Mexico	Per 101 pounds, $4	Same	None
New Granada	1 kilogramme, (2⅕ pounds,) 50 cents	Same	None
Norway	Rough, free; split, 5¼ cents per pound	Same	None
Papal States	1 centinajo, (74.86 pounds,) 60 cents	Same	In the direct trade, none.
Peru	Work d. 20 per cent. on a valuation of 75 cents 1.014 pound.	Same	None
ortugal	Per 101 pounds, 34 cents. Hereto is to be added a new duty of 10 per cent. ad valorem for the abolition of the Lisbon bank notes, and one of 3 per cent. ad valorem for fees.	Same	As American product direct from the U. States, none; Portuguese colonial products pay only the fifth part of these duties.
Russia	1 pound, 7½ cents	Same	None
Sandwich Islands	5 per cent. ad valorem	Same	None
Sardinia	No definition in the tariff	Same.	
Spain and possessions	In national vessels, per 1 lb. 3 drs., 2 cents; in foreign vessels, 2¾ cents.		¾ of 1 cent per lb. in favor of Spanish vessels against American.
	Cuba—		
	On a valuation of $62 50 per quintal (101 lbs.):— Foreign produce, direct from the country of production, in Spanish vessels, 19½ per cent.; in foreign vessels, 27½ per cent.; from Spain, in Spanish vessels, 19½ per cent. Spanish produce, in foreign vessels, 14½ per cent.; in Spanish vessels, 7½ per cent.		20 per cent. on the fixed value in favor of Spanish products under Spanish flag against those of the United States under American flag.

DUTIES—Continued.

COUNTRIES.	PRODUCT OF THE SEA. WHALEBONE. United States fishery.	National fishery.	Descrimination.
Spain and possessions	*Porto Rico*— On a valuation of $62 50 per quintal (101 lbs.):— Foreign produce, direct from the country of production, in Spanish vessels, 16 per cent.; in foreign vessels, 23 per cent.; from Spain, in Spanish vessels, 16 per cent. Spanish produce, in foreign vessels, 12 per cent.; in Spanish vessels, 7 per cent. *Philippine Islands*— No definition given in the tariffs.		16 per cent. on the fixed value in favor of Spanish products under Spanish flag against those of the United States under American flag.
Sweden	Free	Same	None
Switzerland	Per 110¼ pounds, 37 cents	Same	None
Turkey	5 per cent. ad valorem, (including the 2 per cent. internal duty.)	Same	None
Tuscany	1 pound, 1 cent	Same	None
Two Sicilies	Per 192½ pounds, $3 20	Same	If imported direct from U. S. fisheries, a deduction of 10 per ct. ad val.; otherwise subjected to tonnage and discriminating duties.
Uruguay	Not being specially named in the tariff, 20 per cent. ad valorem.	Same	None
Venezuela	1.014 pound, 2 cents	Same	None
Zollverein	Free	Same	None

DUTIES—Continued.

COUNTRIES.	PRODUCT OF THE FOREST.		
	TIMBER.		
	United States.	Other countries.	Discrimination.
Argentine Republic	5 per cent. ad valorem	Same	None
Austria	Per 100 cubic feet, 36⅝ cents	If imported from the Zollverein, free.	By sea, none
Belgium	Direct from the United States, in United States or Belgian vessels, per tonneau, (52$\frac{9}{10}$ square feet,) 37½ cents. Indirect, or from other countries, United States vessels pay, per tonneau, 73½ cents. Oak, with the bark on, unsawn, per tonneau, 18¾ cents.	Same	In the direct trade, none. In the indirect trade, however, United States vessels have to pay 37 cents per tonneau more than Belgian.
Bolivia	Free	Free	
Brazil	5 per cent. ad valorem	Same	None
Central America	Costa Rica.—Not named in the tariff Guatemala.—Not named in the tariff.	Same	None
Chili	Pine, oak, &c., on the valuation of 25 cents per square foot, free.	Same	None
China	10 per cent. ad valorem	Same	None
Denmark and colonies	Per 100 cubic feet, $1 57½.—(See Comparative Tariffs.)	Same	None
Dominican Republic	No definition given	Same	None
Equador	No definition given in the tariff	Same	None
France and possessions	Pine, squared, hewn, 2 cents per 1 stère, (35.31 square feet.)		
	Corsica.—Pine, squared, hewn, 2 cents per 1 stère	Same	None
	Algiers.—Free.		
Great Britain and possessions.	Duties various; say $2 40 per load of 50 cubic feet.	From the North American colonies duties various; say 96 cts. per load of 50 cub. feet, and 5 per cent. additional.	$1 44 per load of 50 cubic feet, less 5 per cent. on the whole value.
	North American provinces.—Generally free. In Canada, 12½ per cent. prior to reciprocity treaty; now free.	From other North American provinces and United States, free.	None
	West Indies.—Duties various; say $2 88 per 1,000 feet.	Same	None
	Australian possessions.—Generally 60 cents per 40 cubic feet.	Same	None
	East Indies.—Generally 5 per cent	Same	None

DUTIES—Continued.

COUNTRIES.	PRODUCT OF THE FOREST.		
	TIMBER.		
	United States.	Other countries.	Discrimination.
Hayti	Hard wood, squared, per 1,000 pounds, equal to 1,080 pounds English, $3. Soft wood, squared, per 1,000 pounds, equal to 1,080 pounds English, $2.	Same	10 per cent. wharfage duty, $1 per ton tonnage duty, and 6 per cent. ad valorem consignment duty. Haytien ships are exempt from these duties, with the exception of 2 per cent. consignment duty.
Hanse Towns	Hamburg.—½ of 1 per cent. ad valorem		
	Bremen.—⅝ of 1 per cent. ad valorem	Same	None
	Lubeck.—½ of 1 per cent. ad valorem		
Holland and colonies	For ship building, with the bark on, per ton, (2,200 pounds,) 10 cents. Sawn, with the bark on, per ton, 60 cents. Dutch East Indies.—In Hollandish and equalized vessels, 6 per cent. ad valorem; in other, 12 per cent. ad valorem. Dutch Guiana and West Indies.—In Hollandish and equalized vessels, 3 per cent. ad valorem; other, 6 per cent. ad valorem.	Same	If not the produce of the United States, subject to discriminating duties.
Mexico	For building, free	Same	
New Granada	Free	Same	None
Norway	Free	Same	None
Papal States	In trunks 7 to 12 inches in diameter, 100, $7 77. In trunks 12 to 18 inches in diameter, 100, $23 33. In trunks 18 to 24 inches in diameter, 100, $93 33, (masts.) Over 24 inches in diameter, 100, $280.	Same	If imported direct from the United States, none.
Peru	Free	Same	None
Portugal	100 arratels, (101 pounds,) 11¼ cents, to which is to be added an additional duty of 13 per cent. ad valorem.	Same	If direct from the United States, none. Portuguese colonial products pay only ⅓ of the whole duty.
Russia	In the ports of the Baltic sea, per arshine, (0.77 yard,) 1⅓ cent.	Same	None
Sandwich Islands	5 per cent. ad valorem	Same	None
Sardinia	1 per cent. ad valorem	Same	None
Spain and possessions	Joists and beams, in national vessels, 5¼ cents per cubic foot; in foreign vessels, 7¼ cents per cubic foot. Spanish colonial products pay only one-fourth of the above duties.		Spanish vessels are in favor by 2 cents per cubic foot.

DUTIES—Continued.

COUNTRIES.	PRODUCT OF THE FOREST.		
	TIMBER.		
	United States.	Other countries.	Discrimination.
Spain and possessions—Continued.	*Cuba*—		
	On valuation		26 per ct. on the fixed value in favor of Spanish woods, in Spanish vessels, against the United States.
	Foreign produce, direct, from the country of production, in Spanish vessels, 23½ per cent.; in foreign vessels, 33½ per cent.; from Spain, in Spanish vessels, 23½ per ct.		
	Spanish produce, from Spain, in foreign vessels, 17½ per cent.; in Spanish vessels, 7½ per cent.		
	Porto Rico—		
	On valuation		22 per ct. on the fixed value in favor of the Spanish flag and produce against those of the United States.
	Foreign produce, direct from the country of production, in Spanish vessels, 20 per ct.; in foreign vessels, 29 per cent.; from Spain, in Spanish vessels, 20 per cent.		
	Spanish produce, from Spain, in foreign vessels, 15 per cent.; in Spanish vessels, 7 per cent.		
	Philippine Islands.—No definition given in the tariff.		
Sweden	Free	Same	None
Switzerland	Per 110 pounds, 11 cents	Same	None
Turkey	5 per cent. ad valorem, (including 2 per cent. ad valorem internal duty.)	Same	None
Tuscany	Per 74.86 pounds, 2 cents.		
Two Sicilies	20 per cent. ad valorem, in addition to a small specific duty, graduated according to kind.	Same	Sicilian and equalized vessels, on direct voyage, have a deduction of 10 per cent. ad val.; also American vessels.
Uruguay	5 per cent. ad valorem	Same	None
Venezuela	$9 per 1,000 feet for pine beams	Same	None
Zollverein	Oak, ash, acorn, &c., per 1 schifflast, or 4,125 pounds, 69 cents; pine, do., 100 square feet, 23 cents.		

DUTIES—Continued.

COUNTRIES.	PRODUCT OF THE FOREST.		
	LUMBER.		
	United States.	Other countries.	Discrimination.
Argentine Republic	5 per cent. ad valorem	Same	None
Austria	Per centner, or 110 pounds, 36⅝ cents; fine sorts, not European, free.	If imported from the Zollverein, free.	By sea, none
Belgium	All kinds, direct from the United States, in United States or Belgian vessels, per tonneau, (52$\frac{9}{10}$ square feet,) $1 67½; indirect, or in other foreign vessels, $2 04½ per tonneau.	Same	In the direct trade, none; in the indirect, Belgian vessels, 37 cents per tonneau in favor of Belgian against United States vessels.
Bolivia	Free	Free.	
Brazil	Fir wood, in boards of 1 inch thick, every 1,000 palmos, (8½ inches,) $4 23; all others, 30 per cent. ad valorem. (By latest tariff, lumber is rated from 5 to 30 per cent. ad valorem.)	Same	None
Central America	Costa Rica.—Not named in the tariff. Guatemala—Not named in the tariff.	Same	None
Chili	Pine, oak, in planks, boards, &c., free; valuation of, $35 per 1,000 feet.	Same	None
China	10 per cent. ad valorem	Same	None
Denmark and colonies	$1 57½ per last of 2 tons, ship's burden	Same	None
Dominican Republic	25 per ct. on fixed valuation, as follows: boards, pine, 1,000 feet, $10; boards, pitch pine, 1,000 feet, $12.	Same	None
Equador	Boards, 1 inch thick, 2 cents per foot	Same	None
France and possessions.	Boards and planks, over 80 millimetres thick, 2$\frac{7}{10}$ cts. per 100 metres length, or 110 yards; boards and planks, from 34 to 80 millimetres thick, 18⅝ cents per 100 metres length, or 110 yards. *Corsica*— Boards and planks, over 80 millimetres thick, 2$\frac{7}{10}$ cents per 100 metres, or 110 yards length; boards and planks, under 80 millimetres thick, 18⅝ cents per 100 metres, or 110 yards. *Algiers.*—Free. *Martinique*— Per 110 yards, 23⅛ cents; boards and planks, over 80 millimetres thick, pay 2$\frac{7}{10}$ cents per piece of 100 metres, or 110 yards long. Boards and planks, 34 to 80 millimetres thick, pay 18⅝ cents per piece of 100 metres, or 110 yards long. 1 millimetre = 0.039 inch; 1 metre = 1.093 yd.		None

DUTIES—Continued.

COUNTRIES.	PRODUCT OF THE FOREST.		
	LUMBER.		
	United States.	Other countries.	Discrimination.
Great Britain and possessions.	Generally same as timber, (which see)	See Timber	See Timber
	North American possessions.—See Timber	See Timber	See Timber
	West Indies.—See Timber	See Timber	See Timber
	Australian possessions.—See Timber	See Timber	See Timber
	East Indies.—See Timber	See Timber	See Timber
Hayti	Pine, per 1,000 feet, $1 75; pitch pine, per 1,000 feet, $2 50; fir, deal boards, per 1,000 feet, $1 75; oak boards, per 1,000 feet, $3 50.	Same	10 per cent. ad val. wharfage duty; $1 per ton tonnage, and 6 per cent. ad val. consignment duty. Haytien vessels are, with the exception of 2 per cent. ad val. consignment duty, exempt from these duties.
Hanse Towns	Hamburg.—½ of 1 per cent. ad valorem Bremen.—⅔ of 1 per cent. ad valorem Lubeck.—½ of 1 per cent. ad valorem	Same	None
Holland and colonies	Per ton, (2,200 pounds,) 30 cents	Same	If not the produce of the United States, subject to discriminating duties.
	Dutch East Indies— In Hollandish or equalized vessels, 6 per cent. ad valorem; in other, 12 per cent. Dutch Guiana, and West Indies— In Dutch and equalized vessels, 3 per cent. ad valorem; other, 6 per cent.		
Mexico	Boards, for building, in a rough state, free; boards, already worked, 25 per cent. ad val.	Same.	
New Granada	Free	Same	None
Norway	Free	Same	None
Papal States	Boards, and other sawed wood, under 2 inches thick, per 100, $2 33; 2 to 3 inches thick, $4 66; 3 to 6 inches thick, $12 43; over 6 inches thick, $24 88.	Same	If imported direct from the United States, none.
Peru	Free	Same	None
Portugal	Boards, under 1 inch thick, per square foot, ⅓ of a cent; under 2 inches thick, ⅔ of a cent; under 3 inches thick, 1 cent; more than 3 inches thick, 1⅓ cent.	Same	If direct from the United States, none; Portuguese colonial products only one-fifth of the duty.
Russia	Boards of all kinds, 1½ cent	Same	None
Sandwich Islands	5 per cent. ad valorem	Same	None
Sardinia	Boards, under 2 inches thick, per 1 yard, ⅔ of a cent; over 2 inches thick, ⅔ of a cent.	Same	None

DUTIES—Continued.

COUNTRIES.	PRODUCT OF THE FOREST.		
	LUMBER.		
	United States.	Other countries.	Discrimination.
Spain and possessions..	For building ships, &c.: in national vessels, 2 per cent. ad val.; in foreign vessels, 3 per cent. ad val.	----------------	1 per ct. in favor of Spanish vessels against those of the United States.
	Cuba—		
	Boards, cedar, on a valuation of $25 per 1,000 feet; maple, on a valuation of $25 per 1,000 feet; pine, on a valuation of $20 per 1,000 feet.	----------------	Cedar pays 26 per cent. less, in favor of Spain against the United States; maple and pine pay 20 per cent. less on the fixed value in favor of Spain against the United States.
	Foreign produce, direct from the country of production, in Spanish vessels, cedar, 23½ per cent., pine and maple, 19½ per cent.; in foreign vessels, cedar, 33½ per cent., pine and maple, 27½ per cent.; from Spain, in Spanish vessels, cedar, 23½ per cent., pine and maple, 19½ per cent.		
	Spanish produce, in foreign vessels, cedar, 17½ per cent, pine and maple, 14½ per cent.; in Spanish vessels, cedar, 7½ per cent., pine and maple, 7½ per cent.		
	Porto Rico—		
	Boards, cedar, on a valuation of $25 per 1,000 feet; maple, on a valuation of $25 per 1,000 feet; pitch pine, on a valuation of $20 per 1,000 feet; white pine, on a valuation of $15 per 1,000 feet.		
	Foreign produce, direct from the country of production, in Spanish vessels, cedar, 20 per cent., maple and white pine, 16 per cent., pitch pine, 17½ per cent.; in foreign vessels, cedar, 29 per cent., maple and white pine, 23 per cent., pitch pine 23½ per cent.; from Spain, in Spanish vessels, cedar, 20 per cent., maple and white pine, 16 per cent., pitch pine, 14½ per cent.	----------------	Cedar, 22 per cent. in favor of Spanish product and shipping; maple and white pine, 16 per cent.; pitch pine, 16¾ per cent.
	Spanish produce, in foreign vessels, cedar, 15 per cent., maple and white pine, 12 per cent., pitch pine, 15 per cent.; in Spanish vessels, cedar, 7 per cent., maple and white pine, 7 per cent.; pitch pine, 6¾ per cent.		
	Philippine Islands —No definition given in the tariff.		
Sweden...........	Free....................................	Same.........	None..................
Switzerland..........	Per 110 pounds, 11 cents..................	Same.........	None..................

DUTIES—Continued.

COUNTRIES.	PRODUCT OF THE FOREST.		
	LUMBER.		
	United States.	Other countries.	Discrimination.
Turkey	5 per cent. ad valorem, (including the 2 per cent. internal duty.)	Same	None
Tuscany	Per 74. 86 pounds, 72 cents	Same	None
Two Sicilies	Pine boards, 16 to 22 inches, per 100, $1 60; 12 to 15 inches, per 100, 72 cents; 8 to 11 inches, per 100, 56 cents.	Same	Sicilian and American vessels on direct voyage pay 10 per cent. ad valorem less than given in the tariff.
Uruguay	25 per cent. ad valorem	Same	None
Venezuela	Pine boards, per 1,000 feet, $6	Same	None
Zollverein	Boards and planks, pine, per 100 square feet, 23 cents; oak, do., 69 cents.	Same	None

DUTIES—Continued.

COUNTRIES.	PRODUCT OF THE FOREST.		
	STAVES.		
	United States.	Other countries.	Discrimination.
Argentine Republic	5 per cent. at valorem	Same	None
Austria	1 centner, (110 lbs.,) 36⅝ cents	If imported from the Zollverein, free.	By sea, none
Belgium	$1 67½ per 100 pieces, for hogsheads, &c.; 40 cents per 100 pieces, common staves.	Same	To the direct trade, none
Bolivia	Free	Same	None
Brazil	30 per cent. ad valorem. (By latest tariff, staves range from 5 to 30 per cent. ad valorem.)	Same	None
Central America	*Costa Rica.*—Free	Same	None
	Guatamala.—Free		
	San Salvador.—Free		
Chili	Worked or not, free	Same	None
China	5 per cent. ad valorem	Same	None
Denmark and colonies	Of 7-4 yard in length and upwards, 24 cents per 120 pieces; between 7-4 and 4-4 yard in length, 4⅗ cents per 120 pieces; of less than 4-4 yard in length, 2⅓ cents per 120 pieces; of headings, two are reckoned for one stave.	Same	None
Dominican Republic	25 per cent. on a fixed valuation of $30 per 1,000	Same	None
Equador	For pipes, per 100, 80 cents; for barrels, per 100, 24 cents.	Same	None
France and possessions	Over 1,299 millimetres (1 millimetre = 0.39 inch) long, 37⅓ cents per 1,000; 1,299 to 974 millimetres long, $27\frac{9}{10}$ per 1,000; under 974 millimetres long, 18⅗ cents per 1,000.		None
	Algiers.—Free		
	Martinique.—$1 12 per 1,000		
Great Britain and possessions.	Exceeding 72 inches in length, 7 inches in breadth, or 3½ in thickness, $2 16 per load of 50 cubic feet.	From the North American colonies, exceeding 72 inches in length, 7 in. in breadth, or 3½ in thickness, 48 cents per load of 50 cubic feet, and 5 per cent. additional.	$1 68 per load of 50 cubic feet in favor of colonies.
	North American possessions, generally free; in Canada, 12½ per cent.	From other British N. American possessions, free.	Generally from 3½ to 12½ per cent.

DUTIES—Continued.

COUNTRIES.	PRODUCT OF THE FOREST.		
	STAVES.		
	United States.	Other countries.	Discrimination.
Great Britain and possessions—Cont'd.	West Indies: From 96 cents to $2 per 1,000	Same	None
	Australian possessions: From 24 to 36 cts. per 1,000	Same	None
	East Indies: Generally 5 per cent	Same	None
Hayti	Per M, 75 cents	Same	10 per cent. wharfage duty, $1 per ton tonnage duty, and 6 per cent. ad valorem consignment duty. Haytien vessels are exempt from these duties, with the exception of 2 per cent. ad valorem consignment duty.
Hanse Towns	Hamburg: ½ of 1 per cent. ad valorem. Bremen: ⅝ of 1 per cent. ad valorem. Lubeck: ½ of 1 per cent. ad valorem.	Same	None
Holland and colonies	Per ton of 2,200 lbs., 40 cents	Same	If not the produce of the United States, subject to discriminating duties.
	Dutch East Indies.—National and equalized vessels, 6 per cent. ad valorem; other foreign vessels, 12 per cent. ad valorem.		
	Dutch Guiana and West Indies.—In national and equalized vessels, 3 per cent. ad valorem; in other foreign vessels, 6 per cent.		
Mexico	Per 101 lbs., 30 cents	Same	None
New Granada	No definition given in the tariff	Same	None
Norway	⅝ ells (1 ell = ⅝ of a yard) long, 120 pieces, $1 59		
	⅞ ells to ⅝ ells long ..do.. 1 06		
	For barrels, ⅘ to ⅞ ells long ..do..26½ cts.	Same	None
	Through the custom-houses of Hammerfest, Vardoe, and Vadsoe only, 13¼ cents.		
Papal States	Under 6 inches, per 100, 23 cents	Same	None
	Over..do..do..46 cents	Same	None
Peru	Free	Same	None
Portugal	For barrels, per 100, 12 cents	Same	If direct from the United States, none; from Portuguese colonies, only one-fifth of the duties to be paid.
	Up to 29 inches, per 100, 12 cents.		
	30 to 37 inches, per 100, 14 cents; to which duties 13 per cent. ad valorem is to be added.		
Russia	Free	Same	None
Sardinia	1.09 yard long, oak, each, ⅝ of a cent	Same	None
	Do..other wood, each, ½ of a cent	Same	None

DUTIES—Continued.

COUNTRIES.	PRODUCT OF THE FOREST.		
	STAVES.		
	United States.	Other countries.	Discrimination.
Spain and possessions	From Hamburg, in national vessels, \$2 65 pr. 1,000 Do foreign do 3 53 do From other places, national do 1 32½ do Do foreign do 2 65 do		Staves from Hamburg pay in national vessels 90 cents per 1,000, and from other countries 22¼ cents per 1,000 less than in American or other foreign ships.
	Cuba—On a valuation of \$25 per 1,000:— Foreign produce, direct from the country of production, in Spanish vessels, 19½ per ct.; in foreign vessels, 27½ per cent.; from Spain, in Spanish vessels, 19½ per cent. Spanish produce, in foreign vessels, 14½ per cent.; in Spanish vessels, 7½ per cent.		20 per cent. on the fixed value in favor of Spanish products and shipping.
	Porto Rico—On a valuation of \$12 per 1,000:— Foreign produce, direct from the country of production, in Spanish vessels, 17¼ per ct; in foreign vessels, 23½ per cent; from Spain, in Spanish vessels, 14¼ per cent. Spanish produce, in foreign vessels, 15 per cent.; in Spanish vessels, 6¾ per cent.		16¾ per cent. on the fixed value in favor of Spanish products and shipping.
	Philippine Islands—No definition given in the tariff.		
Sweden	Free	Same	None
Switzerland	1,100 lbs., 11 cents	Same	None
Turkey	5 per cent. ad valorem, (including the 2 per cent. internal duty.)	Same	None
Tuscany	One carriage load, 19 cents	Same	None
Two Sicilies	Oak, 5 palmi per 100, \$22 40 and 20 per cent.		
Uruguay	Not named in the tariff		
Venezuela	Free	Same	None
Zollverein	1 schiffslast, 37½ centner, (1 centner = 110 lbs.,) oak, 92 cents; pine, 46 cents.		

DUTIES—Continued.

COUNTRIES.	PRODUCT OF THE FOREST.		
	SHINGLES.		
	United States.	Other countries.	Discrimination.
Argentine Republic	5 per cent. ad valorem	Same	None
Austria	1 per centner, (110 lbs.,) 36⅝ cents	If imported from the Zollverein, free.	By sea, none
Belgium	Direct from the United States, in United States or Belgian vessels, per M, $3 88.	Same	In the direct trade, none.
Bolivia	Free	Same	None
Brazil	30 per cent. ad valorem. (By latest tariff, from 5 to 30 per cent. ad valorem.)	Same	None
Central America	Costa Rica: Free	Same	None
	Guatemala: Free		
Chili	Worked or not, 25 per cent. on a valuation of $14 per 1,000.	Same	None
China	5 per cent. ad valorem	Same	None
Denmark and colonies	$1 57½ per last of 2 tons of ship's burden.—(See this article in Comparative Tariffs.)	Same	None
Dominican Republic	25 per cent. on a fixed valuation of $5 per 1,000	Same	None
Equador	Per 1,000, $3 36	Same	None
France and possessions	Under 2 metres, (1 metre = 1.093 yard,) 9$\frac{3}{10}$ cts. per 1,000; 2 to 4 metres, 37⅕ cts. per 1,000; 4 and over, 77⅘ cts. per 1,000.	Same	None
	Algiers: Free		
	Martinique: 13$\frac{95}{100}$ cts. per 1,000		
Great Britain and possessions.	$2 40 per load of 50 cubic feet	North American colonial possessions, 48 cents per load of 50 cubic feet, and 5 per cent. additional.	In favor of North American colonies and ag'st the United States, $1 92 per load of 50 cubic feet.
	North American possessions: From 6¼ to 12½ per cent.	From other North American possessions, free.	From 6¼ to 12½ per cent. against the United States.
	Newfoundland: 24 cents per 1,000		
	West Indies: Generally $1 44 per 1,000	Same	None
	Australian possessions: Generally $1 44 per 1,000	Same	None
	East Indies: Generally 5 per cent	Same	None
Hayti	No definition given in the tariff		
Hanse Towns	Hamburg: ½ of 1 per cent. ad valorem Bremen: ⅜ of 1 per cent. ad valorem Lubec: ½ of 1 per cent. ad valorem	Same	None
Holland and colonies	Not defined in the tariff	Same	If not the produce of the United States, subject to discriminating duties.
	Dutch East Indies.—National and equalized vessels, 6 per cent. ad valorem. Other foreign vessels, 12½ per cent. ad valorem.		
	Dutch Guiana and West Indies: Per 1,000, 12 cts.		

DUTIES—Continued.

COUNTRIES.	PRODUCT OF THE FOREST.		
	SHINGLES.		
	United States.	Other countries.	Discrimination.
Mexico	Free	Same	None
New Granada	Per 1,000, $2	Same	None
Norway	$52\frac{2}{3}$ cents per 1,000	Same	None
Papal States	No definition in the tariff	Same	None
Peru	Free	Same	None
Portugal	No definition in the Portuguese tariff	Same	None
Russia	Free	Same	None
Sandwich Islands	5 per cent. ad valorem	Same	None
Sardinia	No definition given in the tariff	Same	None
Spain and possessions	Not named in the Spanish tariff	Same	
	Cuba.—On a valuation of $3 75 per 1,000 Foreign produce— Direct from the country of production, in Spanish vessels, $19\frac{1}{2}$ per cent. Direct from the country of production, in foreign vessels, $27\frac{1}{2}$ per cent. From Spain, in Spanish vessels, $19\frac{1}{2}$ per cent. Spanish produce— In foreign vessels, $14\frac{1}{2}$ per cent. In Spanish vessels, $7\frac{1}{2}$ per cent.		20 per cent. on the fixed value in favor of Spanish products and shipping.
	Porto Rico.—On a valuation of $3 per 1,000 Foreign produce— Direct from the country of production, in Spanish vessels, $17\frac{1}{4}$ per cent. Direct from the country of production, in foreign vessels, $23\frac{1}{2}$ per cent. From Spain, in Spanish vessels, $14\frac{1}{4}$ per cent. Spanish produce— In foreign vessels, 15 per cent. In Spanish vessels, $6\frac{3}{4}$ per cent.		$16\frac{3}{4}$ per cent. on the fixed value in favor of Spain.
	Philippine Islands.—No definition given.		
Sweden	Free	Same	None
Switzerland	Per 1,100 lbs., (10 centners,) 12 cents	Same	None
Turkey	5 per cent. ad valorem, (including the 2 per cent. internal duty.)	Same	None
Tuscany	Not named in the tariff	Same	None
Two Sicilies	Not named in the tariff		
Uruguay	5 per cent. ad valorem	Same	None
Venezuela	Per 1,000, $1	Same	None
Zollverein	Not given in the tariff, unless charged as *staves*.		

DUTIES—Continued.

COUNTRIES.	PRODUCT OF THE FOREST.		
	TAR.		
	United States.	Other countries.	Discrimination.
Argentine Republic	15 per cent. ad valorem	Same	None
Austria	Free	Same	None
Belgium	Free	Same	None
Bolivia	28 per cent. ad valorem	Same	None
Brazil	American, 1 barrel, 38 cents Swedish, 1 barrel, 94 cents. (By latest tariff, 10 per cent. ad valorem.)	Same	American products in favor of, 56 cts. against Swedish.
Central America	Costa Rica: Per quintal, (101 lbs.,) $1 Guatemala: Per arroba, (25 lbs.,) 50 cents.	Same	None
Chili	Free	Same	None
China	5 per cent. ad valorem	Same	None
Denmark and colonies	Per barrel, 26¼ cents	Same	None
Dominican Republic	25 per cent. on fixed valuation of $2 per barrel	Same	None
Equador	Per 101 pounds, 25 cents	Same	None
France and possessions	Mineral tar, 2 cts. per 220 pounds; vegetable tar, in national vessels, 64⅗ cents per 220 pounds; in foreign vessels, $1 02$\frac{3}{10}$ per 220 pounds. Martinique: Mineral tar, $\frac{93}{100}$ cents per 220 lbs.; vegetable do, 13$\frac{95}{100}$ cents per 100 kilogrammes.	Same	If as American produce and imported direct in United States vessels, none; but if imported indirectly, United States vessels pay the same as other foreign vessels.
Great Britain and possessions.	Free	Free	None
	North American possessions: From 2 to 5 per ct. generally, prior to reciprocity treaty; now free.	Free	None
	West Indies: Generally from 50 cents per barrel to 4 per cent. ad valorem.	Same	None
	Australian possessions: Generally 24 cents per barrel.	Same	None
	East Indies: Generally free	Same	None
Hayti	Per barrel, 75 cents	Same	10 per ct. ad valorem wharfage, $1 per ton tonnage duty, and 6 per cent. ad valorem consignment duty. Haytien vessels are exempt from these duties, with the exception of 2 per cent. consignment duty.
Hanse Towns	Hamburg: ½ of 1 per cent. ad valorem Bremen: ⅗ of 1 per cent. ad valorem Lubec: Per tonne of 200 pounds, 1⅗ cent	Same	None
Holland and colonies	Free Dutch East Indies: Dutch and equalized vessels, 6 per cent. ad val. Other foreign vessels, 12 per cent. ad valorem. Dutch Guiana and West Indies:	Same	If not the produce of the United States, subject to discriminating duties.

DUTIES—Continued.

COUNTRIES.	PRODUCT OF THE FOREST.		
	TAR.		
	United States.	Other countries.	Discrimination.
Holland and colonies—Continued.	Hollandish and equalized vessels, 4 cents per 221 pounds; other foreign vessels, 8 cents per 221 pounds.		
Mexico	No definition given in the tariff	Same	None
New Granada	Per 1 miriágramo, (26 lbs. 9 oz,) 8 cents	Same	None
Norway	Per toende, (34⅝ gallons,) 79½ cents; through the ports of Hammerfest, Vardoe, Vadsoe, only 39¾ cents.	Same	None
Papal States	Per 74.86 pounds, 2 cents	Same	If direct from the United States, none.
Peru	Free	Same	None
Portugal	Per 128 pounds, 12 cents; to which is to be added a duty of 13 per cent. ad valorem.	Same	If imported direct from the United States, none; from Portuguese colonies, only one-fifth of these duties is to be paid.
Russia	On the Baltic Sea, per ton, 35 cents; on the Black Sea, per ton, 30 cents.	Same	None
Sandwich Islands	5 per cent. ad valorem	Same	None
Sardinia	Per 220 pounds, 18½ cents	Same	None
Spain and possessions	In Spanish vessels, 12¾ cts. per quintal, (101 lbs.;) in foreign vessels, 17 cents per quintal.		4¼ cents per quintal in favor of Spanish vessels against other nations.
	Cuba—		
	On a valuation of $3 per barrel of 200 pounds:— Foreign produce, direct from the country of production, in Spanish vessels, 19½ per cent.; in foreign vessels, 27⅓ per cent. From Spain, in Spanish vessels, 19½ per ct. Spanish produce in foreign vessels, 14½ per cent.; in Spanish vessels, 7½ per cent.		20 per cent. on the fixed value in favor of Spanish product and shipping against that of other nations.
	Porto Rico—		
	On the valuation of $3 per barrel:— Foreign produce, direct from the country of production, in Spanish vessels, 16 per cent.; in foreign vessels, 23 per cent. From Spain, in Spanish vessels, 16 per cent. Spanish produce, in foreign vessels, 12 per cent.; in Spanish vessels, 7 per cent.		16 per cent. on the fixed value in favor of Spanish product and shipping against that of other countries.
	Philippine Islands—		
	Not named in the tariff		
Sweden	1 barrel, 53⅓ cents	Same	None
Switzerland	Per 110 pounds, 6 cents	Same	None

DUTIES—Continued.

COUNTRIES.	PRODUCT OF THE FOREST.		
	TAR.		
	United States.	Other countries.	Discrimination.
Turkey	5 per cent. ad valorem, (including the 2 per cent. internal duty.)	Same	None
Tuscany	Per 74.86 pounds, 5 cents	Same	None
Two Sicilies	Per 192½ pounds, 68 cents	Same	In Sicilian and United tates vessels, direct from United States, a deduction of 10 per cent. ad valorem will be made; bu if indirect, and not in equalized vessels, tonnage and discriminating duties to be paid.
Uruguay	5 per cent. ad valorem	Same	None
Venezuela	Per barrel of 8 arrobas, = 16 gallons, $1	Same	None
Zollverein	Per 110 pounds, 11½ cents	Same	None

DUTIES Continued.

COUNTRIES.	PRODUCT OF THE FOREST.		
	PITCH.		
	United States.	Other countries.	Discrimination.
Argentine Republic	15 per cent. ad valorem	Same	None
Austria	Free	Same	None
Belgium	Per 44,000 pounds, 71⅛ cents	Same	None
Bolivia	28 per cent. ad valorem	Same	None
Brazil	American, 1 barrel, 49⅓ cents. (By latest tariff, 10 per cent. ad valorem.)	From other counries, $1 31 per barrel.	82 cents in favor of American product against that of other countries.
Central America	Costa Rica: Per quintal, (101 pounds,) $1	Same	None
	Guatemala: Per arroba, (25 pounds,) 50 cents		
Chili	Free	Same	None
China	5 per cent. ad valorem	Same	None
Denmark and colonies	Per barrel of 224 pounds, $10 52½	Same	None
Dominican Republic	25 per cent. on fixed valuation of $2 per barrel	Same	None
Equador	Per quintal, 30 cents	Same	None
France and possessions	In national vessels, 93 cents per 220 pounds; in foreign vessels, $1 02$\frac{3}{10}$ per 220 pounds.	Same	As American produce, and imported direct into France in United States vessels, none; but indirectly, not as American produce, United States vessels pay the same as other foreign vessels.
	Martinique: Per 220 pounds, 13.95 cents		
Great Britan and possessions.	Free	Free	None
	North American possessions: From 50 cents per barrel to 2½ per cent. prior to reciprocity treaty; now, free.	Same	None
	West Indies: From 12 to 50 cents per barrel	Same	None
	Australian possessions: Generally 24 cents per barrel.	Same	None
	East Indies: Free	Free	None
Hayti	1 barrel, 50 cents	Same	10 per cent. ad valorem wharfage, $1 per ton tonnage, and 6 per cent. ad valorem consignment duty. Haytien vessels are exempt from these duties, with the exception of 2 per cent. consignment duty.
Hanse Towns	Hamburg: ½ of 1 per cent. ad valorem Bremen: ⅔ of 1 per cent. ad valorem Lubec: Per tonne of 200 pounds, 1⅜ cent	Same	None
Holland and colonies	Free	Same	If not the product of the United States, subject to discriminating duties.

DUTIES—Continued.

COUNTRIES.	PRODUCT OF THE FOREST.		
	PITCH.		
	United States.	Other countries.	Discrimination.
Holland and colonies—Continued.	Dutch East Indies: Dutch and equalized vessels 6 per cent. ad valorem; other foreign vessels 12 per cent.		
	Dutch Guiana and West Indies: Hollandish and equalized vessels 3 per cent. ad valorem; other foreign vessels 6 per cent.		
Mexico	No definition given in the tariff		
New Granada	Per 1.014 pound, ½ cent	Same	None
Norway	Per pound, ¾ cent	Same	None
Papal States	Per 74.86 pounds, 2 cents	Same	If imported direct from the United States, none.
Peru	Free	Same	None
Portugal	Per 128 pounds, 24 cents, to which is to be added a duty of 13 per cent. ad valorem.	Same	If imported direct from the United States, none. From Portuguese possessions only one fifth of said duties to be paid.
Russia	On the Baltic Sea, per ton, 35 cents	Same	None
	Do. Black Sea, per ton, 30 cents	Same	None
Sandwich Islands	5 per cent. ad valorem	Same	None
Sardinia	Per 220 pounds, 18½ cents	Same	None
Spain and possessions	In Spanish vessels, 25 cents per quintal, (101 lbs.) In foreign vessels, 34 cents per quintal.		8½ cents per quintal in favor of the Spanish flag against other countries.
	Cuba.—On a valuation of $3 per barrel of 200 lbs. Foreign produce, direct from the country of production, in Spanish vessels, 19½ per ct.; in foreign vessels, 27½ per cent.; from Spain, in Spanish vessels, 19½ per cent. Spanish produce, in foreign vessels, 14½ per cent.; in Spanish vessels, 7½ per cent.		20 per cent. on the fixed value in favor of Spanish shipping and produce, against that of other countries.
	Porto Rico.—On a valuation of $3 per barrel. Foreign produce, direct from the country of production, in Spanish vessels, 16 per cent.; in foreign vessels, 23 per cent.; from Spain, in Spanish vessels, 16 per cent. Spanish produce, in foreign vessels, 12 per cent.; in Spanish vessels 8 per cent.		16 per cent. on the fixed value in favor of Spanish produce and shipping against other countries.
	Philippine Islands.—Not named in the tariff.		
Sweden	Per 18¾ pounds, (lispund,) 8⅓ cents	Same	None
Switzerland	Per 110 pounds, 6 cents	Same	None
Turkey	5 per cent. ad valorem (including the 2 per cent. internal duty.)	Same	None
Tuscany	Per 74.86 pounds, 5 cents	Same	None

DUTIES—Continued.

COUNTRIES.	PRODUCT OF THE FOREST.		
	PITCH		
	United States.	Other countries.	Discrimination.
Two Sicilies	Per 192½ pounds, 68 cents	Same	In Sicilian and United States vessels, direct from the United States, a deduction of 10 per cent. ad valorem will be made; but if indirect, or not in equalized vessels, tonnage and other discriminating duties are levied.
Uruguay	5 per cent. ad valorem	Same	None
Venezuela	Free	Same	None
Zollverein	Per 110 pounds, 11⅓ cents	Same	None

DUTIES—Continued.

COUNTRIES.	PRODUCT OF THE FOREST.		
	ASHES.		
	United States.	Other countries	Discrimination.
Argentine Republic	By sea, 15 per cent. ad val.; by land, free	Same	None
Austria	$4\frac{1}{2}$ cents per 110 pounds	Same	None
Belgium	Pot and pearl ashes, free	Same	None
Bolivia	28 per cent. ad valorem	Same	None
Brazil	Potassium, purified, per pound, 6 cents. (By latest tariff, 5 to 30 per cent. ad val.)		
Central America	Costa Rica.—Not named in the tariff. Guatemala —Not named in the tariff.		
Chili	Pot and pearl ashes, 25 per cent. on a valuation of $5 per quintal, (101 pounds.)	Same	None
China	5 per cent. ad valorem	Same	None
Denmark and colonies	Free	Same	None
Dominican Republic	Not defined in the tariff, and, therefore, 25 per cent. ad valorem.	Same	None
Equador	Pot ash, 60 cents per 1.014 pound	Same	None
France and possessions	Common vegetable, in national vessels, $18\frac{3}{10}$ per 220 pounds; in foreign vessels, $20\frac{3}{10}$ per 220 pounds.	Same	As American produce, in American vessels direct to France, none; indirect, and not as American produce, United States vessels pay the same as foreign vessels.
Great Britain and possessions.	Free	Free	None
	North American possessions, free	Free	None
	West Indies, from $3\frac{1}{2}$ to 5 per cent	Same	None
	Australian possessions, generally, 5 per cent	Same	None
	East Indies, generally, 4 per cent	Same	None
Hayti	Not named in the tariff.		
Hanse Towns	Hamburg, $\frac{1}{2}$ of 1 per cent. ad valorem	Same	None
	Bremen, $\frac{3}{8}$ of do do	Same	None
	Lubeck, $\frac{1}{2}$ of do do	Same	None
Holland and colonies	Pot and pearl, weed ashes, and soda, free	Same	If not the produce of the United States, subject to discriminating duties.
	Dutch East Indies. Hollandish and equalized vessels, 6 per cent. ad valorem; other foreign, 12 per cent.		
	Dutch Guiana and West Indies. Hollandish and equalized vessels, 2 per cent. ad val.; other foreign vessels, 6 per cent. ad val.		
Mexico	Not named in the tariff.		
New Granada	Pot ash, 25 per cent. ad valorem	Same	None
Norway	Per pound, $\frac{1}{8}$ of a cent	Same	None
Papal States	Pot ash, per 74.86 pounds, 5 cents	Same	None, if imported direct from the United States.
Peru	Pot ash, 25 per cent. on a valuation of 9 cents per 1.014 pound.	Same	None

DUTIES—Continued.

COUNTRIES.	PRODUCT OF THE FOREST.		
	ASHES.		
	United States.	Other countries.	Discrimination.
Portugal	Per 100 arratels, or 101 pounds, 43 cts., to which is to be added an ad valorem duty of 13 per ct.		If direct from the United States in United States vessels, none; Portuguese colonies pay only one-fifth of the whole duty.
Russia	Free	Same	None
Sandwich Islands	5 per cent. ad valorem	Same	None
Sardinia	No definition given in the tariff	Same	None
Spain and possessions.	Pot and pearl ashes, in Spanish vessels, 53 cents per quintal, (101 pounds;) in foreign vessels, 63½ cents.		9½ cents per quintal in favor of the Spanish flag against foreign.
	Cuba—		
	Pot ash, on a valuation of 37½ cts. per pound; common wood, 75 cents per quintal.		20 per cent. in favor of Spanish vessels and produce, against foreign.
	Foreign produce, direct from the country of production, in Spanish vessels, 19½ per ct; in foreign vessels, 27½ per cent.; from Spain, in Spanish vessels, 19½ per cent.		
	Spanish produce, in foreign vessels, 14½ per cent.; in Spanish vessels, 7½ per cent.		
	Porto Rico—		
	Pot ash, on a valuation of 37½ cts. per pound; common wood, 75 cents per quintal.		
	Foreign produce, direct from the country of production, in Spanish vessels, 16 per cent; in foreign vessels, 23 per cent.; from Spain, in Spanish vessels, 16 per cent.		
	Spanish produce, in foreign vessels, 12 per cent.; in Spanish vessels, 7 per cent.		
	Philippine Islands —Not named in the tariff.		
Sweden	Pot ash, not refined, and all wood ashes, free	Same	None
Switzerland	Pot ash, per 110 pounds, 6 cents; common wood ash, 110 pounds, 6 cents.	Same	None
Turkey	5 per cent. ad val., (including the 2 per cent. internal duty.)	Same	None
Tuscany	Common, per 74.86 pounds, 40 cents	Same	None
Two Sicilies	Free	Same	None
Uruguay	Free	Same	None
Venezuela	Not named in the tariff.		
Zollverein	Pot ash, per 110 pounds, 11½ cents; common wood, free.	Same	None

DUTIES—Continued.

COUNTRIES.	PRODUCT OF THE SOIL.		
	WHEAT.		
	United States.	Other countries.	Discrimination.
Argentine Republic	Per fanega, (2½ bushels,) $1 44	Free	Not to be exactly defined.
Austria	Per centner, (110 pounds,) 16⅓ cents	Same	None
Belgium	18¾ cents per 220 pounds	Same	Same
Bolivia	28 per cent. ad valorem	Same	None
Brazil	20 per cent. ad valorem	Same	None
Central America	Costa Rica, free Guatemala, not defined in the tariff	Same	None
Chili	If the price is under $3 per fanega, (2½ bushels,) 25 per cent. ad valorem; otherwise, free.	Same	None
China	5 per cent. ad valorem	Same	None
Denmark and colonies	Per toende, 3.94 bushels, 26⅔ cents	Same	None
Dominican Republic	For seed, free	Same	None
Equador	Per quintal, (101 pounds,) $2; for seed, free	Same	None
France and possessions	The tariff on cereals of all descriptions in France, whether imported or exported, is regulated by the average monthly prices of wheat in the principal markets. These markets, or "customs frontier," are divided into four classes: Toulouse being one of the markets of the 1st class, Gray being one of those of the 2d class, Paris being one of those of the 3d class, and Nantes being one of those of the 4th class; into which classified cities alone cereals are suffered to be imported, or from which to be exported. When, therefore, for sake of example, the average price of the hectolitre of wheat in Marseilles is 28 francs or more, in Bordeaux 26 or more, in Paris 24 or more, and in Nantes 22 or more, the tariff on a hectolitre of *barley*, in each place, in French or equalized vessels and by land, is 12½ centimes, and on its flour 30 centimes per 100 kilogrammes; on a hectolitre of *buckwheat* 10 centimes, and on 100 kilogrammes of its flour 25 centimes; on a hectolitre of *Indian corn* 13¾ centimes, and on 100 kilogrammes of its flour or meal 30 centimes; on a hectolitre of *oats* 8¾ centimes, and on 100 kilogrammes of its flour 27½ centimes; on a hectolitre of *rye* 15 centimes, and on 100 kilogrammes of its flour, 32½ centimes; and, finally, on the hectolitre of *wheat* 25 centimes, and on 100 kilogrammes of flour, 50 centimes. If the importation takes place in foreign vessels or vessels not equalized, the tariff is, of course, much higher. On this system the duty on cereals goes on increasing as the price of wheat in the standard markets *decreases;* and when wheat is down so low as to be worth less than 22 francs the hectolitre in Marseilles, 20 in Bordeaux, 18 in Paris, and 16 in Nantes, the tariff *increases*, by 1.50 francs on each hectolitre of wheat, by the decrease of each franc in the price of wheat per hectolitre, and 4.50 francs on every 100 kilogrammes of flour; and by 82½ centimes on each hectolitre of Indian corn, and 2.20 francs on every 100 kilogrammes of meal.		As produce of the United States and imported direct into France in United States ships, the same duty is paid as in French ships. Imported indirectly, not as American produce, subjected to the same duty as in other foreign ships.

DUTIES—Continued.

COUNTRIES.	PRODUCT OF THE SOIL.		
	WHEAT.		
	United States.	Other countries.	Discrimination.
France & possessions—Continued.	The prices which regulate the averages for each class of the four into which the frontier customs bureaus of all France are divided are fixed by the minister of commerce, according to the average prices of the regulating markets for each class. These prices and the corresponding duties are published on the first day of each month in the Bulletin of Laws, and these duties are levied until the first day of the succeeding month. The hectolitre contains 2.84 bushels. The kilogramme weighs 2 20 pounds. The present sliding scale of French corn duties seems to have continued much the same for many years, the past 12 years at least. The 1st class of market cities in France comprises Toulouse, Gray, Lyons, and Marseilles. The 2d comprises Marans, Bordeaux, Toulouse, Gray, Saint Laurent pris Mâçon, le Grand-Lemps. The 3d comprises Mulhausen, Strasbourg, Bergues, Arras, Roye, Soissons, Paris, Rouen, Saumur, Nantes, and Marans. The 4th comprises Metz, Verdum, Charleville, Soissons, Saint Lô, Laimpol, Quimper, Hennebon, and Nantes.		

A table of French corn duties, exhibiting the prices and rates of duties on wheat, as regulated by the prices of wheat.

Regulating prices, per hectolitre of 2.84 bushels, of wheat in each of the four classes of the customs frontier.				WHEAT.					
				IMPORT DUTIES.				EXPORT DUTIES.	
				Upon grain.		Upon flour.			
1st class.	2d class.	3d class.	4th class.	French vessels, or by land.	Foreign vessels.	French vessels, or by land.	Foreign vessels.	Grain.	Flour.
Price above.	*Price above.*	*Price above.*	*Price above.*	*Per hecto'e.*	*Per hecto'e.*	*Per 100 kil.*	*Per 100 kil.*	*For each*	*fr. above.*
Frs. 28	Frs. 26	Frs. 24	Frs. 22	$0 04 3/5	$0 04 3/5	$0 09 3/10	$0 09 3/10	$0 37 1/5	$0 74 2/5
28 to 27	26 to 25	24 to 23	22 to 21	4 3/5	27 9/10	9 3/10	40	1 11 3/5	2 23 1/2
27 to 26	25 to 24	23 to 22	21 to 20	4 3/5	27 9/10	9 3/10	40	74 2/5	1 48 4/5
26 to 25	24 to 23	22 to 21	20 to 19	23 1/5	46 1/2	65 1/10	95 1/2	37 1/5	74 2/5
25 to 24	23 to 22	21 to 20	19 to 18	41 4/5	65	1 20	1 51	4 3/5	9 3/5
24 to 23	22 to 21	20 to 19	18 to 17	60 2/5	83 7/10	1 77 4/5	2 66	4 3/5	9 3/5
23 to 22	21 to 20	19 to 18	17 to 16	87 9/10	1 11 3/5	2 59	2 90	4 3/5	9 3/5
Under.	Under.	Under.	Under.	For each	franc less.	For each	franc less.	For each	fr. less.
22	20	18	16	27 9/10	27 9/10	83 1/5	83 1/5	4 3/5	9 3/5

Martinique, the hectolitre, (2.84 bushels,) 37 1-5 cents.

DUTIES—Continued.

COUNTRIES.	PRODUCT OF THE SOIL.		
	WHEAT.		
	United States.	Other countries.	Discrimination.
Great Britain and possessions.	24 cents per quarter, (8 bushels)	Same	None
	North American possessions: Generally free	Same	None
	West Indies: From 5 to 6 cents per bushel	Same	None
	Australian possessions: In some free; others 36 cents per quarter.	Same	None
	East Indies: Generally 14 cents per bushel	Same	None
Hayti	No definition given in the tariff	Same	
Hanse Towns	Hamburg: ½ of 1 per cent. ad valorem Bremen: ⅜ of 1 per cent. ad valorem Lubeck: 1 last, (91 bushels,) 43$\frac{1}{10}$ cts	Same	None
Holland and colonies	1 last, or 85. 20 bushels, $3 20	Same	If not the produce of the United States, subjected to discriminating duties.
	Dutch East Indies: 24 per cent. ad valorem; national and equalized vessels, 12 per cent. ad valorem.		
	Dutch Guiana and West Indies: 6 per cent. ad valorem; national and equalized vessels 3 per cent. ad valorem.		
Mexico	Prohibited, except for consumption of the frontier inhabitants, through the ports of Matamoras, Acapulco, and La Paz, in Lower California, and the custom-houses of Camargo, Mier, Piedras, Negras, Monterey, Laredo, and Paso del Norte.	Same	None
New Granada	Free	Same	None
Norway	1 toende, (3. 94 bushels,) 63 cts	Same	None
Papal States	If the price per rubbio (8. 36 bushels) is under $14, prohibited; under $15, $2; over $16, free.	Same	None
Peru	Specific duty of 75 cts. on a fanega of 135 bushels.	Same	None
Portugal	Wheat, and all other grain, are admitted only in small quantities for seed, and then they have to pay per 101 pounds $1 12, to which is to be added additional duty of 13 per cent. ad valorem.	Same	Portuguese colonial products pay only a fifth part of the duties.
Russia	On the Baltic sea, per chetwert, (5. 95 bushels,) $1 52; on the Black sea, 14 cts.	Same	None
Sandwich Islands	5 per cent. ad valorem	Same	None
Sardinia	Pr. hectolitre, (2. 84,) 46½ cts	Same	None

DUTIES—Continued.

COUNTRIES.	PRODUCT OF THE SOIL.		
	WHEAT.		
	United States.	Other countries.	Discrimination.
Spain and possessions	Prohibited, unless permitted by special order of the government.	Same	
	Cuba.—On a valuation of $5 per quintal (101 lbs.) Foreign produce, direct form the country of production, in Spanish vessels, 23½ per ct.; in foreign vessels, 33½ per cent.; from Spain, in Spanish vessels, 23½ per cent. Spanish produce, in foreign vessels, 17½ per cent.; in Spanish vessels, 7½ per cent.		26 per cent. on the fixed value in favor of Spanish wheat in Spanish vessels, against American wheat in American vessels.
	Porto Rico.—On a valuation of $5 per quintal. Foreign produce, direct from the country of production, in Spanish vessels, 20 per cent.; in foreign vessels, 29 per cent.; from Spain, in Spanish vessels, 20 per cent. Spanish produce, in foreign vessels, 15 per cent.; in Spanish vessels, 7 per cent.		22 per cent. on the fixed value in favor of Spanish against American vessels.
	Philippine Islands.—No definition given in the tariff.		
Sweden	Per 4. 157 bushels, 60 cents	Same	None
Switzerland	Per 110¼ pounds, 3 cents	Same	None
Turkey	5 per cent. ad valorem, (including the 2 per cent. ad valorem internal duty.)	Same	None
Tuscany	Per sack of 180 pounds, 92 cents	Same	None
Two Sicilies	Direct from the United States, in United States ships, or in national ships, per 192 pounds, 80 cents; in foreign and not equalized vessels, per 192 pounds, $1 60.		National and equalized vessels, on direct voyage, pay only half of what equalized and other foreign vessels, on indirect voyage, pay.
Uruguay	20 per cent. ad valorem	Same	None
Venezuela	For seed, free; otherwise, no definition given	Same	None
Zollverein	Per scheffel, 1½ bushels, 11½ cents	Same	None

DUTIES—Continued.

COUNTRIES.	PRODUCT OF THE SOIL.		
	FLOUR.		
	United States.	Other countries.	Discrimination
Argentine Republic	Foreign flour, per 101 pounds, $1 44	Free	Not exactly defined
Austria	Per centner, (110 pounds,) 36⅝ cents	Same	None
Belgium	Per 220 pounds, 57 cents; if not by a royal decree, entirely free, as, for example, from Aug. 28, 1853, until July 31, 1854, and from the last named period until December 31, 1855.	Same	None
Bolivia	28 per cent. ad valorem	Same	None
Brazil	25 per cent. ad valorem; (by latest tariff, 30 per cent. ad valorem.)	Same	None
Central America	*Costa Rica.*—Free *Guatemala.*—Per arroba, (25 pounds,) 25 cents *San Salvador.*—24 per cent. on a fixed value of $4 per quintal.	Same	None
Chili	If the price is under $4 per quintal, 25 per cent. ad valorem, and if over $4, free.	Same	None
China	5 per cent. ad valorem	Same	None
Denmark and colonies	Per toende, or 3. 94 bushels, 78 cents At St. Croix, per 110⅓ pounds, 60 cents	Same	None
Dominican Republic	25 per cent. on fixed valuation as follows: per barrel of 150 to 200 pounds, $5; Indian corn meal, per barrel of 150 to 200 pounds, $2.	Same	None
Equador	Per barrel or sack of 190 to 200 pounds, $7 50; of Indian corn, per barrel, $2.	Same	None
France and possessions	See Wheat In Algiers the same duties are levied as in the cities of class No. 2, (on the Mediterranean.) Martinique, per 220 pounds, $3 44½.		See Wheat
Great Britain and possessions.	9 cents per cwt	Same	None
	North American possessions.—In some free, in others 20 per cent. ad valorem, prior to reciprocity treaty.	Canada, 20 p. ct.	20 per cent. in favor of Great Great Britain, in Canada.
	West Indies.—Generally $1 44 per barrel		None
	Australian possessions.—Generally 36 cents per quarter, or 8 bushels.	Same	None
	East Indies.—Generally 5 per cent	Same	None
Hayti	Per barrel, $2	Same	10 per cent. ad val. wharfage duty, $1 per ton tonnage duty, and 6 per cent. consignment duty. Haytien ships are, with the exception of 2 per cent. consignment duty, exempt from these duties.

DUTIES—Continued.

COUNTRIES.	PRODUCT OF THE SOIL. FLOUR. United States.	Other countries.	Discrimination.
Hanse Towns	Hamburg.—½ of 1 per cent. ad valorem Bremen.—⅜ of 1 per cent. ad valorem Lubeck.—Per tonne, or 200 pounds, 3½ cents	Same	None
Holland and colonies	Per 221 pounds, $1 80 Dutch East Indies.—In national and equalized vessels, 12 per cent. ad valorem. Dutch Guiana and West Indies.—Per 221 pounds, 12 cts.; foreign, not equalized vessels, 24 cts.		If not the produce of the United States, and imported direct into Holland in American vessels, subject to discriminating duties.
Mexico	Prohibited, except for Yucatan, Tampico, Matamoras, and the custom-houses of the northern frontiers.	Same	None
New Granada	Free	Same	None
Norway	17.615 pounds, 14¼ cents; rye meal, free	Same	None
Papal States	If the price per rubbio, (8.36 bushels,) is under $16, prohibited; if over $16, $1 50; if over $17, 75 cents; if over $18, free.	Same	None
Peru	Specific duty of $2 per 101 pounds	Same	None
Portugal	No definition given in the late tariff, and most likely prohibited.		
Russia	On the Baltic sea, per chetwert, (5.95 bushels,) $3 37½; on the Black sea, 33⅜ cents.	Same	None
Sandwich Islands	5 per cent. ad valorem	Same	None
Sardinia	Per 220 pounds, 84 cents	Same	None
Spain and possessions	Prohibited, unless permitted by special order of the government.	Same	None
	Cuba— Spanish flour, in Spanish ships, a specific duty of $2 per barrel; in foreign ships, per barrel, $6. Foreign flour, in Spanish ships, per barrel, $8 50; in foreign vessels, per barrel, $9 50. To which is to be added, for foreign flour, an additional duty of 2 per cent. ad val, and 1 per cent. "balanza."		Here the duties on American produce amount almost to prohibition, as the discrimination between Spanish and American is alone in the tariff already $7 50 in favor of the former, besides 2 per cent. ad val. additional, 1 per cent. "balanza," tonnage, port charges, &c.
	Porto Rico— On a valuation of $12 50 per barrel Foreign flour, direct from the country of production, in Spanish vessels, 35¼ per cent.; in foreign vessels, 43¾ per ct.; from Spain, in Spanish vessels, 23¼ per cent. Spanish flour, in foreign vessels, 33 per cent.; in Spanish vessels, 6¾ per cent.		The customs duties, without considering port chargesand light-house dues, amount to 28½ per cent. ad val. in favor of Spain against the Unit.d States.

DUTIES—Continued.

COUNTRIES.	PRODUCT OF THE SOIL.		
	FLOUR.		
	United States.	Other countries.	Discrimination.
Spain and possess'ns—Continued.	To which is to be added, if consumed in the city of Porto Rico, a new duty of 88 cents per barrel, exclusive of light-house dues *Philippine Islands.*—No definition given in the tariff.		
Sweden	The same duty as that on the grain of which it is made, with the addition of 10 per cent. for grinding.	ame	None
Switzerland	Per 110¼ pounds, 9 cents	Same	None
Turkey	5 per cent. ad valorem, (including the 2 per cent. internal duty.)	Same	None
Tuscany	Per 74.86 pounds, 80 cents.		
Two Sicilies	In Sicilian or equalized vessels, per 192½ pounds, 80 cents; in foreign, not equalized vessels, per 192½ pounds, $1 60.	Same	If direct from United States, a deduction of 10 per cent. ad val.; if indirect, subjected to tonnage and other discriminating duties.
Uruguay	35 per cent. ad valorem	Same	None
Venezuela	Per barrel of 150 to 200 pounds, $4	Same	None
Zollverein	Per 110 pounds, $1 38	Same	None

DUTIES—Continued.

COUNTRIES.	PRODUCT OF THE SOIL.		
	INDIAN CORN.		
	United States.	Other countries.	Discrimination.
Argentine Republic	Per fanega, (2½ bushels,) 96 cents	Same	None
Austria	1 centner, (110 lbs.,) 12⅛ cents	Same	None
Belgium	Per 220 lbs., 13 cents	Same	None
Bolivia	28 per cent. ad valorem; if imported into the port of Iquique, only one half, viz: 14 per ct.	Same	None
Brazil	20 per cent. ad valorem	Same	None
Central America	Cost Rica.—Free Guatemala.—24 per cent. on the invoice value with an addition of 20 per cent.		
Chili	If the price is under $3 per fanega, (2.57 bush.,) 25 per cent. ad valorem, and if over $3, free.	Same	None
China	Free	Same	None
Denmark and colonies.	1 toende, or 3.94 bushels, 22⅛ cents	Same	None
Dominican Republic	25 per cent. on fixed valuation of $1 per barrel	Same	None
Equador	Per 101 lbs., $1	Same	None
France and possessions.	When wheat is 28 francs or more ($5 24.34) in the first class markets of France, 26 or more ($4 86.88) in the second, 24 or more ($4 49.42) in the third, and 22 or more ($4 11.98) in the the fourth, per hectolitre, (2.83$\frac{1}{10}$ bushels,) then the duty on Indian corn is 34¾ centimes (2.45 cents) per hectolitre, in each of those markets, and the duty on meal, per 100 kilograms, (220 lbs.,) is 30 centimes, (5.63 cents. The duty goes on increasing, in like manner, as the price of wheat decreases; and, when wheat is below 22 francs, ($4 11.98,) 20, ($3 74.53,) 18, ($3 37.07,) and 16, ($2 99.62,) in the standard markets, respectively, then the duty in each of the markets increases by 82½ centimes (15.35 cents) on each hectolitre of corn, by the decrease of each franc (18.73 cts.) in the price of the hectolitre of wheat, and by francs 2.20 (41.19 cents) on every kilogramme (2.20 pounds) of meal. See Wheat.		As product of the United States, and imported direct into France in the United States ships, the same duty is paid as in French ships. Imported indirectly, not as American produce, subjected to the same duty as in other foreign ships.

A table of French corn duties, exhibiting the prices and rates of duties on Indian corn, as regulated by the prices of wheat.

Regulating prices, per hectolitre of 2.84 bushels of Indian corn, in each of the four classes of customs frontier.				INDIAN CORN.					
				IMPORT DUTIES.				EXPORT DUTIES.	
				Upon Grain.		Upon Meal.			
1st class.	2d class.	3d class.	4th class.	French vessels or by land.	Foreign vessels.	French vessels or by land.	Foreign vessels.	Grain.	Meal.
Price above	*Price above*	*Price above*	*Price above*	*Per hectolitre*	*Per hectolitre.*	*Per* 100 *kil.*	*Per* 100 *kil.*	For each	fr. above.
Frs. 28	Frs. 26	Frs. 24	Frs. 22	\$0 $2\frac{3}{5}$	\$0 $2\frac{3}{5}$	\$0 $5\frac{1}{2}$	\$0 $5\frac{1}{2}$	\$0 $20\frac{2}{5}$	\$0 $44\frac{2}{5}$
28 to 27	26 to 25	24 to 23	22 to 21	$2\frac{3}{5}$	$25\frac{7}{10}$	$5\frac{1}{2}$	$34\frac{1}{2}$	61 [illegible]/10	1. 33
27 to 26	25 to 24	23 to 22	21 to 20	$2\frac{3}{5}$	$25\frac{7}{10}$	$5\frac{1}{2}$	$34\frac{1}{2}$	$40\frac{7}{10}$	$88\frac{4}{5}$
26 to 25	24 to 23	22 to 21	20 to 19	$12\frac{7}{10}$	$35\frac{9}{10}$	$38\frac{4}{5}$	$69\frac{3}{5}$	$20\frac{2}{5}$	$44\frac{2}{5}$
25 to 24	23 to 22	21 to 20	19 to 18	$22\frac{9}{10}$	$46\frac{1}{10}$	$72\frac{1}{5}$	1. $02\frac{9}{10}$	$2\frac{1}{2}$	$5\frac{1}{2}$
24 to 23	22 to 21	20 to 19	18 to 17	$33\frac{4}{5}$	$56\frac{3}{10}$	1. $05\frac{1}{2}$	1. 36	$2\frac{1}{2}$	$5\frac{1}{2}$
23 to 22	21 to 20	19 to 18	17 to 16	$48\frac{3}{10}$	$71\frac{2}{5}$	1. $55\frac{1}{2}$	1. 86	$2\frac{1}{2}$	$5\frac{1}{2}$
Under	Under	Under	Under	For each	franc less.	For each	franc less.	For each	fr. less.
22	20	18	16	$15\frac{1}{10}$	$15\frac{1}{10}$	50	50	$2\frac{1}{2}$	$2\frac{1}{2}$

In Algiers the same duties are levied as in the cities of class No. 2.

DUTIES—Continued.

COUNTRIES.	PRODUCT OF THE SOIL.		
	INDIAN CORN.		
	United States.	Other countries.	Discrimination.
Great Britain and possessions.	24 cents per quarter, = 8 bushels	Same	None
	North American possessions: Free	Free	None
	West Indies: Generally 6 cents per bushel	Same	None
	Australian possessions: Generally 24 cents per quarter, or 8 bushel.	Same	None
	East Indies: Generally 5 per cent	Same	None
Hayti	Per barrel, $1	Same	10 per cent. wharfage duty; $1 per ton, tonnage duty; and 6 per cent. ad valorem, consignment duty; of which duties Haytien vessels are free, with the exception of 2 per cent. consignment duty.
Hanse Towns	Hamburg: ½ of 1 per cent. ad valorem Bremen: ⅔ of 1 per cent. ad valorem Lubeck: ½ of 1 per cent. ad valorem	Same	None
Holland and colonies	Per last of 85. 20 bushels, $2 40	Same	If produce of the United States, and imported direct in United States vessels, none; otherwise, subject to discrimination duties.
	Dutch East Indies: 24 per cent ad valorem; national and equalized vessels, 12 per cent. ad valorem.		
	Dutch Guiana and West Indies: In Hollandish and equalized vessels, per 221 pounds, 4 cents; in foreign, not equalized, vessels, 8 cents.		
Mexico	Prohibited, except for the consumption of the inhabitants of the northern frontiers, and through the same custom-houses as are designated under the article Wheat.	Same	None
New Granada	Free	Same	None
Norway	1 ton or 300 bushels, 14 cents	Same	None
Papal States	If the price per rubbio (8. 36 bushels) is under $10, prohibited; over $10, $1 50; over $11, 75 cents; over $12, free.	Same	None
Peru	20 per cent. on a valuation of $1 50 per quintal, (101 pounds.)	Same	None
Portugal	Grain, in general, admitted only in small quantities for seed; the government, however, has lately been empowered by the Cortez to admit Indian corn, on account of the scarcity of this article in the country.	Same	From Portuguese colonies, free; American, $1 12 per 101 pounds.

DUTIES—Continued.

COUNTRIES.	PRODUCT OF THE SOIL.		
	INDIAN CORN.		
	United States.	Other countries.	Discrimination.
Russia	On the Baltic sea: Per chetwert, (5. 95 bushels,) \$1 87½. On the Black sea: Per chetwert, (5. 95 bushels,) 15 cents.	Same	None
Sandwich islands	5 per cent. ad valorem	Same	None
Sardinia	Per 100 kilogrammes, (220 pounds,) 18½ cents	Same	None
Spain and possessions	Prohibited, unless permitted by special order of the government.		
	Cuba—		
	Grain, on the valuation of \$4 per barrel of 200 pounds; meal, on the valuation of \$5 per barrel of 200 pounds.		26 per cent. on the fixed value in favor of Spanish product in Spanish vessels, against that of the United States in American vessels.
	Foreign produce, direct from the country of production, in Spanish ships, 23½ per cent.; in foreign ships, 33½ per cent.; from Spain, in Spanish ships, 23½ per cent.		
	Spanish produce, in foreign ships, 17½ per cent.; in Spanish ships, 7½ per cent.		
	Porto Rico—		
	Grain, on the valuation of \$2 50 per 3 bushels		22 per cent. on the fixed value in favor of Spain, against the United States.
	Foreign produce, direct from the country of production, in Spanish vessels, 20 per cent; in foreign vessels, 29 per cent.; from Spain, in Spanish vessels, 20 per cent.		
	Spanish produce, in foreign vessels, 15 per cent.; in Spanish vessels, 7 per cent.		
	Philippine Islands—		
	No definition given in the tariff.		
Sweden	1 tunna or 4. 157 bushels, 10 cents	Same	None
Switzerland	Per 110¼ pounds, 3 cents	Same	None
Turkey	5 per cent. ad valorem, (including the 2 per cent. ad valorem internal duty.)	Same	None
Tuscany	Per sack of 155 pounds, \$1 92	Same	None
Two Sicilies	Not defined in the tariff.		
Uruguay	30 per cent. ad valorem	Same	None
Venezuela	Free	Same	None
Zollverein	Per scheffel, (1½ bushel,) 11½ cents	Same	None

DUTIES—Continued.

COUNTRIES.	PRODUCT OF THE SOIL.		
	RICE.		
	United States.	Other countries.	Discrimination.
Argentine Republic	20 per cent. ad valorem	Same	None
Austria	Rice, per centner, 110 pounds, 36⅝ cents; paddy, per centner, 12½ cents.	Same	None
Belgium	From the United States, in United States vessels, per 220 pounds, 1.52 cent. The same in Belgian vessels.	Not equalized vessels have to pay per 220 pounds, $1 80.	For the direct trade, none; but for the indirect trade, 28 cents against the United States in favor of Belgium.
Bolivia	28 per cent. ad valorem	Same	None
Brazil	Most probably no importation at all. (By latest tariff, 20 per cent. ad valorem.)		
Central America	*Costa Rica.*—Not named in the tariff. *Guatemala.*—Per arroba, (25 pounds,) 24 cents. *San Salvador.*—24 per cent. on a fixed value of $3 per arroba, (25 pounds.)		
Chili	Carolina, 25 per cent on the valuation of $5 50 per 101 pounds; from other places, 25 per cent. on a valuation of $3 50 per 101 pounds.	Same	None
China	Free	Same	None
Denmark and colonies	Paddy, per 110¼ pounds, 43⅝ cents; rice meal, per 110¼ pounds, 96⅙ cents.	Same	None
Dominican Republic	25 per cent. on a fixed valuation of $3 per 101 lbs.	Same	None
Equador	Per 101 pounds, $3	Same	None
France and possessions	From the country of production, in national vessels, 46½ cents per 220 pounds. The same in foreign vessels, $1 67⅝ per 220 pounds. From Europe, in national vessels, 72⅝ per 220 pounds. The same in foreign vessels, $1 67⅝ per 220 pounds. From entrepots, in national vessels, $1 11⅞ per 220 pounds. The same in foreign vessels, $1 67⅝ per 220 pounds. Paddy is charged only one half of said duties. At Corsica, in national vessels, 18⅝ cents per 220 pounds; in foreign vessels, 20⅝ cents per 220 pounds. Algiers, Sardinian rice, in French vessels, 55⅝ cents per 220 pounds; Sardinian vessels, $1 48⅝ per 220 pounds; foreign vessels, $1 74⅝ per 220 pounds; from other places, the same as in France. Martinique, per 220 pounds, 75 cents.		As American produce, and imported direct in American bottoms, none; otherwise, subjected to the duty on foreign vessels.
Great Britain and possessions.	9 cents per cwt	Same	None
	North American Possessions: Generally free	Same	None

DUTIES—Continued.

COUNTRIES.	PRODUCT OF THE SOIL.		
	RICE.		
	United States.	Other countries.	Discrimination.
Great Britain and possessions—Cont'd.	West Indies: From 24 cents to 48 cents per cwt.	Same	None
	Australian Possessions: Generally 24 cents per cwt.	Same	None
	East Indies: Generally 14 cents per bushel	Same	None
Hayti	Per 108 pounds, 75 cents	Same	10 per cent. wharfage duty; $1 per ton tonnage duty, and 6 per cent. ad valorem consignment duty. Of these duties Haytien vessels are free, with the exception of 2 per cent. consignment duties.
Hanse Towns	Hamburg: ½ of 1 per cent. ad valorem Bremen: ⅜ of 1 per cent. ad valorem Lubec: ½ of 1 per cent. ad valorem	Same	None
Holland and colonies	Per 221 pounds, 12 cents	Same	If not the product of the United States, subject to discriminating duties.
	Dutch East Indies: No importation	Same	
	Dutch Guiana and West Indies: Per 221 pounds, 10 cents; foreign, not equalized vessels, 20 cts.		
Mexico	Prohibited	Same	None
New Granada	Free	Same	None
Norway	Paddy, per tunna, or 3 bushels, 72 cents; rice flour, 1 pound, 1¼ cent.	Same	None
Papal States	Per 74.86 pounds, 60 cents. *Note.*—Duty regulated by market price.	Same	None
Peru	Specific duty of $2 per quintal of 101 pounds	Same	None
Portugal	Per 101 pounds, $1 39; to which is to be added 13 per cent. ad valorem.	Same	From Portuguese colonies only a fifth part of the whole duty is to be levied.
Russia	On the Baltic Sea, per pood, (36 pounds,) 45 cts.; on the Black Sea, per pood, 15 cents.	Same	None
Sandwich Islands	5 per cent. ad valorem	Same	None
Sardinia	Per 220 pounds, 55½ cents	Same	None
Spain and possessions	Under the national flag, $1 69½ per quintal; under the foreign flag, $2 12.	Same	42½ cents per quintal in favor of Spain against the United States.
	Cuba—		
	On the valuation of $1 25 per arroba, (25 lbs.) Foreign produce, direct from the country of production, in Spanish vessels, 23½ per cent.; in foreign vessels, 33½ per cent.; from Spain, in Spanish vessels, 23½ per cent.		26 per cent. in favor of Spanish produce and flag against American.

DUTIES—Continued.

COUNTRIES.	PRODUCT OF THE SOIL.		
	RICE.		
	United States.	Other countries.	Discrimination.
Spain and possessions—Continued.	*Cuba*— Spanish produce, in foreign vessels, 17½ per cent.; in Spanish vessels, 7½ per cent. *Porto Rico*— On a valuation of $4 50 per quintal, (101 lbs.) Foreign produce, direct from the country of production, in Spanish vessels, 20 per cent.; in foreign vessels, 29 per cent.; from Spain, in Spanish vessels, 20 per cent. Spanish produce, in foreign vessels, 15 per cent.; in Spanish vessels, 7 per cent.	----------	22 per cent. on the fixed value in favor of Spain against the United States.
	Philippine Islands.—No definition given in the tariff.	Same	----------
Sweden	Paddy, 4. 157 bushels, 50 cents	Same	None
Switzerland	Per 110¼ pounds, 3 cents	Same	None
Turkey	5 per cent. ad valorem, (including the 2 per cent. internal duty.)	Same	None
Tuscany	Per 74. 86 pounds, 16 cents	Same	None
Two Sicilies	192½ pounds, $1 60	Same	If direct from the United States in United States vessels, a deduction of 10 per cent. ad valorem will be made; if indirect, subject to tonnage and other discriminating duties.
Urugay	20 per cent. ad valorem	Same	None
Venezuela	Free	Same	None
Zollverein	69 cents per 110 pounds; paddy, 46 cents per 110 pounds.	Same	None

DUTIES—Continued.

COUNTRIES.	PRODUCT OF THE SOIL.		
	TOBACCO.		
	United States.	Other countries.	Discrimination.
Argentine Republic	20 per cent. ad valorem	From Paraguay or from Corrientes, 10 per cent ad val.	14 per cent. ad val. against the United States in favor of Paraguay and Corrientes.
Austria	Being a monopoly of the government, it can only be imported by permission of the same. Leaf, per 110 pounds, $4 85; smoking, in rolls and cigars, per 110 pounds, $12 12½.	Same	Its monopoly of course in favor of Austria against all other countries.
Belgium	Leaf from Havana, Porto Rico, Columbia, in foreign vessels, per 220 pounds, $3 13; in Belgian or equalized vessels, per 220 pounds, $2 79. As produce of the United States, direct in United States or Belgian vessels, $1 86 per 220 pounds. Cigars, direct from the United States in Belgian vessels, $39; in vessels of countries of production, $41 80 per 220 pounds; indirect, or by other foreign vessels, $45 60 per 220 pounds.	Same	For product of the United States, in a direct trade, the United States vessels pay the same duties as Belgian. In the indirect trade, however, Belgian vessels are in favor against those of the United States. For products from Havana, Columbia, and any other country, Belgian vessels enjoy a discrimination over Am'n.
Bolivia	28 per cent. ad valorem	Same	None
Brazil	60 per cent. ad valorem. (By latest tariff, 30 to 40 per cent. ad valorem.)	Same	None
Central America	*Costa Rica.*—Tobacco can be imported on account of the government only, as it is a monopoly of the same. *Guatemala.*—24 per cent. on the invoice value, with an addition of 20 per cent. *San Salvador.*—A government monopoly.		
Chili	Tobacco, raw and unmanufactured, is a monopoly of the government. Paper cigars, 25 per cent. on a valuation of 31¼ cents per 1.014 pounds. Chewing tobacco, 25 per cent. on the valuation of 20 cents per 1.014 pounds. All other cigars pay a specific duty of 75 cents per 1.014 lbs.	Same	Raw tobacco as a monopoly of the government.
China	Tobacco, of all kinds, per picul, or 133⅓ pounds, 29⅗ cents.	Same	None
Denmark and colonies	Leaf, per 110⅓ pounds, 89⅗ cents; manufactured, per 110⅓ pounds, $3 15.	Same	None
Dominican Republic	25 per cent. on fixed value as follows:— Virginia, raw, per quintal, $16; in cigars, per mille, $5. Other, raw, per quintal, $20; in cigars, per mille, $10.	Same	None
Equador	Unmanufactured, per quintal, (101 pounds,) $10. Cigars from Cuba, per 1,000, $5.	Same	None

DUTIES—Continued.

COUNTRIES.	PRODUCT OF THE SOIL.		
	TOBACCO.		
	United States.	Other countries.	Discrimination.
France and possessions.	Tobacco is a monopoly in France, and imported for the government.	----------------	If American produce, and imported in American vessels direct to France, the same duties as on French vessels are to be paid; if, however, of foreign produce, or imported indirectly, American vessels have to pay the duty of foreign vessels.
	In leaves, from other than European countries on national ships, free.		
	Same in foreign ships, 1$\frac{4}{5}$ cts per 220 pounds....		
	From entrepots in national vessels, 93 cts. per 220 pounds.		
	From entrepots in foreign vessels, $1 01$\frac{4}{5}$ per 220 pounds.		
	Cigars and other manufactured tobacco, from other than European countries in national ships, free.		
	The same in foreign ships, $2 77$\frac{7}{10}$ per 220 pounds.		
	From entrepots in national vessels, $1 30$\frac{1}{5}$ per 220 pounds.	Same	
	From entrepots in foreign vessels, $2 77$\frac{7}{10}$ per 220 pounds.		
	All tobacco, whether in leaves or manufactured, if imported for private account, prohibited.		
	Corsica: Manufactured tobacco in national vessels, $18 52 per 100 kilogrammes, (220 lbs.;) in foreign vessels, $19 90 per 100 kilogrammes, (220 lbs.)		
	Algiers: From French entrepots 20 per cent. ad valorem; from foreign places, 25 per cent. ad valorem.		
	Martinique: In leaves, $3 72 per 220 pounds; manufactured, $5 58 per 220 pounds.		
Great Britain and possessions.	72 cents per lb., and 5 per cent. additional	Same	None ....
	North American possessions: From 2 to 3 cents per lb.	Same	None ....
	West Indies: From 6 cents per lb. to 20 per cent. ad valorem.	Same	None ....
	Australian possessions: From 12 to 18 cts. per lb.	Same	None ....
	East Indies: Generally $2 40 per cwt.	Same	None ....
Hayti	Leaf, per 1.014 lbs., 4 cents	Same	10 per cent. wharfage duty, $1 per ton tonnage duty, and 6 per cent. consignment duty. Haytien vessels are exempt from these duties, except 2 per cent. consignment duty.
	Chewing ... do ...... 3 cents		
	Cigars ..... do ..... 25 cents		

DUTIES—Continued.

COUNTRIES.	PRODUCT OF THE SOIL.		
	TOBACCO.		
	United States.	Other countries.	Discrimination.
Hanse Towns	Hamburg: ½ of 1 per cent. ad valorem		
	Bremen: ⅜ of 1 per cent. ad valorem	Same	None
	Lubeck: ½ of 1 per cent. ad valorem		
Holland and colonies	Leaf, per 221 lbs., 28 cents	Same	If not imported direct from the United States, subject to discriminating duties.
	Cigars, per 221 lbs., $16		
	Other manufactures, per 221 lbs., $4 80		
	Dutch East Indies: Leaf, 1.037 lb., 6¼ cents		
	Cigars, Havana, 1.037 lbs., 80 cents		
	Cigars, other, 1.037 lbs., 20 cents		
	Dutch Guiana and West Indies: National and equalized vessels, 12 cents per 221 lbs.		
Mexico	Tobacco of all kinds can be imported on demand only, or by special license, of the government, being a monopoly.	Same	None
New Granada	Cigars, per 1 kilogramme, (2⅕ lbs.,) $0 80		
	Cigarillos....do............do.... 1 00	Same	None
	Tobacco, unmanufactured....do.... 20		
Norway	Leaf, 1 lb., 4½ cents	Same	None
	Manufactured, per lb., $8\frac{9}{10}$ cents	Same	None
Papal States	Leaf, per 74.86 lbs., $8 10		
	In rolls....do......10 00		
Peru	Specific duty of $20 on a quintal of 101 lbs	Same	None
Portugal	The importation of tobacco belongs exclusively to the Royal Contract Company.	Same	No privilege exists for United States shipping.
Russia	On the Baltic Sea, leaf, per 36 lbs., $4 50	Same	None
	On the Black Sea......do........93¾ cents	Same	None
	On the Baltic, manufactured, 1 lb., 45 cents	Same	None
	On the Black.......do......do..7½ to 18½ cts.	Same	None
Sandwich Islands	5 per cent. ad valorem	Same	None
Sardinia	Snuff, Spanish, per kilogramme, (2.204 lbs.,) $2 22	Same	None
	Cigars, Havana......do.........do...... 3 70	Same	None
Spain and possessions	Prohibited.—Virginia cigars and tobacco are admitted in the port of Malaga at the following rates of duty: Cigars, in Spanish vessels, 25 cents; in American vessels, 33⅓ cents per lb; raw tobacco, in Spanish vessels, 15 cents; in American vessels, 20 cents per pound.	Same	None
	Cuba—Leaf can be imported at the deposit only, and then on a valuation of $6 per quintal—2 per cent. from all countries. Snuff, on a valuation of $25 per quintal. Foreign produce, direct from the country of production, in Spanish vessels, 23½ per ct.; in foreign vessels, 33½ per cent.; from Spain, in Spanish vessels, 23½ per cent.		On the importation of leaf tobacco, none. Snuff pays, as Spanish product and in Spanish vessels, 26 per ct. on the fixed value less than American produce on American vessels.

DUTIES—Continued.

COUNTRIES.	PRODUCT OF THE SOIL.		
	TOBACCO.		
	United States.	Other countries.	Discrimination.
Spain and possessions—Continued.	*Cuba*—Continued. Spanish produce, in foreign vessels, 17½ per cent.; in Spanish vessels, 7½ per cent.		
	Porto Rico—Leaf tobacco from Virginia pays a fixed duty of $4 per quintal; from St. Domingo, $5 per quintal; from Cuba, $3 per quintal; manufactured in cigars, from foreign countries, $5 per 1,000; from Cuba, $2 per 1,000.	....	Leaf tobacco in Cuba is in favor by $1 on a valuation of $20 per quintal, against that of the United States on a valuation of only $8 per quintal. Cigars from Cuba pay, on a valuation of $10 per 1,000, $3 less than American, on a valuation of only $3 per 1,000.
	Philippine Islands—Tobacco, as product of the foreign possessions of Asia, can be admitted in entrepot only.		
Sweden	Leaf, 1 pound, 5⅝ cents; manufactures of, per pound, 11⅜ cents.	Same	None
Switzerland	Leaf, per 110¼ pounds, 64 cents; smoking, in rolls, do., $1 48; cigars, do., $2 78.		
Turkey	Virginia, in leaf, 5 per cent. ad valorem, including the 2 per cent. ad valorem.	Same	None
Tuscany	Leaf, $1 10½ per 74.86 pounds.		
Two Sicilies	Leaf prohibited.—Manufactures of, per 192½ lbs., $14 40.	Same	If in Sicilian vessels or direct from the United States in United States vessels, a deduction of 10 per cent. will be made; otherwise, tonnage and discriminating duties are to be paid.
Uruguay	Leaf, 25 per cent. ad valorem; snuff and other, 30 per cent. ad valorem.	Same	None
Venezuela	Cigars, from Havana, per 1,000, $3; raw tobacco, 1.014 pound, 10 cents. Virginia, St. Domingo, Porto Rico, in cigars, per 1,000, $2; same, not manufactured, 101 lbs., $6.	Same	None
Zollverein	Leaf, $2 76 per 110 pounds; smoking, in rolls, $7 59 per 110 pounds; cigars and snuff, $13 80 per 110 pounds.	Same	None

DUTIES—Continued.

COUNTRIES.	PRODUCT OF THE SOIL.		
	COTTON—RAW.		
	United States.	Other countries.	Discrimination.
Argentine Republic	15 per cent. ad valorem	Same	None
Austria	Free	Same	None
Belgium	In Belgian and United States vessels, *direct* from the United States, per 220 pounds, ⅛ cent; in United States vessels, *indirect*, from other places, per 220 pounds, 31½ cents. (*Note.*—By law of 12th April, 1854, cotton (raw) is made free of duty.)	In vessels of the countries of production, not equalized, per 220 lbs., 31½ cts.	In the direct trade, and as home produce, none. In the indirect trade 31⅝ cts. per 110 lbs. against the United States in favor of Belgium.
Bolivia	28 per cent. ad valorem	Same	None
Brazil	Not named, as there is no importation. (By latest tariff, 5 per cent. ad valorem.)	Same	None
Central America	*Costa Rica.*—Per quintal, $1 (with the seed)	From Central America, 25 cts.	Discrimination in favor of Central America, 75 cents.
	Per quintal, $3 (without seed)	From Central America, 75 cts.	Discrimination in favor of Central America, $2 25.
	Guatemala.—No importation. *San Salvador.*—Not defined.		
Chili	Not picked, 25 per cent. on the valuation of $4 per quintal, (101 pounds,) and picked, 25 per cent. on the valuation of $8 per quintal.	Same	None
China	Per picul, (133⅓ pounds,) 59⅝ cents	Same	None
Denmark and colonies	Free	Same	None
Dominican Republic	Not mentioned in the tariff, as there is no importation of raw cotton.	Same	None
Equador	Per quintal, 50 cents	Same	None
France and possessions	From French colonies, in national vessels, free. From countries out of Europe, in national vessels, $3 72 per 220 pounds; the same in foreign vessels, $6 51 per 220 pounds; from entrepots, in national vessels, $5 58 per 220 pounds; in foreign vessels, $6 51 per 220 pounds. Corsica and Algiers the same as in France.		American cotton imported in American bottoms direct to France pays the same duties as in French vessels; on indirect trade it pays the same as in other foreign vessels. If, however, the vessel touch at a British port, it will in this instance be considered as if on direct voyage.
Great Britain and possessions.	North American possessions: Free	Free	None
	West Indies: Generally free	Free	None
	Australian possessions: Generally 5 per cent	Same	None
	East Indies: Generally 5 per cent	Same	None
Hayti	Cotton is a monopoly of the government and a home product of the island; therefore no importation.	Same	None

DUTIES—Continued.

COUNTRIES.	PRODUCT OF THE SOIL.		
	COTTON—RAW.		
	United States.	Other countries.	Discrimination.
Hanse Towns	Hamburg: ½ of 1 per cent. ad valorem Bremen: ⅔ of 1 per cent. ad valorem Lubeck: ¼ of 1 per cent. ad valorem	Same	
Holland and colonies	Free Dutch East Indies: 2 per ct. ad val.; Hollandish and equalized vessels, one-half of these duties. Dutch Guiana and West Indies: National and equalized vessels, 3 per cent. ad valorem; other foreign, 6 per cent. ad valorem.	Same	If not the produce of the United States, subject to discriminating duties.
Mexico	Free of internal taxes; external, $1 50 per quintal, (101 pounds.)	Same	None
New Granada	Picked, per kilogramme, (2⅕ pounds,) 15 cents; not picked, per kilogramme, 5 cents.	Same	None
Norway	1 pound, ½ cent	Same	None
Papal States	Per 74.78 pounds, 10 cents	Same	None
eru	Not picked, 1 per cent. on a valuation of $4 per quintal, (101 pounds;) picked, 1 per cent. on a valuation of $8 per quintal.	Same	None
Portugal	Per 100 arratels, or 101 pounds, 2⅔ cents, to which is to be added 13 per cent. ad valorem extra duty.	Portuguese colonial product, free.	None if imported direct
Russia	On the Baltic sea, per 36 pounds, 18¾ cents; Black sea, free.	Same	None
Sandwich Islands	5 per cent. ad valorem	Same	None
Sardinia	Free	Same	None
Spain and possessions	From Spanish colonies.—In Spanish vessels, 37 cents per quintal; in foreign vessels, $1 32½ per quintal. From countries producing cotton.—In Spanish vessels, 79½ cents per quintal; in foreign vessels, $1 85 per quintal. From countries not producing cotton.—In Spanish vessels, $2 12 per quintal; in foreign vessels, $3 20 per quintal. Cotton not picked pays only ½ of these duties.		Cotton from the Spanish colonies, if imported in Spanish vessels, pays $1 48 per quintal less than American, in United States vessels.
	Cuba— Picked, on a valuation of $10 per quintal, (101 pounds;) not picked, do., $5 per do. Foreign produce, direct from the country of production, in Spanish ships, 19½ per cent.; in foreign ships, 27½ per cent.; from Spain, in Spanish ships, 19½ per cent. Spanish or colonial produce, in foreign ships, 14½ per cent.; in Spanish ships, 7½ per ct.		20 per ct. on the fixed value in favor of Spanish production on Spanish vessels, against production of the United States in United States vessels.

DUTIES—Continued.

COUNTRIES.	PRODUCT OF THE SOIL.		
	COTTON.		
	United States.	Other countries.	Discrimination.
Spain and possess'ns—Continued.	*Porto Rico—* Picked, on a valuation of $10 per quintal, (101 pounds;) not picked, do., $5 per do. Foreign produce, direct from the country of production, in Spanish vessels, 16 per ct.; in foreign vessels, 23 per cent.; from Spain, in Spanish vessels, 16 per cent. Spanish or colonial produce, in foreign vessels, 12 per cent.; in Spanish ships, 7 per cent. *Philippine Islands.*—No definition given in the tariff.		16 per ct. on the fixed value in favor of Spain against the United States.
Sweden	Free	Same	None
Switzerland	110¼ pounds, 6 cents	Same	None
Turkey	5 per cent. ad valorem, (including the 2 per cent. ad valorem internal duty.)		
Tuscany	Free	Same	None
Two Sicilies	In national or American vessels, direct from the United States, per 192½ pounds, $8; American vessels, indirect, or other foreign vessels, $16 per 192½ pounds.	Same	Equalized vessels, on direct voyage with products of their countries, enjoy a deduction of 10 per cent. ad valorem.
Uruguay	20 per cent. ad valorem	Same	None
Venezuela	No definition given in the tariff	Same	None
Zollverein	Free	Same	None

DUTIES—Continued.

COUNTRIES.	PROVISIONS.		
	BEEF.		
	United States.	Other countries.	Discrimination.
Argentine Republic	By sea, 20 per cent. ad valorem; by land, jerked beef, free.	Same	None
Austria	Fresh or salted, 110 pounds, 36⅝ cents; smoked do., $1 21¼.	Same	None
Belgium	Per 220 pounds, 93 cents	Same	None
Bolivia	Free	Same	None
Brazil	Dry, 1 arroba, (25 pounds,) 23½ cents; salted, do, 35¼ cents. (By latest tariff from 15 to 30 per cent. ad valorem.)	Same	None
Central America	Costa Rica, per 101 pounds, 62½ cents	Same	None
	Guatemala, salted, 1 arroba, (25 pounds,) 48 cts.		
Chili	Salted, free	Same	None
China	5 per cent. ad valorem	Same	None
Denmark and colonies	Smoked, $1 09¾ for 133⅓ pounds	Same	None
Dominician Republic	25 per cent. on fixed valuation, as follows: Salted, per barrel, $12; smoked, per 101 pounds, $18; on St. Croix, smoked, salted, dried, per 110⅓ pounds, $1 25.	Same	None
Equador	Salted, per quintal, (101 pounds,) $2	Same	None
France and possessions	Salted, per 100 kilogrammes, (220 pounds,) 9$\frac{3}{10}$ cents.	Same	None
	Martinique, salt beef $1 86 per 220 pounds	Same	None
Great Britain and possessions.	Free	Free	None
	North American possessions: Free	Same	None
	West Indies: Generally $2 40 per cwt.	Same	None
	Australian possessions: Generally 36 cts. per cwt	Same	None
	East Indies: Generally free	Same	None
Hayti	Salted, per barrel, $1	Same	10 per cent. ad valorem wharfage; $1 per ton, tonnage; and 6 per cent. ad valorem consignment duty. Haytien vessels are exempt from these duties, with the exception of 2 per cent. consignment duty.
	Smoked, per 108 lbs., $1 50		
Hanse Towns	Hamburg: ½ of 1 per cent. ad valorem	Same	None
	Bremen: ⅝ of 1 per cent. ad valorem	Same	None
	Lubeck: ½ of 1 per cent. ad valorem	Same	None
Holland and colonies	Salted, $2 40 per 221 lbs.	Same	If not the produce of the United States, subject to discriminating duties.
	Smoked, $3 20 per 221 lbs		
	Dutch East Indies: Hollandish and equalized vessels, 24 per cent.; other, foreign, 24 per ct.	Same	

DUTIES—Continued.

COUNTRIES.	PROVISIONS.		
	BEEF.		
	United States.	Other countries.	Discrimination.
Holland and colonies—Continued.	Dutch Guiana and West Indies: Dutch and equalized vessels, 16 cents per 221 lbs.; other, foreign, 30 cents per 221 lbs.		
Mexico	$5 per 101 lbs	Same	None
New Granada	Free	Same	None
Norway	Dried, 1 lb., 1⅓ cent	Same	None
Papal States	Prohibited	Same	None
Peru	3 per cent. on a valuation of $6 50 per quintal, (101 lbs.;) salted, free.	Same	None
Portugal	Salted and smoked, per 101 lbs., $3 36	Same	If direct from the United States, in United States vessels, none; but from the Portuguese colonies in national vessels, only one-fifth of the duties is levied.
Russia	Per 1 pood, (36 lbs.,) $1 50, on the Baltic Sea	Same	None
	Do do 45 cts., on the Black Sea	Same	None
Sandwich Islands	5 per cent. ad valorem	Same	None
Sardinia	Fresh, per 100 kilogrammes or 220 lbs., 92½ cts.	Same	None
	Salted do do $1 80½	Same	None
Spain and possessions	Salted, on national vessels, 31¾ cents per arroba, (25 pounds 7 oz.;) on foreign vessels, 38¼ cts., per arroba.		6½ cents per arroba in favor of the Spanish flag against that of other nations.
	Cuba.—Salted, on a valuation of $9 per barrel of 200 pounds; smoked, $1 75 per arroba (25 lbs. 7 oz.)— Foreign produce, direct from the country of production, in Spanish vessels, 23½ per cent.; in foreign vessels, 33½ per ct.; from Spain, in Spanish vessels, 23½ per cent. Spanish produce, in foreign vessels, 17½ per cent.; in Spanish vessels, 7½ per cent.		26 per cent. on the fixed value in favor of Spanish products and shipping against other nations.
	Jerked, from Buenos Ayres and Brazil, on a valuation of $5 50 per quintal; from Campeche, Costa Firma, and Tampico, $1 25 per arroba, (25 pounds 7 oz.;) from the United States, $6 50 per quintal, 101 lbs.: Direct from the country of production, in Spanish vessels, 19½ per cent.; in foreign vessels, 27½ per cent.		8 per cent. on the fixed value in favor of the Spanish flag against other nations.

DUTIES—Continued.

COUNTRIES.	PROVISIONS.		
	BEEF.		
	United States.	Other countries.	Discrimination.
Spain and possessions—Continued	*Cuba.*—Continued.		
	Upon jerked beef from the United States and Campeche, Costa Firma and Tampico, there is a deduction of 6 per cent., and upon that from Buenos Ayres and Brazil a deduction of 14 per cent.		On jerked beef, 8 per cent. in favor of Buenos Ayres against the United States.
	Porto Rico —Salted, on a valuation of $9 per bbl. Foreign produce, direct from the country of production, in Spanish vessels, 17½ per cent.; in foreign vessels, 23½ per cent.; from Spain, in Spanish vessels, 14¼ per ct. Spanish produce, in foreign vessels, 15 per cent; in Spanish vessels, 7 per cent.		16½ per cent. on the fixed value in favor of Spanish vessels and produce against those of other nations.
	Jerked beef from the United States on a valuation of $7 per quintal; from Buenos Ayres and Brazil, $6; from Campeche, Costa Firma, and Tampico, $5 per quintal: Foreign produce, direct from the country of production, in Spanish vessels, 16 per ct.; in foreign vessels, 23 per cent.		7 per cent. in favor of Spanish against foreign shipping.
	Jerked beef from the United States and Campeche, Costa Firma and Tampico, is subject to a deduction of 6 per cent., and from Buenos Ayres and Brazil to a deduction 14 per cent.		Upon jerked beef, 8 per cent. in favor of Buenos Ayres against the United States.
	Philippine Islands.—Not named in the tariff		
Sweden	Per lispund, (18¾ pounds,) 6⅔ cents	Same	None
Switzerland	Salted or smoked, per 110¼ pounds, 65 cents	Same	None
Turkey	Salted, 1 cantar = 127 pounds, 7½ cents, and 2 per cent. ad valorem internal duty.	Same	None
Tuscany	Fresh, per 74.86 pounds, 50¼ cents; salted or smoked, per 74.86 pounds, $1 20.	Same	None
Two Sicilies	Free	Same	None
Uruguay	30 per cent. ad valorem	Same	None
Venezuela	Per 1.014 pound, 2 cents	Same	None
Zollverein	Salted, per 110 pounds, $1 38	Same	None

DUTIES—Continued.

COUNTRIES.	PROVISIONS.		
	PORK.		
	United States.	Other countries.	Discrimination.
Argentine Republic	20 per cent. ad valorem	Same	None
Austria	Fresh and salted, per 110 pounds, 36⅝ cents; smoked, per 110 pounds, $1 21¼.	Same	None
Belgium	Smoked ham, per 220 pounds, $2 77	Same	None
	Lard and other, per 220 pounds, 93 cents	Same	None
Bolivia	Free	Same	None
Brazil	Salted, per arroba, (25 pounds,) 47 cts.; smoked, per pound, 2¾ cts. (By latest tariff from 15 to 30 per cent. ad valorem.)	Same	None
Central America	*Costa Rica:* Per 101 pounds, 62½ cts.	Same	None
	Guatemala: Salted, per arroba, (25 pounds,) 50 cts.	Same	None
	San Salvador: 24 per cent. on a fixed value of $5 per quintal.	Same	None
Chili	Salted; free	Same	None
China	5 per cent. ad valorem	Same	None
Denmark and colonies	Salted, per 110⅓ pounds, 54½ cents; smoked, per 110⅓ pounds, $1 09¼.	Same	None
	On St. Croix bacon, smoked or salted, 80 cents per 110⅓ pounds.	Same	None
Dominican Republic	Salted, 25 per cent. on fixed value of $12 per barrel.	Same	None
Equador	Salted, per 101 pounds, $2	Same	None
France and possessions	Salted, per 220 pounds, 9$\frac{3}{10}$ cents; bacon, per 220 pounds, 9$\frac{3}{10}$ cents.	Same	As American produce in U. S. vessels direct to France, none; indirectly, and not as American produce, U. S. vessels pay the same duty as other foreign ships.
	Corsica: Salted, on national vessels, $1 86 per 220 pounds; on foreign vessels, $2 04⅗ per 220 pounds.		
	Martinique: Salted, on national vessels, $1 86 per 220 pounds; on foreign vessels, $2 04⅗ per 220 pounds.		
Great Britain and possessions.	Free	Free	None
	North American possessions: Free	Free	None
	West Indies: Generally $4 80 per barrel of 200 pounds.	Same	None
	Australian possessions: Generally 48 cents per barrel.	Same	None
	East Indies: Generally 5 per cent	Same	None
Hayti	Same as Beef.		
Hanse Towns	Hamburg: ½ of 1 per cent. ad valorem Bremen: ⅚ of 1 per cent. ad valorem Lubeck: ½ of 1 per cent. ad valorem	Same	None

DUTIES—Continued.

COUNTRIES.	PROVISIONS.		
	PORK.		
	United States.	Other countries.	Discrimination.
Holland and colonies	Salted, per 221 pounds, 20 cents; smoked, per 221 pounds, 26 cents. Dutch East Indies: Free. Dutch Guiana and West Indies: Hollandish and equalized vessels, 20 cents per 221 pounds; other foreign, not equalized, 40 cents per 221 pounds.	Same	If not the product of the United States, subjected to discriminating duties.
Mexico	$5 per 101 pounds		None
New Granada	Free	Same	None
Norway	Salted, $2\frac{1}{4}$ cents	Same	None
Papal States	Smoked, per 74.86 pounds, $2 50	Same	None, if imported direct from the United States.
Peru	3 per cent. on a valuation of $7 per 101 pounds; salted, free.	Same	None
Portugal	Salted, $3 36 per 101 pounds	Same	If direct from the United States, on United States ships, none; from Portuguese possessions, only one-fifth of the whole duty is to be paid.
Russia	On the Baltic sea: Salted, per pood, (36 pounds,) $1 50. On the Black sea: Salted, per pood, (36 pounds,) 45 cents.	Same	None
Sandwich Islands	5 per cent. ad valorem	Same	None
Sardinia	Fresh, per 100 kilogrammes, (220 pounds,) $92\frac{1}{2}$ cents; salted, per 100 kilogrammes, (220 pounds,) $1 86.	Same	None
Spain and possessions	Salted, in Spanish vessels, $31\frac{3}{4}$ cents per arroba, (25 pounds 7 oz.;) salted, in foreign vessels, $38\frac{1}{4}$ cents per arroba, (25 pounds 7 oz.;) smoked, in Spanish vessels, $63\frac{1}{2}$ cents per arroba, (25 pounds 7 oz.;) smoked, in foreign vessels, $76\frac{1}{4}$ cents per arroba, (25 pounds 7 oz.) *Cuba*— Salted, on a valuation of $12 per barrel of 200 pounds; smoked, on a valuation of $2 per arroba, (25 pounds 7 oz.)		Salted, $6\frac{1}{2}$ cents per arroba; smoked, $12\frac{3}{4}$ per cent. in favor of the Spanish against foreign flags.
	Foreign produce, direct from the country of production, in Spanish vessels, $23\frac{1}{2}$ per cent.; in foreign vessels, $33\frac{1}{2}$ per cent.; from Spain, in Spanish vessels, $23\frac{1}{2}$ per cent. Spanish produce, in foreign vessels, $17\frac{1}{2}$ per cent.; in Spanish vessels, $7\frac{1}{2}$ per cent.		26 per cent. on the fixed value in favor of Spanish produce and shipping against that of other nations.

DUTIES—Continued.

COUNTRIES.	PROVISIONS.		
	PORK.		
	United States.	Other countries.	Discrimination.
Spain and possessions—Continued.	*Porto Rico—*		
	Salted, on a valuation of $15 per barrel		16½ per cent. on the fixed value in favor of Spanish produce and shipping against the United States.
	Foreign produce, direct from the country of production, in Spanish vessels, 17¼ per cent.; in foreign vessels, 23½ per cent.; from Spain, in Spanish vessels, 14½ per cent.		
	Spanish produce, in foreign vessels, 15 per cent.; in Spanish vessels, 7 per cent.		
	Smoked, on a valuation of $9 per quintal, (101 pounds.)		22 per cent. in favor of Spanish products and shipping against other nations.
	Foreign produce, direct from the country of production, in Spanish vessels, 20 per cent.; in foreign vessels, 29 per cent.; from Spain, in Spanish vessels, 20 per cent.		
	Spanish produce, in foreign vessels, 15 per cent.; in Spanish vessels, 7 per cent.		
	Philippine Islands—		
	Not named in the tariff.		
Sweden	Per lispund, (18¾ pounds,) 20 cents	Same	None
Switzerland	Salted, per 110¼ pounds, 27½ cents	Same	None
Turkey	5 per cent. ad valorem, (including the 2 per cent. internal duty.)	Same	None
Tuscany	Salted, per 74. 86 pounds, 80 cents	Same	None
Two Sicilies	Salted, free	Same	None
Uruguay	30 per cent. ad valorem.		
Venezuela	Salted or smoked, per 1. 014 pound, 2½ cents	Same	None
Zollverein	Salted, per 110 pounds, $1 38	Same	None

DUTIES—Continued.

COUNTRIES.	MANUFACTURES.		
	COTTON GOODS.		
	United States.	Other countries.	Discrimination.
Argentine Republic	Fustians, 15 per cent. ad valorem	Same	None
Austria	Yarn, unmixed, or mixed with wool or linen, one or two threads, 110 pounds, $2 91; common manufactures, 110 pounds, $20; fine, $40.	Same	None
Belgium	Plain, not colored, 220 pounds, $33 37; colored and printed, 220 pounds, $60 18; drills, 220 pounds, $25 92.	Same	None
Bolivia	28 per cent. ad valorem	Same	None
Brazil	30 per cent. ad valorem. (By latest tariff, 10 to 30 per cent. ad valorem.)	Same	None
Central America	*Costa Rica.*—Manufactured, bleached, 1.014 lbs., 7 cents; drills, white, 1.014 pounds, 8 cents; 'rills, striped and printed, 8 cents. Cotton oods, unbleached, 1.014 pounds, 5 cents. Lace, per 1. 4 pounds, 25 cents. *Guatemala.*—Handkerchiefs, common. $1 per doz.; fine, $2. Stockings, common, 42 cents per dozen; fine, 72 cents. Stockings for women, common, 30 cents per dozen; fine, 48 cents. Drill, up to 32 inches wide, per yard, 2½ cents; drill, colored, up to 32 inches wide, per yard, 3 cents.	Same	None
Chili	25 per cent. ad valorem	Same	None
China	Cambrics and muslins, 20 to 24 yards long, and 40 to 46 inches wide, per piece, 22½ cents; gray, or unbleached, viz: long cloth, domestics, &c., &c., 30 to 40 yards long, and 28 to 40 inches wide, per piece, 14⅘ cents.	Same	None
Denmark and colonies	Printed manufactures, per 110⅓ pounds, $17 45; bleached and unbleached, per 110⅓ pounds, $8 17½. On St. Croix, 12½ per cent. ad val.	Same	None
Dominican Republic	25 per cent. on fixed valuation as follows:— Fustian, per yard, 4 cents; finer sort, 5 cents. alico, fine, per yard, 6 cents; common, 4 cents. Bleached or unbleached, according to breadth, per yard, 2 to 8 cents.	Same	None
Equador	Drills, per yard, 2½ cents; shirtings, per yard, 2 cents; Osnaburgs, per yard, 2 cents.	Same	None
France and possessions	Nankeen, except from India and in French vessels, prohibited. Laces and tulles, 5 per cent. ad valorem both for French and foreign vessels. All other kinds are prohibited.		If direct from the United States as home productions and in United States ships, and not prohibited, the same duty as in French.

DUTIES—Continued.

COUNTRIES.	MANUFACTURES.		
	COTTON GOODS.		
	United States.	Other countries.	Discrimination.
France and possessions—Continued.	*Algiers.*—White, of 15 to 20 threads, on French vessels, $25\frac{9}{10}$ cents per $2\frac{1}{4}$ pounds; on foreign vessels, $27\frac{9}{10}$ cents per $2\frac{1}{4}$ pounds. White, 20 to 25 threads, on French vessels, $55\frac{4}{5}$ cents per $2\frac{1}{4}$ pounds; on foreign vessels, $56\frac{2}{5}$ cents per $2\frac{1}{4}$ pounds. White, 25 threads and upwards, on French vessels, \$1 54 per $2\frac{1}{4}$ pounds; on foreign vessels, \$1 69 per $2\frac{1}{4}$ pounds. Colored and printed, of 15 to 20 threads, on French vessels, $31\frac{1}{2}$ cents per $2\frac{1}{4}$ pounds; on foreign vessels, $33\frac{1}{2}$ cents per $2\frac{1}{4}$ pounds. 20 to 25 threads, on French vessels, $46\frac{1}{2}$ cents per $2\frac{1}{4}$ pounds; on foreign vessels, $50\frac{1}{2}$ cents per $2\frac{1}{4}$ pounds. 25 threads and upwards, on French vessels, 93 cents per $2\frac{1}{4}$ pounds; on foreign vessels, \$1 $02\frac{1}{3}$ per $2\frac{1}{4}$ pounds. *Martinique.*—Prohibited importation in other than French vessels.		vessels. If, however, of foreign production, and not direct from the United States, the duties designed for foreign ships must be paid.
Great Britain and possessions.	5 per cent.	Same	None
	North American possessions: $12\frac{1}{2}$ per cent.	Same	None
	West Indies: From $3\frac{1}{2}$ to 5 per cent.	Same	None
	Australian possessions: Generally 10 per cent.	Same	None
	East Indies: Generally 5 per cent.	Same	None
Hayti	Fustian, 24 inches broad, per yard 4 cents; do., of superior quality, 5 cents. Bleached or unbleached cloths, according to breadth, 2 to 8 cents per yard. Calico, fine, 6 cents per yard; common, 4 cents per yard.	Same	10 per cent. wharfage duty, \$1 per ton tonnage duty, 6 per cent. consignment duty; of which duties, except 2 per cent. consignment duty, Haytien vessels are free.
Hanse Towns	Hamburg: $\frac{1}{2}$ of 1 per cent. ad valorem Bremen: $\frac{2}{3}$ of do do Lubeck: $\frac{1}{2}$ of do do	Same	None
Holland and colonies	6 per cent. ad valorem	Same	If not the production of the United States, subject to discriminating duties.
	Dutch East Indies: 25 per cent. ad valorem. Hollandish and equalized vessels pay only one half of this duty. Dutch Guiana and West Indies: 6 per cent. ad valorem. Hollandish and equalized vessels only 3 per cent.		

DUTIES—Continued.

COUNTRIES.	MANUFACTURES.		
	COTTON GOODS.		
	United States.	Other countries.	Discrimination.
Mexico	Bleached and unbleached cloths, ribbed and plain, not exceeding thirty threads, at and under one vara wide, per vara, (yard,) 3 cents. The same, exceeding thirty threads, 5 cents per yard. Stockings of all kinds, for grown persons, from 30 to 48 cents per dozen.		None
New Granada	Manufactured into shawls, stockings, gloves, &c., 25 cents per 1.014 pound; muslins, gauzes, shawls, &c., 34⅝ cents per 1.014 pound; all other manufactures 14 cents per pound.	Same	None
Norway	Bleached and unbleached, from 9 to 22 cents per 1.014 pound.	Same	None
Papal States	Spun, not colored, 74.86 pounds, $1; threaded and colored, do., $3; all articles of, do., $12.	Same	None
Peru	Manufactures of, as fustians up to 4 yards width, the dozen yards, 15 per cent. on a valuation of $6.		None
Portugal	Manufactures of, 1 pound, 6 to 70 cents; to which is to be added an additional duty of 13 per cent. ad valorem.	Same	As American produce, imported direct from the United States, none. Goods from Portuguese colonies pay only the fifth part of these duties.
Russia	Printed, 1 pound, 56¼ cents to $1 20; bleached and unbleached, 36 cents to $1 20.	Same	None
Sandwich Islands	5 per cent. ad valorem.	Same	None
Sardinia	Mixed with linen or wool, plain, twilled, or in any way wrought: Bleached, per pound, 8½ cents; unbleached, do., 8½ cents.	Same	None
Spain and possessions	Common cloth under national flag, 29¾ cents to 55¾ cents per 1 lb. 3 drs.; under foreign flag, 35½ cents to 66¾ cents per 1 lb. 3 drs.		5¾ to 11 cents per pound in favor of Spanish against American vessels.
	Cuba— On valuation Foreign produce, direct from the country of production, in Spanish vessels, 23½ per ct ad valorem; in foreign vessels, 33½ per ct. ad valorem; from Spain, in Spanish vessels, 23½ per cent. ad valorem. Spanish produce, in foreign vessels, 17½ per cent. ad valorem; in Spanish vessels, 7½ per cent. ad valorem.		26 per cent. on the fixed value in favor of Spanish products in Spanish vessels against those of the United States in United States vessels.

DUTIES—Continued.

COUNTRIES.	MANUFACTURES.		
	COTTON GOODS.		
	United States.	Other countries.	Discrimination.
Spain and possessions—Continued.	*Porto Rico—*		
	On valuation		22 per cent. on the fixed value in favor of Spanish products under Spanish flag against United States vessels under American flag.
	Foreign produce, direct from the country of production, in Spanish vessels, 20 per cent. ad valorem; in foreign vessels, 29 per cent. ad valorem; from Spain, in Spanish vessels, 20 per cent. ad valorem.		
	Spanish produce, in foreign vessels, 15 per cent. ad valorem; in Spanish vessels, 7 per cent. ad valorem.		
	Philippine Islands—		
	All goods, with the exception of cambayas		11 per cent. in favor of Spanish products under Spanish flag against American products under American flag.
	Under Spanish flag, Spanish product, 3 per cent. ad valorem; foreign product, 8 per cent. ad valorem.		
	Under foreign flag, Spanish product, 7 per cent. ad valorem; foreign product, 14 per cent. ad valorem.		
Sweden	Printed manufactures, 1 lb., 26⅔ cents; bleached and unbleached, 1 lb., 20 cents.	Same	None
Switzerland	Unbleached yarn, three threads and upwards, per 110¼ lbs., 64 cents; one or two threads, per 110¼ lbs., 37 cents.	Same	None
Turkey	Calicoes, gray, 2⅜ cents per 2¾ lbs.; American drill, 3 per cent. ad valorem; fustian, 23-27 inches wide, 3 per cent. ad valorem; hereto are to be added 2 per cent. ad valorem internal duty.	Same	None
Tuscany	Simply spun, 20 cents per 74. 86 lbs.; colored and threaded, 40 cents per 74. 86 lbs.	Same	None
Two Sicilies	Printed, striped, or mixed with linen, 2. 306 yards, 47 cents to 64 cents.	Same	If by direct trade, a deduction of 10 per cent. ad valorem; indirect, subject to tonnage and discriminating duties.
Uruguay	20 per cent. ad valorem; cambrics, 10 per cent. ad valorem.	Same	None
Venezuela	For lamps, wicks, per 1. 014 lb., 18 cents; yarn, per 1. 014 lb., 18 cents; batiste, per yard, 3 cents.	Same	None
Zollverein	Yarn, mixed or unmixed with wool or linen, one or two threads, per 110¼, $2 07; unbleached, three threads and upwards, $5 52.	Same	None

TABULAR STATEMENT

SHOWING

THE RATES OF DUTIES LEVIED

ON

LEADING STAPLES OF THE UNITED STATES

IN

GREAT BRITAIN AND IN THE PRINCIPAL BRITISH POSSESSIONS THROUGHOUT THE WORLD;

NOTING SUCH DISCRIMINATIONS AS EXIST IN FAVOR OF ANY OTHER NATION.

DUTIES

ON

STAPLE PRODUCTS OF THE UNITED STATES,

IN

GREAT BRITAIN, ETC.

COUNTRIES.	PRODUCT OF THE SEA.		
	CURED FISH.		
	United States.	Other countries.	Discrimination.
Great Britain	Free	Free	None
North American possessions—			
Canada	Free	12½ per cent. ad valorem	12½ per cent. in favor of United States.
Nova Scotia	Free	Free	None
New Brunswick	Free	Free	None
Prince Edward's Island	Free	(Dried,) 36 cents per 100 pounds.	36 cents per 100 pounds in favor of United States.
Newfoundland	Free	Free	None
West Indies—			
Jamaica	48 cts. to 96 cts., per cwt.	48 cts to 96 cts. per cwt.	None
British Guiana	Dried, 25 cents per cwt.; mackerel, $1 per barrel; other, 75 cts. per barrel.	Same	None
Trinidad	Dried or salted, 24 cents per 100 pounds; pickled, 60 cents per barrel.	Same	None
Antigua	Dried or salted, 24 cents per 100 pounds; pickled, 48 cents per barrel.	Same	None
Honduras	2½ per cent. ad valorem	Same	None
Australian colonies—			
New South Wales	24 cents per cwt	Same	None
Van Dieman's Land	Not defined	Not defined	
Australia South	24 cents per cwt	24 per cent	None
Victoria	Free	Free	None
New Zealand	48 cents per cwt	Same	None
East Indies—			
Bombay	5 per cent. ad valorem	Same	None
Bengal	5 per cent. ad valorem	Same	None
Ceylon	36 cents per pound	Same	None

DUTIES—Continued.

COUNTRIES.	PRODUCT OF THE SEA.		
	WHALE OIL.		
	United States.	Other countries.	Discrimination.
Great Britain	Free	Free	None
North American possessions—			
Canada	Free	12½ per cent. ad valorem	12½ per cent. in favor of the United States.
Nova Scotia	Free	Free	None
New Brunswick	Free	20 per cent. ad valorem	20 per cent. in favor of the United States.
Prince Edward's Island	Free	Free	None
Newfoundland	Free	10 per cent. ad valorem	10 per cent. in favor of the United States.
West Indies—			
Jamaica	4 per cent	Same	None
British Guiana	15 cents per gallon	Same	None
Trinidad	3½ per cent	Same	None
Antigua	12 cents per gallon	Same	None
Honduras	2½ per cent	Same	None
Australian colonies—			
New South Wales	Not defined in tariff		
Van Dieman's Land	Free	Free	
Australia South	6 cents per gallon	Same	None
Victoria	Free	Free	
New Zealand	Free	Free	
East Indies—			
Bombay	5 per cent	Same	None
Bengal	5 per cent	Same	None
Ceylon	5 per cent	Same	None

DUTIES—Continued.

COUNTRIES.	PRODUCT OF THE SEA. WHALEBONE.		
	United States.	Other countries.	Discrimination.
Great Britain	Free	Free	None
North American possessions—			
Canada	Free	12½ per cent. ad valorem	12½ per cent. in favor of the United States.
Nova Scotia	Free	Free	None
New Brunswick	Free	Free	None
Prince Edward's Island	Free	10 per cent	10 per cent. in favor of the United States.
Newfoundland	Free	5 per cent	5 per cent. in favor of the United States.
West Indies—			
Jamaica	5 per cent. ad valorem	Same	None
British Guiana	4 ..do.......do	Same	None
Trinidad	3½..do.......do	Same	None
Antigua	4½..do.......do	Same	None
Honduras	2½ per cent.	Same	None
Australian colonies—			
New South Wales	Not defined		
Van Dieman's Land	Not defined		
Australia South	Free	Same	None
Victoria	Free	Same	None
New Zealand	10 per cent.	Same	None
East Indies—			
Bombay and Bengal	5 per cent. ad valorem	Same	None
Ceylon	......do.......do	Same	None

DUTIES—Continued.

COUNTRIES.	MANUFACTURES.		
	COTTON GOODS.		
	United States.	Other countries.	Discrimination.
Great Britain	Free	Free	None
North American possessions—			
Canada	12½ per cent. ad valorem	Same	None
Nova Scotia	6¼ do do	Same	None
New Brunswick	7½ do do	Same	None
Prince Edward's Island	5 do do	Same	None
Newfoundland	7½ do do	Same	None
West Indies—			
Jamaica	4 do do	Same	None
British Guiana	4 do do	Same	None
Trinidad	3½ do do	Same	None
Antigua	4½ do do	Same	None
Honduras	1 do do	Same	None
Australian colonies—			
New South Wales	Not specified		
Van Dieman's Land	Not specified		
Australia South	10 per cent. ad valorem	Same	None
Victoria	Not specified		
New Zealand	From 1½ cent per yard to 10 per cent.	Same	None
East Indies—			
Bombay and Bengal	10 per cent. ad valorem	Same, except from Great Britain, on which 5 per cent. is levied.	5 per cent. in favor of England.
Ceylon	5 per cent	Same	None

DUTIES—Continued.

COUNTRIES.	PRODUCT OF THE SOIL.		
	WHEAT.		
	United States.	Other countries.	Discrimination.
Great Britain	24 cents per 8 bushels	Same	None
North American possessions—			
Canada	Free	Same	None
Nova Scotia	Free	Same	None
New Brunswick	Free	4 cents per bushel	4 cents in favor of the United States.
Prince Edward's Island	Free	Free	None
Newfoundland	Free	5 per cent. ad valorem	5 per cent. in favor of the United States.
West Indies—			
Jamaica	6 cents per bushel	Same	None
British Guiana	5 cents per bushel	Same	None
Trinidad	3½ per cent	Same	None
Antigua	6 cents per bushel	Same	None
Honduras	2½ per cent	Same	None
Australian colonies—			
New South Wales	Not defined in tariff		
Van Dieman's Land	do		
Australia South	36 cents per 8 bushels	Same	None
Victoria	Free	Free	
New Zealand	Free	Free	
East Indies—			
Bombay	Free	Free	
Bengal	Free	Free	
Ceylon	5 per cent	Same	None

DUTIES—Continued.

COUNTRIES.	PRODUCT OF THE SOIL.		
	FLOUR.		
	United States.	Other countries.	Discrimination.
Great Britain	9 cents per cwt.	Same	None
North American possessions—			
Canada	Free	Same	None
Nova Scotia	Free	Same	None
New Brunswick	Free	72 cents per barrel	72 cents per barrel in favor of United States.
Prince Edward's Island	Free	$1 20 per barrel	$1 20 per barrel in favor of United States.
Newfoundland	Free	36 cents per barrel	36 cents per barrel in favor of United States.
West Indies—			
Jamaica	$1 44 per barrel	Same	None
British Guiana	$1 00 per barrel	Same	None
Trinidad	$1 20 per barrel	Same	None
Antigua	do	Same	None
Honduras	2½ per cent. ad valorem	Same	None
Australian colonies—			
New South Wales	Not defined		
Van Dieman's Land	do		
Australia South	24 cents per 100 pounds	Same	None
Victoria	Not defined		
New Zealand	Free	Free	None
East Indies—			
Bombay and Bengal	5 per cent. ad valorem	Same	None
Ceylon	do	Same	None

DUTIES—Continued.

COUNTRIES.	PRODUCT OF THE SOIL.		
	INDIAN CORN.		
	United States.	Other countries.	Descrimination.
Great Britain	24 cents per quarter, (8 bushels.)	Same	None
North American possessions—			
Canada	Free	Free	None
Nova Scotia	Free	Free	None
New Brunswick	Free	Free	None
Prince Edward's Island	Free	5 per cent. ad valorem	5 per cent. in favor of U. S.
Newfoundland	Free	Same	Same
West Indies—			
Jamaica	6 cents per bushel	Same	None
British Guiana	5 cents per bushel	Same	None
Trinidad	5 cents per bushel	Same	None
Antigua	6 cents per bushel	Same	None
Honduras	2½ per cent. ad valorem	Same	None
Australian colonies—			
New South Wales	Not defined in tariff		
Van Dieman's Land	Not defined in tariff		
Australia South	24 cents per 8 bushels	Same	None
Victoria	Not defined		
New Zealand	6 cents per bushel	Same	None
East Indies—			
Bombay and Bengal	5 per cent. ad valorem	Same	None
Ceylon	5 per cent. ad valorem	Same	None

DUTIES—Continued.

COUNTRIES.	PRODUCT OF THE SOIL.		
	RICE.		
	United States.	Other countries.	Discrimination.
Great Britain	9 cents per cwt	Same	None
North American possessions—			
Canada	Free	Same	None
Nova Scotia	Free	Same	None
New Brunswick	Free	Same	None
Prince Edward's Island	Free	5 per cent. ad valorem	5 per cent. ad valorem in favor of United States.
Newfoundland	Free	Same	None
West Indies—			
Jamaica	48 cents per cwt	Same	None
British Guiana	25 cents per 100 pounds	Same	None
Trinidad	48 cents per 100 pounds	Same	None
Antigua	48 cents per 100 pounds	Same	None
Honduras	2½ per cent. ad valorem	Same	None
Australian colonies—			
New South Wales	Not defined		
Van Dieman's Land	Not defined		
Australia South	24 cents per cwt	Same	None
Victoria	Not defined		
New Zealand	48 cents per cwt	Same	None
East Indies—			
Bombay and Bengal	5 per cent. ad valorem	Same	None
Ceylon	14 cents per bushels	Same	None

DUTIES—Continued.

COUNTRIES.	PRODUCT OF THE SOIL.		
	COTTON.		
	United States.	Other countries..	Discrimination.
Great Britain	Free	Same	None
North American possessions—			
Canada	Free	Same	None
Nova Scotia	Free	6¼ per cent	6¼ per cent. in favor of the United States.
New Brunswick	Free	1 per cent	1 per cent. in favor of United States.
Prince Edward's Island	Free	5 per cent	5 per cent. in favor of United United States.
Newfoundland	Free	10 per cent. ad valorem	10 per ct. in favor of United States.
West Indies—			
Jamaica	Free	Free	None
British Guiana	4 per cent. ad valorem	Same	None
Trinidad	3½ per cent. ad valorem	Same	None
Antigua	4½ per cent. ad valorem	Same	None
Honduras	2½ per cent. ad valorem	Same	None
Australian Colonies—			
New South Wales	Not defined		
Van Deiman's Land	Not defined		
Australia South	5 per cent. ad valorem	Same	None
Victoria	Not defined		
New Zealand	10 per cent. ad valorem	Same	None
East Indies—			
Bombay and Bengal	Not defined		
Ceylon	Not defined		

DUTIES—Continued.

COUNTRIES.	PRODUCT OF THE SOIL.		
	TOBACCO.		
	United States.	Other countries.	Discrimination.
Great Britain	72 cents per pound, and 5 per cent. additional.	Same	None
North American possessions—			
Canada	Free	1 cent per pound, and 5 per cent. additional.	In favor of the United States to the amount noted.
Nova Scotia	Free	Same	None
New Brunswick	Free	1 per cent. ad valorem	1 per cent. in favor of United States.
Prince Edward's Island	Free	4 cents per pound	4 cents per pound in favor of United States.
Newfoundland	Free	4 cents per pound	4 cents per pound in favor of United States.
West Indies—			
Jamaica	4 cents per pound (including Cavendish.)	Same	None
British Guiana	5 cents per pound	Same	None
Trinidad	6 cents per pound	Same	None
Antigua	4 cents per pound	Same	None
Honduras	$2 88 per 100 pounds	Same	None
Australian Colonies—			
New South Wales	16 cents per pound	Same	None
Van Dieman's Land	48 cents per pound	Same	None
Australia South	12 cents per pound	Same	None
Victoria	16 cents per pound	Same	None
New Zealand	18 cents per pound	Same	None
East Indies—			
Bombay and Bengal	5 per cent. ad valorem	Same	None
Ceylon	$2 40 per cwt	Same	None

DUTIES—Continued.

COUNTRIES.	PRODUCT OF THE FOREST.		
	TIMBER.		
	United States.	Other countries.	Discrimination.
Great Britain	For ship building, free; for other kinds, see Comparative Tariffs.	From British colonies, see Comparative Tariffs.	
North American possessions—			
Canada	Free	2½ per cent., (saw logs)	2½ per cent. (saw logs) in favor of United States.
Nova Scotia	Free	Free	None
New Brunswick	Free	Generally free	None
Prince Edward's Island	Free	5 per cent. ad valorem	5 per cent. in favor of United States.
Newfoundland	Free	24 cents per ton	24 cents per ton in favor of United States.
West Indies—			
Jamaica	From $1 92 to $2 88 per 1,000 feet, 1 inch thick.	Same	None
British Guiana	$2 per 1,000 feet, board measure.	Same	None
Trinidad	Spruce and pine, (white,) $1 50 per 1,000 feet.	Same	None
Antigua	White pine, $2, and pitch pine, $3 per 1,000 feet, 1 inch thick.	Same	None
Honduras	$1 92 per 1,000 feet	Same	None
Australian colonies—			
New South Wales	Not defined in tariff		
Van Dieman's Land	Not defined in tariff		
Australia South	Sawn or split, 60 cents per 40 cubic feet.	Same	None
Victoria	Not defined in tariff		
New Zealand	Not defined in tariff		
East Indies—			
Bombay and Bengal	Not defined in tariff		
Ceylon	5 per cent. ad valorem	Same	None

DUTIES—Continued.

COUNTRIES.	PRODUCT OF THE FOREST.		
	LUMBER.		
	United States.	Other countries.	Discrimination.
Great Britain	See Timber		
North American possessions—			
Canada	Free	2½ per cent	2½ per cent. in favor of United States.
Nova Scotia	Free	Same	None
New Brunswick	Free	Same	None
Prince Edward's Island	Free	60 cents per 1,000 feet	60 cents per 1,000 feet in favor of United States.
Newfoundland	Free	30 cents per M, (except from the other colonies.)	30 cents per M in favor of United States, unless from the other colonies.
West Indies—			
Jamaica	See Timber		
British Guiana	$2 per 1,000 feet	Same	None
Trinidad	See Timber		
Antigua	See Timber		
Honduras	See Timber		
Australian colonies—			
New South Wales	Not defined		
Van Dieman's Land	Not defined		
Australia South	60 cents per 40 cubic feet	Same	None
Victoria	Not defined		
New Zealand	24 cents per 100 feet	Same	None
East Indies—			
Bombay and Bengal	Generally 5 per cent	Same	None
Ceylon	Generally 5 per cent	Same	None

DUTIES—Continued.

COUNTRIES.	PRODUCT OF THE FOREST.		
	STAVES.		
	United States.	Other countries.	Discrimination.
Great Britain	See Comparative Tariffs		
North American possessions—			
Canada	12½ per cent. ad valorem	Same	None
Nova Scotia	Free	Same	None
New Brunswick	7½ per cent	Same	None
Prince Edward's Island	Free	Same	None
Newfoundland	5 per cent., (and at the port of St. John's, 10 per cent. on the amount of duty.)	Same	None
West Indies—			
Jamaica	96 cents per 1,000	Same	None
British Guiana	White oak, $2 ; all others, $1 50 per 1,000.	Same	None
Trinidad	$2 40 per 1,000	Same	None
Antigua	$2 50 per 1,000	Same	None
Honduras	2½ per cent. ad valorem	Same	None
Australian colonies—			
New South Wales	Not defined		
Van Dieman's Land	Not defined		
Australia South	60 cents per 40 cubic feet	Same	None
Victoria	Not defined		
New Zealand	10 per cent. ad valorem	Same	None
East Indies—			
Bombay and Bengal	Not defined		
Ceylon	Not defined		

DUTIES—Continued.

COUNTRIES.	PRODUCT OF THE FOREST. SHINGLES.		
	United States.	Other countries.	Discrimination.
Great Britain	$2 40 per load of 50 cubic feet.	48 cents per load of 50 cubic feet, and 5 per cent. additional from British colonies.	Nearly 400 per cent. in favor of colonies.
North American possessions—			
Canada	12½ per cent. ad valorem	Same	None
Nova Scotia	Free	Same	None
New Brunswick	7½ per cent. ad valorem	Same	None
Prince Edward's Island	5 per cent. ad valorem	Same	None
Newfoundland	24 cents per 1,000	Same	None
West Indies—			
Jamaica	From 72 cents to $1 44 per 1,000.	Same	None
British Guiana	50 cents per 1,000	Same	None
Trinidad	24 cents per 1,000	Same	None
Antigua	From 50 cents to $1 50 per 1,000.	Same	None
Honduras	48 cents per 1,000	Same	None
Australian colonies—			
New South Wales	Not defined		
Van Dieman's Land	Not defined		
Australia South	12 cents per 1,000	Same	None
Victoria	Not defined		
New Zealand	24 cents per 1,000	Same	None
East Indies—			
Bombay and Bengal	Not defined		
Ceylon	5 per cent. ad valorem	Same	None

DUTIES—Continued.

COUNTRIES.	PRODUCT OF THE FOREST.		
	TAR.		
	United States.	Other countries.	Discrimination.
Great Britain	Free	Same	None
North American possessions—			
Canada	Free	2½ per cent.	2½ per cent. in favor of the United States.
Nova Scotia	Free	Free	None
New Brunswick	Free	1 per cent.	1 per cent. in favor of the United States.
Prince Edward's Island	Free	2 per cent.	2 per cent. in favor of the United States.
Newfoundland	Free	5 per cent.	5 per cent. in favor of the United States.
West Indies—			
Jamaica	4 per cent. ad valorem	Same	None
British Guiana	50 cents per barrel	Same	None
Trinidad	12 cents per barrel	Same	None
Antigua	4½ per cent.	Same	None
Honduras	2½ per cent.	Same	None
Australian colonies—			
New South Wales	Not defined		
Van Dieman's Land	Not defined		
Australia South	24 cents per barrel	Same	None
Victoria	Not defined		
New Zealand	Free	Same	None
East Indies—			
Bombay and Bengal	Generally free		
Ceylon	Generally free		

DUTIES—Continued.

COUNTRIES.	PRODUCT OF THE FOREST.		
	PITCH.		
	United States.	Other countries.	Discrimination.
Great Britain	Free	Same	None
North American possessions—			
Canada	Free	2½ per cent	2½ per cent. in favor of the United States.
Nova Scotia	Free	2½ per cent	2½ per cent. in favor of the United States.
New Brunswick	Free	1 per cent	1 per cent. in favor of the United States.
Prince Edward's Island	Free	2 per cent	2 per cent. in favor of the United States.
Newfoundland	Free	5 per cent	5 per cent. in favor of the United States.
West Indies—			
Jamaica	4 per cent	Same	None
British Guiana	50 cents per barrel	Same	None
Trinidad	12 cents per barrel	Same	None
Antigua	4½ per cent	Same	None
Honduras	2½ per cent	Same	None
Australian colonies—			
New South Wales	Not defined		
Van Dieman's Land	Not defined		
Australia South	24 cents per barrel	Same	None
Victoria	Not defined		
New Zealand	Free	Same	None
East Indies—			
Bombay and Bengal	Free	Same	None
Ceylon	Free	Same	None

DUTIES ontinued.

COUNTRIES.	PROVISIONS.		
	BEEF.		
	United States.	Other countries.	Discrimination.
Great Britain	Free	Free	None
North American possessions—			
Canada	Free	20 per cent	20 per cent. in favor of the United States.
Nova Scotia	Free	$1 44 per cwt	$1 44 in favor of the United States, (per cwt.)
New Brunswick	Free	$1 96 per cwt	$1 96 per cwt. in favor of the United States.
Prince Edward's Island	Free	Free	None
Newfoundland	Free	48 cents per barrel of 200 pounds.	48 cents per barrel in favor of the United States.
West Indies—			
Jamaica	$2 40 per cwt	Same	None
British Guiana	$1 50 per barrel, (200 lbs.)	Same	None
Trinidad	$2 per barrel, (200 lbs.)	Same	None
Antigua	$3 84 per barrel, (200 lbs.)	Same	None
Honduras	2½ per cent	Same	None
Australian colonies—			
New South Wales	Not defined		
Van Dieman's Land	Not defined		
Australia South	36 cents per cwt	Same	None
Victoria	Not defined		
New Zealand	96 cents per barrel	Same	None
East Indies—			
Bombay and Bengal	Generally free	Same	None
Ceylon	Generally free	Same	None

DUTIES—Continued.

COUNTRIES.	PROVISIONS.		
	PORK.		
	United States.	Other countries.	Discrimination.
Great Britain	Free	Free	None
North American possessions—			
Canada	Free	Mess pork, 12½ per cent.; other kinds, 20 per cent.	In favor of the United States 12½ and 20 per cent., as in the preceding column.
Nova Scotia	Free	$1 44 per cwt.	$1 44 per cwt. in favor of United States.
New Brunswick	Free	$1 96 per cwt.	In favor of United States $1 96 per cwt.
Prince Edward's Island	Free	$1 44 per cwt.	In favor of United States $1 44 per cwt.
Newfoundland	Free	72 cents per bbl.	72 cents per barrel in favor of United States.
West Indies—			
Jamaica	$2 40 per barrel of 200 lbs.	Same	None
British Guiana	1 50 do do	Same	None
Trinidad	2 00 per barrel	Same	None
Antigua	3 84 per barrel of 200 lbs.	Same	None
Honduras	2½ per cent.	Same	None
Australian colonies—			
New South Wales	Not defined		
Van Dieman's Land	Not defined		
Australia South	36 cents per cwt.	Same	None
Victoria	Free	Same	None
New Zealand	$1 20 per barrel	Same	None
East Indies—			
Bengal	Generally 5 per cent.	Same	None
Bombay	do do	Same	None
Ceylon	do do	Same	None

COMMERCE.

IMPORTS INTO AND EXPORTS FROM FOREIGN COUNTRIES.

SPECIAL PRIVILEGES AND RESTRICTIONS.

74 □

COMMERCE.

IMPORTS INTO FOREIGN COUNTRIES—DUTIES AND CHARGES.

(GENERALLY BY TREATY.)

COUNTRIES.	PRODUCE OF THE UNITED STATES.
Argentine Republic	Same as on similar produce of all equalized foreign nations.
Austria	Same duties as on the produce of all other foreign nations, whether imported in United States or national vessels.
Belgium	Same duties as on similar produce of other equalized countries. No discrimination between the vessels of the United States and Belgium on direct importation into either country. Premiums, drawbacks, &c., allowed to national vessels on imports or exports to be allowed to the vessels of either country in the ports of the other ; this privilege not to apply to salt, or the produce of the national fisheries. Steam vessels of the United States and of Belgium, engaged in regular navigation between the two countries, are exempt in both countries from all duties of tonnage, anchorage, buoys, and light-houses.
Bolivia	The same duties as on the produce of the most favored nations.
Brazil	Same duties as on similar produce from other foreign nations, (Portugal excepted,) and no discrimination in respect of tonnage of the vessel and her cargo between Brazilian vessels and those of the United States. Coasting trade not permitted, but American vessels may touch at different ports to discharge or receive freight on giving notice to the proper officer at the first port.
Central America—	
Costa Rica	Same duties as on the produce of the most favored nation, whether imported in Costa Rican vessels or in those of the United States.
Nicaragua	Same duties as on similar produce of the most favored nations.
San Salvador	Same duties as on similar produce of all other foreign nations. No discrimination in favor of national vessels over those of the United States.
Guatemala	Same duties as when imported either in the vessels of all foreign nations or in national vessels on such produce, manufacture, or merchandise, as may be lawfully imported into either country, respectively. Whatever may be lawfully exported or re-exported from Guatemala in its own vessels to any foreign country, may be exported or re-exported in vessels of the other country, with the privilege of all bounties, duties, and drawbacks.
Honduras	Same as on similar imports in vessels of all other countries, or of Honduras.
Chili	The same duties as are levied on similar importations from all other foreign nations, except Bolivia, the republics of Central America, Columbia, Mexico, Peru, the Argentine Republic, Uruguay, Paraguay, New Granada, Venezuela, Equador, and all new nations that may be formed out of the ancient territory of Spanish America.
China	Same duties as are levied on vessels of the most favored nations. No additional tonnage duties to be paid by vessels going from one to another of the five ports. These ports are Canton, Amoy, Foochow, Ningpo, and Shanghai. No other ports in China are open to foreign trade. Tariff and other duties are prescribed in treaty.
Denmark	Same duties as are levied on similar imports from all other foreign nations, whether in United States or national vessels.

IMPORTS INTO FOREIGN COUNTRIES, &c—Continued.

COUNTRIES.	PRODUCE OF THE UNITED STATES.
Danish possessions	Whatever can be lawfully imported into or exported from the West India possessions of Denmark in national vessels from or to the ports of the United States, or from or to the ports of any other foreign country, may, in like manner, and with the same duties and charges, be imported into or exported from the said possessions in vessels of the United States. The direct trade between Denmark and these possessions is reserved to the Danish government by the treaty of 1826.
Dominican Republic	No treaty.
Equador	Same duties as on similar produce from other foreign countries. Certain port privileges reserved for vessels built at the dockyard of Guayaquil, to which vessels of the United States are not admitted, but to which they shall be entitled if they shall at any time hereafter be extended to vessels belonging to Spain, Mexico, or any other Hispano-American republic.
France	Same duties, whether in American or French vessels, in *direct* voyage; cotton, the same in *indirect* voyage also, if shipped for France. Raw tin and products of fisheries are liable to same duties as in foreign vessels, being by treaty exempted from equalization.
West India possessions	Same duties as on similar produce, whether national or foreign, of other nations, and no distinction between United States or French vessels.
East Indies	Same tonnage duties as on French vessels; cargoes, free.
Great Britain	Same duties as on similar products of the most favored nation, and no discrimination in favor of national vessels.
American possessions	Same duties and charges, whether imported in national or in United States bottoms.
East India possessions	Same duties, charges, &c., as are levied on vessels and imports of all other foreign nations.
Hayti	Same duties as on similar imports from other nations having accredited commercial agents near the Haytien government, or having recognized its independence.
Hanse Towns, viz:	
Lubeck, Bremen, and Hamburg.	Same duties as are levied on similar produce of the most favored nation, and no distinction between Hanseatic and United States vessels. Whatever may be lawfully exported or re-exported from the Hanse Towns, in national vessels, to any foreign country, may also be exported or re-exported in United States vessels, with the privilege of all bounties, drawbacks, &c.
Holland	Same duties as are levied on imports from the most favored nations, and whether in national or United States vessels. All bounties, drawbacks, &c., granted to national vessels, on imports or exports, from or to the ports of the United States, to be also extended to vessels of the United States.
Possessions	Same as on similar produce imported in national vessels.
Mexico	The same duties as are levied on similar produce of any other foreign nation, and no distinction, whether imported in national or United States vessels.
New Granada	Same duties as on like produce of all foreign nations, and, whether with national or foreign produce, American vessels are subject to no higher or other duties than the vessels of New Granada.
Norway and Sweden	Same duties and charges, whether imported in United States or Norwegian vessels; and the same equality is applicable, whether the vessel is freighted with national or foreign produce, if not entirely prohibited.
Papal States	Same duties as when imported in vessels belonging to the Papal States.—(*Vide* President's proclamation, June 7, 1827.)
Peru	Same duties as are levied on similar produce of the most favored nations; no distinction, whether imported in Peruvian or United States vessels of the burden of two hundred tons and upwards.
Portugal	Same duties as are levied on similar imports from the most favored nations, and no distinction between national and United States vessels.
Possessions	The above regulations apply equally to the possessions of Portugal to which foreign trade is allowed.

IMPORTS INTO FOREIGN COUNTRIES, &c.—Continued.

COUNTRIES.	PRODUCE OF THE UNITED STATES.
Russia	The same duties, charges, and port dues as on similar produce of the most favored nation; no distinction, whether imported in national or United States vessels, or as to origin of produce, unless entirely prohibited.
Sardinia	Same duties as on similar produce of all other foreign nations, and no distinction, whether imported in United States or Sardinian vessels, or as respects the origin of imports, if not prohibited.
Spain	Commercial intercourse regulated by legislation, and subject to various prohibitions and restrictions, which, so far as the department is informed, are applicable to all foreign vessels.
Possessions—Cuba and Porto Rico.	Same as above.
Sweden	*Vide* Norway.
Turkey	The same duties as on similar products of the most favored nations.
Tuscany	Same duties as on similar imports from all other nations, and no distinction between national and United States vessels.
Two Sicilies	Same duties as on similar products of all other nations, and no distinction between national and United States vessels.
Uruguay	No reciprocal treaty.
Venezuela	Same duties as are levied on similar produce from other foreign nations, and no distinction, whether imported in United States or Venezuelan vessels.
Zollverein	No treaty with the confederated States of—
Prussia	Same duties as on similar imports, the produce of other nations, and whether imported in Prussian or United States vessels, (treaty May 1, 1828.)
Bavaria	No commercial treaty.
Saxony	Same.
Hanover	Same duties as on similar produce from other nations, and no distinction between United States and Hanoverian bottoms.

IMPORTS INTO FOREIGN COUNTRIES, &c.—Continued.

COUNTRIES.	PRODUCE OF FOREIGN COUNTRIES.
Argentine Republic	Same duties as when imported in the vessels of all other nations having treaties with the republic.
Austria	Same duties and charges as when imported in national vessels, and whether direct from the United States or from any other country.
Belgium	Same duties as on similar imports from any other nation, and no distinction between United States and national vessels.
Bolivia	Same duties as in vessels of the most favored nations.
Brazil	Same duties as when imported in vessels of any other nation, except Portugal.
Central America—	
Costa Rica	Same duty as when imported in the vessels of the most favored nation.
Nicaragua	Same as Costa Rica.
San Salvador	Same duties as when imported in vessels of any other nation, or in national vessels.
Guatemala	Same duties and other charges as when imported in national vessels.
Honduras	Same as above.
Chili	Same duties as when imported in vessels of the most favored nations, except such as have been or may be formed out of the ancient territory of South America.
China	Same duties as are levied on vessels of the most favored nation. Trade restricted to the five ports.
Denmark	Same duties as if imported in national vessels.
Possessions	Direct trade with the West India colonies is reserved to Denmark; but, whatever produce, &c., Danish vessels can lawfully import into or export from these colonies, from or to the ports of the United States, may, in like manner, with similar duties and charges, be imported into or exported from said colonies in vessels of the United States.
Dominican Republic	No treaty.
Equador	Same duties as if imported in vessels of the most favored nations, or in national vessels.
France	Admitted on payment of a discriminating duty in favor of similar imports in French vessels.
Possessions—	
West India	On same terms as apply to all other foreign flags. French produce can be imported only in French vessels.
East India	Same as on similar imports in all other vessels.
Great Britain	Same charges, duties, &c., as on similar imports in vessels of all other nations, and of national vessels.
American possessions	Same duties and charges in United States vessels as in all other foreign or national vessels.
East India possessions	Same duties as in vessels of all other nations.
Hayti	Same duties as in vessels of other foreign nations which have accredited consular agents, or have acknowledged the independence of Hayti.
Hanse Towns	Same charges and duties as in national vessels.
Holland	Same charges as are levied on similar imports in national vessels.
Possessions	Same duties and charges as on imports in national vessels.
Mexico	Same charges and duties as in national vessels.
New Granada	Same as in national bottoms.
Norway	Same duties and charges as in Norwegian vessels.
Papal States	Same duties as are levied on similar produce in all other foreign bottoms.
Peru	Same duties, charges, &c., as when imported in national vessels.
Portugal	Same as when imported in vessels of the most favored nations, other than the producing country, and a discrimination of 20 per cent. in favor of national vessels in the indirect trade.
Possessions	Same as above.
Russia	Same charges, duties, &c., as when imported in national vessels.
Sardinia	Same charges and duties on all foreign produce not prohibited, whether imported in Sardinian or United States vessels.

IMPORTS INTO FOREIGN COUNTRIES, &c.—Continued.

COUNTRIES.	PRODUCE OF FOREIGN COUNTRIES.
Spain	Discrimination in favor of national vessels.
Possessions	Same charges as when imported under other foreign flags.
Sweden	Same duties and charges as when imported in Swedish vessels.
Turkey	Same duties and charges as when imported in national vessels.
Tuscany	Same as in national vessels.
Two Sicilies	Same duties and charges as when imported in vessels of the most favored nation, or in national vessels.
Uruguay	No reciprocal treaty.
Venezuela	Same duties as when imported in Venezuelan ships.
Zoll-Verein—	
Prussia	Same duties as when imported in Prussian vessels on all merchandise that may be lawfully imported.
Bavaria	No commercial treaty.
Saxony	Same.
Hanover	Same duties as when imported in Hanoverian bottoms.

EXPORTS FROM FOREIGN COUNTRIES.

COUNTRIES.	DUTIES. (GENERALLY BY TREATY.)
Argentine Republic	Same as if exported in the vessels of any other foreign nation having a treaty with the republic.
Austria	Same duties and charges as if exported or re-exported in national vessels, without regard to origin of merchandise or produce.
Belgium	Same duties and charges as if exported in national vessels.
Bolivia	Same duties as when exported in vessels of the most favored nation.
Brazil	Same duties as on exports in vessels of all other nations, except Portugal.
Central America—	
Costa Rica	Same duties as when exported in vessels of the most favored nation.
Nicaragua	Same as Costa Rica.
San Salvador	Same duties as when exported in vessels of any other nation, or in national vessels.
Guatemala	Same duties as are payable on similar merchandise, or produce, in other foreign vessels.
Honduras	No export duties.
Chili	Same duties as when exported in vessels of the most favored nations, except the countries formed out of the ancient territory of Spanish America.
China	The same duties as when exported in the vessels of other foreign countries having treaties.
Denmark	Same as when exported in national vessels, and to any country.
Possessions	Same duties and charges as if exported in national vessels, as to all produce, or other merchandise, which can be lawfully exported to the United States.
Dominican Republic	The same as to other foreign countries.
Equador	Same charges and duties as when exported in the vessels of the most favored nation.
France	Same duties as when exported to all other foreign nations, and whether in United States or national vessels.
Possessions—West Indies	In Algiers and Corsica the same duties, whether in United States or in national vessels. In Guiana, in favor of French shipping.
East Indies	In the West and East Indies no exportation duties levied.
Great Britain	Same duties as are charged in all other bottoms, and no distinction between United States and British vessels.
American possessions	Same duties and charges as on exports to all other foreign countries, (certain exemptions in favor of Great Britain and other British possessions excepted,) and whether in United States or national vessels.
East India possessions	Same duties as when exported in the vessels of all other foreign nations. National vessels are charged generally only one-half of said duties.
Hayti	Subject to various duties, which are applicable to all foreign vessels. Acajou, campeche, cacao, cotton, and ox hides, are the only articles paying export duties.
Hanse Towns	Same duties and charges, whether exported to United States or any other foreign nation, or in United States or Hanseatic vessels.
Holland	Same duties as on similar exports, whether in United States or national vessels.
Possessions	Same duties as on similar exports in national vessels.
Mexico	Same duties and charges as when exported in Mexican vessels.
New Granada	Same as when exported in vessels of New Granada, and to any country.
Norway	Same duties and charges in United States as in national bottoms.
Papal States	Same duties and charges as when exported in vessels of other foreign nations.
Peru	Same duties and charges, whether in United States or Peruvian vessels.
Portugal	Same duties and charges as when exported in national vessels.
Possessions	Same as in national vessels.
Russia	No distinction as to exports between United States and Russian vessels.
Sardinia	Same duties and charges as on exports to all other nations, and whether in United State or Sardinian vessels.
Spain	The same duties and charges as when exported to other foreign nations.
Possessions	Same as in vessels of other foreign nations.
Sweden	Same charges and duties as on similar exports in national bottoms.

EXPORTS FROM FOREIGN COUNTRIES—Continued.

COUNTRIES.	DUTIES. (GENERALLY BY TREATY.)
Turkey	Same charges and duties as when exported in national vessels.
Tuscany	Duties and charges the same as in national vessels.
Two Sicilies	Same duties and charges as on exports to the most favored nations, and no distinction between national and United States vessels when exporting Sicilian produce, &c.
Uruguay	No reciprocal treaty.
Venezuela	Same charges and duties as when exported to all other foreign nations.
Zollverein—	
Prussia	Same duties and charges, whether exported in Prussian or United States vessels, without regard to origin of merchandise.
Hanover	Same charges and duties as when exported in Hanoverian vessels, whether the exports consist of Hanoverian or foreign produce.

EXPORTS FROM FOREIGN COUNTRIES—Continued.

COUNTRIES.	BOUNTIES. (GENERALLY BY TREATY.)
Argentine Republic	Not provided for in treaty, but no privileges allowed to any foreign nation over the United States
Austria	Same as when exported or re-exported in national vessels.
Belgium	Same as when exported in Belgian vessels, either to the United States or to any other foreign country; (salt, and the produce of the national fisheries, are exempted from this reciprocity.)
Bolivia	The same as are allowed to the most favored nation.
Brazil	The same bounties as are allowed on exportations in vessels of all other nations, (Portugal excepted.)
Central America—	
Costa Rica	The same as are allowed on the exportation of similar produce in Costa Rican vessels.
Nicaragua	The same as Costa Rica.
San Salvador	Same as are allowed on exportations or re-exportations in vessels of San Salvador.
Guatemala	The same bounties as when exported or re-exported in vessels of Guatemala.
Chili	Same bounties as are allowed on exportations or re-exportations in vessels of all other nations, except those formed out of the ancient territory of Spain.
China	None provided for in treaty, but United States vessels enjoy equal privileges with all other foreign nations.
Denmark	Same as are allowed on similar exportations or re-exportations in Danish vessels.
Possessions	Same as on exportations in Danish vessels, as to all produce that can be lawfully exported or re-exported to the United States, or to other foreign countries.
Dominican Republic	No treaty.
Equador	Same bounties are allowed as on similar exportations in vessels of Equador.
France	A discrimination is made on the exportation of some articles, (by legislation.)
Possessions—	
West Indies	United States vessels enjoy similar privileges with other foreign vessels.
East Indies	United States vessels enjoy similar privileges with other foreign vessels.
Great Britain	Same bounties on exportation of British goods exported direct to the United States, whether in United States or British vessels.
American possessions	Same.
East India possessions	Same as in other foreign vessels.
Hayti	The vessels of all nations that have accredited commercial agents at Hayti, or have acknowledged its independence, enjoy equal privileges, in all respects.
Hanse Towns	Same as when exported or re-exported in Hanseatic vessels.
Holland	Same as when exported or re-exported in Dutch vessels.
Possessions	Same bounties as when exported or re-exported in national vessels.
Mexico	Same as on exports in national vessels.
New Granada	Same bounties as on exports in the vessels of New Granada.
Norway	Same bounties as on exports in Norwegian vessels.
Papal States	Same as are allowed on exportation in the vessels of other foreign nations.
Peru	Same as on exports in Peruvian vessels.
Portugal	Same bounties as when exported in national vessels.
Russia	Same bounties as when exported or re-exported in Russian vessels.
Sardinia	Same as when exported in vessels of the most favored nation.
Spain	Bounties expressly forbidden by the organic regulations of Spain.
Possessions	No discrimination between American and other foreign vessels.
Sweden	Same as on exports in Swedish vessels.
Turkey	Same as on exportations in vessels of the most favored nations.
Tuscany	Same as on exports in national vessels.

EXPORTS FROM FOREIGN COUNTRIES—Continued.

COUNTRIES.	BOUNTIES. (GENERALLY BY TREATY.)
Two Sicilies	Same as on similar exports in Sicilian vessels.
Uruguay	Same as in other foreign vessels.
Venezuela	Same bounties as on exports in Venezuelan vessels.
Zollverein—	
Prussia	Same bounties as on exports in Prussian vessels.
Hanover	Same as in Hanoverian vessels.

EXPORTS FROM FOREIGN COUNTRIES—Continued.

COUNTRIES.	DRAWBACKS. (GENERALLY BY TREATY.)
Argentine Republic	Same as on similar exports in the vessels of all other nations.
Austria	Same as on exportations or re-exportations in national vessels.
Belgium	Same as on re-exportation in national vessels.
Bolivia	Same drawbacks as on exportations or re-exportations in vessels of the most favored nation.
Brazil	Same as on re-exportation in vessels of any nation except Portugal.
Central America—	
Costa Rica	Same as are allowed on re-exportation in vessels of Costa Rica.
Nicaragua	Same as are allowed on re-exportation in vessels of the most favored nation.
San Salvador	Same drawbacks as are allowed on re-exportation in vessels of San Salvador.
Guatemala	Same as are allowed on exportations or re-exportations in vessels of the most favored nation.
Honduras	Same as allowed on re-exportation in vessels of the most favored nations.
Chili	Same drawbacks as are allowed on exportations or re-exportations in vessels of all other nations. Special favors to vessels belonging to countries formed out of ancient Spanish territories.
China	Vessels of United States enjoy equal privileges granted to vessels of all other nations.
Denmark	Same as are allowed on re-exportations in vessels of Denmark.
Possessions	Same as in Danish vessels.
Dominican Republic	No treaty.
Equador	Same drawbacks as are allowed on exportations or re-exportations in vessels of Equador.
France	The same as are allowed on exportations or re-exportations in vessels of all other nations.
Possessions—	
West Indies	Same as on exportations in vessels of other nations.
East Indies	Same as above.
Great Britain	Same as are allowed to national vessels.
American possessions	Same as above.
East Indies	Same as allowed to vessels of all other foreign nations.
Hayti	Same as are allowed on exportations in vessels of all other foreign nations.
Hanse Towns	Same as are allowed on exportations or re-exportations in Hanseatic vessels.
Holland	Same as are allowed on exportations or re-exportations in Dutch vessels.
Possessions	Same as are allowed on similar exportations in national vessels.
Mexico	Same as on exportations or re-exportations in national vessels.
New Granada	Same as on exportations in national vessels.
Norway	Same as on exportations or re-exportations in national vessels.
Papal States	Same as are allowed on similar exportations in other foreign vessels.
Peru	Same as on exportation in Peruvian vessels.
Portugal	Same as are allowed on similar exportations in national vessels.
Russia	Same drawbacks as are allowed on similar exportations in Russian vessels.
Sardinia	Same as on similar exportations in vessels of the most favored nations.
Spain	Drawbacks prohibited by Spanish law.
Possessions	Same as to other foreign vessels.
Sweden	Same as on similar exportations in Swedish vessels.
Turkey	Same as on similar exportations in vessels of the most favored nations.

EXPORTS FROM FOREIGN COUNTRIES—Continued.

COUNTRIES.	DRAWBACKS. (GENERALLY BY TREATY.)
Tuscany	Same as on similar exportations in vessels of Tuscany.
Two Sicilies	Same as on similar exportations in vessels of the Two Sicilies.
Uruguay	Same as in other foreign vessels.
Venezuela	Same drawbacks as are allowed on exportations in national vessels.
Zollverein—	
Prussia	Same drawbacks as are allowed on exportations in Prussian vessels.
Hanover	Same drawbacks as are allowed on exportations in Hanoverian vessels.

SPECIAL PRIVILEGES.

COUNTRIES.	SPECIAL PRIVILEGES.
Argentine Republic	The commerce of the United States enjoys none over that of other foreign countries. A decree has been published, (May 1, 1854,) by which no port charges are to be levied on vessels entering the rivers and ports of that republic until buoys have been laid down and wharves established.
Austria	United States vessels enjoy all the privileges of commerce granted to Austrian vessels, both in the direct and indirect trade.
Belgium	United States vessels pay tonnage duty once a year only, same as national vessels—a privilege denied to these countries with whom reciprocal treaties do not exist.
Bolivia	The same as other equalized countries.
Brazil	None.
Central America—	
Costa Rica	None over the vessels of all other foreign nations.
Nicaragua	None.
San Salvador	None.
Guatemala	None.
Honduras	Americans or other foreigners who settle in Honduras are allowed to own Honduras built vessels and employ them, with all the privileges of national vessels, in the foreign or coasting trade and on the rivers of the interior.
Chili	Coasting trade permitted to foreign steamers, and in the following articles to all vessels, viz: stone coal, fire bricks, iron, lumber, and earth for foundry purposes.
China	Tonnage duties payable only at one port, with the privilege of visiting any of the other five ports to dispose of or discharge cargo, subject only to the established duty thereon. Rice and other grains exempt from import duty.
Denmark	None.
Possessions	A discrimination in tonnage duties over all European vessels, even those of the mother country.—See "Actual duty," &c , *postea*.
Dominican Republic	None.
Equador	United States vessels are allowed to convey salt from Punta Santa Helena to Guayaquil.
France	None, except as guaranteed by treaty. Raw cotton imported from the United States, indirectly into France, enjoys the same privileges as other American produce imported directly.
Possessions—	
West Indies, &c.	None.
East Indies	None.
Great Britain	None.
American possessions	American vessels admitted to privileges in the navigation of the St. Lawrence not conceded to other foreign vessels, by local authority.
East India	None.
Hayti	Steam vessels may touch at Haytien ports to discharge merchandise and deliver letters free of port charges, tonnage dues, &c.
Hanse Towns—	
Bremen	American vessels can enter without employing a broker, which is incumbent on captains of all other foreign countries not having a treaty with Bremen. The expense of such an agent is $8 for all vessels over 150 tons.—(Decision of the Senate of Bremen, 1852, under treaty of 1827.)
Hamburg	None.
Holland	None.
Possessions	None.
Mexico	None.
New Granada	None, except such as are granted to the Panama Railroad Company by charter.—See "Actual duty," &c., *postea*.
Norway	None.
Papal States	Coasting trade is permitted, and American, French, and Austrian vessels are assimilated to those of the Pontifical States with respect to port duties.

SPECIAL PRIVILEGES—Continued.

COUNTRIES.	SPECIAL PRIVILEGES.
Peru	None.
Portugal	None.
Possessions	None.
Russia	None.
Sandwich Islands	All goods imported from the United States, except sugar, coffee, molasses, syrups, rice, and spiritous liquors, pay an import duty of 10 per cent. less than similar goods imported from China or the Philippine Islands.
Sardinia	None.
Spain	None.
Possessions	None.
Sweden	None.
Switzerland	None.
Turkey	None.
Tuscany	None.
Two Sicilies	None.
Uruguay	None.
Venezuela	None.
Zollverein—	
Prussia	Coasting trade allowed to all foreign vessels between Stettin and Memel to the 1st July, 1855.
Hanover	None.

SPECIAL RESTRICTIONS.

COUNTRIES.	SPECIAL RESTRICTIONS.
Argentine Republic	Should war at any time exist between any of the states, republics, or provinces of the river Platte, or its confluents, the importation of munitions of war, arms of all kinds, gunpowder, lead and cannon balls, is prohibited.
Austria	Tobacco and salt cannot be imported without a license from the government.
Belgium	The direct trade between the United States and Belgium is subject to no restrictions, except such as are alike applicable to national as well as to United States vessels. Salt and the produce of the national fisheries are excepted by treaty from this reciprocity. In the indirect trade, United States vessels are on the same footing with the vessels of all other foreign nations. (Our treaty with Belgium is violated in this: masters of American vessels are compelled to note their protests before the tribunal of commerce, whereas Belgian masters in ports of the United States, or in any foreign port, must note such protests before the consul of their nation.)
Bolivia	Commerce between the United States and Bolivia is regulated by the Peru-Bolivian treaty of November 30, 1836. American commerce is subject to no special restrictions.
Brazil	The Brazilian government claims that the treaty of 1828 has no longer any binding effect, the notice to terminate it, provided for in article 23, having, as alleged, been long since given to the government of the United States; hence the commerce of the United States is subject to such restrictions as may, at any time, be imposed by legislation. The privileges guarantied by articles 11 and 13 of that treaty are withheld, and, in one case, have been officially refused.
Central America—	
Costa Rica	Tobacco and gunpowder are government monopolies, and can only be sold to government and landed in public stores. Spirits pay a duty of 6¼ cents per 25 pounds gross weight for storage in government stores; before consignee can take it thence he must pay $300 per annum for privilege of selling either wholesale or retail.
Nicaragua	None exist.
San Salvador	None exist.
Guatemala	None exist.
Honduras	None exist.
Chili	None, except as to the coasting trade, from which foreign vessels are excluded, see "Special Privileges." The vessels of nations that have not accepted the reciprocity system, adopted by the Chilian government in 1851, are subjected to an extra tonnage duty of 75 cents per ton. (NOTE.—By act of Congress, January 7, 1824, the President of the United States is empowered to declare by proclamation a suspension of all discriminating duties of tonnage, &c., upon the vessels of any nation allowing the same terms to American vessels.)
China	Before cargo can be discharged, a permit must be obtained from the Chinese authority, under penalty of $500 and confiscation of goods so discharged. Opium is declared contraband.
Denmark	None, unless the Sound dues, which are applicable to all other foreign flags, be considered such. These duties are, on raw cotton, 20 cents per 100 pounds; tobacco, 17½ cents per 112 pounds; rice, 11 cents per 112 pounds.
Possessions	None.
Dominican Republic	A discriminating tonnage duty against the United States in favor of those nations that have treaties, or have recognized the independence of the republic.
Equador	None.
France	None.
Possessions—	
West Indies	Trade restricted to certain enumerated merchandise and produce, both of import and export. American vessels are compelled to employ and pay an interpreter at Martinique.

SPECIAL RESTRICTIONS—Continued.

COUNTRIES.	SPECIAL RESTRICTIONS.
French East Indies	
Great Britain	None, except as are usual in time of war.
Possessions—American	None.
East Indies	Discriminations allowed in direct trade in favor of British bottoms.
Hayti	The government claims one-fifth of all coffee exported, for which it pays a mere nominal price.
Hanse Towns	None.
Holland	None.
Possessions	In the East Indies certain ports and islands not open to foreign commerce.
Mexico	None, if we except the utmost rigor.
New Granada	None, with respect to commerce.
Norway	None.
Papal States	None ascertained over other foreign vessels
Peru	None.
Portugal	None.
Possessions	Sanitary restrictions rigid with respect to vessels coming from southern port
Russia	None.
Sandwich Islands	None.
Sardinia	None.
Spain	None.
Possessions	None.
Sweden	None.
Switzerland	None.
Turkey	None.
Tuscany	None.
Two Sicilies	None.
Uruguay	None.
Venezuela	None.
Zollverein	None.
Prussia	None.
Hanover	None.

NAVIGATION.

TONNAGE DUTIES AND CHARGES,

MODE OF MEASURING TONNAGE,

SANITARY RESTRICTIONS,

AND

COLONIAL TRADE.

NAVIGATION.

COUNTRIES.	TONNAGE DUTIES AND CHARGES. (GENERALLY BY TREATY.)
Argentine Republic	Same as levied on all other equalized bottoms.
Austria	Same as on national vessels coming from the same place as to tonnage, light, pilotage, port charges, and fees.
Belgium	Same as on Belgian vessels, but the tonnage is rated according to Belgian measurement.—(*Vide* "Mode of measuring tonnage"—Belgium.)
Bolivia	Same as on vessels of the most favored nation.
Brazil	Same as are levied on Brazilian vessels.
Central America—	
Costa Rica	Same as on Costa Rican vessels as to tonnage, light, or harbor dues, pilotage, or any other local charges.
Nicaragua	Same as on the vessels of the most favored nations.
San Salvador	Tonnage and other duties the same as are levied on the vessels of San Salvador.
Guatemala	Same as on national vessels.
Honduras	Same as on vessels of the most favored nations.
Chili	Same tonnage and other dues as on vessels of the most favored nation. (Certain privileges are reserved to vessels from countries formed out of ancient Spanish territories in South America.)
China	Same as on vessels of the most favored nation.
Denmark	Same as on Danish vessels. Sound dues same on United States vessels and their cargoes as on the vessels and cargoes of the most favored nation.
Possessions	Same duties and charges as on Danish vessels, except in the direct trade between Denmark and her West India colonies, which is reserved.
Dominican Republic	Same as other foreign nations.
Equador	Same as on national vessels.
France	Not to exceed five francs per ton of American register over and above tonnage dues on national vessels.
French possessions—	
West Indies	The same as on French vessels, (by legislation.) Direct trade reserved to mother country.
East Indies	Same as on French vessels, (by legislation.)
Great Britain	Same duties and charges as on national vessels.
American possessions	Same as on national vessels.
East India possessions	Same duties and charges as on vessels of the most favored nations.
Hayti	Same as on vessels of most favored nations having accredited consular or commercial agents near the government, or that have acknowledged its independence.
Hanse Towns	Same as on Hanseatic vessels.
Holland	Same as on national vessels.
Possessions	Same as on national vessels.
Mexico	Same tonnage and other dues as are levied on Mexican vessels arriving from foreign countries.
New Granada	Same as on New Granadian vessels.
Norway	Same as on national vessels with respect to all duties or charges in the shape of tonnage, light money, pilotage, and port charges.
Papal States	Same as on other foreign vessels, and in the direct trade as on national vessels.

TONNAGE DUTIES AND CHARGES—Continued.

COUNTRIES.	TONNAGE DUTIES AND CHARGES. (GENERALLY BY TREATY.)
Peru	The same duties of tonnage, light, harbor, pilotage, quarantine, and other local charges, (vessels not to be under 200 tons,) as on national vessels.
Portugal	Same duties and charges as on Portuguese vessels.
Russia	Tonnage duties same as on Russian vessels coming from same ports. In regard to light-house duties, pilotage, and port charges, as well as to the fees and perquisites of public officers, and all other duties and charges whatsoever, same as on the vessels of the most favored nations with which Russia has no existing treaty of entire reciprocity.
Sardinia	Same duties and charges as on Sardinian vessels.
Spain	Same as Spanish vessels from Spanish ports in Europe pay in the United States.
Possessions	Discriminating duties largely in favor of Spanish vessels. Regulated by royal decrees of the Spanish government.
Sweden	Same duties and charges, of every description, as on national vessels.
Turkey	Same as on vessels of the most friendly powers.
Tuscany	Same as on national vessels.
Two Sicilies	Same duties of tonnage, harbor, light-houses, pilotage, quarantine, and all other duties in respect of voyages between the United States and the Two Sicilies, if laden, or in respect of any voyage, if in ballast, as on national vessels.
Uruguay	No treaty.
Venezuela	S me as on Venezuelan vessels.
Zollverein—	
Prussia	Same duties and charges as on Prussian vessels.
Hanover	Same as on Hanoverian vessels; and same amount of toll at Bruns-hausen, or Stade, on the river Elbe, as on other foreign vessels.

TONNAGE DUTIES AND CHARGES—Continued.

COUNTRIES.	ACTUAL RATE OF DUTY BY LOCAL LEGISLATION.		
	On United States shipping.	On national shipping.	Discrimination.
Argentine Republic	$2 08 per ton, with cargo; in ballast, 12 cents per ton; health officer's visit, $6; and other dues, $2 per ton, (entrance and clearance.)		
Austria	Anchorage 4 kreutzers, and lights ⅜ kreutzer per ton; both equal to nearly 6 cents per ton; port charges on a vessel of 300 tons amount to $24.	Same	None
Belgium	95⅝ centimes inwards and the same outwards per ton, and 16 per cent. additional, to be paid but once a year, from 1st January to 31st December, whether one or more voyages be made; 95⅝ centimes = 17¾ cents which, with the 16 per cent. added, will amount to 20½ cents per ton entrance duty, the clearance duty being the same.	Same	None
Bolivia	Not ascertained		
Brazil	300 reis, = 15 cents, per ton Brazilian measurement, which, in ordinary cases, exceeds United States measurement about 25 per cent.; and vessels making more than two voyages in the same year are exempt from tonnage duty for all voyages over that number.	Same	None
Central America—			
Costa Rica	No tonnage duties except for light-houses—*i. e.*, 6¼ cents per ton, and $3 from each vessel for port captain's fees, including entry, clearance, and for apprehending deserters.	Same	None
Nicaragua			
San Salvador	All sea-going vessels, without distinction of burden or flag, pay $17 in full of tonnage, anchorage, and other port dues; there are no pilots.		
Guatemala			
Honduras	One dollar per ton, and register fees; sealed paper, fort pass, &c., about $20 per vessel, on clearing with cargo; in ballast, these clearance duties amount to about $1 25.	25 cents per ton.	75 cents per ton.
Chili	Tonnage, 25 cents per ton; anchorage and roll of vessel's crew, $2 each.—(*Vide* "Special Restrictions.")	Same	None
China	Over 150 tons, 5 mace per ton; 150 tons or under, 1 mace per ton; all other port dues or fees are abolished. The mace equals 14⅘ cents.		
Denmark	According to weight of cargo. In Copenhagen the whole expenses on a vessel of 250 tons, including pilotage, Sound dues, from ports north of Cape Finisterre, $264; south of Cape Finisterre, $384.	Same	None
Possessions	Tonnage duty, 19 cents per ton; pilotage, from $7 to $50	45 cents per ton.	Discrimination in favor of United States vessels 25 cts. per ton.

TONNAGE DUTIES AND CHARGES—Continued.

COUNTRIES.	ACTUAL RATE OF DUTY BY LOCAL LEGISLATION.		
	On United States shipping.	On national shipping.	Discrimination.
Dominican Republic	One dollar per ton in port, and 50 cents additional for the coast; light money, 6¼ cents per ton; pilotage, 6 Spanish dollars entering, and 10 Spanish dollars anchoring; wharfage, 6 Spanish dollars; interpreter, 2 Spanish dollars; doctor's visit, 2 Spanish dollars.		
Equador	Every vessel entering Guayaquil, or any other of the larger ports of the republic, has to pay tonnage duty, per ton, 25 cents; light-house duty, per ton, 6¼ cents; anchorage, for every 20 tons, $10; for clearing the port, for every 20 tons, $4; with the exception of light-house dues, whaling, steam, and packet boats are free of all port charges.	Same	None
France	Tonnage duties, per ton, 93½ cents, as per register; clearance duty, for vessels above 300 tons, $2 77; declaration at the custom-house, each, $2\frac{7}{10}$ cents; passport duty, each, 18⅗ cents; permission for loading or discharging, $2\frac{7}{10}$ cents; vessels arriving in distress are free of all these duties; same duties for both direct and indirect voyage.	Free	93½ cents per ton.
Possessions—			
West Indies	With general cargo, 53¾ cents per ton; with wood, 29⅝ cents per ton; various other charges, amounting in the aggregate to about $5 66, exclusive of pilotage and interpreter's fee; the two latter, on a vessel of 300 tons, amount to $35 57.	Same	None.—(See "Special Restrictions," France and possessions.)
East Indies	4 cents per ton, and in port of Pondicherry an additional light duty of 3 cents per ton.	Same	None
Great Britain	The only tonnage charges are port or dock dues and light dues, which vary in the different ports of Great Britain, and in no case are higher than those charged on British vessels; a vessel pays only for such lights as she has to pass in reaching her port; those duties on a vessel of 500 tons burden entering Liverpool are lights, 11½ cents per ton, $57 50; dock dues, 33 cents per ton, $165; whole tonnage dues, $222 50.	Same	None
Possessions—			
American	Port and light duties vary in different colonies; Newfoundland, no tonnage duty; light, 12 cents per ton; these duties vary from 12 cents to 40 cents per ton, and in no case can there be a discrimination in favor of British ships.	Same	None
East Indies	Port charges, including pilotage, in proportion as tonnage increases over 100; 300 tons, about $25; 1,200 tons, $50; Cape Town, no tonnage duty; Australian possessions, generally not exceeding 25 cents per ton.	Same	None
	$1 per ton	Free	$1 per ton

TONNAGE DUTIES AND CHARGES—Continued.

COUNTRIES.	ACTUAL RATE OF DUTY BY LOCAL LEGISLATION.		
	On United States shipping.	On national shipping.	Discrimination.
Hanse Towns—			
Bremen	Port dues, whilst lying in harbor on a vessel of 120 tons, $12 ; and, from 120 up to 450 tons and over, the port dues increase to $38 40.	Same	None
Hamburg	On a loaded vessel, tonnage dues are 14 cents per last = 3 tons; in ballast or with coals, 7 cents per last. Pilotage from Bosch to Hamburg, 48 cents per foot. No other port charges except a fee of $1 68 to harbor master.	Same	None
Holland	90 cents per ton, paid only once per annum. Light money 16 cents per ton, inward; 5 cents per ton, outward. Harbor dues at New Deep, $2\frac{1}{2}$ cents per ton. Canal dues, inward, 20 cents per ton; outward, 12 cents per ton. Dock and harbor dues at Amsterdam, 10 cents per ton for 3 months. NOTE.—Tonnage dues were abolished in 1855.	Same	None
Possessions	East Indies: Anchorage, 30 cents per last of 3 tons. Pilotage not exceeding $8 per 6 feet draught, and for every additional foot about $1 40.		
	West Indies: Tonnage on a vessel of 25 tons, 5 cents per ton; of 50 tons, 8 cents per ton; of 100 and over, 10 cts. per ton.	Same	None
Mexico	In practice, $1 50 per ton is charged on entrance of vessels. Mexican vessels pay the same tonnage duties as foreign, if coming from, and loaded with the produce of, foreign countries. Pilotage, $2 50 per foot of draught; hospital dues, $10; captain of the port, $3 50; stamps for entering and clearing, $8 50. By decree of 1851, the following are the only duties which can be legally charged, viz: Pilotage at Matamoras, Tampico, and Tabasco, in and out each time, $2 50 per foot of draught; in all other ports open to foreign trade, $1 75 per foot of draught, with an additional for pilot's boats in the 1st class of ports, $6; in the 2d class of ports, $3. Fees of captain of port, $3 50. All other duties, anchorage, certificates, signatures, &c., are abolished.	Same	None
New Granada	All port charges at Aspinwall, $6 40, from which vessels bringing cargoes for Panama railroad are exempt. (Charges in other ports not ascertained, but it is presumed do not exceed the above.)	Same	None
Norway	Tonnage, $47\frac{7}{10}$ cents per last, of 2 tons nearly. Light dues $14\frac{2}{15}$ cents per last.	Same	None
Papal States	3 bajocchi (3 cents) per ton	Same	None
Peru	Tonnage, 25 cents per ton. Total expenses and charges from entry to clearance, (tonnage excluded) not exceeding $43 75. This includes shore agency, expense on cargo, &c.	Same	None

TONNAGE DUTIES AND CHARGES—Continued.

COUNTRIES.	ACTUAL RATE OF DUTY BY LOCAL LEGISLATION.		
	On United States shipping.	On national shipping.	Discrimination.
Portugal	Tonnage 28 cents; bar dues, 11⅛ cents. Exchange building contribution, 5 mills and an additional charge of 15 per cent. on tonnage and bar dues.	Same	None
Possessions	No tonnage duties, light or hospital money on shipping. Port charges, including all expenses at the Azores, $19 80. If the vessel has crossed the line, $23 40.	Same	None
Russia	75 cents per last, (about 2 tons;) pilotage and other charges are levied either on the draught or cargo of the vessel.	Same	None
Sandwich Islands	Tonnage duties abolished. Port charges for pilotage at Honolulu and Hilo, $1 per foot each way. Health certificate, buoys, harbor master's fee, and clearance, $7. At Lahaina, total charges, $9; at Kealakeakua, Hawaii and Kauai, $6 total charges.	If engaged in foreign trade, same.	None
Sardinia	Tonnage duties are abolished. Anchorage, 33 tons or under, 18 cents 6 mills per ton annually; from 36 to 80 tons, 3 cents 8 mills per ton; over 81 tons, 5 cents 7 mills per ton.	Same	None
Spain	10 cents per ton for anchorage; 10 cents per ton for light dues; ⅛ of 10 cents or 1¼ cents per cwt. of cargo for landing. The port dues and other charges on any foreign vessel belonging to a nation having reciprocal treaty with Spain, on national vessels, and, (by royal decree of 1852, put in force in 1854,) on United States vessels in the peninsula and the adjacent islands, are $3 58 on a vessel of 200 tons, exclusive of pilotage, on which there is no discrimination.	Half of these duties.	5 cents per ton on anchorage and light duty, each.
Cuba	$1 50 cents per ton, (including 1 per cent. balanza duty.) Light dues, 6¼ cents per ton. Health visit, 3 cents per ton. Vessels arriving in ballast and clearing in the same state are free of tonnage duties. Other charges differ at the different ports. At Havana, 21⅞ cents per ton is to be paid for the dredging machine. Vessels leaving the island with a *full* cargo of molasses are free of tonnage duties.	62½ cts. per ton, and 1 per cent. balanza.	87½ cents per ton.
Porto Rico	Tonnage, $1 per ton; mud machine, 12½ cents per ton; light duty, 3 cents per ton. Foreign vessels arriving with a full cargo of coal pay a tonnage duty of only 50 cents per ton, provided they carry no other merchandise besides. All vessels are free of tonnage duty clearing with a full cargo of molasses, or arriving and clearing again in ballast.	37½ cents per ton	62½ cents per ton.
Philippine Islands	25 cents per ton, if cargo is landed or shipped; if bulk is not broken the tonnage duty is only 12½ cents per ton. Mud machine 5 cents per ton, if bulk is not broken 2½ cents per ton. In ballast, entering and clearing, nothing. Light dues, ½ real (6¼ cents) per ton.	12½ cts. per ton. National vessels pay one-half of all these dues.	12½ cents per ton.

TONNAGE DUTIES AND CHARGES—Continued.

COUNTRIES.	ACTUAL RATE OF DUTY BY LOCAL LEGISLATION.		
	On United States shipping.	On national shipping.	Discrimination.
Sweden	10 cents (nearly) per last, or 5 cents per ton each way. There are other charges, the total of which may be gathered from the following actual charges on a ship of 500 tons burden, viz: Port and cargo expenses, 562 bco. rx. dollars, 12 skillings, or nearly $225.	Same	None
Turkey	No tonnage dues except for anchorage and pilotage, which amount to 12 cents per 20 tons.	8 cents per 20 tons.	4 cts. per 20 tons.
Tuscany	Anchorage on a vessel of 175 to 200 tons, $10 93; over that tonnage, $1 15 for each 25 tons additional.	Same	None
Two Sicilies	Indirect voyage 40 grains (23 cents) per ton. Direct, or in ballast, 3⅜ cents per ton. Pilots are not licensed. The charge for bringing into port and mooring varies from $10 to $15, according to size of vessel.	3⅜ cents per ton.	Indirect voyage, 19⅝ cts. per ton; direct voyage, or in ballast, none.
Uruguay	31 cents per ton	15½ cts. per ton	15½ cents per ton.
	Pilotage in, $8	$4	$4
	Pilotage out, $4	$4	None
	The expenses on entrance are $42, exclusive of tonnage	$19	$23
Venezuela	Tonnage duty, 37½ cents per ton; light duty, 6 cents per ton; entrance duty, 7 cents per ton; anchorage, 18 cents per ton; water, 12 cents per ton.	Same	None
Zollverein	Prussia, 30 cents, nearly, per last of 2 tons. There are other charges on entering a port, amounting altogether to about $6. Pilotage is levied on the draught of a vessel, and is paid per foot—from $1 to $2 75 per foot, according to size of vessel.	Same	None
Hanover			

MODE OF MEASURING TONNAGE, ETC.

COUNTRIES.	MODE OF MEASURING TONNAGE	SANITARY RESTRICTIONS.
Argentine Confederation.	American register is admitted.	Vessels are visited by port physician and subjected to quarantine when necessary.
Austria	The length, breadth, and depth, are multiplied in Paris feet and divided by 94.	Vessels with clean bills of health are admitted to immediate pratique. With suspicious bills of health, or having touched at suspected places, 10 days quarantine; no bills, or foul bills of health, 15 days, do. Quarantine charges, entry and departure on a ship of 100 tons and upwards, $4 32, and 72 cents per diem to gondolier.
Belgium	Multiply the length, breadth, and depth, (deducting one-third for curves,) in cubic metres, and reduce them into tons of one and a half metre, by deducting one third. The difference between this mode of measurement and that adopted in the United States may be seen from the following example: Ship "Jenny Lind"—American tonnage, 522 $\frac{87}{95}$. Belgian tonnage, 490.	Quarantine is only required from vessels coming from sickly places, and seldom exceeds 5 days. A bill of health from the medical authorities or the Belgian consul at sickly places is required. The charge for each visit is 8 francs = 93½ cents, and for detaining pilot on board, 4 francs 23 centimes.
Bolivia		
Brazil	The length is multiplied by the average breadth, and that again by six-tenths of the depth, and the remainder is divided by 100.	All vessels subject to visitation by health officers, and, when deemed necessary, to quarantine. Hospital fees are levied on vessels and their crews.
Central America—		
Costa Rica	No rules of measuring tonnage prevail. The ship's register is accepted as sufficient.	No quarantine regulations. Each vessel pays a hospital fee of $1 per head.
Nicaragua		
San Salvador		
Guatemala		
Honduras	Tonnage taken as per American register; when doubt exists, American mode of measurement resorted to.	No quarantine regulations exist, but, in cases of necessity, a visiting committee is appointed.
Chili	The length is taken from the after part of the stem to the forward part of the stern post, this multiplied by the depth, and the product by the breadth at the wales, and this product divided by 95 for the tonnage. This mode conforms to the American carpenter's measurement.	Vessels from sea, known to have infectious diseases on board, are quarantined from 10 to 40 days, at the discretion of the authorities. No bills of health are required.
China	None prescribed; American register accepted as sufficient.	None prescribed in treaty; vessels arriving at any of the five ports are exclusively under control of the consuls of their respective nations.
Denmark	See Possessions, *postea*	Clean bill of health and a certificate (both signed by Danish consul) attesting nationality of vessel, and if laden with cotton the origin of cargo. Quarantine examinations are made at Elsineur.

MODE OF MEASURING TONNAGE, ETC.—Continued.

COUNTRIES.	MODE OF MEASURING TONNAGE.	SANITARY RESTRICTIONS.
Danish Possessions	Measure the length from stem to stern into 4 equal parts, (which will make 3 dividing lines,) the breadth taken inside at the three divisions added together and divided by 3 gives the breadth; a string line drawn under the deck beams to the ceiling along side of the kelson, the medium taken as in breadth; length, breadth, and depth, reduced to inches and multiplied with each other and then divided by 322,767, gives the burden in lasts of 4,000 pounds, or 2 tons. Six inches are allowed in measuring depth for variation.	At some periods, as at present, the regulations are very strict, and oftentimes unnecessarily embarrass commerce; at other times relaxed and frequently entirely neglected. There is no fixed or permanent rule.
	The foot consists of 11 inches	
Dominican Republic	Not ascertained	A bill of health, properly authenticated, is required.
Equador	The medium between length of keel and deck multiplied by extreme breadth of beam, multiplied by depth of hold and product divided by 95, will give the number of tons.	There are no quarantine regulations. Bills of health are obtained from a medical board.
France	Tonnage of American vessels computed as per ship's register. Mode of French measurement, average length multiplied by greatest width (or widest beam taken from inside to inside,) multiply this product by depth of hold and divide by 3.80, cut off the millimetres, and the French tonnage is given.	A bill of health granted by the authorities of the place whence the vessel has sailed, signed by the French consul, is sufficient to exempt a vessel from quarantine. Should the vessel be subjected to quarantine, the charges in Havre are thus: From United States, 15 centimes per ton per day; from Europe, 10 centimes per ton per day; lazaretto duty, 3 centimes per ton per day, and 2 francs for each person daily.
Possessions—		
West Indies	Same as above	
East Indies	Same as above	
Great Britain	Multiply the sum of the depths by the sum of the breadths, and the product by the length, and divide the final product by 3,500, which will give the number of tons register.	A bill of health is required signed by the British consul, or in his absence by some competent authority at the port whence the vessel cleared.
In all British dominions	The above rule prevails.	
Hayti	Multiply the length, width, and depth into each other, in feet; divide by 94, and the product will give the tonnage.	Arbitrary and frequently oppressive.
Hanse Towns.		
Bremen	Multiply the length, breadth, and depth into each other, and divide the product, for vessels built in usual manner, by 240; for clipper built ships, by 280. The quotient gives the the lastage; 2 lasts are equal to 3 American tons, or 6,000 pounds.	Bremen has no quarantine regulations; but the usual precautionary measures are adopted when vessels arrive from ports where great sickness prevails.

MODE OF MEASURING TONNAGE, ETC.—Continued.

COUNTRIES.	MODE OF MEASURING TONNAGE.	SANITARY RESTRICTIONS.
Hanse Towns—Contin'd.		
Hamburg	Same as above; but the custom-house surveyors adopt the American mode.	Vessels from the Mediterranean, west coast of Africa, West Indies, southern ports of the United States, South America, and all ports where contagious diseases exist, must pass quarantine examination. A bill of health is sufficient if properly authenticated.
Holland	The length, breadth and depth, taken in Netherland ells, (each ell = $3\frac{28}{100}$ English feet,) are multiplied by each other; the product multiplied by 4, and divided by 9, will give tonnage.	Vessels having a clean bill of health permitted to immediate entry, otherwise they are detained, 3 days at least, at quarantine.
Possessions	Same as above.	
Mexico	One-half length from stem to stern, and half length of kelson, multiplied by $\frac{3}{4}$ of breadth of beam, $\frac{1}{2}$ breadth of bottom, and $\frac{1}{2}$ depth of hold, and the product divided by $70\frac{19}{100}$, gives the tonnage.	The usual bill of health from the last port is required. No quarantine is exacted, unless when a contagious disease exists on board.
New Granada	Given, the three dimensions, (length, width and depth,) multiply them into each other, in cubic metres and parts thereof, and divide by 3,222, the quotient will give the tonnage.	At Aspinwall no quarantine restrictions or regulations of any kind.
Norway	Length multiplied by breadth, and its product by the height of depression. The sum to be divided by one of eight different numbers, (corresponding with eight classes, into which all vessels are ranged,) the application of either depending on kind and shape of vessel. The result is the number of heavy lasts, one of which is equal to 5,376 American pounds.	From an infected place, 10 days' quarantine; from a suspected place, 5 days; charge on vessel, 1 cent per ton each day, and certificate of officer, 75 cents. A bill of health is required.
Papal States	Registered tonnage is admitted	Clean bill of health must be produced and attested, for which one scudo ($1) is charged. Examination charges amount to about 16 cents.
Peru	The length from the stem to the stern, multiplied by the breadth, and this result multiplied by the depth, gives the tonnage; cutting off 2 figures for hundreths. Difference between this mode and that of United States: Peruvian, $987\frac{70}{100}$ tons. American, $1,070\frac{25}{95}$ tons.	Clean bill of health admits vessels to immediate entrance. When on quarantine no charges, except physician's fees.
Portugal	Multiply length, width, and depth by each other, (in Portuguese "palms,") and divide by 324. The quotient will be the tonnage. The palm is equal to 22 French centimetres. This mode gives a result of about 15 per cent. less than United States measurement.	A clean bill of health, legalized by the Portuguese consul, at the port of departure, admits a vessel to immediate *pratique*. Quarantine, in cases of contagious diseases, cannot be performed at Oporto. Vessels in such circumstances must remove to some other port.

MODE OF MEASURING TONNAGE, ETC.—Continued.

COUNTRIES.	MODE OF MEASURING TONNAGE.	SANITARY RESTRICTIONS.
Russia	The length and breadth are multiplied together, and the product multiplied by the difference between light and load water lines. The sum thus obtained is divided by such divisor as the class to which the vessel belongs may determine, and the product is the tonnage, (in lasts, one of which is equal to about 2 tons,) supposing all to be on board that belongs to the vessel, proper, and crew. The particulars for ascertaining the difference between light and load water lines, as well as the classification of vessels, &c., may be found in detail by having reference to Consular Return from the port of Helsingfors, in Finland, in reply to circular of October 8, 1854.—("Returns," vol. 4.)	For Cronstadt and St. Petersburgh a passport through the sound is required; a bill of health given at Elsineur must be exhibited at the first guard-ship. Quarantine is exacted, in all cases of contagious disease, at places fixed for that purpose.
Sandwich Islands	American register of tonnage sufficient, though tonnage measurement is not required at these islands, charge being levied either upon vessel or draught in feet.	Health certificate is required to be furnished and signed by the pilot, for which is charged $1.
Sardinia	Given, the three dimensions, (length, width and depth,) in French feet, multiply them into each other, and divide by 94.	
Spain	To the length add three times the exterior breadth, from the product take the fourth part, multiply result by the interior breadth and depth, and then divide by $70\frac{19}{100}$; the result will be number of tons. The Spanish mode gives a result about $22\frac{1}{2}$ per cent. less than that of the United States; but tonnage is usually taken as per ship's register. The above dimensions are taken in Spanish feet.	Vessels proceeding from foreign countries must be provided with a bill of health, certifying that the port from which they proceed was in a healthy state, and not in free intercourse with any unhealthy country, which must be legalized by the Spanish consul. In default of such a document, the captain is subject to a fine of ten dollars, (in the port of Barcelona four dollars.) The quarantine observation (three days) heretofore existing is abolished by royal order of May 24, 1852.
Possessions—		
Cuba	Same as above	All vessels must have a clean bill of health, signed by the Spanish consul at their last port, else they are subject to an expensive and tedious quarantine.
Sweden	Length multiplied by pth, and its product by the height of depression, the sum to be divided by one of eight different numbers, (corresponding with eight classes, in which all vessels must be ranged,) the application of either depending on the helm and shape of the vessel; the result is the number of heavy lasts, each last being equal to about 5,376 American pounds.	Bill of health required with the visa of the Spanish consul from the last port. Vessels coming from an infected or suspected place are quarantined 10 days from the former, and 5 days from the latter. Charges in quarantine 1 cent per ton per day, and 75 cents for certificate of health.

MODE OF MEASURING TONNAGE, ETC.—Continued.

COUNTRIES.	MODE OF MEASURING TONNAGE.	SANITARY RESTRICTIONS.
Turkey	None exists; vessels are measured by comparison with others whose capacity is known.	Bill of health is required.
Tuscany	Not ascertained	Quarantine of from 7 to 20 days required; not having clean bills of health, the period depends on the nation of the vessel and the port whence she sails.
Two Sicilies	Multiply length in feet by width, and the product by depth, and divide the result by 94, and tonnage is given.	Bills of health signed by Sicilian consuls at the last port must be produced. Quarantine dues are arbitrary and oppressive, not being fixed by law.
Uruguay	The same as in the United States, with the difference of taking the real depth of hold, instead of breadth of beam, and allowing, according to the judgment of the measurer, for difference of build, whether sharp or full.	A bill of health from an Uruguay consul, or, in his absence, from custom-house authority, must be produced, else the vessel is liable to quarantine at a charge of $4 per diem.
Venezuela	Multiply length by width, and the product by depth, divide result by 94, and tonnage is given; instead of 95, 94 is used as a divisor, as the Spanish foot equals only 11 English inches.	A clean bill of health is required, signed by Venezuelan consul, or, if there be no such consul, by the consul of any nation. Penalty, 40 days quarantine, counting from the day the vessel sailed from last port.
Zoll-Verein— Prussia Hanover		Clean bills of health required.

COLONIAL TRADE.

COUNTRIES.	COLONIAL TRADE.
Argentine Confederation	
Austria	
Belgium	
Bolivia	
Brazil	
Central America	
Chili	
China	
Denmark	Direct trade between Denmark and her northern possessions, viz: the Faroe Islands, Greenland, and the West India colonies, reserved; but between the West Indies and foreign countries, allowed on same terms as to duties and charges, applicable to vessel and cargo, as in national vessels. By treaty.—(See "Special Privileges.")
Equador	
France	Permitted by legislation, under certain restrictions as to merchandise imported.—(See "Possessions," below.)
Possessions—	
West Indies	Direct trade reserved to French vessels. Principal trade allowed to United States vessels consists in importing tobacco, wood, beef, Indian corn, and other staples. American vessels usually leave in ballast, the French law prohibiting the exportation of leading staples, except direct to France and in French vessels. All the articles prohibited in the trade between the United States and the West Indies may be imported in French vessels from certain bonded warehouses in France.
East Indies	Direct trade reserved to national vessels.
Great Britain	Permitted by treaty and by legislation.
Possessions—	
American	Open to all nations.
East Indian	Open to all nations.
Hayti	None.
Hanse Towns	None.
Holland	Direct trade open to vessels of the United States. (By treaty.)
Possessions	Permitted to United States vessels on same terms as to national vessels.
Mexico	None.
New Granada	None.
Norway	None.
Papal States	None.
Peru	None.
Portugal and possessions	Permitted by treaty on same terms (as to productions of the United States) as to national vessels.
Russia	
Sandwich Islands	None.
Sardinia	None.
Spain	Permitted.
Possessions—	
Cuba	Regulated by orders of the Captain General of Cuba, with the approval of the home government. This also applies to Porto Rico.
Sweden	Permitted to St. Bartholomew.

COLONIAL TRADE—Continued.

COUNTRIES.	COLONIAL TRADE.
Turkey	None.
Tuscany	None.
Two Sicilies	None.
Uruguay	None.
Venezuela	None.
Zollverein—	
Prussia	None.
Hanover	None.

INDEX.

INDEX.

www.ingramcontent.com/pod-product-compliance
Lightning Source LLC
LaVergne TN
LVHW021058110826
845150LV00001B/113